Opening the Gates

Opening the Gates

The Lip Affair, 1968–1981

Donald Reid

VERSO

London • New York

First published by Verso 2018
© Donald Reid 2018

1 3 5 7 9 10 8 6 4 2

Verso
UK: 6 Meard Street, London W1F 0EG
US: 20 Jay Street, Suite 1010, Brooklyn, NY 11201
versobooks.com

Verso is the imprint of New Left Books

ISBN-13: 978-1-78663-540-2
ISBN-13: 978-1-78663-542-6 (US EBK)
ISBN-13: 978-1-78663-543-3 (UK EBK)

British Library Cataloguing in Publication Data
A catalogue record for this book is available from the British Library

Library of Congress Cataloging-in-Publication Data

Names: Reid, Donald.
Title: Opening the gates : the Lip affair, 1968–1981 / Donald Reid.
Description: New York : Verso, 2018.
Identifiers: LCCN 2017058612 | ISBN 9781786635402 (hardback)
Subjects: LCSH: LIP (Firm) | Lip, Fred, 1905– | Clock and watch
  industry—France—History—20th century. | Strikes and
  lockouts—France—History—20th century. | Industrial management—Employee
  participation—France—History—20th century. | Industrial
  relations—France—History—20th century. | BISAC: POLITICAL SCIENCE /
  History & Theory. | POLITICAL SCIENCE / Political Ideologies / Communism &
  Socialism.
Classification: LCC HD9999.C584 L576 2018 | DDC 331.892/88113094446—dc23
LC record available at https://lccn.loc.gov/2017058612

Typeset in Minion Pro by MJ & N Gavan, Truro, Cornwall
Printed in the UK by CPI Group (UK) Ltd, Croydon, CR0 4YY

For Holly, Hadley and Otis,
who made it possible

Contents

Acknowledgments

All who work on Lip are indebted to Michel Jeanningros. He had an office at the entry to the occupied factory and welcomed visitors, introducing them to workers inside. As I can attest, he has continued to play this welcoming role. In 1973, he was the Lip employee who took responsibility for compiling a wall mural of press coverage of the movement and a wide diversity of other documentation. Jeanningros has never stopped, creating an archive that one militant at the time referred to as "manna for a university thesis," now housed in the Archives départementales du Doubs (ADD).

I am deeply grateful to leading figures in the Lip conflict I interviewed—Jacky Burtz, Dominique Bondu, Raymond Burgy, Fatima Demougeot, Michel Jeanningros, Claude Neuschwander, Charles Piaget, Jeannine Pierre-Émile, Monique Piton, and Roland Vittot—and to all who spoke to me about these events. Charles Piaget and Dominique Bondu let me consult their papers; Claude Neuschwander shared his unpublished manuscript, "Ils ont tué Lip"; Anne-Marie Martin provided transcripts of her films on Lip. Over the course of researching this project, I have benefited from assistance that I found myself thinking of as expressions of support characteristic of, and in some cases rooted in, the Lip experience. I would like to thank Gaston Bordet, Pierre Bouvier, Richard Copans, Caroline Dehedin, Dominique Dubosc, Thomas Faverjon, Mathieu Firmin, Frank Georgi, Guillaume Gourgues, Laurent Kondratuk, Dominique Ladoge, Sébastien Layerle, Anne-Marie Martin, Joëlle Mauerhan, and Pierre Thomé. In true acts of scholarly solidarity,

Joëlle Beurier and Christian Rouaud shared transcripts of interviews they conducted with important figures in the Lip Affair.

I want to express my deep appreciation to a number of archivists, including Myriam Cour-Drouhard and the director of the ADD Nathalie Rogeaux; Camille Abbiateci, Bérénice Hartwig, and Michel Hitter of the Archives municipales de Besançon (AMB); Rosa Olmos of the Bibliothèque de Documentation Internationale Contemporaine (BDIC); Marie Eugénie Mougel of the Confédération Française Démocratique du Travail (ACFDT); Élise Mavraganis of the Fédération Générale de la Métallurgie of the CFDT (FGM-CFDT); and Aurélie Mazet of the Confédération Générale du Travail (ACGT). Brooke Andrade of the National Humanities Center (NHC) and the interlibrary loan department of the University of North Carolina at Chapel Hill (UNC-CH) fulfilled my seemingly insatiable desires.

I benefited greatly from discussions of my work with the French History and Culture Carolina Seminar at UNC-CH and the Joint French History Seminar at the University of Toronto/York University. I am indebted to Dominique Bondu, Hélène Chuquet and Holly Russell, who read a draft of the manuscript and provided very helpful critiques. It gives me special pleasure to thank Patrick Fridenson and Jacques Rancière—scholars who have shaped and inspired my work since the very years I examine in this book—for their readings and perceptive comments on the manuscript.

I would also like to thank the NHC for the John G. Medlin, Jr. Senior Fellowship, and UNC-CH for the W.N. Reynolds Leave, which provided me with the opportunity to complete this project. I am deeply appreciative to my editor, Sebastian Budgen, for his support and guidance, and to Mark Martin and the staff at Verso Books who brought this book into existence.

List of Acronyms

2AL Association des Amis de Lip
4M Micro-mécanique et matériel médical
AB Archives Beurier. Transcripts of interviews done by Joëlle Beurier
ACFDT Archives of the CFDT
ACGT Archives of the CGT
ACN Archives of Claude Neuschwander
ACO Action Catholique Ouvrière
ADD Archives départementales du Doubs
ADELS Association pour la Démocratie et l'Éducation Locale et Sociale
AFGM-CFDT Archives of the Fédération Générale de la Métallurgie-CFDT
AFP Agence France-Presse
AG Assemblée Générale (General Assembly)
AM Archives of Anne-Marie Martin
AMB Archives municipales de Besançon
ANPE Agence Nationale Pour l'Emploi
AR Archives Rouaud. Transcripts of interviews done by Christian Rouaud
ASSEDIC Association pour l'emploi dans l'industrie et le commerce
ASUAG Allgemeine Schweizerische Uhrenindustrie Aktiengesellschaft
BDIC Bibliothèque de la Documentation Internationale Contemporaine
BSN Boussois-Souchon-Neuvesel
CA Comité d'Action (Action Committee)
CAMIF Coopérative des adhérents à la mutuelle des instituteurs de France

CAP Commissions Artisanales de Palente
CCPPO Centre Culturel Populaire de Palente-les Orchamps
CE Comité d'entreprise (works council)
CEH Compagnie Européenne d'Horlogerie
CESI Centre des Études Supérieures Industrielles
CFDT Confédération Française Démocratique du Travail
CFTC Confédération Française des Travailleurs Chrétiens
CGC Confédération Générale des Cadres
CGE Compagnie Générale de l'Électricité
CGT Confédération Générale du Travail
CIASI Comité Interministériel de l'Aménagement des Structures Industrielles
CJP Centre des Jeunes Patrons
CLEF Collectif de Liaison, Études et Formation
CNPF Conseil National du Patronat Français
CREPAC Centre de Recherche pour l'Éducation Permanente et l'Action Culturelle
CRS Compagnies Républicaines de Sécurité
DEUG Diplôme d'études universitaires générales
EDF Électricité de France
EHESS École des Hautes Études en Sciences Sociales
FGM-CFDT Fédération Générale de la Métallurgie-CFDT
FTM-CGT Fédération des Travailleurs de la Métallurgie-CGT
GIMM Groupement des Industries Métallurgiques et Minières
GOP/PLC Gauche Ouvrière et Paysanne/Pour le Communisme
GP Gauche Prolétarienne [ex-GP is the party after its dissolution by the state in 1970]
GROP Groupe de Recherche Ouvrier et Paysan
HBJO Horlogers, Bijoutiers, Joailliers, Orfèvres
IDI Institut de Développement de l'Industrie
INA Institut National de l'Audiovisuel
JEC Jeunesse Étudiante Chrétienne
L.I.P. Les Industries de Palente
LPI Lip Précision Industrie
MI Ministère de l'Intérieur
MNEF Mutuelle Nationale des Étudiants de France
MT Ministère du Travail
OP Ouvrier professionnel
ORTF Office de Radiodiffusion-Télévision Française
OS Ouvrier spécialisé

PCF Parti Communiste Français
PD Préfet du Doubs
PM Premier ministre
PR Préfet de la Région de Franche-Comté et du Doubs
PS Parti Socialiste
PSU Parti Socialiste Unifié
RG Renseignements Généraux
SA Société Anonyme
SCEIP Société Coopérative des Études Industrielles de Palente
SCOP Société coopérative et participative
SEHEM Société Européenne d'Horlogerie et d'Équipement Mécanique
SNIAS Société nationale industrielle aérospatiale
UDR Union des Démocrates pour la République
UEC Union des Étudiants Communistes
UIMM Union des Industries et Métiers de la Métallurgie
UNCLA Union Nationale des Comités de Lutte d'Ateliers
UNEF Union Nationale des Étudiants de France
VLR Vive la Révolution!

List of Illustrations

1. Charles Piaget speaking in Besançon, August 1973. Photo by Barnard Faille. © Bibliothèque municipale de Besançon.

2. Children demonstrate in Besançon, June 1973. © AFP/Getty Images.

3. Watch worker, 1974. Photo used with the tagline, "Nothing Is Done Well Without Passion" in a CEH advertisement (1974) and on the cover of *Lip au féminin* (Syros, 1977) with the response, "Our Passion Is the Fight." Photo by Marc Riboud. © Marc Riboud/Magnum Photos.

4a. "It Is Possible. We Produce, We Sell, We Pay Ourselves." Sign on the Jean Zay School in Besançon, August 1973. Photo by Jean-Paul Margnac. © Jean-Paul Margnac.

4b. Watch sales at Palente, August 1973. Photo by Bernard Faille. © Bibliothèque municipale de Besançon.

5. The Pay Commission counts money on the eve of the first payroll, August 1973. Photo by Patrick Meney. © P. MENEY/AFP/Getty Images.

6. Lip workers at a meeting, 1973. Photo by Henri Cartier-Bresson. © Henri Cartier-Bresson/Magnum Photos.

7. Claude Neuschwander, 1974. Photo by Marc Riboud. © Marc Riboud/Magnum Photos.

8a. Les Lip approve the Dole accords, January 1974. Photo by Bernard Faille. © Bibliothèque municipale de Besançon.

8b. Workers put "Lip Will Live" stickers on a train in Besançon, June 1976. Photo Bernard Faille. © Bibliothèque municipale de Besançon.

Timeline

1867: Emmanuel Lipmann founds the Comptoir Lipmann

1962: Lip moves to Palente

May 1968: Occupation of Palente by workers

April 17, 1973: Departure of the president-director general of Lip, Jacques Saintesprit

April 20, 1973: Creation of the Action Committee

June 10, 1973: Occupation of Palente

June 12–13, 1973: Sequestration of provisional administrators; sequestration of watches

June 18, 1973: General Assembly of workers votes to begin watch production

June 20, 1973: Sale of watches begins at Palente

August 2, 1973: Workers pay themselves for the first time

August 7, 1973: Workers first meet with negotiator Henri Giraud

August 14, 1973: Expulsion of Lip workers from Palente

September 29, 1973: March of supporters of Lip at Besançon

October 12, 1973: Workers vote to reject the Giraud offer

January 29, 1974: Workers vote to accept the Dole accords

March 11, 1974: Palente reopens

December 1974: Remaining Lip workers are offered employment at their previous rank (and begin work by March 1975)

February 8, 1976: Claude Neuschwander is forced to resign as president-director general

April 13, 1976: SEHEM declares bankruptcy

May 5, 1976: The General Assembly votes to occupy Palente

May 8–9, 1976: Open House at Palente

July 26, 1976: Workers sequester watches

May 31, 1977: Workers vote to begin watch production, sales, and payment of their salaries

November 28, 1977: General Assembly votes to establish Les Industries de Palente (L.I.P.)

February 1979: To meet conditions for the legalization of L.I.P., a director from the outside is hired; lists A, B, and C are released.

July 1979: Creation of the Commissions Artisanales de Palente

October–November 1979: General Assembly votes to pursue negotiations and to accept conditions set by the state for legalization of L.I.P.

June 1980: Legalization of L.I.P.

March 20, 1981: Departure from Palente

Introduction

Lip has become the opportunity for a general discussion of the aspirations of workers faced with capitalist society. To engage with Lip thus became a means to engage more with one's own situation. The meaning of solidarity then becomes different. Solidarity with Lip often marked a solidarity with one's own aspirations that, sometimes, one had not believed possible. "It is possible" ... allowed certain audacious aspirations of May 1968 to reawaken. Like the events of May 1968, the Lip event is first and foremost the fruit of this recognition of another possible.

—Pierre Rosanvallon[1]

Social reality is aptly made of founding events, like Lip or May '68, that introduce a breach in the system and renew the conditions of its evolution ... The event is inseparable from a desire and a social imagination, for it does not exist in itself, like a thing ... The Lip conflict became the Lip event only in the interpretation that was made of it.

—Pierre Rosanvallon[2]

We lived on Lip time ... What came to us from there, from Besançon, it was a kind of leaven that made the dough rise like nothing else. We saw they had found a collective alchemy, with their leaders, something rare.

---

1 "Quand un conflit devient un événement," *CFDT Aujourd'hui* 4 (November–December 1973): 3–6 (unsigned, but there is a later version in Rosanvallon's *L'Âge de l'autogestion*).

2 Pierre Rosanvallon, *L'Âge de l'autogestion* (Paris, 1976), 95–7.

> But they convinced us that it was reproducible! And that exemplarity for
> other struggles communicated an incredible force.
>
> —Martine Thomas Rousset[3]

The long 1968 in France—with its roots a decade earlier in opposition
to the Algerian War and in the search by the new left for alternatives to
the Socialist and the Communist parties—extended from May '68 until
the election of François Mitterrand in 1981. It saw the last widespread
expression in France of a belief in the creativity and moral universe of
workers engaged in labor conflicts as the driving force of social transformation. The most remarkable of these suspensions of subordination
occurred at the Lip factory in Besançon, where a planned mass layoff in
1973 deprived workers of the ability to withhold their labor.[4] The media
used the term struggle, *lutte,* for the actions of new social actors that took
their place alongside strikes by workers after May 1968.[5] In the case of
Lip, the strike that was not a strike, *lutte* became the way of identifying
this innovative form of *lutte des classes,* class struggle. "At Lip," a worker
explained, "we aren't 'on strike', but 'in struggle.'"[6] The absence of a boss
with whom to negotiate—unusual at the time, but increasingly common-
place in firms going under in succeeding years—demanded of workers
that they tell and enact a story in which all French people were invited
to participate. Lip workers occupied their factory, produced and sold
watches, and paid their own salaries. They revealed, to use the concept
Jean-Paul Sartre voiced in May 1968, "the extension of the field of possibilities," not just for workers, but for all who lived their struggle and
gave it support and meaning.[7] What mattered at Lip, as Karl Marx said
of the Paris Commune, was "its own working existence."[8] Lip quickly

---

3   Rousset was a member of a Lip support committee in the Paris suburbs. ADD
45J101 Martine Thomas Rousset, "Lip Lip Lip Hourrah!!!," *Le Pigeon* 19 (November
2013): 14.

4   "Suspensions of subordination" is a term used by Emmanuel Dockès, "Insubordination, propriété et action collective," *Semaine sociale Lamy,* supplement to no. 1631
(May 19, 2014): 42.

5   Hélène Hatzfeld, *Faire de la politique autrement. Les expériences inachevées des
années 1970* (Rennes, 2005), 249–51. See also Lilian Mathieu, *Les années 70, un âge d'or
des luttes?* (Paris: Textuel, 2009). Using the Google n-gram of books published in French,
lutte(s) (whether referring to social conflict or some other struggle) doubled in usage
from 1958 to 1977, declined by one-third in 1981, and was back to the 1958 level in
1989. *Lutte des classes* accounts for less than 5 percent of the usage of *lutte* in these years.

6   *Rouge,* September 28, 1973.

7   *Le Nouvel observateur,* May 20, 1968.

8   See Kristin Ross' revealing analysis in this tradition in *Communal Luxury: The
Political Imaginary of the Paris Commune* (London, 2015).

became an *affaire* in the French sense of the term: it was a political and social conflict that preoccupied and divided France and led the French to confront major issues and to engage politically.

The business press referred to the Lip Affair as "the May 1968 of the workers"; "their action calls into question a number of fundamental principles of capitalist market society: in this sense, it is more subversive than was May 1968."[9] A new vocabulary developed: *lipistes* for *L'Express* and *lipiser* for *Libération*. But for all, the workers were *les Lip*. When, much later, Jean-Claude Sensemat bought the brand name Lip, he complained that in addition to taking watches, the workers had, in taking this name, infringed on the trademark. Workers' identification with what they produce can be read as a sign of the alienating nature of labor in capitalism, but as Sensemat recognized, *les Lip* had become "in everyday language the symbol of workers on strike with stubbornness."[10] Repeated acts of unity and solidarity constituted and affirmed the collectivity of *les Lip*. Expressed in the General Assembly, it was organized and led by the unions. Community was the social and cultural expression of this collectivity constructed by the rank and file through their daily participation in the movement.

The narrative of Lip would go on to have "more plot twists, more alternations of sky high hopes and bitter disappointments than any Hollywood screenplay."[11] In 1974, a group of industrialists reopened Lip under the direction of a socialist. The project was shepherded through by Jean Charbonnel, whose dismissal as Minister of Industry at the time the workers were preparing to return to their jobs made the Lip Affair a turning point in the history of the left Gaullism he championed, and its reformist aspirations. To pull off their project, these capitalists worked with the Second Left—leaders of the Confédération Française Démocratique du Travail (CFDT), Michel Rocard of the Parti Socialiste Unifié (PSU), and individuals who had been engaged in the broad alternative democratic political and economic project nurtured in associations and clubs born of opposition to the Algerian War and to the all-encompassing nature of the state in the Fifth Republic.[12] However,

---

9 *Les Informations*, August 20, 1973.

10 Jean-Claude Sensemat, *Comment j'ai sauvé LIP* (Paris, 2005), 48–9. The name of the enterprise is written LIP and Lip. The latter is used in this text to refer both to the enterprise in operation until the summer of 1973 and to the community, projects, and struggles of its workers beginning that year.

11 Jonah D. Levy, *Tocqueville's Revenge: State, Society, and Economy in Contemporary France* (Cambridge, 1999), 119.

12 Hatzfeld, *Faire de la politique autrement*, 68. See Frank Georgi and Antoine

the firm lasted only two years, marking a beginning of the end of the enterprise as the organizing principle of capitalist production in France. The French state played a more active role in quelling projects of the 1968 years, both radical and reformist, than is generally recognized. At Lip, the state reasserted its power, starting with rebellious workers and moving to the "modern" businessmen in 1975–6, before returning to the steadfast workers.

Charles Piaget and Roland Vittot, leaders of the local (*la section syndicale*) CFDT-Lip, call the struggle at Lip in 1973 "the last conflict of the 'thirty glorious years'"—the years of postwar growth that made conceivable both the aspirations of 1968 and the Lip workers' assertion of the possible five years later. They refer to the conflict beginning in 1976, after the collapse of the new firm, as "the first of the crisis" that followed.[13] Initially, there was a sense that Lip had negotiated a path between the two periods, mobilizing the practices and communities rooted in 1968 to deal with the recession that confronted workers in the 1970s. In 1975, social planners saw Lip as a model for a large number of bankrupt firms being taken over and successfully operated by workers throughout Europe.[14] However, the world of 1968 receded and re-centered, giving way to market nostrums and to the Common Program, a nostalgic reiteration of past generations' Socialist and Communist projects, a "diplodocus text" in the words of Pierre Rosanvallon.[15] Neither had a place for the Lip workers' community, making it the utopia it did not want to be. Several hundred Lip workers found themselves establishing a cooperative against their will, and remained in the occupied factory until 1981, in the longest labor conflict in French history.

Imagination in power at Lip had a national as well as a class component. A member of the Resistance, Maurice Clavel, identified with the de Gaulle of June 18, 1940 and placed the events of Lip in this tradition:

Prost, *L'invention de la CFDT, 1957–1970. Syndicalisme, catholicisme, et politique dans la France de l'expansion* (Ivry-sur-Seine, 1995). Nicolas Defaud, *La CFDT (1968–1995). De l'autogestion au syndicalisme de proposition* (Paris, 2009). Frank Georgi, *CFDT: Identité en questions?* (Nancy, 2014). *Le Parti socialiste unifié. Histoire et postérité*, eds. Noëlline Castagnez, Laurent Jalabert, Marc Lazar, Gilles Morin, and Jean-François Sirinelli (Rennes, 2013). *Le PSU. Des idées pour un socialisme du XXIᵉ siècle?*, ed. Jacques Sauvageot (Rennes, 2013). Bernard Ravenel, *Quand la gauche se réinventait. Le PSU, histoire d'un parti visionnaire 1960–1989* (Paris, 2016).

13   Charles Piaget and Roland Vittot, "LIP: une lutte riche d'enseignements" in *Parti et mouvement social. Le chantier ouvert par le PSU*, eds. Jean-Claude Gillet and Michel Mousel (Paris, 2011), 283.

14   "Les 'lip' en Europe," *Intersocial* 5 (May 1975): 3–12.

15   Hervé Hamon and Patrick Rotman, *L'effet Rocard* (Paris, 1980), 132.

"It was the first dream of the people in thirty years"; failure to remember the story of Lip "would be, alas, the sign that our people have renounced their identity."[16] For André Frossard—son of the first secretary-general of the French Communist Party, but himself a convert to Catholicism and a prominent conservative intellectual—"if there exists the possibility of escaping the alternative unbridled capitalism-totalitarian socialism, one must look to the experience of Lip."[17] A resister captured and tortured by Klaus Barbie, Frossard was not speaking to the "realists": "since June 1940, I have seen them too often get the realities wrong."[18] In the 1970s, France faced challenges to fundamental national narratives of the French as having been a people in resistance during the war and French workers as class-conscious proletarians. *Les Lip* offered the response many craved: they showed resistance and embodied radical working-class action.

In 1976, Sartre told Benny Lévy, "With the technical object, we must do what we do with the aesthetic object. Lip is in effect *Madame Bovary*."[19] Like *Madame Bovary*, Lip is a text that created a world from the world that created it, confronted the legality of its day, and continues to challenge, inspire and haunt our imaginations. Leftists and capitalists, political parties and unions, responded to the issues posed in May 1968 and the next decade through their engagements with developments at Lip. Support for the workers of Lip, like that for the farmers of Larzac contesting the army's seizure of their land, was a site where 1968 was to be found through the 1970s.[20] A broad swath of French men and women attributed national qualities to the native French workers of Franche-Comté as they did to the farmers of Larzac. Leftists were surprised to find in the Lip conflict "the beginning of a great messianic movement … the center of attraction of a France in germination, of an alternative France."[21] The workers of Lip posed a welcome challenge to the depersonalized, hierarchical society to which '68ers feared they were condemned.

Central to these developments in 1973 and the succeeding years

16   Maurice Clavel, *Les Paroissiens de Palente* (Paris, 1974), 145, 413.

17   Monique Bel, *Maurice Clavel* (Paris, 1992), 293.

18   *Le Figaro*, May 27, 1977, 1.

19   Benny Lévy, *Pouvoir et Liberté*, ed. Gilles Hanus (Paris, 2007), 66 (October 16, 1976).

20   Larzac was infused with left Catholicism and shared many traits with the struggle at Lip. See Donald Reid, "Larzac in the Broad 1968 and After," *French Politics, Culture & Society* 32:2 (Summer 2014): 99–122.

21   *Libération*, June 1, 1977, 4. Leftists is the translation of *gauchistes*: those on the radical left who rejected the goals and practices of the "old left" Socialist and Communist parties in favor of working to achieve socialism in alternative organizations and parties.

was the opening of the Lip factory gates (closed by the Confédération Générale du Travail (CGT) at Lip and throughout France in May 1968) to those who came to see and speak with the workers. When the gates opened, many who identified with the aspirations of 1968 entered. In 1973, a Nanterre student, Dominique Barbier, walked down a passerelle in the occupied factory adorned with posters made by the workers: "All of a sudden I had the feeling of a transposition, as if I was leaving Nanterre and there was a continuation, that I was going from the student movement to the workers' movement." She planned to spend a week in Besançon, but stayed a year, active in the struggle and with her wages paid by *les Lip*.[22] Another student deeply engaged in the movement, Dominique Bondu, found a shared language with those with whom he worked at Lip.[23] As with the farmers at Larzac, groups of supporters throughout France, drawn from students and young professionals, often without the mediation of parties or national union confederations, established relationships with the workers. Each revealed new worlds to the other.

Xavier Vigna and Michelle Zancarini-Fournel rightly contend that the historiography of the 1968 years has denied historical legitimacy to such "improbable encounters."[24] Historians who want to present French intellectuals as abandoning Marxist politics in the 1970s have no place for the ways in which the innovative workers they met helped take them there.[25] In turn, historians of labor have rarely discussed the workers' experience of a cultural revolution in the post-1968 era, and the new challenges and practices that arose from their interactions with a diversity of partisans. However, such improbable encounters played a particularly important role throughout the Lip Affair. Because the Lip workers did not think that a vanguard party would take their movement from them, they did not fear sullying that movement in these encounters:

> Without this fertile encounter, would we ever have spoken, imagined, created as we have done? Without it, would we have had the audacity to

22   Hélène Fleckinger, "Des *Cahiers de mai* au documentaire. Entretien avec Dominique Barbier," *Revue documentaires* 22–3 (2010): 208.

23   Dominique Bondu, "L'Élaboration d'une langue commune: LIP-GP," *Les Temps modernes* 684–85 (July–October 2015): 69–80.

24   Xavier Vigna and Michelle Zancarini-Fournel, "Les rencontres improbables dans les 'années 68,'" *Vingtième siècle* 101 (2000): 163–77. For an insightful examination of these "meetings," see Kristin Ross, *May '68 and its Afterlives* (Chicago, 2002), ch. 2. Jacques Rancière's *La Nuit des prolétaires* (Paris, 1981), a remarkable work about such improbable encounters, inspired this study of Lip.

25   Donald Reid, "Well-Behaved Workers Seldom Make History: Reviewing Insubordination in French Factories during the Long 1968," *South Central Review* 29:1–2 (Spring-Summer 2012): 68–85.

launch ourselves into the reanimation of our factory? Without a doubt, certainly not in the same way. For it is the fruit of our experience that at each decisive moment, for each important choice, we called on others than ourselves. Not that we lacked imagination and audacity, but because we were convinced that the idea is always the outcome of a birth [assisted by a midwife].[26]

Some of the most important of the improbable encounters at Besançon brought socialist feminists together with female workers, spurring each to reflect and act on their situation as women in new ways.

The Lip workers' relationships with the men and women who entered through the open gates led to what Staughton Lynd calls "accompanying," predicated on mutually recognized expertise.[27] Rather than offering a social history of a labor force or an economic history of the watch industry, this study pays particular attention to the accompanying of workers like Charles Piaget and Fatima Demougeot and the intellectuals who lived and worked with them—like Jean Raguénès, Dominique Bondu, and the many veterans of May '68 whom *les Lip* questioned and who questioned *les Lip*. Lip workers and those who embraced their cause acted as catalysts for one another, allowing developments already present in each to manifest themselves in new, unexpected ways, seemingly spontaneously (although they were anything but). Workers' organization and activism spurred by engagement with supporters in turn awakened and answered a desire among leftists to escape the solipsistic elements of their own practice. Maoists found workers who did not need their theories in order to challenge the system. When no longer Maoists, they could still pass through the open gates, as Lip helped them explore other possible futures. Piaget commented that, like Monsieur Jourdain, Lip workers did not know theory, but found they were practicing it.[28] Sartre averred that leftist papers needed more theory, but not theory from books like his: the theory of Lip, he contended, could be found only by talking with Lip workers.[29] What might come of this? Several years later, Lip workers and their supporters called a meeting to discuss launching a periodical: "the synthesis of the century will be made ... [Emmanuel] Mounier and

26   *L'Heure*, 4 [supplement to *Lip Unité*, December 1977]. The article is unsigned, but bears the mark of Jean Raguénès.

27   Staughton Lynd, *Accompanying: Pathways to Social Change* (Oakland, 2013).

28   Bernard Ravenel, "Un militant ouvrier autogestionnaire. Entretien avec Charles Piaget," *Mouvements* 8 (March–April 2000): 119.

29   *Paris Match*, July 14, 1973.

Sartre surpassed … better, unity realized and purified! Read the Great 'quarterly': The Spirit of Modern Times."[30]

During the first decade of the Fifth Republic, many on the radical left had turned from factories in France to movements outside the West as the site of the audacity needed to make a new world. However, as Bethany Keenan has argued, the possibilities that May 1968 revealed brought the aspirations of French radicals back home.[31] No event was more important in returning to the Hexagon the imagination invested in national liberation movements in Vietnam and elsewhere than the conflict at Lip. The Maoists spoke of "One, two, three Vietnams in France. In French: one, two, three Lips";[32] "Vietnam is not the prerogative of the Vietnamese. In Franc-Comtoise they say: Lip."[33] For the then Maoist Bondu, "Lip made of our fantasies a reality, synthesizing our goals, like the creation of a liberated zone in Vietnam."[34] In July 1973, Alphonse Veronese, national leader of the Fédération des Travailleurs de la Métallurgie of the Confédération Générale du Travail (FTM-CGT), visited Lip. To make his point to a meeting of his national federation that they must be "extremely vigilant" in the face of the risks being taken by the CFDT-Lip, he reported their militants as saying "We consider ourselves to be a little VIETNAM."[35] A poster displayed in the occupied factory, made by one of the workers, showed a plane dropping tools in place of bombs and read, "In VIETNAM it's over … At LIP it is beginning."[36]

"I dreamed of the liberation of peoples," said Raguénès. "And I thought that one liberated a factory like one liberated a people."[37] This was how he envisaged the path from today's society to one that placed men and women rather than capital at its center:

30   BDIC F delta rés 702/15/1 "Projet de Journal 2AL," December 22 [1979]. Mounier had launched the journal *Ésprit* (Spirit) and Sartre *Les Temps modernes* (Modern Times).

31   Bethany Keenan, "'Vietnam is Fighting for Us': French Identities and the US-Vietnam War, 1965–1973." PhD thesis, University of North Carolina at Chapel Hill, 2009.

32   "Pour un mouvement du 12 octobre, en quelque sorte," *Cahiers prolétariens* 3 (January 1974): 22.

33   *La Cause du peuple*, September 13, 1973, 7.

34   Virginie Linhart, *Volontaires pour l'usine. Vies d'établis 1967–1977* (Paris, 1994), 197.

35   ACGT Lip Box 4 Procès-verbaux de la réunion des camarades du bureau fédéral [of FGM-CGT], July 30, 1973.

36   "L'Imagination au pouvoir: les affiches de Lip," *Libération* special issue, August 10, 1973, 6.

37   Jean Raguénès in Christian Rouaud, *Les Lip, L'Imagination au pouvoir* (Les Films d'Ici, 2007).

Creating Vietnams, Vietnam-factory, Vietnam-Church, Vietnam-justice, Vietnam-police … Vietnam-Lip … The Vietnams, it does not have to be solely at the level of factories. It is just as important that there be Vietnams at the level of justice, of the police, of the Church, at all levels. The day when there will be enough Vietnams, when the relations of power will be destroyed between the powerful and the governed, the teacher and his students, between the priest and his flocks, that day there will inevitably be a change in society.[38]

The Gaullist minister Charbonnel was taken aback by what he saw as Raguénès' effort "to transform the Lip Affair into a little Vietnam for a calm French province."[39] But what developed in Besançon drew on the energy and dreams the left had devoted to Vietnam, not the arms Lip workers had been making.[40] Like Vietnam, reference to Lip became a way to talk about what the many struggles in France shared and could offer one another.[41] In 1980, Raguénès said that when he had referred to Vietnams throughout France in 1973, what he meant was the many "autonomous centers," open to others, which one could see being formed during the Lip struggle. This was his idea of a revolutionary future, in which the interminable war in Vietnam revealed the non-violent uprisings that would never lose this quality: "it is in this dynamic—a little in the image of the fires of St. John which light up everywhere in the plain on June 24—it is in this dynamic—made of little groups, little communities, at once autonomous and open—that the future is created."[42] These sites, were, in Raguénès' evocation of what admirers sensed at Lip, "filled with the perfume of self-management."[43]

For supporters of the Lip struggle, the slogan "it is possible," written on a banner hung on the factory, referred to the workers' democratic self-management (*autogestion*), as a prefiguring of socialism. For the skilled workers who initiated the movement, however, "it is possible" referred to a firm with no layoffs, no dismantling and no loss of benefits,

---

38 *Libération*, October 19, 1973, 3.

39 Jean Charbonnel, *À la gauche du général* (Paris, 1998), 232.

40 The minutes of a meeting of Lip unions in January 1973 read, "There is little chance of advancing the [armaments] branch given the end of the war in Vietnam." Jean Divo, *L'Affaire Lip et les catholiques de Franche-Comté* (Saint-Gingolph, 2003), 34.

41 See, for example, "Un Lip judiciaire," *Les Temps modernes* 31 (1976): 1007–37.

42 ADD 45J108 Lip Livre Dialogue [hereafter Lip Livre] Part 1/Conversation 4, 8. This is an unpublished manuscript in three parts composed of texts by and conversations among Pierre Besançon, Dominique Bondu, Marc Géhin and Jean Raguénès, between 1980 and 1983. This reference is to page 8 of Conversation 4 in Part 1.

43 Jean Raguénès, "Oublier Lip?," *Autrement* 126 (January 1992): 188.

and not initially to a change in the exercise of authority and practices on the shopfloor. The Lip Affair did not begin as a classic 1968-era strike, where workers rejected the terms of the Fordist trade-off of higher productivity for higher wages, a trade-off that had fueled the final decade of the "thirty glorious years" of postwar growth. But the Lip skilled workers' demand for what the market did not confer was equally radical. While the conflict was launched to save jobs, the support for it across France came from those who embraced the tactics used, what *les Lip* referred to as their self-management of the struggle. And that struggle in turn changed the Lip workers; it had a particular impact on youths and on women, who made up half of the labor force. Although they were largely unskilled workers burdened with responsibility for the household, women played a leading role on the self-governing commissions that ran all elements of the movement. Some among them exemplified the "workers' insubordination" of the long 1968 by taking the next step and challenging the male union leadership.[44] The community born of the struggle, with its aspirations to live and work differently, resonated in France for close to a decade. And in turn it was community, rather than simply jobs, that became what *les Lip* fought for and the means they used to do so.

The impetus for the workers' imagination at Lip was condemnation of the global capitalism that deprived them of employment, but their supporters also saw in their initiatives a response to the alienation, centralization, and authoritarian hierarchies upon which capitalism depended. They spoke in terms of self-management as a participatory democratic practice in enterprises and neighborhoods conceived as an alternative to the bureaucratic structures of business and union confederations and to the technocratic rule of experts in the Fifth Republic.[45] Theoreticians posited that self-management was not fully possible as long as capitalism, not workers' democracy, made the decisions. However, from their efforts to respond to the failure of the works council (*comité d'entreprise*) to keep workers informed before 1973, through their work with economists in 1973 on an alternative business strategy for their enterprise and

---

44   See Xavier Vigna's groundbreaking *L'Insubordination ouvrière dans les années 68* (Rennes, 2007) and Vincent Porhel, *Ouvriers bretons. Conflits d'usines, conflits identitaires en Bretagne dans les années 1968* (Rennes, 2008).

45   The best work on self-management in France is *Autogestion. La dernière utopie?*, ed. Frank Georgi (Paris 2003). See also by Frank Georgi: "L'autogestion en France des 'années 1968' aux années 1980. Essor et déclin d'une utopie politique," *La Pensée* 356 (October–December 2008): 87–101; and "L'autogestion: une utopie chrétienne?" in *À la Gauche du Christ*, eds. Denis Pelletier and Jean-Louis Schlegel (Paris, 2012), 373–98.

their later efforts to rethink responsibility and decision-making in the cooperative, Lip workers pursued a social critique of capitalism with self-management qualities.

Like workers elsewhere, the Lip workers did not speak of self-management.[46] However, they showed what CFDT-Lip leader Raymond Burgy called a "capacity for self-management."[47] And, as Frank Georgi has recognized, for partisans of self-management, Lip supplied what they had previously lacked: an image and apparent incarnation of self-management in France.[48] But self-management interpreted as a workers' practice applicable to all facets of society largely disappeared from French political discourse after 1981, at the same time as did its representation in France: the Lip workers' factory occupation. The national memory of events at Lip today remains rooted in the images developed in campaigns to popularize the struggle in the 1970s, existing uneasily with memories among the Lip workers themselves of the risks taken and the dreams betrayed. The Lip Affair was the last national expression of workers as the creators of a new world. The idea of Lip workers practicing self-management was an effort to capture this. At the time, French Communists attacked the Lip workers as promoting "the ideas of another age,"[49] and this is how the non-Communist left has come to think of Lip as well. The sociologist Michel Freyssenet played an important role in the conflict through his work in the *Les Cahiers de mai*. He saw that "defeat in the Lip conflict, bearer of alternative practices and perspectives developed over ten years, sounded the death knell of the hopes placed in the invention of the future by those who want to change it."[50] For Robert Castel, the Lip Affair marked the end in France of situating a revolutionary alternative in the working class.[51] PSU leader Huguette Bouchardeau, an active supporter of *les Lip* and author of a novel set in Besançon at the time of the struggle in 1973–4, concurred: "Worker romanticism, for me, is over, and Lip is the last resurgence. I see in it the defeat of all my activist existence.

46   Danièle Kergoat, *Bulledor ou l'histoire d'une mobilisation ouvrière* (Paris, 1973), 92.

47   ACGT Lip Box 9 "Extraits intervention Burgy CFDT Lip le 29.9.73."

48   Frank Georgi, "Vivre la lutte, incarner l'utopie: les conflits Lip et leurs représentations, 1973–1981," *D'Ailleurs* 1 (2015): 20–35.

49   Jean-Claude Poulain, "Se débarrasser des idées d'un autre âge," *Economie et politique* 256 (November 1975): 25.

50   Michel Freyssenet, "Vers une sociologie des rapports sociaux," CSU, 2001, at freyssenet.com.

51   Robert Castel, *Les Métamorphoses de la question sociale* (Paris, 1995), 361–2n4. See also Pierre Lantz, 'Lip et l'utopie', *Politique d'aujourd'hui* 11–12 (December 1980): 97–104.

I can no longer describe it except with the deep feeling of a collective defeat, of a sustained illusion."[52]

Bouchardeau spoke like a mourner at a wake. Lip workers never made reference to the Church, nor did the Church make Lip a cause, but the workers drew important elements of their vision and their initiation into participatory democracy from left Catholicism, quite different from the Catholic social thought that informed the industrialists who reopened Lip in 1974 to show they had what it took to modernize French business.[53] One can see why Charbonnel thought historians of the future would see the Lip Affair less as a social conflict "than as testimony to the crisis of the Church in the second half of the twentieth century."[54] The left Catholicism that nurtured opposition to the Algerian War in the late 1950s only to recede after 1981 is a fundamental element of the long 1968.[55] Coming from a left Catholic culture, the workers of Lip spoke a powerful language of social justice, largely lost to us now. For Piaget, mass layoffs from enterprises that workers had made are "a regulator inherent in the capitalist regime, but are absolutely not necessary in an economy made for man."[56] *Les Lip* demanded rights in a language infused with Catholic humanism: "The layoff is the greatest violence that a worker undergoes. It is an incarceration in a world where his value and his dignity have disappeared."[57]

In the workplace, what Lip workers drew from left Catholic culture could be more radical than the efforts organized by the Communists. But rather than the condemnation of Communist organizations at the core of many narratives of the long 1968, the defining event at Lip was the failure of the capitalist enterprise to fulfill workers' expectations. In a nod to Jacques Maritain, Frossard wrote to Piaget, "Dear Sir, you have tried ... to change a company [*une société anonyme*] into a society of people."[58] In language antithetical to market ideology, workers spoke frequently of their struggle to confront "egoism" in themselves in order to construct a collectivity, as well as to realize themselves in communities

---

52   *L'Événement du jeudi*, October 31, 1991, 15. Huguette Bouchardeau, *La Grande Verrière* (Paris, 1991).

53   Denis Pelletier, *La crise catholique. Religion, société, politique* (Paris, 2002), 270, 272–3.

54   *La Croix*, October 27, 1973, 5.

55   On Catholic humanism and left Catholic culture in postwar France, see *À la gauche du Christ*, ed. Pelletier and Schlegel.

56   *Le Monde*, September 18, 1973, 40.

57   *Libération*, April 7, 1976, 8–9.

58   *Le Point*, July 18, 1977, 55.

in ways seemingly impossible in the society in which they lived. Workers had long contested the insecurity at the heart of capitalism, but *les Lip* brought the values and practices of 1968 to their confrontation with business mergers and industrial downsizing in a new era of globalization. They did so by defending the enterprise as a geographically situated space, the imagined site of worker self-management, where employees could build communities, contest the untrammeled mobility of capital and labor, and exercise control over their future. Lip was a movement of factory workers that spoke to and brought together a broad alternative left, the unfulfilled legacy of 1968. This is a legacy that can continue to challenge and inspire us today.

1

Lip, Lip, Lip, Hurray!

The endeavor of *les Lip* began many years ago, when some men and women, each with the will to change their lives, to put their Christianity into practice beyond the traditional ways, met at Lip ... To confront what the 'system' had always instilled in them: egoism, domination, sanctions ... What a workshop for a Christian!

—Roland Vittot[1]

To mark the hundredth anniversary of his watchmaking firm in 1967, Fred Lip had a fresco, six meters long and two-and-a-half meters high, painted inside the entrance to the factory in Besançon. It traced the history of measuring time from the ancient world, where master architects are shown examining parchments while laborers toil in the background, to the modern era, where managers appear in front of male and female workers from whom a plethora of watch parts emerge. In the middle of the fresco are portraits of eminent scientists, including Copernicus, Galileo, Newton and Einstein. Dressed in Renaissance garb, Fred Lip apparently stands with them.[2]

Fred Lip was the grandson of Emmanuel Lipmann, an Alsatian Jew who opened a watchmaking workshop in Besançon in 1867. At the time, farmers and their families in rural Franche-Comté devoted their

---

1   Roland Vittot, "La longue marche des Lip!," *Notre combat* 191 (December 1977–January 1978): 7–8.

2   The figure with Einstein was taken by all to be Fred Lip, but much later he said it was his grandfather, Emmanuel Lipmann. "Les révélations de Fred Lip," *Le Meilleur*, October 21, 1989, 10.

evenings and winters to making the well over 100 parts needed to construct a mechanical watch. Artisans in Besançon, like those employed by Emmanuel Lipmann, assembled the watches. This division of labor between the production of parts in the countryside and their assembly in Besançon continued to characterize watchmaking a century later. The population of Besançon doubled in size during the three-decade-long postwar boom to 120,000; Franche-Comté was second only to the Nord in the percentage of industrial workers in the population. In 1972, the region was home to 82 percent of the employees and 84 percent of the sales revenue in watchmaking in France.[3] In 1976, there were 213 watchmaking enterprises in Franche-Comté, about half of which made parts while the rest assembled watches; 160 had fewer than fifty employees. Only three, including Lip, manufactured parts, assembled watches, and had more than 500 employees.[4]

Another fresco could have been devoted to the many agricultural and industrial cooperatives in Franche-Comté, including the *fruitières*, peasant cooperatives that produced cheese, described by Besançon-native Victor Hugo in *Les Misérables*. Socialists Charles Fourier and Pierre-Joseph Proudhon were also born and grew up in Besançon.[5] In 1941, Marcel Barbu founded the Boimondau "labor community" in Valence following his expulsion from Besançon (where, in 1936, he had set up a firm to make watchcases for Lip) at the beginning of the Occupation. Boimondau was predicated on the active participation of all in the community through a network of neighborhood and workplace groups. Pay for workers and their unemployed spouses were based on seven elements of a member's "human values": a means of assessing their contribution to the community beyond solely that of production.[6] Not far from the Lip factory, in the first decade and a half of the Fifth Republic, the extraordinary Centre Culturel Populaire de Palente-les Orchamps (CCPPO)

3   Jean-Claude Daumas, "Le système productif localisé et la manufacture. L'industrie horlogère en Franche-Comté au début des années 1970," *Semaine sociale Lamy*, supplement to no. 1631 (May 19, 2014): 11. Watchmaking refers to a set of businesses, from producing watch parts to making finished watches or a combination of these. Watch worker encompasses the diversity of employees who make parts, assemble watches, and work on them.

4   ADD 45J111 Syndex, "Rapport au comité d'entreprise de la Compagnie Européenne d'Horlogerie sur les comptes de 1975," May 1976.

5   However, the Communists were pleased to report that neither Fourier nor Proudhon were known to workers in Besançon in 1973. *L'Humanité dimanche*, August 22, 1973, 9.

6   Michel Chaudy, *Faire des hommes libres. Boimondau et les communautés de travail à Valence* (Valence, 2008).

brought cultural revolution to workers, imbricating militancy and the arts, from films and filmmaking to theatre and book discussions, with the idea that "to introduce Bach to workers is a kind of factory occupation."[7]

In 1906, when anarcho-syndicalists organized workers in the Lipmann firm, the founder's son, Ernest Lipmann, overcame their forty-five-day strike, despite the strikers' use of whistles to harass scabs—whistles that the firm had provided workers in 1900, to wreak havoc at a meeting of opponents of another Alsatian Jew, Alfred Dreyfus.[8] This was a period when Ernest Lipmann differentiated his company from others in Besançon in several ways. He created a manufactory composed of a network of workshops on the rue des Chalets. Although the firm continued to purchase watchcases and some other components from the network of local producers, it came to make four-fifths of the watch parts itself. Ernest Lipmann was equally innovative in marketing. He registered the brand name Lip in 1908 and launched an advertising campaign in mass circulation magazines. This broke with the existing system in which vendors bought watches from producers and sold them under their own name. The firm put Lip on each watch face and gave selected watch seller-jewelers the right to offer them. It set prices and took responsibility for the warranty, in lieu of the practice of having the merchant decide on the price and guarantee the product.[9]

By 1931, with 245 employees and an annual production of 40,000 watches, the Lipmann firm was the largest watch manufacturer in France. It stood out in a Besançon with 4,000 artisans making watches in workshops and 1,000 others whom the extension of electricity allowed to work in their homes.[10] That year the firm reorganized as a joint stock

7   Donald Reid, "Well-Behaved Workers Seldom Make History: Reviewing Insubordination in French Factories during the Long 1968," *South Central Review* 29:1–2 (Spring–Summer 2012): 69–75. The CCPPO was active from 1959 until the eve of the Lip conflict in 1973. The cultural life of *les Lip* during the 1970s shares important qualities with the CCPPO experience. Charles Piaget, among others, appreciated and attended CCPPO productions. "La Palente de Charles Piaget," *Besançon Votre Ville*, May 2007, 25. However, if Lip workers were peripheral to the direction of the CCPPO, this may have been due in part to conflicts between the CCPPO and the CFDT in the city, which saw the CCPPO as too aligned with the Communists. ADD 43J18 CFDT-Union locale to CCPPO, December 9, 1970.

8   Joseph Pinard, "Lip: mettre les montres à l'heure," *Besançon Votre Ville*, September 2013, 42. Jean Charles, *Les Débuts du mouvement syndical à Besançon. La Fédération ouvrière (1891–1914)* (Paris, 1962), 138, 145.

9   Marie-Pia Auschitzky Coustans, *Lip, des heures à conter* (Seyssinet, 2000), 19–20. "Watch seller-jewelers" is a translation of the professional category of "*Horlogers, Bijoutiers, Joailliers, Orfèvres.*"

10   Claude Cuénot, "Ouvriers et mouvement ouvrier dans le Doubs de la fin de la

company, Lip SA d'Horlogerie, initially selling stock to vendors of its watches and using the funds to expand along the rue des Chalets. Ernest Lipmann's son, Fred, joined the firm as the director of production. He had been an indifferent student, more interested in rebuilding and racing motorcycles than school; for several years, he held a world speed record. When he failed his baccalaureate exam, he was sent to the École nationale d'horlogerie in Besançon and received a degree specially designed for him. However, in coming to work in the family business he sought to avoid, in his words, "behaving like a crass residue of capitalism." Fred Lipmann later framed his arrival in the firm as "the beginning of my great revolution: the struggle of the forces of youth and the future against those of tradition, or else of inertia."[11]

The Swiss began industrializing the fabrication of watches in the late nineteenth century, and had well surpassed the French in sales by the interwar years. The Lipmanns stood out among French watchmakers by responding with the standardization and rationalization of production. The firm mechanized, broke down the work process to establish worker specialization in a single operation, speeded up production, and increased the use of piece work such that 89 percent of workers were paid by output in 1930. Workers struck for a month that year against the new production norms and the replacement of skilled workers (*ouvriers professionnels* (OP)) by unskilled workers (*ouvriers spécialisés* (OS)) performing one task repetitively for less pay; 60 percent of both male and female workers participated in the movement. Fred Lipmann negotiated with the workers in place of his father, and held the line against reversing these changes. In 1934, the firm claimed that worker productivity had increased three-fold in recent years.[12]

As an element of his project to enact the modern employer, Fred Lipmann embraced a theatrical paternalism. In the early 1930s, he ordered workers making watches to replace their traditional black smocks with white ones, and had them exchange their shoes for white slippers when they entered the factory to avoid tracking in dirt. To signal

première guerre mondiale au début des années 1950." Thèse, Université de Bourgogne, 2000, 1: 83. Pierre Daclin, *La Crise des années 30 à Besançon* (Paris, 1968), 16–24. Olivier Borraz, *Gouverner une ville Besançon 1959–1989* (Rennes, 1998), 34.

11   "Fred Lip: l'enfant terrible du patronat français," *L'Entreprise*, September 20, 1958, 29–31.

12   Cuénot, "Ouvriers," 1: 207–8, 213–14, 259. Daclin, *La Crise*, 26–7, 104–5. Claude Fohlen, *Histoire de Besançon* (Paris, 1965), 441. Aimée Moutet, *Les Logiques de l'entreprise. La rationalisation dans l'industrie française de l'entre-deux-guerres* (Paris, 1997), 122.

their membership in the community devoted to production, managers, including the director, wore white smocks as well.[13] Because visibility and cleanliness were of paramount importance, Fred Lipmann installed fluorescent lights and jointless flooring. The firm opened the factory to the public, allowing it to visit the workshops and there to be impressed with their order and modern technology. In 1934 Lip claimed to be the first French firm to provide paid vacations.[14] After the victory of the Popular Front in 1936, Fred Lipmann got up on the roof of a car and harangued his workers to resist the bosses. During the workers' brief occupation of what he considered *his* factory, he went to the locked gate and asked to join them, but they turned him away.[15] Tales like this may be apocryphal, but the fact that they were widely repeated is a testament to Fred Lipmann's projection of the image of a boss, a *patron*, unlike any other.

Lip had used its expertise in precision mechanics and timers to make armaments for France in World War I. When the Germans occupied Besançon in 1940, they requisitioned the factory to produce parts for their own armed forces. After Fred Lipmann's efforts to get his parents to Switzerland failed, they were deported and died in Auschwitz in 1943.[16] At the Liberation, Fred Lipmann showed up gun in hand to take back the Aryanized factory.[17] He changed his name to Lip and took sole direction of the company. Under his leadership, Lip diversified. The firm took compensatory damages from Germany in the form of machine-tools and developed a department devoted to precision mechanics that was key to the operation of other elements of Lip in both technical and accounting

13   Pierre Vitoux, "Lip. Montres à la chaîne," *Essor* 2 (August 1953): 73.

14   However, Lip was pushed in this direction by its workers. In 1930, workers struck to receive four paid vacation days (and got two). Pinard, "Lip: mettre les montres à l'heure," 42.

15   Auschitzky Coustans, *Lip*, 21–2. ADD 45J1 Michel Jeanningros, "Contribution à l'histoire de LIP 1867–1972 (hiver 1980)," 6.

16   Fred Lip, *Conter mes heures* (Paris, 1973), 91–2. After the war, Fred Lip did not mention his parents' fate in interviews, and his religion did not figure in accounts of his business or conflicts with his workforce. However, he did tell reporters of a painting by Jean Oberlé of his great grand-uncle Isaac David Lipmann, president of the Jewish consistory in Besançon, who offered a watch he had made in the name of the Jewish community of Besançon to Napoléon when the emperor visited Besançon. "Fred Lip: l'enfant terrible du patronat français," 29. *Le Télégramme de Franche-Comté*, March 16, 1968, 6. Vitoux, "Lip," 72. But Fred Lip was neither from "an old Jewish family from Franche-Comté," as he claimed, nor was he related to Isaac David Lipmann. The one time Fred Lip evoked anti-Semitism in France, it was through another's voice. He closed his memoir with an eleven-page letter from a friend containing a brief mention that he was exposed to criticism because he was the only Jewish owner among French watchmakers. "You are now charged with all the sins of Israel." Lip, *Conter*, 157.

17   ADD 45J105 Aimé Holtzer, "Lip SA, vu de l'intérieur, 1938–1968."

terms; it supported fixed charges without which other departments would run a deficit. Lip moved successfully into new markets like parts for semi-conductors and silicon coatings for IBM. Armaments sales to NATO and to France during the Algerian War provided close to 30 percent of the firm's revenue in the mid-1950s. Although only a small element of production, profits from this sector provided Fred Lip the funds to reestablish his firm as the preeminent name in French watches. In 1970, 75 percent of Lip's turnover was in watches with the remainder in armaments, precision mechanics, and machine-tools (made in a small factory in nearby Ornans). The symbiotic relationship between the different divisions was one basis of the company's prosperity.[18]

Fred Lipmann had gone to the United States to observe factory management in 1928, before beginning work in the firm, and he took pride in the soubriquet, "the French Ford of the watch"; he even adopted the American slogan, "Keep on smiling."[19] After the war Lip introduced aptitude tests to assign workers to posts, and established in-house job training for employees.[20] Charles Piaget dubbed Lip "paternalist and modern" when he began there in 1948, a place where the work week included one and a half hours of sport, but production was pushed.[21] That same year, Fred Lip claimed to have introduced assembly line production to watchmaking before Switzerland or the United States.[22] In 1962, the firm produced 600,000 watches, making it the seventh largest producer in the world.

Unlike other French watchmakers, Lip supported a renowned research staff which registered numerous patents. A diverse body of skilled workers and the vertical integration of watch-part production and watch assembly gave the Lip scientists a flexibility and an overview that helped make possible successes in research and the initial phases of implementation. Fred Lip was proud to present the first electronic watch made in France to General de Gaulle in 1952; in the 1960s, the firm

18 Although armaments remained the only profitable sector when the firm declared bankruptcy in 1973, the decline in arms sales took away this cushion for the watch industry around 1970. Évelyne Ternant, "L'affaiblissement du SPL horloger franc-comtois depuis le milieu des années 70: mythes et réalités historiques" in *Les Systèmes productifs dans l'Arc Jurassien. Acteurs, pratiques et territoires*, ed. Jean-Claude Daumas (Besançon, 2004), 124–5. On the mechanics workshop, see Auschitzky Coustans, *Lip*, 39.

19 Vitoux, "Lip," 65–6.

20 Cuénot, "Ouvriers," 1: 472. Edgar Hirschi, *Fred Lip Innovateur Social* (1990).

21 "Charles Piaget: un témoignage d'engagement syndical" (August 1999), at peuple-et-culture.org.

22 AMB 5Z13 Fred Lip to Directeur de la Banque de France (Besançon), April 1, 1967.

produced and marketed them. By the end of that decade, it was clear that the future of the watch lay in quartz technology, and Lip produced the first quartz watch in France in 1971.[23] However, since the vertical integration at Lip was on a much smaller scale than at other watch manufactories in the world, this limited the company's ability to take full advantage of these advances.[24]

This did not stop Fred Lip from embedding Lip in postwar consumer culture. In the words of a consultant in 1976, "The Lip brand is *tradition*, the strength of custom, seriousness; it is tied to *the family*, to childhood, to traditional values; it is *French*."[25] Lip was known as the First Communion watch—"for that great day a great brand," in the words of one of their advertisements. In 1949, Lip arranged with Radio Luxembourg (RTL) that the hour would be announced with the line, "RTL has chosen Lip to give you the exact time." The firm came to similar agreements with Radio Monte-Carlo and Europe 1. Lip also sponsored sporting events, including the Tour de France in 1959, for which it served as official timekeeper and promoted itself during the race with the slogan, "Lip, Lip, Lip, hurray!" In 1968, Lip collaborated with Omega to provide the timekeeping for the Winter Olympics in Grenoble.[26] In 1962, Fred Lip called upon the public relations firm Publicis to develop the firm's identity. Publicis assigned its rising star Claude Neuschwander to the account. Neuschwander built the Oscar-winning campaign around the slogan, "Fred Lip is infallible!" Fred Lip later defiantly explained to the president of the watch seller-jewelers' association that their sales depended on his image: if Lip stopped advertising, he warned him, "there will be no more Lip prestige, there will be no more Fred Lip."[27]

The factory complex on the rue des Chalets grew from 1,000 to 10,000 square meters, spread out over 167 workshops and offices in twenty-six buildings on both sides of the street. It was "a maze of corridors, of staircases and of rooms" that isolated workers, who could not leave their

23   Évelyne Ternant, "Le milieu horloger français face à la mutation de la montre à quartz: 1965–1975" in *De l'horlogerie aux microtechniques: 1965–1975: acts du colloque ... Besançon, 9–10 février 1995* (Besançon, 1996), 30–2.

24   Évelyne Ternant, "La Dynamique longue d'un système productif localisé: l'industrie de la montre en Franche-Comté." Thèse de doctorat, Université Pierre Mendès-France, 2004, 401–6.

25   ADD 1026W19 Bernard Julhiet Conseils, "Dossier Industriel CEH-Lip" (September 1976).

26   "Fred Lipmann: une page se tourne," *Le Bijoutier* (December 1996), 37. For a selection of print ads, see lip-blog.com.

27   AMB 5Z14 Fred Lip to F. Danielou, Président du Syndicat des HBJO, December 2, 1968.

workplace without permission.[28] Fred Lip's crowning achievement was to replace this hodge-podge in 1962 with a new 22,000 square meter factory with large glass windows, situated on the extensive lawns of a nine-hectare park in Palente, a quartier of Besançon and the site of a large housing development built in the 1950s. A decade after the move, 40 percent of the firm's employees lived in Palente. The firm provided free bus service for employees who did not live near the new factory. A large company restaurant—where Fred Lip assured that the same meal was served to all, from production workers and the clerical staff through the director—allowed the firm to introduce the continuous work day. All workers entered through a vestiary where they changed into their work clothes and then rushed to workshops through a 128-meter long aerial passerelle constructed to keep out dust and humidity.[29]

Fred Lip and his firm had troubled relationships with other watch companies and with the watch seller-jewelers who marketed Lip watches. While Lip continued to make most of the parts for its watches, it drew upon workshops in rural Haut-Doubs for watchcases, watchbands, and glass coverings.[30] However, this independence from much of the watch trade in Franche-Comté did not stop Fred Lip from condemning the makers of watch movements, the intermediaries between parts producers and producers of finished watches. About the time Lip moved to Palente, the makers of watch movements set up a cartel that used its control of the market to squeeze watch producers, most of whom lacked Lip's autonomy as a manufactory, forcing them to compete almost solely on price, rather than quality or new features. In an angry letter in January 1968, Fred Lip charged the cartel with having "no ambition but money" and of wanting only to "make the usual everyday little second-hands for watches." As the cartel would not use the profit that its control of the market gave it to encourage innovation, he concluded that the French watch trade would find itself unable to compete with developments elsewhere.[31]

---

28   Charles Piaget, "Les luttes de LIP de 1948 à 1983" [2005], at alencontre.org. AMB 7Z47 Gérard Falin, "Rapport de stage, août–septembre 1966." ADD 45J105 Holtzer, "Lip SA"

29   Association de Palente, *Palente au fil du temps. Du village à la cité* (Besançon, 2011), 253, 256. Cuénot, "Ouvriers," 1: 75. Françoise Dumayet, "22 femmes … à la chaîne," *Elle*, October 7, 1968, 109. "Fred Lipmann: une page se tourne," 37. François-Henri de Virieu, *Lip: 100.000 montres sans patron* (Paris, 1973), 234.

30   Jean-Marc Holz, "Crise, restructuration et adaptation du capital industriel à Besançon," *Revue géographique de l'est* 21 (1981): 65–80.

31   Daumas, "Le système productif localisé," 14–15.

Of a different nature were Fred Lip's conflicts with Kelton, a French firm bought by Timex, that opened a factory in Besançon a couple of years after he had set up operations in Palente. Kelton manufactured inexpensive watches which it sold in outlets ranging from tobacconists to department stores, rather than through a network of watch seller-jewelers. Kelton, which in 1971 made 1,500,000 watches—three times the production of Lip—challenged Lip's longstanding dominance of watch production in Besançon. Kelton, Fred Lip explained to the prefect and the mayor, was just a factory, not an enterprise with roots in Besançon like Lip. He raised questions about "the stability and the morality of the workforce" such an operation would attract, and added that "the big boss in New York" could wave his "magic wand" and "it is very possible that in two months, he moves his factory to Italy … to make a few cents more."[32]

Lip made several unsuccessful efforts to market less expensive watches, including a children's watch, the Minilip, in 1969, sold in department stores and intended to get young consumers to think of Lip when they became adults.[33] However, Fred Lip's primary tactic was to condemn Kelton timepieces to all who would listen as "a convenience-store watch," wholly American in nature, not French.[34] In 1967, he wrote General Pierre de Bénouville, director of *Jours de France*, "the gauge of women's fashion above all others," to say that readers are "deceived" when they see "with Dior and Givenchy, in *Jours de France*, tobacco shop watches on elegant people, in evening dresses or tuxedos": if the cultured clientèle of *Jours de France* is misled into buying Kelton watches, they will have it in for the magazine.[35] The next year, Fred Lip warned François Dalle, president of L'Oréal, that if Kelton was successful in marketing "junk under the fallacious name of 'watch,'" who knew what would be next? "In these conditions, it could perfectly well happen tomorrow that an enormous American firm, wishing to establish itself in the market, would sell distilled water with three drops of salt in it, saying that this lotion is a real hair care panacea."[36] In the company's annual report in 1968, Fred Lip

---

32   ADD 1026W8 Fred Lip to PD, March 28, 1966. AMB 5Z14 Fred Lip to Jean Minjoz, January 15, 1968. To top it all off, the go-between that Kelton used with French authorities had worked for the Comité d'Organisation de la Montre of the Vichy Regime. ADD 2377W180 Fred Lip to PD, May 10, 1967.

33   The Minilip was made in Switzerland by the Ébauches SA. AMB 5Z15 Fred Lip to Leo DuPasquier (Ébauches SA), March 17, 1969. Hervé Jannic, "Lip en veut pas perdre pied," *L'Expansion* 25 (December 1969): 76.

34   AMB 5Z14 Fred Lip to Gaston Cathiard, August 26, 1968.

35   AMB 5Z13 Fred Lip to Général Pierre de Bénouville, December 19, 1967.

36   AMB 5Z14 Fred Lip to François Dalle, March 14, 1968.

refused to "apologize and adopt modern sales methods."[37] He would not follow Kelton's lead and demean Lip watches by making them available in stationery shops, tobacconists or department stores. When Fred Lip decided to develop a campaign against Kelton, Claude Neuschwander of Publicis warned him against it and he was forced to go to another firm. In 1969, Lip placed ads with the slogan, "Some watches bought in stationery shops [*papeteries*] end up in the waste basket [*une corbeille à papiers*]." Kelton sued for slander. Fred Lip lost and had to pay 250,000 francs in damages.[38]

Although Lip stuck to the existing network of the (at its height) 8,000 watch seller-jewelers authorized to sell Lip watches, these small businessmen resented the conditions Lip imposed. Some of the firm's requirements were anodyne: all Lip sellers had to set watches to 10:10, so that the hands would be in the shape of a smile.[39] The real conflict came over Fred Lip's effort to convince the sellers that they too were menaced by Kelton and should share in the cost of promoting the Lip brand. In January 1968, he wrote to the president of the watchmakers' association, the Chambre Française de l'Horlogerie, that the French watch trade was "the republic of the past, with Daladier. Everything was going badly, Daladier accepted everything ... and you are Daladier."[40] Fred Lip was an ardent Gaullist—"When I speak of Him, I do not speak of God. It was and still is General de Gaulle"[41]—and in March 1968 he wrote to the publisher of the trade review, *La France horlogère*, that if Charles de Gaulle had not fought during the war, the Americans would have occupied France, and the French would not be free. Fred Lip was taking de Gaulle's place now in the struggle to defend the French against the new American invasion. The Americans may have liberated France in 1944, but "this is not a reason to let them occupy us through the tobacconists."[42]

The conflict with the watch seller-jewelers heated up when Lip turned to television advertising in 1969 in the face of competition from Kelton. Lip raised the cost at which the firm provided watches to watch seller-jewelers by 3 percent, without raising the price at which the watches could be sold. It put this 3 percent into what Fred Lip told the merchants was a "propaganda fund for watch seller-jewelers and for Lip," which

37   ADD 1026W3 Société anonyme d'horlogerie Lip. "Rapport annuel 1968," 10.
38   Interview with Neuschwander by Reid, June 7, 2013.
39   Jean-Claude Sensemat, *Comment j'ai sauvé LIP* (Paris, 2005), 103.
40   AMB 5Z14 Fred Lip to André Augé [January 1968].
41   Jannic, "Lip ne veut pas perdre pied," 70. Lip, *Conter*, 97.
42   AMB 5Z14 Fred Lip to Millot [March 1968].

Lip would use for television advertising that was intended to bring customers to their shops to buy Lip watches.[43] The watch seller-jewelers would get only 42 percent of the sale price versus the 45 or 50 percent they received when they sold other firms' watches. Fred Lip responded to complaints by saying that because of Lip's advertising, it took only eight minutes to sell a Lip watch, but twenty-two minutes for a watch made by any other firm.[44] The problem was compounded because Lip believed that its advertising brought customers to the shops of the watch seller-jewelers, who then used the opportunity to show other companies' watches to clients who had asked to see a Lip. In December 1968, Fred Lip found himself asking McCann Erickson to develop advertising to help consumers get over their "timidity" when they asked for a Lip watch and were offered another brand.[45]

In 1969, when the French were asked which watch brands they knew, more than 90 percent named Lip.[46] However, name recognition did not translate into increased sales following the move to Palente. Although watch production at Lip declined only slightly, competition from mass market watches reduced its share of the national market from 20 percent to 7 percent between 1962 and 1970. Lip remained a brand with a primarily French market; it exported less than 10 percent of its production. As Lip celebrated its 100th anniversary in 1967, it faced a set of commercial challenges in a new environment in which multinational firms were coming to play a dominant role. That year, after having been turned down by Timex, Fred Lip sold one-quarter of the firm to Ébauches SA, an element of the Swiss watch trust Allgemeine Schweizerische Uhrenindustrie Aktiengesellschaft (ASUAG), one of the largest watch firms in the world.[47] ASUAG (now Swatch) was a holding company which at the time

---

43   AMB 5Z14 Fred Lip to La Guilde des Orfèvres (Paris), November 23, 1968. Those who raised their sales of Lip watches 30 percent in 1969 would get this 3 percent back.

44   Minutes of the Lip board of directors, February 26, 1970, in BDIC F delta rés 578/40 CFDT-LIP, "Lip en lutte vous Informe …" [1973].

45   AMB 5Z14 Fred Lip to McCann Erikson (L.B. & A Tréard), December 18, 1968.

46   Jannic, "Lip ne veut pas perdre pied," 72.

47   In 1967, Ébauches SA signed an accord with Lip to eventually acquire a 52 percent share of Lip, but the French state initially set the limit at 25 percent. ACFDT 8H561 Ébauches SA, "Industrie horlogère européenne. Une expérience suisse. Ébauches SA-Lip 1967–1973," 12, 22. That year the Ministry for the Economy and Finance required that Lip use funds from the sale, and its facilities at Palente, to bring together a number of small, struggling watchmakers. However, Electra, this effort to make Lip the core of a project to aid the French watch industry, failed. Minutes of Lip board of directors, February 26, 1970, in BDIC F delta rés 578/40 CFDT-LIP, "Lip en Lutte Vous Informe …" [1973]. Auschitzky Coustans, Lip, 34–6.

of its acquisition of Lip—within a few years it exercised a controlling share—did two-thirds of its business in watch parts and one-third in watches like Longines. It was a marriage, in the words of *Le Figaro*, of a tightrope walker, Fred Lip, and a diplodocus, for Ébauches SA's irresolute, ponderous behavior at Lip would reveal "the same gigantism, the same slowness of response, the same unsuitability for evolution."[48] But Fred Lip denied that it was an objectionable arrangement. He said that he had seen de Gaulle, who told him he could sell to the Swiss, but not to the Americans.[49]

While analysts saw ASUAG as seeking an entry into the French market, Fred Lip framed the transaction as a (never realized) means for Lip to develop sales outside of France. He explained that around the world people thought favorably of Swiss watches, but spurned French watches because they did not think of France as a watchmaking nation, just as they would not want Turkish champagne or Brazilian perfume. Fred Lip's plan was to build a Lip factory in Switzerland and to penetrate foreign markets with watches marked "Lip-Genève," in the expectation that little by little they would then buy watches simply marked Lip and made in Besançon. In fact, he explained, no one would know if the "Lip-Genève" watches were made in Besançon or in Switzerland: "what is important, is the advertising of the brand."[50] Not surprisingly, the transaction further alienated Fred Lip from other French watchmakers. In 1967, in the Chambre Française de l'Horlogerie, partisans of a national solution to the watch industry's problems refused to consider collaborating with Fred Lip, whom they had never liked nor trusted. However, having excluded him from their plans, they then held it against him that he had brought the Swiss into his firm.[51]

The Employees

Who were Fred Lip's employees and how did they respond to his authoritarian paternalism? Although in 1913 one-third of the Lip workforce were Swiss immigrants, and five of the seven workers identified by the police as leaders of the strike in 1930 had been Swiss, the workforce after the war came largely from Franche-Comté, with very few foreign

---

48 *Le Figaro*, August 13, 1973, 3.
49 *L'Est républicain*, October 4, 1975.
50 *Le Télégramme de Franche-Comté*, March 16, 1968, 6.
51 de Virieu, *Lip*, 30–1.

workers.[52] From 200 employees after the war, Lip grew to 800 in 1952 and 1,427 in 1973 (110 of whom worked at the machine-tools factory in Ornans), including 691 workers (of whom 300 were unskilled OS), 269 technicians, 175 white-collar employees and office staff, seventy supervisors (*chefs d'équipe*), sixty-six managers, research scientists and engineers (*cadres*), thirty-four salesmen and twelve directors. The average age of an employee was thirty-one.[53] As working conditions and benefits were better than at comparable factories in Besançon, staff turnover was low. For one mechanic, the stability made it "practically the civil service of mechanics."[54] It was estimated in 1980 that half the Lip workers owned, were renovating or constructing an individual home.[55] Most workers were hired with the sponsorship of a relative or friend who worked at Lip. Some 200 Lip employees were married to another Lip employee. This contributed to the homogeneity and stability of the workforce, as well as to an insularity that cut Lip workers off from other workers in Besançon.[56] And in turn it led to a strong identity and pride shared by workers in all departments of the firm.

In the postwar penury, Fred Lip cemented his power by hiring from within current employees' families and by helping arrange housing. "Everyone," explained union leader Charles Piaget, "was indebted to him." Fred Lip visited the ateliers to talk with workers, and frequently hopped on his motorbike to see employees at their homes.[57] Many appreciated his generosity in settling cases involving individual workers, although they recognized that he used the employment of several members of a single family to put pressure on workers he saw as resisting his authority. Beginning in 1945, the firm distributed a monthly magazine to employees about the life of the firm, *Horizons nouveaux* (later renamed *InterLip*). In the workshops in Besançon and at Palente, Fred Lip installed loudspeakers in each workshop and office. This allowed him to speak to employees

---

52   Alain Gagnieux, *Etrangers de chez nous—L'immigration dans le Doubs et à Colombier-Fontaine (1850–1950)* (Besançon, 2008). Cuénot, "Ouvriers," 1: 259.

53   ADD 45J10 Commission Popularisation des travailleurs de Lip, "Dossier d'information," August 29, 1973, 3. The number of factory workers and office personnel at Palente was closer to 1,200.

54   AR Interview with Jacky Burtz by Rouaud, May 6, 2004, 10.

55   Dominique Bondu, "De l'usine à la communauté. L'Institution du lien social dans le monde de l'usine." Thèse de 3ème cycle, EHESS, 1981, 118

56   Jean Raguénès, *De Mai 68 à Lip. Un dominicain au coeur des luttes* (Paris, 2008), 137. AB Interview with Michel Garcin by Beurier (1992), 5.

57   A later example of Fred Lip's paternalism was his request to Noëlle Dartevelle, secretary of the works council, to find a child of a Lip employee whom he could support to pursue a college education. AMB 5Z14 Fred Lip to Noëlle Dartevelle, June 29, 1968.

every Friday afternoon. Periodically, he gathered all personnel from OS to engineers in the restaurant at Palente to convey news of the firm and its plans.[58] Piaget recognized that the unions at Lip learned from Fred Lip the importance of disseminating information and engaging with workers. He had, Piaget explained, "tried to create a big family, and in our opinion, he succeeded."[59]

The prefect of Doubs reported that when telephoning, Fred Lip was known to identify himself by saying, "God the father on the line."[60] However, in keeping with a paternalism that would not speak its name, Fred Lip asked workers not to call him *patron*.[61] In 1958, 10 percent of the firm's stock was in the hands of employees, primarily the senior staff, including salesmen for whom it was used as an incentive.[62] However, Fred Lip had no intention of sharing authority with his employees. He was proud of his relationship with them and like all autocrats mistrusted those who stood between him and his people. This could take the form of a faux populism: as workers were not allowed to smoke in the factory for security reasons, neither could managers.[63] However, what struck workers was Fred Lip's regal relationship with his "court" of ten or twelve directors, generally promoted from within rather than drawn from engineering school graduates. He would introduce them to visitors with the words "Here are my slaves …"[64] Employees circulated stories of Fred Lip's humiliation of the directors because they disliked them, but found direct opposition difficult.[65] They told the tale of Fred Lip hiding under the table before the directors arrived for a meeting—thinking he was late, they began speaking frankly about him. After a couple of minutes he popped up to chastise them.[66] Fred Lip expected his directors to be beholden to him. Each year he would take them to the mountains to

---

58   Thomas Lacoste, *Lip, une école de la lutte à l'usage des jeunes generations. Un film-entretien de Thomas Lacoste avec Charles Piaget* (L'Autre association, 2008). Catherine Chaillet and Pierre Laurent, *Besançon. Un temps d'avance* (Paris, 2007), 106.

59   Charles Piaget in Bernard Gauthier, *Lip. Le rêve et l'histoire* (Beau Comme Une Image, 2005). In support of Fred Lip's nomination to the Légion d'honneur, the state police reported that, in response to the request of the government, he made evident "financial sacrifices" for several years after the war so as to not lay off any personnel. ADD 1485W91 RG to PD, June 22, 1948. Lip was named chevalier in September 1948.

60   ADD 1026W8 PD, December 2, 1966.

61   Dumayet, "22 femmes … à la chaîne," 109.

62   "Fred Lip: l'enfant terrible du patronat français," 29–31.

63   Jannic, "Lip ne veut pas perdre pied," 73.

64   Gil Baillod, "Une longue histoire," *L'Impartiel*, May 14, 1973.

65   Interview with Bondu by Reid, June 20, 2011.

66   Fred Lip denied the story, saying that if he had wanted to know what they were saying he could have used hidden microphones. "Les Révélations de Fred Lip," 10.

ski for two weeks—he was an avid skier—and they were expected to ski when he skied, eat what he ate, etc. The workers claimed that after each of these trips, one director was fired.[67] In Maurice Clavel's novel, *Les Paroissiens de Palente*, Fred Lip appears as the "capitalist Caligula" who "had not made his horse a consul, but had reduced his consuls, his most important department heads, to the status of beasts of burden before the personnel, in order to humiliate them."[68] Sometimes, Fred Lip fired directors, gave them a handsome severance package, and then hired them back shortly afterwards. They were well remunerated for their servitude, but rarely lasted more than a year or two. The transience of the higher staff contrasted with the stability of the workforce, many of whom were career employees.[69] Subject to the whims and tyrannical abuse of Fred Lip, dishonored for accepting this in exchange for good pay, the directors abused workers in turn and forfeited the workers' respect.

Outsiders remarked on the particular relationship Fred Lip had with the workers. Jean Raguénès, who began work at Lip in June 1971, a few months after Fred Lip retired, remarked: "I was struck by the impact he had retained in the minds of the Lip personnel, of all inclinations. There was a little bit of fascination. In spite of himself, he must have inculcated something in the Lip personnel, the confrontational side, the independence, the imagination."[70] Jacques Chéréque, the secretary-general of the Fédération Générale de la Métallurgie of the CFDT (FGM-CFDT), to which the CFDT-Lip belonged, remarked on the "love/hate relations between the leaders of the local and the boss [Fred Lip]. They constantly insult one another, but they adore one another."[71]

About half of the factory workers and office personnel at Lip were women, and close to half of them were single, widowed, divorced, or unmarried mothers.[72] Seventy-seven per cent of the unskilled workers were female in 1972; women who were skilled (OP) or office staff were

---

67   "Fred Lip: L'enfant terrible du patronat français," 29–31. Interview with Jean-ningros by Reid, June 1, 2011.

68   Clavel, *Les Paroissiens de Palente*, 25.

69   ADD 1026W19 Bernard Julhiet Conseils, "Dossier Industriel CEH-Lip" (September 1976). However, dismissal by Lip was often the prelude to a very successful career elsewhere. De Virieu, *Lip*, 199–200.

70   *L'Est républicain*, June 27, 1993, 12.

71   Jacques Chéréque, *La Rage de faire* (Paris, 2007), 71.

72   Pauline Brangolo, "Les filles de Lip (1968–1981): trajectoires de salariées, mobilisations féminines et conflits sociaux." Mémoire, Université de Paris 1, 2015, 53. This is an excellent study, notable for its presentation of demographic and occupational data on women workers.

congregated in the lowest ranks.[73] Males dominated the positions as skilled workers, technicians and supervisory personnel. At one time, promotion had been based on qualifications attained on the job, but in the 1960s the firm moved to having workers take classes outside work hours and pass exams to move up the ranks. Most women had responsibility for their households and few were able to pursue this route; many held the same job and remained unskilled workers for twenty or more years. As Lip worker Alice Carpena put it, the many "female heads of family" could not get "a head of family position," precisely because they had responsibility for their family.[74] Men rarely stayed in a low job classification for so long, and some who did the same work as women had a higher rank and were therefore better paid.[75] In 1973, nine-tenths of the personnel with the title *chef* were male. The proportion of male to female technicians and foremen was in the range of 15 to 1.[76]

Older women who started work, or went back to work, when their children were of school age, or because they had divorced or become widows, were assigned to production where they made watch parts, working in heat and noise, driven by cadences, with their hands in oil all day.[77] Young women were assigned to the assembly lines, housed in a clean, air-conditioned shop. However, nowhere else in the factory were employees as tightly managed, with one supervisor for every twenty to thirty workers. For Piaget, "The first vision of the watch workshop was a shock: backs bowed over at the same angle, with the boss on a platform who was watching over his world in a total silence."[78] Supervisors pushed production, mixing threats with talk of bonuses, nurturing an environment of submission.[79] Some female OS—unskilled in the sense of specialized in doing just one operation—performed the same gesture 8,000 times a day: "you have the cadence embedded in you." They often developed eye problems. Each workstation had three light switches. At the end of the line the supervisor sat in front of a board that indicated which lights were on, as well as a counter that showed the production

73   This figure did not include workers at the machine tool plant at Ornans. *Lip au féminin*, supplement to *Combat socialiste* 16 (February 1975): 8

74   AM "Débat avec les femmes de LIP, LYON juin 1975."

75   Jeanne Z., non-unionized OS, in "Comment 'l'affaire' nous a changés," *Preuves* 16 (1973): 64–5.

76   Brangolo, "Les filles de Lip," 40–1.

77   Pascale Werner, "La Question des femmes dans la lutte des classes. L'Expérience Lip (Avril 73–Mars 74)," *Les Temps modernes* 336 (July 1974): 2446–8. *Lip au féminin*, 56.

78   *Libération*, April 29, 2000.

79   *Lip au féminin*, 10–11. Ravenel, "Un militant ouvrier autogestionnaire," 114–15.

of each worker. A worker lit the first light to indicate she was beginning work; the second when she needed a part or assistance, and the third when she had to absent herself and a worker was sent to take her place. Foremen prevented workers from speaking to one another.[80] Although their wages were among the lowest in the factory, women on the line developed a sense that they were "less worker" than the women making watch parts because they did not work in dirt and din. Classical music accompanied the movement of the line. The combination of the workers' pride in their status and close monitoring made the assembly line the site of the least resistance to management.[81]

As one employee said, it was not just a question of obeying managers, but "of pleasing as well in how one submitted to commands." Male managers used their position to pit female workers against one another, favoring some with better posts and humiliating others.[82] Women throughout the factory and offices, found that, in the words of a young office worker, "the bosses, confident in their power, 'flirted' with each new arrival." Female workers complained that sexual relationships were the only path to advancement.[83] Fatima Demougeot reported that

> The pressure to engage in unwanted sexual activity is horrible in women's workshops. A girl who goes out with the boss is well regarded and could get a better assignment. For the promotion of women, all depends on the boss: you please him or you don't. From this the beauty contests on the line, stories, jealousies, the division of women, allowing yet more exploitation.[84]

Others spoke of "women who put on makeup from A to Z, who spent an hour before the mirror in the lavatory, who passed before M. J ... with radiant smiles."[85]

---

80   Interview with Charles Piaget by Auguste Dubourg [1998] in *La Subversion démocratique* (Pantin, 2000), 310–11 [quoted]. Gérard Terrieux, "L'expérience Lip." Thèse de 3ème cycle, Université de Paris I, 1983, 105. BDIC F delta rés 578/36 "Débat entre les travailleurs de la Redoute et de Lip," November 10, 1973, 4.

81   "Quand les ouvriers se mêlent de tout," supplement to *Libération*, February 7, 1974, B [quoted]. Werner, "La Question des femmes," 2447–9.

82   *Lip au féminin*, 10–11, 49. However, Lip employee Monique Piton believed that no woman in the Lip conflict ever experienced sexual harassment or violence from male comrades. Monique Piton, "Lip de l'intérieur: 'Je suis de Doubs, j'ai participé à une lutte ouvrière qui a sécoué la France entière'" in *Les Affranchies: Franc-comtoises sans frontières*, ed. Nella Arambasin (Besançon, 2013), 216.

83   Bondu, "De l'usine à la communauté," 477 [quoted]. *L'Outil des travailleurs*, December 1973–January 1974, 11.

84   *Lip au féminin*, 57.

85   *L'Outil des travailleurs*, December 1973–January 1974, 11.

With limited access to the job-training classes, women had few chances for promotion. An OS could advance to the lowest rank of skilled worker, OP1 (*professionnel-maison*) by developing the skills to do several jobs performed by OS. Promotion achieved on the job was possible only for a worker whose supervisors arranged for her to work long enough at several posts to achieve competence at them. The manager in charge assessed the worker's proficiency. Those who pursued this track were considered to be beneficiaries of supervisors' favoritism and were consequently seen as dependent on them.[86] This was a constant source of friction, because an OP1 was better paid than an OS who did the same work. In any case, the rank of OP1 was not certified by a diploma, and the women who were promoted from within feared that this higher job status would not be recognized by other employers;[87] this was a factor for some male skilled workers as well, and would provide a further reason for workers to fight for the survival of Lip.[88] Sociologists who visited Lip in 1973 reported that many female workers, whether they worked on the line or in the production of watch parts, aspired to become office workers, a position they saw as an escape from the degradation they experienced on the job.[89] Very few ever made this transition, but it helps to explain the feeling of liberation female factory workers had when doing clerical work in the occupied factory.

The unions were male bastions and efforts to address the situation of the female unskilled workers were problematic. Union tracts spoke of the specific situation of the OS, but not of female workers.[90] In 1968 the unions won the right for female OS who were fifty-five and held the exhausting jobs on the presses producing watch parts to be transferred to other jobs. But this "turned into a fiasco" because although the women had complained of conditions on the presses, they had worked so long on them that they felt out of place elsewhere and returned to their former jobs. Piaget later recognized that this revealed "our major deficiency.

86   BDIC F delta rés 702/20/2 CESI, "Plan d'intervention pour le changement et le développement de la C.E.H. Enquête diagnostique janvier 1975-mai 1975," May 20, 1975, 11–12, 15. Vittot believed that promotion from OS to OP was done by "favoritism" 95 percent of the time. Terrieux, "L'Expérience Lip," 39.

87   Anne, an OP promoted from within, in Annick Le Floc'hmoan, "Chez Lip, les femmes," *Antoinette* 111 (October 1973): 42.

88   François B., non-unionized OP in "Comment 'l'affaire' nous a changés," 67.

89   Marie-France Cristofari, "Lip à Besançon et le mouvement des 'groupes femmes'" in *Travail et rapports sociaux de sexe*, eds. Xavier Dunezat, Jacqueline Heinen, Helena Hirsta, and Roland Pfefferkorn. (Paris, 2010), 189.

90   Interview with Demougeot by Reid, June 12, 2013.

The male delegates spoke for the women, thinking they were doing the right thing."[91]

But the unions had little success addressing the issue. Lacking training and experience, few women had the confidence to stand for election as delegates.[92] The CFDT-Lip's admirable practice of using the hours of paid work time allotted to delegates after May 1968 to engage with workers, while meeting outside work hours for union business, made the position particularly difficult for women workers with childcare responsibilities they could not pass off. The few women active in the unions understood that the male camaraderie which was a source of union strength worked to marginalize women. This made the union, in the CFDT-Lip member Monique Piton's words, "masculinized and a little disdainful of women."[93] Not surprisingly, when TF1 did a show and *Elle* an article on assembly line workers at Lip in October 1968, only two of twenty-two interviewed expressed any interest in unions.[94] Female workers at Lip were used to class and patriarchal oppression, and it would take the world-turned-upside-down of 1973 for them to challenge it.

The only female union leader at Lip before then, and the only union leader who made male managers' *droit du seigneur* an issue, was Noëlle Dartevelle of the CGT-Lip. Dartevelle came from a peasant family and had been active in the Jeunesse Agricole Chrétienne—"That's the basis of my activism"—until she was twenty-one, when she moved to Besançon and found employment at Lip.[95] A dedicated autodidact, she began as an OS1, the lowest rank, but worked her way up. For twenty years, she was on the works council of the firm and served as its secretary. Dartevelle was deeply admired by women at Lip across the political spectrum. OS Alice Carpena was not alone in recognizing that Dartevelle was "the only woman who dared to assert herself, to speak up ... I admired her guts."[96]

Dartevelle was known for speaking out against the sexual harassment of female employees. This, she told a leader of the rival CFDT-Lip, explained why she received votes in elections for the works council from

---

91   Daniella Chaillet, Marie-Odile Crabbé-Diawara and Jacques Fontaine, "Entretien avec Charles Piaget. 'Notre lutte, nos objectifs, c'est à nous seuls de les contrôler,'" *Contretemps* 22 (2014): 122

92   Maria-Antonietta Macciocchi, *De la France* (Paris, 1977), 429.

93   ADD 45J96 Notes manuscrites of Père Zinty, vicaire général, "Affaire Lip" [October 1973].

94   Dumayet, "22 femmes ... à la chaîne," 106–9.

95   Divo, *L'affaire Lip*, 57–8.

96   *Lip au féminin*, 49, 60.

women across the political spectrum, including female CFDT-Lip members.[97] Piton was not alone in preferring to speak with Dartevelle about personal and workplace issues, rather than with the leaders of her union. Emblematic were the events at a General Assembly of workers held in February 1973 to discuss the difficulties women workers were having getting their grievances about excessive production demands addressed. A few months earlier, the managers' union, the Confédération Générale des Cadres (CGC-Lip), had joined forces with the workers' unions to get its concerns addressed. However, when the CGC-Lip representative chimed in that "our charming companions have other arms to defend themselves," the Assembly, led by an infuriated Dartevelle, condemned him. Although the national CGT favored cooperation with the CGC as part of its effort to build the cross-class alliances necessary to win support for the Common Program in the legislative elections the following month, Dartevelle's defense of women took precedence at Palente and helped bring an end to this relationship of the CGC-Lip with the workers' unions at Lip.[98]

Charles Piaget and the CFDT-Lip

Charles Piaget was the CFDT-Lip leader who had spoken with Dartevelle. He believed her appeal to female workers at Lip came not from her efforts to counter sexual harassment, but from her role as secretary of the works council, involved in activities that engaged with important elements of the household economy for which women were responsible.[99] Piaget was the son of a Swiss watch worker who had moved to Besançon. His parents divorced and he was raised by his father and never knew his mother. In 1943, when Piaget was fifteen, his father died, and he was taken in by a family of naturalized Italian immigrants. Piaget graduated from the École nationale d'horlogerie to which Fred Lip had been sent, and was hired by Lip as a skilled mechanic. He was known for the exceptional quality of his work and the expectation that other workers should work just as well and as hard as he did.[100]

97   AB Interview with Dartevelle by Beurier (1992), 2, 4, 35. AR Interview with Piaget by Rouaud, May 5, 2004, 1.

98   Monique Piton, C'est possible! (Paris, 1975), 21–2, 145–6.

99   Tribune Socialiste, May 28, 1970, 7.

100   Interview with Piton in BDIC F delta rés 707/9(1) Fonds Michel Duyrat Bande UNCLA 3 Cahier no. 1.

Fred Lip had found resisters with Communist ties in the factory when he returned in 1944, but he got rid of the "superresistant delegates" over the next three years and had established firm control by the time Piaget began work in 1948.[101] Piaget identified himself as having been "egoistic" and "very individualist" at the time; in 1949 he was the sort who broke ranks by working overtime at the regular pay. However, he was transformed after experiencing the egoism of others on the shopfloor. He had hoped to learn from the experienced mechanics, but when he went to see them they would not share the tricks of the trade, covering their hands with a white rag and not saying a word. The skilled workers at the time sought to protect their pay and status. Piaget and the other young mechanics responded by keeping individual notebooks and writing down the problems they confronted on the job and how they handled them. The novices passed these notebooks among themselves, discussed their experiences and formed a group. When the company reduced a bonus that affected the young mechanics much more than the well-paid veterans, the latter did not react. Their junior colleagues talked over the situation and walked out. After two days, management asked to see two representatives of those on strike, and the workers chose Piaget as one of them. The company had a pressing order and the bonus was restored. The young mechanics who had worked together came from the Communist-led CGT and the Catholic Confédération Française des Travailleurs Chrétiens (CFTC), as well as the non-unionized. Such experiences were at the origin of the distinctive union culture which would develop later at Lip.

The CFTC and the CGT were very weak at Lip in the early 1950s and, in line with the policies of their national federations, frequently butted heads. When the watch workers in Besançon struck in 1950 for an increase in the cost-of-living allowance, the personnel director went through the workshops at Lip talking to individuals about loans, housing, and jobs for their sons. Participation in the strike was minimal and took the form of what Piaget termed a "strike by proxy," in which union representatives told workers to stay home while the union negotiated for them. Every morning, the unions held a public meeting for strikers, told them where things stood, and sent them home. The strike lasted ten days and ended with Lip mailing each worker a letter telling them to come to work and vote on the company's meager offer: "the return to work

---

101   "Lip: Charles Piaget et Monique Piton Racontent," November 16, 2013, at autogestion.asso.fr.

was a debacle." Only 5 percent of the workforce was unionized in the mid-1950s.[102]

Piaget joined the CFTC-Lip just to please his future brother-in-law. As the older, more skilled workers sought simply to protect their own situations, it was the younger skilled workers who ran for union office in the factory. Piaget himself had initially resisted taking this step because he too wanted to ascend the hierarchy and was afraid union activity would harm his prospects.[103] However, once he was elected personnel delegate in 1954, Piaget pursued the cooperation with the CGT-Lip that had characterized his work with other young workers. In the CFTC-Lip, Piaget rejected the union leaders' practice of meeting primarily among themselves, believing that this isolated them. He made a point of going to where the workers gathered, at breaks and at lunch and on the bus, and listening to what they had to say about work, talking with them and taking notes: "To listen. That was our secret, an open secret. Tell them: 'Speak among yourselves if you don't dare speak before everyone.'" He got other delegates to adopt this practice and they then met to put together demands and strategies that responded to workers' concerns. Their grievances became the basis for short leaflets, written without union jargon, that the CFTC-Lip and its successor in 1964, the CFDT-Lip, distributed to workers as they left the factory. Workers came to see that problems they had thought were particular to their workshop or office were in fact a widespread concern in the factory.[104]

In the late 1950s, Piaget used this understanding of shopfloor culture in successful confrontations with management, despite the low union membership at Lip. When he realized that the company was not including agreed-upon production bonuses in overtime pay, Piaget laid out the situation and then asked workers what they thought, whether they were union members or not. That a union would solicit the ideas of non-members was unheard of. The precision mechanic Raymond Burgy remembered, "I was astounded, so I got my union card!"[105] The CFTC-

102   Good accounts by Piaget of these years include Piaget, "Les luttes de LIP." Lacoste, *Lip, une école de la lutte.* AR Interview with Piaget by Rouaud, September 11, 2003, 3–7, 16, 33. Réseau Citoyens Résistants, *La Force du collectif. Entretien avec Charles Piaget* (Paris, 2012), 10, 40–1.

103   Interview with Piaget by Dominique Féret, "A voix nue," France Culture (2011), at franceculture.fr.

104   Ravenel, "Un militant ouvrier autogestionnaire," 114–15. Chaillet and Laurent, *Besançon,* 106–7 [quoted]. Archives Piaget, Charles Piaget and Raymond Burgy, "LIP. L'avant 1973 ... La construction d'une force des travailleurs ... Vers l'autogestion ..." [November 2007].

105   Pierre Thomé, *Créateurs d'utopies* (Paris, 2011), 185.

Lip put out a leaflet showing that the company was not following the law, and the state labor inspector agreed with the union's analysis. The firm was forced to pay every worker a year of missing bonuses. That Fred Lip had been shown to be acting illegally and had been forced to make restitution was a shock to the autocratic culture of the firm.

Management fostered numerous individual arrangements to make workers feel that they were recipients of special treatment. Workers hid their pay slips from one another. To counter this effort to divide them, thirty mechanics from all ranks agreed to share their pay slips with the individual names crossed out. Using these, the CFTC-Lip put together a leaflet pointing out inconsistencies and inequalities. Workers could see that there was favoritism and numerous blatant injustices in the way pay was determined. In Piaget's words, "Individualism turns against the boss." However, it was collective action that gave workers the power to address individual injustices. The firm was forced to establish and make known common criteria for the determination of mechanics' wages. The union then applied this tactic to other areas of the factory and the management ended up making the pay range for each category of worker public for the first time.[106]

Piaget came from the mechanics workshop that produced a disproportionate number of CFDT-Lip delegates; the management referred to it as "the Latin Quarter."[107] It was a place where workers displayed self-respect and control of their workplace, evidenced by their reading leaflets at their machines before starting work, and stopping work five minutes early to wash their hands—this in a factory where each minute late was multiplied by five. During the conflict in 1973, the CFDT-Lip sought to determine why most of its leaders were mechanics. It realized that work in the mechanics workshop required workers to move about and talk to one another in order to complete jobs involving work on several machines. This, they concluded, made the mechanics more accustomed to working collectively than were the women bound to their place on an assembly line or the men and women hunched over a single machine making watch parts.[108] The mechanic Roland Vittot remarked that, whether due to his diverse skills or because he was a CFDT-Lip delegate, he was moved to seventeen different workshops over twenty-three

---

106   AR Interview with Piaget by Rouaud, September 11, 2003, 15. Lacoste, *Lip, une école de la lutte*. Archives Piaget, Piaget and Burgy, "LIP. L'avant 1973 …," 5.

107   Charles Piaget, *Lip. Charles Piaget et les Lip racontent* (Paris, 1973), 170.

108   Werner, "La Question des femmes," 2449–50. Réseau Citoyens Résistants, *La Force*, 18; Terrieux, "L'Expérience Lip," 36.

years: "They needed a fitter, but didn't need a delegate."[109] In his case, this effort to put a check on a union leader ironically enabled him to build up his network of contacts within the factory.

When operations moved to Palente, the CFTC-Lip acquired a detailed map of the new factory and constructed a scale model of it so that they could be sure they had a "correspondent" in every work area. Many of these remained clandestine out of fear of Fred Lip, but they provided information to the union that served as the basis for analyses of what was going on throughout the factory.[110] Fred Lip in turn sought to use the move to Palente to assert control in the precision mechanics workshop. In 1963, he got rid of the many individual machines used to prepare the tools used in making watches. He replaced them with large all-purpose machines and, assigning mechanics to make-work jobs, brought in a complete new team of employees, from secretary to engineer, to set them up. The operation was a fiasco; after a few months the firm sold the new machines and sought out the original equipment wherever it could be found. The mechanics returned to their work.[111]

Stymied in this effort to get union leaders to leave, Fred Lip pursued another strategy. He promoted them to supervisory positions—from the "first" to the "second" collège, to use the legal categories; engineers and managers, the cadres, were in the third collège—in the expectation that this would change their allegiances. Most prominent was Piaget, who was made a supervisor and put in charge of his workshop. Piaget spoke of himself as someone who might well have become a cadre in a different situation, but he never wavered in his desire to work for the union.[112] He got union approval to take up the new post and became the first Lip employee to be a shop supervisor and union delegate at the same time.[113] These efforts to align union leaders with the company well-being may have made them more attuned to the interests of the enterprise and not solely those of its proprietors.

Fred Lip was more successful in exercising control over the unskilled workers through extension of the use of piece rates in line with earlier practices at Lip. First-generation workers from the countryside were willing to accept the increased production pace that could raise wages by

---

109   AB Interview with Vittot by Beurier (1992), 2.
110   Piaget, "Les luttes de LIP." Lacoste, *Lip, une école de la lutte.*
111   Piaget and Vittot, "LIP," 277.
112   France Culture, "Nous les Lip," November 22, 2003.
113   Ravenel, "Un militant ouvrier autogestionnaire," 115. In an indirect critique of the CFDT-Lip leadership, *L'Humanité* later remarked that two CGT-Lip militants had refused such promotions. *L'Humanité*, August 6, 1973, 3.

10 to 15 percent, though it also created new opportunities for supervisors to pit workers against one another.[114] The system shaped the outlook of the unskilled labor force, making it initially resistant to union organization. When workers had been paid by the hour, allowance had been made for technical problems that impeded production. However, with piece rates, dealing with such situations became the workers' responsibility as though they were subcontractors. If parts were defective and this slowed down production or forced work to be redone, the workers suffered the consequences. As pay was also based on the quality of production—runs that did not require a controller to check them saved the firm money—this increased the stress on the OS.[115]

Job security was another sore point for the unskilled workers in particular. Piaget estimated that Fred Lip went through one production director every twenty months. In 1967, he dismissed a director whom the cadres liked because he treated them with respect. They struck for the first time and asked the workers to join them. The workers themselves had a longstanding grievance about Lip's practice of hiring in July to step up production for Christmas sales and then letting workers go in January.[116] Faced with 110 layoffs, workers led by CFDT-Lip and CGT-Lip joined the cadres and shut the factory down for three days. Piaget made a point of telling striking workers not to go home but to stay in the street in front of the factory, remain informed about the strike, and discuss it among themselves. Although Lip did not take the director back, the firm instituted provisions to reduce seasonal turnover.

This strike marked a significant change at Lip. Union strength when workers walked out was at a nadir. During what Vittot refers to as a "no man's land," the CFTC-Lip had gone from 250 members in 1960 to thirty in the CFDT-Lip in 1967.[117] Before 1967, managers and workers had never cooperated. Furthermore, until then, workers had seen layoffs as inexorable, not believing they could do anything about them. That forty workers still lost their jobs deeply affected the workforce. What

---

114   Jacques Roy, "Lip 1973: l'entreprise transformée," *Que Faire Aujourd'hui?* 22 (1982): 21. Fatima Demougeot in *Lip au féminin*, 10.

115   "Lip des militants du comité d'action parlent," supplement to *Revolution!* 35 (1973): 27–8. AB Interview with Dartevelle by Beurier (1992), 64–5. Interview with Piaget in Dubourg, *La Subversion*, 310.

116   Workers compared their frequent reductions in hours and layoffs to the severance pay given to the managers regularly fired by Fred Lip. ADD 1812W34 *Cité Fraternelle* [the diocesan weekly], December 20, 1963.

117   *Tribune socialiste*, June 1978, 6–7. Piaget, *Lip. Charles Piaget et les Lip racontent*, 127.

had been seen as a problem for those dismissed became the concern of all and led to a resolution that there should be no layoffs in future.[118] The unions infuriated Fred Lip by gathering information about the economic situation of the company from workers, both unionized and non-unionized, as well as from supervisors and even some managers, to make their case.

The Works Council

The preamble of the 1946 constitution of the Fourth Republic stipulated that "all workers participate, through the intermediary of their delegates, in the management of enterprises." Every large firm had to have a works council (*comité d'entreprise*) composed of union delegates and representatives elected by employees, presided over by the director of the firm. The works council had to be informed and consulted on all questions concerning the operation of the business, and in particular those affecting employment and working conditions.[119] The works council was in part a response to employees' takeover and operation of a number of enterprises after the Liberation, but in its early years the Lip works council had a different agenda. It did things like send letters of reprimand to women workers who refused supplemental work on Saturdays.[120] During the decades before 1968, the works council at Lip served primarily to fund and manage a diversity of social works such as buying coal and foodstuffs wholesale to sell to employees, negotiating with summer camps for employees' children, and selecting Christmas gifts for them.[121] However, after the strike in 1967, the works council turned to examining the economic situation of the company. Although the CGT-Lip was reticent about engaging in such activities, believing that dealing with the capitalist system should be left to capitalists, within a few years the CFDT-Lip had ten militants taking economics courses at the Bureau d'étude économique inter-syndicale de Franche-Comté.[122]

---

118   BDIC KA 214 1 *Les Cahiers de mai* interview with Piaget [1973].
119   "Lip, les faits et le droit" in *Universalia* (Paris, 1974), 383.
120   Piaget, "Les luttes de LIP." Lacoste, *Lip, une école de la lutte.*
121   Piaget and Vittot, "LIP," 276.
122   Ibid., 276–7. *Politique hebdo*, December 20, 1973, 16. "Bande son du film *Non au démantèlement! Non aux licenciements!*" in Saoura Cassou, "Lip, La Construction d'un mythe." Mémoire, Université de Paris I, 2002, 192–3. AMB 5Z221 CFDT, "Le Dossier du comité d'entreprise LIP," 1973.

Confrontations between the works council and management over the provision of information would become an important element of conflicts at Lip after 1968. In the late 1960s, the new left championed worker control of production as a socialist alternative to a union strategy limited to the fight for higher wages. At Lip, however, workers' concern over the future of the firm led the CFDT-Lip to places where unions had rarely gone before, as they demanded that workers be kept fully aware of the financial state of the enterprise and that their voices be heard and their interests recognized in the owners' deliberations. If self-management was an ideology developed in an economy of full employment, the Lip workers' efforts to have a major role in decisions concerning their livelihood would make this the radical alternative during the national recession of the 1970s.

Political Choices

In the 1950s, the CFTC-Lip was governed by the decisions of its members rather than fealty to the national organization. It held weekly meetings with the CGT-Lip and the two locals prepared together for their monthly meetings with management. They established a good working relationship, despite the heated conflicts between the national confederations. This accord was only strengthened when the CFTC-Lip rejected the company's offer to negotiate and sign accords with it alone. In 1959, the CGT took note of the cooperative relationship of the unions at Lip and invited Piaget to Moscow, an offer the CFTC-Lip voted to accept. However, the regional CFTC leadership said he should not go. The CFTC-Lip resisted and the CFTC metalworkers' federation convoked "a kind of disciplinary council" to reiterate that Piaget should reject the invitation. Despite this, he followed the mandate of his own local and made the trip to the Soviet Union. On his return, the CGT asked Piaget to go on a speaking tour it had arranged, but when he told them what he planned to say, the confederation withdrew its offer. A few years later, the CFTC-Lip wrote to protest when the secretary-general of the CFTC, Eugène Descamps, attended a reception held by the American general in command of NATO.[123]

Such experiences opened Lip militants up to the ways in which new

---

123   Piaget, "Les luttes de LIP." AR Interview with Piaget by Rouaud, September 11, 2003, 7, 12.

causes might relate to their own. Emblematic of the roots of the long 1968 a decade earlier was Piaget's attendance at a talk by the radical Catholic opponent of the Algerian War and *Témoignage chrétien* editor, Robert Barrat. The meeting was banned and had to be held in a barn. Piaget was taken with Barrat's exposition of an "employers' colonialism," which Piaget felt he knew at Lip: "We quickly came to feel that the Algerians' problems were also our problems." In a discussion with comrades in the Action Catholique Ouvrière (ACO) about causes to which Christians should devote themselves, he decided that "the most disadvantaged at that time were the Algerians, struggling for 'their dignity.'"[124] This led him to the Union de la Gauche Socialiste and from there to the Parti Socialiste Unifié (PSU), the core of the new left in France which became the party of the CFDT-Lip leadership.

Catholic Workers' Actions

Franche-Comté had a relatively high level of Catholic religious observance. In 1962, in the diocese of Besançon, 35 percent went to mass weekly and 45 percent at Easter.[125] This strongly marked the Lip workers' social and political culture. Jeannine Pierre-Émile first heard Charles Piaget when she worked as an OS assembling watches at another firm, before coming to work at Lip. He came to call on workers to strike in May 1968: Piaget spoke "a Christian language as I conceived it in 'the ideal' ... putting into acts religion as I thought of it."[126] Jean Raguénès, the Dominican priest who worked at Lip, explained in 1973: "Here, it is a little a workshop of priests. Everyone follows Piaget because he resembles a priest."[127] He added that during the conflict of that year, the Lip workers formed "a parish similar to those that must have existed in the early days of Christianity."[128]

The leaders of the CFTC-Lip and then the CFDT-Lip were practicing Catholics. Most were active in one or another of the twenty ACO groups in Besançon. Piaget was a longtime member of an ACO group in his

---

124   *Témoignage chrétien*, August 30, 1973, 6. Ravenel, "Un militant ouvrier auto-gestionnaire," 114. AR Interview with Piaget by Rouaud, September 11, 2003, 13.

125   Pelletier, *La crise catholique*, 271.

126   Daniel Jacquin, "Lip 1973–1981 (Analyse sociologique)." Thèse de 3ème cycle, EHESS, 1982, 176.

127   *Le Point*, August 6, 1973, 20.

128   *Le Nouvel observateur*, July 30, 1973, 30.

neighborhood as well as another at Lip.[129] In monthly meetings, an ACO group brought together its ten or so members to discuss issues of public concern and develop responses to them in light of the Gospel. Although the CFDT-Lip had many more ACO members, members of the CGT-Lip participated as well, turning certain groups into sites where the union cooperation particular to Lip could be developed. A priest who worked with the ACO in Besançon commented that the presence of members of both unions "helped us a lot in not making absolute an analysis or an ideology, and the grouping was better achieved."[130] Several of the women workers most active in 1973 were active ACO members, as were the wives of a number of the union leaders.[131]

Future CFDT-Lip militant Burgy had returned from the Algerian war "completely bewildered," with a need to speak and act. He found a place he could do so in the ACO. Fellow CFDT-Lip leader Vittot explained that he came from a countryside marked by numerous strong prejudices: "It was the ACO that taught me the acceptance of the other, tolerance … My need to be a militant with passion came from the ACO."[132] At the height of the conflict in 1973, Piaget explained that the ACO "is a movement that leads you to ask questions of yourself. For six months, this has been crucial in helping us to never take ourselves for chiefs, for stars."[133] Union leaders drew on practices developed in the ACO, with its imperative to "see, judge, act"—to consider an issue raised by a member, judge it with reference to Christ's teaching and example, and decide what action to take. Collective discussion led to collective action. These reflective practices, "reviews of life," gave workers the tools to question the social order and defend alternatives to it.[134] ACO members developed an ethos that provided the basis for a participatory democratic culture at Lip. During ACO meetings, Piaget came to understand

> how important it was to respect others and to say to oneself, 'There, he said something that I think isn't good; but I am not going to say it like that; I am going to say to him "Listen, yes, you have an idea there. Perhaps we should go more deeply into that together so we can see."'

---

129   Charles Piaget, "L'ACO, une pratique de vie," *Oxygene* 17 (June 2000): 18.

130   Michel Droz-Vincent, "Lip," *Masses ouvrières* 313 (October 1974): 53.

131   Interview with Vittot by Reid, June 3, 2011. Piaget and Vittot, "LIP," 277.

132   Thomé, *Créateurs d'utopies*, 183, 184.

133   *Le Monde*, October 31, 1973 [quoted]. Droz-Vincent, "Lip," 47. Dominique Féret, *Les Yeux rouges* (Besançon, 1998), 75.

134   Divo, *L'affaire Lip*, 75–6, 102.

With experience, one perceives that sometimes there are a few problems. But don't say, as I've seen so many times, whether it is CGT or CFDT militants, 'You don't get it. The union fight isn't like that!'[135]

Success came from getting workers engaged and nurturing their ability and confidence to challenge those in charge. The ACO, Piaget explained: "reminds us that our objective is to get others involved. That they themselves take in hand their own affairs. In each man, there is a capacity to develop. The problem is to awaken it. What good will it do? If it is different from us, we must accept it; if it supplants us, that too: that is its value."[136] "Unions," said Piaget, "must be there to gather the experiences of workers' struggles, capitalize on them, analyze them, but certainly not to direct them!"[137]

Piaget practiced a particular form of leadership. He wrote the unsigned CFDT-Lip tracts, and was admired for his success at presenting a synthesis of discussions in the local, rather than necessarily what he thought best.[138] Clavel captured this element of Piaget's direction: "What is admirable in Piaget is that he is a sort of mediator between each and every one. He is the inspirer, the organizer, and has authority only because he returns to each a little of what he received from him."[139] Clavel evoked "the phrase of Mao, who 'collectivizes Socrates': 'Politics is the art of teaching clearly to the masses what they themselves teach us confusedly.' It's a collective existential maieutics."[140]

Throughout the conflict, participants spoke in terms of egoism and collectivity. CFDT-Lip militant Marc Géhin used the language of the struggle when he said, "There is something I lost in the conflict, my egoism."[141] One non-unionized worker said of Piaget that he had "a rare quality: he thinks only of others."[142] In the occupied factory, Piaget swept

---

135   AR Interview with Piaget by Rouaud, December 2, 2003, 17.

136   Jean-Pierre Barou, *Gilda je t'aime, à bas le travail!* (Paris, 1975), 216.

137   Thomé, *Créateurs d'utopies*, 193.

138   Raymond Burgy, cited in Thomas Champeau, "Lip: Le Conflit et l'affaire (1973)." Mémoire, EHESS, 2007, 12–13.

139   *Libération*, May 25, 1974, 2.

140   *Le Monde*, June 12, 1974, 21.

141   Piaget, *Lip. Charles Piaget et les Lip racontent*, 171. Asked what he feared losing with the end of the conflict, an OS responded in these terms as well: "Until now, I led quite an egotistical life; the conflict led me to join the struggle with the others, but would I have the courage? Egoism always remains a little latent." Claude Goure, "'Conversation avec des 'petits lip,'" *Panorama aujourd'hui*, November 1, 1973, 22. For other discussions of egoism, see Piton in *L'Outil des travailleurs*, February 1974, 10; and Vittot, "La longue marche des Lip!," 8.

142   "Comment 'l'affaire' nous a changés," 63, 65.

the courtyard most days, picked up the trash and re-taped posters that were coming off. Reflecting on this, one worker explained: "In the structural struggle of society, each has a place: the one who thinks, the one who puts up posters, the one who picks up trash … Piaget, it's amazing to see how he would cover the scale from top to bottom. There wasn't a distinction between the brains and the guys who were working."[143] For Piaget, it is "the inner history of everyone, torn between belief in the collective and fending for themselves." He had no doubt that "a wage earner will never spontaneously choose the collective."[144] This is why the struggle itself was so important for him and why it was crucial to keep workers engaged. Piaget's years in the ACO gave him the tools to do so.

In 1964, a large majority of the CFTC, including the CFTC-Lip, set aside its formal relationship to the Catholic Church and reformed as the Confédération française démocratique du travail (CFDT). The new organization spoke of its democratic, decentralizing project of self-management in which economic planning responds to human needs and the means to meet them are decided by the producers. This allowed the CFDT to make the CFTC values of humanism, community, and responsibility its own, while affirming its differentiation from the CGT project of effecting change through state action. At Lip, the transition from CFTC to CFDT saw a shift in how the hours allotted to workers' representatives were used—moving away from the social projects of the works council and even more clearly toward meeting workers at work in order to explore their grievances and how to address them.[145] Such direct engagement formed the core of CFDT-Lip action.

Conclusion

Contemporaries thought Fred Lip eccentric, but his firm was a pioneer in production and research, as well as in the development and defense of a brand name. It was in this environment—based on the projects of a family firm, rooted in its place of birth—that the Lip workers would cultivate a social imagination, develop new forms and styles of communication to engage the citizen-consumers of France, foster the brand

---

143   Michel Rocard, "Postface" to Piaget, *Lip. Charles Piaget et les Lip racontent*, 181–2.

144   Réseau Citoyens Résistants, *La Force*, 11.

145   ADD 45J102 "Militant chez Lip, Roland Vittot répond à nos questions," *Retraité Actif* 36 (December 2014): 9.

name of their struggle and control of what was said in its name, and fight to protect the factory at Palente that they saw themselves inheriting. Communists attributed "the reformist self-management current" they saw in Lip to the "little privileges" accorded by Fred Lip. But the self-management of which the CFDT spoke required a commitment by workers to their place of work, and it was this that both the subjugated female unskilled workers and the male skilled workers took from Fred Lip.[146] They also inherited his conflicts with the watch industry in Franche-Comté and with the watch seller-jewelers. His relations to national business organizations were of a piece with the CFTC-Lip/CFDT-Lip's acts of independence in dealing with the national union confederations. As Dominique Bondu, who worked at Lip for a decade during the struggle, remarked: "It is because there had been a big boss [*grand patron*], that there was, I believe, a big movement."[147]

This was the context in which Catholic organizations gave the Lip workers and their leaders the means to think and dream and organize in terms that were neither capitalist nor orthodox Communist. And, as Piaget recognized in conversation with local Communist leaders (after he himself had broken with the Church), workers led by the CFDT-Lip with their "halo of Christians" could take radical actions without immediately attracting the forces of repression the CGT would have for engaging in the same acts.[148] The CFTC-Lip and the CFDT-Lip were both stronger in relation to the CGT-Lip than was the case in most French factories, and they were more successful in cooperating with the CGT-Lip than the national confederations were with one another.

Piaget saw a special role for workers in the fulfilment of a humanism consonant with what he took from left Catholic political culture: "We, the workers, we are bearers of another society that will be made for man."[149] For him, in engaging in struggles like that at Lip, "we get back to what God wanted: the complete fulfillment of the person. At Lip, we really felt this. Certainly, we could not go far enough, but we glimpsed the prefiguration of such a society … We discover the 'collective', men among men, capable of opening up, of turning toward something other than egoism."[150] This humanist project, initially expressed with reference

---

146   Yann Le Masson and Paul Seban, "La question du Parti, et quelques autres," *Cinéma Militant* 5/6 (March–April 1976): 176.

147   Linhart, *Volontaires pour l'usine*, 198.

148   ADD 177J13 Transcript of a discussion between Lip leadership and local PCF leaders at Palente [1977].

149   *Le Monde*, September 18, 1973, 40.

150   *Témoignage chrétien*, February 7, 1974, 6.

to religion, would provide Lip employees in and out of the unions with a shared language of liberation to counter the resignation and egoism that factory closings usually elicited with an assertion of the collectivity as both the means to respond to economic fatalism and a manifestation of solidarity to be defended in itself. Equally important was the experience of union leaders in Catholic organizations, where they learned to value discussion and self-analysis; these became the bases of a particularly successful union culture at Lip. Vittot came to believe more, he explained, but to go to Sunday mass less since it meant sitting with bosses for whom Christian values had no place in their professional lives.

> The faith in Jesus Christ requires that we never stop fighting for truth and justice, whatever the cost. This excludes certain concessions, certain compromises, all the 'gimmicks'. Thus our faith marks our struggle and the way we conduct it … We sought to have decisions taken by the greatest number … after wide-ranging discussions in which all can express their views. And in our local there is no official to run things. We are all co-responsible. We feel this is a Christian value.[151]

When *les Lip* met and acted together, they came to feel that another world was possible.

---

151   The speaker is not identified, but is Vittot. Aimé Savard, "LIP: les chrétiens partagés entre leur sens de l'absolu et le souci du réalisme," *Informations catholiques internationales* 443 (November 1, 1973): 2.

2
The Serpent

"What got us going," said CGT-Lip leader Noëlle Dartevelle, "was to see all those students marching: it was huge."[1] On May 13, 1968 the national union confederations called a one-day general strike to protest the brutality of the Compagnies Républicaines de Sécurité (CRS) in their repression of student demonstrations. This triggered wildcat factory occupations across France, though not at Lip, where the employees went back to work. The CGT scrambled to assert leadership. The morning of Monday May 20, 1968, bruisers from the CGT in Besançon (CGT-UL) showed up with cudgels and pick handles and blocked the entrance to Palente, saying there was a strike, so no one could enter. They were following instructions from the national confederation and had not informed the CGT-Lip that they were coming.

However, the unions at Lip saw things differently. The previous Saturday, CFDT-Lip leaders had met all day to discuss the situation. The next day, they contacted the CGT-Lip and the two unions agreed on a plan of action. On the morning of May 20, the CFDT-Lip and CGT-Lip leaders told the CGT-UL that it was up to workers to "reflect together."[2] The unions directed all workers as they arrived, not just those in unions, to enter the factory and meet in the company restaurant. A delegate from each union addressed the General Assembly, making clear that if the workers voted to strike, they were agreeing that all would participate in daily meetings and in the organization of every facet of the strike:

---

1   Jean-Baptiste Quiot, "'Mai 68 m'a ouvert les yeux," *Politis*, July 26, 2007, 27.
2   BDIC KA 214 1 *Les Cahiers de mai* interview with Piaget [1973].

this was "the end of the strike as it had been done up to now, when one went fishing," in the words of CFDT-Lip militants, reiterating their goal in the strike at Lip the year before.[3] Furthermore, when it came to a vote being held on whether to accept or reject a settlement, each worker should be prepared to assess the situation and not simply follow their leaders. The union delegates then passed around a portable microphone, but with managers present no workers would speak. The CFDT-Lip had anticipated this and responded by calling a forty-five-minute break to allow the workers to meet in groups of five or ten in their workshops and offices, in hallways and on the lawn, without the managers present. Union delegates circulated, intervening only to provide information when asked. When the workers reconvened, they discussed the situation for two hours. "The guys from the CGT[-UL] behind the gates, outside," Piaget recalled, "did not stop shouting 'hurry up, what's going on?'" When the workers decided they were ready, they voted overwhelmingly by a show of hands to strike and occupy the factory. Those who did not support the strike were not booed, and one of the Assembly's first decisions was that no one would be criticized for voicing opposition to the strike and that opponents would be allowed to enter the factory and be given the opportunity to speak to strikers. The workers went on strike not because the union had told them to, but following, in Piaget's words, "a whole series of reflections."[4] The key to this and succeeding movements at Lip was the belief that strength came not solely from a handful of gifted leaders and a disciplined workforce, but from the engagement of the collectivity of individual workers who saw that their views had been solicited and heard.[5]

Hoping to engage in preemptive talks, Fred Lip had shown up when the CFDT-Lip began to distribute handouts early on the morning of May 20. He told the union delegates to come to his office in order to negotiate. They declined, saying the workers would decide what they would

---

3   *Le Monde libertaire*, February 16, 1978, 8.

4   Piaget, *Lip. Charles Piaget et les Lip racontent*, 130. *Il était une fois la révolution* (Paris, 1974), 22. Roland Vittot, "La longue marche des Lip!," *Notre combat* 191 (December 1977–January 1978): 7. *Lip Unité*, Second Trimester 1983, 8. Ravenel, "Un militant ouvrier autogestionnaire, 114. Piaget, "Les luttes de LIP." "On n'imagine pas tout ce que 68 peut faire pour nous!," *École émancipée* numéro spécial (May 2008), 14. Piaget and Vittot, "LIP," 285. Thomas Zurbach, "1968: le Mai des travailleurs à Besançon." Mémoire, Université de Franche-Comté, 2002, annexe 5. AB Interview with Piaget by Beurier (1992), 28; AR Interview with Piaget by Rouaud, September 11, 2003, 17–19.

5   Piaget in Stéphane Paris and Jean-Louis Genest, "Ce que démontre Lip," *Les idées en mouvement* 147 (March 2007): 19.

do.[6] However, if he had a leaflet to circulate as well, Piaget added, he was welcome to give it out. The General Assembly voted to allow Fred Lip to go to his office, as long as he did not interfere with the strike. Later that day, Fred Lip wrote the company board of directors, "I'm not afraid. Courage consists of being in one's factory, not letting it be occupied, and defending it in person."[7] Armed with a semi-automatic pistol that he told his managers he was ready to use, he sought to block worker access to certain offices; each case was negotiated with a strike committee composed of unionized and non-unionized workers.[8] In Dartevelle's words, "Speaking as equals with hierarchical superiors made the movement of May '68 blossom."[9] The strike committee allowed a group of directors and secretarial and security staff to join Fred Lip in the factory as long as they stayed in agreed-upon areas. Fred Lip explained to the president of the Ébauches SA that it was the occupiers who had been limited to certain parts of the factory in "a *gentlemen's agreement*, if one can believe that the Lip management and the strikers were gentlemen."[10] For Fred Lip, May 1968 was, in Piaget's words, clearly "a world turned upside down." He called Piaget and Dartevelle into his office and told them his suitcase was packed and he would be joining other bosses in Switzerland if this was a revolution.[11]

At the time of the strike, a team of Lip researchers was getting close to completing development of a watch that used a quartz crystal oscillator. They planned to present it at the international watch show in Geneva in the fall. Lip was racing against the Swiss to be the first to show such a watch. After Fred Lip explained the situation, the strike committee authorized a group of thirty employees to go back to work in order to assure expeditious completion of the watch. This exercise of an "embryonic dual power" revealed the Lip workers' embrace of the firm's technological innovation as the source of their power as well.[12]

In the occupied factory, workers continued to meet and debate. The General Assembly convened each morning, but exchanges took place throughout the day. One CFDT-Lip leader summed up May 1968 at Lip:

---

6 Interview with Piaget by Féret, "A voix nue," France Culture (2011).

7 AMB 5Z14 Fred Lip, "Note à messieurs les Administrateurs," May 20, 1968.

8 "On n'imagine pas tout ce que 68 peut faire pour nous!," 14–15.

9 Quiot, "Mai 68 m'a ouvert les yeux," 27.

10 AMB 5Z14 Fred Lip to President of Ébauches SA, June 6, 1968.

11 Quiot, "Mai 68 m'a ouvert les yeux," 27.

12 Claude Neuschwander, *Claude Neuschwander: une vie de militance[s]* (Gap, 2011), 135–6. Georges Ubbiali, "Mai 68 à Besançon," *Dissidences* 5 (2009): 52 [quoted].

"What happens in the conflict is that people begin to talk."[13] However, the General Assembly voted to follow the nationwide CGT policy of not allowing students into the occupied factory. Piaget spoke with them through the gates. He later called this "extremely unpleasant" and contrary to the liberation of speech that characterized life within the factory.[14]

Workers created some fifteen committees to handle factory responsibilities, drawing on both unionized and non-unionized workers. Each morning the committees reported to the General Assembly on their activities. Employees also met in their places of work and formulated particular demands relevant to their situation. Union delegates went around the workshops to make sure things were going smoothly, but did not join in.[15] Each workshop selected a delegate, some of whom were union members and others not, and formed a committee to collate these demands. "So they had a set of demands," Piaget explained, "which probably resembled the *cahiers de doléances* of 1789."[16]

Although the strike committee made clear that the movement would not end until a national agreement was reached, Fred Lip, ever the iconoclast, infuriated owners in Besançon and in the nation by signing an accord with the unions a week before the national Grenelle Accords. It included a number of provisions that went beyond what the national agreement and what other firms in the area would offer, including a paid day off for mothers on their child's first day at school, an additional vacation week between Christmas and New Year, time during the work day for three ninety-minute union-run general assemblies each year (this was paid time after 1970), a higher minimum monthly salary (the "mini-Lip," which primarily benefited the youngest workers), and an early retirement benefit at 60 percent of a worker's salary (at age sixty for women and sixty-three for men). Most significantly, Lip broke ranks with other employers and established a periodic cost-of-living adjustment based on agreed-upon price indices. The total amount for the workforce was divided evenly among employees, rather than allocated according to an individual's pay. This caused "a brief uprising among the OP," Piaget would recall, but raised the salaries of unskilled workers in comparison with those in other factories in Besançon, while keeping managers' pay in line with that offered elsewhere. Regional CFDT

13 Piaget, *Lip. Charles Piaget et les Lip racontent*, epigraph.
14 Zurbach, "1968," 76, 86.
15 Interview with Piaget by Féret, "A voix nue," France Culture.
16 Zurbach, "1968," 128.

officials circulated the accord as a model of the maximum that could be attained. The prefect observed that in signing the first such agreement in Franche-Comté, "Fred Lip aims to show that he continues to be at the lead in social policy." It may have also been a product of the competition of Fred Lip and the Ébauches SA for control of the firm after 1967, a conflict that offered workers at Lip a certain power.[17]

Workers at Lip did not want things to be as they had been before May. When it came time to return to work, fifteen conflicts broke out in individual offices and workshops over supervisors' treatment of employees. The state labor inspector asked the union leadership to work with him and the management to handle these situations. But the unions refused. Pointing to the discussions among workers that had been going on since the beginning of the strike, they said it would have to be the employees in the workshops and offices themselves who made the decisions. In response to each sit-down strike, two union delegates got all the employees at the affected site to sit in a circle and discuss their grievances. In what Piaget termed "a school for struggle," union delegates explained how specific issues related to national accords and the law, and got the demands particular to each work area put down in writing.[18] Prior to going to see management, the delegates explained to representatives chosen by the workshop that managers would try to impress and ridicule them, but they should not respond to these provocations. The union delegates accompanied them to see the bosses. The representatives then went back to their workshop or office to explain the results of their talks and the work group decided whether or not to pursue the work stoppage.[19] This exercise of collective action bore fruit beyond securing responses to particular grievances. Although the situation of women workers did not fundamentally change, one woman on the assembly line explained to a reporter from *Elle* that, after May, she "no longer trembled" when she talked to her supervisor.[20]

---

17   Ibid., 164–5. Chaillet, et al. "Entretien avec Charles Piget," 122. ADD 2377W180 PD to MI, February 18, 1969. AMB 5Z15 Fred Lip to Directeur de la Banque de France (Besançon), May 2, 1969. ADD 45J10 Commission Popularisation des travailleurs de Lip, "Dossier d'information," August 29, 1973, 15. Gaston Bordet on France Culture, "Arc-et-Senans, 1: LIP-Palente, 1973–1976, l'histoire d'un conflit," at inamediapro.com. Jean-François Belhoste and Pierre Metge, *Premières Observations sur des rapports de la transformation de propriété. Lip et l'industrie horlogère française 1944–1974* (Paris, 1978), 102. Hirschi, *Fred Lip Innovateur Social.*

18   Lacoste, *Lip, une école de la lutte.*

19   Piaget, "Les luttes de LIP." AR Interview with Piaget by Rouaud, September 11, 2003, 21–2.

20   Françoise Dumayet, "22 femmes ... à la chaîne," *Elle*, October 7, 1968, 109.

Divisions among employees broke down in the occupied factory. For Fatima Demougeot:

> What struck me in the movement is the fact that we all got together: blue collar, white collar, mechanics, watch workers, unskilled workers, supervisors. That was important, the mix of people, of men and women, of different socio-professional categories. It was quite striking. In my case at least, this marked me … The meetings between people and the idea that we can get together, all rise up at the same time. Yes, the feeling of belonging to a group, that was May '68, more than anything else.[21]

Piaget concurred, "We began by getting to know each other in '68. The mechanics had the watch workers visit their workshop. The watch workers said, come, we'll show you ours as well. We were in the same factory, we had different jobs, and the folks didn't know each other."[22] Piaget reflected that collective movements reduced violence because individuals in groups developed confidence and perspective by assessing proposed actions together. Thinking of Fred Lip and another boss he had met in May 1968 armed with a hunting rifle, Piaget explained that the bosses turned to violence because they felt alone. Fred Lip had no "counter-power," while he, Piaget, required others in the form of "counter-powers" in order to lead effectively.[23]

Events in May 1968 and succeeding years brought more workers to the unions. One quarter of *les Lip* were unionized after May, and by 1973 the number had risen to half—twice the rate in France as a whole. However, the unionization rate remained significantly higher among skilled workers and supervisors than unskilled workers. The increase in CFDT-Lip membership was particularly dramatic and it overtook the CGT-Lip in size, though they secured equal numbers of delegates in workplace elections.[24] The CGC established a local at Lip in 1968, and, faced with directors' harsh treatment of the managerial staff, forty-eight of fifty-one cadres joined.[25] Ninety per cent of workers exercised a right won in May by coming to the periodic general assemblies called by the

---

21   Sophie D'Houtaud, "L'héritage de mai 68 à Besançon vu par ses propres acteurs," Mémoire, Université de Franche Comté, 2006, 68–9.

22   Ibid., 124.

23   AB Interview with Piaget by Beurier (1992), 30, 33–5.

24   ADD 45J1 Michel Jeanningros, "Contribution à l'histoire de LIP 1867–1972 (hiver 1980)," 27. Lacoste, *Lip, une école de la lutte. Tribune socialiste*, June 1978, 6–8.

25   Joëlle Beurier, "La mémoire des Lip." Mémoire, Université de Paris I, 1992, 48.

unions. When the situation warranted it, these followed the format used in May 1968 of having union leaders lay out issues and workers break into small groups to discuss them and reconvene to adopt a position. These assemblies in turn facilitated cooperation between the CFDT-Lip and the CGT-Lip by requiring them to come up with a common agenda. Piaget came to think of his union as the motor and the CGT-Lip as a necessary brake, seeing their ability to work together as the reason the movement at Lip in 1973 did not stall.[26]

Information

Before May 1968, unions had been allowed to post notices in the factory only after they had been vetted by the firm, a process that could take weeks and resulted in out-of-date announcements with many words crossed out. The Grenelle Accords and the subsequent legislation on the rights of locals ended this censorship. The Lip unions took advantage of this new right to post a large poster board—4 by 2.6 meters, approaching the size of the fresco, illuminated by neon lights—in the cloakroom everyone used at the entry to Palente. "For us," Piaget explained, "that was really a big victory," one the Lip union leaders came to consider the most important they had achieved in 1968. Workers' delegates would put up four or five posters written in large characters that could be read and commented on in a minute or two by workers entering and leaving the factory. "More and more," said Piaget, "the culture of discussion established itself and the wage earners got used to speaking in public."[27] Fred Lip responded by having his personnel director rip down what he considered offensive posters. The director then convinced his boss that this had been a mistake, but when Fred Lip tried to put the posters back up, the union delegates prevented him from doing so until the bailiff they had summoned arrived and told the director that he had broken the law. This impressed all involved and the company management never interfered with the poster board again.[28]

---

26   Piaget, *Lip. Charles Piaget et les Lip racontent*, 35.

27   Charles Piaget, "Petit manuel de la lutte collective," at politis.fr.

28   Raguénès, *De Mai 68 à LIP*, 130. Divo, *L'Affaire Lip*, 3. Edmond Maire and Charles Piaget, *Lip 73* (Paris, 1973), 115. Piton, *C'est possible*, 16–17. Guy and Piaget in Piaget, *Lip. Charles Piaget et les Lip racontent*, 19–20, 156–7. Zurbach, "1968," 136, 167. Pierre Izibert, "Charles Piaget: une vie d'engrené," *Pays Comtois* 17 (March–April 1998): 24. AR Interview with Piaget by Rouaud, September 11, 2003, 20.

If, in Vittot's words, the conflict at Lip in 1973 was "born of May '68," he thought that "the principal gain of May" was the provision of information to workers.[29] Conflicts generated by the creation of an informed, participating labor force in a firm facing financial difficulties intensified after May 1968. The works council was a central site for these debates. After a meeting in June 1968, Fred Lip complained to the council secretary Dartevelle that self-management was a bad joke (*une plaisanterie de garçon de bain*), and developed his idea that members of the council like herself were "paid to uphold the company that employed them."[30] In January of that year he had already complained to the works council about union leaflets distributed in the factory and negative information given to newspapers, saying that it was the job of the works council to protect the labor force and the way to do that was to look after the firm's interests.[31] One Lip delegate explained that Fred Lip "looks to use the works council as a means of indoctrination. He recounts his misfortunes: I lost a market, etc. If we are taken in, we are reacting like a manager entirely subject to the interests of the firm, or rather, when it comes down to it, of the boss."[32] In November 1968, Fred Lip implausibly suggested that the works council should participate in punishing "harshly" and in some cases laying off workers who did not make the necessary extra effort, rather than leaving it up to management "to impose discipline and to be unpopular."[33]

Fred Lip's desire to get delegates to carry out his plans was checked by their democratic practices. He chided the works council for treating whatever he told them as public information.[34] He was particularly frustrated that when he made proposals, union representatives would make no decisions before discussing them with their "comrades" in the organization.[35] In December 1970, he wrote Dartevelle that the firm was planning to suppress some activities, but had not decided which ones: "It is clear that if before the meeting of the works council, we see leaflets, new steps taken by your comrades, without there having been execution

---

29   *Tribune socialiste*, June 1978, 6–7. Vittot, "La longue marche des Lip!," 7.

30   AMB 5Z15 Fred Lip, "Note aux membres du Comité," October 24, 1969.

31   AMB 5Z14 Fred Lip to Dartevelle, secretary of the CE, January 25, 1968.

32   *CFDT Syndicalisme hebdo*, September 13, 1973, 13.

33   AMB 5Z14 Fred Lip, "Note à tous les membres du CE," November 18, 1968.

34   ACGT Uncatalogued Papers on Lip. Compte-rendu du CE, March 18, 1970 in "Registre Comité d'Entreprise 6 avril 1962–28 février 1973." AMB 5Z15 Fred Lip to Dartevelle, April 2, 1970; Fred Lip, "Note aux membres du 3e Collège," August 29, 1970.

35   AMB 5Z15 Fred Lip to delegates and members of the CE, May 2, 1969 [quoted]; Fred Lip, "Note à Messieurs les Délégués", December 4, 1969.

[of measures by the company], we would be freed on our part from certain obligations to the works council."[36] A couple of years later, Fred Lip complained that when he had convoked Piaget in July 1970 to tell him of the firm's recent losses, Piaget refused to take what he was told into account and responded by saying that all the bosses offered their workers were "fudged balance sheets."[37] Yet Fred Lip himself had recognized why in an interview in March 1968: "Naturally, in France, after 2,000 years of enslavement of the mass of workers, it appears difficult to think that the works council and personnel delegates can believe what the owners, the capitalists, and heads of business tell them!"[38] But this did not stop him from giving bad news about the firm to union leaders on occasion and then acting shocked that they mistrusted the veracity of these scattered confidences.[39]

By law two representatives of the works council had advisory seats on the board of directors.[40] This was to assure that they had access to the information given to the board. Although bound by law not to reveal to workers what they learned at these meetings if so instructed by the board president, the union delegates refused to be held to this.[41] The firm in turn went to great lengths to assure that the representatives were kept in the dark. Fred Lip contravened the law by arranging for the board to meet secretly without the works council members present to make important decisions. He sought to ensure that the board would appear united when it did meet with them and would "impress representatives of the personnel with their resolution."[42] He worked out with the board what would be discussed in their presence. A note in February 1971

---

36   ADD 177J7 Fred Lip to Dartevelle, December 8, 1970.

37   Hervé Jannic, "Fred Lip s'explique," *L'Expansion* 68 (November 1973): 111.

38   *Le Télégramme de Franche-Comté*, March 16, 1968, 6.

39   Jannic, "Fred Lip s'explique," 111. Hervé Jannic, "Lip en veut pas perdre pied," *L'Expansion* 25 (December 1969): 73. AMB 5Z14 Fred Lip to Dartevelle, June 25, 1968; Fred Lip, "Note au secretariat du comité d'entreprise [Dartevelle]," August 5, 1968; Fred Lip to Piaget, August 9, 1968; Fred Lip, "Note à tous les membres du CE," October 1968; Fred Lip, "Note à tous les membres du CE," November 18, 1968.

40   Dartevelle later said that she learned to be such an effective public speaker by listening to the businessmen on the board. AB Interview with Dartevelle by Beurier (1992), 53–4.

41   Fred Lip to administrateurs de la Société Lip, January 9, 1971, cited in Maire and Piaget, *Lip 73*, 31. *Libération*, December 18, 1973, 8.

42   AMB 5Z17 Fred Lip to Pierre Renaggli, administrateur de la Société Lip à ASUAG, January 25, 1971 [quoted]; Fred Lip to Messieurs les Administrateurs de la Société LIP, February 1, 1971. For the revealing minutes of the February 26, 1970 meeting of the board of directors before and after the entry of the works council representatives, Dartevelle and Piaget, see Maire and Piaget, *Lip 73*, document 10.

reveals the lengths to which directors went to keep worker delegates from raising troubling issues:

> [The works council representatives] are only present in a consultative capacity, but we cannot refuse them the right to speak. To safeguard ourselves, it would be wise to have a very specific agenda, behind which the President can take refuge. This would be a way to prevent certain problems from being raised, without hindering performance of [the board's] regular duties.[43]

If the works council delegates, Dartevelle and Piaget, were going to tell workers what they learned, Fred Lip's goal was to use the board meetings to try to get the unions to convey selected information. At a meeting in April 1970, he explained that in the absence of dividends many benefits accorded to workers came at shareholders' expense; he pointedly said it was important for all to know what would happen if stockholders withdrew their support.[44]

In late September 1973, well into the conflict of that year, President Georges Pompidou told reporters that the Minister of Industry Jean Charbonnel "had taken the trouble to read all the minutes of the works council and he had seen nowhere—since we were speaking of participation—the representatives of the personnel protesting against technical, commercial or personnel policies."[45] Pompidou thought that should put a damper on critics, without asking why there could be no evidence of such participation: workers were denied their legal right to a full range of information about their enterprise and were not consulted on decisions concerning its future and their own.

Participation

Charles de Gaulle favored Catholic social policies of class reconciliation, premised on incorporating rather than empowering workers, and very

---

43   BDIC F delta rés 707/5 FGM-CFDT, "L'affaire LIP," press conference, August 8, 1973.

44   BDIC F delta rés 578/40 CFDT-LIP, "Lip en Lutte Vous Informe ..." [minutes of Lip board of directors meeting of April 29, 1970].

45   Le Figaro, September 20, 1973, 7. An unimpressed Piaget commented that at least "this showed that the thorn remained in his foot." Le Nouvel observateur, October 1, 1973, 32.

unlike those of the Lip trade unionists. After the war, de Gaulle spoke of the association of capital and labor. Fred Lip had touted the ability of each employee to become a "co-owner" of Lip who would be interested in the smooth operation of the firm like every other shareholder. However, this invitation to join the "Capital-Labor association at Lip" attracted few workers, appended as it was to paychecks in June 1958, the first month since de Gaulle's return to power, but a month when workers saw reduced hours and pay.[46] In 1965, de Gaulle returned to the theme, though he replaced association with participation, the term he would use in response to May 1968. Ever the loyal Gaullist, Fred Lip spoke in October 1968 of having workers from one division of the firm visit those in another in terms of participation. For the CGT-Lip, this revealed participation at Lip to be nothing more than "smoke and mirrors with which [Fred Lip] hopes to take the personnel and unions on the road of collaboration."[47]

Frustrated with the union representatives' rejection of his appeals to rally behind him, Fred Lip sought to counter the workers' new-found power after May '68 by asserting that delegates on the works council were too old in spirit, if not in age. In August 1968, he laid out plans for a new committee of four or five workers under the age of twenty-five, preferably half female and from parts of the factory where the unions were weakest. He saw himself leading this committee, which would embody "the ideas, the desires and the projects of the future of all those who represent the dynamic element" at Lip. Fred Lip felt so good about this project that he sent a duplicate of the memo to "my friend Piaget."[48] Although the plan did not come to fruition, in December 1969 Fred Lip explained to the works council that he would like to add one or two representatives to it, ideally women and not workers from the already well-represented mechanics workshop.[49] He held a competition among young workers for the best logo for a promotional campaign and took the two winners, both male, to New York City.[50] He then proposed that

46   ADD 177J7 CGT tract "L'association Capital-Travail chez Lip" [1958].
47   ADD 177J7 Union locale des syndicats d'Ornans (CGT) tract, October 23, 1968.
48   AMB 5Z14 Fred Lip to Ferry ("délégué spécialisé dans les jeunes"), August 27, 1968.
49   AMB 5Z14 Fred Lip, "Note à tous les membres du CE," December 13, 1968.
50   They were part of group that included thirty watch seller-jewelers recognized for their sales (and accompanied by their spouses), and sixty to seventy individuals picked from the 250,000 who had filled out entry forms at the shops of watch seller-jewelers, in an effort by Lip to get potential buyers to stores and win the good will of these merchants. "Fred Lip vous parle," *Interlip*, March 1969, 57–8.

the works council expand by adding these youths to its numbers. Piaget convinced the skeptical workers' representatives to agree, but to Fred Lip's chagrin the unions won over the new representatives. One of these was the twenty-year-old Marc Géhin, who joined the CGT-Lip and later the CFDT-Lip, and would play an active role in events at Lip over the next decade.[51]

Fred Lip and the Image of French Business

Fred Lip identified with the outsider status of those who had taken to the streets in 1968: "The big movement of May 1968, I approved of it, not in its tenor, but in its goals."[52] He attacked French employers and hoped to rally youth to his side. At odds with other employers in the area, other watch-making firms and the general direction of French business, his firm did not belong to the Union patronale du Doubs, the Chambre Française de l'Horlogerie, or the national business organization, the Comité National du Patronat Français (CNPF).[53] On the first day of the strike at Lip, he told his board that workers needed owners who would provide for them "rather than whining all the time while refusing everything to every-body." He condemned "the ruling class in general, and above all French employers; if there are revolutions and radical transformations, it will be their fault." He blamed the CNPF for being "regrettably silent."[54] Fred Lip reiterated these complaints in an article in *Le Monde* in August 1968 in which he adopted a populist tone, condemning bosses who paid less than the minimum wage while enjoying a luxurious lifestyle. He criticized the "bigwigs" who directed the CNPF for being out of touch with "active business leaders" like himself, and lamented the absence of a "big boss" able to talk spontaneously before cameras like the student leaders in May.[55] In June 1968, Fred Lip wrote to André Augé—whom he had always thought unqualified to head up the Chambre Française de l'Horlogerie because his firm made watch springs rather than watches—to tell him "the students have blown off the old professors" and that he should take

---

51   Ravenel, "Un militant ouvrier autogestionnaire," 115.
52   *Le Monde*, June 2, 1973, 32.
53   Bernard Brizay, *Le Patronat: histoire, structure, stratégie du CNPF* (Paris, 1975), 207.
54   AMB 5Z14 Fred Lip, "Note à messieurs les Administrateurs," May 20, 1968.
55   *Le Monde*, August 15, 1968, 13. Fred Lip reduced his own monthly salary after May 1968 by about the pay of an OS, from 16,000 to 14,000 francs. Interview with Jeanningros by Reid, June 1, 2011.

the hint and quit the presidency.[56] He ended an open letter to owners of watchmaking firms in the summer of 1968 by asking, "Messieurs bigwigs, are you waiting for an occupation of your premises ... by the young and the less young business heads, to rid us of your aged presence?"[57]

Although himself born in 1905, Fred Lip still identified with the idea of youth. When asked about the CNPF in 1969, he responded that not only was *patronat* "an out-of-date word," but the current leadership of the CNPF was equally out of date: "Essentially, it is as if, in the Olympic Games parade, they had at the head of the delegation a potbellied president carrying the flag with trembling hands." The president of the CNPF, he added, should be no more than forty-five years old. Speaking in May 1969, he described the kind of representatives business needed: "svelte men, representing a dynamic force, dressed like everybody and not like the bankers of 1914."[58] For Fred Lip, May 1968 had shown that the public image of business was of unprecedented importance in the mediatized world in which his business, and his workers, operated.

After May

The movement at Lip in 1973 developed directly out of May '68. While the Prime Minister Jacques Chaban-Delmas responded by pursuing a "new society" through a limited set of state initiatives, the Lip workers, faced with company backtracking, developed a new society in their workplace. On June 6, 1968, Fred Lip had sent one of his condemnations of the establishment to the organization that negotiated collective contracts for watch producers, the Groupement des Industries Métallurgiques et Minières (GIMM), a branch of the Union des Industries Métallurgiques et Minières (UIMM). His biting letter of resignation concluded that the GIMM's leadership should be thrown out. However, early in 1970, Fred Lip had a change of heart and informed the GIMM orally and confidentially—he reserved public letters for denunciations—that he would stop paying the cost-of-living adjustment and would instead adhere to the conditions in the new contract governing watchmaking in the region that the GIMM had just negotiated. Since he had taken Lip

---

56   AMB 5Z14 Fred Lip to André Augé, June 28, 1968. Ternant, "La Dynamique longue," 246.

57   ADD 1485W91 "Lettre ouverte sur l'industrie de la montre" [summer 1968].

58   Gérard Adam, "Si vous étiez president du CNPF? ...," *Dirigeant* 2 (May 1969): 18–19.

out of the GIMM, the contract did not apply to his firm, but he sought to use this ploy to end application of the payment system his firm alone had introduced after May 1968. He added that he would initiate no new social policies without first taking them up with the GIMM: "a complete disavowal of his social policy," in the words of the state police.[59]

This was one example of Fred Lip's repeated attempts in the face of a 35 percent decline in watch sales between 1968 and 1971 to take back elements of the May 1968 strike settlement and to lay off workers.[60] Drawing on their experience in May, workers responded by developing alternative sites of power in the factory. In December 1969, Lip gave 200 watch workers three unpaid days off, but the workers were able to get two of the three days paid at the mini-Lip, the minimum wage practiced at Lip. The firm was rebuffed again in January 1970 when it attempted to change the cost-of-living adjustment. The next month, in addition to deciding to align itself with the GIMM, the firm announced that it would lay off 200 workers for a month. Workers had held meetings to discuss the situation in their workshops in January; in February, the union-led General Assembly developed a new set of demands having to do with working conditions and pay. Workers responded, as they would to all company measures directed at a minority of the workforce, by making demands that concerned all. Faced with this opposition, management shifted to reducing the workweek of 400 workers by 10 percent without making up the lost salary; workers interpreted this as a prelude to dismissals. They "occupied" their work areas during the hours they had lost. Posters, leaflets, and cassettes, which workers throughout the factory listened to during their breaks, fostered discussion.

That month, in February 1970, a reporter for *L'Est républicain* brought together CGT-Lip and CFDT-Lip delegates with Fred Lip to discuss the situation of young workers. Fred Lip contended that the conflict had been launched by young workers, not the union leadership, and a few months later explained to the board of directors the need to limit the access to reports and minutes of meetings, which Piaget and Dartevelle as works council representatives were legally authorized to see, "out of fear that their unions would be overtaken by wild ones or youths."[61] The union delegates qualified Fred Lip's assessment of the origin of the movement, but recognized that

59   ADD 1485W91 RG, February 17, 1970.

60   Jean-Claude Daumas, "Fred Lip" in *Dictionnaire historique des patrons français* (Paris, 2010), 441.

61   ACGT Uncatalogued Papers on Lip. Fred Lip to Adminstrateurs, April 9, 1970.

the young don't put up with working conditions the way we did twenty years ago ... Before May 1968 there was no dialogue. The same strike launched in 1966 would have failed. The context is different now. And yet Lip is a liberal firm, we don't deny it. But the young are less 'conditioned', that is to say less subject to their conditions than longtime workers. We must teach people to assume their responsibilities.[62]

What might this involve? In February 1970, a number of workers wanted to go on strike immediately and to block entry of all workers to the factory, but Piaget convinced them that they should stick to the democratic practices they had adopted in May 1968: "Preventing people from coming to work, we would break the accord we had made together." Union delegates set up "reflection groups." Workers who wanted to strike came to accept that without strong majority support they would be defeated. From the discussions came the idea of having strikers form a "serpent," which would snake its way in silence through the factory. When the serpent entered a workshop, five strikers would break off to talk to workers they thought they could convince. When a worker put down his tools and joined the serpent, everyone in the moving line clapped. Then the enlarged serpent went on its way, going to every workshop and office. In three days, a strong majority of the workforce had adhered to the movement. The unions taped their negotiations with management and played them for workers during breaks. Workers kept their jobs and won concessions as well on demands concerning the designation of professional categories and annual and vacation bonuses, issues that affected all; an account funded by workers and the firm was established to provide workers whose hours had been cut with two-thirds of the pay they had lost.[63]

A frustrated Fred Lip recognized that the union's dissemination of information in leaflets and posters had been essential in mobilizing workers. He responded by lodging a libel suit against a dozen union delegates for having, he told his managers, "the nerve to post absolutely false information in order to intoxicate the personnel." What most offended him was that the union materials discussed the financial situation of the firm: "this intoxication," he informed his cadres,

---

62 L'Est républicain, February 22, 1970.

63 ADD 2377W181 PD to MI, February 18, 1970; February 19, 1970. ADD 1026W8 "Rappel du déroulement du conflit de Juin 1970." Piaget and Vittot, "LIP," 285. Réseau Citoyens Résistants, La Force, 16–17. For the conflicts of these years see "Un an de lutte chez LIP," supplement to Critique socialiste 5 [1971].

"is a union-political plan that is remote-controlled since no delegate knows about depreciation, taxation, devaluation and such."[64] He could not believe that any worker could understand the financial balance sheets on which their future depended. Fred Lip lost the case, but this would not be the last time that the workers' right and competence to cross the divide and examine the economics of their enterprise would be questioned.

In June 1970, the firm took the offensive again. High inflation induced sporadic strikes. It responded by announcing an across-the-board raise that in fact reduced pay over the long term by folding in the periodic cost-of-living adjustments negotiated in May 1968.[65] Mechanics joined by other workers began taking a fifteen-minute break every hour and used the time to convince those who were still working to join the movement; a continuous discussion with changing participants was held on the lawns of Palente. Workers' delegates argued that pay rates and cost-of-living adjustments should be considered separately. Faced with company intransigence, the General Assembly voted to occupy a part of the factory, including the directors' offices. Workers phoned directors, asking them to meet in their very own, now occupied, offices; employees jeered as they walked by.

Fred Lip was in Geneva at the time and, as was his practice, refused to allow his staff, "when he was not there, to deal with personnel issues of any magnitude."[66] However, this did not stop him from telephoning the prefect and the police repeatedly, asking them to send forces to end occupation of the factory. The prefecture demurred, characterizing the factory occupation as "a sort of village fair." Realizing the importance of bringing their situation to public attention, workers leafleted vehicles in Besançon. Lip had long been proud of its reputation as a firm that offered better pay and benefits than other employers in the city, and Fred Lip was pained to see his image of the firm challenged in public. At Palente, "persuasion pickets," to use the workers' term, sought to convince employees not to work rather than preventing them from doing so. One thousand of the 1,300 employees struck. The CFDT-Lip broke with the standard practice of developing strategy in closed meetings of union delegates working with a staff member from the confederation. Union

64   AMB 5Z15 Fred Lip to Dartevelle, April 2, 1970; Fred Lip, "Note aux membres du 3e Collège," August 29, 1970. [quoted]

65   Charles Piaget, "La formation par l'action collective" in *L'École à perpétuité*, eds. Heinrich Dauber and Étienne Verne (Paris, 1977), 156.

66   ADD 2377W181 Sous-préfet to PD, March 10, 1970.

leaders met with workers, union and non-union, in groups on the lawns of Palente. "We were practicing a reflection open to everyone," Piaget explained. "We sat in a circle with the other workers in the struggle to take stock and then reflect, bringing all the union reflection to bear on the situation." At first, these workers were content to listen, but they soon became active participants. From these meetings came a novel idea that was brought to the General Assembly and approved. Occupation of the factory itself on the eve of the annual vacation in July would not be effective. Instead, strikers threatened the company night guard, who was forced to shut himself in, while others stayed in the factory through the night to block the shipment of finished watches at what was the time of First Communion sales. Piaget later referred to this as "putting a customs system in place." Workers searched managers as well as trash bins when they left the factory, to make sure watches were not being spirited away. Fred Lip called on managers to break through the workers' line at the loading dock, but the union delegates placed themselves between the two sides, preventing workers and managers from exchanging blows and the watches from leaving the factory.[67]

After pursuing a policy of no concessions from afar, Fred Lip returned and quickly gave the workers far more than they had demanded: the firm ended the reduced hours introduced at the beginning of the year, granted an hourly pay increase double what the workers had originally demanded, and raised the mini-Lip. The astonished prefect reported:

In fact, M. Lip had, for more than a week, refused to give a 20 centime per hour raise, saying that if more than 13 centimes, the burden created would jeopardize the equilibrium of the enterprise. Suddenly, on 24 June, he declared that a raise of 40 centimes was possible, even pairing it with other significant complementary benefits. The illogical character, almost thoughtless, of this behavior did not escape the unions, which will not fail to take it into account in upcoming conflicts.[68]

---

67   ADD 1026W8 "Rappel du déroulement du conflit de Juin 1970." BDIC F delta rés 578/40 CFDT-LIP, "Lip en Lutte Vous Informe …" [a company report attached to minutes of the Lip conseil d'administration meetings in 1970]. ADD 45J10 Commission Popularisation, "Dossier d'information," 4. BDIC KA 214 3 *Les Cahiers de mai* interview with Piaget [1973]. Charles Piaget, "LIP. Les effets formateurs d'une lutte collective," *Entropia* 2 (Spring 2007): 145, 152 [quoted]. Interview with Vittot by Reid, June 3, 2011.

68   ADD 1026W8 "Rappel du déroulement du conflit de Juin 1970."

Workers, the prefect recognized, were becoming more receptive to the unions, particularly the CFDT-Lip, than they had been even a few months earlier.[69] Managers lost authority; those who made offensive remarks to workers were named on the poster board. The effects were felt throughout the factory. In August 1970, the largely female press operators successfully used spontaneous work stoppages to get piece rates standardized and their pay raised.[70]

Fred Lip turned his attention to trying to get rid of CFDT-Lip delegates. In November 1970, he sent a letter to the personnel to say that Lip "lacks the means to serve as a laboratory of revolution for a handful of fanatics and incompetent mystics."[71] However, the state labor inspector informed him that he could not fire the delegates without going through a formal legal process. Fred Lip sought to win the inspector over by saying that no stock on the Paris stock exchange had fallen more in 1970 than Lip, but the official was not moved.[72] To build a case for laying off the delegates, Fred Lip decided to close the two mechanics workshops in which most of them worked and sell the machinery. Although recent legislation, part of Chaban-Delmas' "new society" initiative, required him to present such a project to the works council and examine alternatives, he did not, leading workers to post little posters, "F. Lip outlaw," above their machines. Playing off the firm's advertisements, workers told Fred Lip that it was not him, but "Your delegates who have the quality of your watches."[73] Workers set up a system in which a lookout blew a whistle when he saw men coming to get a machine. Thirty mechanics came running and surrounded the machine in question. Arms crossed, the mechanics explained to the movers that what they were about to do was illegal. Half an hour later, the movers left empty handed. The unions also posted workers to prevent machines from being taken after hours. One night two machines were removed, but the workers went to the loading dock and brought them back. In each case, the workers reinstalled the machines; Piaget took advantage of his position as shop supervisor to assign work to the machinists who operated them. After two days, management gave up.[74]

69   ADD 2377W181 PR to MI, June 24, 1970. The prefect of Doubs was also the regional prefect of Franche-Comté and exercised both functions in dealing with Lip. He is referred to as the prefect in the text.

70   "Un an de lutte chez LIP," 18.

71   ADD 177J7 Fred Lip to personnel, November 16, 1970.

72   AMB 5Z17 Fred Lip to Vuillerme, Inspecteur du Travail (Besançon), January 4, 1971.

73   ADD 45J1 Jeanningros, "Contribution à l'histoire," 28.

74   "Lip vivra, Messmer cédera, une nouvelle étape de la lutte, tous avec Lip!,"

In January 1971, Fred Lip set out to fire forty office workers and ten mechanics. As office workers rarely joined in labor actions, he hoped that they would not benefit from the cooperation of workers in the factory. But he was wrong. The layoffs were taken up as the cause of all. Workers and administrative personnel made posters expressing their solidarity and, using a right won in May 1968, put them up in their workshops and offices for all to see. Employees competed for the best slogan, picture and placement. When managers removed them, workers called on their union delegates to get the posters put back up. To protect the posters, workers would take them down each evening, store them in the cloak-room, and put them up again the next morning. Piaget recalled that "disobedience spread throughout the factory. Wage earners refused to provide the usual information on their work. There was a standstill and total chaos."[75] After two weeks, all the fired workers were rehired. Fred Lip's last hope of using the works council to rally workers was put to rest when it voted to reprimand the head of production and instructed him not to maneuver again to fire employees. Thwarted, Fred Lip placed advertisements in local newspapers saying that if a firm needed mechan-ics, he had some available.[76]

A workers' community emerged, animated by a sense of what it considered just. In March 1973, one of the few French workers of Alge-rian origin at Lip, Ouaked Areski, hit another young worker who had used a racial slur against him. The president-director general asked the CGC-Lip what should be done and followed their advice to fire Areski. A month after the confrontation with the CGC-Lip over the treatment of women workers, the workers' unions called a meeting and produced a tract with "elements of reflection": "For ten hours we are closed up in this factory and in view of the tension that reigns there, it happens that words or acts exceed what is right," but putting a young worker who had been defending his honor out on the streets was immoral.[77] Such issues could and should be handled in the workshop. Furthermore, the CFDT-Lip and the CGT-Lip condemned the CGC-Lip for "class collabo-ration," by essentially firing an employee: this was not what a union did.[78] More than 400 workers went to the personnel director and threatened to

L'Internationale 44 (January 1974). Piaget, "Les luttes de LIP."

75   Réseau Citoyens Résistants, *La Force,* 19–20

76   ADD 45J10 Commission Popularisation, "Dossier d'information," 4–6. Divo, *L'affaire,* 10–11, 54. Piaget, *Lip. Charles Piaget et les Lip racontent,* 21. *Politique hebdo,* August 30, 1973, 8. Piaget, "Les luttes de Lip." *Combat socialiste,* February 1971, 2.

77   ADD 1812W34 CFDT/CGT "Licenciement," March 29, 1973.

78   ADD 1812W34 CFDT/CGT, "Chez Lip C'est la CGC qui Licencie," March 1973.

strike if either worker was laid off. Faced with the unity of workers across union lines, management kept both employees.[79] On another occasion, a male and a female worker on a late shift were caught making out. They had kept an eye on the machines and production had not been affected. When the management threatened the pair with dismissal, workers put down their tools and the lovers stayed on.[80]

Workers' sense of belonging to a social and ethical community also encompassed the behavior of managers. Like the women in production, female office workers, often alone with their bosses, experienced sexual harassment. When Monique Piton went to work for Lip in 1970, she was subject to the unwanted attentions of her boss. She responded by hitting him on the head with a wastebasket, an act that would normally have meant immediate dismissal. Machines throughout the factory came to a halt. Piton was moved to a new position, but not fired.[81] Another time a manager slapped a worker. When management did not act, workers struck, leading Fred Lip to suspend the manager. The latter, devastated at having been repudiated by both the workers and the firm, spoke of resigning. At this point, a worker delegate came to see him to explain that the workers respected his abilities and had nothing against him except for the act for which he had been punished. The manager apologized to the worker and returned to his position.[82] Workers considered Palente a community that could itself address the conflicts that arose within it.

The Future of Lip

With the replacement of de Gaulle as president by the banker Georges Pompidou in 1969, French economic policy began moving from national autonomy to international market capitalism. The state did not object in 1970 when Ébauches SA expanded its holdings in Lip through an intermediary firm it controlled. In February 1971 Ébauches SA arranged to replace Fred Lip as president-director general with Jacques Saintesprit, secretary-general at Lip after the war and later Lip vice-president and then president-director general of an enterprise owned by ASUAG—in his new position, "a straw man for the Swiss," in Dartevelle's

79   Piton in BDIC F delta rés 707/9(1) Fonds Michel Duyrat Bande UNCLA 1 Cahier no. 1. *Politique hebdo*, August 30, 1973, 9. Piton, *C'est possible!*, 22–4.

80   Monique Piton, *Mémoires libres* (Paris, 2010), 68–9.

81   Piton in *Lip au féminin*, 13–14, 69

82   Divo, *L'affaire Lip*, 9–10.

words.[83] Back in 1968, when Saintesprit was already working for ASUAG, Fred Lip had dismissed him as a man with cultural capital ("an economic and literary background that allowed him to express himself in an appropriate language since he had occasion to mix with people of quality"), but not the dynamic youth the times required of a business leader.[84] After Saintesprit replaced him, Fred Lip put him in the category of an "ectoplasmatic creature," presumably because he appeared to have been willed into existence by the Ébauches SA, that would in turn make him vanish without a trace two years later when that will disappeared.[85] For his part, Saintesprit referred to the state of "organic decomposition" in which he found the firm.[86]

Lip had an active research department, a modern factory, a well-known and respected brand name, a good sales department, and a stable and skilled labor force. Early in Saintesprit's tenure, the firm presented the first ready-to-market French quartz watch. ASUAG was interested in Lip for its research and particularly its work on the quartz watch, in order to ensure it would not have a competitor using this technology of the future in France. It shifted research in electronic/quartz watches away from Lip in Besançon and used Lip patents and research in its laboratories in Switzerland.[87] With Fred Lip gone, French watchmakers made efforts to get the Institut de développement de l'industrie (IDI), created by Chaban-Delmas in 1970 to assist industrial enterprises that needed funds to modernize (and in some readings, to save them from foreign predators), and large French firms to invest in Lip. Their plan was to wrest Lip from the Swiss and make it a center of regional development as part of a national response to technological and commercial changes in the watch business. André Augé, head of the Chambre Française de l'Horlogerie and the subject of Fred Lip's scorn, offered to direct the transformed Lip. However, the state deferred to the Ébauches SA, which was unwilling to give up control of Lip, leading the Chambre to abandon these efforts.[88]

---

83   AB Interview with Dartevelle by Beurier (1992), 74.
84   ADD 1485W91 Fred Lip, "Lettre ouverte sur l'industrie de la montre" [1968].
85   BDIC F delta rés 702/4/2, Fred Lip to Claude Neuschwander, November 18, 1975.
86   AMB 5Z18 Saintesprit to PD, November 13, 1972.
87   BDIC F delta rés 707/5 FGM-CFDT, "L'affaire LIP," August 8, 1973.
88   Ternant, "L'affaiblissement du SPL," 124–5. Daumas, "Le système productif localisé," 13. An offer by Lip to share its quartz technology with the French watchmakers' research center Cetehor failed as well due to their fear of Lip as a Swiss Trojan horse.

Nevertheless, Ébauches SA retained the idea of seeking funds from the French state for Lip. It had Lip ask the IDI to invest in the firm by taking 35–40 percent of the stock; Ébauches SA could then reduce its share while profiting from the infusion of capital into Lip.[89] Saintesprit recognized that good labor relations were necessary to make a strong case to the IDI. He was tactful and a good listener. When "Saint-es" had been at Lip earlier, workers had found him easier to deal with than Fred Lip and other directors.[90] In the fall of 1970, Saintesprit had contacted Lip unions to warn them of "the consequences of blind agitation."[91] However, when he took control in 1971, he immediately abandoned Fred Lip's plans for layoffs.[92] Reviewing the conflicts of the past two years, he told workers: "You couldn't have done otherwise. We, on the outside, it was making us 'boil'. You were quite right." Saintesprit added: "Freezing wages, that prevents employees from breathing. The word layoffs should not be uttered in this firm."[93] "When there is a difficulty of any kind," he explained, "I call Piaget and everything is fixed up."[94] In 1972, Saintesprit replaced payment by individual production with a system that made wages dependent on total production and a variety of individual criteria. The result was a significant increase in wages, particularly for the OS. After examining the financial situation of the company, the workers' delegates expressed their reservations to him about such an increase in wages, but he put it in place.[95] In Vittot's words, Saintesprit "bought social peace."[96] In October 1972, Saintesprit informed the personnel that the average salary had increased 28.2 percent between February 1971 and September 1972, not counting increases in bonuses—double the rate of inflation.[97] But what happened at Palente needed to stay in Palente. Saintesprit explained that the strength of the unions at Lip was an issue for the IDI, which the CFDT-Lip interpreted as a warning (that it did not intend to heed) to

Ternant, "La Dynamique longue," 410–11, 441–4.

89   AMB 5Z18 Saintesprit to PD, November 13, 1972.

90   ADD 1812W34 *Cité Fraternelle*, December 20, 1963.

91   ADD 1812W33 RG, September 8, 1970.

92   ADD 1812W33 RG, February 8, 1971.

93   ADD 45J2 "Document CFDT, adressé aux différentes personnalités, ainsi qu'à la presse" [February 1973], 4.

94   *La Croix*, August 3, 1973, 12.

95   *CFDT magazine*, November 1993, 18–19. And when the General Assembly rejected the CFDT-Lip delegates' position on this issue, they accepted this affirmation of worker democracy. *CFDT Syndicalisme hebdo*, September 13, 1973, 5.

96   Vittot in Chris Marker's film, *Puisqu'on vous dit que c'est possible*.

97   AMB 5Z220 "Compte rendu de la réunion des délégués du personnel du 24 octobre 1972 à 10 heures."

discontinue the strong support it had been giving workers' movements elsewhere in Besançon, as this would irritate the CNPF.[98]

In any case, the IDI was under the purview of the Minister of Industry Charbonnel and the Minister for the Economy and Finance Valéry Giscard d'Estaing. The latter was particularly unsympathetic to the IDI, this "illegitimate child of the 'new society,' " and its project of investing state and private funds in selected firms.[99] Lip's application to the IDI appeared to remain unanswered. Nor was it fully presented to the works council as by law it should have been.[100] Although workers would have been disappointed if they had known the details of the proposal, it was held out as a salvation to them. Piaget spoke in January 1972 of workers taking "their pilgrim's staff" to see the state authorities and urge action.[101] However, when Saintesprit spoke to the works council at the end of 1972, he made reference to unspecified reforms and closings that the IDI would require. The CFDT-Lip responded that workers would not be sacrificed to the technocrats and capitalists working behind the scene:

> Once again, the 'specialists' are building a 'new future'. Les Lip, the pawns that we are, are hoodwinked in every way to put together solutions that we will not know until they're decided, as usual! Once again, we should count only on ourselves to see that these plans do not adversely affect our interests.[102]

Saintesprit laid out his understanding of the situation to the prefect in November 1972. "The preoccupation with full employment remains the basis of management of this enterprise"; if the IDI did not come through, this "would back Lip into a corner." To keep workers employed, Saintesprit had raised production dramatically—in 1972 it was one-sixth larger than in 1969—leading to a large stock of watches. Saintesprit reported that as director, he "is supposed to present the worst-case scenario, recalling tirelessly the limits of the possible." But he found the workers were imbued with "the acute awareness of belonging to a community unlike any other." Discouraging economic figures did not dull their faith. He concluded by reminding the prefect that workers had been

98   ADD 45J2 "Document CFDT, adressé aux différentes personnalités," 8.
99   Le Monde, May 9, 1973.
100   "L'affaire Lip: emergence de nouveaux droits," Projet 80 (1973): 1202.
101   ADD 45J2 Compte-rendu de la réunion "informations syndicales" du 17.1.72 [quoted]. ADD 1026W11 RG, April 26, 1973.
102   ADD 177J8 CFDT-Lip, "Lip: Quel Avenir?," January 5, 1973.

successful in building support when they took to the streets of Besançon in 1970 and could do so again.[103] The prefect got the point and a couple of days later wrote to the prime minister to support the IDI request with reference to the legislative elections the following spring. CFDT-Lip leaders, he wrote,

> would possess, at the height of the electoral campaign, a platform of the first order to alert public opinion to the deterioration of the economic situation … The population, usually moderate in its judgments, would have difficulty understanding that the government did nothing to avoid the closing of an enterprise of this size. …
>
> The fragile equilibrium between the Majority and the Opposition which marks the first electoral district of Doubs would thus be regrettably compromised on the eve of the election at the beginning of next year [1973].[104]

Whether or not the Swiss thought they had been "tricked" into investing in Lip, as the prefect thought, ASUAG found other ways to profit from its control of Lip while waiting for a reply from the IDI.[105] The Lip commercial network in France sold ASUAG watches made in Switzerland. ASUAG was interested only in watchmaking, and the pursuit of contracts for mechanics in particular lagged; ASUAG's (in)action gave it evidence to make the case that divisions other than watchmaking should be spun off. It wanted to end Lip's production of watch parts and make it an assembly plant using parts made within the ASUAG network. Lip began buying watch parts from ASUAG firms such that the percentage of components made at Palente in watches assembled there dropped from 75 percent in 1967 to 56 percent in 1973.[106] In 1972, Lip bought four times the value in watch parts from ASUAG as it sold to it.[107] Finally, ASUAG saw the future was in quartz not mechanical watches, and sought to use Lip research and patents in Switzerland rather than develop new production facilities at Palente. [108]

Saintesprit realized that his success in maintaining labor peace while preparing for the transformation of Lip into an assembly plant for ASUAG could not last much longer. In September 1972, he told the works

103   AMB 5Z18 Saintesprit to PD, November 13, 1972.
104   ADD 1026W7 PD to PM, November 17, 1972.
105   ADD 2377W181 PD to Ministre Jean Charbonnel, November 17, 1972.
106   Collectif [of Lip employees], Lip: affaire non classée (Paris, 1976), 13.
107   Jannic, "Fred Lip s'explique," 112.
108   Piaget, Lip. Charles Piaget et les Lip racontent, 213. Piton, C'est possible!, 102.

council that he was ready to leave and had asked the board of directors to name a "dauphin" to take his place when the time came. Later that year, the IDI told the Ébauches SA that it would not respond favorably to the firm's request until dramatic changes along the lines of ASUAG's plans for a stripped-down Lip were made. It was not surprising that the IDI recommended disposing of divisions not engaged in watch assembly, since it relied on figures drawn from the period of ASUAG's effort to phase them out.[109] If these sectors appeared unprofitable, this was in ASUAG's interest. However, the IDI informed Ébauches SA that it would say nothing publicly before the elections in March 1973.[110] ASUAG did tell Fred Lip in January 1973 that it would put Saintesprit and his policies to foster labor peace aside in favor "of other more deep-reaching measures." But it did not tell Fred Lip about the IDI's decision, so it could use the need to present a good face to the IDI as a reason to ask him to stop badmouthing the current management of the firm.[111]

Ébauches SA increased its holdings in Lip and came to exercise control of the company, but it had different plans for it than Fred Lip. "Alas, the Don Juan that was Ébauches SA settled for wooing a pretty young woman, in this case Lip. He took me to the theatre and the cinema, but did not consummate the relationship. Not very virile, those Swiss!"[112] Declining armaments sales took away the cushion that had protected watch production, still based on the manufacture of a significant proportion of watch parts at Palente. In 1972, Switzerland sold ten times as many watches in the United Kingdom as in France.[113] A proud Fred Lip would later say the Swiss had bought Lip to do away with a brand name "which cast a shadow on them the world over,"[114] but in fact the Lip name and commercial network were the source of its appeal to the Swiss in their effort to create a place for themselves in France and in the Common Market. However, in 1972, when Switzerland signed a trade agreement with the Common Market that reduced tariffs, the appeal of Lip to ASUAG declined. In any case, ASUAG proved more virile than Fred Lip thought. In June 1973, *Témoignage chrétien* published a drawing entitled "Marianne Lip Confides" depicting Lip as a pregnant Marianne

---

109   BDIC F delta rés 707/5 FGM-CFDT, "L'affaire LIP," August 8, 1973
110   Ébauches SA, "Mémorandum relatif à LIP SA," May 21, 1973, in Maire and Piaget, *Lip 73*, document 4.
111   AMB 5Z223 Directeur Général of ASUAG to Fred Lip, January 4, 1973 (with a note saying a copy of this letter was sent to Charles Piaget in May 1973).
112   Jannic, "Fred Lip s'explique," 111.
113   BDIC F delta rés 707/5 FGM-CFDT, "L'affaire LIP," August 8, 1973
114   "Les Révélations de Fred Lip," *Le Meilleur*, October 21, 1989," 11.

emblematic of a ravaged France. She explains: "Flirting, he took advantage of me. He told me that if there was a pregnancy [*s'il y a ébauche*], 'you will come to my country Switzerland and we'll take care of it.'"[115]

Deprived of the information legally due to it, the works council took advantage of a provision in the law that allowed it to hire an "expert accountant" to analyze the finances of the firm. This research provided the basis for a twenty-one-page memorandum the CFDT-Lip sent to the press and 100 state and elected officials in February 1973. It laid out the situation at Lip and the need for state action. The report showed that the dire situation was the fruit of the Ébauches SA plan to dismantle Lip and make it an assembly plant, while using the Lip name to market its watches: "The Lip firm forms a whole in human and economic terms. It would be unacceptable to see this enterprise dismantled … as is envisaged … It was never our idea to demand the impossible, but today we say: That's enough, we aren't pawns on a chessboard."[116]

The second round of the legislative elections was held on March 11, 1973. The IDI made its decision public on March 19. With the IDI option off the table, Saintesprit had served his purpose and on April 17 he resigned. Workers believed that Saintesprit's departure signaled that layoffs were imminent and that Saintesprit, whom they saw as "a so-called *social patron*," had been judged "too weak" to carry them out.[117] Ébauches SA did not replace Saintesprit, leaving a void that workers would occupy. The Tribunal de Besançon, a bankruptcy court, named two provisional administrators to oversee liquidation of the enterprise. Ébauches SA had been planning to dismantle the firm, including selling the machine-tools and armaments divisions, as part of its plan to make Palente a watch assembly plant. It wanted, Piaget told workers, "to cut all the branches of the Lip tree. All the branches that did not interest them."[118] Although the unions made clear in April that they recognized it was likely that some elements of production would need to be rethought and some workers reassigned, they were adamant that neither layoffs nor

---

115   *Témoignage chrétien*, June 21, 1973, 10. Ébauche means beginning, referring here to pregnancy, to a watch movement that has not been completed, and to Ébauches SA (ASUAG), which had taken control of Lip. At the time abortion was illegal in both France and Switzerland.

116   ADD 45J2 "Document CFDT, adressé aux différentes personnalités" [quoted]. Pierre Jusseaume, "Un succès venu de loin. La 'Popularisation' chez Lip," *Politique aujourd'hui* 3–4 (March–April 1974): 63.

117   BDIC F delta rés 578/36 "Débat entre les travailleurs de la Redoute et de Lip," November 10, 1973.

118   "Notes de Charles Piaget pour des prises de parole en atelier," April 24, 1973, in Cassou, "Lip, La Construction d'un mythe," 181.

the breakup of the firm were necessary and that workers' existing benefits should be maintained.[119] Dismantling the firm would leave individual units more vulnerable to downsizing. In the words of the joint statement of the CFDT-Lip and CGT-Lip in early May, the Ébauches SA plan was to "let the firm go down the drain," to remove "the 'noble' work" from Lip and to reduce the factory to "a performer with the mastermind in Switzerland." It could, they warned, ultimately become a "letter box," with the sole function of allowing Swiss-made watches to be sold under the French trademark of Lip.[120] Workers put up a poster in the factory that read, "Les petits suisses [a cheese] will not eat us. We will eat them."[121]

Pierre Messmer, Chaban-Delmas' successor as prime minister, saw no need for the construction of a "new society" and had no sympathy for the Lip workers, but even he would later characterize Ébauches SA as acting in "a nineteenth-century style."[122] Managers set out to instill fear in workers, while the firm launched what Piaget called a "vast brainwashing operation" in both the local and the national media to render the dismantling of Lip seemingly ineluctable.[123] Workers in turn formed committees in early May to establish regular contact with newspapers and other media to make the case that with investment in the products of Lip research there would be no need for layoffs or breaking up the firm. Ébauches SA's "dramatization on a national scale" brought its own dangers.[124] A few weeks after dismissing Saintesprit, the provisional administrators had to run advertisements in the press and on radio and television to counter the effects of their campaign to scare workers in order to reassure watch seller-jewelers and their customers.[125] On top of this, the prefect reported to the prime minister at the end of May that if effective leadership that took full advantage of the potential at Palente were put in place, it was not clear that the number of layoffs apparently envisaged would be necessary.[126]

---

119   *Le Monde*, September 18, 1973, 40.

120   ADD 45J2 CFDT-Lip/CGT-Lip to Responsables du Groupe Communiste à l'Assemblée Nationale, May 2, 1973.

121   Piton in BDIC F delta rés 707/9(1) Fonds Michel Duyrat Bande UNCLA 1 Cahier no. 1.

122   Pierre Messmer, *Après tant de batailles* (Paris, 1992), 371.

123   "Notes de Charles Piaget," April 18, 1973, in Cassou, "Lip, La Construction d'un mythe," 178.

124   AMB 5Z223 CFDT-Lip and CGT-Lip to deputies in the region, May 2, 1973 [quoted]; Pierre Jusseaume (CFDT) and Jean Vuillaume (CGT) to Deputy Jacques Weinman, April 21, 1973.

125   ADD 1026W7 PD to PM, May 9, 1973.

126   ADD 1026W7 PD to PM, May 31, 1973.

Mobilization of Workers

For three weeks after Saintesprit's resignation, union delegates joined by workers from a newly created Action Committee visited each workshop and office twice a day and held fifteen-minute "mini-assemblies." They produced and distributed a seven-page leaflet on Ébauches SA and its plans for Lip. Equipped with a mobile sound system, they led discussion on all the issues workers raised, with the goal of ensuring the engaged commitment of every worker.[127] Piaget's notes show that as militants went around the factory, they talked workers through an analysis of the situation in order to combat the "constant hammering in the media" aimed at convincing workers that "unemployment is a fatality."[128] The day after Saintesprit's dismissal, Piaget toured the workshops, saying, "They would like to see us be sheep. But no, we must be lions."[129] Referring to workers at other firms in Besançon which had faced a similar situation, Piaget said "they asked of them the best suicide possible," but *les Lip* should not accept this.[130]

To avoid this fate, each worker had to put aside the egotistical first reaction—the hope he or she would not be laid off—in favor of a commitment to the collectivity: "At this time, to attend only to one's work, relying solely on the flip of a coin, heads or tails, I would or would not be affected—this is not the way a man acts ... No one should disengage at such a time. Breaking ranks is to be oblivious or cowardly."[131] Fighting mass layoffs constituted an important break with the standard practice of the CFDT and CGT confederations; they did not directly contest dismissals for economic reasons, but sought better severance pay and employment opportunities elsewhere for those who lost their jobs. Piaget countered that workers needed to refuse "to be the playthings of economic destiny."[132] They had to overcome "the thousand and one facets of our conditioning to subordination" and resist entreaties from family and friends to accept the inevitable.[133] Such resolve, Piaget believed, required group therapy:

---

127   Chaillet et al., "Entretien avec Charles Piaget," 117–18.

128   "Il y a 25 ans ... Lip" [interview with Piaget], *Sud* 85 (September 1998): 8.

129   "Notes de Charles Piaget," April 18, 1973, in Cassou, "Lip, La Construction d'un mythe," 179.

130   "Notes de Charles Piaget," April 24, 1973, in ibid., 181.

131   Ibid., 182. See also *Politique hebdo*, December 20, 1973, 16.

132   "L'affaire Lip: emergence de nouveaux droits," 1201–20.

133   Charles Piaget, "Préface" to Chaudy, *Faire des hommes libres*, 11.

In the general assemblies we have addressed these problems together. Articulating them has helped a lot to resolve them. We found that the expression in a group of the outlook of each really helped overcome fears and concerns. Through all the smiles, all the 'confessions', we could see that one's problem was also that of the neighbor and that of all, that it was not shameful, that this was true, and one has to live with it to overcome it. The feeling of belonging to a collectivity was facilitated, and rendered stronger than individualism.[134]

The unions convened a General Assembly and broke into small groups to discuss what actions to take. When it reassembled, the Assembly voted against going on strike, believing that the company could wait out salary-less striking workers. It then debated the idea of reducing the pace of production, more difficult than striking because managerial personnel constantly harassed workers participating in slowdowns. However, faced with sectors where the company had stopped seeking contracts and which therefore risked running out of work, the Assembly agreed on slowing down production in order to assure continued work and pay for all; this also required individual workers to take action that committed them to the struggle and gave them the chance to reflect together when they were not working.[135] "What is essential," Piaget explained, "is that you reduce the totality of your sense of self in the work because you are beginning to think about something else":[136]

Lowering production rates was a weapon of liberation for us. We knew it wasn't enough to hurt the trust, that it was pinpricks on the hide of a big elephant. But it was essential for the workers, so that gradually they take charge of their strike and have the time they need to reflect while still being paid. Through this, they discovered they were the ones who controlled production.[137]

Employees developed ways to get their colleagues to engage. They moved the desk of a non-participating technician while he was out of his office. What began as an act of shaming ended with his co-workers circling

---

134 Piaget, "La formation par l'action collective," 158.
135 "Lip des militants du comité d'action parlent," supplement to *Révolution!* 35 (1973): 13.
136 AR Interview with Piaget by Rouaud, September 11, 2003, 36 [quoted]. Piaget, *Lip. Charles Piaget et les Lip racontent,* 129. Piaget, "Les luttes de LIP."
137 Piaget, *Lip. Charles Piaget et les Lip racontent,* 24, 27.

the technician "affectionately" and inviting him to join with them. In Piton's telling, "He was relieved and pleased by our intervention. He was suffering staying outside the community," and went on to be an active participant.[138]

Union delegates found it most difficult to get female assembly line and watch-part workers to slow down production. In May 1968, Piaget had been shocked that assembly line workers who had met to talk about how to work "less stupidly, to work differently," told him that if one worker could put both hands on the watch face, that would be an improvement. "There," Charles Piaget realized, "we really saw the invisible chains, the chains that tie each to their workstation, the brain, the hands, everything. It was incredible: their horizon extended only fifty centimeters by fifty centimeters!"[139] A forty-four-year-old female OS would recall: "the day we said that we had to slow down production, I didn't think I could ever do it; 19 years at piece work, and, all at once, you had to do less, whereas before you never did enough!"[140] Mechanics would take a chair and sit for two or three hours with an OS, encouraging her to reduce production, sometimes showing her ways to do so.[141] The goal was to break the hold of the cadence over workers so that they would not be so absorbed by work that they could not think about and discuss the situation they were confronting. A male CFDT-Lip delegate from the machine shop reported that when he first arrived at the assembly lines, "we really felt like strangers ... [W]hen the bosses were there, the women maintained their production rate. When we came, they slowed down, only to pick up the rhythm when we left. You could have the impression that alongside them, we too were playing the role of bosses."[142] "It's horrible, I had the sense of being a cop in charge of breaks. I had to take them one by one from their workstations so that they could come talk with us in the sunshine and rest a little."[143]

However, taking breaks was the idea of the female OS themselves, who felt they could not slow down production and so began to stop work for five or ten minutes an hour instead.[144] This led to heated

138   Piton, C'est possible, 71–2.
139   Féret, Les Yeux rouges, 62–3.
140   Bondu, "De l'usine à la communauté," 480.
141   Burgy in Piaget, Lip. Charles Piaget et les Lip racontent, 46–7. BDIC F delta rés 578/36 "Débat entre les travailleurs," 4.
142   Werner, "La Question des Femmes," 2450.
143   Le Nouvel observateur, June 25, 1973, 18.
144   "LIP, LIP, LIP, hourra!" Program of Daniel Mermet, "Là-bas si j'y suis," November 25, 2013, at franceinter.fr.

confrontations with their bosses. When told to get cracking, they learned to answer that they wanted information and explanations about the company's future. The overseers turned away, giving workers a chance to talk among themselves about the firm's situation.[145] In so doing, they directly and viscerally committed themselves to the movement, without losing their salary. "Through this struggle," Vittot explained, "what is remarkable is that the workers dared to get up, leave their workstations, and speak out, with the bosses always there, and thus affirm that they were not shackled."[146]

The records kept of production presented another hurdle. One militant explained that "We discovered how difficult it was for workers not to fill out their worksheets; these are in fact real chains that attach the worker to his workstation as surely as a galley slave to his oars."[147] Despite this, workers stopped filling out production cards and the office staff took control of the computer cards on which production was entered. Without these, managers were unable to single out and intimidate individual workers.[148] By May 10, watch production was down 50 per cent; in armaments and mechanics, production was at 10 percent of the norm.[149]

Militants encouraged workers throughout the factory to use company materials to make posters and to hang them on their office walls or machines. These took their place alongside the motivational quotations Fred Lip had posted throughout the factory. The posters allowed workers to give individual expression to collective grievances and aspirations. Workers left their workstations and gathered to look at and discuss colleagues' posters. They got to know one another better: "it was euphoric … strong enough to break the production rates. The posters mobilized workers to take them on."[150] A primary subject was the oppressive overseer. The workers' defense of their posters against bosses who sought to take them down further engaged them in the struggle. In the words of one office worker, the posters revealed to colleagues and to employees themselves a creativity hidden in the world of work:

---

145 *L'Outil des travailleurs*, December 1973-January 1974, 10.

146 Roy, "Lip 1973," 21.

147 AMB 5Z221 "Prise de parole pour meeting" [1973]. Piaget made the same point. *Témoignage chrétien*, June 21, 1973, 10.

148 *Rouge*, June 1, 1973, 9. BDIC F delta rés 578/41 "Lip," *L'Anti-brouillard*, trial issue, May 1973, 3.

149 ADD 1026W12 RG, May 10, 1973.

150 Michel in "Lip des militants du comité d'action parlent," 13-14.

Right at the beginning, a lot of people found themselves through the posters. We posted in the factory, on windows. We drew our thoughts, we drew things that were really funny. There, we discovered hidden unknown talents, folks who were working on machines, who were totally unknown. They were there; they put up their small posters, with slogans in the form of short, simple phrases. Little by little people discovered the gifts they had and which had no place in the work they were doing.[151]

In occupied factories the norm was for workers to maintain the means of production, but not to operate company machinery. However, Lip employees had used photocopy machines to run off leaflets in May 1968. In the spring of 1973, they also operated the company's offset machines to reproduce their favorite posters: Crossing the Rubicon, a group of workers later called it.[152]

Faced with the company's strategy of leaving their movement to rot, the importance of applying the "moral pressure" of "public opinion" in the region became clear: "It is our last asset," in the words of one Lip worker.[153] A key was for workers to continue to get paid, even when spreading word of their situation outside of the factory. Without production records, the provisional administrators were reduced to paying workers for hours present.[154] The General Assembly established "a kind of people's court." When workers saw that the factory guards were noting their comings and goings, they decided to make this impossible by painting blue the windows of the guardhouse at the entry to the factory. Office workers did not report colleagues who left to go leafleting, and employees in the payroll office did not record the absences of workers out campaigning.[155]

Employees wore their work clothes to leaflet in Besançon and surrounding communities. Piton realized that the white smocks in which Fred Lip had dressed watch workers and secretaries, and that she would never have worn outside Palente before, had become a source of pride.[156]

---

151   Sylvaine in Piaget, *Lip. Charles Piaget et les Lip racontent*, 93–4.

152   Burgy and Piton in ibid., 47, 144–5. *Libération*, August 10, 1973, 6. Raguénès, *De Mai 68*, 141. "Lip des militants du comité d'action parlent," 13–14. Piaget, "LIP. Les effets formateurs," 146–9.

153   *Politique hebdo*, May 17, 1973, 13.

154   ADD 1026W3 Administrateur provisoire Louis Dufay to Inspecteur du travail (Doubs), May 14, 1973.

155   Piton, *C'est possible!*, 64, 72. ADD 1026W3 Administrateur provisoire Louis Dufay to PD, June 4, 1973. Piton in "Lip des militants du comité d'action parlent," 14.

156   Piton in BDIC F delta rés 707/9(1) Fonds Michel Duyrat Bande UNCLA Cahier no. 1. Piton, *C'est possible!*, 56.

At the beginning of June, workers heard that Paris public transit buses from the 1930s were being sold off. They bought one, decorated it with posters and banners, and mounted loudspeakers on it. On the road from June 8 to 12, the bus took their cause to workers in forty-six firms in Besançon and led a several-hundred-meter-long caravan of workers in their autos around Franche-Comté.[157] *Les Lip* had success in rural communities, though they faced skepticism from small watchmakers in Haut-Doubs, whose antipathy to Lip was not overcome by the workers' contention that their fight was for French watchmaking as a whole.[158]

The Communists

In the first years after May 1968, the CFDT-Lip and the CGT-Lip met each week and produced leaflets signed by both unions. Although the CGT decided this arrangement was too favorable to the CFDT-Lip and ended the intersyndical bulletin, the unions continued a noteworthy cooperation and fended off repeated efforts by both Fred Lip and Saintesprit to divide them.[159] However, the initial threat posed by the dismantling of the firm was to skilled workers in mechanics, where the core of the CFDT-Lip support was based, while OS in watch production, a site of CGT-Lip strength, were apparently at less immediate risk. The prefect noted in mid-February 1973 that this gave the two unions different interests:

> This is why the CGT[-Lip] seemed until now to accept with a certain serenity the prospect of profound changes in operation of the enterprise in the spring, while the CFDT[-Lip] affirmed immediately its opposition to all fragmentation of the unity of production at Lip, in particular any financial or legal separation between watchmaking and other activities.

The prefect believed that "the CFDT[-Lip] therefore adopts a position that amounts to freezing the current structures, in order to make sure its influence is not reduced within the enterprise."[160] As far as the Com-

157   Jusseaume, "Un succès venu de loin," 66. *Lip Unité*, October 1974, 4. Chaillet et al., "Entretien avec Charles Piaget," 118.

158   Piton, *C'est possible!*, 67.

159   BDIC KA 214 1 *Les Cahiers de mai* interview with Piaget [1973]. BDIC KA 214 2 *Les Cahiers de mai* interview with Piaget [1973].

160   ADD 1026W7 PD to PM, February 14, 1973.

munists were concerned, the CFDT-Lip's arguments about the economic possibilities of the firm took the unions where they should not go. In March 1973, *L'Heure LIP*, the bulletin of the party cell in the factory, asserted that it was not up to workers to address the problems of an individual capitalist firm. In keeping with the Common Program, the answer to the Swiss mismanagement of Lip was nationalization (although Lip was not among the firms to be nationalized in the Program).[161]

However, the Parti Communiste Français (PCF) and the regional and national CGT leadership came to fear that the CGT-Lip was cooperating too closely with the CFDT-Lip. Government wiretapping in mid-May 1973 revealed that the CGT and the PCF felt the need to bring in regional leaders to assert their authority over the CGT-Lip in order to ensure that Lip not become a "new 'Joint Français,'" referring to a strike in Bretagne in 1972 which had attracted support from leftists, the bane of the PCF.[162] In mid-May, Claude Curty, the federal secretary of the Union Départementale of the CGT, explained the importance of avoiding a strategy that "would lead to the decay" of the movement, which he believed was happening at Lip. It was important to "bring to Besançon a comrade from the leadership of the federation to draft a model text for the papers of the party cell," to have one or two Communist deputies, and to get the party leadership and *L'Humanité* more involved. He suggested calling in the Jeunesses Communistes: "We need something original and independent."[163]

The CGT favored a strategy of bringing pressure to bear on the state. In line with this, the CGT-Lip got the CFDT-Lip to cosponsor a demonstration of workers from Lip in Paris on May 29. However, when Curty directed the CGT-Lip to put out a leaflet in its own name calling for participation, Claude Mercet, secretary-general of the CGT-Lip, refused: the CFDT-Lip would "kick our asses," saying that the CGT-Lip was trying to operate on its own. To Curty's response that the CGT-Lip would have to take leadership, Mercet explained that this would be the end of the movement at Lip: "You know what the union members said: Curty has come to pollute our movement!"[164] This concern for unity and autonomy would characterize the workers' unions at Lip through the spring and

---

161   AMB 5Z221 *L'Heure LIP* 3 (March 1973).

162   ADD 1026W8 "CGT Affaire Lip," May 15, 1973. Lip workers saw the "moral pressure of all the French" achieved by Joint Français workers as the key to their struggle as well. *Politique hebdo*, May 15, 1973, 13.

163   ADD 1026W8 "PCF Affaire Lip," May 17, 1973.

164   ADD 1026W8 "CGT Affaire Lip," May 17, 1973.

summer of 1973. In late June, the workers heard of a dispute between the CFDT-Lip and the CGT-Lip. They took the initiative and immediately circulated a petition asking that the unions put aside their differences; in an hour or two, more than 200 workers signed the petition and it stopped circulating only because the unions met together immediately and assured workers of their continued unity.[165] This union cooperation appealed particularly to those around France who saw the contesting confederations as a central impediment to the France they hoped to see develop after May 1968.

The Action Committee

The dramatic mobilization of the workers at Lip in the spring of 1973 was in part the work of the Action Committee (*comité d'action*), at the origin of which was the Dominican priest Jean Raguénès. In the words of Lip worker Michel Cugney, Raguénès was "the keystone of informal power at Lip. He does not recognize the structures at all, but he has amazing power!"[166] Raguénès had been the driving force behind the opposition to firing Ouaked Areski.[167] Although a cleric, he had an activist's curriculum vitae: a move from "angelic disengagement to incarnation in a community. From individual history to history in a people (not in the Maoist, but in the Biblical sense)."[168] Doing his military service in Morocco on the eve of that nation's independence, Raguénès worked hard to explain to Moroccans in the French army that they should be on the other side.[169] In 1967 Raguénès was appointed chaplain at the Centre St. Yves, a meeting place for Catholic law students. In May 1968, he set up a loudspeaker inside the center and it became a site where all could come and speak day and night.[170] After May, Raguénès became involved in the fate of the Katangais, working-class youths from the suburbs of Paris who had provided security for student demonstrators in May. As the police took back the occupied campuses and students departed, a dozen or so Katangais decided to train as resisters outside of Paris and so be ready to pursue the revolution when students returned in the fall.

165 *Les Cahiers de Mai hebdo*, July 2, 1973, 4.
166 *Lip Unité*, April-May 1980, 3.
167 ADD 1812W34 RG, April 4, 1973.
168 Léo Lévy, *À la vie* (Lagrasse, 2013), 87.
169 *Le Monde*, April 5, 2007, 20.
170 AR Interview with Raguénès by Rouaud, Transcript no. 1 [2003], 5.

After the group executed a member they felt endangered their security, they fled to the Sorbonne, the last occupied campus in Paris. The student occupation committee included many Catholics and it sent the Katangais to the Centre St. Yves. Raguénès and other clergy sheltered them until they decided to turn themselves in later that summer. Both before and during his time at the Centre St. Yves, Raguénès worked with youth on the margins of society, but after May 1968 he realized it was not sufficient to "go toward"; he must "be with."[171] He was not a worker priest, but took a job at the Peugeot factory at Sochaux to support himself before going to Besançon, where he set up a house for recidivists with the goal of establishing a community based on shared responsibilities. In 1971, Raguénès was hired as an OS in the armaments division at Lip.

Raguénès joined the CFDT-Lip, but initially did not play an active role in it. The union had grown significantly since May 1968 with an influx of young workers. Challenged in September 1972 by one of them—François Laurent, an OS who cleaned the machines with trichloroethylene—Raguénès turned his attention to those marginalized within the union because the existing leadership was so gifted that no one would think of challenging it. Raguénès recognized that the leaders of the CFDT-Lip were not "organization men" cut off from the base like the CGT leaders at Sochaux, but this still did not assure democracy.[172] Raguénès and three union members in their mid-twenties wrote a letter to the CFDT-Lip leadership in which they explained that the trimestrial general assemblies, though attended by a large majority of the personnel, were so well prepared, the tracts distributed were so pertinent, the union delegates so able, clear and active, that workers were daunted: "many male and female workers felt reduced to the role of assenting and admiring spectators, with no real possibility to participate."[173]

The union leadership understood that their very virtues were the problem. The CFDT-Lip opened its doors to a constant flow of workers. Whatever efficiency was lost, the accessibility was "fruitful": "operations got better, the circle enlarged and developed."[174] Piaget constantly interrupted his speeches with questions to the workers, underscoring his message that nothing would be possible without the men and women in

---

171   Raguénès, *De Mai 68*, 71–91, 108 [quoted].

172   Raguénès in "Lip des militants du comité d'action parlent," 10.

173   Raguénès, *De Mai 68*, 131 [quoted]. Beurier, "La Mémoire des Lip," Annexe VIII.

174   Piaget, "LIP. Les effets formateurs," 152.

his audience: "What do you think of this? Do you think it will work?"[175]
For Piaget:

> From the beginning, we asked ourselves: weren't we risking, we, dele-
> gates, being a break on the outpouring of ideas? ... We, in the CFDT-Lip,
> said the day when the personnel as a whole contest us, well, that day, for
> us, that's it, it's won. We had done our work as trade unionists. It means
> that each of the workers was taking an interest, contributing.[176]

In response to the letter sent by Raguénès and the workers, in November 1972 four or five CFDT-Lip leaders began meeting once a week after
work with Raguénès and a comparable number of young union members,
including Marc Géhin, winner of Fred Lip's contest for youth. This group
explained that it did not want to be "purely consultative" or "the good
democratic conscience of the delegates"—"not a simple transmission
belt" between the delegates and the workers, but "a place of reflection
and initiatives."[177] As a result of the rights given to locals in the legislation
of December 27, 1968, union and elected personnel delegates received
fifteen paid hours per month to fulfill their responsibilities. CFDT-Lip
delegates generally used this time to meet workers during the work day,
so as not to take delegates away from those they represented. But with
Saintesprit's resignation on April 17, 1973 the delegates broke with this
practice. Needing more time, they met together at work. Feeling they
were being informed of discussions and decisions made during the day,
Raguénès and a couple of other workers decided to leave work without
permission (or pay) to take part in discussions with the union delegates.
The next day, some fifty workers went to the delegates' meeting. On April
20, it was enlarged to include all workers. Each day, seventy or eighty
and sometimes up to twice that many workers came, drawn from both
unions as well as the non-unionized. A growing number of these workers
presented their concerns and ideas at the meetings. They also joined
union delegates in going about the factory to convince employees to
join the work slowdown. More important, these men and women went
back to their workshops and discussed issues raised at the meetings and

---

175   Champeau, "Lip: Le Conflit et l'affaire," 12–13. Piton in BDIC F delta rés
707/9(4) Fonds Michel Duyrat Bande UNCLA Cahier no. 4 [quoted].

176   *Libération*, September 17, 1973, 4.

177   Raguénès in "Lip des militants du comité d'action parlent," 10–11. Raguénès
in Piaget, *Lip. Charles Piaget et les Lip racontent*, 148. BDIC F delta rés 578/39 *Les Cahiers
de mai* to chers camarades [their members], November 27, 1973.

presented the workers' responses the next day, thus assuring "a more collective way of thinking" and making the daily meetings themselves "an instrument of collective reflection."[178]

When the CGT-Lip delegates, followed by those of CFDT-Lip, decided to meet on their own, the new group followed suit and adopted the name Action Committee. The Action Committee emerged in a time of crisis and Piaget recognized that its first job "was to fight the defeatism and fatalism," which workers in such situations naturally feel.[179] Insisting "we do not want to be the OS of the action," and "we are all delegates in potential," the Action Committee held meetings of 100 or so workers without union delegates, fearing that their presence would impede discussion. Although the CGT-Lip initially considered meetings that excluded delegates as perforce anti-union, it soon came to accept the new development.[180] Raguénès believed the heterogeneity of participants made these gatherings a place that "destroyed the parochialism one found among the delegates."[181] The Action Committee functioned as the workers had earlier at the delegates' meetings, assuring discussion of a diversity of ideas at the General Assembly, in place of the respectful reception previously accorded to the union leaders' interventions.[182]

Clavel wrote admiringly that the Action Committee was "a spur to combat complacency" that gave the CFDT-Lip the impetus "to create its own opposition, to contest itself."[183] Vittot said of the Action Committee, "I myself am glad that they call us into question from time to time," and he would say in August 1973 that it was the Action Committee "that had given the struggle its exceptional character."[184] His response had qualities of his experience in the ACO: "Me, I experienced it as something great. I learned to listen. I try to keep my trap shut. There are a whole lot of people with things to say. Not CGT or CFDT in particular. Just as much activists as me."[185] Piaget spoke of the need revealed by the Action

---

178   Jusseaume, "Un succès venu de loin," 65. BDIC F delta rés 578/38 *Les Cahiers de Mai*, nos. 41–2, non-paru (page proofs without page numbers).

179   BDIC F delta rés 578/41 "Entretien avec C. Piaget," *L'Anti-brouillard*, trial issue, May 1973: 3.

180   "Lip des militants du comité d'action parlent," 11. BDIC F delta rés 578/36 "Débat entre les travailleurs," 2–3.

181   *Libération*, June 25, 1973, 3.

182   Piton in BDIC F delta rés 707/9(1) Fonds Michel Duyrat Bande UNCLA 3bis Cahier no. 1.

183   *Libération*, May 25–6, 1974, 2.

184   Piton, *C'est possible!*, 509. *Anti-brouillard*, September 1973, n.p.

185   ADD 177J13 Transcript of a discussion between Lip leadership and local PCF leaders at Palente [1977].

Committee: "to break the divide: the delegates and the union think, the wage earners follow."[186] Piaget welcomed this "counter-power," seeing the Action Committee as born of workers themselves discovering "that it was unacceptable to let the delegates deal with the struggle on their own" and recognized that what was required to contest "the personality, the personalism" that union leaders exercised was a space where all could enter into debates previously left to those leaders, without fear that the latter would condemn their ideas as "daft."[187] OS Paulette Dartevel the essence of this empowerment: "at the Action Committee, if you said something really stupid, never mind, we had a good laugh and moved on, whereas in front of the delegates, we dared less."[188] Raguénès believed the Action Committee created an environment in which the previously silenced spoke up, and their insights, formerly unrecognized by them and by all, emerged to become elements of a productive democratic conversation:[189] "It is a matter of revealing the knowledge that is in each one of us, by word and by reason. The educator and the educated have a shared, inseparable role. The Action Committee was not a defined group, but much more a 'style.'"[190]

For the first time, workers who felt trapped and worthless on the job saw their ideas considered and valued. A male OS who did not belong to a union explained:

> It is there [in the Action Committee] that we proved that a guy who drills holes all day can take initiative, that he has a whole batch of ideas, of riches buried in him. All of this has to come out, one must break the lead wall of alienation, of subjection, of conditioning caused by idiotic work. This condition, we scrutinized, exposed, treated, probed, went through. All at once, you felt guys opening themselves up.[191]

Participants developed ideas and solutions on their own, rather than depending on directives from union delegates. Workers had always been

---

186   Réseau Citoyens Résistants, *La Force*, 31–2.
187   Michel Duyrat in F delta rés 707/9(1) Fonds Michel Duyrat Bande UNCLA 3 Cahier no. 1. Piaget, *Lip. Charles Piaget et les Lip racontent*, 32–3.
188   *Lip au féminin*, 52. Dominique Enfraze makes the same point in *Lip Unité*, First Trimester 1983, 10.
189   Raguénès, *De Mai 68*, 174.
190   "Lip, de Palente au Xingu," *Le Poivron* 89 (March 2007), lepoivron.free.fr.
191   "Comment 'l'affaire' nous a changés," 71. For more such testimony, see Jean Lopez, "Lip Interview [transcript of discussions with CA members]" [November 1973], typescript at BDIC Q Pièce 12.785, 43–6.

called on to produce banners and distribute leaflets, but now they were asked to think about what should be written on them.[192] No one expressed better than Piton the liberation that Action Committee members experienced, speaking in the absence of union delegates—there was "no political know-it-all" whose reference to (his) long experience could censor them. "Unions see nothing but difficulties, reason only in legal and material terms, and don't understand feelings; one could say they have no heart. The Action Committee lets us free our imagination; it was the joy and the sincerity of the struggle."[193] For one female worker, the Action Committee "was a people's militia to maintain the spirit of initiatives."[194]

The Action Committee sought to involve all participants by reaching consensus, rather than resorting to majority vote. Piton explained:

> In the Action Committee, if we have so many difficulties, it is because in the case of differences, we don't go halfway. This has never happened to us. We can be twenty against ten and we continue to fight it out, to the end. Sometimes, nothing comes out of it. We aren't a union. That we don't work things out amicably in order to come up with a compromise, I like that. An Action Committee, that's it; everyone expresses themselves, each holds to their idea. There is exchange, cross-fertilization and it is the cross-fertilization of ideas that makes the Action Committee.[195]

Piaget recognized that in the Action Committee, "people propel themselves; the very fact that they are not in a structure constitutes an advantage that permits the gush of ideas, of forces."[196] Action Committee meetings never had an agenda. As far as Raguénès was concerned, the Action Committee was never an "entity," an institution which existed permanently rather than just when needed.[197] But later, when the CGT-Lip, backed by the CFDT-Lip, sought to make Action Committee participation in negotiations conditional upon affirming in writing that it was an organ of the struggle and would disappear when the conflict was resolved, the Action Committee refused.[198] In the words of one member:

---

192   Piton in L'Outil des travailleurs, December 1973–January 1974, 8.
193   Piton in Werner, "La Question des femmes," 2455–6. Piton. C'est possible!, 475. Piton in "Lip des militants du comité d'action parlent," 12.
194   BDIC F delta rés 707/9(3) Fonds Michel Duyrat Bande UNCLA Cahier no. 3 Bande 6 (AG of 20 June 1973).
195   Il était une fois la révolution, 63.
196   Barou, Gilda je t'aime, 217.
197   L'Outil des travailleurs, April 1974, 16.
198   Guy in Piaget, Lip. Charles Piaget et les Lip racontent, 19.

I found in the Action Committee something other [than in the union]: the Action Committee, it doesn't exist, there is no structure. There is nothing at all. We often discussed, we even tried to make, the embryo of a structure that we rushed to destroy because that didn't work. And so now, when we speak of dissolving the Action Committee, it is extremely difficult, because the Action Committee doesn't exist anywhere.[199]

The Action Committee had particular appeal to young workers, many of whom had begun work and joined a union after May 1968. A number of leaders of the movement over the next decade came from the Action Committee. These included Dominique Enfraze, who at sixteen had started work as an OS in mechanics in 1969; Marc Géhin, a technician in the same workshop as Piaget; as well as Jacky Burtz and François Laurent, talented young workers who had shown the aptitude and commitment to take advantage of the company job-training program. Burtz was a mechanic who had been in the CGT-Lip, but left it for the Action Committee and later joined the CFDT-Lip. If at first male workers from threatened sectors like mechanics and armaments provided most participants, women later became active and often made up the majority at a meeting. In the past, female OS had been most at risk in the annual seasonal layoffs, but now their jobs were on the whole less immediately threatened than the male skilled workers and technicians. However, for many workers, male and female, the liberation within a valued community that the Action Committee and other elements of the experience brought became for them the *raison d'être* of the conflict.

The non-judgmental atmosphere of the Action Committee made it a place where some women workers began to overcome their fear of having their ideas dismissed and learned to express themselves in public.[200] Demougeot recalled that female workers spoke at Action Committee meetings "very quickly, in short phrases, because they weren't sure of themselves"; men, with greater mastery of public speech, still dominated the floor.[201] However, it was in the Action Committee that female employees like Piton and Demougeot emerged as leaders and became prominent voices and faces of the movement. Piton was the

---

199 Lopez, "Lip Interview," 48. See also *Il était une fois la révolution*, 62. French Maoists spoke in these terms as well: "We build the party to destroy it." Michèle Monceaux, *Les maos en France* (Paris, 1972), 66.

200 'Comment 'l'affaire' nous a changés," 71.

201 Demougeot in Caroline Dehedin, "À Lip, les femmes aussi ont une histoire: la lutte des ouvrières de 1973 à 1977." Masters, Université de Rouen, 2011, 78.

daughter of a blacksmith in a village in Doubs. She had begun factory work at sixteen. When she went to work at Lip twenty years later, she was a single mother who had divorced an abusive husband and been fired at Kelton for refusing the advances of her boss. In October 1973, she told a meeting that, in contrast to the union, the Action Committee "had in particular helped women to express themselves."[202]

Fatima Demougeot was born in Algeria. Her father was a harki, a lieutenant in the French army. At age ten she was recruited by the Red Cross to serve as an interpreter in the regroupment camps that the French created in Algeria during the war.[203] In 1962, when she was thirteen, her family left Algeria and went to a refugee camp in southwestern France. At eighteen, Demougeot left for Besançon to escape "parental authority." Later she explained, "I have fought all my life for [my liberty], against my family circle and this lack of liberty."[204] She settled in a hostel for young female workers and the residents elected her to present their grievances on the strict rules for residents. A CFDT militant directed the hostel and through her, Demougeot met ACO members and herself became active in the Jeunesse Ouvrière Chrétienne.[205] She went to work as an OS at Lip in March 1967. Like several of the men active in the Action Committee, Demougeot took full advantage of the evening job-training classes and within a couple of years was promoted to quality-control technician.[206] She joined the CFDT-Lip in May 1968 and was one of a half-dozen young workers whom CFDT delegates took aside and trained to be go-betweens with workers, "to make known the problems in the workshops that the veterans don't always see," at the very time when Fred Lip too was looking for sympathetic young workers.[207] When Demougeot realized that she had not received a raise she was due, she went to see Piaget. He worked with her and got the union to support her, but would not go see the management to present her case. Demougeot felt unable

202   ADD 45J96 Notes manuscrites de Père Zinty, vicaire général, "Affaire Lip" [October 1973].

203   AB, "Fatima Demougeot, une femme laïque et républicaine," *La Presse Bisontin* 91 (September 2008): 10.

204   *Il était une fois la révolution*, 117.

205   Interview with Demougeot by Reid, June 12, 2013.

206   *Le Nouvel observateur*, September 17, 1973, 42–3. AM "Debat avec les femmes de LIP, LYON juin 1975." *Le Matin*, March 4, 1986. *L'Unité*, March 14, 1986, 22. "D'un combat à l'autre," *Pays comtois* 74 (September 20, 2007): 28–30. Robert Gildea et al., *Europe's 1968. Voices of Revolt* (Oxford, 2013), 34.

207   D'Houtaud, "L'héritage," 125. Interview with Demougeot by Reid, June 12, 2013. ADD 45J100 Draft of Thomé, *Créateurs d'utopies*, 13 [quoted].

to do this on her own, but with Piaget's encouragement, she finally did and got satisfaction. "He is the guy," she said, "who gives to the *petits* the means to defend themselves and to express themselves."[208] The Action Committee further developed her confidence.

The national union confederations could not accept the Action Committee. Although CGT-Lip members participated in Action Committee meetings until mid-June, the Action Committee ran counter to the CGT belief that unions should have full responsibility for worker organization. In the words of one Action Committee member reflecting on the hierarchical structure of the CGT: "We were there like black sheep, no place foreseen for us."[209] At the end of June, one national CGT official spoke of the Action Committee as "*démocratouille*," a democratic stew.[210] Later that summer the CGT reasoned that those not in unions could speak in the General Assembly, so there was no need for the Action Committee.[211] For the CGT, the Action Committee could at best carry out material tasks assigned to it by the unions. Mercet, the CGT-Lip secretary-general, offered a milder expression of his confederation's position, saying that members of the Action Committee were "full of good will," but were not "militants," meaning that "they saw things much more superficially than we did. They did not feel their responsibility engaged in the same way."[212]

The CFDT-Lip prided itself on "a certain independence" from the national metallurgical federation and the confederation. "We were not a local that was 'imprinted,'" Piaget explained. "We forged ourselves."[213] Burgy referred to the CFDT-Lip as being an "odd duck" for the national leadership.[214] The national leadership saw strike committees, of which the Action Committee was a variant, as prone to falling in the hands of a few and launching actions that could get out of control. At the national CFDT congress in late May–early June 1973, CFDT-Lip voted with the minority against the condemnation of strike committees.[215] Piaget later explained:

208 Jacquin, "Lip 1973–1981," 180-1.
209 "Comment 'l'affaire' nous a changés," 72.
210 *Le Monde libertaire*, February 16, 1978, 8.
211 ACGT Lip Box 3 "Position CGT sur le comité d'action."
212 *Libération*, September 21, 1973, 3.
213 *Libération*, September 17, 1973, 4.
214 AR Interview with Burgy by Rouaud, May 5, 2004, 1-2.
215 Jacques Chérèque and Edmond Maire, "Les Leçons de Lip" in Maire and Piaget, *Lip 73*, 119.

In '73, the [confederations] were really taken aback that we put our union power at stake in saying that the more circles of autonomous reflection there are, the better it will be. So there were people, unionized or not, who set about reflecting and making proposals, becoming a driving force of the struggle. And we [in the CFDT-Lip] considered ourselves one of the driving forces, but no more than that.[216]

This was not how the CFDT thought things should be. It condemned the Action Committee as "a handful of militants" trying to play the role of a union. The confederation blamed the existence of the Action Committee on the failure of the CFDT-Lip leaders to keep the union rank and file actively involved in decision-making within the union; in this, it echoed the motivations of the founders of the Action Committee.[217] Unable to understand why the CFDT-Lip would tolerate the presence of the Action Committee, the FGM-CFDT dispatched Frédo Moutet, national treasurer and member of the executive commission, to Besançon. Moutet was won over, saying the situation, including the Action Committee, was unionism as he dreamed of it, but he was unable to convert the FGM-CFDT leadership. The federation secretary-general Jacques Chérèque called Piaget to say that Moutet may have been "bamboozled," but he would not be: he reiterated the federation position that mass firings could not be fought and the best that could be done was to seek severance pay for laid-off workers.[218] For Chérèque, the Action Committee, an organization he associated with leftist opponents of unions, and the demands for no layoffs and no dismantling, went hand in hand. Piaget responded that the federation should supply its expertise, but leave control of campaigns like that at Lip in the hands of the workers.[219]

Raguénès referred to himself as an embodiment of the "wise mad men," "that is to say [of] those people who want—right now—something other than this 'stereotyped', conformist society," and to Piaget as the embodiment of the "mad wise men"—the "mechanics of Besançon

---

216   D'Houtaud, "L'héritage," 126.
217   *CFDT Syndicalisme hebdo*, September 13, 1973, 6.
218   Rachida El Azzouzi, "Charles Piaget: une leçon de liberté" (July 6, 2013), mediapart.fr. AR Interview with Piaget by Rouaud, September 11, 2003, 53–4. AR Interview with Burgy by Rouaud, May 5, 2004, 1–2. Lacoste, *Lip, une école de lutte.* "Il y a 25 ans … Lip," 8.
219   Frank Georgi, *Soufflons nous-mêmes notre forge* (Paris, 1991), 170. Charles Piaget, "Lip 1973: Des problématiques toujours d'actualité" [1997] in *Autogestion. Une idée toujours neuve*, ed. Guillaume Davranche (Paris, 2010), 108–9. Ravenel, "Un militant ouvrier autogestionnaire," 114.

with Franche-Comté roots, peasants become workers ... and workers from father to son! Fond also of their little house, creatures of comfort, familial and personal," but "open to adventure, to another possible, etc." The Action Committee and the CFDT-Lip exemplified in different ways the relationship of the two dimensions of May 1968 present in the struggle at Lip—liberation and workers' control. "It is this equilibrium," said Raguénès, "between the wise mad men and the mad wise men, an equilibrium wonderfully proportioned at the time ... that truly created the 'Lip space.'" They were "in an ongoing dialectic"; their "fertilization" produced the particular qualities of the movement at Lip.[220]

Raguénès believed that all institutions functioned such that those in authority thought and gave lessons to the rank and file: "We, on the contrary, must begin with the base. The base must develop itself, structure itself, permanently contest itself or otherwise it ends in a totalitarian regime."[221] Piaget was sympathetic, but recognized the confederation's position that "the informal democracy" exercised by those attending the meetings of the Action Committee differed from that of the union, because they did not concern themselves with whether their views reflected those of the mass of workers. However, the Action Committee mobilized individuals outside of the union hierarchy and served as an invaluable think tank for the movement. It forced the delegates to open up: "perhaps we lose a little efficacy in the short term, but in the long run, we benefit enormously."[222] Piaget recognized that the Action Committee led the CFDT-Lip to pursue policies outside the range of those the confederation considered feasible: "I say it clearly, if we had been an orthodox local, we would never have developed such a conflict."[223]

Lip workers spoke frequently of living in a society where they were conditioned to accept authority. Nowhere was this truer than in the factory itself, though Action Committee militants asked if the CFDT-Lip did not encourage this discipline as well. The Lip conflict asked workers to transform themselves; it demanded "a questioning ... of oneself," in Géhin's words.[224] Ingrained obedience to authority had made workers unused to taking responsibility and deprived them of the will to do so.[225] In 1973, there were some thirty CFDT-Lip and CGT-Lip militants. Piaget

---

220 *Libération*, October 20–1, 1973, 2. ADD 45J108 Lip Livre Part1/Conversation 4, 12–13.
221 *Libération*, October 19, 1973, p. 3.
222 Piaget, *Lip. Charles Piaget et les Lip racontent*, 32.
223 Piaget, "Les luttes de Lip."
224 Marc Géhin in Piaget, *Lip. Charles Piaget et les Lip racontent*, 168.
225 Lopez, "Lip Interview," 43.

knew that they could have led the movement on their own only "by preventing the explosion of ideas, of ideas for actions that came from strong participation. That is to say by bottling up the conflict."[226] The meetings of the Action Committee were a means, Raguénès explained, "for all the workers, unionized or not, to participate in the elaboration and the analysis, and in the responsibilities. Basically, it is a democratic way to live not only union problems, but the problems of responsibility inside an enterprise."[227]

The movement born of experienced unionized skilled workers' activism and assertions of control of the workplace elicited among others at Lip a democratic movement of liberation not rooted in the factory itself. Many younger workers attracted to the Action Committee contrasted their situation with that of union leaders like Piaget and Vittot—skilled workers in supervisory positions "who had come to venerate work": "Piaget thinks that he fulfills himself through meticulous work in production and in the union." Action Committee youth wanted jobs, but did not see work itself as fulfilling; they sought, in the language of May, to "live differently," to see the realization of man and woman elsewhere than in the alienating world of the factory. They distanced themselves from workers whose decades of work had shaped them: those whose "entire existence is built on the Lip myth. And they fought for the restitution of this stolen myth."[228] Although such differences persisted and developed over time, a community born of the struggle itself brought together workers with different aspirations.

Conclusion

The problems Lip confronted beginning in the late 1960s did not result directly from Asian competition or new technologies. Fred Lip had mismanaged his firm's response to a changing watch market. The French state in turn had allowed Ébauches SA to take control of Lip. The Swiss firm wanted the Lip brand name, its sales network and research; it used its position to prevent the transformation of production at Palente on the eve of the emergence of the electronic/quartz watch.[229]

---

226   Piaget, "Lip 1973: des problématiques toujours d'actualité," 108.
227   Raguénès in Piaget, *Lip. Charles Piaget et les Lip racontent*, 149–50.
228   "Le conflit Lip: lutter pour quel travail?," *Frères du monde* 84–5 (1974): 117–21.
229   Daumas, "Le système productif localisé," 11–17. Daumas, "Fred Lip," 441.

Perhaps a movement like that at Lip could have taken place only in France. In the standard telling, British and West German unions called strikes and negotiated directly with employers' organizations contracts governing wages, benefits, and rights for workers in exchange for enforcing no-strike clauses for the length of the contract. Unions in Fifth Republic France, however, were weaker and French workers more combative, or at least appeared more combative because unions could not subject them to the same discipline. Rather than negotiating contracts, competing national unions in France found themselves mobilizing workers who, in the absence of the national bargaining structures in place elsewhere, appeared to act spontaneously.[230] This was the situation that Chaban-Delmas had hoped to address, but he was stymied. Without established practices of negotiation between employers and unions nationally or in individual enterprises, the confederations needed to bring in the state to resolve industrial disputes. And in the absence of those structures of negotiation—particularly at Fred Lip's firm, given his rejection of the employers' organizations—striking workers in individual enterprises could seem to be pursuing victory like an army rather than as potential dealmakers. This is why Daniel Mothé, reflecting on the conflict at Lip in 1973, said labor activists in France were called militants.[231] The apparent powerlessness of workers in a failing firm brought out an exceptional audacity and creativity in the workers of Lip, while making their supporters active participants.

Spontaneity, however, is not the correct term to use in relation to the Lip workers. The insubordination and demand for transparency that characterized the Lip worker movement in 1973 were the fruit of years of union activism. When Lip workers were shown a very sympathetic documentary film of the events of 1973, they withheld their imprimatur because it had not presented the many years of union work that preceded those events, and would therefore mislead viewers seeking to change their own situations.[232] Piaget believed that what May 1968 had shown was that "workers had to be a little bolder."[233] The workers of Lip responded by developing a culture of participatory democracy on the shopfloor and in the firm that offered workers and leftists appealing alternatives to

230 Chris Howell, *Regulating Labor: The State and Industrial Relations Reform in Postwar France* (Princeton, 1992).

231 Daniel Mothé, "Lip: réussite de la lutte, échec de la grève," *Esprit* 430 (December 1973): 890–6.

232 *Idées ouvrières*, September 1977, unpaginated.

233 *Le Monde*, September 18, 1973, 40.

the confederations and the Socialist and Communist parties. In the words of the unionists in a nearby department, while May 1968 did not challenge fundamental principles, the movement at Lip did do so five years later.[234] Lip gave the correct time to those who set their watches in May 1968.

---

234   BDIC F delta rés 578/43 UD CFDT de l'Isère, "2 Éléments pour aider à comprendre et expliquer le conflit de chez LIP" [undated].

3

We Produce, We Sell, We Pay Ourselves

A victory [in the struggle at Lip] is a booster rocket for the idea of worker power contained in Lip.

—Pierre Victor[1]

Imagine that in a country the number of enterprises deciding to engage in an action of the type "we produce and we sell" multiplies by 10 or even by 100; add to this, in the service sectors, other struggles of the type "we provide the service, but we don't charge for it," or "we distribute the products and we pay ourselves," or "we take our money out of the banks." The real mass action able to put political power into crisis is of that nature. Demonstrations in the streets or the classic strike are not enough, any more than before 1968 national days of action were sufficient … The question asked today is the following: how many simultaneous Lips can a central capitalist power confront without entering into a period of grave crisis? Lip cannot remain an accident, an exception. It must be integrated as an essential element and probably determinant in a revolutionary union strategy.

—Frédo Krumnow[2]

The CFDT-Lip and CGT-Lip organized a nocturnal guard in the factory in response to reports that the firm would begin secretly removing machinery and watches as a prelude to declaring bankruptcy. This, the

---

1 Philippe Gavi, Jean-Paul Sartre, and Pierre Victor, *On a raison de se révolter* (Paris, 1974), 238 (July 1973).

2 Frédo Krumnow, *CFDT au coeur* (Paris, 1976), 172, 176–7 [November 1973].

police remarked on May 10, 1973, already constituted "in effect, a sort of occupation of the site."[3] On May 17, the managers went through the workshops, "something they never did," in an effort "to spread panic," saying that "if you act, it means liquidation, everyone laid off."[4] That day, feeling that the provisional administrators were, in Burgy's words, adopting "an ostrich policy" in relation to the future of company,[5] the workers held them for an hour and a half in an unsuccessful effort to get information. The next day the administrators wrote to the personnel to say that only hours worked would be paid.[6] Workers burned the letters, put the ashes in a coffin, and sent it to the administrators. On May 28, the administrators posted a notice reiterating the pay policy. The workers occupied the offices of a director; he telephoned the administrators who authorized him to rescind the policy.[7]

The unions and the Action Committee heard a rumor that the administrators were speaking with potential foreign buyers—"We even wanted to put up a sign at the entrance: 'For purchase of the enterprise, come on Wednesdays from 11 to 12,'" a frustrated Piaget said—but workers were kept in the dark.[8] On June 5, one of the three remaining Lip directors questioned the statement made by an administrator the day before that a contract with a new buyer was about to be signed. The workers responded by telling the three directors to leave their offices and not to re-enter the factory unless they brought back detailed, verifiable information on the future of the enterprise. The state was equally unforthcoming. The unexpected decision by the Minister of National Education to cancel an order for machine tools from Lip and give it to a British firm was not encouraging.[9]

On June 10, the workers occupied the factory in order to "safeguard of the means of production." This standard union language took on a new meaning; with the future of Palente in question, the workers themselves were its true defenders. Two days later, the two provisional administrators, one of the Lip directors, and the president of the Besançon Chamber

3   ADD 1026W8 "Informations confidentielles CGT," Conversation of Claude Curty and Claude Mercet, May 9, 1973. ADD 1026W12 RG, May 10, 1973 [quoted].

4   ADD 1026W8 "Informations confidentielles CGT," Conversation of Buhler (Union départementale, CGT) and Mercet, May 18, 1973.

5   Piaget, *Lip. Charles Piaget et les Lip racontent*, 47.

6   BDIC F delta rés 702/7/3 Administrateurs provisoires to Lip employees, May 18, 1973.

7   *Le Figaro*, May 30, 1973.

8   *Libération*, August 10, 1973, 2.

9   *Politique hebdo*, August 30, 1973, 9.

of Commerce came to Palente to meet with the works council. In the words of a skilled worker who was not a union member and had not been participating in the movement: "And then here they were, the provisional administrators come to act like clowns"; they had done nothing for two months "except dally about with us."[10] The workers' representatives provided a running account of the meeting by phone. Every fifteen minutes an update was broadcast on loudspeakers to the close to 1,000 workers assembled in the courtyard.[11] The administrators expressed ignorance about the fate of the factory, but said that workers would no longer be paid. When they heard this, hundreds of male and female employees burst into the building and sequestered the delegation, making it clear that no one would leave until the bigwigs answered questions about the future of the firm. They said nothing, but the union delegates kept the crowd under control. The elderly president of the Chamber of Commerce was released and the majority of workers were sent home.

One hundred workers and delegates remained with the administrators and the director. A worker opened an administrator's briefcase and found the plan for the future of Lip that the Interfinexa consulting firm had prepared for Ébauches SA. Although the administrators had claimed not to know what Ébauches SA had in store for Lip, there were manuscript notes on the project in the hand of one of them. Ébauches SA was planning to make Palente a watch assembly plant and to sell off the rest of the firm. The board of directors had discussed these plans in the absence of representatives from the works council, in violation of the law. There was a list by name of 480 workers to be laid off, with the severance pay each would receive, as well as a budget of 2 million francs to combat the unions' expected opposition. A report found in the briefcase wrongly anticipated that the actions of Ébauches SA would precipitate a strike in April, that the workers would run out of funds after two months, and the movement would end when the factory closed for vacation in July; this line of action would open the way for the IDI funding which had been denied earlier.[12]

Incensed, the workers then went through papers in the directors' offices. They found evidence that Fred Lip had made special financial arrangements for members of his family and for his own side-businesses using company resources: in the colorful words of Burgy—a supervisor

---

10   François B. in "Comment 'l'affaire' nous a changés," 67.

11   Piton in BDIC F delta rés 707/9(1) Fonds Michel Duyrat Bande UNCLA 1 Cahier no. 1. "Nous les Lip," France Culture, November 22, 2003.

12   Piaget, "Lip 1973: des problématiques toujours d'actualité," 106.

in mechanics, a banker's son, a CFDT-Lip militant, and Dartevelle's successor as works council secretary—they discovered that "Lip was a veritable nest of mafia and each hogged the blanket without any concern for the workers."[13] Other documents revealed that the state and local police had been keeping close tabs on the workers' leaders and informing management of their findings; there was even evidence that Lip sold watches to state police officers at the factory discount.[14] One worker took documents to the ORTF television station in Besançon, where a reporter read the conclusions of the Interfinexa report on the air. Workers who had gone home came back to Palente.

The prefect called in the CRS. They arrived to find a crowd of male and female workers, some armed with table legs and iron bars from the workshops. The state police pushed through the improvised barricades built with office furniture and scuffled with the workers, who refused to let the hostages go. Piaget sought to negotiate their release, saying they could leave in exchange for a ten-day extension of the period salaries would be paid. However, when the departmental director from the labor ministry put the offer to one of the administrators, he refused. Piaget and other union leaders then went to see the prefect, but returned with nothing but the threat that if those being held were not released, the CRS would storm the building. "The rank and file, very riled up since the afternoon"—in the words of the official from the labor ministry—wanted to fight the CRS. He was impressed and relieved to see Piaget and Vittot convince workers to exercise "passive resistance". The administrators and the director made it out to a waiting police car.[15]

Most workers went home. Ten or so militants, predominantly from CFDT-Lip, but including some in the Action Committee as well as a member of CGT-Lip, met in the factory.[16] In the words of one of them, it was 2 a.m. and they found themselves without anything, "stark naked."[17] They would need to counter the discouragement they knew the workers would feel. The group decided to take another hostage that could be used in negotiations: the large stock of finished watches made during Saint-esprit's administration.[18] In the early hours of the morning, a few female

---

13   Burgy in Piaget, *Lip. Charles Piaget et les Lip racontent*, 45.

14   Maire and Piaget, *Lip 73*, 100.

15   ADD 1026W14 Direction départmentale du travail et de main d'oeuvre to PD, June 13, 1973.

16   The CGT-Lip had not favored detaining the delegation, so few CGT members had stayed to confront the police. "Lip des militants du comité d'action parlent," 15–16.

17   The delegate is quoted in Chris Marker's film, *Puisqu'on vous dit que c'est possible*.

18   Consultants brought in by the CFDT in the summer of 1973 said the firm had

workers distracted the factory guard; other workers used a garbage truck and ten cars to take some 30,000 watches out of the factory and past the police. Vittot reports that fifty more cars answered a call for vehicles and they left with the loaded cars. This prevented the police from being able to track the watches that left the factory.[19] Later that day, June 13, the General Assembly enthusiastically approved "the biggest hold-up of the century," to cite the *France-Soir* headline. Burgy took charge of moving the watches to numerous locations where they could be kept in dark, dry spaces and remain in good condition.[20] As more watches were uncovered (and produced) in Palente, he found hiding places for these and for the money from sales as well. For security, Burgy did not reveal to anyone the dozens of attics, basements and barns used, even to Piaget and the other leaders. To prevent their seizure, he oversaw the movement of watches and funds in the summer and the fall, among thirty or forty sites as far away as Chambéry.[21]

Among those to whom *les Lip* turned were priests, who hid watches and funds in churches and rectories. Their backing—and their explanation that the act was, like a starving man's theft of bread, not a sin—assuaged the conscience of the workers and their confederates.[22] This was only one element of the support workers received from Catholic sympathizers in the area. Earlier, the labor inspector at Besançon, a devout Catholic, had written a personal letter to the Archbishop of Besançon, Marc-Armand Lallier, saying that it was important for the Church to take a stand on the hundreds of planned layoffs at Lip. Michel

---

twice the needed stock on hand. The excess stock had a value of 13 million francs. Guy Groux and René Mouriaux, *La CFDT* (Paris, 1989), 174. Jean-François Belhoste and Pierre Metge, *Premières Observations sur des rapports de la transformation de propriété. Lip et l'industrie horlogère française 1944–1974* (Paris, 1978), 94.

19   ADD BC 20893 "Les Sages fous et les fous sages. Un film documentaire de Christian Rouaud," 20. Michel Jeanningros estimates that 25,000 watches were taken the night of June 12–13. Raymond Burgy puts the figure at 30,000. Accounts at the time frequently reported that 32,000 completed watches were taken and that another 32,000 watches were in production. Workers found more watches in the occupied factory. Jeanningros' personal notes say that the General Assembly on June 20, 1973 was told that workers had 65,000 watches. Jeanningros to Reid, August 19, 2016; Burgy to Reid, July 25, 2016.

20   *La Croix*, August 2, 1973, 3.

21   *L'Est républicain*, April 13, 2013; June 12, 2013. In September 1973, several hundred CRS lodged at one of the most important hiding places—a Church building—without realizing it. Interview with Pierre-Émile by Reid, June 4, 2011.

22   Conservative critics of the workers could not resist attributing the firm's problems to "new-style" priests whose rejection of the material side of Church activities had depressed the sale of First Communion watches. René Berger-Perrin, "Les leçons de l'Affaire Lip," *Liberté Économique et progrès social* 34 (April–June 1979): 12.

Jeanningros, a manager on the commercial staff of Lip since 1960, had secretly joined the CFDT-Lip in 1968. He and his wife were active in the ACO. Jeanningros and Bernard Girardot, another Catholic on the commercial staff who had also become a CFDT-Lip member on the quiet, made contacts with Church leaders and convinced the Archbishop to support the workers. The Archbishop sent a pastoral letter on June 3, backing the workers' demands for no layoffs and no dismantling of Lip. "We do not have the right to leave workers ignorant of their fate … God's will, that's what we today call job security"; "All that mutilates man … is not in God's plan." One must not, he said, "make money the master of the world."[23] The Archbishop recognized that standing by the workers was controversial, saying in September: "Like Christ, whom he wishes to serve, the bishop is often 'a sign that provokes the contradiction.'"[24]

On June 15, the Archbishop spoke at a "dead city" demonstration: businesses closed and public transport stopped to dramatize the effects that the layoffs would have on Besançon. Organizers asked Lip workers to engage individually in the popularization of their movement. Each received handwritten invitations to give to friends.[25] Turnout for the demonstration approached 15,000, but *les Lip* were left feeling that they would have to do something more to get the state's attention. Around 550 Lip workers had demonstrated in Paris on May 29, and workers had crossed the border to protest at the Ébauches SA headquarters in Neuchatel. Yet these rallies had not changed anything. Union leaders knew from conflicts elsewhere that in the best of cases strikers could last only eight or nine weeks without pay. With a great deal of effort, they could collect donations covering only 5 to 10 percent of what would be needed to sustain themselves. Furthermore, the annual July vacation was approaching—a difficult time to maintain a movement. PSU militants in Besançon discussed workers making and selling watches to put pressure on the Ébauches SA and the state to negotiate. A Trotskyist Ligue Communiste paper floated the proposal as well.[26]

---

23   In the summer, the manager of a bank where the movement had deposited funds informed Burgy when the police were going to do a search; a unionized Catholic telephone worker warned workers that listening devices had been placed on leaders' phones. Divo, *L'Affaire Lip*, 109–14, 129.

24   ADD 1026W25 Marc Lallier, "Revision de vie …," *Église de Besançon* 16 (September 9, 1973). This is a reference to Luke 2:34.

25   *Les Cahiers de mai hebdo*, June 26, 1973, 4.

26   *La Taupe rouge* presented making and selling watches as a tactic in the May 21 and June 4, 1973 issues. "Un pas vers la révolution," supplement to *Rouge* 231 (1973): 8–9.

The idea of starting up production was in the air. It came up in a conversation between Raguénès and a Parisian journalist from *Politique hebdo*, a leftist paper edited by another Dominican, Paul Blanquart, which had taken an active interest in Lip. The writer told Raguénès that Lip workers were gaining an audience and that launching production would earn them support throughout the nation, the support they needed to break out of the isolation of a provincial factory facing dismantling and layoffs. Almost twenty years later, Raguénès remembered this conversation and the decision to take the proposal to Piaget:

> This idea was at first an ectoplasm at the level of small radical groups, which was becoming now a kind of little bubble that I took hold off [with the journalist]: it must be incarnated, carried out, because you can't just talk about it. But, to carry it out, we must see the Lip movers and shakers. The first one, that's Piaget. Let's go! We went to see Piaget.[27]

Piaget embraced the project. This kind of action, he said, was not one for workers who had only been on strike for a couple of days over their wages—"that would devalue the matter." But this was not the situation at Lip. Sixty-three days after Saintesprit stepped down, workers had received no response to their queries: such action was justified.[28] Union delegates and Action Committee members met and decided to present the idea to the General Assembly on June 18.[29] Raguénès' explanation of how the plan to launch production came to pass is emblematic of how Lip militants thought of their exchanges with visiting leftists: "It took the intervention of someone exterior to the group to make things click and give birth to the idea. In effect, the [Lip] group was pregnant with the idea, but seemed unable to deliver on its own." "The angel Gabriel," in the form of the journalist from Paris, was a catalyst who initiated a chain reaction involving components already present at Palente.[30]

The Call of June 18

Other angels were at work assuring that the issue did not divide the unions. When the union delegates and the Action Committee met to

---

27 Beurier, "La mémoire des Lip," Annexe VIII.
28 BDIC F delta rés 578/36 Transcript of AG, June 18, 1973.
29 Piaget and Vittot, "LIP," 285–6. Raguénès, *De Mai 68*, 152–3.
30 ADD 45J108 Lip Livre Part 1/Conversation 4, 12.

decide what to do, the CGT-Lip leader Mercet came up with the idea of launching production before others had raised it. Perhaps, as Raguénès says, the others laid out the logic for doing so without explicitly suggesting it, so that the leftist-sounding proposal to put the assembly lines in operation did not set off alarms for the CGT-Lip since it had been their idea.[31] On June 18, it was Mercet who proposed making watches to the General Assembly. He used the CGT's standard language when discussing occupied factories, talking of defending the "means of production," in this case by finishing the assembly of incomplete watches and selling these (rather than the completed watches taken earlier) to fund a "subsistence salary." Piaget picked up the argument for protecting the machines, saying that public opinion would make it a lot harder for the police to go into a factory where workers were doing what workers were supposed to do—produce—than one where the owners were liquidating the assets.[32]

While Piaget did not hesitate to place the action in a broader context, telling workers of the British shipyard workers in the Upper Clyde who had occupied the yards of their bankrupt employer and made arrangements to finish and sell ships, he made it clear, as he would later say, that "It's not a question of letting ourselves be taken with the fascination of producing, nor of turning ourselves into merchants."[33] There was no pretense that workers at Lip were performing all the functions of a business. Self-management in the sense of an enterprise run by workers in a capitalist economy was not possible, Piaget explained to the General Assembly: suppliers and merchants would boycott the factory; though, he added, buddies who worked for Électricité de France (EDF) would prevent power from being cut. By making clear that what they proposed was not self-management, the union leaders ensured that the action would not alienate the CGT, which saw self-management as a distraction from the Common Program strategy. At the General Assembly two days later, Mercet asked for twenty volunteers to take "the place of honor" at a Communist demonstration in Paris, "guys strong enough" to spread the word that at Lip they were engaged in self-defense, not self-management. Piaget jumped in to explain that when Mercet said strong guys, he wanted to ensure that "there are a few people who know how to

31   Ibid., Part 1/"L'idée en acte," 4.
32   Unless otherwise noted, material is drawn from BDIC F delta rés 578/36 Transcript of AG, June 18, 1973.
33   Piaget, "La formation par l'action collective," 168–9.

respond to a few traps that journalists could set for them" with questions about self-management.[34]

Mercet presented starting up production as a means for workers to pay themselves while they protected the factory. Piaget saw the action in terms of building support for their local movement to be fought nationally. He underscored the importance of how the public understood the conflict: "the issue of wages is much less important in this operation than the impact on the population and on workers ... It is not a question of saying that we are going to come up with the pay, one way or another." Workers who protest by working could win support from those who associated strikes with slothfulness and disorder. It was important, one worker told the General Assembly, that the public see them working: "it must not turn into a circus here." Daniel Montébelli, a computer programmer active in the Action Committee, chimed in that journalists from around the country would be coming:

> We must show the truest image of our action so as not to put forward
> to the nation base material demands, such as wages, but the struggle
> we are fighting for employment guarantees, isn't that it, and the form of
> improvised struggle at Lip given to all of the workers of France.

The General Assembly broke into small groups to discuss launching production. When they reconvened, the Assembly enthusiastically endorsed what *Libération* termed "the call of June 18," the name given de Gaulle's appeal to resist in 1940.[35] Workers thought that the provocative act of restarting the assembly line would fairly quickly lead the provisional administrators and the government to negotiate, and they would never reach the stage of paying themselves.[36] The stock at Palente included 32,000 watch movements, as well as the needles, cases and watch straps required to complete the watches.[37] Assembly was just a question of placing the watch movement in a case, and putting on the dial and the hands, the glass and the watch strap. There was no rush to complete the job as the act of production itself was more important than the finished

---

34   BDIC F delta rés 707/9(3) Fonds Michel Duyrat Bande UNCLA Cahier no. 3 Bande 6 (AG of June 20, 1973).

35   *Libération*, June 18, 1974, 1. *Lip Unité*, August 2, 1973, 1.

36   BDIC F delta rés 578/36 "Débat entre les travailleurs de la Redoute et de Lip," November 10, 1973, 8–9. "Un pas vers la révolution," 9.

37   ADD 45J10 Commission Popularisation des travailleurs de Lip, "Dossier d'information," August 29, 1973.

product. Piaget told the General Assembly that those who worked would be volunteers and could discuss and set the conditions and hours of their work, knowing this would make the experience all the more appealing to the new left, representing a form of self-management on the shopfloor that prepared the way for an as yet unachievable self-managed economy. In an atmosphere recalled as "an incredible euphoria," a small number of female assembly line workers began work that day.[38] Workers started selling watches two days later. Elsewhere in the factory, union delegates negotiated a contract to produce mechanical parts for a Parisian industrialist with materials he provided. Fifteen workers began the job on June 20. Lip had turned down this business earlier, confirming workers' suspicions that the firm had been declining to take work in activities other than watch assembly in order to make the case for dismantling Lip.[39]

In May, Piton had written and circulated through the factory each day for a week a new chapter of a *feuilleton* which commented on events at Lip through the story of a boat with a leak and its intrepid sailors and none-too-admirable commanders.[40] Decades later, Piaget reflected on the days before June 18: "The bosses had all left, but the subordination that characterizes the wage earner still made us hesitate. Fear was there. We resembled sailors who mutinied in the eighteenth century. None of us knew how to steer the boat and we were forced to give power to the officers."[41] But this changed dramatically with the decision to restart production. A week later, Maurice Clavel commented that the "mutiny of a crew, of the Bounty, whatever," had become the metaphor of choice for "our bourgeois colleagues, who are perhaps touched with clemency by the evidence and in any case do not dare say anything bad about the movement."[42] However, in landlocked Besançon, perhaps Daniel Anselme of *Les Cahiers de mai* was more to the point when he suggested that to tell their story the workers should make what he termed a pirate film in which the pirates seize the "war treasure"—the watches—and hold out on their island, Palente.[43]

---

38   AB Interview with Pierre-Émile by Beurier (1992), 47.

39   *Le Figaro*, June 21, 1973, 10. Barou, *Gilda je t'aime*, 170. ADD 1812W25 RG, June 21, 1973.

40   Piton, *C'est possible!*, 44–55. Workers also wrote many poems and songs. A number of these can be found in *Il était une fois la révolution*.

41   Chaillet et al., "Entretien avec Charles Piaget," 119.

42   *Libération*, June 25, 1973, 4.

43   "Faire voir, ceci et rien d'autre," Interview with Dominique Dubosc by Christine Martin, September 2004, dominiquedubosc.org.

The General Assembly

The occupation of Palente was key to developing workers' participation in the movement, creating a strike culture very different from that Piaget had known when union leaders would tell strikers to go home and let them take care of things. As he explained: "Occupation, that would oblige personnel to come because there is always some little something to do: maintain the machines, greet visitors and the press, prepare sandwiches … In some ways, the personnel had the impression of going to work. They did not stay away as isolated individuals."[44] Lip militants thought of the General Assembly, in Piaget's words, as the site where each individual worker daily affirmed their membership in the collectivity: "The guiding principle of the conflict (its philosophy) was set in the General Assembly," Piaget asserted: "each had to be well imbued with this guiding principle."[45] General Assembly meetings had been held in April and May, but beginning with the occupation of the factory on June 10, one (and sometimes two) were held each weekday until the factory reopened on March 11, 1974: close to 200 meetings over the course of the conflict. Between June 18, 1973 and January 1, 1974, attendance varied from eighty to 1,000 (of the 1050 workers employed at Palente), with an average of 466 present and a median of 450.[46]

Each morning, the delegates of the CGT-Lip and the CFDT-Lip got together separately to discuss the situation, while initially up to 100 employees in the Action Committee gathered in the restaurant. Then the union delegates and the Action Committee together formulated the agenda for the General Assembly. The CFDT-Lip met in a room with glass windows and open doors near the cloakroom that all passed through when they entered the factory. Anyone who wanted could come in to see and hear the delegates. Piaget saw this as helping workers to see that "a discussion" was constructive, not the site of experts' assertion of authority.[47] When officials from the confederation came to Lip in 1973, they were, in Piaget's words, "startled: 'it's not possible to deliberate like

---

44 Étienne Penissat, "Les occupations de locaux dans les années 1960–1970," *Genèses* 59 (June 2005): 78–80.

45 Piaget, "Lip 1973: des problématiques toujours d'actualité," 109.

46 Some fifty of the employees at Palente left early in the movement in 1973. About 100 of the remaining 1,150 employees were senior staff and managers and never attended the General Assembly. For an accounting drawn from police reports, see Champeau, "Lip: le conflit et l'affaire (1973)," 191–3.

47 Brangolo, "Les filles de Lip (1968–1981)," 383–4. Interview with Piaget by Reid, June 7, 2011.

that, with all these people entering and leaving!' "[48] This culture characterized the General Assembly as well. Drawing on a practice developed
in labor conflicts at Lip in 1970, the union delegates presented different positions and deliberated in the Assembly, rather than doing so in
private and presenting the results to workers.

Workers kept the company buses running and employees arrived at
the occupied factory at 8:00 or 8:30 and attended the General Assembly at 9:00 (and sometimes again at 2:00 in the afternoon). Meetings
were generally ninety minutes, although they could last from one
to two-and-a-half hours. They were held in the restaurant at Palente,
which was large enough for the entire workforce and had a good sound
system. Union delegates sat at a tribune and ran the meeting. After laying
out the agenda and answering questions from the floor, the delegates
turned to representatives of the individual commissions managing
the movement at Palente and to Lip workers who had been travelling
through France talking about the struggle. Hearing of support across
the nation was important to maintain morale. Visitors could attend the
General Assembly and those who wished to address the issues under
discussion were encouraged to do so: "We think that the power of information is not real unless it is confronted with a maximum number of
viewpoints."[49]

To facilitate discussion in the General Assembly, a microphone on a
pole was circulated. Piaget thought that "most of the time, you saw many
more women then men" at these meetings.[50] Over the course of time,
more workers, including women, began to participate. For some, speaking in the Action Committee had given them confidence. To encourage
participation, union delegates tried with some success techniques like
asking three or four workers to speak at a time, as one naturally followed
up on another.[51] One worker told Maria-Antonietta Macciocchi: "And
then, by enchantment, in the general assemblies, those who had seemed
most on the margins, the least intelligent, who had never opened their
mouths, made the best proposals."[52] There was an insistence on dignity
and respect: "No fights," workers from Lip told workers at La Redoute

48   "Lip aujourd'hui," *La Barre à tous* 3 (April 1975): 34.
49   *Lip Unité*, January 1975, 3. Monique Piton, "Favoriser l'imagination et la
réflexion collectives," *Politique aujourd'hui* (March–April 1974): 75. Interview with
Piton by Reid, June 6, 2011. *Témoignage chrétien*, June 28, 1973, 4.
50   Brangolo, "Les filles de Lip (1968–1981)," 381.
51   "Charles Piaget et le film 'Lip, l'imagination au pouvoir'. Propos recueillis," at
lucky.blog.lemonde.fr.
52   Macciocchi, *De la France*, 150.

in Roubaix, "no crude language. It was a matter of always being dignified and very polite when you explained something."[53] The General Assembly could have the qualities of an expanded ACO meeting. For Piaget, "There has to be tolerance. For example, when an intervention falls 'flat' or is 'irrelevant', it is necessary to begin by taking up what was of value and then bringing up the inadequacies in such a way as to allow others to offer elements which can enlighten the person."[54] Over the course of the conflict, as the CGT-Lip lost support and faced demands to cede the floor, Piaget insisted that CGT-Lip representatives speak and be respected. On one memorable occasion, when a CGT-Lip member made a statement far from the consensus and an opponent whistled, the assembly turned on the whistler and applauded the speaker.[55]

The assemblies affirmed the lived immediacy of a community at work in the institution of the collectivity: "the whole hall, all were friends," in the words of one non-unionized skilled worker.[56] At Lip, the General Assembly took on a more important role than in movements more tightly run by unions. The sense that unity came from the expression and embrace of a shared discourse rather than a disciplined organization made leaders' mastery of public speaking an important source of power.[57] Piaget's exceptional ability to make all feel that he expressed "what each felt themselves," in the words of Jeannine Pierre-Émile, a CFDT-Lip delegate and member of the works council, was crucial.[58] Another female worker active in the movement, Alice Carpena, evoked the feeling of solidarity the General Assembly could create: "What was great, was to all arrive (more than 1,000 people) at the same analysis, the same ideas. Moreover, we knew our problems too well to let ourselves be duped."[59]

Piaget recognized that in a society that encouraged thinking in terms of the individual, it can be difficult to see that collective sackings require a collective response. Knowing that many workers faced opposition to participation from their families, he spoke of the revivifying effects of the Monday morning assemblies: "Weekends, Lip employees had to deal with the doubts and critiques of their families. This was isolating. But

---

53   BDIC F delta rés 578/36 "Débat entre les travailleurs," 2–3
54   Piaget, "La formation par l'action collective," 156.
55   Piaget, *Lip. Charles Piaget et les Lip racontent*, 36.
56   François B. in "Comment 'l'affaire' nous a changés," 69.
57   Jean-Pic Berry, "Lip 1978." Maîtrise, Centre de Sociologie des Organisations, 1978, 16.
58   Jacquin, "Lip 1973–1981," 186.
59   Alice in *Lip au féminin*, 52.

on Mondays, in the midst of 800, 850 engaged personnel, the anguish disappeared, giving way to action."[60] For many workers, the collectivity which reinforced itself with each meeting of the General Assembly took on emotional attributes previously provided by extended family and friends outside the workplace. This reinforced the workers' dependence on and commitment to the movement. In any case, regular attendance at the General Assembly kept workers informed, able to discuss the movement with visitors to Palente, as well as to answer questions raised in their families.[61]

Before making important decisions, the General Assembly broke into groups for three-quarters of an hour to discuss the issues and responses, a practice facilitated by the small tables in the restaurant, which allowed discussion "in complete tranquility, without the frictions of the general assemblies."[62] It was at this point that the Assembly became what Piaget referred to as "a collective intellectual."[63] Union and Action Committee militants sat in on these discussions, providing information in response to workers' questions. When the small meetings ended, the delegates assembled for ten minutes to talk about what they had heard. If delegates found a clear consensus emerging, it was put to a vote in the General Assembly by raised hand. If not, a vote was put off and discussion continued until accord could be reached. In Piaget's words, "we only offered solutions that were already those of the majority."[64] Pierre-Émile was not alone in seeing that Piaget's apparent selflessness made workers feel that they had been heard when the delegates articulated a position: Piaget "thought only collectively, of the collectivity. He forgot himself totally. I believe he was the most altruistic of all then. That's it. Piaget is fully in Lip and Lip is fully in Piaget."[65] The General Assembly bred a sense of familiarity, a feeling among workers that they knew their union delegates better—"we were on a first-name basis"—that encouraged workers to broach issues frankly, without the deference that might have been used with union authorities before.[66] Only twice did the Assembly vote by secret ballot, at the request of the CGT-Lip. Piaget questioned the secret ballot for privileging egoistic concerns over the collectivity: "With

---

60   Piaget, "Petit manuel de la lutte collective," at politis.fr.
61   Piaget, "LIP. Les effets formateurs," 143–4, 146–7.
62   BDIC F delta rés 578/36 "Débat entre les travailleurs," 2–3, 15.
63   Interview with Charles Piaget [October 2, 2009], at npa209.org.
64   *Libération*, September 20, 1973, 6 [quoted]. Piaget, "La formation par l'action collective," 156.
65   AB Interview with Pierre-Émile by Beurier (1992), 16.
66   *L'Outil des travailleurs*, December 1973-January 1974, 6.

a secret ballot, you think of yourself, of your family. It's like you are in front of your television set. But our struggle is collective, that's where you find courage. Me, when I spend 48 hours at home, I need to return to the collectivity. Once more, I'm less afraid."[67]

Because the union leadership set the agenda and ran the General Assembly, Lip workers recognized that it could reproduce "the hierarchical system of the factory: on one side those who know, who speak and who direct; on the other, those who listen and who follow,"[68] and so understood the need, in Piaget's words, to prevent their struggle "against an oppressive hierarchy ... from creating another ... just as oppressive."[69] Union leaders were aware that the collectivity they frequently evoked was not a natural consequence of the workers' situation. Just as the struggle at Lip was not a product of spontaneity in sociological terms, the same was true in terms of its goals and tactics. The union brought "what it knows of the workers' movement because the workers do not discover it like that in an innate and spontaneous way."[70] The workers' culture at Lip was very much the product of the CFDT-Lip's atypical practice for years of devoting 90 percent of its time to building an autonomous force of workers, well informed and actively engaged in all facets of the movement; it devoted only 10 percent of its time to the tasks that occupied most unions: running an organization, researching issues and meeting with management.[71] Lip workers explained to their colleagues at La Redoute that as the General Assembly approved positions that often had their origins in union delegates' and Action Committee members' conversations with workers, they accepted that the delegates would be best at advancing them and seeing them realized. The delegates' verbal mastery had been seen as an impediment to worker expression and was at the origin of the Action Committee. But it could also be an ally.[72] Delegates presented initiatives to workers not as done deals, but as elements that workers should discuss and for which they should take responsibility. In

67   *Libération*, October 12, 1973, 12.

68   Piaget, "LIP. Les effets formateurs," 144.

69   Piaget, *Lip. Charles Piaget et les Lip racontent*, 34–5.

70   Piaget in "Lip vivra, Messmer cédera, une nouvelle étape de la lutte, tous avec Lip!," *L'Internationale* 44 (January 1974). In his study of a number of strikes in 1971 and 1972, Vigna found that although unions clearly had the most committed militants, they were increasingly seen as organizations with resources and skills to be put at the service of workers acting through general assemblies, rather than assuming the directing role they had exercised in the past. *L'Insubordination ouvrière*, 203.

71   Rachida El Azzouzi, "Charles Piaget: une leçon de liberté" (July 6, 2013), at mediapart.fr.

72   BDIC F delta rés 578/36 "Débat entre les travailleurs," 15

this sense, the power of the movement came from the workers' creation of a collectivity in their response to the leadership.

The Commissions

Yet, with the leaders exercising what Demougeot terms "the deciding word," could the General Assembly be the expression of democratic practice at Palente? It set policy, but discussion was primarily in the form of responses to the agenda laid out by leaders.[73] In the summer of 1973, a visiting leftist saw the General Assembly becoming a "machine to applaud good news and to vote for decisions taken elsewhere." However, he went on to say that the work of the commissions countered the loss of the "democratic character" of the Assembly.[74] It determined policy, but the commissions decided how to carry it out. Commissions reported back to the Assembly, responding to questions and critiques. "In this way," Vittot believed, "it was possible for Lip workers to address all of the problems posed by the struggle, to discuss them collectively, and then to lay out a position."[75] Commissions set their own schedules and these fixed hours replicated the experience of going to work. Like attendance at the General Assembly, this assured employees' active engagement.

Commissions met daily to discuss what needed to be done and how, and who should do what. Each commission elected a coordinator to ensure that all participated in making decisions and did comparable amounts of work.[76] "The commissions are democracy + efficacy," in the words of Piaget and Raguénès. "They decide themselves all of their jobs."[77] Marc Géhin explained that the point was not for others to tell his commission what needed to be done and how—"To act like that is already to lean on an analysis, on a hierarchy"—but for the commission to address issues and work out solutions.[78] Later, the Lip workers' paper L'Heure would say, "The life of the community begins in the commissions … it is there that workers apprentice in the life of the group, there that

---

73   Interview with Demougeot by Reid, June 12, 2013.
74   *La Cause du peuple*, July 6, 1973, 12.
75   Jacques Roy, "Lip 1973," 22.
76   Pierre Saint-Germain and Michel Souletie, "Le voyage à Palente," *Les révoltes logiques* 7 (Summer 1978): 77. A list of workers and the commissions on which they served in the summer of 1973 is in ADD 1812W34.
77   "Lip aujourd'hui," 34.
78   *Libération*, October 19, 1973, 3.

they learn to make decisions and to apply them."[79] The commissions were the clearest expression of the "self-management of the struggle" that the CFDT-Lip spoke of *les Lip* practicing.[80]

The first commissions were set up on June 18. There were eventually thirty-five commissions and a host of subcommissions established to handle all facets of the movement, including production, watch sales, servicing of the watches sold, welcoming visitors, the restaurant, social activities (i.e., evening film screenings), management of personnel and of stocks of watches and parts, defense and upkeep of the factory and grounds, and transportation (the bus service). The largest commission was concerned with popularization— the development of external support. Action Committee members played an important role in the creation of commissions and in making them sites of debate and creative innovation. After the commissions began to meet, the Action Committee itself became "rather episodic, appearing only in a crisis."[81] With the commissions in full swing, only twenty or so workers continued to participate actively in it throughout the summer.[82] "When the workers organized in commissions," Raguénès said, "the Action Committee shut down; it had attained its goal."[83]

The commissions prefigured a world to come in which individuals would not be bound to one task forever, but would be able to change jobs to fulfill the desire to do things they had never done before.[84] Workers joined a commission of their choosing and could change commissions when they liked. Typists sold watches; assembly line workers became telephone operators, and so on. Emancipated from their job designations and from the company hierarchy, workers embraced a new self-respect and confidence, operating the occupied factory without managerial personnel. Doing jobs they had never dreamed of doing in parts of the factory that had been closed to them, OS and office workers developed a new confidence, discovering talents they did not know they had.[85] A young female OS explained,

79   *L'Heure*, 3 [supplement to *Lip Unité*, December 1977].

80   For a use of "self-management of the struggle" in this sense in a CFDT magazine a half-year before Piaget began employing the term, see Vigna, *L'Insubordination ouvrière*, 259.

81   Moustache in BDIC F delta rés 707/9(1) Fonds Michel Duyrat Bande UNCLA 3 Cahier no. 1.

82   *Lip Unité*, September 1978, 4.

83   *L'Outil des travailleurs*, April 1974, 16.

84   Piaget, *Lip. Charles Piaget et les Lip racontent*, 130.

85   Jeanne Z. in "Comment 'l'affaire' nous a changés," 65. François B. in ibid., 70.

Do you realize what this means, for a woman like me, used to remaining bent over, under the same neon light, doing the same thing eight hours a day, to find myself suddenly free with my time, free with my pace of production, free to get up during work, free—this is going to seem ridiculous—to be a seller or a secretary going from one "commission" to another?[86]

Another OS compared the alienation and disengagement of factory labor to working "in complete euphoria" on a commission where "suddenly, I was no longer a number. They asked my advice and listened to me. It was marvelous."[87] For Piton, "We discovered in the struggle that everyone, when they are not confined to a definite task, compartmentalized, parcelized, reveals unexpected gifts. An average secretary becomes a charming organizer … We learned about one another, valued one another."[88] A female assembly line worker who chose to sell watches to visitors exclaimed, "we did not need [the bosses'] 'order'. FOR ONCE, WE HAD THE CHANCE to experience something other than a fixed task!"[89]

Workplace hierarchies were not maintained on the commissions, most of which did things outside the range of activities for which the hierarchies had been designed. Many mechanics—from the most highly unionized sector and the heart of activism before the occupation—already operated in this world and initially appeared, in the words of one of them, "totally disoriented," inactive on the commissions.[90] However, for some women, the commission meetings marked "the apprenticeship of speech" in a public forum.[91] The disappearance of the managerial hierarchy was particularly liberating for female OS and was reflected in the commissions themselves. As one explained: "In fact, when the head of a commission raised her voice a little too much, we said, 'Watch out. We don't want any more heads, no more bosses.' "[92]

As they had in May 1968, mechanics, watch workers and office workers visited one another's workplaces and got to know individuals and their

---

86   *Le Nouvel observateur*, July 30, 1973, 31.
87   Claude Goure, "Conversation avec des 'petits lip,'" *Panorama aujourd'hui*, November 1, 1973, 21.
88   Piton, *C'est possible*, 263–4.
89   Reine H. in *Lip au feminine*, 19.
90   Gérard Cugney in Piaget, *Lip. Charles Piaget et les Lip racontent*, 171.
91   Werner, "La Question des femmes," 2454–5.
92   Groupe de femmes en lutte du 18ème arrondissement, "Lip au féminin," *Les Pétroleuses* [1974]: 3.

jobs, which had been closed off to them in the past.[93] Before the strike, Paulette Dartevel said, "we did not know one another [at Lip]. Now, there is not a workshop or an office in which you don't know someone."[94] Another reported, "Now, I know everyone. I call people by their first name. This was unthinkable before."[95] The breakdown of the separation between workers and work areas was particularly dramatic for women workers. "Gone were the prestigious positions; the end of a hierarchy based on contempt," Lip employee Georgette Plantin remarked.[96] The female OS who toiled in oil and noise had always felt inferior to employees in the cleaner, calmer environments of the assembly line and the office. For the first time these women met and formed relationships of equality working on the commissions and eating together.[97]

The Restaurant

One of the most important institutions in the occupied factory was the restaurant set up in place of the one a contractor had run for the company. The watchparts worker René Mercier, son of a pastry cook, but with no experience in the trade himself, volunteered to assume direction of the restaurant with a commission staffed by Action Committee members. In the words of one of them:

> People no one knew took initiatives ... [René Mercier] began by making snacks, sandwiches. Then he got to cold cuts, then warm meals. We ate just as well as before, if not better. It's incredible. He orders his meat, his bread, other things as though he had done it his whole life. Never misses a beat.[98]

Each day about 600 workers ate an inexpensive lunch in the restaurant. With occasional large gifts of food from sympathizers, and good relations with a diversity of local suppliers, it offered comparable meals at significantly lower prices than those of the contractor.[99] The commission hired the workers laid off by the contractor and paid them

93 Réseau Citoyens Résistants, *La Force*, 17.
94 *Lip au feminine*, 22.
95 *Paris Match*, January 19, 1974, 22.
96 *Lip au féminin*, 33.
97 Reine J. in ibid. 24. Werner, "La question des femmes," 2445, 2450.
98 Sylvaine in Piaget, *Lip. Charles Piaget et les Lip racontent*, 93–4.
99 *La Cause du peuple*, September 13, 1973, 11.

the mini-Lip, which was a higher wage than they had gotten from the contractor.

Before the movement, workers had grouped by profession in the restaurant; there was little contact or discussion with other workers. "This separation," remarked Demougeot, "was something very big in the enterprise."[100] Whereas workers from various sectors had eaten at different times, now, without fixed times for each workshop to go to the restaurant, they shared tables with a diversity of employees; the meal was "a site of discussions, of quarrels, and of camaraderie." The restaurant was recognized as the expression of a new culture of equality and dignity for those preparing the food as well. Gilbert, a Lip worker at the restaurant, explained early in 1974:

> So we didn't allow hierarchical relations any more in the work. The other day, B., one of the union delegates, came to our kitchen to see where we were with the *bûches de Noël*. He came as though on inspection, without even saying hello. I gave him hell. Here we work to render a service. We have a right to acknowledgment.[101]

The restaurant emerged as one of the "living symbols of Lip power": "it is more than a restaurant, it is one the developments of Lip: a laboratory where we think and construct a new society. It is 'the welding of *les Lip*.'"[102]

Female Workers

The CFDT-Lip and the CGT-Lip originally mobilized female workers as mothers in the demonstration they organized in Besançon on June 27, 1973. Two hundred female workers and wives of workers with 100 of their children began by releasing balloons with cards of support to be sent to the factory. They then marched to the prefecture and, speaking as mothers, asked that there be no dismantling or layoffs and that workers receive their June salaries.[103] The very nature of a campaign based on

---

100   "Quand les ouvriers se mêlent de tout," supplement to *Libération*, February 7, 1974, B.

101   *L'Outil des travailleurs*, February 1974, 11–12.

102   *Il était une fois la révolution*, 96.

103   ACGT Lip Box 5 "Mercredi 27 juin 1973 CGT/CFDT travailleuses, femmes des travailleurs et leurs enfants" (tract). ADD 1812W25 Commissaire Central de Besançon to PD, June 27, 1973.

popularization of their struggle valorized activities that could be seen as gendered feminine, like welcoming and hosting visitors, and responding to letters of support. Leadership of the movement was male, and in retrospect a male worker commented that "before the conflict, the women were unskilled OS and the men for the most part were skilled OP. This distribution of tasks was found in the struggle."[104] Yet as producers and sellers of watches, women were the face of the movement for supporters.

In July 1973, the sociologist and *Les Cahiers de mai* militant Danièle Kergoat went to Palente to interview female workers. She categorized the women she met into three groups in terms of their engagement.[105] The first included those who played an active role in all facets of the struggle and were beginning to "fit into the collective of men." Alice Carpena, an OS in the CFDT-Lip, nearing fifty years old and known to sing *The Internationale* when her work area "lacks the right atmosphere"[106], explained: "They looked for volunteers for this or for that and there was no longer a difference between men and women ... We discovered that we could do exactly the same things as the men."[107] Female OS spoke and were listened to. The forty-four-year-old OS Paulette Dartevel explained that "For the first time, we reflected on subjects that we had believed were reserved for men: our role in society, politics."[108] Over time more women spoke in the General Assembly, but they remained a small minority.[109] Kergoat's second group were known to all as the *tricoteuses*. They attended the General Assembly every day and joined commissions. Piton underscores their role as greeters of journalists and other visitors and in finding them places to stay.[110] Although the *tricoteuses* were far from the Madame Defarges of Lip, Michel Garcin, a later leader at Palente, said that they "express tacitly a form of adherence, of solidarity, even of satisfaction that the order of work life be put in question." Silently knitting at the Assembly meetings, they expected to be convinced and in particular to hear "concrete responses" to particular problems. Male leaders came to see the *tricoteuses*' silent approval or disapproval as exercising a form of

---

104 Yves Faucoup, "Que sont devenus les Lip?," *L'Estocade* 20 (September–October 1983): 27.

105 Danièle Kergoat, "Les Pratiques revendicatives ouvrières" (Centre de sociologies des organisations, 1978), 82–3.

106 *Lip au féminin*, 9.

107 *Politique hebdo*, March 6, 1975, 8.

108 *Lip au féminin*, 21.

109 Werner, "La question des femmes," 2456.

110 Interview with Piton by Reid, June 6, 2011.

democratic control over the movement.[111] A third group was composed of female workers and the wives of male workers who stayed at home and whose lack of participation was often attributable to the decisions of the male head of household.

The activism of women affected expressions of sexism and patriarchal authority. One female worker commented that, for once, men solicited women's opinions and did not say "Hey girls, get us something to eat."[112] Georgette Plantin, a social worker employed by Lip and quite active in the movement, was struck by the situation of female workers whose husbands did not work for Lip, but who brought them along when they did guard duty at night at Palente. These evenings, she reported, were marked by long, fruitful discussions. Husbands, who would previously have spoken for their wives, now waited for them to speak and listened to them closely and admiringly.[113] Women felt free to criticize male authority when it threatened to impede participation in the form of a husband preventing his wife from leaving Besançon to participate in national tours, or the worker who sent his mother-in-law along with his wife to keep an eye on her when she went to a demonstration in Paris.[114] When activist women saw individual cases of male domination interfering with the workers' struggle, they reacted. But in the spring and summer of 1973, female workers did not organize on their own for fear of compromising unity, and they therefore had no place to reflect together on issues particular to women outside informal discussions like those over meals in the restaurant.

The issue of setting up a child-care center was proposed by some women in the Action Committee in the summer of 1973, but did not get very far. As workers were still getting paid, many women could maintain the arrangements they had used to look after their children when working.[115] They realized that male leaders saw child care as a female responsibility and were hesitant to pursue what they knew would be seen as a distraction from the fight for jobs.[116] "It is true that in a struggle like this, all is possible," said Demougeot of child care, "but we are limited as well."[117]

---

111   AB Interview with Garcin by Beurier (1992), 32. Forty women knitted during each General Assembly in November 1978, when overall attendance was half of what it had been in 1973. ADD 1026W21 RG, November 2, 1978.

112   AB Interview with Hélène Leidelinger by Beurier (1992), 41.

113   Évelyne Le Garrec, *Les Messagères* (Paris, 1976), 101.

114   Werner, "La question des femmes," 2452. Groupe de femmes, "Lip au féminin," 6.

115   Le Garrec, *Les Messagères*, 102–3.

116   *Politique hebdo*, September 13, 1973, 12.

117   Demougeot in Piaget, *Lip. Charles Piaget et les Lip racontent*, 115.

In the summer of 1973, Piton became the voice of those who felt that with the breakdown in roles and practices at Lip could come a transformation of gender relations as well. Initially, when asked about the difficulties she encountered as a woman, Piton responded, "I laughed at them, asserting that here, we didn't have any."[118] Men ran the movement, but she did not seem concerned: "Our men at Lip don't lead us badly. We have nothing to complain about. And if one day they piss us off, we'll fight back."[119] However, she recognized later that the summer of 1973 was "a time when equality was possible," not one where it had been achieved.[120] In a social space where elocution was so important—the premise behind the idea that the General Assembly, not the unions, was paramount—there were ways of speaking seemingly reserved for men. Men could speak directly, but if a woman "had a suggestion to make, she should do it timidly, saying: 'Don't you think that ...'"[121] And, Piton added, if a woman like herself did speak directly from the floor at the General Assembly, making comments that veered from the agenda, the men on the tribune would not engage with what she said.[122]

Demougeot had a similar experience. She recognized that the act of speaking at Assembly meetings led others to form misconceptions about her: "since I am the only woman on the commissions to speak in the General Assembly, I am therefore adamant, I have definite opinions, I am a dogmatic revolutionary. It's not true. To put it simply: I exist, I question and I ask that they leave me this right."[123] Put in this situation, she analyzed perceptively the difference between asking women to speak and preparing them to do so:

[The men in the union] may have pushed me to express myself, but they did not help me to do so. And these are two quite different things. That is to say that when they needed us, they said to us: you must speak. And then, I wasn't prepared. Psychologically, I wasn't. Yet I had a batch of things to say, but I was speaking up next to these guys who in two words said it all. While if, in a meeting, they had said to me: you have the floor,

---

118   *Politique hebdo*, March 6, 1975, 8.
119   BDIC F delta rés 707/9(1) Fonds Michel Duyrat. Bande UNCLA 3 Cahier no. 1.
120   Piton in *Lip au féminin*, 28.
121   "Les LIP au féminin" in Piaget, *Lip. Charles Piaget et les Lip racontent*, 113–14.
122   Monique Piton, "Lip de l'intérieur: 'Je suis de Doubs, j'ai participé à une lutte ouvrière qui a sécoué la France entière'" in *Les Affranchies: Franc-comtoises sans frontières*, ed. Nella Arambasin (Besançon, 2013), 215.
123   *Lip Unité*, April–May 1980, 11.

speak, we're listening to you, I believe I would have been more assured, I would have found it easier to express myself.[124]

The popularization strategy created a situation in which Piton and Demougeot, though not leaders of the struggle, became crucial figures in the presentation of Lip by sympathetic media. The prominence of Piton in particular could give her the status of a star, resented in a movement that took pride in its collective nature, when the legitimacy of men who spoke up in the Assembly and other public forums was not questioned. In *Les Paroissiens de Palente*, Clavel terms the character based on Piton the "coryphaeus" of the choir of Lip workers.[125] However, this should not obscure the importance of Piton and Demougeot as figures who understood and engaged with concerns of the new left like feminism and consumerism more easily than the male leadership. Piton had a long lunch with Herbert Marcuse and found that they shared a common critique of consumer society.[126] Demougeot frequently discussed with journalists her interpretation of consumerism in terms of egoism and collectivity, defining concepts of the Lip movement. She spoke of becoming aware "that 'I was, despite all, conditioned by and a slave to cash.'" Change was not easy, but she put aside saving for a washing machine and gave money to strikers elsewhere instead: "That's good, isn't it? To not be subject to the consumer society."[127] Making the personal the political was at the heart of the unprecedented mobilization of the women at Lip.

Production

Production was limited so as not to use up the stock of watch parts: "It is more a symbolic than a real production," in Piton's words.[128] Only one

---

124 Le Garrec, *Les Messagères*, 105–6. See AB Interview with Jean Perriau by Beurier (1992), 19, where he talks about union leaders dismissing Demougeot's ideas, and then sometimes reintroducing them without recognizing their provenance.

125 Clavel, *Les Paroissiens*, 172. Edgar Faure, Gaullist deputy of Doubs, asked to see Piton when he made contact with the workers in 1973. Piton, *C'est possible!*, 414. Piton is a good example of an individual who developed in revealing new ways through her "improbable encounters" with leftists and feminists drawn to the Lip conflict. She came to be a figure who was more appreciated in these worlds, to which she spoke in the terms they wanted to hear, than in the community of *les Lip*.

126 Piton, *Mémoires libres*, 83–4.

127 *Le Nouvel observateur*, September 17, 1973, 43.

128 Piton in BDIC F delta rés 707/9(1) Fonds Michel Duyrat. Bande UNCLA 2 Cahier no. 1.

of the four assembly lines operated in late June and two in early August, in response to the continuing demand for watches. On June 20 and 21, the factory assembled about half the 2,500 watches produced daily in normal operation; it quickly shifted to producing 500–600 watches per day in late June and 800–1,000 in early August. The number of female OS putting in partial work days ranged from seventy-six in late June to 150 in early August, although when workers took vacations in July, as few as fifteen or twenty workers assembled watches.[129]

The commission in charge of each element of the production process set the hours and pace of work based on discussions with the workers.[130] Dealing with watches near completion gave little opportunity to rethink radically the way work was done. Daniel Mothé complained that workers' innovation was in the realm of posters, not production, since they did not do away with the assembly line itself.[131] However, female OS introduced changes that were significant to them and in so doing offered a challenge to the submission they had long endured.[132] Workers set their own cadences, took turns doing the most fatiguing work, and ended the use of buttons to call for missing pieces that kept them glued to their places. They introduced the rotation of workers to new stations several times a day and sought to ensure that all workers were engaged in both management and production. Some supervisors even took their turns on the line: "There were no longer any bosses because they were working with us as simple workers."[133] External quality checks showed that the watches produced met Lip's high standards. Workers felt that without managers driving production, the quality was better and workers no longer experienced attacks of nerves that stopped production.[134] While women workers' liaisons with managers had been affected by previous periods of worker activism, several ended abruptly in the summer of 1973.[135] Certainly one of the most important elements of the conflict was the liberation of women at Lip from "macho chiefs" on the shopfloor.[136]

129   ADD 1812W25 RG, June 21, 1973. Burgy estimates that about 25,000 watches were assembled during the conflict. Burgy to Reid, July 25, 2016.

130   "Lip des militants du comité d'action parlent," 28–9. *Politique hebdo*, July 19, 1973, 8. Michel in Piaget, *Lip. Charles Piaget et les Lip racontent*, 143. "'Le monde à l'envers …'," *L'Anti-brouillard* 2 (June 1973): n.p. *Rouge*, June 27, 1973.

131   Roy, "Lip 1973," 21. Mothé, "Lip: réussite de la lutte," 895–6.

132   Jacquin, "Lip 1973–1981," 64.

133   Groupe de femmes, "Lip au féminin," 3.

134   "Lip des militants du comité d'action parlent," 30–1.

135   *Libération*, June 25, 1973, 4. *La Cause du people*, September 13, 1973.

136   Interview with Bondu by Reid, June 20, 2011.

At the General Assembly of June 18, CGT-Lip leader Noëlle Dart-evelle had made a plea for the inclusion of managers who wanted to participate, saying that they had been subject to the abuse of Fred Lip and would be needed when the factory returned to full capacity.[137] A few of the sixty managers initially offered to help with technical aspects of production, believing that the conflict would be resolved before employees paid themselves.[138] But, Piton reported, as workers began to produce watches, "The managers wandered miserably in the factory, talking in the corners, uncomfortable; they were useless."[139] With few exceptions, they followed the CGC line and withdrew on the grounds that watch sales would constitute theft.[140]

The situation of the managers concerned the CGT. In the words of Georges Séguy, CGT secretary-general, Lip showed that the owners need workers, but workers do not need owners. However, managers were another story. Séguy refused to buy a watch made by the workers.[141] When rumors appeared in the national press that *les Lip* would fire their managers, CGT-Lip rushed out a press release, reiterating the lesson that spring of the case of Ouaked Areski: neither workers nor unions dismiss personnel, ever.[142] Communists had no desire to scare off the votes of managers needed to bring a government to power which would enact the Common Program. For Séguy, "It is as absurd to believe that workers can do without foremen as to believe that children can do without teachers, and the ill without doctors."[143] Léon Gingembre, president of the Union des petites et moyennes entreprises, said that in the face of all the talk of self-management at Lip, only Séguy spoke "as a boss [*patron*] ought to."[144]

Watch Sales

Twice a year, at Christmas and at the time of First Communions in May–June, Lip had set up tables in the restaurant and sold watches to employees at the 42 percent discount the watch seller-jewelers received;

137   BDIC F delta rés 578/36 Transcript of AG of June 18, 1973.
138   *Les Cahiers de mai hebdo*, July 9, 1973, 2.
139   Piton, *C'est possible*, 102.
140   ADD 1026W14 PD to PM, June 22, 1973.
141   *Politique hebdo*, September 13, 1973, 10.
142   ACGT Lip Box 3 Communique of CGT-Lip, July 25, 1973.
143   "Quand les ouvriers se mêlent de tout," C.
144   Léon Gingembre, "Introspection de l'Affaire Lip," *Revue politique et parlementaire* 845 (October 1973): 21–2.

these watches were generally models that had not been commercial successes and were being retired.[145] The General Assembly of June 18 decided to sell all watches at this 42 percent discount and the next day cars with loudspeakers drove through Besançon spreading the news.[146] The CGT-Lip had initially sought to have watches sold primarily by the works councils of other firms. With Dartevelle in charge of sales, the works council of Creusot-Loire at Firminy and the Fédération of the Haute-Garonne of the Communist Party (for their festival on June 24) were among the first purchasers. Dartevelle announced sales of 80,000 francs by the end of June 20 and 110,000 francs by noon the next day.[147] Although provision of consumer goods by works councils had never seemed a radical act before, they were well situated to pursue these illicit sales. However, the commission in charge of sales worked through other outlets as well with the goal of furthering popularization of the struggle.[148] Within a couple of weeks, les Lip stopped accepting individual orders by mail, reserving sales for visitors to Palente, individuals who came to rallies around the country at which Lip workers spoke, and collectivities like works councils and unions. An advertisement appeared in the Le Nouvel observateur of July 2 touting the 42 percent discount and instructing buyers to send their orders to the CFDT municipal office in Besançon. The PSU had about ten members at Lip, all members of the CFDT-Lip, including Piaget, Vittot and Burgy.[149] The national party mobilized to sell watches throughout the nation; within a week of the General Assembly's decision to produce and sell watches, the PSU had prepared a catalogue that it sent it to militants in all departments with instructions to make it available to unions, works councils and other interested groups.[150]

---

145   Auschitzky Coustans, Lip, 83.

146   ADD 1812W25, RG, June 19, 1973. The workers took the 30 percent value-added tax from the price it charged and held these funds separately until resolution of the conflict.

147   ADD 1812W25 RG, June 21, 1973.

148   At the General Assembly of June 18, Vittot pointed out that with summer vacations coming up, sales by the works councils would be limited. BDIC F delta rés 578/36 Transcript of AG, June 18, 1973.

149   Piaget and Vittot, "LIP," 279n272. The PCF reported having five members at Lip in 1972. ADD177J11 "Le parti dans la lutte chez Lip" (1972). Fred Lip sought to play the PSU and the PCF against one another. AMB 5Z14 Fred Lip to Dartevelle, June 25, 1968.

150   Piaget and Vittot, "LIP," 285–6. ADD 177J12 PSU-Lip, "Travailleurs en lutte," tract of late June 1973. Les Cahiers de mai hebdo, July 9, 1973, 2. The CGT's initial response was to criticize the PSU for its efforts to coordinate sales as divisive. ACGT Archives Henri Krasucki 7 CFD 102 Rocard to Krasucki, June 28, 1973.

The commission in charge of finances maintained a large poster in the hall that led to the restaurant on which it detailed the amount and origin of funds coming in from watch sales and supporters' contributions, as well as the expenses the movement incurred. The sales funded pay for the workers; contributions were used for popularization activities like national tours of Lip workers.[151] The tabulation was updated each day. "They treated us like dreamers," Piaget said to reporters, "but in two weeks we achieved a turnover better than that of the firm: 250,000 millions in old francs, while they had 6,500 sales points, and we have just one."[152]

Such comments could give the impression that workers sought to sell as many watches as possible, but their goal was to sell their cause. When the Minilip watches had not found a market in France a couple of years earlier, the firm had unloaded them in Kuwait at a loss of 3 million francs. Fortuitously, a merchant from Kuwait showed up in Besançon in July 1973, with suitcases full of cash (since workers did not accept checks). He sought to buy 30,000 watches.[153] However, the sales commission turned him down. Their goal was to garner the public support necessary to pursue their struggle, which is why they were pleased with the decision of the Socialist Party (PS) to purchase 2,000 watches to sell at their national meeting in late June. "Each watch sold should serve as a witness to our fight."[154]

Consumer society produced a new political action, a complement to the boycott. Maurice Clavel wrote of those who bought watches that they were "very numerous and modest Magi kings," who marveled at what was being born at Palente; "they were the donors, as in the corners of old paintings, but this time they squeezed into the middle."[155] The acquisition of a consumer good, the heart of capitalist society in the decades of postwar growth, had been turned into an act of resistance. Watch buyers joined the struggle through their purchase and acquired

Cassou's excellent "La Construction d'un mythe" examines the role of the PSU in watch sales.

151   Initially contributions were also used to compensate workers who had put the most hours into the movement for deductions made from their May 1973 paychecks. *Les Cahiers de mai hebdo*, July 9, 1973, 2.

152   "Les Vacances des ouvriers de Lip," *Libération*, (Spécial Vacances, 1973), 8.

153   *Le Monde*, 4 July 1973. ADD 1812W25 RG, July 18, 1973.

154   ADD 1026W11 RG, July 17, 1973. "Lip=les ouvriers tiennent bonne la barre …," *L'Anti-brouillard* 2 (June 1973): n.p. ADD 45J95 José Gonzalvez, "Les anciens de Lip remontent le temps," *Le Pays*, September 20, 2003, 33 [quoted].

155   Clavel, *Les Paroissiens de Palente*, 148–9.

the knowledge to make the workers' case to others. At first, workers found dealing with visitors to Palente difficult and tended to avoid them. Although the General Assembly voted to open the gates to visitors, the CGT's understanding of outsiders to the factory as alien and potentially dangerous was widespread. This changed with the introduction of watch sales, which became the endpoint of tours of the factory. Buyers may have been attracted by the 42 percent discount, but with each watch sale, workers took the opportunity to explain their movement.[156] To do this, OS learned about the product they made, rather than solely the element of it on which they had worked. They became experts at explaining the particularities of the watches they were selling as well as the struggle they were pursuing.[157] In making the case for more volunteers, the sales commission told the General Assembly that they were needed to assure "genuine discussions": "we are not an ordinary store."[158] A journalist from *Le Nouvel observateur* captured the atmosphere when he wrote that "the Lip factory today partakes of the courtyard of the Sorbonne in May '68 and a meeting of small shopkeepers."[159]

Initially, when the production and sale of watches was seen as a means of giving workers added weight in anticipated negotiations, the idea was to hold hostage the watches taken on the night of June 12–13 rather than sell them. This was the arrangement the CGT-Lip made with the CFDT-Lip, which had taken charge of hiding the watches. Citing promises of secrecy made to those who were holding the watches, the CFDT-Lip would not tell the CGT-Lip where the watches were stashed.[160] Yet, in an instance of the unusual collaboration the unions manifested in the summer of 1973, the CGT-Lip did not go public with its demand that the two unions together do an inventory of the watches.[161] Because production was kept low, the unexpected success of the campaign led to the sale of hidden watches. However, buyers wanted to believe they were

---

156   *Lip Unité*, July 11, 1973; August 2, 1973.

157   *Les Cahiers de mai hebdo*, July 9, 1973, 2. The workers guaranteed the watches they made (but not any that watch seller-jewelers had on hand and sold during the strike). *Lip Unité*, August 9, 1973, 2.

158   "Bande son du film *Non au démantèlement! Non aux licenciements!*" in Cassou, "Lip, La Construction d'un mythe," 204.

159   *Le Nouvel observateur*, July 30, 1973, 31.

160   ACGT Archives Henri Krasucki 7 CFD 102 Claude Mercet to CFDT-Lip, July 10, 1973. ADD 177J8, CGT-Lip to CFDT-Lip, August 3, 1973.

161   ADD 45J5 CGT-Lip to CFDT-Lip, July 10, 1973. ACGT Lip Box 3 CGT-Lip Prise de parole "non effectué," dated July 11, 1973. ADD 45J97 Claude Mercet (CGT-Lip) to Jusseaume (CFDT-Lip), August 6, 1973. ACGT Lip Box 4 CFDT-Lip to CGT-Lip, August 9, 1973.

purchasing watches which had been made after June 18 and initially CFDT-Lip leaders assured them that this was the case.[162]

Through watch sales, the CFDT-Lip wanted to generate a groundswell of interest and support, whereas for the CGT the Common Program, not a nationally supported local movement, was the strategy that would benefit French workers. When it recognized the sale of sequestered watches, the CGT kept quiet to avoid unnecessarily alienating small businessmen whose support was needed for the victory of the Common Program. The CGT-Lip came to reassure itself with the belief that sales were limited to watches not in a particular collection, both to maintain a stock of the most marketable watches that could be sold when the conflict was resolved, and to reduce the opposition of watch seller-jewelers since they might not be so prone to see these as lost sales: the workers were primarily selling "the dead stock," models that the watch seller-jewelers would not be offering (which is why these watches were still at Palente), and that, if not sold at a discount to the personnel, would have ended up in "a crushing machine."[163]

However, such reasoning did not satisfy the watch seller-jewelers. That workers attracted buyers by selling watches at the wholesale price heightened their antagonism.[164] Selling or buying a Lip watch sequestered in June or manufactured after June 18 was unlawful, making buyers complicit in the movement. After the national federation of watch seller-jewelers filed a suit for damages, saying that the sale of Lip watches elsewhere than in their establishments was illegal, supporters followed the precedent of those seeking the legalization of abortion. They signed and published a "manifesto of receivers of stolen goods" in September 1973—"We declare that we have personally and actively participated in the sale of watches that the workers of Lip organized to assure a subsistence salary and to pursue their struggle ... We therefore ask to incur all the legal actions that would be entailed by the plaint against X by the national federation of watch sellers."[165] Workers had sold more than 40,000 watches by the beginning of August, enough to pay salaries for

---

162   *L'Unité*, June 29, 1973.

163   ADD 1026W14 PD to PM, June 22, 1973. AB Interview with Claude Mercet by Beurier (1992), 24. AB Interview with Dartevelle by Beurier (1992), 44, 75. *L'Usine nouvelle*, April 1974, 147.

164   *Revue des bijoutiers horlogers*, October 1973, 157–60.

165   AMB 5Z225 Commission Exécutive de la CFDT to all CFDT governing bodies, September 8, 1973. *Politique hebdo*, September 20, 1973, 16. Rocard in Piaget, *Lip. Charles Piaget et les Lip racontent*, 185 n1.

three months.[166] The police had little success in seizing watches—only forty-nine by October 1973—by which time, Piaget said, 70,000 watches had been sold.[167]

The First Pay

Although the provisional administrators would not pay salaries for June, they sought to break the strike by providing vacation pay for July when the factory closed, as well as the usual vacation bonus. However, they were not successful. Workers spread their vacations out in July and some 300 chose not to take them in order to pursue the struggle.[168] This ensured that 600 workers were always present at Palente. They worked on commissions, welcomed visitors, and stood guard at night in the factory. In July, the general assemblies were held on the lawn. As there was no tribune, participants sat in a circle, which they later recalled had provided the best "pedagogical atmosphere."[169] Over the month, the workers began to fear that the authorities would intervene and the General Assembly of July 18 asked all on vacation to come back as soon as possible. The liquidation of the business on July 31 made it clear to workers that they would never be paid by the company. They made the decision to distribute their first pay at the beginning of August. The General Assembly stipulated on July 31 that each worker was to sign in and work a minimum of four days of normal length each week on a commission in order to receive a salary. Tours of night-guard duty, which all male workers, including the union delegates, undertook (and women did as volunteers), would be counted as a day of commission work.[170]

---

166 *La Croix*, August 2, 1973, 3.

167 BDIC F delta rés 578/36 "Texte de l'intervention de Charles Piaget au cours de meeting qui a eu lieu à la Bourse du Travail de Lyon le 24 octobre 1973." As of November 16, 1973, workers had sold 82,000 watches for a total of 10,889,314 francs, of which 6,630,000 had been used to pay salaries or held to fund social charges deducted by employers. *Lip Unité*, November 16, 1973, unpaginated.

168 "Comment 'l'affaire' nous a changés," 80. See the letter the CGT-Lip sent to members, asking them to shorten or forego their vacations, that begins "you are a member of the CGT, therefore you are naturally more conscious than other workers of the struggle directed against the Power [the state] and Business." ACGT Lip Box 3 CGT-Lip to members, July 6, 1973.

169 Piaget, "LIP. Les effets formateurs," 143.

170 *Lip Unité*, August 2, 1973, 1. Participants were acutely aware that all had been socialized in the very order they were challenging. Not all workers had volunteered for work on a commission. The General Assembly did on occasion assert the collective interest by shaming individuals who failed to do work in the movement, citing the

At the General Assembly of June 18, Piaget had said that for now the movement could think only in terms of assuring to all a "subsistence salary," i.e. the mini-Lip, not full pay. But success in the sale of watches and the lack of progress toward resolution of the conflict raised the issue of what pay workers should give themselves. With the liquidation of the firm, each worker would receive state unemployment insurance, a percentage of their individual salary. The CGT favored using funds from watch sales to supplement this to assure that all received a subsistence pay of 1,100 francs per month; this amounted to a figure slightly higher than the minimum wage in the Common Program. The CGT was wary of Lip becoming a model for workers elsewhere; it believed the modest salary would also discourage *les Lip* from taking a hard line on opening negotiations.

Raguénès, however, did see the conflict as a model and proposed that the level of pay itself reflect the innovative nature of the community taking shape at Palente: "an exceptional pay for an exceptional time," predicated on the nature of a movement run by commissions, in which an individual's place in the company hierarchy was irrelevant.[171] In addition to their unemployment benefits, he favored giving all employees the same lump sum from watch sales and setting a minimum monthly pay at 1,500 francs, well above the pay many OS currently received.[172] Raguénès and his supporters in the Action Committee saw this as a crucial act by which workers could make clear to all that they were engaged in a global critique of a hierarchical society, rather than a movement that would not question the workplace hierarchy—replicated, militant younger workers in the Action Committee remarked, in the leadership of the CFDT-Lip by workers with supervisory responsibilities.[173] Some forty CA members and CFDT-Lip delegates met and hashed out the issue. It had a history at Lip. After May 1968, the CFDT-Lip had been the force behind the levelling involved in the introduction of a cost-of-living adjustment computed on the basis of all salaries paid at Lip, with the total divided equally among all workers, a system opposed by management and the

---

excuse of a sick child or a scheduling conflict when in fact they were moonlighting. Alain Desjardin, *Une vie pour ... Ici et là-bas, solidaire* (Saint Jean des Mauvrets, 2008), 228.

171   Raguénès in Piaget, *Lip. Charles Piaget et les Lip racontent*, 71. Raguénès, *De Mai 68*, 165.

172   BDIC F delta rés 702/7/1 Action Committee, "Un salaire exceptionnel pour un temps et une action exceptionnels" [This was never distributed. See Raguénès' note attached to this document].

173   "Le conflit Lip: lutter pour quel travail?," 119.

CGT.[174] However, much to Raguénès' disappointment, the General Assembly rejected his proposal as well as that of the CGT-Lip, and followed the advice of the majority of the Action Committee and of the CFDT-Lip on salaries. Recognizing that employees had different financial obligations and would stay fully engaged only if they could continue to meet them, the General Assembly voted to take into account the unemployment stipend all received and then pay each employee a supplement such that they received what they had earned when the conflict began.[175] Just three managers worked on commissions and received pay.[176] Knowing the other managers collected only unemployment benefits, one female worker triumphantly observed, "What do they make a month? Not much. Whereas we have our full pay. It was our revenge on them."[177]

At the end of the General Assembly on August 2, Burgy, who handled the money from watch sales, asked that all of the doors be locked and that no one, including journalists, leave. He announced that pay would be distributed. This was a day before the previously announced date in order to thwart the police. The night before, Burgy and members of the commission responsible for pay had used the company computer tapes to calculate the amount to be given to each worker. Funds were set aside for mandatory deductions, including social security. After taking into account what each employee was receiving in unemployment pay (based on their regular pay), the commission put in individual envelopes what was necessary to bring this up to their full pay along with a paystub that laid out the deductions. When workers received their pay envelope, they signed a statement saying that they knew it came from the sale of watches. Their "legitimate worker pay" (not "wild pay," the term used by the press) became emblematic of the struggle.

Conclusion

Confronting factory shutdowns often evokes a ritualized mourning. Jean Godard of the CFDT-Lip explained: "If we had a classic strike on the problem of employment, what would we have done? We would have

---

174   Ibid., 135–6.

175   In Rouaud, *Les Lip. L'Imagination au pouvoir*, Vittot remarks that neither proposal made wages proportional to the level of engagement in the struggle itself.

176   *Le Figaro*, August 3, 1973, 3. The engineer Georges Cuche was preeminent among them. He wanted to protect the research done at Lip from the Swiss. Interview with Jeanningros by Reid, June 1, 2011.

177   Sylvaine in Piaget, *Lip. Charles Piaget et les Lip racontent*, 94–5.

marched through town with a coffin, we would have buried employment, and we would have gone home very quietly. And that would have been that."[178] There had, of course, been strikes directed against closings before, the most famous of which was that of the coal miners of Decazeville in 1961–2, marked by the miners' occupation of the mines.[179] Although the UIMM saw Lip workers as being like miners in France who wanted to remain miners even when the coal was gone,[180] *les Lip* differentiated themselves from protests against mine closings, arguing that the future at Lip was in human, not natural, resources.[181] *Libération* journalist Jean-Pierre Barou concurred, presenting events at Lip as a "response to the extinguished world" of the coal mines in the Lorraine.[182] In Vittot's words, "Lip is not a mine that you close because there isn't any more coal. Lip is a young girl, extremely pretty, that you don't let go of."[183] The community born of the struggle countered the anomie of the unemployed individual and became itself what workers were fighting for. General assemblies, commissions, popularization of the struggle, the restaurant, production, sales and pay responded to the material needs of the movement, but equally important they sustained the community as a living presence.[184]

A strike is based on the premise that production stops in a world predicated on production, and that the resulting world turned upside down will force steps to rectify it in the form of concessions to striking workers. At Lip, however, it was the employer who wanted to put a halt to production in much of the enterprise. In this situation, the conflict at Lip was a world turned upside down because it was not turned upside down. *Les Lip* maintained a semblance of normality: workers worked, took their annual vacation in July, and received their full pay. One female worker said of the "notorious cold room" where watch parts were stored: "It was our *bête noire*. But now, it is our savior, the cold room. If it hadn't been constructed against us, it could not have served us."[185] Management dis-

---

178   *L'Outil des travailleurs*, December 1973–January 1974, 4.

179   Donald Reid, *The Miners of Decazeville: A Genealogy of Deindustrialization* (Cambridge, 1985).

180   BDIC F delta rés 578/41 "L'affaire Lip-la-lune," supplement to *UIMM Actualités*, October 1973.

181   BDIC F delta rés 578/39 "Informations en direct de Besançon" attached to *Lip Unité*, October 23, 1973 [dated October 30, 1973]. Piaget in "Un pas vers la révolution," 27.

182   Barou, *Gilda je t'aime*, 152.

183   *Libération*, November 19, 1973, 12.

184   Piton, "Favoriser l'imagination," 75.

185   BDIC F delta rés 707/9(2) Fonds Michel Duyrat Bande UNCLA Cahier no. 2.

appeared and could be said to have gone on strike. If a strike of workers is in its essence passive, the commissions where workers made decisions about all facets of the movement and carried them out gave the conflict at Lip a very different quality. It also assured that workers maintained and developed connections with one another, crucial in sustaining their commitment in a long job action.

The struggle itself opened workers up to new experiences. Tactics developed to maintain existing employment and benefits became themselves the source of new opportunities of real importance to workers, in particular a breaking down of forms of oppression, subordination, and division by sector and rank that had defined factory life. There were two overlapping conflicts, that of the veteran skilled male workers to maintain their employment and that of the young male skilled and primarily female unskilled to sustain and develop the new possibilities of liberation born of the struggle. That workers had a full salary for the duration of the movement made possible what the sociologist René Lourau referred to as a "vacation from alienated life" in which workers could immerse themselves in a new set of daily practices, and it was this that allowed the development of a culture of radical new aspirations: "This struggle demonstrates that another society is possible, an egalitarian society in which all workers will take charge of their affairs," in the words of an Action Committee tract of July 6, 1973.[186] Perhaps it was not self-management, but there is something to Piaget's assessment that it was, "in short, the beginning of a socialist society."[187]

---

186   René Lourau, *L'Analyseur Lip* (Paris, 1974), 17. ADD BC 20893 "Les Sages fous et les fous sages," 23.
187   *Libération*, December 5, 1973, 3.

4

The Factory Is Where the Workers Are

For an instant, the day when [Pierre Messmer], his eye, his face, his voice strangely hardened, let out in front of the television cameras his famous "Lip, it's over!," I thought I saw a Roman legionnaire pushing back the curious at Calvary and next to the gallows, with a movement of his chin over his shoulder, crying, "Christianity, it's over!"

—André Frossard[1]

All [the CGT] was saying was that we had to normalize the conflict. And they didn't notice that they were using the same word 'normalization' as the USSR did for Czechoslovakia … The CGT always wanted to normalize, to get back on the path of the traditional conflict, with its traditional demands … As soon as the conflict was normalized, they did like the Russians with Dubček and his comrades. They treated us as traitors to the working class and servants of the bosses.

—Charles Piaget[2]

The Lip Affair came at the juncture of "the thirty glorious years" of postwar growth and the beginning of a long recession, marked by debates over how the state should respond to the challenges of May 1968, and of discordant Gaullist and market economic policies. In July 1972, President Georges Pompidou replaced Jacques Chaban-Delmas as prime minister with Pierre Messmer, a man with no taste for the "new society" promoted by his predecessor. But this was not true for all Gaullists. In early June,

---

1   *Le Point*, July 18, 1977, 55.
2   Macciocchi, *De la France*, 146–8, 150.

Michel Habib-Deloncle, political director of *La Lettre de la Nation*, the organ of the Gaullist party, the Union des Démocrates pour la République (UDR), published a severe condemnation of Fred Lip, blaming him for the workers' situation.[3] The secretary of state to the Minister of Labor, Christian Poncelet, told journalists that if he needed a watch, he would consider buying one from the Lip workers. Reminded that this was illegal, Poncelet said that he heard they were selling well: "we're going to be a lot in prison."[4] Alexandre Sanguinetti, assistant secretary-general of the UDR, accepted a watch made by the workers not long after production began.[5] Habib-Deloncle, Poncelet and Sanguinetti were close to Chaban-Delmas and initially saw in the Lip Affair evidence of the need for a "new society."[6]

Not surprisingly, in Piaget's words, "'*la 'participationnite*' was all the rage" among conservative politicians discussing Lip—a means "to restore the virginity of a man of the left" to a man on the right, a Trotskyst observed.[7] Gaullists of all stripes, including Messmer, Sanguinetti, Edgar Faure, and Alain Peyrefitte, were quick to trot out "participation," suggesting that if Fred Lip had been more forthcoming with information, the workers would not have challenged the company analyses and would have left a sinking ship like good market actors.[8] But this came with a realization that it was too late for participation to work its magic. Messmer, for one, wanted to have nothing to do with Lip. After Lip workers started producing watches, he explained that the state could not serve as an arbiter since by his reckoning there was a business failure, not a social conflict.[9]

Before leaving for vacation in August, Pompidou told members of his government that there was no need to do anything: "Lip only interests some Parisians and intellectuals on the left. France doesn't care."[10]

---

3   Daniel Duigou, *Journaliste, psy et prêtre* (Paris, 2005), 24.
4   *Le Figaro*, June 23–4, 1973, 6.
5   *Politique hebdo*, August 23, 1973, 15.
6   Gaullists further to the left enthusiastically supported *les Lip* in the summer of 1973 as champions of national independence and economic democracy. Saying that the workers' actions were not legal, but legitimate, like those of de Gaulle on June 18, 1940, they condemned Pompidou's position as being like that of Adolf Thiers toward the Paris Commune. ACFDT 20F138 Front progressiste tract [1973].
7   *Libération*, August 10, 1973, 2. ACGT Lip Box 15 *La Taupe Rouge*, November 28, 1973.
8   de Virieu, *Lip*, 94. Divo, *L'Affaire Lip*, 30. *Le Monde*, June 27, 1973, 26; June 30, 1973, 29. *La Croix*, September 4, 1973, 3.
9   *Le Figaro*, June 25, 1973, 9.
10 *Le Nouvel observateur*, August 20, 1973, 15.

However, the absence of a company director who could negotiate and the Lip workers' success at generating national support made the government's strategy of letting the movement rot away increasingly untenable. Critics ranging from *Le Figaro* to *L'Humanité*, from PSU leader Michel Rocard to the leftist *Guerre de classes*, characterized the state as playing the role of Pontius Pilate, washing its hands of responsibility.[11] In early July, *Le Point* wrote that "Lip now resonates like original sin in the owners' world" and a month later that "the first Trojan War of self-management is well under way before our eyes."[12] It became the Minister of Industry Jean Charbonnel's task to deal with the Trojan Horse at Palente.

Negotiations with "the Fake Zorro"

An August 1973 poll found 63 percent of the French to be favorable to the actions of Lip workers.[13] Charbonnel, "magician of the month of August," in Fred Lip's words, stepped in on August 1 with a variant of the Ébauches SA's project of dismantling the firm and laying off between 400 and 600 workers. Like the earlier IDI plan, it drew its conclusions from the data Ébauches SA had assembled for 1972–3, which reflected the efforts Ébauches SA was already taking to gut Lip.[14] The General Assembly immediately rejected Charbonnel's proposal. Distribution of the first pay the following day was the workers' response. Even the leader of the CGC-Lip, which opposed the sale of watches and the employees' payment of their salaries, called Charbonnel's plan "a badly botched holiday homework assignment."[15] To keep his initiative alive, Charbonnel dispatched Henri Giraud to Besançon, not as a mediator (between the workers and whom?), but in the difficult-to-harmonize roles of a government delegate and, if he could negotiate successfully with the workers, creator of a new firm he would direct. Giraud was a businessman known for having resuscitated failing metallurgical firms, much smaller than

---

11   *Le Figaro*, August 6, 1973, 3. *Le Monde*, August 2, 1973, 17. *L'Humanité*, August 15, 1973. Rocard in Piaget, *Lip. Charles Piaget et les Lip racontent*, 197. "La nouvelle légalité," *Guerre de classes* 6 (October 1973): 1.

12   *Le Point*, July 2, 1973, 23; August 6, 1973, 19.

13   The Société Française d'Études et de Sondages poll, published in *L'Est républicain* on August 18, 1973, was taken just before the CRS occupation of Palente.

14   BDIC F delta rés 707/5 FGM-CFDT, "L'affaire LIP," August 8, 1973.

15   *Témoignage chrétien*, August 9, 1973, 7.

Lip, including one at nearby Arc-et-Senans in 1972—he was "the Saint-Bernard of ill firms" in the words of *Le Canard enchaîné*.[16] Calling on "the fake Zorro" Giraud allowed the state to avoid dealing directly with the outlaws in Besançon.[17] When asked why he took the job, Giraud told *Le Figaro*, "I am a [practicing] Catholic. I was in the Scouts. I had a chance to do a good deed."[18]

Giraud first met with workers on August 7. They insisted that he come to Palente—"It's not in Paris with dossiers and pencils that you study the issues," Piaget told him, "It's here at the factory in the workshops with the workers!"[19] *La Croix* termed it an "'American style' [meeting] under the lights of TV cameras," but other thoughts crossed Giraud's mind.[20] Referring to the assembled Lip workers, many of whom brought their wives and children, Giraud would recall, "Suddenly, I had the impression of finding myself in the pictures of the revolutionary tribunals in my junior high history book."[21] He told the gathering that he would hold separate meetings with representatives of each union. In a dramatic moment before the assembled workforce, the unions rejected his offer, saying that they would not be divided and would only see him together.

Giraud would not meet with workers at Palente again. In early August, the police increased their presence in an effort to intercept the movement of finished watches out of the factory. The workers responded by trying to figure out what the police knew and how they would act, by doing things like loading vehicles with bread crumbs and seeing which ones were intercepted and taken to the police station.[22] On August 8 the court of appeals ordered the evacuation of Palente and that measures be taken to deny workers entry to the factory or the opportunity to remove materials, in order to secure the machines and stock for creditors. The next day the magistrate came to put seals on the gates of the factory, but was prevented from doing so by the personnel. This was enough for

---

16   Divo, *L'Affaire Lip*, 72. On these negotiations, see Guillaume Gourgues, "Le débat dans la lutte. Changement et 'vérité' économique dans le conflit Lip (1973)" in *Critiques du dialogue: Discussion, traduction, participation*, ed. Sylvain Lavelle (Villeneuve d'Ascq, 2016), 245–74.

17   Paul Maire, "Lip ou les mécanismes de l'horlogerie capitaliste," *Masses ouvrières* 306 (January 1974): 74.

18   *Le Figaro*, August 4–5, 1973, 6.

19   Henri Giraud, *Mon été chez Lip* (Paris, 1974), 32.

20   *La Croix*, August 9, 1973, 3.

21   Giraud, *Mon été*, 37. ADD 1026W11 RG, August 6, 1973.

22   "Un pas vers la révolution," 17.

Messmer. With Pompidou on vacation, he acted, believing that it was time for another form of state intervention than Giraud was providing. Early in the morning of August 14, "like cut-throats in the Middle Ages waiting for travelers in the woods," in CFDT leader Edmond Maire's words, 3,000 state police moved into the factory, overrunning the fifty or so workers standing guard and clearing the way for the CRS to occupy Palente.[23] Messmer presented the expulsion as the government's rejection of "unbridled capitalism," since the occupation was just a consequence of Fred Lip's poor management.[24] Rocard responded that the state's interventions confirmed the void that was Gaullist labor policy: "the Charbonnel Plan and the police intervention at Palente showed to all that participation can be put in the trashcan of history."[25] This was the message of the work stoppages throughout France and of the 587 party and union delegations that went to the l'Hôtel Matignon on August 23 to deliver more than 3,000 motions and petitions of support for the workers of Lip to Messmer.[26] After the expulsion from Palente, *La Croix* referred to the Lip Affair as "a real national psychodrama."[27]

For the new left, the Lip conflict was the expression in France of the global long 1968 and they placed the expulsion in this context. Jean-Pierre Faye saw the police taking Palente as of a piece with the Soviet-led troops' invasion of Prague in 1968: "as a matter of fact, the party of Messmer and [Michel] Debré had a big interest in seeing the revolution of workers' councils at Prague crushed."[28] Another situation occurred to Pierre Audibert of *Libération*: following five years of negotiations in Paris, the Americans and the Vietnamese had spoken of an "imminent peace" in December 1972, followed later in the month by the Americans' massive bombing campaign in North Vietnam; a week after opening negotiations to end the conflict at Lip, the state invaded Palente.[29] Following the overthrow in Chile of the Allende government in September 1973, Bernard Langlois, editor in chief of the PSU weekly, *Tribune socialiste*, developed an analogy between Chile and Lip, what some referred to as Chilip. In Chile, national and international capitalist interests had done what they could to sabotage the economy, and then the army had cited economic failure as its rationale for the coup d'état. In the case of

---

23   *Politique hebdo*, August 23, 1973, 12.
24   *Le Nouvel observateur*, September 3, 1973, 28.
25   Rocard in Piaget, *Lip. Charles Piaget et les Lip racontent*, 202.
26   *L'Humanité*, August 24, 1973, 4.
27   *La Croix*, August 19–20, 1973, 1.
28   Jean-Pierre Faye, "La Grammaire de Lip," *Gulliver* 10 (1973): 34–7.
29   *Libération*, September 19, 1973, 4.

Lip, the state and business interests had done what they could to bankrupt the firm and then pointed to this bankruptcy to justify liquidation.[30] The Ligue Communiste described the expulsion from Palente as "to a certain extent a little Chile" as well.[31]

In Besançon, confrontations took place between the police and youths for several nights after August 14. Although the national media portrayed those confronting the police as leftists from elsewhere, thirty-three of the thirty-four arrested in the following week were workers from Besançon (though few worked at Lip).[32] Piaget lamented that "Palente, it's like a bright light which attracts the moths," and asked supporters to stay away.[33] The unions and the General Assembly distanced themselves from the street-fighting many leftists saw as a political necessity, whether in France or in Chile. In an expression of Catholic humanism, Vittot called out to demonstrators fighting the police: "Behind those helmeted robots ... there are men, there is a human heart beating in each one of them."[34]

Piaget in turn addressed *les Lip*, no longer behind factory walls: "Power ... doesn't know that the factory is where the workers are. The factory, it's not the walls, it is the men and women."[35] In what Maire referred to at the time as "the legality of tomorrow," the workers of Lip championed an alternative to the enterprise as a legal entity defined by ownership of the means of production. Workers' *savoir faire* and creativity, their investment of their lives in the enterprise, gave them rights and responsibilities that trumped those of the stockholders for whom Lip was an abstraction. When Fred Lip ceded control to Ébauches SA, workers saw a space created in which they were the ones who merited the enterprise, not the Swiss who saw it as a means of achieving their own goals rather than those of Lip. Capital would need to adapt to workers' rights rather workers adapting to the dictates of capital. For CFDT theorists

---

30   *Tribune socialiste*, September 12, 1973, 8. For Chilip, see Gavi et al., *On a raison de se révolter*, 244 (October 1973).

31   "Un pas vers la révolution," 20. Messmer responded by questioning why people found it perfectly normal that the state follow a court order to release Alain Krivine, leader of the recently banned Ligue Communiste, but not a court order to enforce evacuation of Palente. *Le Monde*, August 18, 1973, 6.

32   *Anti-brouillard*, September 1973, n.p.

33   *L'Est républicain*, August 20, 1973.

34   Divo, *L'Affaire Lip*, 85.

35   The wording may have been proposed by PSU militants sent by the national party, but it echoed a declaration of the diocesan ACO in 1967: "The enterprise is not first and foremost property, but a community of people." Divo, *L'Affaire Lip*, 102. Piaget and Vittot, "LIP," 285–6.

Pierre Rosanvallon and J.-M. Leduc, Piaget's assertion that the factory is where the workers are, voiced in the face of an apparently mortal blow, "innovates because it puts workers on the offensive faced with problems of employment and no longer only on the defensive."[36]

Expelled from the factory, workers looked to Abbé Marcel Manche of the Saint-Pie parish of Palente, where close to 300 of them lived.[37] He was an admired figure. During the war, Abbé Manche had assumed a false identity as a metalworker in order to be sent to Germany. There he served as a priest for conscripted French workers, to whom the Third Reich denied religious services.[38] During the Lip conflict, Abbé Manche attended meetings of the General Assembly.[39] For the Feast of the Assumption, the day after the expulsion of the workers, he wrote a homily read at mass in each of the five parishes of Palente: "the families at Lip are in the same state of mind as the Virgin on Golgotha confronted with the death of her son. With, at heart, the hope of the Resurrection."[40] The Virgin would hear the prayers of the Lip workers: "Let us recall Cana: 'They have no more wine', said the Virgin, and Jesus found the solution. During a few moments of silent prayer, say and repeat to the Virgin Mary: 'They have no more work, they have no more work tools'. She cannot remain deaf to your appeals."[41] Abbé Manche denounced the "hideous capitalist outlook" of a Lip directed by trusts with no concern for the workers.[42] He helped open Giraud to an understanding of the economic and technological possibilities of Lip that would take him well beyond the Ébauches SA plan cribbed by Charbonnel.[43]

Workers held their daily general assemblies at 9 a.m. in the parish's 981-seat Le Lux cinema, the largest theatre in Besançon. The first took place only four hours after the expulsion from Palente.[44] The city of

36   Maire in Piaget and Maire, *Lip 73*, 121. J.-M. Leduc and Pierre Rosanvallon, "La nouvelle approche des luttes sur l'emploi," *CFDT Aujourd'hui* 9 (September–October 1974): 4.

37   Divo, *L'Affaire Lip*, 75.

38   Association de Palente, *Palente au fil du temps*, 171.

39   Interview with Jeanningros by Reid, June 1, 2011.

40   *L'Express*, August 20, 1973, 13.

41   Divo, *L'Affaire Lip*, 107. *La Croix*, August 17, 1973, 3.

42   *L'Humanité dimanche*, August 22, 1973, 9.

43   Divo, *L'Affaire Lip*, 108.

44   Association de Palente, *Palente au fil du temps*, 188–93. Le Lux had a stage whose elevation threatened the intimacy workers valued in the General Assembly held in the restaurant at Palente. Such distancing ran counter to the culture of the struggle. The table that speakers used was eventually moved to the floor. Lopez, "Lip Interview," 63, 66. *Libération*, December 19, 1973, 3.

Besançon opened up its facilities to *les Lip* as well. On the condition that the workers did not produce watches there, the mayor allowed workers to use the Jean Zay school gymnasium, where they put up partitions to allow commissions to meet. After school began, Lip workers moved to the municipal Maison pour Tous, only a couple of hundred meters from Palente. The city also permitted workers to reopen their restaurant in the abandoned Fort de Bregille on the outskirts of town, and by December it was providing 350 meals a day; for Christmas, the restaurant served 800 meals of turkey with chestnuts and *bûches de Noël* for all.[45] Each day, after the General Assembly, workers met at the restaurant, where large tables encouraged the breakdown of social boundaries.[46] These meals became emblematic for visitors, "the draft [*l'ébauche*] of a new society": "This is not a strike or a demonstration. It is something new. It is a community that withstands a siege by the external world."[47]

Before being kicked out of the factory, workers had hidden parts removed from twenty machines to make them unusable. They had also taken four tons of documents from Palente, including computer tapes, commercial records and client lists, and research studies, most importantly for the quartz watch.[48] Using machines and watch parts taken from Palente in anticipation of expulsion, workers began operating clandestine "phantom workshops," in Piaget's words, where they produced eighty to 100 watches a day at the end of August, one-tenth the total before being ousted from Palente, and 200 a day at the beginning of October. Piton recognized that these workshops were "almost just something for the journalists," but in the face of increased police efforts to find workshops and caches of watches, what was important was to show that the movement lived on. The police searched religious institutions in the area looking for workshops, but had little success.[49] Gaining entry to workers' quarters required more ingenuity. One day the police arrived at the Maison pour Tous disguised as handicapped individuals; once inside, they jumped out of their wheelchairs brandishing their police identity cards.[50] They tracked workers who they thought were taking precautions as they carried bags through the streets.[51]

45   *Libération*, December 20, 1973, 3. *Il était une fois la révolution*, 95.
46   Le Garrec, *Les Messagères*, 109.
47   *Paris Match*, January 19, 1974, 22. *L'ébauche* also means watch movements.
48   *La Croix*, August 15–16, 1973, 3.
49   *Le Monde*, August 31, 1973. *L'Est républicain*, October 2, 1973.
50   Christine Friedel, "Lip, la fête: solidarité, culture et sandwiches à toute heure. Témoignage de Michel Jeanningros" (2001), at theatre-contemporain.net.
51   ADD 1026W11 RG, January 12, 1974.

Watch sales became difficult in the fall and occurred primarily through works councils. Although some ninety meetings of support were held across the country in the three weeks after the expulsion, in only the last of these were workers, protected by the audience, able to sell watches.[52] However, workers still had funds from sales in the summer and had taken the records needed to determine pay and deductions.[53] On August 31, workers locked the doors and distributed a second pay in the Lux cinema, where *Sometimes a Great Notion* was playing and posters were up for the next film, Woody Allen's *Take the Money and Run*.

Giraud had not been informed of the decision to seize Palente. After the CRS occupied the factory, he moved talks to the Saline royale d'Arc-et-Senans, a site built in the eighteenth century as a utopian community, with the director's office in the center and workers' housing in a semi-circle around it. The Saline royale was thirty-five kilometers from Besançon. Giraud hoped that this would allow him to deal with union representatives, away from the mass of workers. The prefect, like Giraud, welcomed the presence of representatives of the national confederations at Arc-et-Senans, seeing them as open to concessions on layoffs and dismantling which were anathema to the local unions. The CFDT and the CGT were motivated to reach a resolution, both because they saw the attention given to the Lip conflict interfering with their own national campaigns for the fall, and because they feared that Lip workers could lose all in seeking to win all. In an emblematic action, the national union offices in Paris stopped participating in the sale of watches.[54]

A revived Action Committee thwarted efforts to distance workers from the talks. It mistrusted negotiations as an opportunity for unions to put their interests ahead of those of the workers.[55] However, it was at the insistence of the CFDT-Lip that Giraud admitted a small Action Committee delegation to the talks at Arc-et-Senans.[56] For Raguénès, the Action Committee could counter the representatives of the confederations, whom he saw as experts speaking in the place of workers.[57]

---

52   *Politique hebdo*, September 6, 1973, 7.

53   ADD 1026W11 RG, August 27, 1973.

54   ADD 1026W14 PD to PM, September 4, 1973. *Politique hebdo*, August 30, 1973, 6.

55   See the Action Committee tract cited in Charles Reeves, *Lip: une brèche dans le mouvement ouvrier traditionnel* (Bois-Colombes, 1974), 34.

56   However, the unions did not allow the Action Committee to sign the communiqués on the talks that they released periodically. Piton, *C'est possible!*, 260.

57   *Il était une fois la révolution*, 236.

Union delegates, representatives from the confederations, and members of the Action Committee made for some forty to sixty participants at each meeting with Giraud.[58] Because the Action Committee saw the delegation of authority as antithetical to its *raison d'être*, it named no permanent delegates to the talks. Much to Giraud's irritation, the Action Committee representatives at the negotiating table changed from day to day.[59] Furthermore, some days a dozen and other days well over 100 workers made their way to Arc-et-Senans. They waited outside, tanning themselves, playing *pétanque* and knitting. Every half-hour a negotiator came out with a loud speaker and informed them about the talks inside. The workers discussed what they heard and often held spontaneous assemblies at the end of the day.[60] As far as Giraud was concerned, this was evidence that the Lip workers had forgotten "real work": "They had abandoned basic everyday work, hard, conventional, tedious perhaps, certainly not glamorous: 'you will earn your bread by the sweat of your brow'. What a difference from this profession of folkloric stars and sales in the wild [*ventes sauvages*] funding pay in the wild [*payes sauvages*]!"[61]

Lip union representatives refused to honor the secrecy in which negotiations usually took place. Each union recorded the totality of the seventy hours of negotiations with Giraud.[62] After each session, the tape was played at the General Assembly in Besançon so that workers could discuss it. The unions also disseminated transcriptions of the "integral text" of the discussions in three booklets. This gave workers information that was generally reserved for union leaders; they could hear and read the nitty-gritty of negotiations without the union or political jargon in which these were usually presented.[63] The recordings also played a role in the negotiations. When Giraud denied having said something, the union representatives played the tape back to him.[64] At first, he had not noticed that the Lip delegates had been recording the negotiations and asked that they stop. The union negotiators responded that they would either tape the talks or take stenographic notes of all that was said. Giraud retaliated

58   BDIC F delta rés 578/38 *Les Cahiers de mai* nos. 41–2 (unpublished). Raguénès, *De Mai 68*, 176. Piaget, "Les luttes de Lip."

59   Guy in Piaget, *Lip. Charles Piaget et les Lip racontent*, 156–7.

60   *Le Nouvel observateur*, September 10, 1973, 19.

61   Giraud, *Mon été*, 133.

62   *Le Nouvel observateur*, September 10, 1973, 19.

63   *Idées ouvrières*, September 1977, unpaginated. The brochures of "Lip. Texte intégral des négociations" are in BDIC F delta rés 578/37.

64   *Le Monde*, August 30, 1973, 19.

by bringing his own more imposing tape recorder to future meetings.[65] The tape deck became both a means for delegates to exercise control in negotiations and for the rank and file to participate.[66] The whole procedure was anathema to Giraud, who thought workers should let union representatives speak for them. Workers, he believed, should work and look after their families rather than spend time in general assemblies where passions ruled and "activist minorities" could hold the workers prisoners to their radical ideas, "like a girl you would seduce."[67]

Messmer told the press in mid-August that perhaps the Charbonnel plan was not perfect, but it had the merit of existing: "there is not a Lip personnel plan."[68] Workers in a capitalist economy are made to feel powerless when faced with the apparent inexorability of information about business viability and employment, as interpreted by the owners. Lip workers refused to accept this. To understand and act on information in the documents they had taken from the factory, they drew on the resources of Syndex, a consulting firm operated by the CFDT that specialized in providing assistance to works councils. At the time, Syndex had about thirty employees and was involved in one way or another with 100 firms. At Lip, Piaget saw Syndex as taking documentation reserved for the minority with a higher education and initiating workers in its decoding and interpretation.[69]

In August and September five Syndex specialists worked full time with Lip workers to put out three detailed reports in the form of booklets on the situation at Lip. Syndex convincingly refuted the charge that high salaries had been the cause of Lip's problems and analyzed poor decisions made by Fred Lip (i.e., too many watch models, failure to respond to changes in the market, and too much spent on advertising), and the systematic pillage of Lip first by Fred Lip and then by Ébauches SA. Lip was not inherently unprofitable; decisions taken by Ébauches SA to further its own interests and not those of Lip made it so. Syndex developed a business plan which showed that the diversity of enterprises at Lip could provide new owners with opportunities for development and workers with full employment. This would require state funds, but,

65   BDIC F delta rés 578/36 "Texte de l'intervention de Ch. Piaget," 6. Piaget, *Lip. Charles Piaget et les Lip racontent*, 30. Piton, *C'est possible!*, 252.

66   For a similar use of a tape deck during negotiations of a strike in May 1968, see Vigna, *L'Insubordination ouvrière*, 64.

67   Giraud, *Mon été*, 138, 160–1, 166.

68   *L'Humanité*, August 21, 1973, 5.

69   Piaget, "LIP. Les effets formateurs," 149–50.

Rocard argued, as workers had no control over bad business decisions, the state should indemnify them through such investment as it indemnified farmers for "acts of God."[70]

The Syndex plan addressed the various components of Lip. Incorporation of Lip into the Ébauches SA behemoth was counter-productive: parts bought from Ébauches SA were more expensive than those made at Palente. The workers' success selling watches showed there were commercial alternatives to reliance on watch seller-jewelers and that increased sales were possible, not to mention the opportunity sales had given to unload excess stock, to provide information on the "junk" and the "favorites" among the excess of watch models, and to increase publicity for the brand. Lip research in electronic/quartz watches made it a site the state needed to nurture in the national interest of maintaining the watch industry in France. As recently as 1972, Lip had applied its expertise in precision mechanics developed in watchmaking to other areas of production in contracts with a number of leading firms, including the Société nationale industrielle aérospatiale (SNIAS) and Dassault, and could continue to do so, thus addressing a deficiency in precision mechanics in France that the state itself had identified in the current Sixth Plan for economic development.[71]

The Syndex plan revealed a growing division between the national confederations. CFDT leaders had particular reason to tout the work of Syndex because it showed what the confederation could provide for a local it thought was too impressed by the support workers received on tours of France. Working with Syndex, they said, Lip workers "discovered that imagination and taking on responsibilities were not sufficient: this had to be joined with competence."[72] The FTM-CGT initially saw Syndex as a CFDT attempt to "make Lip an example of the experience of self-management" and later as an effort to show that capitalism was viable; it saw no reason for unions to "develop projects likely to compete with business in the capitalist management of firms."[73] The CGT interpreted the situation at Lip in terms of the state's complicity with the multinational capitalism of Ébauches SA. It had already proposed in late July that the state provide the majority of capital for a new firm, a variant of

---

70   *Témoignage chrétien*, September 6, 1973, 6–7.
71   BDIC F delta rés 707/5 FGM-CFDT, "L'affaire LIP," August 8, 1973.
72   Piaget and Maire, *Lip 73*, 18, 123.
73   ACGT Lip Box 4 Procès-verbaux de la réunion des camarades du bureau fédéral [of FTM-CGT], July 30, 1973. FTM-CGT, "La CGT et Lip: des faits, des enseignements," *Le Guide du militant de la métallurgie* 94 (April 1974): 31.

its usual nostrum of nationalization, and framed this with reference to the Common Program.[74]

The CFDT-Lip celebrated the "the profoundly revolutionary character of control of the account books. Our victory will be the first big victory of the workers' movement over multinational firms."[75] But, as Piaget made clear, they were unwilling to sacrifice the union's mission to accountants:

> We asked the [Syndex] team to examine the enterprise with us, but we had decided that if we arrived at the conclusion that "the coal mine was exhausted," I'm using a metaphor, then it would be necessary to look for other arguments. It was out of the question to say "we're going to face the facts, that's the capitalist system," but let's say that in the present case we at least had the chance to get to a place where, in union terms, it was valid. So from there, we made use of the situation, but otherwise we would have looked for another line of argument.[76]

The CFDT-Lip recognized that in laying out a business plan, there was "a very real risk of American-style integration" in the management.[77] At one point, the union told Syndex it had gone far enough—"that we do not want to go any further in the demonstration because it was a dangerous demonstration in the [current economic] system."[78]

That said, the Syndex plan did become a basis for negotiations with Giraud. A three-hour presentation of the plan to the General Assembly in August gave workers renewed confidence. It allowed them to present Giraud with an industrial strategy involving specific propositions relating to markets and business structure, a terrain usually left to owners, rather than solely defending their interests in whatever scenario the owners laid out.[79] The Lip delegation clearly knew the firm much better than Giraud and could now speak in the financial, commercial, and technical terms that business used.[80] For Le Figaro, this suggested that "participation" was not just a means of making workers face economic realities. It could

---

74   Lip Unité, July 27, 1973.

75   Le Nouvel observateur, August 27, 1973, 29.

76   "Un pas vers la révolution," 27.

77   Le Nouvel observateur, August 27, 1973, 29. Mothé critiqued the Syndex plan because it did not contain a hint of self-management. "Lip: réussite de la lutte," 895.

78   "Un pas vers la révolution," 27.

79   Gilles Martinet, L'avenir depuis vingt ans (Paris, 1974), 137–40.

80   Leduc and Rosanvallon, "La nouvelle approche," 6–7. Syndex economists participated in the negotiations as well. Giraud, Mon été, 65–7.

enable workers to make employers do the same: "one of the originalities of the Lip conflict—among many others—will have been precisely to show that when they dispose of sufficient elements of information, union leaders in the enterprise can discuss economic dossiers at the same level as managers." [81]

However, the government had no desire to recognize that the workers it had expelled from Palente might have been correct. This would encourage others to contest layoffs.[82] Lip workers met with Giraud fourteen times.[83] They came to feel that he was seeking to take advantage of what Piaget called the "the reassuring and magical character" of negotiations,[84] and was trying to wait out the movement in a Besançon where, since the workers' expulsion from Palente, the population tolerated "the Lip Affair, a little like a cow puts up with the enticements of a fly."[85] There were long intervals between meetings; at one point Giraud went to the Soviet Union to handle business affairs. He came back with word that the Soviets wanted to secure technical assistance from Lip to enter into joint production of a quartz watch, but, he added, only after a "normalization" of affairs at Lip.[86] There were also frequent interruptions during meetings because Giraud had to check on major issues with the government.[87] For Piaget, this showed "to what extent, [Giraud] was a manager," in the sense that he appeared ready to make concessions, but would say he had to make a phone call first and then come back the next morning to announce that the concessions were impossible.[88] The "marathon talks" at Arc-et-Senans were "Vietnamese-style negotiations," Piaget said, referring to the long peace talks held in Paris. The CGT-Lip secretary-general Mercet added that les Lip had the role of North Vietnam, leading to references to Giraud as "a poor man's Kissinger."[89]

In August and September workers withstood a number of efforts to sap their confidence and solidarity. As with the expulsion from Palente, Giraud was not informed of these in advance, though workers noted that

81   Le Figaro, September 26, 1973, 10.
82   Libération, September 17, 1973, 4. Le Monde, September 18, 1973, 40.
83   Interview with Piaget by Féret, "A voix nue," France Culture (2011).
84   Macciocchi, De la France, 144–5.
85   Le Monde, September 15, 1973, 41.
86   La Croix, August 30, 1973, 3. In 1936 Fred Lip had worked under contract with the Soviet Union to establish a watch industry.
87   Le Nouvel observateur, September 3, 1973, 27.
88   BDIC F delta rés 578/36 "Texte de l'intervention de Ch. Piaget," 7.
89   "Un pas vers la révolution," 26. For other references in this sense, see Libération, September 19, 1973, 4; September 21, 1973, 3. Macciocchi, De la France, 144–5.

they often came shortly before or after the two parties met.[90] The plan Charbonnel offered on August 1 had sweetened the rehashing of earlier plans with what the unions and the Action Committee referred to as "jam"—payment of a termination of contract benefit, possible employment in new firms formed by the breakup of Lip, and training for new jobs. The unions warned against what they saw as efforts to "prime the pump" in order to break the workers' unity: "it is only in the General Assembly that we will make decisions. Never act alone, that's our death in a very short time."[91] On the eve of Giraud's arrival in Besançon, the syndic handling liquidation had sent workers letters saying that they had been laid off. But the workers refused to sign up for unemployment, saying that they had jobs at Lip; all they lacked was an employer. Later in August, the IDI sent letters to about one-third of the workers, predominantly female OS in watch assembly, indicating that they would be rehired. Self-addressed stamped envelopes were included for replies. CGT-Lip leader Dartevelle rallied workers to respond by writing on these letters, "We will return together in the same enterprise." The letters were bundled and sent collectively.[92] In negotiations later, when Piaget asked Giraud why these letters had not been sent to the other workers, Dartevelle answered sarcastically for him that at Palente "there are state police to do the work in their place."[93]

In mid-September, workers were told they would not receive their social security benefits if they continued to refuse to sign up for unemployment. In an act of solidarity, union members at the local social security office worked after hours each Tuesday and Friday evening at the Jean Zay gymnasium to maintain records for workers who incurred medical expenses, and calculated the reimbursement to which they were entitled. Workers were then paid from the kitty funded by the deductions for social security made by the pay commission.[94] Furthermore, doctors at the city hospital let it be known that any Lip employee who came to see them would be treated for free.[95]

---

90 Piton, *C'est possible!*, 282.

91 BDIC F delta rés 578/43 CFDT/CGT/CA letter set to all Lip employees, August 2, 1973.

92 *L'Humanité*, August 25, 1973, 3. *Politique hebdo*, August 30, 1973, 7. ADD 1026W11 RG, August 24, 1973.

93 BDIC F delta rés 578/37 "Lip. Texte intégral des négociations (21 Août 21-9 Sept)."

94 *Le Figaro*, September 22–3, 1973, 6. *Lip Unité*, September 28, 1973, 2. *Libération*, September 20, 1973, 6; October 4, 1973, 12. *L'Unité*, September 7, 1973.

95 BDIC F delta rés 578/36 "Texte de l'intervention de Ch. Piaget," 14.

In line with the Ébauches SA plan, Charbonnel had originally pro-posed breaking Lip into four separate firms—watchmaking, military and non-military equipment, and machine-tools. At Arc-et-Senans, Giraud was taken aback when a woman from the Action Committee intervened—he had expected only union delegates to speak. She asked if he had ever been sick and he replied no. She said she thought so, on hearing him make an analogy between a sick firm and a sick man: "You are sick. They cut you in four the better to take care of you …"[96] Though he defended the need for such surgical operations at the time, Giraud took up the issue with the government and fairly quickly established that Lip would not be dismantled. Although there would be three separate companies, they would be under an umbrella firm directed by Giraud that would lease space at Palente to the firms and in which workers would have the same rights and benefits, although all would lose the numerous fruits of conflicts since 1968, including various bonuses and the cost-of-living adjustment.[97]

On the central issue of the number of layoffs, Giraud went from 480 to 330 to 159, but he stopped there: "159 layoffs, that's the number of the owners' ukaze," in Piaget's words.[98] The Lip delegation saw these changes in Giraud's position, and his unacknowledged plans for fewer workers to do more work without an explanation of how, as further evidence that he had poor mastery of the particular situation at Lip.[99] When, in response to a question about Lip, Pompidou told reporters at the end of Septem-ber that if the employer's right to make decisions about employment was threatened, the prosperity of France would be put in peril, this only confirmed for workers that this concern drove Giraud's intransigence.[100] Those affected by Giraud's plan were primarily managers (twenty-three of sixty), skilled workers and supervisors, not the OS who assembled watches.[101] For the 159, the state would make up any difference in their pay at new jobs for six months; they would receive priority if jobs opened up in the successor firm to Lip, but no guarantees.[102] Giraud did not plan

96   BDIC F delta rés 578/37 "Lip. Texte intégral des négociations (21 août–9 sept.)." Session of August 30, 1973, 13.

97   BDIC F delta rés 578/36 "Débat entre les travailleurs," 10–11.

98   *Libération*, October 10, 1973, 6. Collectif, *Lip: affaire non classée*, 29.

99   BDIC F delta rés 707/5 FGM-CFDT, "LIP. L'emploi pour tous," press confe-rence, September 26, 1973.

100   *Lip Unité*, September 28, 1973, 2.

101   ADD 1026W7 PD, announcement of meeting for potential employers of Lip workers, September 17, 1973. *Le Figaro*, October 6–7, 1973, 5.

102   ADD 1026W7 "Lip Giraud. Dispositions à prendre pour le personnel non repris (159 personnes)."

to keep the mechanics workshop, home of the core of the CFDT-Lip leadership, as a separate unit. Three-quarters of those employed in this sector, seventy-two workers, were among those to be laid off. Surreptitiously, managers went door to door to talk at length to workers in armaments and machine tools, sites of new enterprises in Giraud's plan, telling them that Lip was finished and that their chance for a job was to break with the other Lip workers.[103]

When Piaget told the General Assembly on September 12, as he did each day, that "We will be unwavering on the layoffs. Everyone must be taken back," he was recognizing that the community created in the conflict rejected the confederations' practice of responding to layoffs by negotiating for severance pay, retraining and jobs elsewhere for laid-off workers.[104] Business was shocked at the depth of the opposition to these palliatives shown at Lip.[105] So were the confederations. The CFDT believed it was saving the workers from themselves and the CGT that the Lip conflict was an impediment to the only solution for the national collectivity of workers—the election of a government that could implement the Common Program. It was time, both confederations believed, for resolution of the Lip Affair. The CFDT-Lip had pursued actions throughout the strike which were not in line with CFDT policy, and it was more resistant than the CGT-Lip to confederation efforts to reign it in.[106] At the end of August, the secretary-general of the CGT, Georges Séguy, sent a letter to each member of CGT-Lip saying that it was their responsibility to themselves and to the workers of France to engage in the give and take of veritable negotiations, like those in the shoemaking industry held in Romans that summer and mediated by José Bidegain.[107] The CGT found the CFDT-Lip too punctilious at the negotiations: "You would think they were in a corner café debating the sex of angels."[108]

The March of September 29

On September 7, the CGT and the CFDT held a march in Paris to support *les Lip* and to remind all that the confederations were essential

103   BDIC F delta rés 578/36 "Texte de l'intervention de Ch. Piaget," 6, 16.

104   ADD 1026W11 RG, September 12, 1973.

105   Bernard Brizay, *Le Patronat: histoire, structure, stratégie du CNPF* (Paris, 1975), 208–9.

106   *Politique hebdo*, October 3, 1974, 21.

107   ADD 177J7 Georges Séguy to members of CGT-Lip, August 28, 1973.

108   FTM-CGT, "La CGT et Lip," 43.

to achieving a satisfactory result in Besançon.[109] But the demonstration had been hastily called and poorly prepared. Two weeks earlier, a very successful large gathering at Larzac had brought together supporters of farmers fighting the army's appropriation of their land. The CFDT-Union départementale of the Rhône was not alone in comparing the demonstrations, saying that labor confederations had not called on anyone to go to Larzac and yet 80,000 had showed up; the CFDT should not ignore those who had gone there if it wanted to play a leading role in contemporary struggles.[110] Two hundred Lip workers had gone to Larzac and returned quite impressed. Frustrated with the negotiations with Giraud, the General Assembly voted to hold a march in Besançon on September 29 to show that *les Lip* retained national support. The CFDT executive commission was not enthusiastic, fearing that leftists would make the march "a kind of union Larzac."[111] Besançon itself turned a cold shoulder to the demonstration. The city was led by an increasingly unsympathetic mayor, Jean Minjoz, a traditional Socialist whose vestigial anticlericalism prevented him from warming to the Catholic left. Contractors with Lip had not been paid and the population feared the march would bring disorder.[112] Most stores closed on September 29, but this time it was a "dead city" in opposition to the demonstration. This prompted from Clavel a reference to Matthew 25:42: "For I was hungry and you gave me nothing to eat, I was thirsty and you gave me nothing to drink."[113]

Although the CGT-Lip refused to allow the Action Committee to sign the call for the demonstration or any but union representatives to speak at it, the Committee played a leading role in the nineteen commissions directed by a coordinating commission which organized the event.[114] Using lists of subscribers to sympathetic periodicals, visitors to Palente, purchasers of watches, supporters who had written letters, and names gathered in some 130 meetings of support that had been held in France and elsewhere in Europe, organizers sent tens of thousands of letters of invitation.[115] Calls were made for workers to come, but, as the confedera-

---

109 *Le Figaro*, September 9, 1973, 1.

110 ACFDT 8H561 CFDT UD Rhône to Commission Exécutive of the CFDT, September 17, 1973.

111 ACFDT 8H561 Commission Exécutive CFDT, September 22, 1973.

112 AMB 5Z223 Mairie de Besançon, "Procès-verbal de la réunion du 24 septembre 1973." Olivier Borraz, *Gouverner une ville Besançon 1959–1989* (Rennes, 1998), 100.

113 *Libération*, October 1, 1973, 6.

114 *Politique hebdo*, September 20, 1973, 15; September 27, 1973, 4.

115 *Le Nouvel observateur*, September 24, 1973, 29.

tions had feared, a good number of those who attended were '68ers, like those who had gone to the gathering at Larzac. The CGT-Lip condition for participation was that the demonstration be solely union in nature and it withdrew its stand rather than appear with leftists, with whom, CGT officials complained, the CFDT-Lip had been "complaisant."[116] The Maoist leader Alain Geismar characterized Lip workers as "storming the heavens and like their ancestors of the Commune one hundred years ago, they experienced a certain isolation that the great march of September 29 temporarily broke."[117] Michel Rocard later referred to the march as "a high point of leftism."[118] And the state may have seen it as a leftist event as well, without strong support from the confederations, and been encouraged to take a hard line in negotiations.[119]

The number who braved a pouring rain to participate was somewhere between the prefecture's estimate of 30,000 and the figure of 100,000 given by the organizers of the march; 210,000 francs worth of watches were sold.[120] The Action Committee slogan for the demonstration was "Enlarge the Lip space!," which they hoped to do by bringing in other struggles.[121] Piaget asked for workers confronted with restructuring and employment issues elsewhere to share their experiences as a basis for cooperation in the future: "the festival of imagination in struggles, the festival of all that was a little Lip and already carries on in other enterprises."[122] Yet many who came to Besançon were disappointed. They wanted to hold the "Estates General of worker and peasant contestation," to engage in the open discussion and debate which they valued in the conflict at Lip.[123] "We realized," Piaget said later, "that a number of the workers who came to the march expected something else than [simply a demonstration], that there was a thirst to discuss that was not quenched, far from it."[124] In any case, the deluge limited the opportunities for discussion. Nor did the march reinvigorate the movement at Lip. Attendance at the daily General Assembly following the march fell to two

---

116   ACGT Lip Box 9 Curty to Union régionale CFDT de Franche-Comté, September 29, 1973.

117   *Libération*, May 17, 1974, 9.

118   *Le Monde*, March 21, 2007, 28.

119   "Lip Larzac," *Cahiers pour le communisme* 1 (February 1974): 47–8.

120   Piton, *C'est possible!*, 260, 290 [quoted], 293. *Politique hebdo*, September 20, 1973, 15.

121   de Virieu, *Lip*, 155.

122   *Le Monde*, September 18, 1973, 40.

123   *Libération*, October 1, 1973, 6.

124   *L'Outil des travailleurs*, December 1973–January 1974, 5.

to three hundred,[125] leading to the requirement that each worker sign in at the General Assembly in the morning and at the Maison pour Tous de Palente for commission work in the afternoon, on the grounds, Piaget explained, that "our strike was special, aristocratic in the sense that we got paid." The workers had a commitment to those who supported them: "For those who back us, we have the minimum duty to be present, to sign up for the work to do."[126] Whether due to monitoring or to the realization that matters were coming to a head, attendance picked up, averaging 746 from October 5 to 31, with 801 present on October 12.[127]

October 12

In this environment, the CFDT turned its attention to bringing closure to the movement in Besançon. The FGM-CFDT had never been comfortable with the illegal actions of CFDT-Lip. After workers took the watches and began production, FGM-CFDT secretary-general Jacques Chérèque called Piaget. He was furious. "What is this mess?," he wanted to know.[128] At the end of September, he warned that worker intransigence could "end up badly."[129] For Daniel Mothé, federation representatives at Arc-et-Senans were like lawyers trying to convince their clients to accept a plea bargain.[130]

In a conversation published in the October 1 issue of the Communist magazine *France nouvelle*, CFDT secretary-general Edmond Maire agreed with his counterpart in the CGT, Georges Séguy, that "one must not idealize this conflict [Lip] to the extent of making it the national or universal center of gravity of class struggle."[131] A week later, Maire wrote to the CFDT-Lip to share the "in-depth analysis of the Lip conflict" that the Executive Commission of the confederation had just completed. After acknowledging that Lip workers had the financial reserves to hold out for a long time, he told the leadership of the local that they should not be misled by the tens of thousands of supporters at the September

125   *Lip Unité*, September 1978, 4.
126   *Libération*, October 4, 1973, 12. *Le Figaro*, October 4, 1973, 13.
127   ACGT Uncatalogued Papers on Lip. "Personnel pointé aux AG Octobre 1973."
128   Benoît Collombat, "Lip, 1973: la grande peur du patronat" in *Histoire secrète du patronat de 1945 à nos jours*, ed. Benoît Collombat and David Servenay (Paris, 2009), 219.
129   *Témoignage chrétien*, October 4, 1973, 7.
130   Mothé, "Lip: réussite de la lutte," 890–6.
131   *Le Figaro*, October 2, 1973, 16.

29 demonstration: "If there remains strong support for Lip workers, it is especially made up of activists. The mass of workers are more concerned with their own demands and show only the slightest interest in a struggle which has lasted nearly six months." Maire warned that "a defeat will be that of all the CFDT" and concluded by saying that the local should recognize that the state was hardening its stance. Concerned that the CFDT-Lip not be held responsible for a rupture in the negotiations in what had become a national political issue, the Executive Commission recommended that Giraud's plan, which included the layoff of 159 workers, serve as the basis of a response on which a settlement could be reached.[132]

That same day, October 8, the CGT-Lip, faced with pressure from the CGT, met on its own and voted to pursue negotiations on the basis of Giraud's offer—a betrayal of the trade union unity on the local level that Piaget had always considered "indispensable."[133] However, the General Assembly voted by acclamation (not the secret ballot asked for by the CGT-Lip) to reject the CGT-Lip proposal to put aside for now discussion of the number of jobs in order to negotiate the benefits of those who would be employed in Giraud's new firm, while affirming the position of no layoffs. When there was no movement in negotiations with Giraud that day, 100 workers harassed him as he left, presenting him with a harness with blinders to shouts of "Giraud is nothing but a stubborn mule." An offended Giraud responded that this was the last meeting. The state labor inspector convinced him to hold one more, the next day, but this time the meeting would be in Dijon in a new effort to distance talks from the workers.[134] FGM-CFDT secretary-general Chérèque came to Besançon that night to convince the CFDT-Lip to compromise. "Piaget has a double behavior," Chérèque would later say. "On the spot, he is ultra self-management. At the same time, he is grown-up enough to know that, after a couple of months of crazy agapes, they are still on the bluff and will not pull through."[135] As he always had, Piaget believed CFDT-Lip/CGT-Lip cooperation was necessary to achieve victory.[136] Working with Chérèque, the CFDT-Lip put together a new plan: no layoffs without the guarantee of a new job elsewhere with the same conditions and benefits,

---

132   ADD 177J7 Edmond Maire to CFDT-Lip, October 8, 1973.
133   Piaget, *Lip. Charles Piaget et les Lip racontent*, 36. The CFDT-Lip had long complained that national CGT leaders set the agenda for the CGT-Lip when the unions met together. ACGT Lip Box 4 CFDT-Lip to CGT-Lip, August 9, 1973.
134   *Le Figaro*, October 9, 1973, 14.
135   Jacques Chérèque, *La Rage de faire* (Paris, 2007), 73.
136   *Libération*, October 20–1, 1973, 2.

arranged on a case-by-case basis, with a priority for those who had been laid off in hiring at Lip as openings occurred there. The CGT-Lip accepted this and the unions presented their intersyndical proposal to Giraud in Dijon.[137]

Giraud asked lots of questions, had his lawyers review the proposal, then went and made a phone call and came back to say no.[138] He said that he could not guarantee employment for those not given jobs, and he set a deadline for workers to accept his plan with its 159 layoffs. Giraud's assertion that he would personally look after the fate of those who lost their jobs was reiterated by the Minister of Labor, Georges Gorse, in a last ditch effort to offer an antiquated paternalism as a salve for the workings of markets and bureaucracies. National leaders on the left contended that Giraud's refusal to pursue a settlement when offered the first significant concession by workers since talks began was evidence that he was not free to negotiate. Rocard came to feel that the limit on hires, 989, was set by the government—"It was necessary to punish the workers"—and contended that Giraud realized his plan for the reopened factory was unworkable and so sought the failure of the negotiations.[139]

The CGT saw things differently. It would not judge the viability of a capitalist enterprise, but presented the Giraud plan as a victory for workers. The state could not tolerate this, so it instructed its agent Giraud to get the workers to reject it. In its analysis, later distributed to militants, the FTM-CGT explained that, "presented in a provocative form, the text baptized 'the Giraud plan' corresponded in fact to a sum of setbacks for Giraud and the government [which had started with 480 layoffs] ... It was a provocation and a trap at the same time, in the hopes of a reaction of rejection which would make the workers lose sight of their victory."[140] The CGT threw its weight behind bringing the strike to an end. In words reminiscent of the Communist Party leader Maurice Thorez in 1936, that workers must know how to end a strike, Séguy told L'Humanité on October 11 that the CFDT-Lip, unlike the national CFDT, did not have a "realistic attitude." Pursuit of the movement was contrary to the interests of the workers at Lip: "There always comes a time when it is necessary to know it is time to end. We have the impression that this time has come."[141]

---

137   AMB 5Z221 CFDT tract, "LIP c'est possible. Ils peuvent gagner" [October 1973].

138   BDIC F delta rés 578/36 "Texte de l'intervention de Charles Piaget."

139   ACFDT 8H561 "Intervention de Michel Rocard," November 26, 1973. *Tribune socialiste*, January 30, 1974, 2.

140   FTM-CGT, "La CGT et Lip," 15.

141   *L'Humanité*, October 11, 1973, 6. Mercet had been quoted earlier saying,

CGT-Lip secretary-general Mercet did not like the role of orator, and Dartevelle was given the task of making this case to the workers.[142] A week before the march Mercet had talked of the Common Program in a way no national CGT leader would have: "the Lip conflict and perhaps other ongoing conflicts can demonstrate that the Common Program is perhaps out-of-date in its original form."[143] However, in her closing speech to the assembled workers and supporters at the demonstration on September 29, Dartevelle braved hoots of derision to reiterate that *les Lip* might very well not have all their demands met, but what was important was that the movement had weakened the nexus of power, a step toward the only real resolution, a government that could enact the Common Program.[144] A few days later, she responded to Piaget's affirmation that workers would continue the fight even if Giraud pulled out by saying, "Any position that leads to a prolongation of the conflict will have adverse repercussions for workers."[145] Dartevelle later reiterated Séguy's position: "*Les Lip* were not able to fight capitalism all alone, and having obtained the retention of the factory and 160 instead of 600 layoffs, this was an unprecedented victory."[146]

A reinvigorated Action Committee rejected the intersyndical proposal that Giraud had found unacceptable as well. The General Assembly had given union representatives the authority to defend its position, not to bargain it away: "We want to negotiate, but not to be negotiated," in Raguénès' words.[147] A product of the struggle, the Lip community was a whole, not a collection of individuals; the exile of some would betray that community. Raguénès and Marc Géhin, who had quit the CGT when he learned it was discussing severance pay for laid-off workers, penned and distributed a document for the Action Committee, "Lip: Hope of the Working Class?"[148] It echoed the contention of the general secretaries of the CGT and of the CFDT, that the conflict had become such that the Lip workers were fighting for all workers. For Séguy and Maire, this meant that the workers had to accept compromise; for the Action Committee, it meant that the Lip workers needed to pursue their struggle.

"What do you want, Maurice Thorez said you have to know how to end a strike!" "Lip: les dernières montres," *Valeurs actuelles*, August 13, 1973, 10.

142   *L'Expansion*, September 1973, 98.
143   *Libération*, September 21, 1973, 3.
144   *Libération*, October 1, 1973, 7.
145   *Le Figaro*, October 6–7, 1973, 5.
146   *Le Nouvel observateur*, October 15, 1973, 35.
147   *Libération*, October 12, 1973, 12.
148   *Libération*, October 18, 1973, 3.

The confederations had always feared that the Action Committee would contest the unions' right to set the agenda. The Committee saw in the inter-syndical proposal the work of the national union leaders and sought to rally the base to stop the possibility of "accords done behind our backs."[149] It reiterated that workers should not leave their fate in the hands of union delegates. The Committee questioned Piaget's professed need to work with the CGT-Lip, seeing this instead as the faltering of an exhausted militant.[150] It rejected the intersyndical proposal, affirming that the Syndex plan showed the economic viability of the totality of Lip. Raguénès said of the Action Committee's manifesto: "The objective of this text was to denounce all union compromise."[151] "Lip: Hope of the Working Class?" reaffirmed the position of no dismantling, no layoffs, and maintenance of benefits, and said it was the right of all workers "to know the degree of determination and combative-ness" of their union with respect to these demands. What, the leaflet asked, would a worker say to

> our laid-off comrade who fought with us from the beginning, who *hoped*
> *with us* … and who now finds himself far from us (because he had the
> misfortune, for example, to be in the mechanics shop!); to our laid-off
> comrade … who was perhaps the one who yesterday, produced, sold,
> popularized? … WILL WE BE ABLE to speak sincerely of VICTORY
> when many of our comrades will not be at our side?[152]

The Action Committee convinced the CFDT-Lip that before the General Assembly met to decide what to do, workers should discuss the Giraud and intersyndical proposals as well as that of the Committee. On the after-noon of October 11, nine groups of fifty to 150 workers, including CGT and CFDT delegates, met for two-and-a-half to three hours to discuss the proposals at the Maison pour Tous de Palente, in the basement of the Pie X church and at the Fort de Bregille. Each worker received a twelve-page dossier prepared by the intersyndical committee that laid out the unions' position and the results of negotiations with Giraud, as well as a copy of "Lip: Hope of the Working Class?"[153]

The CFDT-Lip met on the night of October 11 to assess what it had

---

149   *Il était une fois la révolution*, 236.

150   Lopez, "Lip Interview," 6–7.

151   *Il était une fois la révolution*, 226–7.

152   BDIC F delta rés 702/7/1 CA, "Lip: espoir de la classe ouvrière?," October 11, 1973.

153   *Lip Unité dépêche quotidienne*, October 11, 1973. *Lip Unité*, October 23, 1973, 2. *Tribune socialiste*, October 17, 1973, 7. *Politique hebdo*, October 18, 1973, 15.

learned from these meetings. Realizing that the intersyndical proposal had little support and knowing that Giraud had rejected it, the CFDT-Lip withdrew its endorsement of this accord with the CGT-Lip. This was in keeping with what Piaget had said a few weeks before: "We have always been with the workers at the forefront of the struggle, but that is because we have accepted at times being surpassed. To refuse, that would have been to put a brake on the struggle. We must accept being surpassed to remain the organization of the workers at the service of all the workers."[154] However, this was anathema to the CGT, which condemned the CFDT-Lip for changing its position overnight to the original stance, the consequence of what it saw as the unchecked leftism of the Action Committee that was contrary to workers' interests and would alienate public support.[155] Faced with the divisions in Besançon, the confederations themselves worked unsuccessfully on October 11 to develop a common position.

On October 12, the General Assembly was asked to choose between a motion to accept the Giraud plan and one to stick to the demands *les Lip* had begun with. The intersyndical position was not offered as an option. The CGT-Lip endorsed the first position, but was frustrated that it was not presented as continuing the fight over workers' benefits after the return to work. The CFDT-Lip and the Action Committee supported the second. An emotional debate followed. A member of the Committee made a strong impression when he asked workers to imagine they were walking in Indian file and counting off 1, 2, 3, 4 and every fourth had to leave.[156] Piaget was unable to stop workers from whistling and calling out "Giraud-CGT same fight" and "Only one solution, lower your shorts," when the CGT delegates took the floor.[157] But, the prefect reported, after Mercet warned the General Assembly of the consequences of a rejection, Piaget went on to make "unprecedented critiques of the CGT, accusing it of dishonesty, of irresponsibility. His accusations created a particularly heated atmosphere until the time of the vote."[158] According to the police, Piaget's words created "an indescribably rowdy atmosphere" in which some members of the CGT-Lip tore up their membership cards in front of the assembly.[159]

When it came time for the vote, Mercet, recognizing that "the room

---

154   *Tribune socialiste*, September 25, 1973, n.p. [special issue for September 29 march].

155   *L'Humanité*, October 11, 1973, 6 [quoted]; October 15, 1973, 5.

156   Raguénès, *De Mai 68*, 186.

157   *Libération*, October 13–14, 1973, 1.

158   ADD 1026W14 PD to PM, October 12, 1973.

159   ADD 1026W14 RG, October 12, 1973.

had been rendered white-hot" by the attacks on his union,[160] demanded the assembly break its usual practice and vote by secret ballot, a provision Giraud had asked for as well. Workers were given two ballots and officials verified their status as Lip employees when they cast their votes. Because the "yes" ballot was larger than the "no" ballot, Mercet contended, the absence of voting booths or envelopes for the ballots made it hardly a secret ballot. But this does not explain the lopsided tally. The vote was 626 for the Action Committee/CFDT-Lip motion vs. 174 for the motion to accept Giraud's proposal and return to work.[161] "What a celebration after the refusal of the plan," one female OS said: "we felt that it had been really OUR vote."[162]

Although most female OS would have been re-hired, many rejected the Giraud plan. Some voted against it because they felt they would be left defenseless with the dismissal of virtually all the CFDT-Lip leadership.[163] And not demanding jobs at Lip for all would have destroyed the community based on the new forms of sociability and the relationships established between workers in different parts of the factory which had taken shape over the course of the conflict. More than individual jobs or benefits, this is what many now saw themselves fighting to protect.[164] In this sense, the vote marked a shift from defense of an earlier situation to defense of what had developed in the struggle. One female OS explained that as a result of the movement, "we are even more attached to our factory than before: now, it is really more than a livelihood, it is our life, truly our place."[165] Recriminations from their extended families after the vote only made the workers all the more committed to the new community born of the struggle.[166] For one young Action Committee militant, "If we had accepted the layoffs, I would have never believed in socialism! For me, socialism, it is the possibility of a thousand sacrificing so as not to abandon 150."[167]

---

160   *L'Humanité*, October 15, 1973, 5.

161   There were perhaps 150 employees—not including managers, the commercial staff in Paris, and workers on the road drumming up support—who were unaccounted for in the balloting, but this still revealed a high level of engagement for a six-month old movement. Barou, *Gilda je t'aime*, 196. The seventy-seven workers at the Ornans machine tools plant, never an integral part of Lip and where the CGT and FO were dominant, voted to return to work under a new employer. The General Assembly approved this arrangement and work started there on November 19, 1973.

162   Marie-Christine in *Lip au féminin*, 52.

163   *Politique hebdo*, October 18, 1973, 16.

164   *Lip Unité dépêche quotidienne*, October 12, 1973.

165   Jeanne Z. in "Comment 'l'affaire' nous a changés," 66.

166   Werner, "La question des femmes," 2453.

167   *Le Nouvel observateur*, October 29, 1973, 33.

Lip was a national movement in the sense that it had nurtured and was dependent on widespread support, but it refused, in the case of the CFDT-Lip, to follow blindly the directives of national union organizations: "At Besançon," Piaget later said, "we did not forget that the important decisions, throughout the Lip conflict, were made by us against the views of the federal directors [of the FGM-CFDT]."[168] For one Action Committee member, "we had an enemy: the owners and the power, and one brake: the CGT which was almost an enemy. It is an enemy as long as it serves as a brake. It's a little like at Waterloo—they wait for Grouchy ... and it is Blücher who arrives."[169] Workers embraced the slogan, "Lip will not be Grenelle," referring to the agreement that the confederations had negotiated which ended the May 1968 strikes. Back then, Piaget added, only a minority of workers had rejected the accords, but this time at Lip a majority did.[170] Action Committee members reciprocated the hostility shown them by the confederations, believing that a movement rooted in a democratic affirmation of local power was incompatible with assertions of discipline and expertise by national leaderships. In his novel *Les Paroissiens de Palente*, Clavel has a character speak of the involvement of the feds in "the tone of a bad gangster film."[171]

The workers' decision disoriented business, the state, and the confederations. From his arrival in Besançon, Giraud had sought to deal with unions whose job, he believed, was to convince workers to follow them. Just as he felt that Lip needed a director who could impose his authority, he made the same critique of the unions at Lip, which "were not followed by their troops and therefore did not fulfill what I understand to be the role of the leader, which is to direct."[172] Only Fred Lip showed satisfaction, seeing in Giraud's situation evidence that others could do no better than he had at Lip. Referring to the rabbits he saw Giraud drawing from his hat, Fred Lip pronounced them "slaughtered one after the other by the union's arms."[173] Of the CFDT-Lip's withdrawal of the intersyndical proposal (rather than Giraud's rejection of it), Charbonnel revealed the depth of his disappointment in denying it when he wrote in his memoirs: "I will not spend my life dwelling on the conspiracy of Charles Piaget, as long ago Cicero did telling of his consulate."[174]

---

168   *Politique hebdo*, October 3, 1974, 21.
169   *L'Outil des travailleurs*, December 1973–January 1974, 8.
170   *Libération*, November 10–11, 1973, 3.
171   Clavel, *Les Paroissiens*, 47.
172   Giraud, *Mon été*, 110.
173   Lip, *Conter mes heures*, 12.
174   Jean Charbonnel, *L'Aventure de la fidelité* (Paris, 1976), 224.

The FGM-CFDT had been shocked as well at what it saw as the local union losing control to the Action Committee. "If this continues," Chérèque said, "we will have unions but not union members."[175] No longer having access to the national CGT network for its popularization activities, Lip workers became more dependent on autonomous groups of leftist supporters, which further upset the CFDT. Evoking the CFDT's repudiation of leftism at its national congress in May–June 1973, Chérèque told a meeting of the FGM-CFDT's leaders a week after October 12 that Lip was now the "battlefield" in the confrontation with leftists and that eventually a disavowal of the CFDT-Lip might be necessary.[176] In November, Piaget recognized that the PSU and the parties of the extreme left were "the only political allies" of *les Lip* and that they worked much more for them than the mainstream left, but he went on to ask that leftist parties "not appear too often." This was important to keep the CFDT confederation on board; too close an association with leftists "is not what is going to take us out of the ghetto."[177]

Crossing the Desert

An important element in the national appeal of the Lip struggle had been the cooperation between the CGT-Lip and the CFDT-Lip. This was lost. After the vote of October 12, the CGT-Lip took its members off the commissions and met separately, no longer as part of the General Assembly.[178] It pursued a more traditional strategy, intervening with deputies and other elected officials to say that what had been possible with the Giraud plan on October 12 was still possible.[179] It called on Lip workers to write or telegraph President Pompidou to ask that Lip not be dismantled and that employment be protected.[180] While the CGT preferred to blame the CFDT-Lip for the failure of the Giraud negotiations and took pleasure in spreading word of Maire's letter of warning to the CFDT-Lip of October 8—"this intervention right on target"—it also condemned the CFDT for its failure to follow through on resolutions passed at its

175 *L'Express*, October 22, 1973, 75.
176 Frank Georgi, *Soufflons nous-mêmes notre forge* (Paris, 1991), 171.
177 "Un pas vers la révolution," 31.
178 *Lip Unité dépêche quotidienne*, November 6, 1973.
179 *L'Humanité*, October 23, 1973, 6. ADD 43J30 Telegram from Claude Curty, secrétaire général CGT-Doubs, to CFDT-LIP, October 23, 1973.
180 *Lip Unité dépêche quotidienne*, October 30, 1973.

last national congress and root out what it saw as the leftism of its local at Lip.[181] To reply to the steady drumbeat of criticism from the CGT, the CFDT-Lip took the unusual step of publishing a half-page advertisement in *Le Monde* to refute the CGT's interpretation of events at Lip, saying that because Giraud had rejected the intersyndical accord it could not have been offered to the General Assembly as a choice. Furthermore, the CFDT-Lip reiterated that it had never felt confident in Giraud's business plan—in Piaget's words, "truly a patched-up job, the whole thing held together by little bits of wire," the apparent result of helter-skelter decisions.[182] Economic success required greater watch production and more non-armaments equipment production; this explained the need for all to be employed and the maintenance of the mechanics division.[183]

While endorsing this position, the FGM-CFDT wrote to the CFDT-Lip on October 17 to tell them that they were not "the exclusive owners of the conflict." Press coverage made it appear that the Action Committee was in charge and that the extreme left was calling the shots, which "did not favor the brand name of your struggle." The state would do nothing and political and union support was frittering away, evident in the "weak union content" of recent popularization efforts. The only solution was to work out an agreement with the CGT-Lip on the basis of the intersyndical position.[184] However, this was easier said than done. The CFDT-Lip voted on October 19 to restart negotiations on the basis of the intersyndical accord, but these efforts were stymied by the Action Committee's hostility to this move coupled with the CGT-Lip's insistence that the Committee play no role in the future.[185] The CGT-Lip rejected the explanation offered by a representative of the CFDT-Lip that the Committee was no longer an active presence of the sort the CGT repudiated. "Currently, the Action Committee is mainly a state of mind, but it is impossible to dissolve a state of mind with a text."[186] The General Assembly rebuffed the CGT-Lip position as well, recognizing that its desire to eliminate those outside of the union leadership challenged the premise that had been central since the beginning of the conflict: that the General Assembly was considered "as supreme" by the unions and

181   ACGT Lip Box 6 CGT, "La situation chez Lip et ses Répercussions" [after October 12, 1973].

182   *Témoignage chrétien*, February 7, 1974, 4.

183   *Le Monde*, October 21–2, 1973, 10.

184   ACFDT 8H561 FGM-CFDT [Chérèque] to CFDT Lip, October 17, 1973.

185   Interview with Charles Piaget and Action Committee members, *Front Rouge*, October 25, 1973.

186   *Lip Unité dépêche quotidienne*, November 12, 1973.

that the unions were not to pursue policies without the agreement of the personnel, as reflected by the Assembly.[187]

Although the Action Committee proved to be more than a "state of mind" after October 12, the General Assembly was no more willing to surrender its position to the Committee than to the CGT-Lip. The Action Committee meeting of November 5 attracted more than fifty participants: "the Action Committee functions a little like a ballon, inflating in ebb periods."[188] The CFDT-Lip returned to the practice of meeting with the Committee before the General Assembly convened.[189] Raguénès recognized that in the uncertainty which followed October 12, a number of young Action Committee members were becoming the workers seeking answers that leftists had earlier sought without success at Lip. However, when Committee members presented radical ideas they had gleaned from these contacts to the General Assembly they were discussed, but not accepted.[190]

In a play Lip workers later wrote about their experience, they referred to the barren spell from late October to late December 1973 as "crossing the desert."[191] Faced with the division of the unions Piaget had always feared, efforts turned to developing the vitality of the General Assembly. It sent a letter to those who came irregularly, assuring them that a solution would be found and that for the success of the struggle, they should attend, "for you are with us and in fact, you are a Lip." Members of a new commission, called "Presence in the Struggle," visited employees who had not been coming to Assembly meetings.[192] Four to five hundred workers participated in the daily general assemblies in late November, and 600 in December.[193] This led to a reaffirmation that the General Assembly was most successful when it existed in a symbiotic relationship with informal discussions or work on commissions: "If you return home brooding after the General Assembly, you are often depressed … It's just the opposite if you go to the Maison pour Tous and if you have an activity in the struggle."[194]

---

187   Lip Unité dépêche quotidienne, November 7, 1973.

188   Politique hebdo, November 8, 1973, 14.

189   Lip Unité dépêche quotidienne, November 22, 1973.

190   "Un pas vers la révolution," 28, 31.

191   "Refuser la fatalité et vivre ensemble au pays [Historique de la lutte présenté par les travailleurs]" in Terrieux, "L'Expérience Lip," Partie I, episode 3.

192   Lip Unité dépêche quotidienne, October 26, 1973 [quoted]. BDIC F delta rés 578/44 "Commission présence dans le conflit" [c. January 1974].

193   Libération, December 20, 1973, 3.

194   Lip Unité dépêche quotidienne, November 7, 1973.

After the October 12 vote, a relieved Prime Minister Messmer announced: "Lip, it's over, as far as I'm concerned." Adding that "Lip workers do not merit the woe in which blind leaders, carried away by passion, have plunged them," Messmer forbade Charbonnel from talking with the unions.[195] On October 18, workers distributed their fourth pay, discreetly in small groups in different places, sometimes even to individuals or at a worker's home. This spurred the police to launch a raid on the workers' headquarters.[196] On October 23, the CRS and the police forced their way into the Maison pour Tous looking for sequestered watches and cash. However, the workers had hidden the watches and most of the money, and the police came up with only thirty-nine watches and two weeks' worth of pay.[197] More effective was the threat to cut off family allowances and social security benefits to Lip workers who did not sign up as unemployed looking for work with the Agence nationale pour l'emploi (ANPE) by November 13, a date picked because the vote on October 12 was taken as the end of their rights to social benefits as strikers and the beginning of the period in which they could claim them only if registered with the ANPE.[198] The CGT-Lip immediately encouraged members to sign up, but the CFDT-Lip followed the General Assembly decision to refuse, concerned that this would be taken as a sign of defeat.

In this period of uncertainty, the community's fears of division and the loss of its mission focused on a woman. Though the movement had profound effects on a number of women and brought several in the Action Committee to prominence, Noëlle Dartevelle was still the only female union leader. Whereas the CGT-Lip secretary-general Mercet was inclined to cooperate with the (male) leadership of the CFDT-Lip, Dartevelle was often the voice of less popular CGT policies.[199] One Action Committee member accused her of using the freedom of expression in the General Assembly to provoke them: "You have seen her with her chewing gum, that is something, with her ironic smile. I think that she waits to be targeted, that she actually waits for people to prevent her from speaking and this will be her victory—You see it each time when

---

195   *L'Humanité*, October 13, 1973, 6.
196   ADD 1026W2 PD, October 23, 1973.
197   BDIC F delta rés 578/36 "Texte de l'intervention de Ch. Piaget," 32.
198   ADD 1026W10 Ministre de la Santé Publique to Direction de la Sécurité Sociale de Bourgogne, November 1, 1973.
199   In Clavel's *Les Paroissiens de Palente* this division is clear. Blandel (Claude Marcel) frequently questions CGT policies. However, Mère Poudevigne (Noëlle Dartevelle) is ridiculed and scorned by sympathetic characters in the novel.

Piaget says 'Let her speak, be quiet', she smiles as if to say: 'See, you aren't democratic.'"[200] Dartevelle had been the most prominent voice challenging the CFDT-Lip leadership by saying it was time to settle the conflict in September and early October. This division continued after October 12. In her role as representative of her union, Dartevelle spoke in favor of signing up with the ANPE and was attacked in crude terms.[201] General Assembly participants began chanting "Bêe, Bêe, look at the goat of Monsieur Séguy."[202] Neither CGT-Lip nor CFDT-Lip leaders told them to stop. Angry and frustrated, Dartevelle said "Shit," something that would have been acceptable from a male delegate whose honor had been challenged, but was considered unacceptable coming from a woman. Mercet took the microphone away from her and would not let her apologize. She was not allowed to speak for two days in the General Assembly and was never forgiven for this breach of decorum. Whatever steps had been taken to bring women into the public forum, the woman with the most prominent public role became a figure of antipathy, condemned as a woman for her behavior. Later, when workers held new elections, the CGT-Lip would not put her up as a candidate for the works council, despite her two decades of experience on it, telling her "you'll be scratched out" by voters.[203]

The issue of registering with the ANPE was resolved on November 12, when Piaget and Mercet together convinced the General Assembly to vote for workers to sign up collectively. In response to the question about what employment they were seeking, workers wrote down the job they had held at Palente and explained that they had lost work when the CRS occupied the factory. With the forms complete, they went off together to the ANPE office in Besançon on November 13.[204] As many workers had feared, the prefect took this as putting an end to "the fiction carefully maintained" that Lip workers were not unemployed.[205] However, there was an advantage to acquiescing. With benefits secured, workers would continue to be able to pay themselves and receive the equivalent of their full salary for several more months. "Something to make the authorities

---

200   Lopez, "Lip Interview," 59.

201   AB Interview with Dartevelle by Beurier (1992), 11.

202   Piton, C'est possible!, 479. This is a reference to the story by Alphonse Daudet, "La chèvre de M. Seguin," with the head of the CGT taking the farmer's place.

203   AB Interview with Dartevelle by Beurier (1992), 16, 60, 62.

204   Lip Unité dépêche quotidienne, November 13, 1973. Libération, November 15, 1973, 6.

205   ADD 1026W13 PD to PM, November 12, 1973.

reflect," Piaget told the General Assembly.[206] Furthermore, the ANPE employees showed no interest in cracking down on *les Lip*. The regional director said that for at least three months, workers' unemployment benefits would not be affected by the salaries they paid themselves. And workers could be reimbursed for social benefits whose payment had been on hold since early September. He also promised that Lip workers would not be directed to other job opportunities until the end of December, nor would they have to check in at the employment office like others receiving benefits.[207]

Confronting Layoffs in France

The Lip Affair had the national impact it did because neither the parties nor the confederations were prepared for the issues it raised. It was a 1968-style movement dealing with what would become the central issue in France during the 1970s: unemployment. Neither the IDI nor the Charbonnel plan did more than reiterate that of the Swiss multinational. Giraud had a political, not an economic mission. Socialists and Communists were supportive of *les Lip*, but kept their distance. The confederations were stymied by a movement that did not see its future in securing individual benefits for those laid off or in the nationalizations of the Common Program.

The most innovative national institutional response was the CFDT dispatch of economists from Syndex. During the conflict, the CFDT-Lip, in deference to the CGT, had referred to self-management of the struggle rather than self-management of production or the economy. However, many supporters of the Lip workers saw their conflict in terms of the self-management of production, an original impetus of self-management developed during the postwar boom to make the workplace more responsive to human needs. However, self-management reached a turning point in the Lip conflict by bringing workers into debates over the investments and strategies necessary to provide jobs for workers. In future conflicts, the CFDT made frequent use of consultants like those of Syndex, though, as at Lip, locals never went on to seek a role in management.[208] The plan Syndex came up with in cooperation with Lip workers was the first of

---

206   ADD 45J16 Wall poster of November 19, 1973.
207   *Lip Unité dépêche quotidienne*, November 12, 1973.
208   Albert Mercier, "Les conflits de longue durée," *CFDT aujourd'hui* 22 (November–December 1976): 8.

forty such plans developed by consultants working with locals to address the specific problems of French firms making mass layoffs at individual sites between 1973 and 1980; these represented a working-class response to the inadequacies of the works councils in failing businesses, so evident in the final years of Lip.[209] When Nicole Notat, secretary-general of the CFDT, came to Besançon in 1993 to address the question of unemployment on the twentieth anniversary of the Lip summer, what she took from it was the role of the CFDT in the elaboration of "industrial counterproposals," not the creativity or imagination of *les Lip* themselves.[210] Yet, as one Syndex accountant asked, did this reliance on experts—to whom locals deferred because they said what the locals wanted to hear—introduce a trade union technocracy in place of self-management? Did it amount "in fact to having enter by the window what we want to make leave by the door, namely the maintenance of workers in ignorance of the fundamental mechanisms of exploitation?"[211]

Lip workers, however, had their own expertise to offer. They believed that movements rooted in communities born of struggle were not an impediment to national organizations, but catalysts for action. Instead of a demonstration along the lines of that of September 29, CFDT-Lip began organizing after October 12 a national colloquium on employment in cooperation with the CFDT. While the confederation emphasized the theme, "No layoffs without an offer of equivalent employment up front," the CFDT-Lip drew on two distinctive elements of their conflict: the exchange between intellectuals and workers, and the desire for direct cooperation between movements contesting layoffs, rather than depending on communication through the national federations. In December 1973, the colloquium brought together economists, doctors, architects, jurists, and psychologists with workers from firms across France faced with layoffs and restructuring like those at Lip. One hundred and fifty Lip workers joined the more than 100 CFDT delegations at the gathering; the CGT declined to participate. The colloquium was not to be a place for workers to pose questions and for intellectuals to answer them. From the beginning of the conflict, Lip workers had depended on external support, but they in turn had no doubt that they had important

---

209   Jean-Pierre Huiban, "La contre proposition industrielle comme élément de stratégie syndicale (1973–1980)" in *1968–1982: le mouvement ouvrier français*, eds. Mark Kesselman and Guy Groux (Paris, 1984), 302.

210   ACFDT CSG/5/3 Nicole Notat, "Il y a 20 ans, LIP …," September 29, 1993.

211   Maurice Najman, "Syndicats: la fin de l'homme de marbre," *Autrement* 29 (1981): 214.

experiences and insights to offer others. The idea of the colloquium was to allow workers from Lip, who had "for seven months conducted an intense common reflection," to exchange their experiences with those of workers in other employment conflicts and for all to engage with the information and concepts supplied by intellectuals.[212]

Syndex had provided one innovative form of cooperation between intellectuals and workers, but in the colloquium the CFDT-Lip proposed another. A central issue after May 1968, the colloquium organizers recognized, was "to clarify what work groups of intellectuals might contribute to a discussion among workers' delegations."[213] This was the period when intellectuals in the Groupe d'information sur les prisons were working with inmates to analyze the long-ignored carceral universe. During the decades of postwar expansion, the unemployed were another group both unheard from and unexamined. Speaking of the colloquium, Piaget said, "This will be the equivalent for employment of what the Conversations at Bichat are for medicine. The difference will be that workers will speak as much as experts."[214] Intellectuals had knowledge of a variety of subjects that led them to "cut up" employment in certain ways, but the exchanges between Lip workers and workers engaged in struggles over employment elsewhere would show that the issues they raised "can and must be cut up in other ways." To take an example of what could be done, Lip workers suggested that in conjunction with doctors and medical students, they study the effects on participants' health of long conflicts like theirs.[215] Not surprisingly, these conversations between experts trained in the academy and experts trained in struggle had their disappointments. Workers were frustrated with the intellectuals' practice of speaking about employment issues in generalities. They felt that this devalued their particular situations and efforts to confront them.[216]

The CFDT-Lip also began working with other unions engaged in fights over employment to plan common actions. The popularization commission asked its national network to establish contacts and discuss actions that enterprises involved in struggles could take. *Lip Unité*, the workers' newsletter, began devoting significant space to campaigns against mass

212   BDIC F delta rés 578/52/10 "Préparation du colloque sur l'emploi. Compte-rendu d'une réunion tenue à Besançon les samedi 10 et dimanche 11 novembre."
213   Ibid.
214   *Libération*, October 16, 1973, 6. The Conversations at Bichat are an annual continuing education program for medical professionals.
215   BDIC F delta rés 578/52/10 "Préparation du colloque sur l'emploi."
216   "Lip Larzac, " 53. Collectif, *Lip: affaire non classée*, 25.

layoffs elsewhere.[217] The confederations responded by throwing up obstacles to what they saw as challenges to their authority.[218] Marie-Noëlle Thibault of the CFDT remarked that the colloquium revealed the parochialism that the national confederation saw in the project: "When we speak of the crisis at the national economic level, the participants had the impression that we were dispossessing them of their conflict, and that this was managed in the enterprise."[219] However, from the perspective of the colloquium organizers, the challenge to capitalist decision-making went where academic experts and the confederations refused to go, leaving it to workers like those at Lip to question "a certain type of economic development and to prefigure the ways in which economic orientations could be implemented [differently]."[220]

Palente and Parliament

Conservative legislators recognized that the Lip Affair had revealed problems, even if their efforts were limited to preserving the existing order by dealing with the consequences. Lip's creditors had contravened the law by laying off the workforce without giving the requisite notice, as well as by paying, after bankruptcy was declared, certain creditors and some employees who had not joined the walkout. In September 1973, in response to Lip, President Pompidou asked his staff to review the legislation to assure that workers were better defended in the case of bankruptcies. François Ceyrac, head of the CNPF, concurred with this effort to make certain, in his words, that "defunct enterprises would be able to pay for their burial."[221] Workers were to be privileged creditors. And if that was insufficient, the Minister of Labor Georges Gorse, another left Gaullist like Charbonnel, signed a decree at the end of December 1973 that established a reserve funded by employers' dues to pay salaries owed

---

217   BDIC F delta rés 578/48 Coordination Technique des Commissions Lip to Commissions Lip, January 6, 1974. *Politique hebdo*, December 13, 1973, 14. On meetings of workers in these enterprises held in succeeding months, see Jusseaume, "Un succès venu de loin," 70.

218   *Les Cahiers de mai hebdo*, January 14, 1974, 4.

219   "Lip: les Raisons d'un succès," *Politique aujourd'hui* (March–April 1974), 27. On Thibault, see Donald Reid, "The Red and the Black: Marie-Noëlle Thibault and the Novels of Dominique Manotti," *French Cultural Studies* 26:3 (August 2015): 1–12.

220   BDIC F delta rés 2074 *Les Cahiers de mai*, 'Projet de texte à la suite des discussions que nous avons eues à Besançon le 1 et le 2 décembre."

221   *Le Figaro*, September 20, 1973, 7; September 21, 1973, 1. Henri Weber, *Le Parti des patrons* (Paris, 1991), 267 [quoted].

workers promptly in the event of the bankruptcy of their employer. This, future Lip leader Michel Garcin explained, "thereby dissipates the risks of collective revolt."[222] A law of October 1974 set unemployment benefits at 90 percent of the previous salary for the first year (with a possible extension of up to four months) for workers who lost work in financially troubled firms. Workers receiving this level of pay were unlikely to start up production to support themselves. Finally, in January 1975, new legislation required that employers receive administrative approval from labor inspectors to lay off workers for economic reasons. This body of legislation was a direct response to the Lip Affair, even if it was far from the "legality of tomorrow" of which Maire had spoken.

---

222   *Le Point,* January 25, 2007.

5

Because We Tell You It Is Possible

The standard course of action for workers involved in a conflict in a medium-sized provincial factory would be to call on the support and guidance of national union confederations. Workers at Lip did this, but more central and innovative was their project of popularization based on opening up Palente to visitors and journalists, and taking their struggle on the road. *Les Lip* nurtured the mainstream press, created their own media, and established good working relationships with leftist militants and their papers. The particular appeal of the Lip struggle was that not only its leaders, but a large number of male and female workers also spoke to reporters and to supporters about their cause. And in turn, as the prefect noted, Lip workers themselves were an important, if unacknowledged, audience for these diverse popularization efforts.[1]

Piaget told the General Assembly on June 18, 1973:

> The principal focus is popularization. The sales, production, management, stocks commissions are simply for survival, to sustain the struggle. The principal commission is popularization because we do not think that it is by producing and selling watches that we will win the struggle we are conducting. What will win the struggle is popularization, is solidarity, is the balance of power we will be capable of creating on the local, regional and national levels.[2]

1   ADD 1026W6 PD, September 14, 1973.
2   BDIC F delta rés 578/46 "Film réalisé sous la responsabilité de la Commission Popularisation des Travailleurs de Lip et financé par elle. Texte intégral de la bande son."

A couple of weeks later, *Le Figaro* recognized the workers' success when it termed the sale of watches "the most successful advertising campaign of the year."[3] The popularization commission soon had some 200 members in nine subcommissions which dealt with a range of activities, including the reception of journalists, a review of press coverage, film production, responses to the hundreds of letters received daily, publication of a newsletter, and the organization of national tours of Lip workers. Yet, if popularization was more important than the production and sale of watches for the success of the campaign, it was dependent on the interest that these acts generated in television and the press.

Television

On no issue were '68ers more united than in their condemnation of the state's use of television to control debate in France. The state-run Office de Radiodiffusion-Télévision Française (ORTF) was the site of constant conflicts after 1968 between the government and reporters, who sought the freedom they believed press journalists enjoyed; the Lip conflict became an important site of this fight.[4] Pierre Desgraupes, ORTF director during a brief period of liberalization in 1969, considered the Lip Affair "a little like the Spanish Civil War; it served as an experience for a whole lot of people to test their ideological weapons in combat."[5] Lip militants were aware of the importance of television coverage from the beginning of the conflict. In May 1973 workers sent a delegation to the ORTF in Besançon to discuss the amount of airtime given to events at Palente and the objectivity of the coverage.[6] Yet, at the end of May, when the ORTF proposed to do a report on Lip, it was the provisional administrators who wrote to the ORTF regional director in Besançon to ask that this project be shelved.[7] However, they were not able to stop coverage altogether. On the night of June 12, the ORTF station in Besançon read on air from the documents that workers had found at Palente. From then on, the ORTF was a contested terrain. Vittot told the General Assembly on June 18 that though the unions thought 15,000 had been at the demonstration on June 15, the ORTF planned to use the figure of 5,000

---

3   Divo, *L'Affaire Lip*, 22.
4   Evelyne Cohen, *La Télévision sur la scène du politique* (Paris, 2009), 157.
5   *Le Point*, January 20, 1975, 81.
6   Cassou, "Lip, la Construction d'un mythe," 22.
7   Administrateurs provisoires to Directeur régional of the ORTF, May 29, 1973, in Maire and Piaget, *Lip 73*, 26.

and backed down only when the mayor of Besançon said there had not been as many on the streets of Besançon since de Gaulle's visit after the city's liberation in 1944; that got the ORTF to boost the figure to 12,000.[8]

As the conflict took on a national dimension, the ORTF sought to shape the narrative. In mid-June 1973, reporter Daniel Duigou was sent to Besançon with instructions to file sympathetic reports on the workers in line with an initial response among Gaullists to make Fred Lip responsible for the workers' situation. Duigou arrived in Besançon just as the workers voted to start up production and sales. The Gaullist deputy for Doubs, Edgar Faure, gave a televised interview, calling the cause "just," but the next day he took Duigou aside to tell him the Lip workers were "dangerous" and must be stopped as soon as possible. Duigou himself was congratulated by his superiors for his reporting favorable to les Lip, but the government's position changed after June 18 and Duigou was dispatched to cover a travelling army air show with a bevy of actresses. Duigou's replacement immediately began running reports harshly critical of the workers.[9] But the events at Besançon were the kind of spectacle for which television news coverage was made. The ORTF could not resist filming and broadcasting events like the padlocks being cut on the refrigerated room in which watch parts were kept at Palente in June, and a clandestine workshop after the expulsion from Palente (which the General Assembly was assured had been moved as soon as the filming was done) in August.[10]

No one believed that the ORTF provided balanced reporting. In late July, the prefect examined the coverage of the syndic's report on the liquidation of the business; he found that little airtime was given to the syndic in comparison with that given to CFDT-Lip leader Vittot's condemnation of the report. He saw this as one more instance of the ORTF's continued "lack of objectivity" in covering the conflict. However, he understood why. In the absence of Lip management, there was no one to respond to the unions, since, the prefect lamented, when the government did, it looked authoritarian.[11] In August the ORTF personnel held

---

8   BDIC F delta rés 578/36 Transcript of AG, June 18, 1973.

9   Daniel Duigou, *Journaliste, psy et prêtre* (Paris, 2005), 24–9.

10   ADD 45J96 Interview with Pierre-Émile by Beurier (c. 1992), 12. ADD 1026W11 RG, August 29, 1973. The ORTF could handle events at Lip as a human interest story, even giving cameras to workers and editing their footage into a final product. See the ORTF show, "Magazine 52," broadcast July 13, 1973: "Du côté de chez Lip," at www.ina.fr.

11   ADD 1026W14 PD to PM, July 24, 1973. In December 1973, two FR3 (ORTF) journalists in Besançon, whom the prefect found too sympathetic to les Lip, were

a twenty-four-hour work stoppage to protest the expulsion of workers from Palente. The next week an ORTF journalist from Paris spoke to the General Assembly to express his support and to say that the reporting on Lip was frequently censored (although there was no question about the quality of this reporting because the ORTF was selling the excised footage to foreign networks). A representative from the ORTF station in Besançon joined him to express the personnel's solidarity with their cause.[12]

The heads of the CGT and the CFDT, Séguy and Maire, joined the fray. They wrote to Arthur Conte, the director of the ORTF, on August 21, 1973, to complain that the network presented only representatives of business and of the government, not of the unions.[13] Ten days later, when they had not had a response from Conte, who was on a business trip in Gabon, they led a demonstration at the ORTF offices in Paris. Yet the situation was more complicated than it appeared. The ORTF let *Le Figaro* know that an accounting of the airtime given to Lip union leaders vindicated the network, but this, of course, was the problem for Séguy and Maire, who were concerned that the national coverage of Lip militants was making it all the more difficult for the national confederations to control them.[14] In any case, confederation grievances did not save Conte from the ire of Prime Minister Messmer, who complained that the presentation of Lip on television was "absolutely detestable." He criticized Conte for not doing his job, which was to come up with a "trick" to challenge the workers. As it was, he said, the coverage was like a television serial in which the repeated appearance of the bad boss or politician began to have its effect (although it was the absence of a boss or politicians willing to go on camera to confront the workers that was the problem). Conte defended the ORTF. Referring to Lip in a public communiqué in October 1973, he called on ORTF journalists to reject without hesitation all efforts to influence their reporting. Later that month, Messmer decided not to renew Conte's appointment.[15] The Lip

---

transferred at his request. Claude Neuschwander and Gaston Bordet, *Lip 20 ans après (propos sur le chômage)* (Paris, 1993), 99.

12   ADD 1026W11 RG, August 23, 1973.

13   ACGT Archives Henri Krasucki 7 CFD 102 Georges Séguy to Arthur Conte, August 21, 1973.

14   *Le Figaro*, August 31, 1973.

15   Cohen, *La Télévision*, 157. Jacques Foccart, *La Fin du gaullisme*, 5 vols. (Paris, 2001), vol. 5, 304–5. Frank Georgi, "Un 'conflit autogestionnaire' sous Georges Pompidou: les pouvoirs publics face à l'affaire Lip (1973-1974)" in *Action et pensée sociales chez Georges Pompidou*, eds. Alain Beltran, Gilles Le Béguec, and Jean-Pierre Williot (Paris, 2004), 171-3.

Affair revealed one set of contradictions concerning the role of the state in the economy of the Fifth Republic; coverage of it on state television revealed another.

The Press

Maintaining the national attention and sympathy their movement garnered was crucial for *les Lip* in a conflict in which the strategy of the Ébauches SA and the French state was to wait the workers out. Nothing frustrated opponents of the movement more than that it had become, in the words of a friend of Fred Lip, "the Loch Ness monster of August," a slow news time.[16] A Lip workers subcommission prepared material for journalists and met with them individually and in press conferences, in an effort to provide "uniform information," based on the decisions of the General Assembly. It also sought to counter the focus on charismatic leaders like Piaget, who thought "the press, as it is shaped by the system, looks for an individual explanation of events, rather than a collective one." Furthermore, the press threatened to create figures whose power made them a threat to democracy; Piaget noted with a certain pride that the General Assembly had once forbidden him to speak to the media for two weeks for a "slippage" during an interview.[17] In any case, having a commission deal with the press enabled Piaget and other leaders to spend more time with workers.[18] The CFDT-Lip's distribution of seized company documents in July, and the FGM-CFDT's publication the next month of twenty-five-page booklets containing material from files found at Lip and analyses of it drawn from the Syndex report, were crucial in getting the movement's message in the press.[19] Sympathetic national reporting in turn influenced the local papers. Favorable coverage in *Le Monde* "usually benefits from great credibility" and was immediately picked up by the local press, much to the prefect's irritation.[20]

Free access to workers and to Palente made the story particularly appealing to the print and audio-visual media. This openness itself became central to the story. Reporters ate with the workers in the

---

16 Lip, *Conter mes heures*, 159.

17 Piaget, "Lip 1973," 110.

18 *Témoignage chrétien*, February 7, 1974, 6 [quoted]. *Lip Unité*, January 1975, 3–4.

19 Later in the summer, the movement published documents seized in June in Piaget and Maire, *Lip 73*.

20 ADD 1026W2 PD, December 3, 1973.

restaurant. Some slept in the factory. They came to meetings of the Action Committee and the General Assembly. "By our mark of confidence, we want to win yours," one employee explained to a reporter from Agence France-Presse (AFP) who spent the night at Palente. At one point, AFP photographer Patrick Meney, sympathetic to the workers, helped get Piaget released from police custody.[21] A group of Parisian journalists marveled in late June: "An OS who uses 'tu' with the special correspondent of *Le Monde*, employees in Fred Lip's office explaining to an Italian journalist the place of the firm in the financial markets, these are just two examples of a reciprocal confidence that was established between journalists and Lip workers."[22] Even those from unsympathetic papers expressed support for the workers. The reporter from *L'Aurore* explained that each day he submitted a dispatch "and the editors make an introduction and a conclusion that screws thing up."[23] And though *Le Figaro* was critical of *les Lip*, fifty of the paper's staff sent a motion of support for the workers in August 1973.[24]

Workers learned to read the press coverage carefully. Beginning June 12, members of the Action Committee started buying daily papers and weekly reviews. They clipped articles on the conflict and posted them. The press subcommission followed this up by gluing articles about Lip on rolls of one-meter wide computer paper and then hanging them up in the passerelle for all to read. The scroll included notes each day on how events were covered on the radio and television as well as in the press. Occasional individual letters of support were also included. By June 22, the scroll was already eighteen meters long. From then on, the subcommission posted an average of ten meters a day with more on days following big events. Workers saved these scrolls on the advice of Paul Blanquart of *Politique hebdo*.[25] They rescued the scroll when the CRS occupied Palente and continued to post it daily at the Jean Zay gymnasium and the Maison pour Tous, hiding it each night in several places. By mid-February 1974, the accumulated rolls were more than two kilometers long.[26]

The head of the popularization commission suggested that this wall mural enabled workers to know what the journalists they met were

21   Interview with Pierre-Émile by Reid, June 4, 2011.
22   *Libération*, June 27, 1973, 3.
23   AR Interview with Pierre-Émile by Rouaud, July 6, 2005, 12.
24   Champeau, "Lip: le Conflit et l'Affaire (1973)," 136.
25   Divo, *L'Affaire Lip*, 17.
26   Record days followed the first workers' pay (20 meters) and the invasion of the factory on August 14 (22 meters). *L'Outil des travailleurs*, February 1974, 13.

writing and to respond to them: "then we think that certain ones will pay attention to what they write."[27] The leadership recognized that it could have presented a critique of media coverage at the beginning of each General Assembly, but they decided it would be more effective to have workers analyze the coverage on their own.[28] Like the bulletin board put up after May 1968, the posted press coverage became a site of discussion and debate which kept workers engaged and informed. Piaget explained: "You understand, during strikes, it is important that folks don't get bored. You always need to give them something to do. That's why we made the wall panels" of articles on Lip.[29] Handwritten posters commenting on the coverage of events often accompanied the mural of press clippings, particularly when coverage tailed off in the late fall of 1973.[30] Of the added material, Jeanningros said: "It is widely read because we carry, a little in the style of Le Canard enchaîné, what's being said in Besançon, the best moments of the meetings, the dirty tricks we had been able to play on the CRS, the reactions of the prefect, the bishop, the mayor, etc."[31]

Visitors

Palente was distinctive for its large glass windows. In the summer of 1973, its appellation, "Glass House," took on a new meaning when workers opened the occupied factory to visitors. The CGT-Lip initially sought to limit entry to representatives of organized labor. Early in the summer, Lip workers met ten to fifteen delegations from works councils from around the country, many led by the CGT.[32] However, the General Assembly voted to let in all visitors, and when the CFDT-Lip talked of soldering the gates open, the CGT-Lip backed down. Unlike the CGT-Lip, the CFDT-Lip welcomed the support of everyone, including leftists. It believed that democratic debate at Lip would winnow the good ideas leftists might introduce from the bad and would in turn offer a response to the leftists' standard repertoire of reproaches to union bureaucracies.[33]

---

27   Jusseaume, "Un succès venu de loin," 68–9.
28   Piaget, "LIP. Les effets formateurs," 157.
29   Le Quotidien de Paris, October 27, 1975.
30   Some of these handwritten posters appeared in Libération in a series "Les murs de Lip ont la parole," in January 1974.
31   L'Outil des travailleurs, February 1974, 13.
32   Les Cahiers de mai hebdo, July 9, 1973, 1.
33   Piaget and Maire, Lip 73, 130–1.

A group of Lip workers explained the value of considering ideas that had their origins outside the factory and the unions: "Since 1968, activists of the CFDT section in Besançon who participated in different struggles realized that the wealth of imagination and of creativity increased with the diversity of participants, especially if they came from different professions." They went on to say that a strong union was necessary to make this exchange of ideas work, however, for only then would workers foster "a collective creation," without losing control of their fight. "It is important that they not be buffeted by the waves, but that they master the current." It was this confidence that made the unusual openness to leftists possible.[34]

In the summer of 1973, two to three thousand men and women came to Palente each day to visit what Françoise Giroud called "the battleship Potemkin in the Bay of Besançon."[35] After the expulsion, workers continued to welcome visitors to their new quarters.[36] Women staffed the welcoming commission and took visitors around the factory, talking about the struggle and ending the tour with an opportunity to buy a watch. Those who came "want to see, to touch like Thomas."[37] One worker on the commission commented: "It is already a little Lourdes and Mecca at the same time."[38] And sure enough one day two buses of Belgian pilgrims returning from Lourdes stopped and toured the factory.[39] The General Assembly and commission meetings were open to visitors as well. They could ask questions and share their ideas and experiences at these meetings, but were more likely to do so at the small Action Committee gatherings, held until the expulsion from the factory in the late afternoon on the lawns of Palente.[40] Visitors were not restricted to guided tours and were struck by what they saw. "A visit to Lip is extraordinary," said Rocard, "not a cigarette butt in 10,000 square

---

34   Piaget, "LIP. Les effets formateurs," 150. During the first years of the Lip Affair, Pierre Rosanvallon made Lip a central element of his "training of CFDT staff to teach them resistance to leftism." Pierre Rosanvallon, "Témoignage," *Revue française d'histoire des idées politiques* 2 (1995): 367.

35   *L'Express*, August 6, 1973, 12. Later, a Lip worker said that workers visited Palente in 1973 as she imagined they had visited Russia in 1917 and 1918. AM Transcript of the film, "Lip au féminin," pt. 2.

36   *Il était une fois la révolution*, 156. They also received as many as 300 letters daily. At its peak, the commission in charge of correspondence wrote individual responses to 200 letters each day. *Lip Unité*, July 19, 1973, 2.

37   *Témoignage chrétien*, August 9, 1973, 4.

38   *Lip Unité*, January–February 1978, 9.

39   Thomé, *Créateurs d'utopies*, 191.

40   Two or three times, meetings of the General Assembly, limited to one hour, were opened to workers only. Piaget, "LIP. Les effets formateurs," 151–2.

meters; the working class expresses its dignity in this way" as well as in workers' creativity and imagination.[41] Visitors could walk about freely, observe production, and talk with any worker they wished, rather than solely designated individuals like union delegates. "At the refreshment bar under the lindens ... visitors and Lip workers discuss over a can of beer. Tourists unlike any others, it is the workers who take these visitors to their workshops."[42] That any worker could be a spokesperson for the movement challenged the belief that solidarity always required speaking in one voice: "As a result, the workers were not afraid to reveal their differences as well as their unity," journalists wrote in June.[43]

And in turn, workers learned from the visitors. They often stayed with workers' families, and the women who put them up, including Demougeot and Piton, were struck by young men who participated in household chores and by the possibility that a woman could leave her house with her chores undone to attend a political meeting, putting participation in the public sphere over domesticity.[44] Piton discovered Marxism with a Maoist who she in turn taught to cook: "And I had to convince him that cooking was neither less useful nor less difficult than reading *Capital*."[45] Visitors became "great propagandists,"[46] but they in turn had a transformative effect on *les Lip*.

Les Cahiers de mai and Lip Unité

The leftists had ideas, but what was most valued by *les Lip* was their technical assistance. Thinking of *Les Cahiers de mai* militants, Piaget said that supporters "contributed in this way to giving their style to the conflict. You could say that the paper *Lip Unité*, the films, the 'spoken paper' on cassettes and a whole series of initiatives were taken and came from exterior supporters."[47] Daniel Anselme directed *Les Cahiers de mai*, a group of about 100 militants nationwide that published its own paper, but repudiated any effort to bring the science of revolution to benighted workers.[48] Their goal was to present information to

41 ACFDT 8H561 "Intervention de Michel Rocard," November 26, 1973.
42 "Les vacances des ouvriers de Lip," *Libération* (Spécial Vacances, 1973), 8.
43 *Libération*, June 27, 1973, 3.
44 Féret, *Les Yeux rouges*, 48–9.
45 Champeau, "Lip: Le Conflit et l'Affaire (1973)," 66.
46 *Libération*, September 20, 1973, 6.
47 Piaget, *Lip. Charles Piaget et les Lip racontent*, 37.
48 Donald Reid, "Daniel Anselme: On Leave with the Unknown Famous," *South*

workers about the experience and innovations of struggles throughout France that they could not get elsewhere and to encourage direct liaisons between workers involved in them.[49] Referring to *Les Cahiers de mai*, Piaget explained that

> the principal reproach we made to information from the [national] unions was that it did not speak of struggles. It told us of the results, a batch of things, but not the struggles, what happened in the struggle and what problems there were, why they lost, no analysis, nothing; in other words, each in his corner remade the world rather than already benefiting from a certain knowledge.[50]

Piaget began subscribing to *Les Cahiers de mai* in 1968, the year it began. When he spoke of the Lip struggle as having been "impregnated" by the strike at Joint Français in Brittany in 1972, where workers developed new techniques of building support, he was drawing on what he had learned from *Les Cahiers de mai*.[51] The group had made contact with workers at Lip during earlier conflicts and this facilitated the recreation of relations in 1973.[52] This was the time that the original monthly *Les Cahiers de mai* was replaced by a weekly version with shorter texts, 90 percent of which were written by workers.[53] It ran until April 1974 and no subject was nearly as well covered in it as the Lip conflict. For *Les Cahiers de mai*

Central Review 32:2 (Summer 2015): 109–30. *Les Cahiers de mai hebdo*, May 28, 1973, 4. Mathieu Firmin, "*Les Cahiers de mai* 1968/1974. Entre journalisme et syndicalisme." Mémoire, Université de Paris 1, 1998, 71–91. Jacques Wajnsztejn, "Bilan critique de l'activité des *Cahiers de mai*" (May 2011), at rebellyon.info.

49   How might such liaisons work? Anselme explained that at the request of *les Lip*, workers elsewhere had secretly compiled a report on Claude Arbel, who was at that time the director of Spemelip, which sought to purchase the armaments division of Lip and thus dismantle the firm. ADD 1026W1 "Note d'exploitation" on "milieux gauchistes," February 25, 1974.

50   AR Interview with Piaget by Rouaud, December 2, 2003, 18 [quoted]. Champeau, "Lip: le conflit et l'affaire (1973)," 26. Well before 1968, the Trotskyist *Voix ouvrière* was distributed for several years at Lip. It was highly critical of the unions. Rather than rejecting it outright, Piaget read the paper and found that its critiques helped him reflect productively on democracy within the union and led to fruitful discussions with the CGT-Lip. BDIC KA 214 1 *Les Cahiers de mai* Interview with Piaget [1973].

51   Interview with Yves Lichtenberger in Firmin, "*Les Cahiers de mai*. Entretiens" [a second volume of Firmin, "*Les Cahiers de mai*"], 45. Piaget in *L'Outil des travailleurs*, February 1974, 8. AR Interview with Piaget by Rouaud, December 2, 2003, 8, 18 [quoted].

52   Firmin, "*Les Cahiers de mai*. Entretiens," 101.

53   Firmin, "*Les Cahiers de mai*," 98–9.

militant Jean-Louis Péninou, "the methods of the struggle [at Lip] were the absolute concretization of the work of *Les Cahiers de mai*."[54]

Les Cahiers de mai played a particularly important role in providing assistance to the newsletter, *Lip Unité*, in making the film *Non au démantèlement! Non aux licenciements!* ("No to Dismantling! No to Layoffs!"), and in the creation of support committees, called mini-commissions.[55] "With Lip," the amazed *Les Cahiers de mai* militant Tewfik Allal remarked, "to put it bluntly, we are an ad agency."[56] If each of these three projects had a precedent in their work in earlier strikes, they took much more expansive forms at Lip. Not long after workers began production in the occupied factory, *Les Cahiers de mai* militant Michel Freyssenet went to Besançon, where he met with the press subcommission and explained the project of *Les Cahiers de mai*. He proposed that with the assistance of *Les Cahiers de mai*, Lip workers put out a newsletter for workers and supporters; "and then, to my great astonishment, something quite revealing of the time, they told me to do it." Anselme and three other *Les Cahiers de mai* militants moved to Besançon, where they stayed for a year and lodged with workers.[57] They were paid the mini-Lip base pay from funds collected for popularization. In *Les Cahiers de mai* militant Yves Lichtenberger's words, "it is no longer *Les Cahiers de mai*. They are activists completely integrated in the actions of Lip." For Tewfik Allal, these militants "squarely became Lip workers."[58] In any case, *Les Cahiers de mai* was very concerned that *Lip Unité* maintain a separate identity. *Les Cahiers de mai* saw its role as providing technical assistance to workers, but not guidance or an ideology, as did most leftist groups. In November 1973 militants put together an issue of *Les Cahiers de mai* with extensive coverage of the struggle at Lip, but held back on publishing it because they were afraid that "insertion of the activists of the *Les Cahiers de mai* in the Lip struggle" would feed suspicions that they were steering a movement whose strength and

54   Firmin, "*Les Cahiers de mai*. Entretiens," 158.

55   In a similar fashion, Lip militants were very appreciative of La Gauche ouvrière et paysanne/Pour le Communisme (GOP/PLC). Created by militants who had broken with the PSU, they used their experience organizing the gathering at Larzac in August 1973 to work with the popularization commission to prepare the September 29 march in Besançon. "They came not as sermonisers, but as people who possessed a tool of use to workers," Raguénès said. *L'Outil des travailleurs*, April 1974, 17.

56   Firmin, "*Les Cahiers de mai*. Entretiens," 19.

57   Ibid., 119–20.

58   Ibid., 21, 70. BDIC delta rés 578/9 "Film in Recent Workers' Struggles in France" [interview with Dominique Dubosc], 20.

appeal came from its expression of workers' imagination and control of their struggle.[59]

With help from *Les Cahiers de mai*, a twenty-worker subcommission of the popularization commission began to produce *Lip Unité*. Three thousand copies of the first issue, dated July 11, 1973, were distributed and circulation went up over the summer. *Lip Unité* initially came out every week or so; there were fourteen numbers in this initial run. The CGT-Lip had opposed accepting the assistance of *Les Cahiers de mai*, but faced with the approval of the General Assembly, it settled for reviewing the page proofs before publication.[60] *Lip Unité* had two audiences—Lip workers and their backers. That both received the same newsletter was important in making supporters feel they were an integral part of the movement. *Lip Unité* presented a "synthesis" of what was said in the General Assembly—"it is on this that all are in principle in agreement; it is therefore a unitary platform renewed day by day"—as well as on the activities of particular commissions.[61] Raguénès described the meetings to put together each issue as self-analysis by workers of recent developments and their significance.[62] *Lip Unité* not only kept supporters apprised of the general will of the collectivity, but also played a crucial role in the democratic culture of Palente, by keeping workers informed and encouraging reflection and debate among them. Summing up what was said in the General Assembly, *Lip Unité*, in the words of *Les Cahiers de mai* militant Dominique Dubosc, "permitted all to better reflect on, and therefore to participate better in the struggle."[63]

Lip Unité subcommission members went through the factory, using tape recorders to collect the "worker thought" of the base.[64] For any one number of the newsletter, perhaps 100 workers took part in such sessions. A portion of the material collected became the basis of the lead article of the issue, with the aim of presenting the principal subjects confronting *les Lip* at the time. The texts were composed collectively and drew on information gathered by the subcommission and on the transcription of

---

59   BDIC F delta rés 578/39 *Les Cahiers de mai* to chers camarades, November 27, 1973.

60   CFDT-Lip militants in "Comment 'l'affaire' nous a changés," 80–1.

61   "Faire voir, ceci et rien d'autre," Interview with Dubosc by Christine Martin, September 2004, at dominiquedubosc.org.

62   BDIC F delta rés 702/15/1 "Débat du 20 janvier 1979," 3–4. This was for the first issue of *La Passerelle*, a journal that was never published.

63   Dubosc to Reid, May 21, 2014.

64   ADD 1026W1 "Note d'exploitation" on "milieux gauchistes," February 25, 1974.

recordings of the General Assembly as well as reports by commissions.[65] Accounts of the work of individual commissions, including production and sales figures, were prepared as well. Before going to press, the *Lip Unité* subcommission edited each text and then presented them to the contributing commissions for their review and critique.[66] One half of the subcommission edited materials and supervised printing and the other half handled distribution; the two groups alternated responsibilities with each issue.[67] *Les Cahiers de mai* helped make the bulletin possible, but they were not the ventriloquists some leftists charged them with being. Although closer to the CFDT-Lip than to the episodic voice of dissent that was the Action Committee, *Les Cahiers de mai* militants were, Demougeot contends, aware that a core of Lip militants played a disproportionate role in decision-making and they sought to encourage a greater democratization.[68] As Dubosc explained, "To write up *Lip Unité* very quickly required the qualities of journalistic synthesis workers would not have. Daniel [Anselme] therefore made an essential contribution, but he had no room to maneuver: he told me often that if he betrayed in the slightest what the General Assembly said, he would have been dropped immediately."[69]

Freyssenet made his proposal for *Lip Unité* on the eve of the workers' annual vacation in July 1973. The provisional administrators hoped that by providing vacation pay, they would get workers to leave and the movement to disintegrate. To keep workers who left Besançon abreast of developments, the *Lip Unité* subcommission collected vacation addresses and sent the bulletin to workers while they were away. Worker delegations on tour phoned in questions they were getting to guide the staff in deciding what to include in upcoming issues.[70] The popularization commission also made *Lip Unité* available to visitors and by subscription to supporters. In an act of solidarity, postmen delivered the bulletin in Besançon outside their working hours

---

65   Cassou, "Lip, la Construction d'un mythe," 58. Firmin, "*Les Cahiers de mai*," 146. *Idées ouvrières*, September 1977, unpaginated.

66   *Politique hedbo*, August 23, 1973, 10.

67   *Lip Unité*, September 28, 1973, 2.

68   Champeau, "Lip: le Conflit et l'Affaire (1973)," 114. However, Action Committee members recognized that *Lip Unité* did not publish material the unions opposed. Lopez, "Lip Interview," 15, 17.

69   Dubosc to Reid, May 21, 2014. Similarly, Lip worker Alice Carpena speaks of the women proposing ideas and men writing them up in *Lip Unité*. Macciocchi, *De la France*, 431.

70   For an example, see BDIC F delta rés 578/48 Commissions Lip de Lyon, "Pour une campagne de popularisation de l'appréciation de l'accord de Dole," February 2, 1974.

At the end of August, *Lip Unité* began producing mini-cassettes, "Radio Lip," on a weekly basis (although only four were produced and distributed). The "Journal-parlé-Lip" drew on recordings of the general assemblies as well as interviews with workers, with the goal of furthering the virtual community of supporters.[71] These were distributed nationally through the same channels as *Lip Unité*. The subcommission responsible for them encouraged the making and distribution of copies from the cassettes sent from Lip, individual and group listening, and broadcasts from loudspeakers mounted on cars. Supporters would play the tapes on speakers as they distributed materials to workers as they left factories.[72] The popularization commission also put out a 45 rpm record, "LIP, un combat, un espoir" ("Lip, a Combat, a Hope"), which featured the songs "On fabrique, on vend" ("We Produce, We Sell") and "On se paie" ("We Pay Ourselves") performed by the Besançon PSU militant Claire; the flip side had extracts from a recording of the General Assembly of June 18, 1973.[73]

Film

In the new media world of the 1970s, film took on a central role in the self-presentation of social movements. René Vautier, director of the groundbreaking film on the Algerian War of Independence, *Avoir 20 ans dans les Aurès* ("To Be Twenty Years Old in the Aurès") (1972), contacted Lip workers in the summer of 1973. He explained that several years before he had been engaged in the effort to save the Forges d'Hennebont in the Morbihan. Twelve hundred workers fought to maintain their factory in Brittany, but finally accepted dismantling in exchange for a "rescue plan" put together by the government which involved breaking the enterprise into five separate firms: "All that had been promised them was revealed to be false, simply a means, as it were, to kill them … They had the bitter experience that this rescue plan was just a ruse to divide them and to

---

71   *Lip Unité*, September 3, 1973, 2. Tapes of "Radio Lip" are in BDIC KA 199 and KA 214.

72   Thierry Lefebvre, "Radio Entonnoir et Radio Lip, deux expériences pilotes," *Cahiers d'histoire de la radiodiffusion* 78 (October–December 2003): 133. Postal workers in the Paris region reproduced and distributed copies of *Lip Unité* and held public listenings of Radio Lip cassettes and discussions with touring Lip workers. *Les Cahiers de mai hebdo*, September 10, 1973, 4.

73   *Lip Unité*, September 14, 1973, 2. A copy of the record is in BDIC F delta rés 578/46.

obtain, without too much upheaval, the firing of all the personnel and the complete shutdown of their enterprise." The workers of Hennebont had asked Vautier to help them to share their experience—"how they had been had"—with *les Lip.*[74] The thirteen-minute film *Transmission d'experience ouvriere* ("Transmission of Worker Experience") arrived during the negotiations with Giraud and was shown three times in the General Assembly: "it was extraordinary," reported the commission cooperating with workers engaged in struggles to save factories elsewhere, "to see to what extent, in all the conversations of all the personnel, it served as a means of reflection ... and after a couple of days, everyone said, 'Ah, it's the coup of the Forges d'Hennebont ... it's like at the Forges d'Hennebont ...'"[75]

Film played a leading role in allowing people around France to speak of Lip in the same way. In the 1960s and 1970s portable film cameras and video tape recorders increased access at reduced cost. The popularization commission put it bluntly: "We have to leave the nineteenth century!"[76] Film offered the most effective counter to the coverage of the conflict on television. Development of film distribution outside of state-controlled television and the commercial circuit of movie theatres made this possible. Viewers watched television as individuals or in cinemas as a collection of individuals who left without discussing what they had seen together afterwards. Films on the Lip conflict were viewed in a different social context. They were not shown on television and, lacking state screening licenses, could not be shown in commercial theatres. However, mini-commissions of supporters, locals and works councils arranged projections of films on Lip. Viewers came with an interest in the Lip conflict and stayed after screenings to talk.

Of the many films made about the Lip conflict in 1973, the most important were those of Chris Marker, Alain Dhouailly, Dominique Dubosc and Carole and Paul Roussopoulos. Each played a different role in popularization. Besançon had been the site of Chris Marker's remarkable documentary on the strike and month-long occupation of the Rhodia textile factory by workers in 1967, *À bientôt, j'espère* ("Soon, I Hope"). His film on the Lip Affair, *Puisqu'on vous dit que c'est possible*

<hr />

74   Porhel, *Ouvriers bretons*, 50. BDIC F delta rés 578/36 "Transcription de la discussion du 1e Février 74 d'un collectif de la commission popularisation Lip sur ce que peut être le travail des mini-commissions dans cette nouvelle phase de la lutte des Lip," 11 [quoted].

75   BDIC F delta rés 578/46 Commission Liaison avec les usines en lutte [1973].

76   BDIC F delta rés 702/7/3 Commission Popularisation, November 23, 1973.

("Because We Tell You It Is Possible"), was rooted in new forms of media creation and distribution. Roger Louis was an ORTF journalist who resigned in solidarity with staff laid off for their criticism of the network in May 1968. He brought them together in the Centre de Recherche pour l'Éducation Permanente et l'Action Culturelle (CREPAC) to foster an alternative to the censorship of state-run television. To disseminate their work, Louis assembled a variety of progressive cultural organizations and the union confederations in a cooperative, Scopcolor. Lip workers contacted the CREPAC in the spring of 1973. The CREPAC sent a team to film events in Besançon and it returned at the end of the summer with eight hours of footage which had escaped police efforts to destroy it.[77] *Puisqu'on vous dit que c'est possible* opens with Louis telling viewers that that there was debate among the member institutions of Scopcolor as to how to present events at Lip, a reflection of the different positions on the Lip conflict on the left. Marker had been called in to assemble and edit the film and did so in a week. The film was screened and debated widely in the Scopcolor network in the fall of 1973.

Puisqu'on vous dit que c'est possible was the antithesis of ORTF news coverage. It undercut established authority, beginning with the genealogy of the Lip(mann) family recited before a still of Moses from Cecil B. DeMille's *The Ten Commandments*. Clips from a television interview with Fred Lip allowed "le Fred" to become the voice of a critique of Ébauches SA and French business. Charbonnel and Giraud enunciate market platitudes, but the figure given authority as the narrator of events is not a minister, businessman or journalist, but Vittot, the CFDT-Lip leader. The film moves from Vittot's account of women workers bound to their machines at the beginning of the conflict in spring 1973 to Piton on women's active participation in demonstrations and meetings. Piaget confronts Giraud before the General Assembly and individual workers speak about the factory becoming a place of fulfillment, not alienation. Marker handled the conflicts that had brought him into the project by constructing a film in which the clips build on one another through their heterogeneity, making different positions part of a discussion. This is clearest in the presentation of the confrontations with police in the week after the expulsion from Palente. Moving footage of Vittot preaching the virtues of solidarity to the police and non-violence to protestors is paired with street-fighting male and female workers, apparently not young leftists, but all the more revered by these radicals for this very

---

77   Daniel Urbain, "Cinéma 'Lip,'" *Cinéma* 181 (November 1973): 17–18.

reason. In a gesture of 1968 irreverence, one woman tells a police agent that his mother should have taken the pill. *Puisqu'on vous dit que c'est possible* ends with the gathering at Larzac at the end of August 1973. The film was important in generating participation in the march at Besançon on September 29 that Larzac inspired.

The CGT had never been comfortable with developments at Besançon. In mid-December 1973, the CGT released *Lip, Les Réalités de la Lutte* ("Lip, The Realities of the Struggle"), which can be seen as a response to *Puisqu'on vous dit que c'est possible*. Directed by Alain Dhouailly, the film drew on CREPAC footage. It begins with a critique of the ORTF coverage of the Lip Affair, but midway through it circles around to argue that the media was particularly remiss in its coverage of the CGT at Lip. This was evident in the media's infatuation with the flamboyant nature of CFDT-Lip, despite what the narrator in the film contends was the equal importance of CGT-Lip in the conflict.[78] Remarkably little of the film is devoted to production, sales and self-pay or to the expulsion from Palente and succeeding confrontations. The point of the film is not to enthrall viewers like *Puisqu'on vous dit que c'est possible*, but to convince them of the correctness of the CGT analysis.

A half dozen CGT-Lip leaders make the case that the situation at Lip was not due to Fred Lip's managerial errors, but to the decisions of Ébauches SA, presented as one of a number of foreign capitalist firms buying up and liquidating French companies with the assent of the state. Piaget is the only CFDT-Lip leader shown. Viewers learn that he is a supervisor, but that none of the CGT-Lip leaders are. A leader of the CGT at the Lip machine-tools plant at Ornans, where the CGT was dominant, explains that it has commissions to deal with every facet of the occupied factory—the CGT can do what the CFDT-led workforce did at Palente—and goes on to say that Ornans workers are better able to maintain the machines than workers at Palente. Protection of the equipment had been the CGT justification of factory occupations since 1936, not the opportunity this gave to operate them.

The film concludes with a clip from the evening news in which the Minister of Labor Gorse says that the government does not foresee any talks after October 12. A voiceover follows, introducing a critique of the

---

78 Reporters did speak primarily with workers in the Action Committee and the CFDT-Lip. The CGT-Lip complained of this. It was particularly critical of *Le Monde*, saying "It is certain that everyone makes an analysis of the situation as a function of their class position," and of *L'Est républicain*. ACGT Lip Box 3 CGT Lip, "Ce qu'il faut savoir" [early August 1973].

workers' decision on October 12 and the media coverage of it: "Let us imagine another Television. Here is what you could hear." Jean Breteau, FTM-CGT secretary-general, then explains that what Giraud offered would have been a victory in this new period of capitalist restructuration and that CFDT-Lip intransigence saved the state and the owners from a defeat that would have provided a precedent of benefit to all workers in France.

Non au démantèlement! Non aux licenciements! was different in origin and nature from either *Puisqu'on vous dit que c'est possible* or *Lip, Les Réalités de la Lutte*. It was not a montage of footage from a variety of sources. The film was made at the request of and under the supervision of a Lip subcommission, which paid the costs of production.[79] Dominique Dubosc, a *Les Cahiers de mai* militant, had made a film to support a strike in 1972 of workers who cut open old car batteries to extract lead.[80] Although the unskilled, unorganized immigrant labor force in the Penarroya plant in Lyon was unlike that at Lip, *Les Cahiers de mai* developed techniques there that they would bring to Palente, including the establishment of support committees and a bulletin which provided a model for *Lip Unité*.[81] Dubosc and Antelme had put together a twenty-minute film, *Penarroya, les deux visages du trust* ("Penarroya, the Two Faces of the Trust"), in response to a worker's observation that Penarroya was a firm that projected a modernity to the public totally at odds with their lives in the factory. Completed before the strike began, the film set owners' pronouncements against worker experience and was widely distributed by *Les Cahiers de mai*. It was what *Les Cahiers de mai* militants termed an "inserted film," made "to fill a strictly determined role [in the struggle], as a function of the strategy decided by the workers."[82]

The Lip popularization commission decided to ask for such a film to be made after seeing it and talking to workers from Penarroya. What convinced them was the workers' explanation of the film's origin. When Penarroya workers took to the road to speak about their strike, they had not wanted only the few who spoke French well to participate in discussions with the men and women who came to see them. The Penarroya strike committee asked for a film that would make the strikers' essential

79   BDIC 578/15 Brochure on *Non au démantèlement! Non aux licenciements!*
80   Laure Pitti, "Penarroya, 1971–1972: deux films, deux regards, une mobilisation" in Tangui Perron, *Histoire d'un film, mémoire d'une lutte* (Paris, 2009), 152–73. Daniel Anselme, 'Penarroya' in *4 grèves significatives* (Paris, 1972), 143–73.
81   Dubosc to Reid, May 21, 2014.
82   "Faire voir, ceci et rien d'autre."

points and then let all respond to questions after the projection "without being an orator." "For us, the film is a rifle."[83]

Lip workers knew that their cause would be successful only if they developed national support. Initially, when the emphasis was on making their case in the region, experienced militants left for the day and presented the workers' position clearly and answered questions. However, as attention shifted to sites further away, it became clear the campaign would suffer if leading militants had to spend so much time on the road away from Palente:

> We had not sufficiently thought out that with ten or twelve delegations of many people, gone for several days, we were going to find ourselves short of activists experienced enough to run a public meeting, for the factory (the center of the struggle) could not strip itself of its best activists. Actually, most of the workers active in the struggle could have very well 'run' a meeting and showed this, but, at least in the beginning, many did not feel capable of presenting the positions and the results of the conflict with the accuracy and the clarity of a Piaget.[84]

"From this was born the idea to 'put Piaget in a box,'" Dubosc explained, "in such a way that all the delegations can leave, as it were, with the best activist, the one who speaks the best, the one who expresses best the collective point of view."[85]

At the end of July, the popularization commission asked Dubosc to make a film centered on Piaget. Dubosc asked workers what they told visitors and made this the template for the film. Working with the commission, Anselme penned a "scenario," in Dubosc's words, "quite dull of a guided visit of the factory (by Piaget)": "Piaget, symbolically surrounded by CGT-Lip delegates and members of the Action Committee [and the CFDT-Lip], explaining all the elements of the struggle during a fake visit of the factory."[86] Following this, there is footage of the General Assembly of July 31. This meeting marked the return of the Lip workers from vacation, a scene that allowed viewers to learn about recent events as these workers had. Through the words of Piaget and

83 *Les Cahiers de mai hebdo*, June 18, 1973, 1.

84 Dominique Dubosc, "Un itinéraire militant" in *Jeune, dure et pure!: une histoire de cinéma d'avant-garde et expérimental en France*, ed. Nicole Brenez and Christian Lebrat (Paris, 2001), 340–1.

85 "Faire voir, ceci et rien d'autre."

86 BDIC F delta rés 578/9 "Film in Recent Workers' Struggles," 20. Dubosc, "Un Itinéraire militant," 340–1 [quoted].

other leaders, the film explained the reasons for the conflict, the tactics workers had chosen and their forms of collective organization. Although the CGT was wary of self-management, the unusual degree of coop-eration between the workers' unions at Lip in the summer of 1973 is underscored when Mercet, CGT-Lip leader, says: "Now it is the workers themselves who choose the production rates, who determine the number of pieces they have to get out and who determine their hours as well."[87] *Non au démantèlement! Non aux licenciements!* was more concerned to establish a bond with the audience than to make an agit-prop presenta-tion like the film on Penarroya. Unlike Marker's *Puisqu'on vous dit que c'est possible*, the radical nature of events in Dubosc's *Non au démantè-lement! Non aux licenciements!* is conveyed not in dramatic footage of confrontations, but in the "serenity" and "calm" of the leaders as they narrate events and convey "the spirit" of the workers at Palente.[88] The two films of 1973 capture the transition of the May 1968 project from a revolutionary narrative of the old order overthrown, and the confronta-tion of street-fighting men and women with the state this entailed, to the creation of self-governing communities that prefigure the world to come.

Dubosc completed filming in five days, and finished *Non au démantèlement! Non aux licenciements!* in two weeks, shortly after the expulsion from Palente. It was screened three times a day at the Jean Zay "factory."[89] An itinerant team of workers with a projector and screen showed the film wherever a viewing was asked for in the area. Groups of supporters and Lip workers made wide use of the film at meetings throughout France. Delegations reported that it worked as intended by presenting the broad outline of events and allowing workers to draw on their experience to answer questions.[90] The popularization commission made close to 100 copies of *Non au démantèlement! Non aux licencie-ments!* and circulated them around the country, particularly to works councils. By their estimate, it was seen by more than 300,000 people.[91]

The feminist Carole Roussopoulos produced a set of films on *les Lip*, very different in content and form from others on the conflict. Noëlle Dartevelle has the uncomfortable role in *Lip, Les Réalités de la Lutte* as the voice of compromise at the September 29 march and, as Piton noted,

---

87   Dubosc, "Bande son du film *Non au démantèlement! Non aux licenciements!*" in Annexe 4 of Cassou, "Lip, la construction d'un mythe," 201.

88   BDIC F delta rés 578/15 Brochure on *Non au démantèlement! Non aux licenciements!*

89   *Lip Unité*, September 3, 1973.

90   *Les Cahiers de mai hebdo supplément*, January 14, 1974, unpaginated.

91   "Faire voir, ceci et rien d'autre."

women are absent from *Non au démantèlement! Non aux licenciements!*[92] However, in Roussopoulos' films on the conflict, individual women have a central role. When she was laid off by *Vogue* magazine, Roussopoulos took her friend Jean Genet's advice and used her severance pay to buy the second portable video camera sold in France; Jean-Luc Godard had bought the first. With her husband Paul Roussopoulos, a refugee from the military dictatorship in Greece, she founded a militant collective, Vidéo-Out, in 1971. Their interest was in the acts and discourses of liberation of the marginalized within society and within social movements.

Working with her husband, Carole Roussopoulos made a half-dozen short videos on Lip, drawing on dozens of hours of footage.[93] They worked in video, not the 16mm film that Marker, Douailly and Dubosc used. An individual could take video footage; there was no need for the team that a filmmaker required. And, unlike film, video could be screened immediately. This offered the possibility "of a control of the image by the people filmed." As Dominique Barbier, who worked with Roussopoulos at Lip, said, "this was an ethical and political preoccupation."[94] Video could also be shown on a portable monitor to small groups or in impromptu screenings. "Video", in the words of Anne-Marie Duguet, "ventured into that genre of dissemination-happenings in the wake of a movement that was contesting traditional cultural spaces." She used one of Roussopoulos' videos on the Lip conflict being shown at the Convention Street market in Paris as her example.[95]

Films took the Lip collectivity as their subject; videos could focus on the particular expressed or repressed within it. Liberation is individual as well as collective, and if individual accounts are not representative, concepts like "collective" and "representative" may themselves work in exclusionary ways.[96] Marker and Dubosc sought to present the collective at work in scenes of demonstrations and the General Assembly with Vittot and Piaget as the voice of this collective. Workers who were not union leaders appear only in quick clips to confirm the consensus, but not as individuals. Piton explained that journalists and filmmakers usually wanted to talk to men, the leaders, and she felt that when

---

92   Piton, *C'est possible!*, 356.

93   Two of these are lost. François Bovier, "Images de Lip: de la Commission Popularisation au Groupe Vidéo-Out" in *Caméra militante. Luttes de libération des années 1970* (Geneva, 2010), 92–3, n62.

94   Hélène Fleckinger, "Des *Cahiers de mai* au documentaire. Entretien avec Dominique Barbier," *La Revue documentaire* 22–3 (2010): 210.

95   Anne-Marie Duguet, *Vidéo, la mémoire au poing* (Paris, 1981), 53–4, 67–8.

96   Ibid., 48–50.

interviewed, the rank and file, and particularly women, were rushed along, never allowed to finish what they had to say. [97] However, Roussopoulos made a series of very different works, in which Lip employees, primarily women and not union leaders, spoke at length about their experience in the conflict. Referring to their work at Lip, Paul Roussopoulos said they saw "that there existed many 'contradictory positions' from those that rejected work and the capitalist system to those who sought on the contrary to protect the equipment, etc. … I believe that what gives life to a film is bringing out the real contradictions."[98]

Carole Roussopoulos came to Besançon and served as an interviewer for the third Radio Lip, asking female employees what the struggle had brought them as women and examining women's growing participation at meetings.[99] She pursued these questions in her filmmaking. Although Radio Lip had been the work of the popularization commission, Roussopoulos did not make her films under its control. Her model at Lip was the testimony of women in consciousness-raising groups, whose witnessing was intended to allow others, including viewers, to come to consciousness of their situation.[100] This was more suited to video than film.[101] As Dubosc himself explained, "The big advantage of video tapes is that they allow capture of the expression of an idea, its application, while the 16mm camera often shows only the outcome of an idea: Piaget behind the microphone."[102] Discussing their oppression as women and as workers, Lip women workers were clearly part of a liberation struggle, but less clearly instruments of the Lip struggle itself. If all militant filmmaking sought to show that the ORTF suppressed the full story in order to protect the interests of the state and capital, Roussopoulos complemented this with a critique of the movement's presentation of itself through male union leaders. Her *Lip-Monique* (1973) contributed to the establishment of Piton as a figure with broad national appeal, particularly to feminists and critics of union hegemony. Piton tells the story of her liberation through participation in the movement. Although Piton speaks of women and of the Action Committee, Roussopoulos does not make her solely a representative of these groups in the way that Marker's

97   Piton in a statement read to a seminar led by Fleckinger in April 2013 on film and the Lip conflicts. See archive.org/details/SminaireVido08042013.

98   *Cinéma et politique* (Paris, 1980), 26.

99   Cassou, "Lip, La Construction d'un mythe," 142–3.

100   Hélène Fleckinger, "Une caméra à soi. Quand les féministes s'emparent de la vidéo" in *Caméra militante*, 40–1.

101   Dominique Barbier in archive.org/details/SminaireVido08042013.

102   *Libération*, March 30, 1977.

use of clips of Piton does in *Puisqu'on vous dit que c'est possible*. As a result, Roussopoulos' films have a different relation to the collectivity. In keeping with the mission of *Les Cahiers de mai*, Dubosc sought to present the struggle as it asked to be presented. From his perspective, focusing on individuals or women changed the dynamic of the struggle; this in turn was Roussopoulos' goal.[103]

Video equipment is easier to learn to use than film cameras. Carole Roussopoulos lent her video camera to *Les Cahiers de mai* militant Dominique Barbier, who, working with the cinema subcommission, filmed General Assembly meetings in the morning and screened them in the afternoon for workers who had not been able to attend, so that they could be brought up to speed immediately.[104] However, Carole Roussopoulos' decision in November 1973 to let three members of the Action Committee use her video equipment created a conflict with the popularization commission when it questioned why these individuals had been chosen. The individual nature of video production threatened the unitary and collective ethos the commission sought to project to the public.[105] Anselme of *Les Cahiers de mai* concurred: because video made by Lip workers would likely be taken as an expression of the workers as a whole, it should be done under the direction of a commission created for the project that answered to the General Assembly.[106] Although in this case the lending of the cameras did not lead to the creation of any videos, it revealed how new forms of technology could challenge movement practices and ideology. The leadership was reluctant to arrange the screening of Roussopoulos' videos to *les Lip*, but these played an important role in generating interest and support among feminists, who were rooted in the left in France but without strong ties to the institutions of the working class.

The films of Marker, Dhouailly, Dubosc and Roussopoulos capture four elements in the interpretation and accompanying popularization of the conflict at Lip. Marker depicted a workers' struggle that took national

103 Dubosc and Fleckinger in archive.org/details/SminaireVido08042013. Paul Roussopoulos said that he and Carole had filmed a lot of footage at Lip in 1973 critical of the union leadership, but they had not used it so as not to impede the movement. Vidéo Out, "'Vidéo Out': attaquer la société bourgeoise par les toits," *Cinéma Militant* 5/6 (March–April 1976): 142.

104 Fleckinger, "Des *Cahiers de mai* au documentaire," 209.

105 BDIC F delta rés 578/46 Unsigned, uncompleted letter to "Cher camarades [Carole and Paul Roussopoulos]," November 25, 1973.

106 BDIC F delta rés 578/46 Handwritten unsigned notes of a meeting appended to the letter to Carole and Paul Roussopoulos [c. November 10, 1973].

confederations where they would not have gone, rather than, as in the May 1968 narratives, choking worker radicalism. Dhouailly shows that individual conflicts must not be allowed to infringe upon the CGT's authority. Dubosc presents the Lip workers' collectivity as it wanted to present itself. Roussopoulos explores the effect of the conflict on individual men and women. Each film and video drew viewers into different understandings of the world of *les Lip*.

Theatre

Film and periodicals were not the only media used to convey the Lip story. French children grew up with comic strips (BDs) like *Lucky Luke*. One Lip worker characterized the series of dramatic events at Lip as "a story in comic strips where one jumps from one image to the next, from one shot to the next. We were playing *Lucky Luke* …"[107] But in the years following May 1968, the BD experienced a cultural revolution. Sixty-eighters made the BD a chosen means of expression. The engaged artists Wiaz and Piotr drew the widely circulated BD account of the conflict in 1973, *Les Hors-la-loi de Palente* ("The Outlaws of Palente"). To remind readers of the world Lip left behind, the last panel features Lucky Luke.[108]

The stage was another site of popularization. Like *Les Cahiers de mai*, the theater group Troupe Z developed new means for workers to tell their story and broke down the division between workers and artists. When Troupe Z came to Palente in the summer of 1973, workers provided rehearsal space and covered some of their expenses. Together with workers, the group carried out an investigation into the culture and practices, the dreams and concerns of *les Lip*. Troupe Z worked what they learned into one-half hour of skits that they performed for workers the first time on July 14. The actors then engaged in discussions with the workers. From these, late in the fall of 1973, came the play *Arthur, où t'as mis les montres?* ("Arthur, Where Did You Put the Watches?"). Colloquies followed each performance for an audience of *les Lip*. These had the qualities of direct democracy: representatives, in the sense of those who enacted *la représentation*, the performance, were subject to the critique of the audience of workers they were representing. One can see this in the conversation with Lip workers at the end of a performance in February

---

107   "Préface des ouvriers de Lip" to Emile Zola, *Le Travail* (Lagrasse, 1979), 30.
108   Wiaz [Pierre Wiazemsky] and Piotr [Piotr Barsony], *Les Hors-la-loi de Palente* (n.p., 1974).

1974. They were appreciative of elements particular to the situation at Lip that had been gleaned from engagement with workers and kept the play from taking on a generic agitprop nature. When one worker compared the piece unfavorably to films like Dubosc's *Non au démantèlement! Non aux licenciements!*, a female worker countered that these films were "strictly unionist," whereas *Arthur, où t'as mis les montres?* "is a reflection of the base." Troupe Z itself participated, responding to comments at one point that it would "review the play completely with your critique in mind." Through these debates young male and female workers sought to contribute to a national representation of *les Lip* and their conflict distinct from the dominant portrayal in *Lip Unité* and Dubosc's film.

Troupe Z toured France, putting on *Arthur, où t'as mis les montres?* sixty times in a variety of settings over the next two years. Integral to each performance was the often heated discussion at the end, assuring that it fostered a participatory politics and art. Drawing on these discussions and those following return performances at Besançon, Troupe Z continuously reworked the piece, thus allowing it to serve for audiences as a source of information on developments in the conflict. The piece treated workers with respect and at a certain distance, to avoid stereotypical presentations of manual laborers in their blue overalls. Scenes drawn from Lip were interspersed with ones of satire and parody directed against bosses and CGT delegates championing the cure-all of the Common Program. Performances after October 12 at "6 heures avec Lip" and other gatherings were an important part of the effort to secure and expand popular support following the break with the Communists and the CGT.[109]

Participation in the Lip conflict was in turn the impetus for a new cultural politics among others. The acting company Al Assifa had its origins in a meeting with Lip workers who were on a speaking tour in 1973. Militants in the Mouvement des travailleurs arabes had aspirations to form a troupe, but had not figured out how. After talking with these workers about their ongoing struggles, the Lip delegation invited them to Palente. They drew on their experiences for a set of sketches on their situation in France. If the Lip workers began by asking why they did not return to their land of origin, they ended by telling the actors that

109 Luc Meyer and La Troupe Z, "Les Z d'une lutte à l'autre" in *Le Théâtre d'intervention depuis 1968*, eds. Jonny Ebstein and Philippe Ivernel (Lausanne, 1983), I: 124–36. Olivier Neveux, *Théâtres en lutte* (Paris, 2007), 110, 112–14, 144. Emile Copfermann, *Vers un théâtre différent* (Paris, 1976), 174–5. Théâtre Z, "La Troupe Z," *Travail théâtrical* 2 (January–March 1976): 130–9. The script of *Arthur, où t'as mis les montres?* is in ADD 45J22.

192 OPENING THE GATES

their story was deeply revealing and they had to find a means to convey it to everyone. Al Assifa was born of these discussions. The troupe first performed its inaugural piece, *Ça travaille, ça travaille mais ça ferme sa gueule* ("Work, Work, but Shut Your Trap"), in August 1973 "in the midst of tear gas bombs during the confrontations at Palente," in the words of one of Al Assifa's founders. Over the next three years, they performed this piece before hundreds of audiences, continually integrating contemporary events into it.[110]

Mini-Commissions

In the weeks after the expulsion from Palente, the CGT took the lead in organizing a campaign of national solidarity in the form of work stoppages and public meetings.[111] However, with the end of the summer, visits and watch sales declined. Both the CGT and the CFDT feared that the Lip campaign would hinder mobilization on issues of national concern. In mid-September, the state blocked the bank account that contained contributions and had been used for public outreach activities. The mass media began to lose interest as the negotiations with Giraud dragged on. Support in *Le Monde* faltered beginning in mid-September when the correspondent who had spent the summer in Besançon was replaced.[112] After October 12, the CGT withdrew active support for popularization events around the country. On their return from national tours, delegations reported to the General Assembly that it was evident that the CGT discouraged members from attending.[113]

The Lip workers' openness to a variety of leftists presented a challenge to the confederations and constituted an important element of radical political culture in post-1968 France. The CGT had always been hostile to leftists. The CFDT was initially more circumspect, but when it drew lessons from the Lip conflict in September 1973, it warned against the type of cooperation that Lip workers had established with *Les Cahiers de mai*: "the CFDT ended by sounding the alarm: *les Lip* rely too much on others in the affair."[114] After October 12, the CFDT grew increasingly

110 Geneviève Clancy and Philippe Tancelin, *Les Tiers idées* (Paris, 1977), 181, 187–8, 258–60.
111 *Politique hebdo*, August 30, 1973, 7.
112 François-Marie Samuelson, *Il était une fois Libération* (Paris, 1979), 241–3. De Virieu, *Lip*, 153, 209–10.
113 *Lip Unité dépêche quotidienne*, November 20, 1973.
114 *CFDT Syndicalisme hebdo*, September 13, 1973, 9.

concerned with insulating itself from association with a leftism it saw unchecked at Lip.[115]

Faced with state repression in August 1973 and later, Lip workers needed new means of popularization to make up for the loss of access to the CGT network and to respond to critiques by the CFDT. The day after Palente was seized, a new issue of *Lip Unité* appeared. The commission at Lip in charge of the bulletin took the occasion to ask locals and support committees around the nation to use stencils and offset printing plates of the bulletin to make additional copies at their own expense and distribute them.[116] This became a regular practice. The commission required that unions and committees print the integral text of *Lip Unité*, rather than producing their own tracts in support of the cause because the Lip workers wanted to keep full control over their message and prevent their struggle from becoming the subject of debates within and between unions and parties. Groups that made reproductions were asked to send copies with information on the number distributed to the commission in Besançon.[117] In mid-September, support groups in Paris and surrounding areas reported distributing 25,000 copies of an issue of *Lip Unité* in markets one Sunday and another 3,000 at subway entrances the next week.[118] Partisans in the postal sorting center at Montparnasse in Paris themselves ensured the distribution of *Lip Unité* in branch offices.[119] *Les Cahiers de mai* reported in early October that in addition to the 30,000 to 50,000 copies of *Lip Unité* produced in Besançon, including copies sent to 5,000 subscribers, more than 300,000 were reproduced and distributed by supporters.[120]

---

115 Piton had contacts with leftists who organized a meeting for Lip workers to speak at the Palais de Mutualité in Paris on December 12, 1973. It was funded by figures like Simone Signoret. The state police reported that the CFDT "had taken offense at this initiative that it considered harmful to the union brand image." The CFDT-Lip initially approved this meeting, but the severe warning the CFDT sent to Piaget led it to issue a statement saying that the meeting had not been arranged at the initiative of Lip workers, although they had no objection to Lip workers participating. ADD 1026W11 RG, December 6, 1973. *Lip unité dépêche quotidienne*, December 5, 1973.

116 BDIC F delta rés 578/43 *Les Cahiers de mai*, Groupe de Lyon, August 14, 1973. BDIC F delta rés 578/15 Projet d'Institut ouvrier pour le développement des pratiques collectives. *Cahier de discussion* 1 (December 1974): 20.

117 BDIC F delta rés 578/51/9 "Note sur la contribution des militants des *Cahiers de mai* à la diffusion de *Lip Unité* (rédigé par les camarades des 'Cahiers' de groupes de Paris et de Lyon, actuellement à Besançon)" [August 1973].

118 BDIC F delta rés 578/43 *Cahiers de mai* (Groupe Paris), "Bilan au 16.9.73 au soir."

119 AMB 5Z223 Armand Plas to Commission Popularisation Lip, September 20, 1973.

120 *Les Cahiers de mai hebdo*, October 10, 1973, 2. ADD 45J15 "Bases et objectifs des mini-commissions Lip." A figure of 450,000 copies of a single issue was reported later. BDIC F delta rés 578/15 Projet d'Institut ouvrier in *Cahier de discussion*, 20.

Mini-commissions around France were born of the efforts after the expulsion from Palente to reproduce and distribute copies of *Lip Unité*. In mid-September, the General Assembly put out a call for groups of militants to develop support throughout France. Their very name, mini-commission, was intended to show a lineage as well as subordination to the commissions at Lip. *Les Cahiers de mai* militants provided leadership for a number of mini-commissions. They established links between them and served as "the intermediary" between the mini-commissions and the popularization commission.[121] The mini-commissions became an important element of the Lip movement and, like the support committees for the farmers of Larzac which developed at the same time, a locus of post-1968 activism. In November 1973, a note put up on the newsboard maintained by Lip workers at the Maison pour Tous said there were seventy-five mini-commissions in France, including thirty-two in the Paris region; there were close to half that many in the Lyon area. Roubaix was another important center of activity.[122] An accompanying message read "Here is enough to keep the RG [state police] busy."[123]

As *Les Cahiers de mai* had done when working with the Penarroya strikers to establish support committees, it sought to assure that the mini-commissions were inclusive and that they followed the directives of Lip workers.[124] In line with the practice of the earlier Vietnam support committees, which had found it "indecent … to dare give advice to those who found themselves in the front lines," each mini-commission signed a contract saying that "their initiatives are under the exclusive control" of the General Assembly as transmitted by the popularization commission.[125] Particular efforts were made to ensure that the mini-commissions did not align with political parties or union confederations. Although a number were associated with locals, they were explicitly instructed not to identify with a particular confederation; their support was to be for the workers of Lip.[126]

---

121   Jusseaume, "Un succès venu de loin," 69–70.

122   BDIC F delta rés 578/48 Commission Lip de Lyon, "Un appel pressant." Earlier in November, *Politique hebdo* reported that there were seventy mini-commissions with close to 1,000 members. *Politique hebdo*, November 8, 1973, 14. For documents of the mini-commissions in Paris, Lyon and throughout France, see BDIC F delta rés 578/43; 578/45; and 578/48.

123   ADD 45J15, Newsboard.

124   *Les Cahiers de mai hebdo*, May 28, 1973, 2. BDIC F delta rés 578/48 *Les Cahiers de mai*, Groupe de Lyon to camarades, September 11, 1973.

125   Léo Lévy, *À la vie* (Lagrasse, 2013), 52. BDIC F delta rés 578/39 "Les 'Commissions Lip' popularisent la lutte des travailleurs de Lip."

126   CGT militants remained active in some mini-commissions. CFDT locals

A *Les Cahiers de mai* militant in Lyon described the strategy of his mini-commission in distributing *Lip Unité*:

We did not favor distribution at the entry or exit of factories. This seemed to us too markedly far left. Enlightened avant-garde. Rather, we wanted distribution by people who were known in the enterprise, who had ... well, who were identified as people of the enterprise and therefore who themselves, because they distributed it, created right away a relation of confidence in what was printed. So the paper was introduced to readers by persons assuring the distribution who were encouraged to identify themselves by adding on the copies they handed out the phrase "this text distributed by ..."[127]

The mini-commissions distributed only materials that came from the popularization commission, "leaving what is said squarely to the workers of Lip."[128] One Sunday morning in September 1973, extreme left groups handed out a tract in markets of the fifteenth arrondissement of Paris with a reproduction of an issue of *Lip Unité* on the front and an announcement of the formation of a support committee; they put their own demands on the back. *Les Cahiers de mai* militants immediately intervened and got militants from these groups to hand out 1,200 copies of *Lip Unité* without additional material in place of the bowdlerized version.[129]

The mini-commissions did not collect funds for the workers of Lip, but fully supported themselves through contributions solicited in their own name. Mini-commissions in large cities shared expenses. An extension of the Lip movement, mini-commissions made themselves models of transparency. Financial records were posted in their offices and could be consulted at any time. Mini-commissions regularly sent accounts of their activities and their financial records to the popularization commission, with copies to the CGT and the CFDT organizations in Besançon.[130] As a result of this close cooperation the mini-commissions represented

sought to avoid situations in which positions on Lip interfered with efforts to develop unity of action with the CGT. BDIC F delta rés 578/48 Commissions Lip de Lyon et banlieue, "Compte rendu adressé à la Commission Popularisation de Besançon," November 22, 1973.

127   Cassou, "Lip, La construction d'un mythe," 66.

128   BDIC F delta rés 578/39 *"Dépêches quotidennes Lip Unité* 5 dec–18 fev."

129   BDIC F delta rés 548/43 *Les Cahiers de mai* Groupe Paris, "Bilan au 16.9.73 au soir."

130   ADD 45J15 "Bases et objectifs des mini-commissions Lip." For an example, see the financial records of the mini-commissions in Lyon in BDIC F delta rés 578/49.

the fullest integration of leftists and workers in a struggle in the post-1968 years in France.

After October 12, 1973

The October 12 vote presented the popularization campaign with a crisis. Conservative media embraced the state and employers' interpretation. *L'Aurore* referred to "the suicide vote," *Le Figaro* to "Operation suicide," *France-Soir* to "Collective suicide," and *L'Express* to "the watch workers–kamikazes of Besançon."[131] In mid-October, the press subcommission reported that "the mainstream press dropped us," as evidenced by the decline in the length of the press coverage posted on the rolls of computer paper to three or four meters a day.[132] Local press coverage became quite hostile as well, as detailed by the analyses contained in the issues of *Lip-Verité*, a companion to *Lip Unité* put out by the press subcommission in the fall of 1973. *L'Est républicain*, the only daily in the department, abandoned its comprehensive and fairly sympathetic coverage; the editor advised workers, "Lay down your arms."[133]

To refute media presentations of Lip workers as "die-hards," the General Assembly voted to have the popularization commission publish a daily bulletin—"a DAILY counter-news"—beginning on October 10, to supplement *Lip Unité*: *Lip Unité dépêche quotidienne*. When there was particular news or possibilities for distribution, the mini-commissions would reproduce and distribute more copies of the bulletin. To respond to any effort to use reports of workers' signing up collectively with the ANPE in November to demobilize supporters, the mini-commissions printed thousands of extra copies of the bulletin for distribution in open-air markets.[134] When Prime Minister Messmer visited Lyon in November, the mini-commissions there handed out 20,000 copies of the daily *Lip Unité*.[135] In addition, the bulletin was directed to engaged partisans whose

---

131   *Libération*, October 15, 1973, 1. *L'Express*, October 15, 1973, 70.

132   BDIC F delta rés 578/43 "La revue de presse."

133   BDIC F delta rés 578/39 Issues of *Lip-Vérité* analyzing local press, October and November 1973. BDIC F delta rés 578/41 "Pour un mensuel populaire à Besançon: Projet" [November 21, 1973]; "Le Journal-Monopole: *L'Est républicain*."

134   BDIC F delta rés 578/48 Commissions Lip de Lyon et banlieue, "Compte rendu," November 22, 1973. Every few days, the popularization commission sent copies of the bulletin to about 500 CFDT organizations and locals that had requested it. *Idées ouvrières*, March–April 1980, 9.

135   The Commission Lip de Lyon distributed as many as 40,000 tracts on occasion. BDIC F delta rés 578/48 Commission Lip de Lyon, "Un appel pressant."

support became all the more important. A *Les Cahiers de mai* militant wrote to Anselme that "something extraordinary is happening." When the arrival of the bulletin was interrupted or late, "It was as if we hadn't eaten for 3 days ... We fear the worst—we could even believe we were in the same valley of tears as Chile. Lip, Chile, same hankie!"[136]

The daily bulletin reflected the agenda and debates of the General Assembly and the meetings of the commissions held that day.[137] However, the popularization commission solicited concerns supporters had so it could address these as well; mini-commissions collected questions after film screenings and telephoned them to Besançon to aid in preparing future issues.[138] A subcommission of two dozen workers separate from that for *Lip Unité* handled production of the daily bulletin.[139] Commission members discussed the contents and wrote the bulletin each afternoon at the same time and in the same place in the Maison pour Tous. Workers were encouraged to stop by and fill in writers as to what individual commissions wanted to say about their activities. Each night between 6 p.m. and 8 p.m., members of the subcommission telephoned "'zero' points" in Roubaix, Lyon, Paris, and Chambéry, and read the bulletin. Supporters recorded it on cassettes, repeating back sentence by sentence. They then typed transcripts and stenciled the bulletin using paper with the Lip letterhead, and prepared them for mini-commission members to pick up and deliver.[140] A CFDT delegate in Roubaux spoke of "the effervescence every night because we were receiving the news from Besançon" and "the revitalization" that preparing the daily bulletin brought to many locals.[141] Every night militants in Paris and Lyon in turn phoned mini-commissions throughout France to transmit the text of the bulletin for reproduction and distribution early the next

136   BDIC F delta rés 578/51/9 Marie to Daniel [Anselme], undated [1973].

137   Cassou shows that the *Lip Unité dépêche quotidienne* did not reflect the totality of divergence in General Assembly meetings, i.e. the tenor of Action Committee members' attacks on the CGT or concerns about keeping all Lip workers mobilized. "Lip, la Construction d'un mythe," 62.

138   See *Idées ouvrières*, December 1977, 30–5, for several pages of questions raised at film screenings and "6 heures avec Lip" events that the central mini-commission in Lyon sent to the popularization commission.

139   *Lip Unité dépêche quotidienne*, December 12, 1973. For the experience of one female OS who worked on the bulletin—taping the General Assembly, typing up articles drawn from these recordings, and presenting these to the General Assembly for approval—see Werner, "La question des femmes," 2454.

140   BDIC F delta rés 578/43 Cahiers de mai [Lyon] to "Chers camarades" [undated].

141   Cassou, "Lip, la construction d'un mythe," 70.

morning.[142] Mini-commissions played cassettes of the bulletin at their meetings, where it served as a basis of discussion.[143]

In Lyon, the neighborhood mini-commissions identified some 240 sites for daily postings, including union bulletin boards, bus stops, train stations, hospitals and the entrances to schools. They put up posters in color reading "DIRECT NEWS OF LIP." In one neighborhood in Lyon, there were ten postings of the daily bulletin within an hour after receiving the call from Besançon. The goal was to encourage groups of people to follow the movement by reading the bulletin each day and to discuss the contents with one another. By late November several hundred individuals picked up 1,500 copies each night for posting throughout the Lyon area. A further 150 supporters provided the central Lyon mini-commission with stamped envelopes so that between 1,000 and 6,000 bulletins could be sent daily to a list of more than 500 subscribers for distribution and posting. Each midnight, postal employees, working closely with the central mini-commission in Lyon, assured that the dispatch went out as quickly as possible. In Paris, militants came by the mini-commission sites in the 14th, 15th, and 19th arrondissements by 7 p.m. each evening to pick up copies for distribution and posting. And in Besançon, the daily bulletin was in turn distributed to all Lip workers in the morning before the General Assembly. *Les Lip* and their supporters throughout the country received the same information at the same time each day.[144]

To truly understand and absorb the collective practice of *les Lip*, the mini-commissions in Lyon said that a collective reading of the daily bulletin was necessary.[145] In addition to producing and distributing *Lip Unité* and the daily bulletin, the mini-commissions organized meetings to listen to audio-cassettes produced by Lip workers and arranged numerous screenings of *Non au démantèlement! Non aux licenciements!* The mini-commissions in the Lyon area reported in mid-January 1974 that they had held around fifty projections of the film.[146] Yet their goal was not

---

142   BDIC F delta rés 578/43 "Rapport de la Commission 'Communiqué Quotidien'" [October 13, 1973].

143   *Les Cahiers de mai hebdo*, November 22, 1973, 1, 4.

144   BDIC F delta rés 578/43 "Rapport de la Commission 'Communiqué Quotidien'" [October 13, 1973]. BDIC F delta rés 578/47 "Appel" du Coordination Technique des Commissions LIP [Lyon], January 13, 1974. BDIC F delta rés 578/48 Commissions Lip de Lyon et banlieue, "Compte rendu," November 22, 1973. Commission Lip de Lyon, 'Un appel pressant." Jusseaume, "Un succès venu de loin," 70.

145   BDIC F delta rés 578/48 Commissions de Lyon, "Urgent: Informations communiquées à tous les membres de commissions Lip," November 29, 1973.

146   BDIC F delta rés 578/48 Commissions Lip de Lyon, "Un appel pressant." BDIC

to "'show a film'"; they sought to spur discussion and to get viewers to think about what they could do to aid Lip workers as well as to reflect on events at Lip to advance their own demands.[147] As rentals proved difficult to manage, the popularization commission encouraged purchases and by October 23 had already sold forty copies of Dubosc's film.[148]

The mini-commissions spread word of the September 29 demonstration and set up transportation for participants.[149] They also worked with the popularization commission to arrange supporters' visits to Lip. Drawing on the "6 heures pour le Vietnam" ("6 Hours for Vietnam") demonstrations several years earlier, the mini-commissions organized "6 heures avec Lip" ("6 Hours with Lip") on Saturdays throughout France. Preparation included a delegation of two or three Lip workers going to each city the Monday before the demonstration. There they played an active role, meeting with the neighborhood mini-commissions and unions, and participating in meetings, "snack-discussions in the canteens," the distribution of tracts, and press conferences to build interest in the event. On the Saturday a contingent of up to a dozen Lip workers would arrive, put up posters with forty photos and explanatory text and run film screenings, meetings, and discussions.[150] On November 10 mini-commissions organized "6 heures avec Lip" which attracted some 20,000 participants in the Paris region, Lyon, Roubaix, Marseille, Bordeaux, Strasbourg, Saint-Etienne, Toulouse, Valence, Colmar, Cannes, Rennes, Caen, Carcassonne, Troyes, Saint-Brieuc, Soissons, and elsewhere.[151] Faced with lukewarm support from the national confederations, Piaget told those gathered for the "6 heures avec Lip" at Toulouse that what Lip workers needed was to "fuse all the different struggles

---

F delta rés 578/46 has records of the hundreds of showings of the film throughout France.

147　BDIC F delta rés 578/48 Commissions Lip de Lyon, "Pour donner un nouvel élan," January 11, 1974.

148　BDIC F delta rés 578/39 "Informations en direct de Besançon" attached to *Lip Unité*, October 23, 1973 [dated October 30, 1973].

149　BDIC F delta rés 578/49 "Bilan d'activités des 'Commissions Lip' de Lyon à la date du 24 nov. 73."

150　Jusseaume, "Un succès venu de loin," 70. *Politique hebdo*, October 18, 1973, 16 [quoted]. AMB 5Z224 "Préparation des '6 heures avec Lip' 19 oct. 1973." For the "6 heures avec Lip" held at the Bourse du travail in Lyon in November, the Lip commissions put up 2,500 posters and handed out 20,000 flyers in advance, and that day passed out 25,000 copies of the most recent *Lip Unité* and thousands of the most important daily bulletins. The mini-commission in turn staffed a table that attracted new supporters. BDIC F delta rés 578/49 "Bilan d'activités des 'Commissions Lip' de Lyon à la date du 24 novembre 73."

151　*Combat*, December 4, 1973, 5.

about employment" around the country: "To support us, we need to create Vietnam-Lip[s] everywhere …"[152]

Representatives on Mission

Newspapers interviewed Lip workers, and books like Lip. *Charles Piaget et les Lip racontent* allowed workers to get their story across in their own words, but nothing had as much impact as meetings across the nation at which Lip workers spoke.[153] The popularization commission planned several dramatic actions reminiscent of Fred Lip's advertising campaigns; seven workers accompanied the Tour de France in a van and held meetings that attracted from 250 to 600 people at each stopover city along the way. Far more widespread and important was the popularization commission's success putting workers on the road for meetings in cities throughout France—some ninety went to fifty-four localities in France and elsewhere in Europe in the last two weeks in August 1973.[154] Workers explained that it was by making their case to their extended families that they developed the expertise to present the workers' position to visitors and on tour.[155] These meetings brought the innovation and imagination of the Lip struggle to sympathizers throughout France. One worker told how, when it came time for questions, someone asked, after having listened to him, what national union he directed. "'Me?'" the Lip worker responded. "'I'm an OS!' The guys were flabbergasted!"[156]

Delegations did not limit themselves to multiple visits to Paris and Lyon; they went to smaller cities like Charleville-Mezières, Bourg-en-Bresse, Annecy, Châteauroux, Saint-Brieuc, and Gap as well.[157] The mini-commissions hosted Lip workers on tour and publicized their appearances. One worker estimated that he had traveled 16,000 kilometers in July and August speaking about Lip.[158] Workers often brought watches to sell, although police efforts to find the watches led to

---

152   *Libération*, November 12, 1973, 1, 12.

153   *Lip. Charles Piaget et les Lip racontent*, published in the "Lutter" series of the radical priest Jean-Claude Barreau, had sold 25,000 copies by mid-November. *Tribune socialiste*, November 19, 1973, 12.

154   Commission Popularisation, "Dossier d'information," 13–14.

155   BDIC F delta rés 578/36 "Débat entre les travailleurs de la Redoute et de Lip," November 10, 1973, 12.

156   Claude Goure, "Conversation avec des 'petits lip,'" *Panorama aujourd'hui*, November 1, 1973, 20.

157   Paris and Genest, "Ce que démontre Lip," 19.

158   *Lip Unité*, September 3, 1973.

harassment.[159] On their return to Besançon, travelers reported on their experiences to the General Assembly. Like the reports of visiting delegations or the reading of letters and telegrams of support, this played an important role in bolstering workers' spirits.[160]

The experience of speaking throughout France to support the struggle could have a real effect on Lip workers. Georgette Plantin recognized the liberation that came from speaking from one's heart about an experience; she saw this as a triumph over the bourgeoisie who kept workers silent with the idea that there was a perfect way to formulate a thought, one that workers believed they could never attain.[161] Many female workers developed a new sense of themselves. Speaking in public assemblies is something they would not have imagined doing before. "It's that," explained Piton, "which is beautiful in our struggle; there are not just delegates, the knowledgeable who go at the invitation of workers. Each can go; each does their best; and in this way timid ones reveal themselves capable of explaining at a microphone before hundreds or thousands of people, a conflict like Lip."[162] She remembered being at a meeting of striking sales women in Lyon, where CGT and PCF members sought to "trap" the representatives from Lip. She herself ran out of arguments. Then Christiane André, who had never dared say anything at a meeting, seized the microphone and responded point by point. "She was really awesome. You had to see the hall, it was sensational."[163]

These large public gatherings differed from union or party meetings. Many women were in attendance and they wanted to hear rank-and-file female workers. In the words of one female worker, "The women were in fact much more appreciated in meetings than the men."[164] Paulette Dartevel, OS in the armaments warehouse, told of going to her third meeting on a national tour, this one in Choisy-le-roi, a suburb of Paris. She had not spoken at previous meetings, but was asked a question and began to answer it. A male worker cut her off, but women at the meeting shouted that they had asked her the question and wanted to hear her answer. This made her feel that her views were valued and she was shocked to find herself speaking freely and confidently.[165] Audiences

---

159   Piton, *C'est possible!*, 356.

160   Piaget, "La formation par l'action collective," 156–7. Champeau, "Lip: le conflit et l'affaire (1973)," 71.

161   *Lip au féminin*, 17.

162   Piton, *C'est possible!*, 471.

163   Piton in *Lip au féminin*, 16–17.

164   Odette in Piaget, *Lip. Charles Piaget et les Lip racontent*, 116.

165   Groupe de femmes, "Lip au féminin," 4. Renée Ducey reports a similar experience in Féret, *Les Yeux rouges*, 41.

were clearly struck by women speaking for the cause, experienced as a challenge to the norm of a working class that spoke through men. It gave a different image of the conflict at Lip. The union leadership was male, but half of the workforce was female. Women speaking in public meetings was an important element in the representation of the movement and won it needed support outside of the confederations.

However, it was precisely this recognition that could be difficult for some male workers to accept. A few male Action Committee members saw in it a threat to the collective they affirmed each day in the General Assembly. In November 1973, one expressed concern that the supporters focused on women as a particular group; he compared it to the national CGT style of organization: "Effectively, it goes back to the CGT way of doing things, of grouping the CGT men, the CGT women, the CGT dogs, you name it."[166] Another dismissed questions addressed to Lip women by women at a meeting in Vitry about their condition as women, terming it a "problem à la mode," which distracted from discussion in terms of class and jobs. Action Committee women objected to women's problems being labeled "à la mode" (although some agreed that the questions posed had fit this description).[167] In any case, active participation in popularization did not necessarily prepare women for leadership in the movement. Demougeot would later reflect that women who spoke with ease at large public meetings would not speak in the General Assembly or meetings of commissions at Besançon in front of men they knew.[168]

Les Lip and Workers in Other Factories

Lip workers met with groups of employees as well as speaking at public meetings. Some of their most successful union-organized meetings were with CGT locals. In early September, the CGT staged walkouts of metalworkers in Roanne to express solidarity with the workers of Lip and to present their own grievances to their employers. Eight hundred workers came to hear the Lip delegation. Lip workers then spoke individually with employees and distributed copies of Lip Unité: "Workers literally

166 Lopez, "Lip Interview," 50. And it is true that Piton said that just as metalworkers and textile workers have different problems and their own federations, the same should be true for women. "Pour les femmes: les syndicats s'attaquent," Parents 61 (March 1974): 120–1.

167 Lopez, "Lip Interview," 51–2.

168 Interview with Demougeot by Reid, June 12, 2013.

ripped the leaflets from our hands and asked for bundles to distribute."[169] On occasion, worker delegations could overcome the hostility of the CGT confederation. Shortly after the October 12 vote, 200 workers at the majority CGT computer research center at Rocquencourt (Île-de-France) met with a Lip delegation. Inspired by a female worker's account of the serpent, they left the meeting and snaked their way through the offices to recruit support on their way to present their demands to management.[170]

At the time of the "6 heures avec Lip" on November 10, 1973 in Roubaix, a delegation of Lip workers met with employees, both unionized and non-unionized, at La Redoute, a large mail-order clothing business. The discussion focused on the strike at La Redoute in April 1973, which had begun when women who handled packing had discussed their grievances and put them on paper, leading other workshops to do the same. The CGT and CFDT unions at La Redoute held daily general assemblies, but little more, and the movement ended in a week. Workers wanted to know from the Lip delegation what else they could have done. Individual workshops met, came up with questions, and picked a representative to pose them to *les Lip*. The La Redoute workers raised issues journalists rarely addressed. How in the spring of 1973 had mechanics at Lip, who were to be laid off, gotten female assembly line workers, whose jobs were not on the line, to see that this was their struggle too? How, after the vote of October 12, "faced with the solitude and isolation of each one of you, with respect to family, friends, the others … how did you hold out?" Workers from other firms also attended the discussion with the delegation from Lip. Militants from the *Les Cahiers de mai* rented a video camera and filmed the discussion. A committee of workers was selected to choose twenty minutes from the footage to make a video to screen and discuss in individual workshops at La Redoute. [171]

169   BDIC F delta rés 578/48 Commission Popularisation Lyon, "Note d'information groupe de Lyon-propositions reproduction-diffusion *Lip Unité* Lyon le 7 septembre 1973."

170   BDIC F delta rés 578/48 "Compte rendu délégation Lip à Paris du 12 au 20 octobre." For a meeting in Vitry after October 12 where Lip workers won over CGT members primed to oppose them, see "Témoignage d'un membre du CA de Lip," *Front Rouge*, October 25, 1973, 7.

171   *Les Cahiers de mai*, May–June 1973, 10–12. For a complete transcript of the discussion with the Lip workers, see BDIC F delta rés 578/36 "Débat entre les travailleurs."

Conclusion

The struggle mobilized *les Lip*, workers elsewhere, and sympathetic youth who rediscovered in their support of Lip workers and Larzac farmers the possibilities that May 1968 had revealed. The community that developed among *les Lip* rejected the managerial authority and alienating environment that had preceded the conflict; many supporters saw it as prefiguring an alternative future to those of capitalism and the Common Program. The popularization strategy fed "a collective imaginary that superimposed itself on the limited objectives" of *les Lip*.[172] This affected both supporters and the Lip workers. For Dominique Bondu, the radical student who had become one of *les Lip*:

> The pleasant pressure of a friendly crowd constitutes in effect an irreplaceable stimulant for *les Lip* transformed into "heroes". In the astonished look, a mite admiring, of the visitor, each knew how to read a charming image of oneself and the phenomenon of the mirror could only reinforce the individual feeling of belonging to a community.[173]

While the union leadership at Lip appreciated the power that this attention could give the movement, many workers, and not just those in the Action Committee, took these representations as an unadulterated reality. Gaston Jouffroy, a cabinet-maker active in the Lip community at the end of the 1970s, felt that the workers' failure to undertake a self-analysis—"Lip gave itself the image of a novel"—came back to haunt them when conditions changed but they still saw themselves in the depictions others had made of them:

> I am persuaded that at the time of the struggle, the 'allies' ... described the situation of the troops from the front, in a manner wholly different from what it really was ... I just ask myself if this exterior support did not lead us sometimes to dispossess ourselves of our own image, to make us forego our own analysis.[174]

---

172   Pierre Lantz, "'Une espèce de flou paradisiaque, un désir sorti de l'enfance' : Les Lip" in *La Gauche, le pouvoir, le socialisme*, ed. Christine Buci-Glucksmann (Paris, 1983), 181.

173   Bondu, "De l'usine à la communauté," 437–8.

174   BDIC F delta rés 702/15/1 "Débat du 20 janvier 1979," 21–2. Daniel Jacquin makes a similar observation in "Lip 1973–1981," 261, 266, 268, 270, 273–4.

If one problem was the Lip workers' identification with the representations sympathetic media created of them, another difficulty would be getting the press to change these representations as the situation changed in succeeding years. Raguénès said in conversation with a group of Lip workers in 1978:

> The public has a weakness for Mandrin, Cartouche, the exploits of the Israelis. But perhaps the support the French [gave Lip] was essentially based on the appealing actions of "a victim who sought to defend himself" without the long-term reasons for the struggle being understood and endorsed … Perhaps it is because the support of the public was rapid and drastic in May–June '73, but based on misunderstandings, that we have so much trouble accepting that in 1978 the press covers us imperfectly and only for spectacular actions. We have to kidnap the prefect or burn cars to get the journalists to show up. This incapacity of the press to take on the substance of the problem, this desire to have impressive events, affects our action and condemns us to perform spectacular acts at the risk of letting the sign take precedence over the message.

The workers responded that their unique place in the left social imagination—"Are we a 'chosen people', charismatic, endowed with a 'national destiny'?"—that had once allowed them to represent the workers of France, could isolate them as well, leaving *les Lip* apparently not different enough for potential supporters and too different for workers elsewhere.[175] This contradiction was never absent in the later chapters of Lip's history.

---

175   BDIC F delta rés 702/4/4 Transcript of discussion of Lip employees in which participants are identified by initials or unidentified [1978].

6

From Besançon to the Chingkang Mountains

They asked me if I discovered the importance of the "creative initiative of the masses" with the Lip conflict. Of course not! It was studying Lenin, twenty-five years ago, that I began to understand it in a profound sense, like many worker militants of my generation.

—Georges Séguy[1]

I speak of myself, precisely because Lip is going to coincide with a change in my position ... There were certain conservative aspects of traditional Marxist thought in my mind, that I had not succeeded in putting in question in May 1968, in particular the big, massive and redoubtable concept of organization such as it had been bequeathed by the supposed heirs to Leninism ... As long as the working class does not speak of organization, you can always be tempted to have recourse to a very old Marxist discourse, very conservative. You can claim that it is worker discourse, which it is in part. It took the worker event, Lip, for me to put into question certain things, very profound, about organization, therefore on theory and power, and to get back on my feet.

—Pierre Victor[2]

Le Télégramme économique, a newspaper read by employers, reflected in July 1973 on events in Besançon: "French society, as those who govern the country and the majority of the ruling classes conceive it, has rarely been as menaced in its principles as it is currently if one goes by the Lip

---

1   *Le Monde*, September 14, 1973, 32.
2   Gavi et al., *On a raison de se révolter*, 12–13 (February 26, 1974).

affair." Workers were defying owners and the state. They had widespread national support. The situation was, the paper concluded, more serious than the events of May 1968, which, after all, had not "infringed on principles."[3] Six months later, the business think tank, the Centre d'Études des Entreprises, compared the situation at Lip to that of the Bolsheviks early in 1917:

> Lip, from now on, it is 600+ people perfectly trained, practiced and organized to propagate permanent revolution in France. Lip is henceforth a reserve of full-time revolutionaries.
>
> It is no longer a question of the survival or the disappearance of an industrial enterprise. It is a matter of a platform of subversive action, installed in France, lavishly subsidized, capable of fomenting or fueling subversive actions, even terrorist ones anywhere in the country.
>
> It is the Sorbonne of 1968, but serious in a different way … by the means of action and pressure that extend everywhere in France. Agitators trained at Lip have brought their support to Noguères, Larzac, Cerizay, Dole, Dunkerque, Nantes … As soon as a weak point appears, agitators are available and come as reinforcements.[4]

Perhaps the author had read the article by Serge July, editor of *Libération*, who wrote of Lip a few days before publication of this report: "Soviet is a Russian word, and community a French word. But these mean, in some ways, the same thing."[5]

Yet it was precisely what was lost in translation that troubled many on the far left. The workers at Lip were not the unskilled, unorganized immigrants working in automobile factories that Maoists and other leftists had identified as the vectors of revolution; they were not, Jean Daniel said when writing about Lip, North African workers, "the lepers without which Christ is not possible."[6] This did not stop Communist Party intellectuals from working overtime to explain that if Lip workers talked with leftists and many leftists found them appealing, it was because the labor force was made up of recent arrivals from the Catholic countryside, another group of immigrants who had not yet learned to be proletarians; if they had, they would recognize that the PCF was the only party

---

3   Article from *Le Télégramme économique*, July 25, 1973, reprinted in *Politique hebdo*, August 23, 1973, 15.

4   ADD 1026W9 "Information-CEE," January 15, 1974.

5   *Libération*, January 10, 1974, 3.

6   *Le Nouvel observateur*, June 3, 1974, 69.

that represented their interests.[7] Situationists joined in questioning what went on at Palente. For them, militants from *Les Cahiers de mai* acted as censors of what they knew to be the workers' true insubordination. Perhaps most radical, many French Maoists, unlike the Situationists, let the Lip workers' actions question them. They saw *les Lip* bringing imagination to power without the Bolsheviks of old or a new generation of revolutionary guides.

"Four Million Young Workers" Come to Besançon

In early January 1974, on the eve of Pierre Messmer's final "Lip, it's over" pronouncement, hundreds of copies of an issue of *Lip Unité*, ostensibly the work of Quatre Millions de Jeunes Travailleurs ("Four Million Young Workers"), mysteriously appeared in Besançon. The police identified a Situationist in Besançon as the source of the paper.[8] The paper had the same masthead and layout as *Lip Unité*, but proclaimed that it had displaced "the strange workerists of *Les Cahiers de mai*," who were "stripping away the story that is in reality our struggle of what it retains that is still profoundly subversive."[9] Declaring "Never Work" in bold type, the pirated edition of *Lip Unité* claimed to speak in the name of the workers. Striking in order to work was an oxymoron; *les Lip* "had self-managed their own alienation." The paper condemned leaders at Lip, "new impresarios of class struggle, for staging a spectacle, contributing in this way to burial of the fight against the system [of alienated wage labor] instead of developing it"; the unions, "owners of the working class," opposed dismantling and layoffs only to preserve their corporate interests and

---

7   Jean-Claude Poulain, "Se débarrasser des idées d'un autre âge," *Économie et politique* 256 (November 1975): 31–2. Conservatives agreed that Lip workers' origins made it "easy to trot out the Aladdin's lamp of socialist utopia." *Le Figaro*, August 22, 1973, 1.

8   ADD 1812W27 RG, January 4, 1974. The pirate edition came in a sixty-five-page text with twelve articles, as well as a copy that was the length of issues of *Lip Unité*. Most of the quotations cited here are from "Contribution à une critique radicale du conflit de Lip" in the long version. This drew extensively from earlier Situationist works on the conflict: *Lip La 25e heure. Adresse aux travailleurs de Besançon* (Paris, October 1973) and "Splendeurs et misères du salariat" [tract of May 20, 1973] (in ACGT Uncatalogued Papers on Lip).

9   After the October 12 vote, the FGM-CFDT made the same charge that *Lip Unité* was the tool of *Les Cahiers de mai*. BDIC F delta rés 578/42 PSU cellule Lip, "Travailleurs en lutte" [October 1973]. However, the FTM-CGT did not differentiate among leftists and presented the pirate *Lip Unité* as proof that *Les Cahiers de mai* controlled what was said in all the issues of the newsletter, including that one. FTM-CGT, "La CGT et Lip," 47.

maintain their monopoly on the sale of workers' labor. Leftists, "stock-holders of the working class," exhibited "a neurotic acquiescence" to the apparently irreproachable unions. As for "the Jesuits of *Les Cahiers de mai*" and the rest of the leftists, "the safeguard of local capital is their Jansenism and the preservation of the salary system their hidden god." The gathering on September 29 "recruited by the unions" had been the "folkloric burial of the movement."

A sociologist at Vincennes, Rémi Hess, shared this outlook. He came to Palente in the summer of 1973 and observed that a minority of workers were actively engaged in the self-management of their conflict, but for "most workers, desertion is the most appealing activity. Rich with war treasure (the hidden watches), *les Lip* prefer to sun themselves than to continue production."[10] Capitalist critics may have harped on the small number of workers engaged in production, but for Hess the problem was that these men and women reinforced the representation of the worker as producer. Nor did he accept the idea that what was most radical at Lip was the large number of workers on commissions who ran the strike and made it their own. The Situationist leader Raoul Vaneigem recognized the spectacle that was Lip in order to dismiss it: *les Lip* had shown that workers were the only group able to "definitively change the world," but they had not.[11]

Anarchists and Marxist purists were eager to show they too had not been taken in by the happening in Besançon.[12] As far as they were concerned, unions opposed layoffs because it would mean a reduction in delegates and dues.[13] The seemingly radical nature of events at Lip secured the existing order of business and union power, showing that "Capital can operate the means of production without private property."[14]

---

10   Rémi Hess, "Information et autogestion," *Autogestion et socialisme* 28–9 (October 1974-January 1975): 73. This was Lourou's view as well. *L'Analyseur Lip*, 135. An Action Committee member explained that workers with nothing to do in the factory sunned themselves on the lawns ("it's normal"), but when the commissions were estab-lished, everyone joined in. "Lip des militants du comité d'action parlent," 29–30.

11   Raoul Vaneigem, "Contributions à la lutte des ouvriers révolutionnaires, des-tinées à être discutées, corrigées et principalement mises en pratique sans trop tarder" (1974), ch. 2, point 62. at libcom.org.

12   For a presentation of several of these critiques, see 'Lip revu et corrigé," *La Lanterne noire* 2 (December 1974-January 1975), at la-presse-anarchiste.net. See also Charles Reeve, *Lip: une brèche dans le mouvement ouvrier traditionnel* (Paris, 1974). Nathan Brown returns to the Situationist and orthodox Marxist perspectives in "Red years. Althusser's Lesson, Rancière's Error and the Real Movement of History," *Radical Philosophy* 170 (November-December 2011): 16–24.

13   "Lip c'est bien fini," *Lutte de classe* (March 1974), 7, 9.

14   "A Lip au pays des réveils," *Lutte continue* 8 (September 10, 1973): 8.

In this "self-management counter-revolution," workers managed and accumulated the capital of a bankrupt enterprise, rather than appropriating it. Instead, Lip workers maintained wage labor and acted as traveling salesmen using modern marketing techniques: "'*les Lip*' are selling their watches in public meetings or at friends' homes, exactly as Tupperware is sold in fashionable living rooms or by hitting on a neighbor."[15]

What, they asked, lay behind this charade? Skilled workers already exercised a certain control over their work and they wanted to maintain the existing system: "self-management maintains the capitalist mode of production."[16] *Les Lip* questioned neither hierarchy nor wage labor.[17] Unions took advantage of workers' "need for the security of the union straitjacket."[18] Leftists' flattery and fetishization of workers' tactics led to "the isolation of Lip by its glorification," rather than the imperative of social revolution.[19] Parties "were vampires drinking the blood" of what workers were creating at Palente.[20] The Action Committee was not the answer: it was "to Lip unions what the university is to the state, its imaginary surety ... The Action Committee, on the whole, gives the impression of a good lapdog."[21] Although there were and remained throughout the conflict important differences on the place of work in the fulfilled life between the veteran skilled mechanics who led the CFDT-Lip and the young and unskilled workers who engaged with the leftists and questioned the idea that workers could realize themselves through work well done, there was little support among *les Lip* for dismissals of the institutions of the struggle.[22]

---

15   "Lip et la contre-révolution autogestionnaire," *Négation* 3 (1974), at meeting. communisation.net.

16   P. Laurent (Mouvement Communiste), "Critique du Conflit Lip et Tentative de Dépassement" [November 1973], 7 [at the International Institute of Social History, IISG Bro 1564/12 fo].

17   Capitalism, Claude Berger explained, is based on the atomization of the individual as worker and as consumer. *Les Lip* had put an end to this: "they collectively recomposed their existence." "Lip et après," *Les Temps modernes* 327 (October 1973): 561. The only way Berger could explain their failure to take the last step and abolish wage labor was by blaming the unions' subversion of the radical impulse at Lip. *Marx, l'association, l'anti-Lénine* (Paris, 1974), 112–19.

18   "Lip: combativité et mystification," *Révolution internationale* 5 (October–November 1973): 11.

19   Ibid., 9, 14.

20   Lourau, *L'Analyseur Lip*, 37. See Jean-François Marchat, "*L'Analyseur Lip* (1974)" in *Institution et implication. L'oeuvre de René Lourau*, ed. Ahmed Lamihi and Gilles Monceau (Paris, 2002), 85–97.

21   Laurent, "Critique du Conflit Lip," 4.

22   See Action Committee members' repudiation of "Supplément à *Lip Unité*,"

French Maoists

Situationists and anarchists saw apparent expressions of workers' imagination and creativity at Lip as rooted in and reproducing the existing system, while mass left parties and the small Bolshevik parties saw workers' imagination and creativity as impediments to their leadership. The opening of the factory gates, rather than providing the entryway to a new world, only confirmed for these critics all they feared. However, other leftists, represented most clearly by *Les Cahiers de mai* militants and Maoists of the ex-Gauche Prolétarienne (ex-GP, legally disbanded in 1970), were quite receptive to what was new in Besançon.

Several CFDT-Lip leaders were members of the PSU. The PSU was more open to consideration of currents on the radical left than any of the other established parties and this created a basis for exchange lacking in other factories. Most locals, following the lead of the CGT, sought to keep leftists away from workers. However, the CFDT-Lip, believing it had the political acumen to assure workers did not get swept away by leftist adventurism, invited all supporters to come to Besançon and meet with workers.[23] Tewfik Allal of *Les Cahiers de mai* explained: "Piaget said that he supported everyone, all the groups that want an office there will have one. It is like Jerusalem. There are all the groups, 'Cathos', Muslims, all were there with their billboards."[24] There were things both workers and supporters could learn from one another. Reflecting on May 1968 and succeeding years, Piaget recognized that "It is in good part spurred by 'leftists' that we relearned democratic practices in struggles."[25] But in the words of one CFDT-Lip militant, it was the leftists who were "overwhelmed" at Lip.[26] The Gauche ouvrière et paysanne/Pour le Communisme (GOP/PLC) read Piaget as "studded with camouflaged references to Mao Zedong,"[27] but Piaget thought that leftists "had learned much more than they had brought," adding that "this is not a bad thing."[28]

---

distributed in September 1973, that attacked unions and defended the "No Work" position. ADD 1812W26, RG, September 21, 1973. Lopez, "Lip Interview," 39–40.

23   *Témoignage chrétien*, February 7, 1974, 5. And when Piaget did feel that the Action Committee members were taking from leftists they met while speaking throughout France too simple a view of the situation after the vote of October 12, he did not seem too concerned: "Anyways I believe it was Lenin who said this: 'only the truth is revolutionary.'" "Un pas vers la révolution," 28.

24   Firmin, "*Les Cahiers de mai.* Entretiens," 20.

25   *Politique hebdo*, October 3, 1974, 21.

26   *CFDT Syndicalisme hebdo*, September 13, 1973, 9.

27   "Lip Larzac," 34.

28   *Politique hebdo*, January 24, 1974, 9.

As time passed, he noted that "the inopportune leaflets of the beginning of the conflict, now we don't see any more of them."[29] Piaget could not help but hope that some of the leftists who came to Besançon sure that trade union impediments to workers' activism were the cause of all problems in a labor conflict would revise their thinking.[30]

No leftist group was more affected by events at Lip than the ex-GP, whose goal, under the leadership of Pierre Victor, the nom de guerre of Benny Lévy, was to enter the masses, to "enlarge the Resistance." More than anything else, the ex-GP was defined by the memory of the exclusion of students from occupied factories in 1968. For the ex-GP *La Cause du peuple*, "We had to wait five years for all to see the scar is closed up: the workers do not have to exclude, but to attract, to draw in. Lip announces to all that the times have changed."[31]

A primary strategy of the ex-GP and other Maoist-influenced groups like Vive la Révolution! (VLR) was the "establishment" of militants as workers in factories: *établis*.[32] Michel Chemin had been a VLR militant working in the Renault car factory in Flins for three years, when he went to Palente on June 18, 1973.

> I expect to find a factory on strike, like those I had always known: strike pickets, edgy workers, union speeches. And I found myself in another world. The people smiled, I have never seen a worker at Flins really and sincerely smile. Guys talked. There was fraternity in the air. It is the beginning of a love story between me and Lip.[33]

For leftists, the idea of a happy worker was an oxymoron. A poster made by Lip workers that read "If you've never seen happy workers, go see them at Lip" captured the world-turned-upside-down quality that Palente manifested in the summer of 1973.

---

29   Not surprisingly, Bernard Girardot, like other CFDT-Lip militants, resented it when he read in leftists' tracts recommendations that they presented as their own but that he believed they had taken from the workers of Lip. *L'Outil des travailleurs*, April 1974, 17.

30   *Politique hebdo*, January 24, 1974, 9. *Témoignage chrétien*, February 7, 1974, 5.

31   *La Cause du peuple*, September 13, 1973, 8.

32   There is an extensive literature on the *établis*. See Donald Reid, "*Établissement*: Working in the Factory to Make Revolution in France," *Radical History Review* 88 (Winter 2004): 83–111. Linhart, *Volontaires pour l'usine*. Marnix Dressen, *De l'amphi à l'établi: Les étudiants maoïstes à l'usine 1967–1989* (Paris, 2000). "Ouvriers volontaires. Les années 68. L'Établissement' en usine," *Les Temps Modernes* 684–5 (July–October 2015).

33   Michel Chemin, "Dix ans ventre à terre," *Autrement* 12 (February 1978): 261.

The ex-GP had a minimal presence at Lip before 1973.[34] However, many Lip workers remember warmly the young Maoists who came that summer. "They believed in *les Lip* … and they LISTENED to us … You could spend a whole day or evening with a Maoist. He didn't open his mouth, he listened to you."[35] The OS Alice Carpena differentiated these young radicals from intellectuals with their big words: "These people listened to us, as if we were masters of something. Because, me, I think we brought them a response to questions they were asking in theory, and then we brought them the practice."[36] Of course, not all such interactions left warm memories. Emblematic was Monique Piton's love affair in the summer of 1973 with a Maoist militant, a lycée professor who wrote for *La Cause du peuple*.[37] He loved being in love with the emblem of worker radicalism at Lip, but, she realized, he was more devoted to worker causes than to her.[38] And in the fall, he went off with a bourgeoise who had come to Besançon, "wanting to mix with workers."[39]

Maoists identified "the commune of Lip" as "the most important event since May '68":[40] "as in 1968 workers penetrated into the Sorbonne for the first time in their lives, in 1973 intellectuals penetrated into the factory for the first time."[41] "Five years had been needed for the undermining that started from the Sorbonne to propagate through the whole social body, by the intermediary of innumerable and often 'surprising' mediations, up to this 'strange' location, unforeseeable: Besançon."[42] For the ex-GP

---

34   Lip workers rejected ex-GP intervention in the strike of June 1970. ADD 2377W181 PR to MI, June 24, 1970. A member of the ex-GP in the mechanics shop was fired for bringing banned issues of *La Cause du peuple* into Palente in November 1970, one of several Maoists laid off by Lip about the same time. ADD 1812W34 RG, December 9, 1970. ADD 1812W33 RG, April 28, 1971. This worker remained active in the ex-GP and is apparently "the comrade Maoist of Besançon" castigated by fellow Maoists in August 1973 for talking of Lip as would a CFDT-Lip delegate: "He did not speak like a Maoist. He must be spoken to about this." BDIC F delta rés 576/3/4 "Notes sur l'école Mao Août 1973." But one never knows how a Maoist will speak. Several months later, the police identified him as helping with production of the faux *Lip Unité*. ADD 1812W27 RG, January 4, 1974.

35   Beurier, "La mémoire des Lip," Annexe VIII.

36   Werner, "La question des femmes," 2458.

37   He is an author of *Il était une fois la révolution*.

38   Piton, *C'est possible!*, 294.

39   Piton, *Mémoires libres*, 82. See Clavel, *Les Paroissiens*, 157, 345, 388, for critical portraits of upper-class female Maoist supporters of Lip who came to Besançon, writers for *Libération* like Piton's rival.

40   *La Cause du peuple*, July 6, 1973, 10.

41   "Pour un mouvement du 12 octobre, en quelque sorte," *Cahiers prolétariens* 3 (January 1974): 20.

42   "De Besançon aux Monts Tsingkiang," *Cahiers prolétariens* 2 (January 1974): 39. This issue had been prepared for release a few months earlier.

fellow traveler, *Les Cahiers de mai* and then *Libération* journalist Philippe Gavi, "the resonance of Lip is due as well to the fact that Lip became a discussion site, a site of speech, exactly as in May 1968 the center of Paris was transformed into a public forum." Pierre Victor agreed: "At Lip now, they discuss anything"; "imagination is no longer just at the Sorbonne."[43]

Pierre Victor first went to Besançon on June 12, 1973 and remained for more than a week through the sequestration of the watches and the beginning of production. On his return to Paris he called a meeting of the cadres of the ex-GP to discuss his epiphany: "I see in Lip the agony of our revolutionary discourse ... What Lip questions is our *raison d'être*."[44] Lip may be a singular movement, Pierre Victor said in July 1973, but it represented a significant change: "To take an expression of Marx in *Capital*, the perpetuation of social relations is put in question ... Even if there is not another factory that does what Lip is doing, there is a symbolic power Lip exercises across all the working class."[45] Drawing on Mao's analysis of the revolution in China in 1928, the ex-GP presented Palente as a liberated site from which the attack on the central power of the state would come:

> In a word, the unlikely 'folly' of red flags flying in the Chingkang mountains, far from the industrial and political centers of China, surrounded by a tide of government soldiers and warlords, is in France the folly of 'Liberated Republics as it were', like Lip, not having the same territorial reality as the red bases of the Chinese Revolution, but playing the same function of a time bomb against the central power, whose end it announces, and in the conscience of the people, which it invites to take power, and to learn the new power, and to defend it.[46]

The workers at Besançon who practiced the illegality preached by the ex-GP were native French, Catholic and unionized; leaders like Piaget were supervisors. Contrary to leftist orthodoxy, the union did not impede worker action; the CFDT-Lip promoted democracy in the General Assembly and nurtured the Action Committee as a check on its own power. To this Denis Clodic, an *établi* at Renault, added:

---

43   Gavi et al., *On a raison de se révolter*, 228 (July 1973), 277–8 (October 1973).
44   Hervé Hamon and Patrick Rotman, *Génération. 2. Les années de poudre* (Paris, 1988), 490–1.
45   Gavi et al., *On a raison de se révolter*, 233 (July 1973).
46   "De Besançon aux Monts Tsingkiang," 39–40.

With Benny [Pierre Victor], we went several times [to Besançon], and we were knocked off our feet. The permeation of Catholicism is enormous. They were priests, leaders dressed in white, who organize a community in revolt. They are achieving what we had dreamed, but in a very different way; they never envisaged civil war for a single moment. In sum, we saw that we had taken the wrong route.[47]

The Maoists had always seen illegal acts as necessary and castigated unions for opposing them in order to protect their position. Illegality had seemed confined to activists on the margins of the working class. Yet here was a union—led by Catholics no less—that broke laws fundamental to capitalism and did so while repudiating the violence Maoists had also thought essential.[48] The authorities could not dismiss Catholic workers as delinquents. This led, Clodic believed, to "a new relation between what is outside of unions and unions," in line with the aspirations of May 1968 to transform the system, rather than solely to get the most out of the existing one.[49]

This involved rethinking the politics of revolution. The final issue of *La Cause du peuple* in September 1973 was entitled "Drawing from the Stock of Lip." Workers revealed a new world to leftist intellectuals like Pierre Victor. He came to believe that "the great invention of Lip" was "a microphysics of the revolution," that took assessment of the situation and decision-making from "the specialists of the workers' movement, the chiefs of staff" and gave it to workers: "the more you particularize the revolution in the community, the more you produce singularity in the community, the better this sense will appear, the better prepared will be the great convulsions, the fevers that shake the body social."[50] The model was no longer class, in which all come together as one, a legacy of factory discipline, but a community with "its power of contagion" which, with the opening of the factory gates, spills out in thousands of individual currents, "dismantles class" as Communists understood it, and "liberates the multiplicities."[51] Lip workers were the ones able "to topple that ideal with the name 'workers' movement.'"[52] They had cut off the heads of the bronze steles of Fred Lip's father and grandfather, near the fresco at the

---

47 Jean Birnbaum, *Les Maoccidents* (Paris, 2009), 55–6.
48 Gavi et al., *On a raison de se révolter*, 311–13 (November 1973).
49 *Libération*, November 9, 1973, 5.
50 Jean Raguénès, Pierre Victor, and Denis Clodic, "Lip 1973–1976," *Les Temps modernes* 367 (February 1977): 1258.
51 Pierre Victor, "Lip acéphale," *Les Temps modernes* 367 (February 1977): 1265.
52 Raguénès et al., "Lip 1973–1976," 1256–7.

entry to Palente. Pierre Victor saw in this a "decapitated thought" marked by a "communal logic" that had no place for "worship of the state" or authority given to a single figure, whether in the form of a director or a political leader: "*les Lip* invented (reinvented because they are not the first) a headless totality."[53] (And Pierre Victor would have felt all the more this way if he had known that Fred Lip learned of the beheading of the statues when a solicitous Claude Mercet, CGT-Lip secretary-general, telephoned him with the news.[54])

Pierre Victor was particularly taken with Piaget's precept: "Each time you have a power, it is necessary immediately to set up a counter-power, so that you are really contested, in such a way as to keep us in our place and not be tempted to dominate others."[55] The year after the statues were decapitated, Piaget imagined himself the rightful target of a cultural revolution: "That's the way that I opened myself up to these critiques: a very painful operation. To be truly open, to confront oneself with the views of others, to see if their ideas aren't better than ours. This is how I imagine the Chinese Cultural Revolution, a constant dialectic coming from the rank-and-file, which attacks and questions ...."[56]

Ex-GP Alain Geismar castigated the CFDT and PSU for talking about self-management endlessly until *les Lip* acted; then they could only recall that self-management was impossible under capitalism:

> But is the future society born of struggles in current society or is it born of a decree at the time of the revolution? We need to begin by recognizing that there is new social action. That we set restrictions later. If we do not do this, there will be a 'progressive' class of the ENA [École Nationale d'Administration] which will make, when the day comes, a beautiful model of self-management.[57]

Geismar could not resist telling the Socialist Jean-Pierre Chevènement that the time for the political parties of the left was over: travel agencies to take the French to Palente and Larzac were needed more than

---

53 Victor, "Lip acéphale," 1266–7.

54 BDIC F delta rés 702/4/2 Fred Lip to Claude Neuschwander, June 12, 1975. And in turn, Fred Lip, determined not to be "guillotined," had "casing, half steel and half concrete" put around the neck of his stele, though it was not on display with the others. Fred Lip to Antoine Riboud in Victor, "Lip acéphale," 1263.

55 *Libération*, December 5, 1973, 3. Gavi et al., *On a raison de se révolter*, 353–4 (November 1973–March 5, 1974).

56 Macciocchi, *De la France*, 151.

57 *Politique hebdo*, August 11, 1974, 19.

Chevènement's PS.[58] If the established parties and unions did not know what to do with the workers of Palente, *les Lip* did not need the leadership of leftist missionaries either. Although the events of May '68 had not led Pierre Victor to question the Leninist party, his engagement with Lip did: "I see in Lip the agony of a revolutionary discourse which year after year, had survived May 1968"; Lip, he said, gave leftists the opportunity, the responsibility, "to transform the whole of the revolutionary movement from top to bottom."[59] For ex-GP members Guy Lardreau and Christian Jambet, the Lip conflict showed that radical intellectuals had nothing more to bring to workers: "it became evident that activism no longer made sense."[60] Ex-GP Léo Lévy said of Lip: "We wanted to put ourselves at the service of the people; here, the people dispensed with our services. There was nothing to do but to disappear."[61] "The dynamic of the struggle at Lip," Chemin wrote, "will end up by removing the last activist and vanguardist illusions from the leadership of the [ex-]GP, which will deserve credit for having this minimum of lucidity."[62]

The revolution taking place in communities like Palente that prefigured the revolutionary society had no need for the revolutionary party of old. The vote of October 12 to reject the Giraud plan was "as if the workers had crossed the Suez Canal to take back possession of their territories occupied by a foreign power," that of the confederations.[63] It led the ex-GP to disband at the beginning of November 1973. "Lip," Pierre Victor (writing as Benny Lévy) explained in 1986, "was our law on the repentants"—referring to the reduction in sentence and the protection given individuals who aid prosecutors by breaking the oath of silence governing certain criminal organizations; it allowed the ex-GP to "quit while ahead" and not turn to terrorism.[64] Gavi said the October

---

58 Alain Geismar, *Mon Mai 1968* (Paris, 2008), 223.

59 Gavi et al., *On a raison de se révolter*, 246 (October 1973), 316 (November 1973).

60 Gilles Hertzog, "L'ange, entre mao et jésus," *Magazine littéraire* 112–13 (1976): 57.

61 Léo Lévy, *À la vie* (Lagrasse, 2017), 76.

62 Chemin, "Dix ans ventre à terre," 261, 262.

63 "Pour un mouvement du 12 octobre, en quelque sorte," 19.

64 Hamon and Rotman, *Géneration*, 2: 530. There was no one single reason for the dissolution of the ex-GP. Sébastien Repaire, *Sartre et Benny Lévy* (Paris, 2013), 109–10, sees the terrorist attack in Munich in 1972, not the Lip conflict, as the reason for its dissolution. This was certainly very important for Pierre Victor, but the breadth of the ex-GP leadership that recognized the significance of Lip in the decision reveals that it was more than a rationale for a decision made for other reasons. See Antoine Liniers, "Objections contre une prise d'armes" in François Furet, Antoine Liniers, and

12 vote "was not a 'rational' vote or, rather, it was that of another 'reason' which had been developed during the months of the strike."[65] For Pierre Victor, the relation of the vote of October 12, "the revolutionary event *par excellence*," to the dominant revolutionary theory in France, which valued only what led to central power, was like that in May 1968 of the March 22 movement to the longstanding practice in France of the general strike followed by compromises.[66] The issue of *Les Cahiers prolétariens* prepared for the meeting when the ex-GP disbanded wrote of "a movement of October 12" that would bring together the diversity of struggles of workers and others in France, as the movement of March 22 had brought together student groups, only to lament that this was, as of yet, "a dream."[67]

The Parishioners of Palente

One-time GP militant Jacques Rancière recognized that *les Lip* were articulating a theory where the ideas of May 1968 met those of nineteenth-century workers' associations, "but where one can also see a 'fusion' of a new type, that of worker experience with Christian ideology."[68] The Catholic humanist concept of man that Lip workers articulated in demanding an economy that serves man was not a bourgeois ideology, but an assertion of equality versus the hierarchies of the factory and political parties. Gavi attributed the criticism/self-criticism practiced by leaders like Piaget and Raguénès not to reading Mao, but to their Catholic faith which, among revolutionaries, gave them "the most developed sense of democracy."[69]

For Rancière and Gavi, the insurgent workers' Catholicism helped explain how they navigated leftist ideologies and practices, but for Maurice Clavel, their faith itself was an inspiration. In December 1972, Pierre Victor had suggested to Sartre that he could be of more use to the revolution if he put aside his study of Flaubert to write a popular

---

Philippe Raynaud, *Terrorisme et démocratie* (Paris, 1985), 193. Jean Rolin, *L'Organisation* (Paris: Gallimard, 1996), 133. Jean-Pierre Barou, *Sartre, le temps des révoltes* (Paris, 2006), 144.

65   Gavi et al., *On a raison de se révolter*, 278 (October 1973).
66   Ibid., 244–6 (October 1973), 316 (November 1973).
67   "Pour un mouvement du 12 octobre, en quelque sorte," 23.
68   Jacques Rancière, *La Leçon d'Althusser* (Paris, 1974), 220.
69   Gavi et al., *On a raison de se révolter*, 325 (November 1973).

novel about a factory occupation.[70] Sartre declined, but Clavel took on this project in *Les Paroissiens de Palente* ("The Parishioners of Palente"). Clavel had seen the Holy Spirit at work in May 1968; his practice of what Jean Daniel referred to as "leftist Christianity" led him to the ex-GP in 1971.[71] Sent to Besançon by *Libération*, Clavel experienced "a revelation" on June 18, 1973 and spent "the happiest time of [his] life" with the workers of Lip:[72] "At Lip, the young OS became for me like spiritual masters."[73] After the sequestration of the provisional administrators and seizure of documents on June 12, *Le Monde* commented that "one could easily make of the Lip Affair a bad novel about industry, full of whisperings, dark places, guarded confidences," but Clavel's novel would be quite different than a "serial" of the sort Rocard told Piaget the Lip Affair was becoming in the summer of 1973.[74]

In *Les Paroissiens de Palente*, Clavel spoke of the conflict as "the epicenter of a mystical tremor," and he saw it as a means of spreading the word in ways that leftist discourse could not. Since Zola, he said, there had not been a novel about workers "that had a chance to convince the other world."[75] But Clavel wrote an anti-*Germinal*. It examines the spiritual rather than material economy of a working-class community. Speaking of the night of June 12, he said that "one of the constant themes of Vittot [Sébastien in the novel] was: 'The factory is made to prevent us from loving one another'—they saw that this time they loved one another. So they had won. It was a very great moment."[76] Fred Lip is Max Lieb in the novel and *Les Paroissiens de Palente* is about taking control of this love.

As Dominique Desanti recognized, *Les Paroissiens de Palente* does not partake of the socialist realism that Sartre saw Pierre Victor as suggesting he undertake: "There is no—Oh Happiness—'positive hero', paragon of revolutionary virtues, bearer of institutional truths."[77] Focusing on eight

---

70 Ibid., 72, 105–6 (December 1972).
71 *Le Nouvel observateur*, June 3, 1974, 69.
72 *Libération*, May 25–6, 1974, 2–3. It is not hard to see why his first articles in *Libération* won him the epithet of "the tearful stork." ADD 45J5 "Le soleil se lève aussi," tract d'un groupe marxiste bisontin, July 3, 1973.
73 *Le Point*, December 30, 1974.
74 *Le Monde*, June 15, 1973, 34. *La Croix*, June 15, 2003, 8. For a study of the novel, see Elisabeth Le Corre "*Les Paroissiens de Palente*: le 'c(h)oeur des militants'" in *Fiction et engagement politique. La représentation du parti et du militant dans le roman et le théâtre du XXe siècle*, ed. Jeanyves Guérin (Paris, 2008), 101–11.
75 Clavel, *Les Paroissiens*, 238.
76 Ibid., 55. *Libération*, May 25–6, 1974, 2 [quoted].
77 *Le Quotiden de Paris*, May 25, 1974, 11.

principal actors, Clavel rewrote their experiences in what he called "a true polyphonic novel," weaving the voices of major actors with whom he had spoken.[78] His interest was activists' psychology, what he saw as "a sort of dialectic between the individual and the collectivity" that journalists' questioning did not reveal.[79] If Carole and Paul Roussopoulos set out to let the marginalized speak, Clavel was interested in what he believed to be the unspoken of the central figures in the movement. At the heart of *Les Paroissiens de Palente* are Mathieu (Piaget), a figure who discovers "on the palms of his hands two red gashes"[80] and whose experiences echo those of Christ in the Garden of Gethsemane,[81] and Simon (Raguénès)—"Lucifer before the Fall" for Claude Mauriac[82]—whose competition with Mathieu for militants' souls is a recurrent theme.[83] The pragmatic national union leaders at the negotiations are the Pharisees. In the central event of the novel, Mathieu himself is tempted. In dealing with Bouthéon (Giraud), he defends workers' interests, not their mission, and when initially opposing the Action Committee position on October 12, he sees himself returning to what he had been before the conflict: "Thus, I saw rise and fall destiny, an exodus aborted. Moses was going to become again the union delegate of the Jews in Egypt and would defend his own until the end of his life ... over the production rates of bricks ..."[84] In Clavel's retelling of the story, the Christ figure Mathieu is rescued by the action of the masses.[85] As Raguénès wrote to Clavel at

---

78   Clavel, *Les Paroissiens*, 9. Marc Géhin appears as the " battered angel" Luc (ibid., 78). Luc is a worker selected for his intellectual qualities by Max Lieb to become a manager. He overcomes the seduction he felt for social advancement, and after seeing the life of good food and easy women, criticizes Lieb and asks to be returned to the shopfloor. For Jean Daniel, "One goes here from the virile fraternity of Malraux to a Christian sensuality at once communitarian and narcissistic, for all these men in struggle love themselves in Christ." *Le Nouvel observateur*, June 3, 1974, 69.

79   Maurice Clavel, interview with France Culture, July 5, 1974, at fabriquedesens. net.

80   Clavel, *Les Paroissiens*, 90.

81   *Libération*, May 25–6, 1974, 3.

82   *Le Figaro littéraire*, May 25, 1974, 13.

83   Clavel reports that at the time of the September 29 demonstration, Piaget said to the *Libération* reporter Jean-Pierre Barou "(truly like [Christ]: 'My father, my father, why have you abandoned me?') Where is Jean, where is Jean, why isn't he here, why doesn't he come?" *Libération*, May 25–6, 1974, 3.

84   Clavel, *Les Paroissiens*, 247.

85   Not surprisingly, Clavel closed *Les Paroissiens* with the events of October 12, 1973. A conflict that found "its happy outcome in the initiative of the providential wing of the owners can appear altered in its meaning, or lost." Clavel, *Les Paroissiens*, 410. All this was too much for Jacques Julliard, aligned with the CFDT and PSU leadership. He saw Clavel's attack on national unions seeking to thwart radical workers

Easter in 1976, "The revolt will have a metaphysical origin. We will write our last chapter together. Soon the Resurrection."[86]

The Communion Table

Reflection on Lip enabled Clavel to play an important role in the discovery by former Maoists "that the social was pregnant with the sacred."[87] Ex-GP were very struck by the role of faith in the conflict. Évelyne Cohen explained:

> For us, Lip represented the extreme of the impetus given by May '68. These were workers like those we had dreamed of, and they were believers. In contact with someone like Raguénès, who told us of his mystical experiences, we understood that we could go no further on the path of politics. And that the domain of engagement was also religious.[88]

That the worker to whom the ex-GP militants felt closest was the Dominican priest Raguènes is significant. Raguénès was an OS and founder of the Action Committee, not a skilled worker or union leader like Piaget or Vittot. It was his spiritual calling that led him to become a manual laborer in order to support himself and not the permanent interloper that the *établis* feared themselves to be. This led a number of ex-GP to see in Catholicism at Lip a gateway to the mystical experience of religion, rather than the site of practices acquired in the ACO that marked the leadership of the CFDT-Lip. Following the dissolution of the ex-GP,

---

as a recourse to the "platitudes of Trotskyist history." *Le Nouvel observateur*, June 17, 1974, 66.

86   *Libération*, May 3, 1976.

87   Pelletier, *La crise catholique*, 294–5.

88   *Le Monde*, May 2, 2008, 17. However, those who did not approve of the dissolution of the ex-GP attributed it to the deleterious influence of Lip: "our great charismatic leader" Pierre Victor had been "transfigured by the mystical revelation of 'Lip'" into Benny Lévy, they lamented. *La Cause du peuple* 1 (November 1974) [nouvelle série]: 2. Looking back decades later, the Maoist Jean-Claude Milner bewailed that "at Lip the doors will open, as before, according to the Gospel, a certain tomb. May, leftism, and the factory were finally united, in peace and in the concert of good wills ... We saw how the Gauche Prolétarienne had wielded this name [Revolution] every which way, going so far as to accept at Lip that the Revolution becomes a variant of the *agape*. But if the Revolution is indistinguishable from the *agape*, if History culminates in the spiritual, then it is not worth the effort." Jean-Claude Milner, *L'Arrogance du présent. Regards sur une décennie 1965–1975* (Paris, 2009), 137–8, 211.

Pierre Victor affirmed his Jewish identity as Benny Lévy. He squared the circle, unlike Fred Lipmann, who had taken the nom de guerre Fred Lip and never looked back.

Raguénès, drawing on his characterization of his relationship to Piaget, described Benny Lévy's relationship to Sartre after the dissolution of the ex-GP as that of the wise mad man and the mad wise man.[89] When Benny Lévy read Hélène Clastres' *La Terre sans mal* in 1975, his first thought was to compare her analysis of the relation of the leader to the prophet among the Tupi-Guarani of Brazil to that of Piaget and Raguénès. Leaders serve society, but the people, accompanied by the prophet, abandon everything to become a community on a journey of liberation to an edenic land of plenty in which the rules and rulers of a confining social order have no place. It was Raguénès who enabled Lévy to see that what took him to Lip was what would take him back to Judaism.[90]

Encounters with the community born of the struggle at Lip brought intellectuals to a new understanding of difference within society. Early in 1974, one-time Maoist André Glucksmann argued that Lip was emblematic of new struggles in which workers and elements of the middle class developed shared interests at the point of production and new forms of democracy in which these alliances could express themselves outside of workplace or union hierarchies.[91] Bernard-Henri Lévy saw the "ideological renewal" of 1968 in a transcendence of the Marxist concept of class and the liberal concept of the individual: in *Les Paroissiens de Palente*, "the plebe of Palente ... prefigures perhaps, and stammers out in any case, the new concept that it will be necessary to properly establish."[92] Benny Lévy recognized through Lip that social movements could build on the recognition of difference and not just the revelation of identity; it was the relation to the other that made Lip radical in a different way than the Maoism which had brought him to Besançon.

Many leftists, drawing on the second volume of Sartre's *La Critique de la raison dialectique*, thought of the Lip workers as a group-in-fusion, coalesced by an existential fear of the death of their factory and their community. Benny Lévy would bring together his two teachers, Sartre and Emmanuel Levinas, saying that Sartre did not understand that the

---

89   ADD 45J108 Lip Livre Part 1/Conversation 4, 12–13.

90   Benny Lévy, *Pouvoir et liberté* (Lagrasse, 2007), 26.

91   André Glucksmann, "Nous ne sommes pas tous prolétaires (fin)," *Les Temps modernes* 331 (March 1974): 1336.

92   *Le Quotiden de Paris*, May 25, 1974, 11.

Apocalypse of the group-in-fusion he imagined would give birth to "the fraternal man" speaking "insurrectional prose" only in dialogue with the other, when "the distant becomes my neighbor."[93] Lévy presents this as the narrative of the bourgeois who seek to come together with the oppressed only to be rejected at the Renault factory gates in 1968, before being granted entry at Palente in 1973—the factory as a "communion table," when the dialogue with the other takes place and the Apocalypse is realized.[94]

Piaget for President

The Common Program haunted the Lip Affair or, more to the point, the Lip Affair haunted the Common Program. The Common Program did not address the crisis in the French watch industry, but that had not stopped the Communists from making their first response to the Lip workers' decision to produce and sell watches that their struggle was a fight for the Common Program.[95] Socialists like Pierre Bérégovoy joined them, saying that the Common Program showed that "the Lip conflict has nicely prefigured the legality of tomorrow."[96] Georges Séguy, secretary-general of the CGT, had briefly attributed to the conflict a magical unifying power when, after the expulsion from Palente, he said some who supported *les Lip* were partisans of the Common Program and others of revolution, meaning the far left: "Indeed, the two are not incompatible."[97]

But this was not how many in the new left or Lip workers themselves saw things. In October 1973, *Libération* had observed that "Lip, by its thousand inventions (self-management, democracy, legitimate illegality, May '68 style contestation …) puts, one has to say, the Common Program at the level of theatre props."[98] For the ex-GP, Lip was the "gravedigger of the Common Program."[99] Lip militants questioned whether working

---

93   Jeannette Colombel refers to "the instant of the apocalypse" with the occupation of the factory, the sequestration of the bosses, the taking of the watches, and the "scandal" of the open doors of the factory after their closure in 1968. *Sartre ou le parti de vivre* (Paris, 1983), 241.

94   Pierre Victor in Raguénès et al., "Lip 1973–1976," 1242. Benny Lévy, "Apocalypse" (1979) in *La Cérémonie de la naissance* (Lagrasse, 2005), 53–4 n2.

95   *L'Humanité*, July 5, 1973, 5.

96   *L'Unité*, February 14, 1974.

97   *L'Express*, August 20, 1973, 11.

98   *Libération*, October 13, 1973, 8.

99   "Pour un mouvement du 12 octobre, en quelque sorte," 23.

through the state would ever unseat the bourgeoisie. For Demougeot, the Common Program was "an illusion given to people, the easiest way to possess us."[100] Radical change was possible only from the power and creativity of struggles from below. The traditional model of turning to local elected officials was no longer viable in the Fifth Republic. "We imagined," said Piaget, "that a mayor or a deputy had a bit of power. And we can see over the course of the conflict to what extent this is not true."[101] Noting that the Socialist mayor of Besançon, Jean Minjoz, distanced himself from the September 29 march in the face of opposition from the prefect and associations of parents of schoolchildren, Piaget added, "This sheds a little light on what the Common Program could be": whatever one thinks of its provisions, the Socialists would be too scared to enact them.[102]

> The Common Program? Chile is there, at this time, to remind us of the problems that poses ... It is not enough to gather together, in great numbers, to prevent a military coup d'état or economic attacks. You also need the most widely spread capacity for imagination, for reflection, in order not to be taken in. What we are doing at Lip is a small step up the stairway in this sense. Chile shuffles the deck of cards. And Lip too shuffles the cards.[103]

Piaget believed that whatever changes were taking place in the rejuvenated PS, "what always characterizes it is that the network of notables (councilors, mayors, parliamentarians) constitutes its true nervous system"; "the workers' sections, the engaged militants are only grafted on."[104] As for the Communists, he believed that after the war they had abandoned the seizure of power as impossible in favor of arriving at socialism by the gradual occupation of government positions, which the bourgeoisie could take back at any time.[105]

But who would go up the stairs with *les Lip*? The GOP/PLC was not alone in criticizing the limitation placed on the mini-commissions around the country to work solely as agents of the Lip General Assembly

---

100   Macciocchi, *De la France*, 434.
101   *Politique hebdo*, December 20, 1973, 17.
102   *Le Monde*, September 18, 1973, 40.
103   *Il Était une fois la révolution*, 139.
104   *Politique hebdo*, October 3, 1974, 21–2.
105   BDIC 578/41 "Piaget s'explique sur son projet de candidature," *L'Anti-brouillard* 7 (May 1974): 1, 3.

rather than becoming involved in building a broad-gauged movement.[106] The leadership of the CFDT-Lip, drawn from the PSU, understood this need. Piaget told the General Assembly in December 1973 that their struggle was one of many: "If we limit ourselves to the issue of employment, we will exclude this vast world. It would be suicide and proof of egoism on our part. We must interest ourselves in the totality of social problems: abortion, national education, the police ..."[107]

Fred Lip had been particularly upset during the conflict in December 1970, when workers thought he was hiding in his office and, with the firm in mind, gathered outside chanting "President Piaget."[108] This was not the last time the call would be heard. On April 3, 1974, the day after the death of the President of the Republic Georges Pompidou, Maoist Alain Geismar, Alain Krivine of the ex-Ligue Communiste (it too had been dissolved), and Isaac Johsua of Révolution! went to Besançon with the support of their organizations and competed in their efforts to convince Piaget to run for president as the "candidate of the struggles."[109] This, they believed, offered the possibility to realize the full potential of the Lip conflict by providing leadership to a large movement of groups pursuing goals for which 1968 served as shorthand. This was the closest that the left would come to the October 12 movement Pierre Victor had hoped would take the place of the ex-GP. A few days later, *Libération* launched an appeal to readers to mobilize in support of Piaget's candidacy: Piaget "will not be the candidate of [leftist] groups or of a party. He will be the spokesman of the France of those at the bottom. He will not speak for us; with him all of us will speak."[110] The paper endorsed Piaget as the candidate who could bring together the diversity of struggles: "the movement born of May '68 grew ... but it is now dispersed, atomized ... Each contestation, each struggle represents a fragment of a new socialist alternative, a small piece of a new socialist project formed by the people themselves."[111] For *Politique hebdo*, "The candidacy of Charles Piaget would have a profoundly subversive sense. It would be the irruption, in the midst of adulterated pairings of chiefs of staff and political apparatuses, of all that is foreign to them and of all who refuse to recognize

---

106 "Lip Larzac," 54.

107 *Libération*, December 9, 1973, 3.

108 AMB 5Z15 Fred Lip to the Comité d'Entreprise, December 9, 1970.

109 Alain Desjardin, *Une vie pour ... Ici et là-bas, solidaire* (Saint Jean des Mauvrets, 2008), 228–9.

110 Jean Guisnel, *Libération la biographie* (Paris, 1999), 61.

111 *Libération*, April 10, 1974, 1.

themselves in them."[112] A presidential campaign would not only give the radical left the appearance of a cohesion it otherwise lacked; leftists realized that it could also "favor a popular regrouping that largely exceeds it," ending their marginality.[113]

Some twenty departmental federations of Piaget's party, the PSU, announced their support for him. Sartre came out for Piaget as well, seeing in his candidacy a reason to put aside his 1968 manifesto, "Elections, traps for idiots," and vote. Piaget would not be elected, but his candidacy, Sartre believed, would give the new forces on the left a chance to develop their ideas before a wide audience. Equally important, "the old left would have to reveal itself by the attacks it will launch against Piaget. We define this old left as an old demonic thing because we present the new in the form of Piaget: a new left that has no chance to take power now but by its assertion will reveal the old." A vote for Piaget, he added, would be "indirectly a complete destruction of the system"; "I think that Piaget comes to destroy the Fifth Republic and it is for this that one must vote for him."[114] The prefect's concerns were more immediate. He saw the campaign for Piaget's candidacy reinforcing the Lip employees' belief that their movement was truly innovative, with national, even international ramifications.[115]

The discussion of a Piaget candidacy brought out conflicts inherent in the Lip Affair. It was the project of those who believed the new world would be built through social struggle, not the dialogue of Chaban-Delmas' "new society" or Common Program nationalizations. Piaget and other Lip leaders were members of the CFDT and PSU. Piaget had been a PSU candidate in the March 1973 legislative elections. For the leadership of the CFDT and the PSU, the determining event in 1973 had been the defeat of the left in this balloting, not the Lip Affair. Both tried to corral the Lip workers in the fall of 1973. Michel Rocard and leaders of the CFDT played important roles in negotiating a settlement to the conflict with representatives of state and capital a few months later. They did not see the future of the left in movements like Lip, but in working with and in the Common Program alliance of the Socialists and Communists.

---

112   *Politique hebdo*, April 11, 1974, 14.
113   Ibid., 15. The only radical left party that did not support the candidacy of Piaget was Lutte Ouvrière, whose candidate Arlette Laguiller came to prominence in the bank employees' strike in 1974. She asked if supporters of Piaget would not back her because bank employees had not financed their movement by printing checks. *Politique hebdo*, April 25, 1974, 13.
114   *Libération*, April 13–14, 1974, 4–5.
115   ADD 1026W1 PD, April 11, 1974.

Chérèque, head of the FGM-CFDT, called Piaget to condemn the idea of his candidacy.[116] CFDT secretary-general Maire made it known that "a rank-and-file union militant, no matter how prestigious, does not perforce have what it takes to become president of the Republic."[117] Piaget had other concerns. He recognized that the logic and success of the Lip movement had been based on the effacement of leaders and that his candidacy would challenge this.[118] Rocard in turn had no place for what he later referred to as the "good-natured prophetism of Charles Piaget."[119] When, in mid-April, with the support of the CFDT leadership, Rocard got the PSU to support the Socialist candidate François Mitterrand in the first round, Piaget decided not to run.[120] Later in 1974 many followed Rocard in abandoning the PSU for the PS, which had made a dramatic comeback since 1968 under Mitterrand's leadership. This left the diminished PSU as what the militant Yves Craipeau called "the party of Lip."[121] In October 1974, Piaget told PSU militants in Paris that what was needed was the establishment "of permanent horizontal connections" among workers engaged in struggles. Only these would allow the free exchange of insights and experiences lost in hierarchical organizations, which exercise "an extraordinary break on the free circulation of ideas!"[122] This became Piaget's project and that of the leadership of *les Lip*.

Libération

The Lip struggle was a turning point in the move from the 1968 narrative of revolution, with which the Centre d'Études des Entreprises had scared itself, to one of liberation. *Libération*, a paper initially produced by Maoists and directed by Sartre, first appeared in kiosks on May 22, 1973. The paper played a crucial role in building interest and support for the workers of Palente. They in turn appreciated the support given them by *Libération*. In September 1973, when *Paris Match* offered 5,000 francs for

116   AR Interview with Piaget by Rouaud, September 11, 2003, 59.

117   *Politique hebdo*, April 11, 1974, 15.

118   Catherine Chaillet and Pierre Laurent, *Besançon. Un temps d'avance* (Paris, 2007), 105.

119   *Le Monde*, March 21, 2007, 28.

120   Nicolas Dufaud, *La CFDT (1968–1995)* (Paris, 2009), 92.

121   *Politique hebdo*, October 10, 1974, 4.

122   Charles Piaget, "Que signifie aujourd'hui militer pour le socialisme, être révolutionnaire?" (presented at PSU meeting on October 24, 1974), reprinted in *Le PSU des idées pour un socialisme du XXIène siècle?* ed. Jacques Sauvageot (Rennes, 2012), 361–2.

a photo of the hidden watches—the "war treasure"—*les Lip* responded by giving it free to *Libération*.[123] In turn, the extensive coverage given to the Lip movement and the interest this created garnered the readership that opened the way to the paper's financial viability in the summer and early fall of 1973.[124]

From the paper's origins, there was a conflict between those like the *basiste* Hélène de Gunzburg, who saw it as a place where the working-class base could speak and be heard, and those who favored the creation of a non-sectarian leftist newspaper that met the standards of professional journalism. In conversations in July 1973, Sartre thought the paper should devote itself to interviews with workers at Lip and elsewhere; Pierre Victor wanted *Libération* to become a place where "communities in struggle" like Lip "would have the right to express themselves without being contested by the omnipotence of the central staff" of the paper. *Libération* editor (and former editor of *La Cause du peuple*) Serge July and reporter Philippe Gavi rejected this idea because they saw that such communities were sites of contradictions as well. Powers established themselves within counter-powers, deciding what could be said and not said; the role of *Libération* should be to contest such censorship.[125]

De Gunzburg was a Maoist who had worked as an *établi* and then for several years at the press agency that preceded *Libération*. She became the chief correspondent at Besançon. A rich heiress who contributed significant funding to the paper, de Gunzburg paid all the costs associated with maintaining a full-time presence of *Libération* at Besançon.[126] In mid-November 1973, she wrote an article based on Piton's contention that workers were rejecting Piaget out of disgust for his support of decisions like signing up with the ANPE.[127] However, others at *Libération* questioned Piton's assertion and the paper published a strong critique of de Gunzburg's article by a journalist from *Politique hebdo*.[128]

Debate about the orientation of the paper and the renewed specter of its bankruptcy marked the months following the vote of October 12.[129]

123   *Le Canard enchaîné*, September 12, 1973.
124   François-Marie Samuelson, *Il Était une fois Libération* (Paris, 1979), 191–2.
125   Gavi et al., *On a raison de se révolter*, 353–4 (November 1973–March 5, 1974).
126   Laurent Martin in conversation with Jean-Noël Jeanneney, November 25, 2006, on France Culture, at fabriquedesens.net. Guisnel, *Libération*, 60–1.
127   *Libération*, November 16, 1973, 6.
128   *Libération*, November 23, 1973, 2.
129   Chérèque, secretary-general of the FGM-CFDT, suggested that the Lip leadership secretly funneled funds from the watch sales to *Libération* to prevent it from going bankrupt. "Mutations industrielles. Entretien avec Jacques Chérèque," May 10, 2010 at del-ly.over.blog.com.

The concentration of *Les Cahiers de mai* on the Lip conflict left it disoriented when a resolution was reached in January 1974. Like July and his allies on *Libération*, they were strong partisans of the candidacy of Piaget: in *Les Cahiers de mai* militant Jean-Louis Péninou's words, "The day Piaget withdrew, he, as it were, killed *Les Cahiers*." It stopped publication in the spring of 1974. *Libération* hired several of its leading lights, with whom July had worked in left politics as a student in opposition to the Algerian War. Péninou, future director-general of *Libération*, explained that July sought the "spirit" of *Lip Unité* for his paper.[130] *Libération* in turn offered *Les Cahiers de mai* militants a political project to take the place of the Piaget candidacy.[131] July's new recruits succeeded *basistes* like de Gunzburg. The method of *Les Cahiers de mai* offered the possibility of a more sophisticated analysis than interviews with individual rank and file. Coverage of the Lip conflict, and then the incorporation of the media which had helped *les Lip* tell their story, played a crucial role in the development of *Libération*, one of the most long-lasting institutional legacies of the 1968 years.

From 1968 to 1981

Not all leftists who came to Palente were looking for the same things. If *Les Cahiers de mai* and Serge July at *Libération* saw in the left-wing unionism of Piaget and Vittot the new forms of democracy and power rooted in developments since 1968 that they sought, others, like the Quatre Millions de Jeunes Travailleurs and the *basistes* at *Libération* saw other legacies of 1968: a rejection of the culture of work and of the union-led collectivity. Both existed. Piaget was the face and voice of the movement, but a number of young Action Committee members were more attracted to the student culture of May 1968 they discovered in the conflict than to Piaget's union and workplace culture. As one explained:

> The leaders of the strike defended the factory, employment, work. The young defended life. The conflict, for them, was a little like a festival. We had much more desire to raise a glass than to speak of the problems posed by the trade unionist. That's the way it was the day the CRS invaded the factory, when we were fifteen charged with its defense, playing cards

---

130   Firmin, "*Les Cahiers de mai*. Entretiens," 158, 160.
131   Guisnel, *Libération*, 67–8.

and listening to records. We were in a state of mind of people who had already deserted the sites of production! It appears to me almost a symbol that that night we found ourselves, like that, in the restaurant [of Palente] celebrating until 4:30 in the morning. This also illustrates the anarchist tendencies that manifested themselves with regard to work.[132]

If the Lip conflict revealed the diversity among workers and of their representations among leftists, it was also a crucial event in the transformation of a number of leftists. "There is a little Lip in the head of more and more people," Gavi said in February 1974, and for no group was this more true than the Maoists, who, in the experience of Lip, thought through their own liberation from faith in a political elite guiding the masses.[133] New Philosopher André Glucksmann paired off Lip workers and Gulag prisoners as bearers of a message of radical democracy for which there was no place in the Marxism of either the Communists or the ex-GP: "Here and there, history is invented by the common workers of Lip, or by the anonymous ones who keep a clear head in the camps of those condemned to death."[134] Clavel looked to the story of Christ to recount the revelations of *les Lip*. A number of Maoists marked by Raguénès journeyed from Palente to prayer. The Lip Affair was a key event in the history of the Second Left as well. If the *basistes* of *Libération* were ousted in favor of the left unionism of *Les Cahiers de mai*, the implementation of this politics on a national scale in the form of a Piaget candidacy was thwarted by the decision of Rocard and CFDT leaders to pursue social change through the candidacy of Mitterrand. The Lip Affair was at once a bridge from the "thirty glorious years" of growth to the long period of recession and unemployment, and from the politics of 1968 to those of 1981.

---

132 "Le conflit Lip: lutter pour quel travail?," 120.
133 Gavi et al., *On a raison de se révolter*, 18–19 (February 26, 1974).
134 André Glucksmann, *La Cuisinière et le mangeur d'hommes* (Paris, 1975), 10–11, 218.

7

Sometimes a Great Notion

In the early 1970s, the split in French business was of a piece with that among Gaullists between Pierre Messmer's assertion of law and order and Jacques Chaban-Delmas' program for a "new society." CNPF leaders were happy to condemn *les Lip*, but none suggested what organized business could do to resolve the situation. Ambroise Roux, vice-president of the CNPF, believed that to put an end to things, Piaget should be arrested and charged with theft.[1] The metaphor of playing Pontius Pilate that critics had used earlier for the state's lack of response came to be directed at business.[2] The CNPF's inaction put it on the defensive, casting doubts on whether it was up to the challenges posed by 1968: "Three years of heavy public relations on the part of the CNPF were swept away by three weeks of Lip," in the words of the CFDT secretary-general Maire.[3] The UIMM referred to "a new religion: la Lipolâtrie" and asked when the yellow or green star would be mandatory for businessmen.[4] Another historical analogy occurred to *L'Express*: "In one word, the CNPF committed the error that was at the origin of all the colonial wars,"

1 *L'Express*, August 6, 1973, 11. Henri Weber, *Le parti des patrons: le CNPF (1946–1986)* (Paris, 1986), 268.

2 "Autour de LIP," *Bulletin d'association de cadres dirigeants de l'industrie pour le progrès social et économique* 287 (October 1973): 432.

3 Bernard Brizay, *Le Patronat: histoire, structure, stratégie du CNPF* (Paris, 1975), 210.

4 BDIC F delta rés 578/41 "L'Affaire Lip-la-Lune," supplement to *UIMM Actualités*, October 1973. See also BDIC F delta rés 578/40 Agence pour le développement de l'information économique, "Après le romantisme de l'été. La vérité sur l'affaire Lip" [1973].

putting the effects—watch production and sales—before analysis of the causes of the conflict at Lip.[5]

However, modernizers in big business with roots in Catholic social thought and some in opposition to the Algerian War—elements one also finds in Lip workers and their supporters—constituted their own oppositional movement within French business that went well beyond Fred Lip's calls for business to adopt an image of youth and found in the Lip Affair a way to forward their goals. They intervened not because they were partisans of worker self-management, but because they were supporters of Chaban-Delmas' "new society" program of seeking to strengthen labor confederations so that they could negotiate contracts that would assure production without disruption as well as predictable wage increases for the life of the contract. The modernizers sought confederations that acted like those the leftists feared already existed. They wanted a strong CFDT with which to negotiate, not one weakened by its inability to control its most famous local. (The CGT would not have openly cooperated with business and, in any case, did not have the CFDT's problem. CGT locals, including the one at Lip, were more obedient to their national leadership.) The creation of a successor firm to Lip was in turn a formative event in the history of the Second Left, as well as a revealing episode in the saga of left Gaullism.

Antoine Riboud

The Lip Affair revealed the importance of networks among France's elites, exemplified by that of Antoine Riboud, director of the glassmaking firm, Boussois-Souchon-Neuvesel (BSN). The Ribouds were an extraordinary family. Marc Riboud had fought in the Resistance and became a world-famous photographer on the left, best known for his shot of a teenage girl confronting troops with a flower at the October 1967 march on the Pentagon. Another brother, Jean, had been a resister held at Buchenwald for two years. He became the president-director general of the very successful oil prospecting firm, Schlumberger. Jean Riboud was close to François Mitterrand. He and his brother Antoine were among the few business leaders to support Mitterrand openly in the presidential campaign in 1974.

---

5   *L'Express*, September 3, 1973, 15.

Unlike most employers, Antoine Riboud appreciated the anti-authoritarian ethos of the students in May 1968. He became a good friend of Serge July at the time: "We had endless conversations about the events, the revolt of the students, the behavior then the strikes of the working class." Riboud took May 1968 as a call to action for business: "May '68 was, for me, the revelation that all the old system was going to be rejected and that this was decidedly going to transform work life. Without that, who would agree to work in our factories in the future? ... Things must no longer be done for people, but 'with' and 'by' them."[6] As part of his effort to develop a humane working environment, Riboud hired a McKinsey consultant to run a program at BSN that encouraged employees to identify problems and come up collectively with solutions. He integrated such efforts with profit-sharing and incentive plans tied to productivity gains.[7] While the CNPF remained hostile to unions, Riboud believed that dialogue with them was essential to the health and stability of the firm: "We cannot manage economically without accepting a counter-power that compels us to reflect, to negotiate and to communicate ... Without unions, we run the risk of having cyclical upheavals that will become uncontrollable."[8]

In 1969, Antoine Riboud came to national prominence when he attempted a public takeover of the larger and more traditional Saint-Gobain glassworks. This novel act of a new capitalism attracted media attention. *Le Figaro* published an article entitled, "The May '68 of Industry": "Imagine a young adventurer jostling a very dignified old lady in a Louis XV salon."[9] Riboud's move was shocking in a France still characterized by family capitalism because it "puts in question the dogma of employer heredity."[10] Though Riboud was ultimately thwarted, the effort won him a reputation as an ambitious, far-sighted entrepreneur.[11] He revealed dexterity in the consumer economy as well, moving his company from glass to what was bottled in glass, taking control of Évian and Kronenbourg, and merging with Danone to form a large food company in 1973. Among those impressed was Fred Lip, who characterized the stockholders of Saint-Gobain as the embodiment of "bourgeois and possessing France." Speaking of "directors of French enterprises,"

---

6   Antoine Riboud, *Le Dernier de la classe* (Paris, 1999), 71–3, 77, 198.

7   Ibid., 69. Pierre Labasse, *Antoine Riboud. Un patron dans la cité* (Paris, 2007), 30, 51–3.

8   Labasse, *Antoine Riboud*, 155.

9   Riboud, *Le Dernier de la classe*, 86.

10   Neuschwander, *Claude Neuschwander*, 256.

11   Labasse, *Antoine Riboud*, 17.

he said: "If there were only Ribouds, France would not be what it is ... In France, for fifty relatively important joint-stock firms, there are forty Vogüé, nine normal individuals, and there is one Riboud"[12]—referring disdainfully to Arnaude de Vogüé, the head of Saint-Gobain, for needing to turn to the public relations firm, Publicis, to save control of his firm from Riboud. In the summer of 1973, workers at Palente were saying that to save their jobs and their industry they needed "a Riboud."[13]

Marked by the Christian personalism of Emmanuel Mounier that he had imbibed at the École des cadres in Uriage during the war, Riboud was known as a Catholic "progressive" owner. When invited in 1970 to the national conference of the Centre français du patronat chrétien for their colloquium, "The Gospel and Industrial Society," he shocked the group by responding, "The Gospel must be rewritten."[14] Two years later, Riboud explained what this might look like when the CNPF asked him to speak at their annual meeting in Marseille. Drawing on personalism, he told the audience that just as directors did economic planning, they should undertake social planning as well. In addition to assuring profitability, management was responsible for countering employees' alienation in the workplace by providing opportunities to take initiative and responsibility. Himself known as "the Garaudy of the patronat,"[15] Riboud ended with soaring lines from his friend, Roger Garaudy: "The true alternative is an activist and creative faith for which the real is not only what is, but all the possibilities of a future that today appear impossible to those who do not have the power of hope."[16] Garaudy was a Catholic and long a leading Communist intellectual. He had been expelled from the party in 1970 for criticizing the Soviet-led invasion of Czechoslovakia. Riboud saw himself in a similar heretical position with respect to the CNPF.

It was Garaudy who provoked Riboud's interest in the Lip Affair over dinner in October 1973.[17] Garaudy saw it as embodying a challenge: the enterprise as a site of workers' rights that were not subordinate to "patrimonial" property rights and of a democracy in which workers participated in determining the goals of the firm and how to achieve them.[18] Listening to Garaudy talk about the Lip workers as the hope of

---

12   Gérard Adam, "Si vous étiez président du CNPF?...," *Dirigeant* 2 (May 1969): 18–19.

13   Hervé Jannic, "Lip victime de Lip," *L'Expansion* 65 (July-August 1973): 35.

14   Labasse, *Antoine Riboud*, 41.

15   Weber, *Le Parti des patrons*, 257.

16   Labasse, *Antoine Riboud*, 70.

17   Riboud, *Le Dernier de la classe*, 99.

18   *Le Monde diplomatique*, March 1974, 13.

socialism made Riboud think about other possibilities they offered. He was indignant that by doing nothing, the CNPF was only worsening public opinion of business: "I wanted business to manifest itself where it had ceased to exist. The scandal in effect lay in the fact that, for the first time, a union was proclaiming, against the view of the owner, that the enterprise was viable and should continue to exist."[19] Thinking of himself as a "consultant," he decided to act in line with the social responsibility of the boss he had outlined at Marseille the year before. Lip would vindicate his ideas about management and secure him the place he sought in French business. Piaget described Riboud's interest as "a demonstration of what he wants to do": a year or two of economic success with no problems with the unions at Lip would be a revelation of the superiority of his ideas that all businessmen would understand.[20] The very element—the reputation of the Lip workers—that discouraged other investors attracted Riboud. Furthermore, given the conflicts between the CFDT-Lip and the CFDT, he believed that the national confederation would be grateful and impressed as well.

Riboud viewed unions as social regulators, able to negotiate wage increases and maintain production for the length of the contract, without the state having to continue to play a dominant role. This was the position of the "modernizers" found in large firms. However, the majority of businesses were opposed to this constituent idea of Chaban-Delmas' "new society," which he had sought to implement as prime minister between 1969 and 1972. For Riboud, resolution of the Lip Affair was a means to show the superiority of his strategy to that of the CNPF. And, in turn, the Lip conflict convinced the CFDT leadership to move from the direct action it had championed since May 1968 to working with employers like Riboud. Riboud himself explained his interventions in the Lip Affair in terms of "the concern to preserve a responsible trade unionism and by sympathy for the national leaders of the CFDT, who found themselves overwhelmed by what was happening on the ground."[21]

Garaudy called Maire, who directed him to Chérèque, secretary-general of the federation to which the CFDT-Lip belonged. Chérèque had been tussling with the local since the spring. The next morning, he met Garaudy at the Gare du Nord in Paris. After their talk, Garaudy called Riboud from a phone booth, prompting Riboud to ask when Chérèque was coming to see him. They met that evening. Chérèque found Riboud

---

19   Riboud, *Le Dernier de la classe*, 100–1.
20   "Lip aujourd'hui," 15.
21   Riboud, *Le Dernier de la classe*, 100–1.

to be "one of the most extraordinary men I ever met."[22] Riboud spoke of "his unsuccessful assault on Saint-Gobain" and the importance of addressing the human dimension in the enterprise; these subjects took him to Lip.[23] He told Chérèque: "Give me proof that the enterprise is economically and socially viable. I adore your lascars, but just the same, you have to keep the lights on! If the deal makes sense, I'm ready to get personally involved."[24] Unlike Giraud's earlier attempt to resolve the conflict, Riboud placed emphasis on finding a firm industrial and financial basis for the company before attempting to reach agreement with the workforce. Many supporters had seen in Lip a new liberation in the workplace, but what interested Riboud was a new form of capitalism. This in turn appealed to important elements in the CFDT, which did not see a response to emerging economic problems in experiences rooted in the labor militancy of 1968.

As much as Riboud spoke of releasing the creativity of his own employees, he made extensive use of consulting firms to plan acquisitions. And he brought into his plans for Lip his friend Renaud Gillet, director of Rhône-Poulenc, a company reliant as well on consulting firms.[25] Consulting firms have an ambiguous position in market economies. They are careful not to share information learned from one client with another, but by establishing close relationships with different firms, they can provide a form of social networking otherwise absent from the market. If Garaudy had led Riboud to look into Lip, the Interfinexa consulting firm worked on a parallel track. Ébauches SA had turned to Interfinexa firm for a solution in the spring and this remained the basis for Charbonnel's plan in early August. With Giraud's failure, the president of Interfinexa took it upon himself to call on Riboud, with whom he had a long relationship, to talk about salvaging Lip. He then went to see Chérèque to talk about Riboud and Gillet's interest in Lip.[26]

The president of Interfinexa also joined Riboud and Gillet when they went to see the president of the CNPF, François Ceyrac. Ceyrac was a "modernizer," aware that he had been chosen to direct a conservative organization. He had played an important role in getting business to

22 Jacques Chérèque, *La Rage de faire* (Paris, 2007), 81–2.
23 *Le Nouvel observateur*, May 16, 2002.
24 Chérèque, *La Rage de faire*, 73–5.
25 See, for example, Riboud, *Le Dernier de la classe*, 58–9. For Rhône-Poulenc's dependence on McKinsey to make strategic decisions, see Christopher D. McKenna, *The World's Newest Profession: Management Consulting in the Twentieth Century* (Cambridge, 2006), 181.
26 *L'Usine nouvelle*, April 1974, 147. *Le Nouvel observateur*, February 4, 1974, 23.

negotiate with the confederations at Grenelle in 1968 (and took plea-sure later in recalling that Fred Lip reproached him for not giving more to wage-earners then). He strongly supported Chaban-Delmas' "new society" and would back Chaban-Delmas' bid for president of the Republic in 1974. Ceyrac was elected vice-president of the CNPF in 1968 and president in 1972. He could tell the press that the CNPF "has only really existed since May '68 ... We must be able to present a social alter-native," but was himself not in a position to do so.[27] Faced with broad support for *les Lip*, the CNPF held back.[28] In July, Ceyrac had criticized Lip workers as conservatives for not accepting change. The General Assembly responded with an open letter, asking him to visit them at Palente.[29] He did not take them up on their offer and told *L'Express* that "We are not a mutual aid society to help the sickly."[30]

However, what concerned Ceyrac was "the weakening of the authority of union organizations in the face of new situations" at Lip and else-where in the summer of 1973.[31] Rejection of the Giraud plan in October struck Ceyrac as having consequences for a system of labor relations predicated on the power of unions to maintain discipline in exchange for material benefits: "If what happened at Lip is not 'exceptional', if this becomes widespread, it can mean that the wage-earners are 'liberating' themselves from union control. I do not believe much in spontaneism, but this is serious. It would be for the unions a loss of authority."[32] In the fall of 1973, Ceyrac saw the situation in Besançon as damaging to the CFDT, and feared that this would strengthen the CGT. He was one of many who interpreted the situation at Lip, where Fred Lip and then the CFDT-Lip had operated out of the control of the national employers' organizations and the national union confederations, as evidence of the shared need to reassert authority.[33] After the October 12 vote, Chérèque appealed to Ceyrac to meet with him, saying "You are a big Catholic." Ceyrac said he could not meet the CFDT leader at the CNPF headquar-ters, so they met secretly at the Saint Philippe du Roule church in Paris. Ceyrac told Chérèque he agreed with his assessment of the debacle in

27   *Libération*, June 11, 1973.
28   Claude Durand and Pierre Dubois, *La Grève* (Paris, 1975), 234.
29   ADD 45J5 "Lettre ouverte des travailleurs de Lip à Monsieur Ceyrac, président du CNPF," July 16, 1973.
30   *L'Express*, August 6, 1973, 11.
31   de Virieu, *Lip*, 104.
32   "Les mises en garde de François Ceyrac," *Les Informations* 1488 (November 5, 1973): 29.
33   *L'Usine nouvelle*, April 1974, 153.

Besançon, but as head of the CNPF, he could not work with the CFDT to resolve it.[34]

José Bidegain

However, what Ceyrac could not do, Riboud and Gillet could. They met with Ceyrac later in October and won his support for a revamped version of the Interfinexa plan which, drawing on the Syndex research, required neither layoffs nor dismantling. Ceyrac reached out to his world of contacts, but in order not to compromise them in discussing the Lip Affair, he met them not in his office, but in a different church in Paris, Saint-Pierre de Chaillot.[35] He approved the choice of José Bidegain, the public face of progressive capitalism, as negotiator.[36] An immigrant from Argentina, Bidegain had served as an officer in the Algerian War in 1956–7. There he commanded some 300 soldiers who had fought, gone home for two weeks and then been sent back to Algeria. He told them, "I am against this war. We must return alive to oppose the politics of those who sent us to Algeria. But to return alive, we must be better organized and more disciplined than our adversaries."[37] When he completed his service, Bidegain denounced the army's use of torture in an article in *L'Express*. This was emblematic of a career Bidegain spent working in employers' organizations with which he disagreed in order to try to change their policies.

As a student, Bidegain had been a militant in the Catholic student organization, the Jeunesse Étudiante Chrétienne (JEC). He co-founded the Association Internationale des Résidents de la Cité Universitaire de Paris in cooperation with Catholic and Marxist activists. They led strikes to protest the quality and price of the food served in the student restaurants of the Cité Universitaire. Bidegain's future wife, Martine Michelland(-Bidegain), had also been active in the JEC and joined the PSU at its creation in 1960. Stricken with tuberculosis as a student, she learned about student health issues and assumed leadership of students in the sanatorium. When Michelland returned to the Institut d'Études Politiques in 1962, she was chosen as president of the Mutuelle Nationale

---

34   "Mutations industrielles. Entretien avec Jacques Chérèque," May 10, 2010, at del-ly.over.blog.com.
35   Gérard Leclerc, *Ils ont traversé le siècle* (Paris, 1994), 159.
36   Brizay, *Le Patronat*, 212.
37   *Libération*, November 7, 1973, 4.

des Étudiants de France (MNEF), whose 300 paid employees managed the social security system for students. Influenced by Félix Guattari, she established a network of psychological clinics for students. The following year, Michelland was elected vice-president of the national students' association, the Union National des Étudiants de France (UNEF). In this capacity, she worked with Michel Rocard on financing student education. Through his wife, Bidegain would establish relations with a number of UNEF veterans.[38]

Fresh from university, Bidegain oversaw the successful expansion of his family's children's shoe factory in Pau (Pyrénees-Atlantiques) from forty employees to 700. Production was handled by autonomous teams (fifteen teams of thirty to seventy workers in 1965) that negotiated production with management every six months; the team bought primary materials and sold finished goods to the firm.[39] The Centre des Jeunes Patrons (CJP), the association of young businessmen, elected Bidegain president, endowing it with an ideology of legitimacy derived from managerial competence rather than the possession of capital, which characterized the CNPF. He was the most important industrialist in the Club Jean Moulin, the paramount laboratory of republican thought in the early years of the Fifth Republic, with members ranging from the then Communist Garaudy to PSU leader Rocard to the banker François Bloch-Lainé. The historian Claire Andrieu writes of Bidegain: "A more complete panoply of the perfect entrepreneur, professional and citizen cannot be imagined."[40] Bidegain was also a member of the Groupe de recherche ouvrier et paysan (GROP), which brought together the Club Jean Moulin, the CFTC and other groups; the GROP was best known for its advocacy of measures to reduce income inequality.[41] He was an active member as well of the Comité national horizon 80, a group drawn from the circles that supported the Socialist Gaston Deferre's presidential ambitions in 1965.[42]

In 1962 Bidegain told the national meeting of the CJP that it was in

38 Interview with Martine Michelland-Bidegain by Jean-Philippe Legois and Camilo Argibay, September 11, 2008, at cme-u.fr. Pierre Rimbert, *Libération de Sartre à Rothschild* (Paris, 2005), 75–6, 93–6.

39 Pierre Bidegain, "'Les Équipes autonomes'" in *Réforme de l'entreprise* (Paris, 1965), 2: 125–30.

40 Claire Andrieu, *Pour l'amour de la République. Le Club Jean Moulin 1958–1970* (Paris, 2002), 207.

41 Hélène Hatzfeld, *Faire de la politique autrement. Les expériences inachevées des années 1970* (Rennes, 2005), 56.

42 Serge Berstein, *The Republic of de Gaulle*, trans. Peter Morris (Cambridge, 1993), 192.

the interests of business to support the youth in the CFTC who would go on to form the CFDT. The following year, the CJP came out in favor of legalizing union sections in the enterprise in order to establish the partners necessary for a dialogue of "constructive contestation."[43] Although the CNPF reviled this position, it admitted Bidegain to its directing committee in his role as CJP president. However, the CNPF's efforts to bring the "*enfant terrible* of the business world" into the fold failed.[44] Two years later, the CNPF removed Bidegain for asserting the longstanding CJP policy of dealing with unions along the lines of François Bloch-Lainé's modernizing manifesto, *Pour une réforme de l'entreprise*, that was anathema to the CNPF.[45]

In May 1968, Bidegain offered the radical student leader Marc Kravetz —a good friend of his wife and a future *Les Cahiers de mai* militant—a truck equipped with loud speakers that Kravetz used to spread the revolutionary message.[46] Bidegain was, in the words of Serge July, "a sort of modern Porthos, ready to face alone a multitude of assailants in order to allow one of his companions to advance more rapidly."[47] The CNPF, shocked by the events of May, invited Bidegain back in July 1968 and named him to the national bureau. However, this arrangement did not last long and Bidegain set out to contest CNPF hegemony. The next year, he launched the association Entreprise et Progrès, which attracted Riboud and Gillet as members. He articulated his understanding of labor/management relations that underlay the group:

> There is class struggle. I don't deny it. It is just that the confrontation must be organized. This is what constitutes one of the motors of society … Certainly, there is a contradictory element. But I think we can perfectly well, step by step, resolve the contradictory things, with temporary accords. Even if we reach the dictatorship of the proletariat, I do not believe we will eliminate the tensions between the directors and the directed. What Marxists call class struggle will remain. It is one of the factors of progress. If we were to get to a situation of perfect unanimity, we would be close to decadence and disappearance.[48]

43   Philippe Bernoux, *Les Nouveaux patrons* (Paris, 1974), 47, 70–3.
44   *Le Figaro*, January 28, 1974, 8.
45   Mette Zolner, *Young Business Leaders Between Utility and Utopia* (Brussels, 2009), 99–100.
46   Jacques Baynac, *Mai retrouvé* (Paris, 1978), 109.
47   *Libération*, October 7, 1999.
48   *Libération*, November 7, 1973, 4.

Charles Piaget speaking in Besançon, August 1973. Photo by Barnard Faille.

Children demonstrate in Besançon, June 1973.

Watch worker, 1974. Photo used with the tagline, "Nothing Is Done Well Without Passion" in a CEH advertisement (1974) and on the cover of *Lip au féminin* (Syros, 1977) with the response "Our Passion Is the Fight." Photo by Marc Riboud.

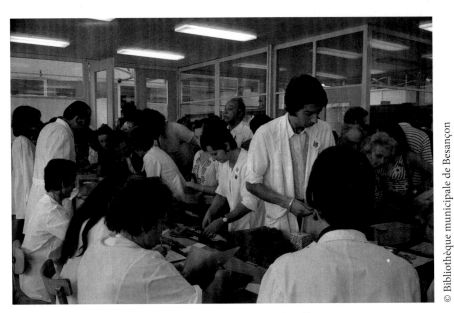

"It Is Possible. We Produce, We Sell, We Pay Ourselves." Sign on the Jean Zay School in Besancon, August 1973. Photo by Jean-Paul Margnac.

Watch sales at Palente, August 1973, photo by Bernard Faille.

The Pay Commission counts money on the eve of the first payroll, August 1973.
Photo by Patrick Meney.

Lip workers at a meeting, 1973. Photo by Henri Cartier-Bresson.

Claude Neuschwander, 1974. Photo by Marc Riboud.

Les Lip approve the Dole Accord, January 1974. Photo by Bernard Faille.

Workers put "Lip Will Live" stickers on a train in Besançon, June 1976. Photo Bernard Faille.

In August 1973, a shoe manufacturing plant in Romans operated by the German firm Salamander closed, leading to the layoff of 327 workers and the workers' occupation of the factory. As at Lip, a foreign firm was destroying French industry and jobs. A delegation of Lip workers went to talk with the Salamander employees, throwing the owners' organization in Romans into panic; it sent a message to members saying "the arrival of outside elements compels us to find a solution rapidly." The owners invited Bidegain, in his capacity as delegate-general of the national association of shoemakers, to resolve the situation.[49] "The Kissinger of footwear" drew on the federation's resources to create a new firm that switched from the manufacture of expensive, fashionable shoes to plastic footwear.[50] There would be no layoffs; workers would be paid to take job-training classes until they were called up to work. Workers would keep their job rank, for example OP2 or OS3, and their benefits, but Bidegain made no promises concerning salaries. He had visited Cuba recently and cited Fidel Castro to the workers: "You will earn what you produce!"[51] The CGT was the majority union in the plant and convinced workers to accept the deal.[52] On August 28, Séguy, secretary-general of the CGT, sent a letter to CGT-Lip members, published the next day in *L'Humanité*, telling them to ask for negotiations like those at Romans.[53] The settlement put pressure on the CNPF as well. The president of Entreprise et Progrès, Paul Appell, wrote Ceyrac to ask why the CNPF was largely absent in a media obsessed with the goings-on at Lip.[54] *Le Figaro* added that Bidegain "came to burnish the owners' blazon," but the CNPF seemed "disoriented" by events.[55] In his news conference on October 13, Maire, secretary-general of the CFDT, asked why there was no Bidegain for the Lip negotiations.[56]

Maire was not alone in asking this question. Ten days after Lip workers rejected Giraud's plan, Bidegain met with Riboud and Gillet for lunch to discuss the situation at Lip. Bidegain's original response, captured in a meeting of the executive council of the CNPF in early August, was orthodox. Labor should not impede the mobility of capital: "such a refusal of geographic and even sectorial mobility [of the Lip workers] would lead

49 *Libération*, December 17, 1974, 4.
50 *Politique hebdo*, June 6, 1974, 4.
51 de Virieu, *Lip*, 281.
52 *Libération*, October 19, 1973, 11. *Le Monde*, January 30, 1974, 31.
53 *L'Humanité*, August 29, 1973, 3.
54 Brizay, *Le Patronat*, 210.
55 *Le Figaro*, August 30, 1973.
56 AFGM-CFDT 1B574 Edmond Maire at press conference, October 13, 1973.

to economic impasses and would stop social progress."[57] However, Bidegain too came to see that the Lip Affair was not so much a question of market orthodoxy, but of the public's assessment of the imagination and creativity of business. When a conflict threatened the political and social order on which the economy depended, Bidegain believed that in the absence of effective state action, business should step in: "the 'firebrand Lip' must be settled quickly."[58] The opportunity for the modernizers to show the superiority of their ideas to those of the conservatives in the CNPF made resolving the situation at Lip what observers later referred to as "a prestige operation."[59] In November 1973, Bidegain became the first owner interviewed by *Libération*: "A boss who says yes to contestation" read the front-page headline.[60]

Bidegain, Gillet, and Riboud formed a group of ten experts which met two or three times a week, working in secrecy on a plan for Lip with the code name "pil."[61] Assured of Bidegain's support, Gillet negotiated with the banks and Riboud with Ébauches SA. They got several other firms to participate, including Jaz, Jaeger, and Thomson-CSF. Although investors wanted government approval before dealing with the unions, Chérèque, following his conversations with Riboud, did not want to wait. He sent Frédo Moutet, the leader in the federation who had gotten to know the Lip workers best and who embraced their cause, to Besançon to convince them to participate if the opportunity arose.[62] Although it would mean abandoning what Riboud called their "'westerns' style," Piaget and the CFDT-Lip leadership decided that this would not be a case of collaborating with business, but a question of exploiting the conflict between modernists and traditionalists within it.[63] What was going on was hidden from workers' view: "the state and the employers abruptly drew the curtains on the rigged theatre of negotiations."[64] However, behind that

57   FTM-CGT, "La CGT et Lip," 29.

58   Patrick Rozenblatt, Francine Tabaton, and Michèle Tallard, "Analyse du conflit Lip et de ses répercussions sur les pratiques ouvrières et les stratégies syndicales." Thèse de 3ème cycle, Paris IX, 1980, 50.

59   Bernard Boucon, André Larceneux, and Georges Magnin, "État, crise, restructuration sectorielle: Un exemple, l'industrie horlogère" in *Sur l'État*, ed. Association pour la critique des sciences économiques et sociales (Brussels, 1977), 316.

60   *Libération*, November 7, 1973, 1.

61   *Paris Match*, February 7, 1974, 33.

62   AMB 5Z221 CFDT [Paris], "La situation chez Lip," November 21, 1973. Chérèque, *La Rage de faire*, 73–5. Piton, *C'est possible!*, 489.

63   *Le Nouvel observateur*, February 4, 1974, 23. *Témoignage chrétien*, February 7, 1974, 5. Riboud, *Le Dernier de la classe*, 101–2.

64   *Lip Unité dépêche quotidienne*, November 15, 1973.

screen were "all those who would be disposed to bring an industrial solution corresponding to our interests." If workers could prevent the breakup of Lip into separate entities—and, in particular, the creation of a separate armaments firm, whose profits were necessary to fund the revival of watchmaking—they believed that competent businessmen, not types like Giraud, would come through.[65] The *Lip Unité* daily bulletin told readers that most workers thought they were in "the final phase of our struggle"; in the General Assembly, some spoke of the "'last quarter of an hour.'" "The great majority among us thought success will go to whoever holds out five minutes longer than the other."[66]

Michel Rocard

If business modernizers and the CFDT saw resolution of the Lip Affair as a way of showing that they were prepared to deal with the unexpected in the post-1968 world, Rocard saw it as a means of making the PSU relevant following its disappointing showing in the March 1973 legislative elections. For Rocard, Lip was, in the words of his biographer, "the Holy Grail" of the "osmosis" between political and social activism.[67] He had come out of the Christian left and been an ardent opponent of the Algerian War and a founding member of the PSU born of this opposition. The PSU was the electoral party most associated with the new left and currents of May 1968 thought. Although the CFDT-Lip leaders were PSU militants, Rocard had different plans for the PSU than they espoused. To be more than a laboratory of radical ideas, the PSU needed a place in the government in order to implement them. An *inspecteur des finances*, Rocard was by profession an elite technocrat, and he believed that for the left to be an alternative and not simply the voice of opposition, it had to prove its mastery of the economy. The PSU had spoken of the nationalization of Lip under worker control, but Rocard came to seek a solution elsewhere.

Rocard framed Lip as a matter of rectifying the effects of poor management, not of dealing with laid-off workers. He argued that Giraud realized that the final plan he had offered was not economically feasible

---

65 *Lip Unité dépêche quotidienne*, November 16, 1973. Charbonnel and the CGT-Lip supported creation of an independent armaments firm. AMB 5Z221 CFDT [Paris], 'La situation chez Lip," November 21, 1973. *Tribune socialiste*, November 28, 1973, 5.

66 *Lip Unité dépêche quotidienne*, November 16, 1973.

67 Jean-Louis Andreani, *Le Mystère Rocard* (Paris, 1993), 470.

and wanted to withdraw it, or, better yet, have the workers do this for him; workers rejected Giraud's plan because the firm it produced was doomed in the marketplace. *Les Lip* were fighting for the "economic revival of a viable enterprise." The demand to rehire all Lip employees was secondary to this goal; these workers were necessary to operate a successful business.[68] Settlement of the Lip conflict could secure Rocard a reputation as a responsible and effective leader, necessary for the positions espoused by the PSU to find a place in mainstream French politics.[69] As was the case for Riboud, the very difficulties that the Lip Affair presented to the establishment made it an opportunity for those on the outside to secure their credentials with the establishment.

Rocard worked closely with the capitalist "modernizers." He knew Bidegain well from their time together in the Club Jean Moulin,[70] and developed a strong affection for Antoine Riboud, who, he said, "did not tolerate workers being punished on the pretext that they lacked a suitable boss."[71] He believed that Bidegain's resolution of the Salamander conflict was an event that "opens new perspectives on the evolution of French capitalism. The state … lets the transformation of economic structures take place in the framework of an employers' solidarity fixing the blunders" which accompany national economic expansion.[72] In November 1973, Rocard explained to the national council of the PSU his support for the efforts of the capitalists engaged in resurrecting Lip, arguing that they sought good relations with unions rather than archaic confrontations.[73]

Jean Charbonnel

If Rocard wanted to develop the place of an alternative on the left through his involvement in the Lip Affair after October 12, the Minister of Industry Charbonnel tried to do the same for Gaullism. Prime Minister Messmer was one face of the state's attitude to Lip with his repetition at each major turning point in the affair that "Lip, it's over." François Mitterrand deemed the phrase to be Messmer's "cock-a-doodle-doo,"

---

68   *Réforme*, March 2, 1974, 11.

69   Neuschwander, *Claude Neuschwander*, 139.

70   Pierre-Emmanuel Guigo, *'Le Chantre de l'opinion'. La communication de Michel Rocard de 1974 à 1981* (Bry-sur-Marne, 2013), 59.

71   *Le Monde*, March 21, 2007, 28.

72   Rocard in Piaget, *Lip. Charles Piaget et les Lip racontent*, 198–9.

73   Jean-Claude Poulain, "Se débarrasser des idées d'un autre âge," *Économie et politique* 256 (November 1975): 27n1. *Tribune socialiste*, January 30, 1974, 2.

spoken in hatred out of weakness: "He is so pleased with it that given the slightest opportunity he would sing it."[74] However, Charbonnel was the minister most closely involved in the Lip conflict. It was Charbonnel, not Messmer, whom Piton invited to visit and see what was really going on at Lip in the summer of 1973.[75] Messmer stood for the Gaullism of order: the state could provide assistance for laid-off workers looking for work and clear workers out of Palente, but that was it. Charbonnel saw a place for the state in addressing social issues and promoting industrial development. His left Gaullism had roots in Catholicism: "The politician who is Christian should not be satisfied with too simplistic a division between the domains of Heaven and Earth," Charbonnel had said in 1972.[76]

In the summer of 1973, Charbonnel resurrected the Gaullist mantra of participation, suggesting it take the form of a cooperative—a solution the Lip workers rejected as simply a way to make them take on problems created by bad management in the past with no resources to deal with them.[77] Faced with the hostility of business, Piaget had no doubt what the fate of such venture would be: "We see what happened in Chile, what economic strangulation there was."[78] In any case, after the expulsion from Palente, Charbonnel changed his tune, saying the situation was so difficult that "it would do a disservice to the idea of participation to compromise it in this affair."[79] He put his faith in Giraud, saying that the problem he confronted was a "sentimental" one; breaking apart the workers' community felt to them like an "injury," but "these moral injuries ... do not prevent life"; once the workers' material situation was addressed "one way or another," they would get over it.[80]

Deeply disappointed by Giraud's failure, Charbonnel elaborated on its consequences and causes in a speech to the Centre français du patronat chrétien in late October 1973. The market had shown that the employment of all Lip workers was impossible. Without the mobility of labor that Lip workers rejected, the French economy was doomed. What was the source of the "persistence of conservative reflexes in the working class," of this "preindustrial mentality," of a penchant for a "France, Rousseauistic and romantic"? A fervent Catholic himself, Charbonnel saw in Lip "the manifestation of a 'clericalism of the left.'" The most important

---

74   François Mitterrand, *La Paille et le grain* (Paris, 1975), 244–5.
75   Carole Roussopoulos, *Monique.*
76   *L'Express*, August 20, 1973, 14.
77   *Le Monde*, August 21, 1973, 21.
78   *Le Monde*, September 18, 1973, 40.
79   *Le Monde*, August 17, 1973, 6.
80   *Le Monde*, August 24, 1973, 15.

element of "the Lip spirit" was "the religious spirit, the desire to make Lip a kind of parish with a daily great mass, a permanent officiating priest, a missionary spirit, a pretension to infallibility and even some intolerance." That said, Charbonnel believed that the shared Catholicism of many workers, employers and agents of the state created "among them a sort of complicity." He concluded that in the face of managerial incompetence— the convenient reference to Fred Lip—the state had to constitute "an urgent intervention fund" and business had to create "a veritable 'club of rescuers', ready to act rapidly and efficaciously" in situations like that at Lip.[81]

After the workers' rejection of Giraud's proposal, Messmer crowed once again that Lip was finished. In Mitterrand's words, "This Cato has found his Carthage. *Delenda est.*"[82] But the situation was more complicated. To calm elements on the right in his majority, Messmer forbade Charbonnel from meeting representatives of the national unions about Lip. However, at the same time, Messmer privately asked Charbonnel to do anything he could to resolve the Lip Affair, fearful that *les Lip* and their supporters would disrupt the national conference of the Gaullist UDR in November.[83] Charbonnel took the opportunity to speak with potential rescuers. After all, the man he had chosen as the alternate for his seat as deputy from the Corrèze, and who took the position when Charbonnel became minister, was Charles Ceyrac, brother of the president of the CNPF.[84] On November 9, François Ceyrac arranged for Riboud and Gillet to meet Charbonnel. The minister proved receptive and meetings followed between the president of Interfinexa and the ministry staff to discuss technical details.[85]

However, the opponents of state intervention held their ground, critical of the extensive borrowing which the Interfinexa plan, like that of Giraud, would require. The Minister for the Economy and Finance, Valéry Giscard d'Estaing, saw modernity in terms of market orthodoxy. Of Lip workers he said: "They must be punished. They must be and remain unemployed. They are going to infect the whole social body."[86] He feared the precedent a resurrection of Lip could create. He told

---

81   *La Croix*, October 27, 1973, 5.

82   Mitterrand, *La Paille et le grain*, 245–6.

83   Jean Charbonnel, *Pour l'honneur du gaullisme. Contre-enquête sur un héritage* (Paris, 2011), 289–90. Jean Charbonnel, *Dictionnaire raisonné d'un gaulliste rebelle* (Chaintreaux, 2014), 146.

84   Collombat, "Lip, 1973," 222.

85   AMB 5Z223 François Ceyrac to Jean Minjoz, November 29, 1973.

86   Charbonnel in Rouaud, *Les Lip. L'imagination au pouvoir.*

Charbonnel at one point, "Lip must be killed!"[87] A man with his own ambitions, Giscard d'Estaing feared an accord between the Gaullists favorable to Chaban-Delmas, like Charbonnel, and the modernist elements of business. He met Riboud and Bidegain to try to persuade them not to intervene in Lip.[88] Ceyrac presented the new Interfinexa plan to President Pompidou, but could not win government support. The state bank, the Société Générale, blocked the project by refusing to provide funding. For, as Messmer was quick to point out, the businessmen getting involved were doing so as individuals, not company directors, and therefore bringing only "symbolic capital."[89] In late November, when Rocard defended working with Riboud to the national council of the PSU, he criticized Charbonnel for not pushing hard enough to get the Société Générale to participate in the project, while calling on party members to close their bank accounts there, as a form of consumer-based activism. Charbonnel, Rocard added, feared that if an industrial solution could be found, "it would show that [Charbonnel] was not competent" since he had not been able to come up with one.[90] These words may have satisfied party militants, but Charbonnel would go on to play an important role in the fruition of Riboud's project.

Claude Neuschwander

After the meeting with Charbonnel in November, Rocard and Riboud had asked Bidegain to approach Claude Neuschwander about directing the new firm. When Neuschwander hesitated, Rocard called him to his apartment on a Sunday morning and won his acceptance with a promise of full support and financing for the project.[91] Bidegain, Rocard and Riboud knew Neuschwander from a variety of experiences. Neuschwander was an ardent Catholic progressive whose formative experience had been as a militant in the JEC. While at the École Centrale des Arts et Manufactures, he had been a leader of the Catholic students who worked with the Socialist students to take control of the UNEF from conservatives in 1956. Neuschwander served as vice-president of

87 *La Croix*, October 23, 2003.

88 Faucoup, "Que sont devenus les Lip?," 20: 24. Jean Charbonnel, *L'Aventure de la fidelité* (Paris, 1976), 240–1.

89 AMB 86W135 "Interview de M. Pierre Messmer" on ORTF Franche-Comté, November 26, 1973.

90 *Tribune socialiste*, November 28, 1973, 5.

91 Neuschwander, *Claude Neuschwander*, 139–41.

the UNEF for eighteen months. There he dealt with the press at a time
the UNEF was taking a leading role in opposition to the Algerian War.
He pursued his opposition to the war, and to statist technocracy, in the
Club Jean Moulin. Neuschwander served on the directing committee of
the Club and launched and ran its book series published by Seuil. He
was also a member of a group within the Club that guarded the presses
of *Le Monde* and the residences of individuals threatened by the French
Algeria terrorist group, the OAS.[92] Neuschwander was an administrator
of the CFDT Fédération des cadres from 1962 to 1970 and a member
of the PSU from 1967 to 1973. He also joined Bidegain's "Entreprise et
Progrès." In fact, it was Neuschwander who had introduced Bidegain to
his future wife, Martine Michelland; she in turn had introduced Neuschwander to Riboud.[93]

The increased power of the state in the Fifth Republic prompted the
creation of the Association pour la démocratie et l'éducation locale et
sociale (ADELS), dedicated to aiding citizens and elected officials in
communes to develop the democratic practices and organizations that
would allow them to run their communities and escape the prefects'
tight control, to "decolonize the provinces" in the words of Rocard, one
of its first presidents. UNEF leaders founded the ADELS. Neuschwander
served as president of the ADELS for several years in the late 1960s.[94]
He and his family lived in the pioneering *grand ensemble* housing
development of Sarcelles in suburban Paris, a social experiment built
to address the housing shortage in postwar France. Neuschwander was
active in the large PSU section there. He was elected president of the
residents' council established through an accord in 1965 with François
Bloch-Lainé, director of the state bank that financed the development.
Neuschwander knew Bloch-Lainé through the Club Jean Moulin and the
GROP. Bloch-Lainé wanted to put into practice in the *grands ensembles*
the participation in governance he also favored in industry. As president of the council, Neuschwander developed what he termed "a form
of self-management" by which residents themselves worked to challenge
financial and technocratic constraints on their community, which, he
believed, had previously been managed without consideration for their
needs and desires.[95]

92   Claude Neuschwander, *La Gauche, sans le PS?* (Paris, 2014), 86.
93   AR Interview with Neuschwander by Rouaud, June 18, 2005, 7. *Libération*,
May 3, 2007.
94   Claude Neuschwander and Jean Cottave, *La Démocratie durable* (La Tour d'Ai-
gues, 2005), 107. Neuschwander, *Claude Neuschwander*, 78–85.
95   Hatzfeld, *Faire de la politique autrement*, 73, 193–4. Neuschwander, *Claude*

Schooled in dealing with the media through his political activities, Neuschwander was hired by the advertising and public relations firm Publicis in 1962. His first account was Lip and he managed it for the next six years. Neuschwander remained politically active while working at Publicis. As vice-president of the Fédération des cadres of the CFDT, he participated in the occupation of the offices of the CNPF in May 1968. The business leaders had no choice but to listen to the cadres tell them that "it is time to think of defending the enterprise, and no longer the interests of the owners," while they waited for the CRS to arrive and clear out the intruders.[96] A frustrated CNPF could not then get the head of Publicis, Marcel Bleustein-Blanchet, to fire Neuschwander: "Claude," he told him, "half of my family was exterminated by the effects of racism in the Nazi camps; my firm will in no way tolerate this sort of racism, of a political character. Continue to think what you want, and, above all, continue to do your work."[97] Neuschwander went on to his greatest success. In 1969, when Saint-Gobain became the target of a public takeover by Riboud's BSN, the company hired Publicis to defend itself. Neuschwander thwarted the BSN by mobilizing the small stockholders of Saint-Gobain in what he and critics referred to as a May 1968 style action. He held very successful "open houses," characterized by some as modern day "estates-general," in which stockholders spoke freely, addressing problems and demanding information.[98] This led to Neuschwander being made secretary-general at Publicis, the second in command, and given responsibility for organizing and directing a network of twenty-three agencies in thirteen European countries.

Neuschwander was a pioneer in rethinking the role of the media in politics in light of the new political culture and new technologies of a mass consumer society. In 1963–4, he played an important role in M. X for president, an innovative campaign for Gaston Defferre which, at the time of the first direct election in France of a president by popular suffrage in more than a century, succeeded in creating a great deal of media interest in the identity of a candidate whose positions, but not name,

---

Neuschwander, 108–22. Claude Neuschwander, "Postface" to Michel Charzat, *Politiquement libre* (Paris, 1999), 211. Claude Neuschwanter, "Patron malgré lui ...," *Semaine sociale Lamy* supplement to no. 1631 (May 19, 2014): 19.

96   Claude Neuschwander, *Patron, mais ...* (Paris, 1975), 72.

97   "Claude Neuschwander" in *Soyons réalistes, demandons l'impossible*, ed. Philippe Godard (Paris, 2008), 81.

98   Neuschwander, *Claude Neuschwander*, 127. David Servenay, "Maurice Lévy, l'oracle du monde des affaires" in *Histoire secrète du patronat de 1945 à nos jours*, ed. Benoît Collombat and David Servenay (Paris, 2009), 556. Henri Hartung, *Les Princes du management. Le patronat français devant ses responsabilités* (Paris, 1970), 82.

were given. Many of the leading figures in the M. X campaign, including Neuschwander and the future Martine Michelland-Bidegain, went on to work with Rocard. Neuschwander applied his talents in political marketing when Rocard ran for deputy in the Yvelines in 1967. Two years later, when Rocard ran for president, Neuschwander used the Publicis recording studios to provide Rocard with training for interviews and televised debates.[99]

From the Dole to Dole

Neuschwander was left in limbo with the rejection of the Interfinexa plan in November 1973, but Riboud did not give up. He turned to the McKinsey consulting firm, with whom he had had a long relationship. McKinsey agreed to develop a much more detailed plan for Lip—and would do it without charge. In mid-December, Riboud got the industrialist to whom the syndic in charge of liquidation of the bankrupt Lip firm had agreed to sell the armaments factory—"this shark without a brain" in the workers' view, if operated independently—to hold off moving machines out of Palente.[100] Riboud also saw Charbonnel and convinced him to ask Neuschwander to work with the McKinsey consultants. As had Syndex, Neuschwander and McKinsey saw the economic success of Lip as dependent on keeping its various elements together. Neuschwander won Charbonnel's support for the increased watch production and diversification of mechanical production of the McKinsey plan. Lip's place would be taken by the Société Européenne d'Horlogerie et d'Équipement Mécanique (SEHEM), a holding company. It would oversee the Compagnie Européenne d'Horlogerie (CEH), which would acquire Palente and the Lip trademark for three years, and Spemelip, which would handle watch parts, armaments, and precision mechanics.[101]

However, having got through the UDR meeting without disruption in November, Messmer expressed disbelief that Charbonnel was aiding and abetting what he referred to in December as "bosses with fantasies."

99   Guigo, 'Le Chantre de l'opinion', 33, 39, 41–2.
100   Politique hebdo, December 5, 1973, 7.
101   The SEHEM met requirements set by France—that the French partners have a majority interest; by Switzerland—that the armaments business be separate from watchmaking; and by French business leaders—that their investment not exceed 5 million francs (of the total of 57 million francs, primarily from long-term bank loans, the French state and ASUAG/Ébauches SA). ADD 1812W28 "Mémorandum justificatif des actionnaires de la SEHEM (14 avril 1976)," attached to RG, April 27, 1976.

He felt that Charbonnel had made, "without speaking to him of it, a last attempt at salvage, against all good sense."[102] In early January 1974 Messmer reminded the world on television that "Lip it's over," and did all he could to ensure that was the case. Ironically this led him to say that maintaining something of Lip did in fact serve the national interest. He stipulated that negotiations could not continue if armaments production had not begun by January 14, 1974. The new manufacturer was ready to start up operation in a building provided by the municipality, but the 120 armaments workers had thus far refused to work without the approval of the General Assembly. However, the General Assembly called Messmer's bluff and voted on January 10 to allow thirty of them to take up work. That did not stop several hundred workers from leaving the General Assembly that day to demonstrate at the building the city had bought to house the armaments factory. Once there, the Action Committee spurred a group of workers to take the building apart, removing and sequestering the doors, windows and a portion of the roof tiles. They made their getaway before the arrival of ten buses of CRS. Piaget then convinced the General Assembly to reject Action Committee plans to prevent the movement of machines from Palente to the new factory, thus allowing armaments production to begin.[103]

Through all of this, Riboud and Neuschwander stood firm, "remaining without moving from [their] positions, Vietnamese style."[104] To Messmer's disappointment, Riboud, Gillet and Charbonnel got the funding needed from French and Swiss banks, ASUAG, and French firms, and from the French state the funds to train workers for the new firm (less expensive, Riboud argued, than having the state pay to create 1,000 jobs in Besançon without a company willing to offer them).[105] The reputations of Riboud and Gillet were more important than their financial contribution: their companies invested only a fraction of the 57 million francs the project required.[106]

Nine hundred participants in a General Assembly in the Lux cinema on January 14 listened to Charbonnel talk with representatives of the confederations in Paris via radio transmission. The confederations could see the light at the end of the tunnel and sent representatives to Besançon

---

102 Pierre Messmer, *Après tant de batailles* (Paris, 1992), 372.

103 BDIC F delta rés 702/1/1 *Lip Unité dépêche quotidienne*, December 14, 1973; January 7, 1974; January 8, 1974; January 11, 1974. *Politique Hebdo*, January 17, 1974, 4. *Les Cahiers de mai hebdo*, January 21, 1974.

104 Neuschwander, *Patron, mais ...*, 33.

105 *L'Usine nouvelle*, April 1974, 147.

106 ADD 45J111 CE of CEH, "Analyse de l'activité de l'entreprise 1974," 41.

to guide discussions. The prefect credited the "personal intervention" of Chérèque with tempering the ardor of the CFDT-Lip leaders and winning their support.[107] The prefect in turn saw the local union maintaining a "conciliatory attitude" on armaments production and other issues so as not to scare off investors.[108] This did not stop them from expressing the desire that Piaget and Vittot not work in the new firm. The PSU and the CFDT offered them positions in their national offices, but they turned these down and stayed at Lip.[109] Anticipating a resolution of the Affair, the General Assembly voted to send letters to the 186 employees who had left Lip and taken jobs elsewhere over the course of the ten-month conflict. They explained that once those who remained had been hired, there was a possibility that those who had left could come back to work in the new firm. In any case, the General Assembly made it clear that the community wanted to maintain contact. It invited former Lip employees to come to the General Assembly and offered to send issues of *Lip Unité* to any who wanted to keep up with events at Palente.[110]

Saying that he was committed to assuring that *les Lip* were not "shot like rabbits," Bidegain went to Dole at the end of January to negotiate an agreement with workers for the newly created firm.[111] Unlike Giraud, he played the role of negotiator, not future boss. Negotiations were non-stop and Bidegain's style differed as well. "Throughout the negotiations at Dole," the Lip delegation told workers with appropriate expressions of wariness, Bidegain "employed, contrary to Giraud, current language, borrowing colloquial expressions from workers, easily speaking famil-iarly to counterparts during breaks in the work sessions."[112] Raguénès noted as well in a discussion with ex-GP the next month that Bidegain had a culture in common with the Catholic workers in the negotiations at Dole: "Twelve times Bidegain cited passages from the Gospel during the negotiations!—and perhaps too the goals overlapped: we see that the role of Christian ideology transforms the 'traditional' relations of workers to owners, without clarifying them, quite the contrary."[113] This may be, but the talks led to an accord.

Although this settlement was the product of business, union and polit-ical elites, not of the forms of engagement and direct action for which

107   ADD 1026W1 PD, January 16, 1974.
108   ADD 1026W1 PD, January 18, 1974.
109   AR Interview with Piaget by Rouaud, December 2, 2003, 10.
110   *Lip Unité dépêche quotidienne*, January 23, 1974.
111   *Libération*, April 7, 1976, 9.
112   *Il Était une fois la révolution*, 23–4.
113   BDIC F delta rés 576/3/4 "Politique dans la classe ouvrière" (February 1974).

Lip workers had become known, the efforts to keep workers informed of what was going on in the talks differentiated it from the standard closed-door labor negotiations. Unions at Lip, the national confederations, and, with Bidegain's consent, Action Committee members, represented workers.[114] More than 100 workers made the trip from Besançon to Dole and every hour a member of the workers' delegation came out to report on the meeting. These reports were recorded on cassettes and played at a union hall in Dole for those who had come from Besançon. There, "a second delegation working on the texts, assessed, measured, indicated, suggested as needed." Updates were telephoned to Besançon, recorded and played over loudspeakers for workers in the Maison pour Tous. Each evening, some fifty members of the CFDT-Lip met in Besançon to talk about the day's developments; the General Assembly in turn discussed these the next morning.[115]

The unions signed the accords on January 29, 1974 and the General Assembly approved them 650 to three, with sixteen abstentions from Action Committee members who, in Piton's words, felt "dispossessed of our struggle" by the way it had been resolved.[116] The day before, workers had paid themselves for the last time. Because workers had not received severance pay, the settlement had the pay they had given themselves take its place. Between two and four in the morning of January 30, workers brought to a municipal garage in Besançon all they had taken, including some 15,000 watches, several tons of documents and commercial records, machine parts removed to disable machines, and computer disks. In return, neither they nor those who had hidden these things would be charged.[117] The same discretion governed transfer of the funds remaining from the sale of watches. Workers drove up to Paris in the middle of the night, arriving at 4 a.m. with two sacks of

114   Raguénès, *De Mai 68 à Lip*, 190.

115   *Les Cahiers de mai hebdo*, January 28, 1974, 1. Collectif, *Lip: affaire non classée*, 29 [quoted]. When employed armaments workers were denied the right to attend the General Assembly, Bidegain stepped in to ensure they could in the future. *Les Cahiers de mai hebdo*, February 4, 1974, 1. After the accords were signed, each morning at 7 a.m. a delegation of workers went to the armaments factory to support workers there in their confrontations with management over issues like the rule that they had to eat their lunch at their workbench. They accompanied the armaments workers to the General Assembly at 8:30 a.m. *Il Était une fois la révolution*, 212.

116   Piton, *C'est possible!*, 603–4. The managers met and voted seventy-one to two with three abstentions in favor, although they found it "largely inferior to the Giraud plan." ADD 1812W34 RG, January 29, 1974. This may have reflected their concerns about working for a socialist director without experience in industry.

117   ADD 1026W11 RG, January 30, 1974; February 22, 1974. Burgy estimates that about 15,000 watches were turned over. Burgy to Reid, July 25, 2016.

banknotes, carefully ordered in old Camembert boxes and smelling of cheese. They gave them to Chérèque. He and a colleague from the FGM-CFDT got on the metro and took the sacks to Riboud in person. He arranged to have the funds counted and put in his firm's safe early that morning.[118]

For Bidegain, the settlement was evidence of the emergence of a progressive business group, one which had taken the initiative in place of the state: "The solution of this affair showed the maturity of business in this country. There is in France a new class of directors who have a sense of their civic responsibilities ... In the private sector, one finds the fighters of the future. The vitality of this private sector is evident, and the future is theirs."[119] He inverted Séguy's words after the expulsion from Palente: "If the boss needs workers, workers sometimes need the boss."[120] Neuschwander thought of the establishment of the new firm in May 1968 terms: "Be reasonable, demand the impossible"; "Lip leads one to say, to take up the slogan of the strike: 'It is possible.' Possible to refuse the false fatality of a cruel and outdated system, where the profit of a few counts for all and man for nothing." He contrasted Riboud and Gillet saving Lip to the multinational firms that had destabilized Chile.[121]

The CFDT was pleased as well. From being a thorn in its side, Lip had become a model of dialogue with owners who could work with unions. Reflecting on the Dole accords, Maire said: "Those who do not see themselves in *les Lip* will tomorrow be outside of the paths of history." Chérèque praised Riboud and Gillet as part of a current of "dynamic industrial politics, a social politics marked by the spirit of dialogue."[122] Pointing to the opposition to the Dole negotiations among the majority of business owners, he could not resist paraphrasing Lenin (only to be told by CGT leader Henri Krasucki this was in fact a *bon mot* of August Bebel): "When the right congratulates you, ask yourself why."[123] Piaget too recognized that there were "two fractions of business. We exploited their contradictions to counter efforts to minimize our

---

118   Riboud, *Le Dernier de la classe*, 102–3. Bernard Ravenel, *Quand la gauche se réinventait. Le PSU, histoire d'un parti visionnaire 1960–1989* (Paris, 2016), 240.

119   "Le patronat et l'affaire Lip," *CFDT aujourd'hui* 7 (May-June 1974): 76.

120   *Libération*, January 31, 1974, 12.

121   Neuschwander, *Patron mais ...*, 22, 113, 127.

122   *Le Nouvel observateur*, February 4, 1974, 23.

123   *Le Figaro*, February 2–3, 1974, 4. Henri Krasucki, "Pourquoi tourner autour du pot?," *Vie ouvrière hebdo*, February 13, 1974, 7. Citing this aphorism of Bebel, the CGT had earlier contended that the flattery of the bourgeois press had gone to the heads of CFDT-Lip leaders and this explained their actions on October 12, 1973. ACGT Lip Box 6 Claude Curty at Ornans, November 19, 1973.

struggle."[124] Following this line of thought, he found himself appreciating the skill of what he saw as the modernist element of the *patronat* "in the line of Chaban-Delmas," in turning the failings of the traditionalists to their advantage: "There is on its part a little judo. Make use of the force of the adversary, examine the fight, apply this to lure in and master the opponent, and take advantage of it."[125]

Not surprisingly, such expertise did not impress most leftists. They joined the Communists and the CGT in criticizing efforts by the CFDT to differentiate between capitalists. The Trotskyist *Lutte ouvrière* contended that the real agenda of the CFDT had been "to select the boss most capable of modernizing the firm among the diverse applicants who appeared." In this telling, the CFDT had let the Action Committee play a role in the negotiations with Giraud because it rejected him as a traditionalist. However, the CFDT took control of the negotiations at Dole because it saw in Bidegain an embodiment of the modern businessmen it sought.[126] Commenting on the press coverage of the accord, *L'Humanité* wrote: "The good bosses have finally gotten here"; "all returns to order when the good boss—José Bidegain—replaces the incompetent head of the enterprise—Fred Lip. The old fable of good and bad bosses is given a little makeup to hide an episode of class struggle." The national confederations had come together in October in an effort to control the errant local union, but now the CGT saw the CFDT bolstering a capitalism in crisis in a misguided effort to further workers' interests. Séguy, secretary-general of the CGT, greeted the signing of the accords with a warning: "The outcome of this conflict cannot end up in a kind of global embrace of workers and allegedly liberal employers, which would bring water to the mill of class collaboration."[127] The CFDT had played the role of "super-revolutionary," before engaging in "class collaboration";[128] Neuschwander had been given the mission of creating "a contagious example of class collaboration."[129]

124 *Libération*, January 31, 1974, 12.
125 *Libération*, December 5, 1973, 3.
126 Groupe de liaison pour l'action des travailleurs, "Lip c'est bien fini," *Lutte de classe*, March 1974, 7.
127 *L'Humanité*, January 30, 1974, 6.
128 *L'Humanité*, January 31, 1974.
129 *L'Humanité*, February 25, 1976, 6. So, when the Tass news agency issued a dispatch on the workers' victory at Lip, picked up by *Le Monde* and other papers, the secretary-general of the CGT in Doubs sent Tass a sharp reprimand: "That your editor understands nothing about class struggle in developed capitalist countries does not, it seems to us, permit him to provide arms to the class adversary, to those whose profession it is to divide the democratic workers' movement." ACGT Uncatalogued Papers on

Including in its accounting the workers at the Lip factory in Ornans, who had accepted Giraud's offer and were therefore not covered by the Dole accords, the CGT reiterated its argument that workers should have accepted Giraud's proposition. After all, he had offered to hire more workers than remained by January 1974 in the Lip workforce, all of whom Neuschwander planned to hire over time, although he had not made a binding commitment to do so.[130] Common Program allies joined in the Communists' critique. For the Socialist Pierre Bérégovoy, the issue was not so much whether Giraud's or Neuschwander's offer was better for the workers of Lip, but that Giraud's offer could be seen as the fruit of the workers' fight, while the Dole accords "put the emphasis on business."[131]

Piaget recognized the danger in such a situation: the progressive minority of employers "looks to integrate the union and the demands, and to show workers that capitalism is capable of responding to all situations and that it is therefore not necessary to change society."[132] However, CFDT-Lip leaders could not help pointing out the inconsistency in the Communists' position. Vittot reminded the General Assembly that the CGT had presented the accord Bidegain reached at Romans in the summer of 1973 as a model for Lip workers, but then condemned the similar agreement reached by Bidegain at Dole.[133] After the Lip workers accepted the accord, the mini-commissions throughout France turned from defending the struggle to defending the resolution reached at Dole from the CGT claims that the Giraud settlement would have been better for workers. Copies of the *Lip Unité* daily bulletin making direct comparisons between the two were widely reproduced and distributed.[134]

Piaget spoke of the accord in terms of buses (perhaps because Giraud had planned to end the company buses that took workers to Palente, which had been interpreted as a way to force workers without transport to leave Lip). Messmer referred to Lip as a bus whose bad driver, Fred

---

Lip. Claude Curty to Director of Tass, March 22, 1974.

130   Krasucki, "Pourquoi tourner autour du pot?," 7. Distributed by the CGT-Lip, this essay engendered heated debate in the General Assembly. ADD 1026W11 RG, February 14, 1974.

131   *L'Unité*, February 14, 1974.

132   *Témoignage chrétien*, February 7, 1974, 5.

133   *Il Était une fois la révolution*, 146.

134   *Lip Unité dépêche quotidienne*, January 30, 1974. BDIC F delta rés 578/36 "Transcription de la discussion du 1e Février 74 d'un collectif de la commission popularisation Lip sur ce que peut être le travail des mini-commissions dans cette nouvelle phase de la lutte des Lip." BDIC F delta rés 578/48 Commissions Lip de Lyon, February 9, 1974. ADD 45J20 Tract of Comité Lip 13th arrondissement (Paris) [February 1974].

Lip, had plunged it into a ravine; the prefect described Giraud as a repair man called after the driver had run away, leaving the workers on board stranded.[135] But for the CFDT-Lip this was just the problem. Giraud had sought to deal with an emergency situation, but had no plan for the future. Speaking to the General Assembly, Piaget described Giraud's plan for the firm as like a bus with a flat tire (the mechanics department) running on empty, which left 160 workers standing at the curb. The "Neuschwander bus," in contrast, was fully fueled and in good shape. All would not be hired immediately, but those not picked up the first time the bus passed through would be taken on board later.[136]

Reopening Palente

In December 1973 one Lip worker had described Palente as "surrounded by rolls of barbed wire ... It makes you think of a concentration camp, of those camps which had already made our grandparents, who remembered too well tough times with the enemy, shed tears."[137] With the CRS occupation ended, another image emerged. Neuschwander said on his arrival at Palente that the factory was like a Sleeping Beauty that he would awaken; he was presented in the press as the Prince Charming whose love would do the trick.[138] The factory had a "flat encephalogram";[139] the machines were "cocooned," each missing a piece.[140] There were only enough parts for five days of watch production.[141]

Far more serious for the future of the CEH were its relations with suppliers in Haut-Doubs and with the watch seller-jewelers. Although the new firm planned, like Lip, to be largely self-sufficient in watch parts, Lip had relied on watch parts makers for a variety of items and for all its watchcases. Although the CEH presented itself as crucial to employment in Franche-Comté and to the future of the region as an engine of technological innovation, the watch trade in the area had always been more hostile to Lip than that in Besançon and viewed the new firm as an

---

135 *L'Express*, September 3, 1973, 16. *New York Times*, September 2, 1973.

136 *Témoignage chrétien*, February 7, 1974, 4–5. Chérèque was blunter: Giraud's plan for Palente was a bus with no wheels and no roof; it could go nowhere. *L'Unité*, February 1, 1974.

137 *Libération*, December 21, 1973, 1.

138 *Le Figaro*, February 3, 1974, 7. Neuschwander, *Patron, mais ...*, 78.

139 Claude Neuschwander, *L'Acteur et le changement* (Paris, 1991), 96.

140 AR Interview with Neuschwander by Rouaud, June 8, 2005, pp. 4–5.

141 Christian Bretagne, "Lip, Lip, Lip, hourra Monsieur Neuschwander!," *Elle*, September 23, 1974, 11.

imposition from the outside.[142] Furthermore, there were about 500 Lip creditors. The Dole accords had not dealt with them, working from the assumption that they would be paid by the liquidation of the old firm.[143] In order to prepare the factory to open, Neuschwander drove to Haut-Doubs to see the discontented suppliers. While they never took to him or to the CEH, it is a testimony to his personal skills and to conversations that the Archbishop of Besançon had with Catholics in the business that Neuschwander returned with a small box containing 200,000 pinhead-sized pieces. However, the commercial court, presided by a watchmaker long hostile to Lip, ordered that the CEH pay the 6 million francs owed to creditors immediately, throwing a wrench into the finances of the new firm.[144]

Reentering to the market presented its own problems. In keeping with the emphasis on quality production, Neuschwander stuck with sales through watch seller-jewelers only, despite their anger over the workers' sale of watches during the strike at the wholesale price. Ébauches SA had bought into Lip with the goal of taking control of its marketing network, and although the CEH held on to the brand name, the Swiss firm had hired away much of the Lip commercial staff in the fall of 1973.[145] Not surprisingly, these salesmen would discourage watch seller-jewelers from selling watches made by the CEH.[146] Neuschwander hired a new sales force and used the skills he had honed at Publicis to address the problem.[147] He began by setting up a Lip train, composed of a loco-motive and six cars.[148] It made twenty-two stops in a three-week trip through France. Neuschwander and CEH managers met with almost 2,600 watch seller-jewelers in an effort to repair relations with them. The train was also, in Neuschwander's words, a successful "public relations operation," garnering favorable press coverage for the new firm as well as the sale of 300,000 watches.[149] By July 1975, he had gotten 5,000 watch

---

142   Ternant, "La dynamique longue," 353.

143   ADD 1026W11 RG, February 11, 1974.

144   AR Interview with Neuschwander by Rouaud, June 8, 2005, 4–5. Neuschwander and Bordet, *Lip 20 ans après*, 72, 112.

145   BDIC F delta rés 578/39 "Informations en direct de Besançon" attached to *Lip Unité*, October 23, 1973 [dated October 30, 1973].

146   Collectif, *Lip: L'affaire non classée*, 150.

147   Bretagne, "Lip, Lip, Lip, hourra Monsieur Neuschwander!," 14.

148   *Revue des bijoutiers horlogers*, October 1974, 110; Gérard Bassand, "M. Neuschwander optimiste par le tour de France du train-forum Lip," *Réalités franc-comtoises* 167 (July–August 1974): 275–8.

149   Neuschwander, *Patron, mais …*, 98. AR Interview with Neuschwander by Rouaud, June 8, 2005, 11.

seller-jewelers to sell CEH watches.[150] When interviewed on the tour, Neuschwander took every opportunity to say that the CEH was now "a normal firm,"[151] "an enterprise like the others."[152] This did not stop a constant drumbeat of demands that CEH not rehire strike leaders. Watch seller-jewelers would visit Palente and stare at Piaget. Neuschwander told an interviewer, "We are tempted to put a wire mesh fence around us with a sign 'Warning Vicious Dog!'" [153]

Not only did Neuschwander come from a background in advertising, but his first client had been Fred Lip. In award-winning advertisements, he had made Fred Lip the image of the firm and the reason for consumers to choose Lip watches. Now he focused attention on a representation of workers and work derived from the conflict. Surveys, he explained, showed that now "the Lip brand enjoys a quite extraordinary coefficient of favor and reputation."[154] With a certain irony, some on the left hostile to advertising could not refrain from speculating in these terms on the impact of the Lip Affair on the public imagination. Yves Bourdet of the PSU reported that advertising firms estimated it would have cost 130 million francs to get such publicity for the Lip brand.[155] Recognizing Piton's exceptional qualities as a publicist during the conflict, Neuschwander hired her to work on advertising in the Paris office of the CEH (and perhaps also, as she believes, because the managers being rehired at Palente did not want her back).

As had Fred Lip, Neuschwander realized that the future of the CEH required the firm to differentiate its watches from cheaper ones available at the tobacconist. Watch seller-jewelers still dominated quality watch sales and the CEH advertising was designed to use public pressure to get them to work with the new firm.[156] In a series of advertisements in the fall of 1974 in the most widely read periodicals, from *Le Monde* and *Le Nouvel observateur* to *Paris Match* and *Elle*, Neuschwander identified the qualities Lip workers had shown in pursuing the conflict with the products they made. Using dramatic photos of Lip workers taken by Marc

150   ACN Neuschwander, "Ils ont tué Lip," II, 14–15. BDIC F delta rés 702/20/1 "Rapport au Comité d'entreprise de la Compagnie européenne d'horlogerie sur les comptes de 1975," 14.

151   Bassand, "M. Neuschwander," 278.

152   *L'Usine nouvelle*, April 1974, 144.

153   "Lip aujourd'hui," 14.

154   Neuschwander, "'Le choix que nous avons fait," 110.

155   Yves Bourdet, "Le conflit Lip 'On fabrique, on vend, on se paye,'" *Critique socialiste* 17 (1974): 72.

156   ADD 45J111 Comité d'Entreprise of CEH, "Analyse de l'activité de l'entreprise 1974," 35.

Riboud, Neuschwander presented Palente as the site not of imagination, as in the May 1968 narrative, but of an artisanal love of craft that many in a modernizing France feared was being lost: "Lip. We hope that you love your job as much as we love ours."[157] An ad with the headline "If Everything Was Made Like a Lip, Things Would Last Longer …," rewrote the Lip conflict in these terms: "In addition, [the workers] had to love to ply their trade at Lip to have defended the life of the factory at all costs and been successful." Those who loved their craft would work constantly to perfect it, "like the employees of Lip who fought to defend Lip and achieved their goal." The struggle became about saving a firm, "but much more about the preservation of an old trade to which a group of men and women were passionately attached." Neuschwander developed the idea that if "the society of abundance" of postwar growth had favored sales of very expensive watches and of the inexpensive, disposable ones abhorred by Fred Lip, "the society of penury" that succeeded it would favor the mid-range watches produced by the CEH.[158]

The CEH needed to create a new market in France where the firm could compete other than on price and which would lead to export sales as well. It sought to make Lip something more than the First Communion watch received as a present. The ads presented the CEH as a place where a mythologized craft culture survived, as an appeal to consumers to escape the technocracy and mass culture feared and despised by both conservatives and radicals. Neuschwander saw the future of the firm in marketing to a new generation of consumers who sought to express their individuality one consumer choice at a time. The CEH campaign embodied the contradictory legacy of 1968: on the one hand emphasizing the unprecedented forms of collectivity among workers, but on the other appealing to the individual all should seek to be in making their purchases.

Michel Garcin, a financial manager who came to the CEH to work with Neuschwander, later described the Lip of Fred Lip as "a family brand with customers living an average life, with a secondary education. But this image was turned upside down by the struggle of 1973, becoming that of 'revolutionary' strikers. Yuppies became our principal customers, we had to adapt."[159] Neuschwander turned to the world of design. In line with the recommendations of Syndex, the CEH reduced

---

157 BDIC F delta rés 702/22/4 CEH 1975 catalogue.
158 *Paris Match*, December 28, 1974, 31.
159 "L'affaire Lip. Entretien avec Michel Garcin, May 17, 2010, at del-ly.over-blog.com.

the number of watch models from 300 to 180 during its first year.[160] Neuschwander sought to establish the new firm's place in the market with fashionable watches: "We are going to use the same marketing practices which, in high fashion, were the key to the success of ready-to-wear boutiques, from Pierre Cardin to Dior to Courrèges."[161] If Fred Lip thought no dedicated follower of fashion would wear Dior with a Kelton watch, Neuschwander turned to Dior itself as a model. He brought in a number of high-profile designers. Roger Tallon created watches with particular attention to ergonomics. They had names like Big TV, Gold Camel, Mafia Moon, and Fridge Fort Knox. He was joined by other prominent designers, including Rudolf Meyer, Marc Held, Michel Boyer, Isabelle Hebey, Michel Kinn, and Jean Dinh Van. Their watches took new forms and in some cases used new materials like aluminum. Producers in the region were not equipped to make the requisite watchcases and the CEH had to invest in the machinery to produce its own.[162] This led to missed deliveries to watch seller-jewelers, who were unaccustomed to an emphasis on design as a selling point for watches; they were still taking the opportunity of getting clients attracted to their stores by the CEH advertising to sell other brands of watches.[163] A study in 1976 not surprisingly showed that the designer watches appealed to highly educated big city managers rather than the traditional Lip market of the middle class in smaller cities.[164] Particularly in a period of recession, the CEH would require time to reach this new clientele. On the other hand, Lip had never developed a large market outside France, but the CEH had some success in exporting these designer watches.[165]

The 844th Unemployed

Michel Debré was not alone in referring to "the disordered action" of the government in dealing with the Lip Affair, and in being shocked by

---

160 *Le Monde*, March 11, 1975, 21.

161 *Paris Match*, June 8, 1974, 81.

162 Neuschwander, *Patron mais ...*, 110. The new firm was encouraged to take this step with the promise that Ébauches SA would buy a significant portion of the production, a commitment on which it reneged. ADD 1026W19 Bernard Julhiet Conseils, "Dossier Industriel CEH-Lip" [September 1976].

163 ADD 35J10 "Position de la Chambre Française de l'Horlogerie sur le problème Lip," April 22, 1976. AB Interview with Garcin by Beurier (1992), 9–10. "Le grand retour de Lip," *Stratégies* 318 (April 5, 1982).

164 ADD 1026W19 Bernard Julhiet Conseils, "Dossier Industriel CEH-Lip."

165 ACN Neuschwander, "Ils ont tué Lip," II, 15.

Messmer's last "Lip, it's over!" announced on television in early January 1974.[166] Charbonnel had stepped into this void. He had initially put his faith in Giraud, but when this effort failed, he emerged as emblematic of a left Gaulism whose influence was receding. Charbonnel saw a role for a state that could encourage investment in the firm rather than limiting itself to helping individual laid-off workers:[167]

> The Lip drama showed that it is necessary to impose a limit on the omnipotence of owners over the means of production, that the workers who contributed to making it also have rights over it and that it is the job of the public authorities, in the face of the owners' failure, to save it, by finding a solution as close as possible to workers' desires.

If, Charbonnel added, Lip was not a site for the participation dear to Gaullists, this was not the workers' fault: "Lip workers demonstrated a search for information about the enterprise and a desire for economic training, that is to say definitively a desire for participation that cannot have left authentic Gaullists indifferent."[168]

And it was true that the Lip Affair had not left Messmer indifferent, if for other reasons. Knowing this, Charbonnel tendered his resignation on January 15, 1974. Although frustrated with Charbonnel for his resistance to finishing off *les Lip*, Messmer refused it. And at the council of ministers on January 30 he passed Charbonnel a handwritten note approving the Dole accords. But at the beginning of March, just when the new firm began hiring back the 843 Lip workers, Messmer forced Charbonnel out, making him, in the words of *L'Est républicain*, "the 844th unemployed of the Lip Affair." The head of the Communist Party, Georges Marchais, said that even a socialist minister would not have done as Charbonnel had done and sacrificed his ministerial portfolio to defend the working class.[169] With the departure of Charbonnel went a left Gaullism that saw the state as having an important role in addressing the failings of the market.[170] Charbonnel proved correct in predicting that Lip redux would not long survive the defeat of Chaban-Delmas' "new society."[171]

---

166   Michel Debré, *Entretiens avec Georges Pompidou 1971–1974* (Paris, 1996), 204 n1.

167   Charbonnel, *L'Aventure*, 227.

168   Jean Charbonnel, "Témoignage sur l'affaire Lip" in Michel Desvignes, *Demain, la participation* (Paris, 1977), 49, 52.

169   Charbonnel, *Dictionnaire raisonné*, 147.

170   Georgi, "Un 'conflit autogestionnaire' sous Georges Pompidou," 174–5.

171   *La Croix*, October 23, 2003, 26.

Conclusion

The individuals and groups involved in the resurrection of Lip reveal the breadth of those who drew on Catholic social thought to pursue alternatives within capitalism before and after 1968. They saw in what May '68 revealed a need and an opportunity for change. In entering the Lip conflict, Riboud, Gillet, and Bidegain made their case for leadership of French business. The Second Left took shape as well in the Lip Affair. For Pierre Rosanvallon:

> The Lip conflict gave back a kind of social and intellectual luster to the CFDT. The CFDT had an intellectual and social luster greater than the CGT in many milieux, but the Lip conflict showed that it had, even inside a traditional type of worker action, the possibility of an innovation in methods and an innovation in themes.[172]

But if the CFDT-Lip innovated in tactics and goals, so did the national confederation. For the CFDT, the resolution of the Lip Affair in 1974 marked a turn away from May 1968 to working with those in the business sector who would work with it. Rocard showed that he represented a force with whom elements of the establishment could engage. The Dole accords were less rewarding for the left Gaullism represented by Charbonnel, whose fate was sealed by the choice of Giscard d'Estaing over Chaban-Delmas as the candidate of the right in the presidential elections of 1974.

In this reconfiguration of movements lay the roots of the end of the long 1968 by 1981. Coverage of the Lip Affair had defined the identity of *Libération* in its first months. The paper revamped its staff with veterans of the Lip conflict in 1974. Its renaissance from the edge of bankruptcy at the dawn of the Mitterrand presidency in 1981 brought together those who had worked to save Lip in 1973–4. Serge July consulted Riboud and accepted his offer to have a BSN manager work with him to revamp the management of the paper.[173] Riboud and his brother Jean Riboud invested in the paper as well. They were joined by Bidegain and his wife Martine Michelland-Bidegain. Bidegain, now a director at Riboud's one-time takeover target Saint Gobain, set up a structure for small investors

---

172 Pierre Rosanvallon, "Témoignage," *Revue française d'histoire des idées politiques* 2 (1995): 367.
173 Riboud, *Le Dernier de la classe*, 199.

in the paper.[174] Michelland-Bidegain, advisor to Rocard at the Ministry of the Plan in 1981, drew on her circle dating from her days in the UNEF and the MNEF to recruit investors as well.[175] The initial resolution of the Lip Affair in the Dole accords in 1974 was the first important project that brought together this elite forged in radical student politics in the early years of the Fifth Republic with prominent business leaders. That the recovery of *Libération*, with *Les Cahiers de mai* veterans Kravetz, Péninou, and Jean-Marcel Bouguereau in leading positions, and funding from those who had revived Lip seven years earlier, came at the very time workers would have to leave Palente, suggested another crucial legacy of the Lip Affair.

174   Jean Guisnel, *Libération, la biographie* (Paris, 1999), 145–9.
175   Rimbert, *Libération*, 65.

8

Take the Money and Run

The enterprise has today become the meeting place of ideas, temperaments and individuals. We ignore one another in neighborhoods and in public housing in the cities. We know one another in the enterprise. It is the parish of the past. There, things happen that question daily life, the perspectives and the hopes of the future, and which suddenly lead on an enlarged scale to the nation itself. There will be other Lip affairs. A reconsideration of traditional notions of social relations is now underway.

—Michel-P. Hamelet[1]

Despite the Dreyfusards' talent, there would have been no Dreyfus Affair if France had been in the midst of war. To condemn and shoot an innocent in the midst of war, the weight of the war makes it such that this cannot stir up the crowds. But in 1975–6 France was at war … economic war, and there could not then be a 'Lip Affair'. The stakes are such that today there would be no resonance in the mass media. The authorities' fight for survival, the weight of unemployment, the uncertainty of employment come into play to prevent such resonance.

—Camarades de Lip[2]

I accepted letting myself be shot so that Lip would survive … Lip is an enterprise they shot … and through the death of Lip, 935 people were condemned to that social death that is unemployment. It is not only murder, it is genocide.

—Claude Neuschwander[3]

---

1   *Le Figaro*, September 4, 1973, 1.
2   *Idées ouvrières*, November 1978, 7.
3   ACN Neuschwander, "Ils ont tué Lip," III, 39; IV, 1. Lines in the script for the

At Palente, the SEHEM began with the community born of the conflict continuing to manifest its egalitarian, participatory qualities in the campaign to assure that it hired all Lip workers. As director, Neuschwander thought of the new enterprise as having the attributes of a community as well. During these years, different ideological and organizational forms of progressive Catholicism informed both the workers' movement and company management in the new firm. The eventual demise of the SEHEM was an element of the end of the enterprise as it had developed over the previous century as a site of worker and managerial contestation and cooperation.

The Cultural Revolution While Waiting for Work

In an unintended use of funds created in 1971 by the Chaban-Delmas government to increase the pool of skilled labor, Lip workers waiting to be recalled were paid their full salary while attending job-training classes. Although these offered most workers little in the way of vocational education, they were important sites of workers' mobilization and the assertion of the community they had created and fought to maintain. Instructors were hampered because the new firm would not explain its personnel needs, saying it did not want competitors to learn of its plans.[4] The female OS were not taught skills that would allow them to advance, and OP waiting to return to their old jobs objected to being taught skills for other employment.[5] Well before the classes began, Piaget said that for four-fifths of the personnel, the classes "will be internships of waiting; we will be a little like merchandise in stock."[6] Workers left classes when they got the call to Palente, rather than when a course ended, encouraging the

---

popularization commission's film, *Lip 76*, read, "There is an anti-Lip racism such that each solution involves elimination." BDIC F delta rés 578/46 Lip 76 script. In another formulation of this idea, state and business were motivated by an "anti-Lip racism": "to be Lip is to be the 'Negroes of South Africa." *Lip Unité*, April 1976, 1.

4   Piaget, "La formation par l'action collective," 180–1.

5   The precedent at the Salamander shoemaking plant was disquieting. There the courses introduced changes required by the move to mass production, without giving workers the opportunity to organize opposition. Philippe Fritsch, "Des Travailleurs dénoncent l'imposture de la 'solution-formation," *Les Temps modernes* 340 (November 1974): 408–20.

6   *Libération*, February 7, 1974, 12. For one worker's thoughts on his experience, see Gérard Cugney, "Une expérience de formation chez LIP en 1974" in *De l'horlogerie aux microtechniques: 1965–1975* (Besançon, 1996), 127–9.

view of the instruction as a stopgap measure.[7] A state official told those in charge to turn a blind eye to tardiness and absences, "provided there aren't waves!" One instructor characterized the experience as "a means to implement a social armistice in the Vietnam of Besançon."[8]

The program began with six weeks of classes in general culture in order to give time for vocational courses to be prepared. Workers were divided into forty-two groups of between twelve to fifteen individuals, which met in fifteen schools spread throughout Besançon. Despite this dispersion, the courses worked to counter the demobilizing effects of inactivity by creating grievances that brought workers together in struggle.[9] They objected to the division of students in these classes by age and without taking into account where they lived. The conflict had engaged all and resulted in fruitful intergenerational exchanges. Georgette Plantin complained of being placed "with those of the same generation as me; this was atrocious; there was a lack of dynamism, of intensity: we ossified."[10] Each of the groups compiled a list of those who wished to change their assignment. A collective composed of union delegates and all interested workers met daily to address issues of immediate concern. It used these lists to create a new set of class assignments. Though the inspector of the Académie du Doubs, charged by the Ministry of Education with administering the program, had refused individual workers' requests to change their classes, he backed down when visited by a delegation from the collective.[11]

When courses began, workers were shocked to find teachers who wanted to name a "sponge supervisor" to clean the board or who put out a box in which students had to place one franc each time they spoke out, unless what they said was deemed "important."[12] Plantin spoke of the "humiliation" skilled workers felt when instructors, with nothing to offer them, taught as they did to their usual audience of teenagers:[13]

---

7   BDIC F delta rés 702/5/2 Michel Préfol, "Perfectionnement Encadrement LIP 16 avril–31 juillet 74" (CESI), September 23, 1974.

8   Michel Préfol, "La formation continue à l'heure lip," *Économie et Humanisme* 231 (September–October 1976): 66. For other assessments of the program, see Léon Vinzier [pseudonym of Gaston Bordet, an organizer of the classes], "L'expérience de Lip," *Esprit* 439 (October 1974): 470–80.

9   Préfol, "La formation continue," 61.

10   BDIC F delta rés 702/5/2 "CESI 5 décembre 1974 Entretien Lip."

11   *Les Cahiers de mai hebdo*, March 18, 1974. *Lip Unité*, June 1974, 3.

12   *Les Cahiers de mai hebdo*, March 18, 1974.

13   Georgette Plantin, "L'accompagnement du service social durant les difficultés vécues par Lip et son rôle actuel," *Rencontre: cahiers du travailleur social* 37 (Spring 1981): 48.

"instruction that infantilized us, that much more in that they did not consider what we had lived through," said Piaget.[14] Workers responded by confronting teachers, asking if they were union members and what their position had been on the conflict. They demanded equality with the instructors, asserting the need to use the familiar *tu* with them to achieve it.[15] A number had success in getting teachers to adapt the curriculum to their situation.[16]

Maoists saw this activism as being in "the best tradition of recent high school and college student movements." Workers' participation in "the revolution against school oppression" was a blow with "an incalculable force and scope" against "the sacrosanct division of manual and intellectual labor, that is to say the very cornerstone of the bourgeois social system."[17] Maoist students who had set themselves to learning from *les Lip* during the conflict found that, when workers became students, there was now a place for them. A Maoist from Lyon discussed a meeting of students and Lip workers who were taking classes:

> *Les Lip* were really edgy about the question of schooling. It electrolyzes them because it was an enormous problem that divided them in a number of ways whose importance they saw, but that they did not know how to address or resolve. In any case, I felt in them a quasi-frenetic need to speak of it, to discuss it, for clarification of the subject. And, in my opinion, only those who have fought in a prolonged way on the school front, who have participated in diverse high school and college movements, would, following an exchange of experiences with *les Lip*, have what is needed to allow them to advance on this question.[18]

Others within this Maoist group "who contest school on the bases of May-June 68" recognized that the exchange went in both directions: "Starting from the struggles we carried out at school, we perceived that

14   Piaget, "La formation par l'action collective," 177–83.
15   AM Transcript of Anne-Marie Martin, *Lip au féminin*, part 2. BDIC F delta rés 702/11/1 Interview with Lip worker Michel C. in the transcript of "Film Lip. La Commune de Palente."
16   ADD 85J56 Les Travailleurs de Lip, "Refuser la fatalité et vivre ensemble au pays" [1979].
17   BDIC F delta rés 576/8 "De la Révolution idéologique à la Révolution culturelle aujourd'hui en France" [1974].
18   BDIC F delta rés 576/8 "2ème Période de la Pratique de Socio/Développement Tâtonnant de la Nouvelle Étude, Matérialiste" [September 1974].

what *les Lip* did to their school is what all high schoolers dream of doing to theirs."[19]

The cultural revolution continued when vocational education courses began in mid-April 1974. The division of workers into those at work and those awaiting work threatened to fragment the community forged in the past year and spurred the formation of new commissions to monitor the fulfillment of the Dole accords and the job-training courses.[20] In June the Action Committee reemerged and put out a leaflet contending that the useless courses were being tested to see if they could discourage workers fighting layoffs in bankrupt enterprises. Denouncing "the demobilizing and castrating effects on the whole of the workforce of Lip," the Action Committee criticized the division of workers into four categories pursuing different programs: OS; skilled workers and some technicians; secretaries and accountants; and other technicians and supervisors. The last of these groups was offered a course with the objectionable name, "management training." "Tell me what your salary is, I will tell you the culture to which you have the right."[21] These class assignments by social class ran contrary to the experience during the conflict, when workers chose commissions on which to work independent of their place in the workplace hierarchy, and developed unexpected interests and skills. The struggle had brought together workers kept apart by rank and job; the training program reintroduced these forms of separation.

The exception to condemnation of the classes as worthless or worse was a class on business and management given by the Centre des Études Supérieures Industrielles (CESI). The course was designed for managers, but the fifty-four students at Lip were almost all technicians and supervisors. This was the group that provided a good portion of the workers' leadership. Instructors noted the frequency with which students missed classes to prepare tracts or for a meeting of the General Assembly, to exercise their mandates as workplace delegates and to attend meetings of the workers' commission on job-training classes.[22] Employees in CESI courses demanded a say in what they studied and how; they went on a successful five-day strike at one point which led to "a reflection together on the role of the leader" and wider distribution of responsibilities

19   BDIC F delta rés 702/5/2 Collectif sur l'école de Lyon, "Enquêtes sur les Lip en stage menées depuis mai 1974" [September 1974].

20   *Il était une fois la révolution*, 212–13.

21   ADD 177J14, Comité d'Action, "Les Paroissiens de Palente hiérarchisés ..." [June 1974].

22   BDIC F delta rés 702/5/2 Préfol, "Perfectionnement encadrement Lip," September 23, 1974.

among participants.²³ Plantin conceived of the struggle itself as having been "a training"; "the CESI training is in a continuum with the training we received in the struggle."²⁴ The CESI staff agreed: "It is what they were looking for in training; a continuation of the conflict that was, in itself, extremely formative."²⁵ Piton was pleased to learn how the CNPF functioned and how to read spreadsheets. Historians of labor taught a history of France that employees had not gotten in school.²⁶ The sociologist Albert Meister led a discussion on self-management in Yugoslavia.²⁷ The CESI course taught the largely male technicians and supervisors who made up the union leadership how to understand and potentially manage an enterprise.²⁸ The participants realized that the instruction they were receiving was "ordinarily reserved for managers and engineers," not lower-level employees like themselves, and they recognized that this "'privileged' training" only heightened the division between leaders and led in the labor force.²⁹

All on Board

The Dole accords had specified that workers would be rehired to meet production needs. Three hundred would be brought back by the end of March 1974 and 500 by September; the remainder of the 830 employees of Lip would be hired as they were needed, but no date was given for the recall of the last workers.³⁰ The first 135 workers, including Burgy, went back to work in March 1974. Burgy had overseen the sale of watches

23   ADD 2032W337 Fifteen employees, including Plantin, to the Directeur régional du travail, October 30, 1974. BDIC F delta rés F 702/5/2 CESI, "Perfectionnement encadrement Lip 2ème session 9 septembre/20 décembre 1974," January 15, 1975, 7, 14.

24   BDIC F delta rés 702/5/2 "CESI 5 décembre 1974 Entretien Lip," 2.

25   BDIC F delta rés 702/5/2 CESI, "Perfectionnement encadrement Lip 2ème session," 10.

26   *Tribune socialiste*, June 21, 1975.

27   BDIC F delta rés 702/5/2 Préfol, "Perfectionnement encadrement Lip," September 23, 1974.

28   "À Lip, des femmes: mille manières de lutter," *Des femmes en mouvement* 5 (May 1978): 33.

29   BDIC F delta rés 702/5/2 "Entreprise Lip CESI," November 19, 1974, 4. The ministry of education would not pay for additional more expensive CESI courses. Jean-Pierre Dumont, "Lip la formation après la grève," *Le Monde de l'éducation* 2 (January 1975): 9.

30   What had happened to the rest of the almost 1,300 employed in April 1973? The sales force had left to work for competitors; 150 workers were employed at the factory in Ornans, now a separate firm; other Lip workers had taken retirement or left to work elsewhere. *Le Point*, January 20, 1975, 77.

during the struggle. Recognizing this, Neuschwander chose him for a new position as the head of human resources—in the face of opposition within the union to the recuperation (and promotion) of someone who had revealed his extraordinary skills in the conflict. Neuschwander charged Burgy with organizing work in the reopened factory. Would all workers be rehired? The prefect did not think so. In April, he wrote that though the unions knew that all would not return to their jobs, they did not tell the workers, preferring "on the contrary to prolong the period of illusions."[31] In June, when Neuschwander proudly told reporters at the news conference held to kick off the national tour of the Lip train that he expected to hire 700 by the end of the year, he unintentionally mobilized the workforce who took this to mean that the remaining 130 employees would not be rehired.[32] A CFDT-Lip representative on the works council asked that Neuschwander show the same "dynamism" in creating jobs as in organizing the trip to lure back watch seller-jewelers.[33]

In making hiring decisions, Neuschwander worked from the criteria of professional level, seniority, and family obligations—which was why the recently hired Dominican OS Raguénès was one of the last rehired— but this left plenty of room for workers' concerns.[34] Groups of women, pregnant women, and the elderly would unexpectedly show up to see Neuschwander in his office to ask when they or family members would be rehired. They stood for the hour he saw them, believing that sitting before the boss put them in a position of submission.[35] The workers' commission on employment discussed news of each hire individually in an effort to assess company actions and to make certain no worker would be left out.[36] The aging OS Alice Carpena knew that continuing in her previous job would be damaging to her eyes, but she decided that when rehired she would not ask to change jobs until all had been

---

31   ADD 1026W1 PD, April 11, 1974. ADD 45J100 Draft of Thomé, *Créateurs d'utopies*, 22.

32   The last 130 included fifty managers and with them in mind Neuschwander spoke of looking for jobs of equal pay in the area. ADD 177J14, Neuschwander to personnel, June 4, 1974.

33   AMB 5Z220 "Compte-rendu de la réunion du Comité d'Entreprise du 13 juin 1974."

34   Their vigilance was heightened by word that the accords governing rehiring that Bidegain had negotiated at Romans were not respected. *Lip Unité dépêche quotidienne*, March 15, 1974. Workers occupied the Salamander plant in May 1974. The new business went bankrupt in November 1974. See note 5 above.

35   Collectif, *Lip: affaire non classée*, 41.

36   AB Interview with Demougeot by Beurier (1992), 24–5.

called back, for fear of taking someone else's place.[37] Neuschwander's decision to hire sixty of the 200 Lip employees who had not participated in the movement, primarily engineers and managers, pitted a valuation based on the organization of production against the one many workers embraced, predicated on participation in the struggle, including voting with the majority on October 12.[38] There was particular concern that Action Committee members and union militants would not be rehired— that managers who had abstained from the conflict would find reasons to not take them back,[39] or that watch seller-jewelers and local businesses would make exclusion of militants the price of doing business. Businessmen in Besançon were so upset when Piaget returned to work in August 1974 that Riboud had to step in to talk sense to them.[40]

Would those who had been rehired fight for the return of the others or not, fearing that this would put the new firm at risk? Those not yet recalled, Piaget said, "continued to print leaflets, to say things that made those with jobs more and more anxious."[41] Faced with this situation, Raguénès lamented that "there was an almost total sclerosis of the imagination."[42] However, the fact that many Action Committee militants were not among those named in the early recalls assured that imagination would resurface.

The incorporation of the Lip struggle into imagery drawn from mass culture had been a way of developing its appeal as a movement that operated outside the strictures of social realism. In *Libération*, Serge July described the Lip community as being "like Astérix and his village of diehard Gauls. Except that the magic potion here is democracy. And from that comes individual and collective liberty."[43] Workers themselves turned to this imagery in their campaign to get everyone rehired. In the summer of 1974, they wrote and printed four issues of the comic strip, *La Gazette Liporum*:

37 *Lip au féminin*, 9.
38 Dumont, "Lip la formation après la grève," 10. AB Interview with Raoul Petitjean by Beurier (1992), 10.
39 For discussion of this concern, see ADD 177J14, CFDT-Lip, "Les Revanchards," May 1974. Collectif, *Lip: affaire non classée*, 38. *Politique hebdo*, October 24, 1974, 6.
40 Neuschwander, *Claude Neuschwander*, 155.
41 *L'Outil des travailleurs*, August 15, 1974, 12.
42 "Lip aujourd'hui," 16.
43 *Libération*, January 10, 1974, 3. July gave Messmer the role of Caesar. In a conflict in 1968 at Brest, workers used figures from Astérix and the slogan, "Our magic potion is unity." Porhel, *Ouvriers bretons*, 78.

At that time, Europe was directed by "Trustus Multinationarum" that moved villages and their inhabitants. But the inhabitants of Liporum refused to submit to these laws. Better, they created their own laws. Then, Multinationarum sent in the troops of social repression [*compagnies de repression sociale* (CRS)].

Neusch Cousinissud Germain secretly does Multinationarum's business after the Giraud character fails in his effort to do it openly. Among the Gauls are Mercéassuranstourix, referring to the CGT-Lip leader Claude Mercet ("I am the tenor in the orchestra of Rue Lafayette [site of the national CGT headquarters in Paris]"), Vitohédéfix, and Piagégoudurix, who rejects Neusch Cousinissud Germain's offer of honey, and triumphs in the end: all the Lipeins, Astérix-Obelix and Obelix-Astérix, are rehired.[44]

When asked in a works council meeting when all would be rehired, Neuschwander responded that he could not perform miracles. In October 1974, the Action Committee responded with a skit in front of the factory. In the morning, they put up a big banner reading "Does it take a miracle for all to return? You will know this evening." Both the employed and those waiting to be recalled came to learn the answer. Five or six workers still in vocational classes, dressed like monks in white albs made of paper, turned to the heavens and begged for a miracle. Raguénès then appeared, not in his alb, but dressed for work with a sign reading: "No need for a miracle for the 830 to enter. It's enough if we pull together." The workers took off their robes and burned them, to show that they saw Neuschwander was not a savior; they did not need such a savior for everyone to be rehired by December.[45]

Efforts were made to foster camaraderie between those with jobs and those as yet without. One day, those waiting to be called back offered aperitifs to employees as they left work. In mid-September 1974, more than 500 workers attended the first General Assembly to be held in the restaurant at Palente since the expulsion in August 1973. Those not yet rehired were not allowed on the factory grounds, so they piled into the old bus that had circulated through the region in the spring of 1973 spreading word of the movement. When the General Assembly ended, they greeted workers at the gates to remind them that all should be present at future assemblies.[46] Once he was rehired, Piaget put up a poster in his workshop

---

44   BDIC F delta rés 702/3/7 *La Gazette de Liporum*.
45   *Lip Unité*, January 18, 1975, 6. *Politique hebdo*, October 24, 1974, 6.
46   *Politique hebdo*, October 24, 1974, 6.

referring individually to each of those not yet back: "We will not stop as long as he is not back." Other workers did so as well, and in an echo of the past, managerial personnel tore these down and workers put them back up.[47] Particular campaigns were launched for the final hires. Each morning workers marked pieces in the shop as work to be carried out by Dominique Enfraze, and labeled his machine and his chair. The department head gave in and recalled him. On the board at the entry to the factory, large group photos of the final 150 workers waiting to be recalled were posted; as they returned, their photos were removed. There were several thermometers in the factory charting the progress toward hiring all 830 employees.[48] In keeping with their position that *les Lip* would have been better off if they had accepted Giraud's offer, the CGT-Lip asked those who had not been called back to lay low and do nothing that might impede recovery of the enterprise, and requested that the firm release the names of those who would not be rehired so that they could look for work elsewhere. However, the CFDT-Lip never gave in. This led the CGT-Lip leader Noëlle Dartevelle, one of the last to be taken back, to say, "If I'm again at Lip, I owe it to the CFDT."[49]

In mid-November, Neuschwander confirmed that all 830 former employees would be rehired, but some of the skilled workers would be taken back as unskilled workers with lower pay. Only preparations for a one-hour walkout at the beginning of December got the management to agree to hire all returning workers at their previous rank. Those who were employed had initially resisted mobilizing for fear that this would hurt the company, but they came to realize that Neuschwander was unusually sensitive to the threat of a job action because it would challenge the image that the modernist businessmen behind the new firm were trying to project. Neuschwander sent letters of employment to the remaining workers, with a start date in March 1975. All workers returned to Palente to do more or less the same work as they had done before.

With the workers back, the General Assembly met only once every two weeks and the collective, composed of union leaders and interested workers, once a week. The CFDT-Lip was the primary site of workers' activism. Five percent of the workforce had been organized in 1956, reaching 50 percent by 1973. After the conflict, 75 percent were unionized,

---

47   *L'Outil des travailleurs*, August 15, 1974, 12.
48   *Politique hebdo*, October 24, 1974, 6.
49   ADD 1812W34 RG, October 25, 1974. ADD 43J19 CFDT-Lip to *L'Humanité*, March 5, 1976. [quoted]

overwhelmingly in the CFDT-Lip.[50] As a result of the workers' rejection of CGT-Lip policies and the departure from the firm of a number of those who had supported them, CGT-Lip membership fell from 220 in June 1973 to seventy-nine in January 1974.[51] Piaget noted an "anti-leader push" after the conflict that caused some workers not to stand in workplace elections, but this was more than made up for by the number of new CFDT-Lip members who sought office. Before 1973, it had been difficult to get the twenty candidates required for personnel delegates and their alternatives, leading some to run for both personnel delegate and the works council. After the conflict, however, the CFDT-Lip leadership identified more than 100 workers it thought could handle these posts.[52] In January 1975, when the first elections under the new firm were held, the union had more than enough candidates. No CGT-Lip members were elected to the works council. Of the ten personnel delegates elected, one each came from the CGT-Lip and the CGC-Lip; the remainder were members of the CFDT-Lip.[53] The power and effectiveness of delegates came from the paid hours they were given to do their job. In the old firm, delegates and their alternates had received the same number of these hours. This was no longer the case in the new firm. To give experience to a wider range of militants, CFDT-Lip delegates allocated a portion of the paid hours they received to elected alternates so that all delegates and alternates had the same number of hours to engage with workers, creating what Piaget called a "collateral [that was] democratic in nature," a security deposit on a "cultural revolution" in the making.[54]

The Enterprise

When Neuschwander was in the UNEF, Gaston Bordet, fellow UNEF board member and native of Franche-Comté, had introduced him to the writings of Fourier and Proudhon. But at the time, Neuschwander

50   Réseau Citoyens Résistants, *La Force*, 20.
51   ADD 1026W11 RG, January 22, 1974. In 1973, *Lip Unité* called itself the bulletin of the Lip workers. When it started up again in 1974, it was as the bulletin of the workers of CFDT-Lip. Guillaume Gourgues, "Occuper son usine et produire: stratégie de lutte ou survie? La fragile politisation des occupations de l'usine Lip (1973–1977)," *Politix* 117 (2017): 135.
52   Interview with Charles Piaget in *Révolution* 48 (March 15, 1974): 11.
53   *Le Monde*, February 2, 1975, 21.
54   "Lip aujourd'hui," 18–19, 24–5. ADD 1812W33 CFDT-Lip, "CFDT: un travail en équipe en service des travailleurs," January 28, 1975.

was taken with one of Fourier's followers, Jean-Baptiste Godin, an industrialist who built a "social palace," the *familistère* in Guise (Aisne) for
his workers. He envied "this idealist ... for having realized, in his life-
time, his utopia."[55] Neuschwander had no such ambitions for Palente,
but he did come with ideas about the nature of the enterprise and "that
another form of management is possible." Although Neuschwander recognized that he was limited in how far he could apply these conceptions
at Palente, he shared with Lip workers the belief that the experiences
there could have an important impact elsewhere.[56]

The enterprise was a building block in the France of the "thirty glorious years" of postwar expansion.[57] "Every worker participates, through
the intermediary of their delegates, in the management of the enterprise," read the preamble of the Constitution of the Fourth Republic
(1946), and the works council had been established with this in mind.
De Gaulle's evocations of participation, whether through profit sharing
or dissemination of information in the firm, were other articulations
of this concept. François Bloch-Lainé developed his thoughts about
the enterprise in the Club Jean Moulin and published them as *Pour
une réforme de l'entreprise* in 1963. His understanding of the enterprise
as providing a "new force of political democracy" had a profound and
lasting impact on Neuschwander.[58] Bloch-Lainé argued that employees and owners should sit on a board that exercised control over the
direction of the enterprise and that the enterprise had responsibilities
not only to shareholders and the state, but to the personnel and to the
sites in which it operated. In line with these ideas, Bloch-Lainé had
created the environment in which the residents' council at Sarcelles
could take responsibility for important elements of community life. In
this spirit, a decade later, Neuschwander promoted "a progressive delegation of responsibility for the improvement of work conditions" to
employees.[59]

The ideology of the enterprise drew on Catholic social ideas of the
firm as a community in which men and women took precedence over
capital. Neuschwander agreed with Bidegain when he said that with

---

55   Neuschwander, *Claude Neuschwander*, 28.
56   Ibid., 141. ACN Neuschwander, "Ils ont tué Lip," V, 10.
57   Alain Chatriot, "'La réforme de l'entreprise'. Du contrôle ouvrier à l'échec du
projet modernisateur," *Vingtième siècle* 114 (2012): 183–97.
58   Neuschwander, *Claude Neuschwander*, 99–100. *Pour une réforme de l'entreprise* "has not aged a bit," Neuschwander wrote in 2014. *La Gauche, sans le PS?* (Paris,
2014), 19.
59   *Le Monde*, January 19–20, 1975, 21.

the transformation of France from a rural to an urban society since the war, "the traditional communities for centuries—villages, parishes, neighborhoods—have burst apart. The factory chimney has replaced the village bell tower. As a result, wage-earners feel part of only one stable community: the enterprise."[60] For Bidegain, "advancing the enterprise is more important than promoting the entrepreneur." In 1968 he had suggested that the CNPF rename itself the Comité National des Entreprises Françaises, and when the CNPF rejected his ideas, he formed Entreprise et Progrès in 1969.[61] Neuschwander believed the enterprise could be other "than the sum of exploiters, polluters and profiteers," the evanescent form taken by financial investments. It could be "the principal site of human activity existing in human civilization."[62] "The enterprise is a collectivity that is quite simply the result of a more and more socialized society."[63]

Neuschwander saw establishments with 300 to 1,500 employees entering a period of crisis. They were often family-owned firms, like Lip, with built-in inefficiencies that had been carried along in the years of postwar prosperity, but they were now increasingly faced with bankruptcy or amalgamation into large firms. However, Neuschwander saw firms of this size under the direction of a management with independence from the owners as "the richest in terms of a social future and therefore in economic effectiveness."[64] Directors, he believed, derive their authority by assuming responsibility for the enterprise and satisfying its multiple interests, only one of which is that of the stockholders; a director is the "accepted coordinator of activities decided collectively for the common good."[65] Neuschwander told business school students in 1974 that "when the disappearance of an enterprise risks bringing harm to the collectivity, a limit should be envisaged to the absolute right of its owners."[66] Dealing with the unions, he similarly talked about "an arbitration between the

---

60 *L'Express*, September 3, 1973, 17. A national association of managers that dismissed the Lip workers as capitalizing on their appeal as the "twin brothers" of television and film heroes fighting authority figures found the workers' attachment to the enterprise "more significant": "The Enterprise *is*," the managers proclaimed. "Autour de Lip," *Association de cadres dirigeants de l'industrie pour le progrès social et économique* 287 (October 1973): 438, 442.

61 *Libération*, November 7, 1973, 4.

62 *Libération*, April 7, 1976, 9.

63 Neuschwander, *Patron, mais ...*, 170.

64 Ibid., 117

65 Ibid., 170.

66 "Innovation sociale: les nouvelles responsabilités. Un débat à l'ESSEC avec M. Claude Neuschwander," *Reflets* (1974), 24.

collective interest of the enterprise and the individual interests of those who work there."[67] Neuschwander expected directors themselves to present three-year plans to their workforce, including projections about employment and conditions of employment: "errors of assessment in the essential area of social forecasting must entail, for the management, the same risks of penalization as errors committed in the assessment of industrial investments."[68]

Although the CFDT and the PSU sought a society based on self-management, they recognized that this would not be possible in a capitalist economy. Neuschwander went further. He was skeptical of self-management and questioned whether medium-sized or large enterprises could ever be run without a managerial hierarchy. He felt that *les Lip* had thought in terms of getting a *patron*, an employer, because they understood that the technological complexity of Lip required a director general.[69] Neuschwander consulted with managers, but refused to allow them to participate in the direction of the enterprise. He saw the director general not as the agent of the board of directors, but as an arbitrator who should have "a total independence vis-à-vis ... the 'triangle'" formed by the personnel, the market and the shareholders. In particular, the director general needed to oppose the owners when doing so was in the interest of the survival and development of the enterprise. To work, all three must be strong. The market and the owners were already strong. Unions were strong at the SEHEM as well, but to apply the lessons of Lip elsewhere, efforts needed to be made to strengthen organized labor in other enterprises.[70]

The Lip conflict in 1973 had seemed exceptional not just for the workers' tactics, but in terms of what Neuschwander identified as a movement "for the defense of their enterprise" rather than simply their jobs.[71] That workers found themselves looking for an employer shocked many, but he believed that their idea of a *patron* was as a component of an enterprise with responsibilities to the personnel, not just to owners and clients. Neuschwander interpreted the enterprise in terms of his sense that "the couple adherence-contestation is slowly but surely overtaking the trio authority-hierarchy-discipline."[72] CFDT-Lip leaders

---

67   ACN Neuschwander, "Ils ont tué Lip," II, 5.
68   *Le Monde*, January 19–20, 1975, 21.
69   Neuschwander, *Claude Neuschwander*, 140, 151–3, 189–90.
70   *Le Monde*, January 19–20, 1975, 21.
71   Neuschwander, *Patron mais ...*, 9.
72   ACN Neuschwander, "Ils ont tué Lip," V, 17–18.

appreciated that what differentiated Neuschwander from other bosses was his recognition, in their words, of "the role and the place workers have in the enterprise."[73] His concept of the enterprise shared traits with that of the Lip workers' community. "An enterprise," Piaget said after the expulsion from Palente, "is first the personnel: it is above all the personnel, with what they have as capital in the form of work, as capital of initiative, as capital in them, which is the only force possible to make the enterprise run."[74] He explained later that "in the occupied factory we reflected on the notion 'of the enterprise,'" asking "What is of a capitalist orientation in the organization and what is not?"[75] Both Neuschwander's and the workers' conceptions of the enterprise were rooted in Catholic humanism. They differed significantly, but shared the sense that the enterprise was where the alternatives to the dominant models of political economy on the left and the right in the Fifth Republic were to be found.

The Shopfloor

Neuschwander's management was predicated on engagement with unions and communication and dialogue with workers. He developed an "apprenticeship" in economics and management for members of the works council and union leaders. Michel Jeanningros recalled later: "Some buddies took full advantage of this to learn about the mechanisms of the operation of enterprises. It was not formalized, but they were able to go anywhere, they were able to talk with the guys in management, with whom they were in a very different relationship than that maintained by previous firms." This nurtured discussion between union leaders and senior management, but could create a distance that Action Committee veterans like Marc Géhin and Demougeot saw, like the CESI classes, as accentuating the division between leaders and led in the collectivity, while conferring on these leaders a new form of legitimacy.[76]

---

73   Jacquin, "Lip 1973–1981," 287–90.
74   *La Cause du peuple*, September 13, 1973, 8.
75   Raymond Burgy and Charles Piaget, "L'aventure des Coopératives LIP" [2007], appendix to Thomé, *Créateurs d'utopies*, at genepi.blog.lemonde.fr.
76   Jacquin, "Lip 1973–1981," 343–4 [quoted]. Bondu, "De l'usine à la communauté," 427.

The case of the militant young workers that managers had not wanted to take back provides an instance of the shared project of the firm's director and the union leadership. Neuschwander kept fourteen of them separate from other workers at Palente by having them do a training internship under Piaget's guidance from March to November 1975. Piaget was pleased to report that at the end they could be reintegrated into the firm. The workers had not changed their politics, but were now concerned as well with developing their skills and doing their work well.[77] Piaget had conceived of this project not as a way of reforming young radicals, but as an alternative to the vocational education workers had experienced the year before. These workers decided to train as a group to achieve the level of skilled worker in tool production. They had "a broad freedom to learn on their own and collectively, to stop the guy in charge when they wanted," and worked from the premise that each of them could bring something to aid the development of the others.[78] Jacky Burtz and François Laurent were among the many in this group who later became worker representatives.[79]

Neuschwander spoke of unions as a necessity: only they could "bring to the enterprise the modernizing and dynamic element that is the pressure of workers for progress." He emphasized this element, rather than Riboud's vision of unions as a source of stability in the firm. A director general, as Neuschwander conceived the position, needed strong unions that would contest management in a "dialectical game between the directors and the unions."[80] "More and more the responsibility of the head of the enterprise will be the management of conflicts, that is to say ... the art of stripping away all that obscures their dialectical meaning."[81] The director general as dialectician led Neuschwander back to what he believed he shared with les Lip: "Is it mandatory," he asked, "especially in an enterprise where the Christian message is appreciated, to forget that for a number of centuries Manicheanism has not been accepted as the basis of Christian reference, and that the law, 'You will love your neighbor' remains valid even if this neighbor is a boss?"[82]

---

77   ACN Neuschwander, "Ils ont tué Lip," II, 7–8.
78   "Lip aujourd'hui," 26. Interview with Jacky Burtz by Reid, June 13, 2017.
79   Collectif, Lip: affaire non classée, 52–3.
80   Neuschwander, Patron, mais ..., 129, 132–3.
81   ACN Neuschwander, "Ils ont tué Lip," V, 19–20.
82   L'Humanité, February 25, 1976, 6.

Neuschwander applied practices from his work at Publicis to the management of the new company. He evoked his own professional past, the organization of "the communication between the enterprise and the social environment," in saying, "You can find there, applied to the enterprise, the outline of a social marketing that risks becoming as indispensable to the enterprise as commercial marketing."[83] He saw in this what differentiated a self-styled left-wing boss (*patron de gauche*) like himself from the traditional boss: "I believe more and more that the function of the boss is a function of social communication … [I] am convinced that communication is much more in the tradition of the spirit of the left than in the tradition of the conservative spirit."[84]

Communication was in sum a response to a widespread crisis in authority.[85] There was a crisis of communication in a society in which "workers feel about as much at ease as university students or army recruits."[86] Neuschwander believed that the medium-sized firm, without too much or too little distance between the executive and employees, facilitated communication.[87] The director general could immediately and widely disseminate information to employees—Neuschwander's posters in the walkway at Palente were almost as large as those of the unions, Piaget commented—and, in turn, management could survey workers' sentiments and solicit ideas and suggestions from them. After all, as Neuschwander recognized, the union often learned from workers of developments in production before he did.[88]

Piaget spoke of a "battle" in the SEHEM with management over the quality and rapidity of the dissemination of information. The firm did away with the paid hour each month when unions could address personnel.[89] But while the Lip firm had sought to suppress the circulation of short bulletins and leaflets, the new company now did nothing about them. With a little ditto machine, the union could make 100 copies and distribute them throughout an entire workshop in an hour.[90] However, such activities took place in a new context. Management was less interested in suppressing concerns than in responding to

83   Neuschwander, "L'entreprise," 21.
84   ADD 45J96 "Claude Neuschwander questions-réponses," *Le Télégramme de Franche-Comté*, June 7, 1974.
85   Neuschwander, *Patron, mais …*, 63.
86   *Le Monde*, January 19–20, 1975, 21.
87   Neuschwander, *Patron, mais …*, 118.
88   AR, Interview with Neuschwander by Rouaud, June 8, 2005, 10–11.
89   ADD 1812W33 RG, June 19, 1974.
90   "Lip aujourd'hui," 9–10.

them.[91] Piaget commented on the effect on employees of Neuschwander's visits twice a day to individual workshops, where he went beyond greetings to ask and answer substantive questions, making sure always to speak to different workers.[92] He would come to the company restaurant and ask workers if he could sit and eat with them, something Fred Lip would never have done. Neuschwander met with the unions and the managers every two weeks; every two or three months he would speak to the labor force as a whole about the situation of the firm. Militants recognized that "these meetings had a big influence on the employees. The fact that the boss talked directly with them helped create a confidence in him among the personnel."[93]

After the long struggle, the factory was a site of greater social interaction and discussion of all aspects of the life of the firm.[94] Neuschwander drew on this to institute hour-long meetings in individual workshops with groups of twenty to thirty workers and the manager with responsibility for the workshop in the presence of members of senior management (to assure that the manager listened and that, when possible, made changes in response to what he heard). The session would begin with every worker saying a little something in an effort to ensure that all would feel comfortable speaking. Workers were encouraged to tell what worked well and what did not and how they thought things could be done differently.[95] Neuschwander saw in these meetings "a small start of self-management."[96] The CFDT-Lip itself produced a report in May 1975 which recognized that job security and "real participation" in the management and plans of the firm were not possible in a capitalist firm, but that there were a number of things which could be done: job enrichment and training leading to advancement; organization of work

---

91   Although Fred Lip saw his practices pursued by Neuschwander, his successor differentiated his understanding of communication from the one-way dissemination of information that characterized Fred Lip's management. BDIC F delta rés 702/4/2, Fred Lip to Claude Neuschwander, November 18, 1975.

92   "Lip aujourd'hui," 8. ACN Neuschwander, "Ils ont tué Lip," II, 12–13. Neuschwander, *Claude Neuschwander*, 54.

93   Collectif, *Lip: affaire non classée*, 62–4. Demougeot spoke of this "charm offensive" as "another way to condition us." *Lip au féminin*, 11.

94   "Lip aujourd'hui," 17.

95   Neuschwander, "Postface" to Michel Charzat, *Politiquement libre* (Paris, 1999), 211. Neuschwander, *Patron, mais …*, 144. Collectif, *Lip: affaire non classée*, 64.

96   "Innovation sociale," 28. Neuschwander, *Patron, mais …*, 149, 172 [quoted]. Unions could participate, but they saw these meetings as an effort to bypass them. Elsewhere, Neuschwander spoke of introducing worker participation in decision-making in workshops as part of a national project. *Le Monde*, January 19–20, 1975, 21.

so as to allow for increased responsibility and exchanges among workers; and encouragement of workers to express their ideas and of supervisors to listen to them.[97]

Skilled male workers and supervisors were the primary beneficiaries of Neuschwander's style of management. Under Fred Lip, managers had little autonomy, but asserted a strict authority, particularly over female OS. Neuschwander rehired many of these managers for their technical competence.[98] They had particular difficulty accepting governance through improved communication, a practice for which their training and experience had not prepared them.[99] A report the CEH commissioned from the CESI referred to these managers as the Achilles heel of the new firm. Workers interviewed for the study contrasted the new director general to the veteran managers who, though traumatized by the conflict, were largely unchanged, unlike those they oversaw. Some told the CESI that maybe these managers "missed their chance in not following the movement." However, Neuschwander's immediate staff, the directors of the new firm, were drawn from consultants who designed the program approved at Dole and from accomplished professionals who gave up secure situations to come to Palente out of a desire to participate in an experience with which they were very much in sympathy. In response to talk of recuperation of the unions by the company, one director commented, "on this subject, I sometimes ask myself: who recuperates who?"[100]

97 ADD 177J14 CFDT-Lip, "Conditions du travail," May 26, 1975.

98 Workers exercised some control over these hires. In September 1974, when Neuschwander decided to hire a manager who had actively fought the workers' movement, the union delegates threatened a conflict and he backed down. Interview with Pierre-Émile in Philippe Alfonsi and Patrick Pesnot, Vivre à gauche (Paris, 1975), 134. However, when Neuschwander did not want to rehire a department head who had behaved particularly badly with personnel in the past, the CFDT-Lip consulted workers in his workshop. Based on their recommendations, it asked that he be taken back with a clear understanding of what would be expected in the future. Jeannine Pierre-Émile, Michel Jeanningros, and Charles Piaget, "Préface" to Divo, L'Affaire Lip, 10.

99 "Claude Neuschwander 'Comment nous allons gagner'," Entreprise, May 31, 1974, 20. Neuschwander, Patron, mais ..., 155. Neuschwander, Claude Neuschwander, 156.

100 BDIC F delta rés 702/20/2 CESI, "Plan d'intervention pour le changement et le développement de la CEH. Enquête diagnostique janvier 1975-mai 1975," May 20, 1975. When women on the line asked once again to put both hands on the watch, Neuschwander responded that he had made calculations and this would not be possible. Piaget thought that Neuschwander said this because of the unwillingness of mid-level managers to change. Parti pris, February 1979, 23.

Although the OS were not subject to the same forms of abusive authority by managers as under Fred Lip, they returned to the same dead-end jobs. For the CFDT-Lip leadership, the conflict was always about jobs. With full employment in the new firm, Piaget recognized that there would be the need to "put up with stuff."[101] But many female OS saw things differently. "We freely agreed to work in the struggle; we did it with joy, in teams and as we thought it should be done."[102] During the conflict workers proved quite capable of doing things above their grade level; they moved to other occupations according to their desires and the needs of the movement. However, with jobs secured, male skilled workers found satisfaction returning to work in a system that recognized their expertise and status. For the female OS, fighting in a different way did not readily translate into working in a different way in the factory.[103]

The 1975 CESI study found a strong desire on the part of the OS assembling watches to meet and talk with other workers and to visit their workshops, as they had been able to do during the conflict. In a response to Neuschwander's emphasis on the provision of economic information to workers, the report explained:

> Beyond information, there is thus a need for knowledge that leads to an implicit desire to form and to keep contacts, meetings. The enterprise should also be a place of this type. One can go so far as to read in these words the desire to create a community. Information is also the knowledge of others and not only of relations of productivity.[104]

A major finding of the study was the aspiration of the OS, making frequent reference to their experience in the conflict, to form teams of workers with different kinds of expertise, and to be given responsibility for production. Neuschwander himself talked of looking ahead to a time when every workshop would set production targets with the directors and each would organize itself, depending on the manager as a technical consultant.[105]

---

101   *Témoignage chrétien*, February 7, 1974, 5.
102   *L'Outil des travailleurs*, February 1974, 10.
103   Bruno Parmentier in *Lip Unité*, February–March 1980, 7.
104   BDIC F delta rés 702/20/2 CESI, "Plan d'intervention," 22.
105   Neuschwander, *Patron, mais ...*, 148. However, union delegates may have discouraged this because they recognized that it made workers within a group discipline their less productive members. AB Interview with Françoise Dromard by Beurier [1992], 11.

Neuschwander called himself a left-wing boss, and did not consider this an oxymoron. He believed that his idea of management, premised on new forms of communication and human relations—an element rooted in Catholic humanism of the "new spirit of capitalism" that Luc Boltanski and Ève Chiapello show developed in response to the 1968-era labor conflicts—was the future in both capitalist and socialist enterprises.[106] But Neuschwander thought that a "left-wing capitalist" was an impossibility.[107] He saw his communication with the labor force at Lip as creating a relationship that could help insulate the enterprise from stockholders. He believed that the exchange of information "between workers and the direction of the enterprise" would create "a sort of consensus which would enable the enterprise to live and develop."[108] This consensus in turn would limit, "to a certain extent, the possibility for stockholders to get rid of one or another person as they wish."[109] In any case, Neuschwander's project presupposed shareholders who did not aggressively intervene in management, a legacy of a generation of postwar economic growth that was to be lost as that era came to a close. Piaget understood the situation better. In March 1975, at the height of the firm's success, he said that Neuschwander was "to capitalism what the good priest of a proletarian parish was to the Vatican powers."[110] But even the good priest could be excommunicated.

The End of the SEHEM

The SEHEM had been born of individuals influenced by Catholic humanism embarking on a rethinking of French business in the context of the dramatic postwar growth. There was reason to be optimistic. The watch industry grew by 3.9 per cent in Franche-Comté between 1973 and 1975.[111] However, the CEH, and with it the SEHEM, succumbed when a changed economic and political environment—the number of unemployed reached 1 million in France in the fall of 1975—revealed that business did not have a place for the kind of management Neuschwander

---

106   Luc Boltanski and Ève Chiapello, *Le Nouvel esprit du capitalisme* (Paris, 1999).
107   ACN Neuschwander, "Ils ont tué Lip," V, 16.
108   Ibid., II, 2, 3.
109   Ibid., V, 38.
110   *Le Quotidien de Paris*, March 13, 1975.
111   Lantz, "Lip et l'utopie," 98.

envisaged or the state for participation in challenges to the uncreative destruction of capitalism.

Neuschwander developed his ideas on management in his book *Patron mais* ... At the book's origin was a conversation with President Valéry Giscard d'Estaing to whom, following a Lip company tradition, Neuschwander presented the first mass-produced quartz watch made in France in the summer of 1975. When Lip had earlier seemed a lame duck, Giscard d'Estaing had no taste for it. However, now that it was back on its feet, the president expressed real interest in Neuschwander's firm. He began his presidency in 1974 as a liberal in both the free market and the Anglo-American political senses of the term. Giscard d'Estaing himself had appointed a committee under the direction of Pierre Sudreau to address reform of the enterprise along the lines Bloch-Lainé had proposed a decade earlier. As a child, Sudreau had been the inspiration for Antoine de Saint-Exupéry's Little Prince. In his report released in February 1975, his suggestion of introducing supervisory boards that would include members elected by the workers was an idea from another world that neither business nor unions wanted to introduce into this one. Giscard d'Estaing saw in Neuschwander the voice of what he hoped would be a reform more acceptable to both parties.[112] He asked him to write up a memorandum with his ideas on management.[113] Riboud himself opposed Sudreau's co-supervision idea and got Neuschwander to turn down Giscard d'Estaing's request and instead to do a book of interviews with a journalist he chose. Riboud went over the manuscript pen in hand before it was published. *Patron mais* ... was composed in July 1975 and it reflects the last of the "thirty glorious years" of postwar growth, when the combativeness of workers in a growing economy was the primary issue. However, by the time the book was published in the fall of 1975, the severity and intractability of the recession and what this entailed led the mad doctor Riboud to doubt the director he had created.

The creation of the SEHEM had given hope to workers elsewhere that their actions could lead to the revival of troubled firms. To stave off this idea, the state turned on the firm. To avoid another Lip Affair,

112   Piaget presents Neuschwander's management as embodying important elements of Sudreau's report as well. "Lip aujourd'hui," 8.

113   Neuschwander, *Claude Neuschwander*, 142–4. When *Patron, mais* ... appeared in the fall, Jean-Pierre Raffarin, the secretary-general of the Mouvement des jeunes giscardiens, praised "the scent of Giscardism" he found in it. He shared "most" of Neuschwander's analyses and was excited "to meet a humanist in the collectivist camp." "Lettre ouverte à Claude Neuschwander," *La Lettre hebdomadaire de GSL*, 375 (December 1975).

Prime Minister Jacques Chirac had created the Comité Interministériel de l'Aménagement des Structures Industrielles (CIASI) in November 1974. It was, in the words of CIASI *inspecteur des finances* Gilles Guitton, "the child of Lip," born of the experience of finding during the Lip Affair that "no one really knew how to manage this crisis."[114] The CIASI brought together technocrats and bankers to analyze and respond to firms in financial difficulties. From an interventionist Gaullist state actively engaged in industrial modernization, the Lip Affair, in the words of Michel Chemin, turned the state into the *médecin malgré lui* of industrial decline—"a sort of emergency medical service that dispenses an expensive medicine and is limited to cases of force majeure." But its goal became to allow the market to function without political interventions such as those the crisis at Lip had encouraged.[115] The CIASI could pursue any number of actions, ranging from mediating among interested parties and reorienting the production of a firm to allowing the reduction of employment in stages or temporarily financing continued employment in mono-industrial areas.[116] However, the affected populations often looked upon CIASI in the Gaullist terms of state direction of industrial development, and this ambiguity played itself out among *les Lip*, who in the mid-1970s continued to address the state in a language it no longer spoke.

The SEHEM did reasonably well until the second half of 1975. Civil and military production were the only sectors that turned a profit, but the Charbonnel and successive plans had all assumed losses in watch sales for several years, and those in 1974 were less than predicted.[117] Imbued with the "thirty glorious years" faith that productivist growth could reconcile the interests of owners and workers, and focused initially on mechanical watches, Neuschwander projected production of more than 1 million watches annually by 1980; as production rose, the factory would be able to take advantage of economies of scale.[118] However, the recession caught up with the firm in the fall of 1975. Too much attention,

---

114   Gilles Guitton in "Faut-il parler de désindustrialisation entre 1974 et 1984?" in *1974-1984. Une décennie de désindustrialisation?*, eds. Pierre Lamard and Nicolas Stoskopf (Paris, 2009), 93–4.

115   Florence Clauzel, "Faillites d'entreprises: les charognards ou les Saint-Bernard?," *Autrement* 40 (May 1982): 149–50.

116   On the CIASI, see Élie Cohen, *L'Etat brancardier. Politiques du déclin industriel (1974-1984)* (Paris, 1989).

117   ADD 45J111 Comite d'Entreprise of CEH, "Analyse de l'activité de l'entreprise 1974," 38.

118   Lantz, "Lip et l'utopie," 102. In 1975, a little less than one-quarter of CEH sales were of electric and quartz watches; the remainder were mechanical watches.

investors were told, had been given to "sexy" elements, like designer and quartz watches.[119] Losses exceeded projections, leaving a nine-month stock of watches. Unexpected expenses like paying off Lip's debts and the introduction of watchcase production contributed to the need for supplemental funding. In addition, the firm had begun with a lease on the assets of the bankrupt Lip, but in 1976 it would have to come up with 42 million francs or relinquish these. Most importantly, faced with the unexpectedly rapid development of quartz and digital watches by foreign competitors, the CEH lacked the funds necessary to take advantage of its advanced research in these areas. An infusion of funds by the owners in February 1976 was insufficient. One stockholder came to Neuschwander with a far-fetched plan. If the CEH could produce triple the average return on capital investment in France at the time, he knew financiers from the Gulf states willing to put up the money to save the firm.[120] Like the Kuwaiti merchant who wanted to buy up the stock of watches in the summer of 1973, such plutocrats could view Lip only as a short-term investment, not a community or an enterprise.

The CEH, and with it the SEHEM, fell victim to a politics of austerity at a time when an active state role in economic development was the only chance for France to meet the challenge posed by the displacement of the mechanical watch by the quartz watch. When Riboud originally promoted the revival of Lip, he was more the social entrepreneur than the empire builder who had established his reputation in the effort to take over Saint-Gobain. Riboud had never invested in Lip with the goal of building an enterprise that, given time and resources, could take a commanding role in its sector. The recession weakened organized labor and the impetus to address the issues he had raised at Marseille in 1972. Riboud and Gillet had supported Chaban-Delmas. When he lost the first round of the presidential elections in 1974 to Giscard d'Estaing, who went on to defeat Mitterrand, investors found less appeal in their association with Lip.[121] Chirac called French shareholders of the SEHEM to the Hôtel Matignon in September 1975, and in the presence of representatives of the CNPF discussed the danger of campaigns for full employment that took the Lip experience as a model.[122] Chirac then conveyed to Riboud

---

119   ADD 1812W28 Mémorandum justificatif des actionnaires de la SEHEM, April 14, 1976.

120   Claude Neuschwanter, "Patron malgré lui …," *Semaine sociale Lamy* supplement to no. 1631 (May 19, 2014): 21.

121   *Libération*, June 22, 1983, 12

122   Neuschwander, "Patron malgré lui …," 20.

and Gillet that it was necessary to do away with what Lip represented because the economic recession was leading to large layoffs and the state and business were afraid of similar conflicts elsewhere.[123] What had been possible in one bankrupt firm in 1974 was not so feasible when there were 200 at the end of the next year. Riboud told Charbonnel that he had no choice but to listen to Chirac. In October 1975, Riboud asked Neuschwander if he would fire 100 workers if Riboud told him to do so. Neuschwander balked, saying this was not on the agenda at Lip, but it made him realize that "Lip as a symbol of full employment posed some problems to stockholders."[124] A crisis began that month with the refusal of the nationalized Crédit Lyonnais, on whose board Riboud sat, to extend a loan to the CEH. In the fall of 1975, state-owned Renault withdrew its order for dashboard clocks from CEH and the Ministry of Industry suspended the 5 million francs that Lip had expected to receive for development of the quartz watch; state banks withheld credit.[125]

Riboud and Gillet had engaged in the Lip Affair to provide a showcase for their ideas about how to deal with labor in the economy of postwar expansion. By the fall of 1975, the recession had clearly taken hold and the BSN and Rhône-Poulenc were themselves laying off workers and closing factories. If resurrecting Lip with full employment of its work-force had been evidence for Riboud, Bidegain and other modernizers of their claim to be the rightful leaders of French business, the project was now a liability to their businesses and in relations with Chirac's government. It was a sign of the times that Bidegain reentered the CNPF in November 1975 as vice-president of its commerce commission. Riboud rejoined the CNPF then as well. When the Lip workers staged the history of their struggle, they said that as a sign that he was reformed, Riboud was asked "give up his dancer Lip."[126]

What Riboud had sought were unions that negotiated and carried out contracts, not enterprises that recognized workers' investment of their lives in the firm. When the CEH did not meet its sales goals in the fall of 1975 and had a larger than expected loss that year, Riboud incorrectly blamed Neuschwander for hiding the financial situation of the firm. This initiated months of scapegoating of Neuschwander, which continued unabated despite a significant turnaround in sales in January

123   *Le Monde*, April 8–9, 2007, 17.
124   ACN Neuschwander, "Ils ont tué Lip," V, 3.
125   Neuschwander, *Claude Neuschwander*, 144–6.
126   "Refuser la fatalité et vivre ensemble au pays" [Historique de la lutte présenté par les travailleurs]" in Terrieux, "L'Expérience Lip," Partie II, épisode 1.

1976.[127] This campaign had attributes of the one that had earlier been directed against Fred Lip as a means of assuring that neither the practices of the state nor those of capitalism per se were questioned.

Meeting in January 1976, the CEH board of directors turned down a plan offered by Neuschwander and set unrealistic financial objectives for the firm accompanied by assaults on the labor force, including thirty-eight early retirements and reduced work weeks for 760 employees. Worse yet, members of the board continued to cast doubt on the firm's future in what CFDT-Lip would call "the largest campaign ever conceived of denigration, of negative public relations."[128] This caused watch seller-jewelers to hold back, reversing the strong sales in January. As Raguénès said, "it's as if M. Riboud told his customers, 'Don't eat my yogurts. They are disgusting.'"[129] The CFDT-Lip negotiated an acceptance of the cutbacks with Neuschwander, with a less severe implementation of the reduction in working hours. That the workers did not strike was evidence of a willingness to work with Neuschwander in a difficult situation.[130] He later said that the Lip unions "always had a sense of responsibility in regards to the survival of the enterprise, to which I pay homage, for if the stockholders had had the same, the enterprise would still be around."[131] However, the Communists, for whom the success of the CEH was problematic, saw this as evidence of "the Neuschwander operation," the creation of relations with personnel and the unions "that would be a contagious example of class collaboration."[132] In an effort to reestablish the place it had forfeited with the signing of the Dole accords two years earlier, the CGT-Lip took the lead in the spring of 1976 in supporting actions by workers with grievances.[133] The state in turn questioned Neuschwander's ability to impose as hard a line on labor as needed.[134]

In any case, Neuschwander had other priorities than squeezing the workforce. The greatest challenge facing the CEH and the French

127   Le Canard enchaîné, April 14, 1976, 4. ADD 1026W19 "Rapport établi à la demande de Monsieur le Préfet par J. Cl. Mayaud dans le cadre de la commission d'expertise chargée d'apprécier l'actif de la CEH" [1976].

128   Lip Unité, April 1976, 1.

129   Libération, April 13, 1976, 7.

130   CFDT-Lip, "LIP 76 Une industrie, une région en danger," April 21, 1976.

131   Les Lip. L'Imagination au pouvoir, booklet accompanying the DVD (Les Films du paradoxe, 2007).

132   L'Humanité, February 25, 1976, 6.

133   ADD 1812W34 RG, March 8, 1976; April 2, 1974.

134   ADD 2032W333 Directeur départemental du Travail to MT, January 26, 1976; February 3, 1976.

watch industry as a whole was the move worldwide to the quartz watch, in which time is kept by thin sheets of synthetic quartz oscillating in response to an electric charge from a battery. Although in 1976 only 11 percent of watches sold in France were quartz, this would soon change. Neuschwander presented saving the CEH in terms of saving the French watch industry. Though the CEH began selling a half-dozen models of quartz watches in September 1975, the move to quartz was a transformation too large for a single French firm to undertake on its own. Starting from the CEH's unique research department inherited from Lip, Neuschwander sought state support to develop a common quartz watch technology that all in the French watch industry could draw on and use. He did not propose a federation of watch producers, along the lines of the ASUAG, but a model where competition among French producers would not be based on technology.[135]

Neuschwander contended that only CEH research could provide the basis for the survival of the large number of small firms in Haut-Doubs. Thinking of the CEH in these terms as well as taking a jab at the CNPF, which had rejected the Sudreau report, President Giscard d'Estaing intervened to play good cop to his rival and his prime minister Chirac's bad cop. He announced a week after the company board of directors met in January 1976 that Quartzelec, a consortium which drew on the research of the CEH, could apply for funds from the CIASI, with the expectation that this would overcome the hesitation of banks to provide credit to the CEH.[136] L'Humanité could not resist the headline the next day, "Giscard d'Estaing flies to the rescue of Neuschwander and Piaget."[137] Stockholders, including Riboud and Gillet, resented this initiative because it came with a requirement that they make new investments in the firm as well. In any case, the initiative did not spur the commitment from banks or the board necessary to put the CEH back on track. However, it did prompt a one-day strike of almost all the small firms involved in the production of watches in Haut-Doubs, accompanied by the villes mortes of shopkeepers and municipal officials, to make the case that the CEH should be abandoned as they were the ones who deserved assistance.[138] Although (and because) quartz technology posed a largely

---

135   AR Interview with Neuschwander by Rouaud, June 18, 2005, 1–3.
136   Le Monde, January 31, 1976, 32.
137   L'Humanité, January 31, 1976.
138   BDIC F delta rés 702/20/1 "Rapport au Comité d'Entreprise de la CEH sur les Comptes de 1975." ADD 2032W333, Directeur régional du travail to MT, February 3, 1976.

unacknowledged threat to small watchmakers, their antipathy to Fred Lip carried over to the CEH. They refused to accept the idea that their future should be dependent on the development by the CEH of a quartz watch technology accessible to all. Chirac, ever an opponent to a revival of Lip, turned to the CIASI as well. As prime minister, the CIASI was within his bailiwick and in mid-February it allocated 8 million francs (1 million more than the CIASI proposed for the CEH) to a research group that had been created in 1971 by firms in the area, but not Lip, to develop watch technology. In the long term, this made no difference. The Société Montrélec (Sociéte pour le developpement de la montre électronique) was a failure.[139]

Giscard d'Estaing's brief dalliance did not save Neuschwander. In fact, Neuschwander's head may have been the price that the CEH board happily paid to remain in Chirac's good graces.[140] The board forced Neuschwander's resignation a couple of days after Giscard d'Estaing's proposal. However, this did not stop it from humiliating Neuschwander by publishing advertisements for his position in Le Monde and Le Figaro without telling him and before publicly announcing his departure. The left-wing boss exemplified by Neuschwander was rooted in a managerial capitalism that had displaced the owner-led family firm, but was unable to survive in the economy that emerged from the recession of the late 1970s. Like all events, the collapse of Lip and later of the CEH can retrospectively be seen as inevitable, the result of the development of quartz watch sales by international competitors, but this is not how it was understood by contemporary actors and observers. In some accounts, blame was placed on the owner-director, Fred Lip, or on the salaried director, Claude Neuschwander, and his understanding of the enterprise. With Fred Lip in mind, André Malterre, national leader of the CGC, spoke of the need for a mechanism to get rid of incompetent directors in order to prevent the creation of "revolutionary situations."[141] In other scenarios, the Ébauches SA or the Riboud-Gillet project are held

139   ADD 45J105 Edgar Hirschi, 'L'industrie française de la montre. Comment on a détruit une industrie en dix ans" (November 1984), 23. Évelyne Ternant argues that funding for Lip technology would not have saved the watch industry—though it, not Montrélec, developed a technology along the lines of that which triumphed worldwide—because watchmakers in France were so averse to innovation and had competing interests that made it difficult to cooperate beyond opposing innovation that came from Lip. Ternant, "L'Affaiblissement du SPL," 107–33. Ternant, "Le milieu horloger français," 25–46.
140   Le Nouvel observateur, February 16, 1976, 25.
141   André Malterre, "La révolution en marche," Le Creuset, September 8, 1973, 2.

responsible. Both used the enterprise for extraneous purposes—to enter the French market or to build up a capital of reputation—and made the future of Lip itself secondary.

In a burst of bravado, Riboud told CFDT representatives the day after Neuschwander's forced resignation: "I rule out the idea of any layoffs. If necessary, I will myself go spend three months at Besançon to take things in hand and accelerate the technological transformation of the enterprise."[142] And as late as the beginning of April, the state police reported that the SEHEM board was divided between hard-liners, including the ASUAG president and representatives of the banks, who wanted a large collective layoff, and a second, less pessimistic, group composed of Bidegain, Riboud, and Gillet, who wanted to buy time in hopes of turning things around.[143] The board replaced Neuschwander with the musical-instrument maker Jean Sargueil, who had first come to prominence as a director of propaganda for the Chantiers de Jeunesse during the Vichy Regime.[144] CFDT-Lip went back to the state with the argument that the new director, though an ally of the hard-liners on the board and dubbed "Mister Coffin" by the union, estimated the funds necessary to maintain the CEH in operation would be half the cost of unemployment benefits for the workforce. This would keep the research, patents and brand name out of the hands of the Swiss. The argument fell on deaf ears.[145] Though Sargueil died of a heart attack in April 1976, he did have time to get the lay of the land: "Never did I expect to meet so much hatred directed against this enterprise."[146]

Sleeping Beauty Once Again

The SEHEM declared bankruptcy in April 1976. Chirac had achieved his aim and confirmed that "The fate of Lip is no longer a government matter."[147] The authorities had expected that workers would undertake "a raid of the stocks or an immediate occupation," something that would give them the pretext to send in the police.[148] However, the workers limited

142 *L'Express*, April 12, 1976, 29.
143 ADD 1812W28 RG, April 1, 1976.
144 Obituary for Jean Sargueil in *Rivarol*, April 29, 1976.
145 AMB 5Z222 Union locale [Besançon] CFDT, "Lip: l'agression", April 5, 1976 [quoted]. *Le Figaro*, April 6, 1976, 6; April 7, 1976, 1.
146 *Libération*, April 6, 1976, 3.
147 *Le Figaro*, April 13, 1976, 8.
148 *Libération*, April 20, 1976.

themselves to securing Palente in order to prevent the syndics from sending in trucks to take away the machines. Substantial night watches composed of workers supplemented by leftists and union members from other firms guarded the factory. Workers hid the finished watches there—the stock had tripled in the past year—but did not prepare to sell them as they could draw on the recently enacted unemployment benefit of 90 percent of their pay for a year.[149] However, employees continued to work in April. In the interest of saving the enterprise, they did not want to alienate the watch seller-jewelers Neuschwander had cultivated: *les Lip* wrote them a letter of assurance.[150] Piaget talked to the 700 present at the General Assembly on April 22, 1976 of "the absolute necessity to give a 'responsible image': all loose behavior, all loitering on the lawns had to be forbidden." Though there was a limited amount of work, Piaget insisted over the objections of the CGT-Lip that "activities started up must be maintained to justify fully wages paid."[151] After the firm was liquidated and the General Assembly decided to occupy Palente in early May, 250 of the 880 employees (830 veterans of Lip and fifty hired by its successor) threw in the towel, leaving 630. Production stopped, but the workers remained committed because they thought employers would not hire workers from Lip and out of loyalty to the community they had formed.[152]

Neuschwander had sought unsuccessfully to build the CEH's future around the technological innovation of its research facilities. With the liquidation of the CEH in May 1976, Lip employees pursued this vision, working with Syndex to develop a plan to draw upon the research facilities and the brand name Lip to make Palente the core of a French watch industry that could compete internationally. Like Neuschwander, they accepted that the CEH could not survive on its own, but the French watchmaking industry in turn could not survive without its research and expertise. The workers wanted the state to invest in the establishment of a Groupement d'Intérêt Économique Horloger Régional dedicated to the innovation and renovation of the failing industry. It would have a federal structure that would preserve the autonomy of the small watchmaking firms of Haut-Doubs.[153] The skills and techniques used in watchmaking were also applicable to a number of areas of growth like micro-mechanics

149 ADD 35J10, Intersyndicale LIP, July 6, 1976. *Le Figaro*, April 14, 1976, 9.
150 *Politique hebdo*, April 29, 1976, 3.
151 ADD 1812W28 RG, April 21, 1976; April 22, 1976; April 23, 1976.
152 *Lip Unité*, August 1977, 5. Burgy and Piaget, "L'aventure des coopératives LIP."
153 ADD 35J10, Intersyndicale Lip, July 6, 1976.

and telecommunications.[154] The goal of *les Lip* was not to sustain a lost cause, but to spur regional development in a diversity of industries: "Thus Lip would become a site of subversion, where responses would be given to new situations."[155]

An expert brought in to assess the facilities at Palente at this time caught the sense of expectation:

> To conclude, I cannot prevent myself from evoking a painful impression born of my recent visits to Lip: a lethargic factory like the château of Sleeping Beauty which awaits the wave of a magic wand, exceptional installations remarkably well maintained, a scientific and technical personnel conscious of the possibilities and that looks to see them utilized in the best general interest, assembly lines that a puff of air would restart.[156]

When workers held an open house at Palente on May 8–9, 1976, it differed from those of the earlier conflict. The large banner at the entry read "We struggle for 900 jobs at Lip and for French watchmaking." Twelve to fifteen thousand visitors came. Workers took them around the factory to see the advanced technology. No watches were sold. Unlike the situation in 1973, the managers and engineers and their union, CGC-Lip, played an important role, actively cooperating with the CFDT-Lip. Managers and engineers, not workers, spoke to the visitors about the technological advances made by the firm and the national and international markets it would have if supported by the state for a few years.[157] Presentations on the quartz watch and on micro-mechanics were intended to show the economic viability of Palente as a center of innovation for the struggling watch industry.[158] At the open house, Raguénès used the metaphor Piaget had called on to characterize Riboud's band of capitalists. He told reporters that now "Lip workers were a little in the position of judo players on the defensive who have to counter the blows."[159] The goal of this open

154   Already at this point, some analysts saw the future of Lip not in watches, but in the skilled mechanics and machinery at Palente. These were viable and could be easily separated from the other sectors of the firm. ADD 1026W19 "Rapport succinct sur le département 'Armement' (Spemelip) de l'ex-société Lip," July 8, 1976.

155   Collectif, *Lip: affaire non classée*, 123.

156   ADD 1026W19 Raymond Chaleat, "Rapport d'expertise concernant la Société Européenne d'Horlogerie," July 8, 1976.

157   *Témoignage chrétien*, May 26, 1976, 9. *Le Figaro*, April 14, 1976, 9.

158   *Libération*, May 11, 1976, 6.

159   *Libération*, May 10, 1976, 8.

house was not so much to impress an audience on the left as to make the case for investment by the state.

This seemed a betrayal to some. Piton asked why workers who made beautiful quartz watches had more right to a job than makers of toilet-bowl chains.[160] A group of Lip workers saw the quartz watch as an example of "the most complete capitalist waste," with no real benefit for consumers, but recognized that in capitalist societies, capitalists decide what is made and Lip was France's only chance to enter this market.[161] Members of the Lip support committee of the Vincennes University faculty went to the open house and were shocked. They wrote an open letter to make clear that they supported the Lip workers, not because of the quality of their watches or technology, but "because the brawl of 1973 has become a symbol of the determination of the French working class."[162] The Communists had never favored opening the doors to the workers' domain, the factory. If they had mistrusted the entrance of leftists, they remained equally suspicious of what they saw as another instance of the Lip workers' desire to choose their exploiters rather than contest them. That the open house was open to all—from capitalists to deputies of parties on the left—led the departmental secretary of the PCF in Doubs to label it "a holy alliance uniting victims and executioners."[163]

In the spring of 1977, in anticipation of the end of the unemployment benefit at 90 percent of the previous salary, the state commissioned reports on future possibilities for Palente, predicated on doing away with the workers' world but drawing on the research department's work on quartz watches to convert it to the production of integrated circuits, a crucial component of modern technology for which France was dependent on foreign producers: "It is the elaboration in progress of a solution to the French problem of integrated circuits that could lift Lip out of the rut." One consultant saw political benefits as well:

Lip has become a symbol that it would be desirable to demystify. To start up this firm would confirm the concern for conciliation of the public authorities and of business, as well as their major preoccupation with

160   "Monique Pitton [sic]: 'Lip 73, oui! Lip 78 … C'est plutôt moche …,'" Commune 20 (June 15, 1978): 21.

161   Collectif, Lip: affaire non classée, 165–73.

162   BDIC F delta rés 702/8/1 Comité de soutien à Lip de la faculté de Vincennes, "Lettre ouverte aux travailleurs de Lip," June 19, 1976.

163   AMB 5Z225 "Déclaration de Serge Paganelli pour le Parti Communiste Français," May 6, 1976.

employment, while to persist in an ostracism on principle would inevitably have the opposite effect.[164]

However, when the management of the Compagnie Générale de l'Électricité (CGE) favored investing in integrated circuits at the former CEH, the firm's president-director general Ambroise Roux overruled it. He had always thought the state showed unjustifiable "leniency" to Lip. Furthermore, to integrate Lip in the CGE would be to "introduce the wolf into the sheep pen," when the CGE was on the Common Program list of firms to be nationalized.[165] But the CEH itself was not on that list. Only the prefect of Doubs saw a place for Lip in the Common Program. He hoped others would project the Lip experience onto it:

> The Lip Affair survives only on the political and social level, where it can perhaps be exploited advantageously during the upcoming elections, to the detriment of the Socialist Party that hesitates between realism and the temptation of an almost unconditional support.
>
> The Lip Affair has bathed since the beginning in a climate of unreality and illusion that prefigures, in large measure, what would prevail if the Common Program of the left one day has a chance to be applied … The opportunity presents itself today, once again, to put those who support *les Lip* in their quixotic obstinacy, fully aware that it is completely unrealistic, in an awkward position before the public.[166]

The Second Left

Palente became a site where Jacques Chirac and Valéry Giscard d'Estaing worked out the move away from Gaullist economic policy premised on a degree of state intervention. Faced with state pressure to do away with the threat posed by the revival of Lip, investors let the firm go bankrupt again in 1976. If these businessmen invested in Lip to save capitalism, they left for the same reason, putting an end to this business response to 1968. As the French watch industry faced the challenge of making the transition from mechanical to quartz watches, it was *les Lip*, drawing on Neuschwander's plan, who fought for an effective response. This was a new dimension of worker power introduced at Lip with the arrival of

---

164   ADD 1026W22 G. Orrand, "Fiche CEH-Lip," May 2, 1977.
165   ADD 1026W22 G. Orrand, "Fiche CEH-Lip," April 26, 1977.
166   ADD 1026W18 PD, "L'affaire Lip en septembre 1977," September 27, 1977.

Syndex at Palente in 1973. That the French watch industry did not meet the challenge should not obscure this element. The fall of Lip was not due solely to the introduction of quartz watches, but the firm's demise was a factor in the decline of the French watch industry in the face of quartz technology.

The Lip conflict in 1973 was a transformative event for leftists; the rise and fall of the SEHEM played the same role for the Second Left. It challenged constituent elements of the Second Left, the PSU and the CFDT, and they backed away from "live tomorrow in the struggles of today"—the mantra on banners at the national CFDT congress held a few weeks before Lip workers began producing watches in June 1973.[167] An initial chapter of the "re-centering" of the CFDT completed in 1978—a trade unionism that participated in creating a capitalism that works for workers without questioning that they work for it[168]—was its involvement in the resolution of the initial Lip struggle in 1973-4; the end of the PSU as a viable alternative on the left began with its opposition to the presidential candidacy of Piaget in April 1974, less than a month after Palente reopened.

Emblematic of these changes were the enduring ties Riboud established with the leading figures of the Second Left. "It is certainly at the time of the Lip Affair," Rocard wrote of Riboud in 2007, "that our convergence of beliefs was put to the test and verified … We thought of saving not only jobs and workers, but the honor of French business as well."[169] These relationships were unaffected by Riboud's abandonment of the SEHEM. Rocard and leaders of the CFDT had played an instrumental role in launching it, but they did not come to the defense of the firm in 1975-6. In May-June 1976, Neuschwander wrote a book for Seuil defending his actions and criticizing Riboud. Riboud read the manuscript and got Rocard and Jacques Julliard—Neuschwander's fellow Catholic student activist in the UNEF and Rocard's close associate—to convince Neuschwander not to publish it.[170] Neuschwander held back when they said the book would hurt the enterprise's prospects.[171] Long afterwards, in recounting the end of the firm, Rocard continued to champion the

---

167   Hélène Hatzfeld, *Faire de la politique autrement. Les expériences inachevées des années 1970* (Rennes, 2005), 249–51. Vigna, *L'Insubordination ouvrière*, nicely encapsulates this as the move from the factory to the state as the center of activity and hopes.

168   Frank Georgi, *Soufflons nous-mêmes notre forge* (Paris, 1991), 171.

169   Michel Rocard, "Préface" to Labasse, *Antoine Riboud*, 8–9.

170   Neuschwander, *Claude Neuschwander*, 159–60. Jacques Chérèque joined in this effort.

171   ACN Neuschwander, "Ils ont tué Lip," III, 49.

position of the by now deceased Riboud over that of Neuschwander. Neuschwander had mismanaged the enterprise, abusing "the generosity of Riboud," who could not be expected to operate without turning a profit: "Neuschwander bankrupted Lip, period." Rocard may have been "sorry," but he had long accepted Riboud's dismissal of Neuschwander.[172] As far as Neuschwander was concerned, Rocard gave "surety" to Riboud when the industrialist carried out the wishes of Chirac and Giscard d'Estaing to put an end to the successor to Lip.[173]

The Lip Affair ultimately did more to bring CFDT leaders together with Riboud than with Piaget or Vittot. Riboud got to know Jacques Chérèque and Albert Mercier, leaders of the FGM-CFDT: "this battle of several years brought us together and we established friendly relations between us." He explained that his engagement in Lip "only reinforced [his] affinities with the national leaders of the CFDT."[174] Chérèque spoke of the resurrection of Lip as a time when "an exceptional partnership fell into place around Riboud's men, like José Bidegain" and leaders of the CFDT and the PSU.[175] The collapse of the SEHEM did not change this. The relationships the confederation and business leaders developed in responding to the crisis at Lip endured. Riboud remained a favorite of CFDT leaders. Nicole Notat gave a glowing encomium at Riboud's funeral in 2002, dating the close ties between Riboud and the CFDT leadership to the Lip Affair.[176] However, Palente, either as *les Lip* or as Neuschwander imagined it, did not find a secure place in the Second Left as it took shape over the course of the Lip Affair.[177] For, as Piaget and

---

172   *Le Monde*, March 21, 2007, 28.

173   *Le Monde*, April 8–9, 2007, 17. Rocard later took back his comment about Neuschwander's responsibility for the collapse of the CEH, saying that he had made it based on his faith in what Riboud had told him, but had since gotten information that made him realize that he was probably wrong. ADD 45J111 Michel Rocard to Wikipedia, February 23, 2012.

174   Riboud, *Le dernier de la classe*, 80, 193.

175   *Le Nouvel observateur*, May 16, 2002.

176   Labasse, *Antoine Riboud*, 12–13, 138–9.

177   The Lip conflict ultimately had as much effect on the CGT as on the CFDT. For the CFDT, it encouraged withdrawal from the radical tactics of the post-1968 years. The Communists and the CGT increasingly embraced them. After the Communist break with the Socialists in 1977, the transfusion from Lip was complete. The CGT adopted what it had condemned in Lip in 1973, including tactics like occupations and economic counter-proposals for troubled firms. Bernard Moss, "Workers and the Common Program (1968–1978): The Failure of French Communism," *Science and Society* 54:1 (Spring 1990): 42–66. This change began the very day workers approved the Dole accords in 1974. Workers under CGT leadership occupied the Rateau turbine manufacturer in Courneuve for twelve days to stop layoffs. After criticizing Syndex for proposing an alternative business plan for Lip, the CGT ventured in the same direction,

Neuschwander and Piaget later recognized, the enterprise itself as the potential site of a social community in a globalizing financial capitalism faltered. "[B]efore," said Neuschwander, "society organized around an economy structured by the enterprise; if the struggles were robust, it remained the site of social identity, of belonging to a class, of worker solidarity. Afterwards, the enterprise is no longer at the heart of the economy."[178] This made the struggle to make the factory where the workers are all the more difficult.

arguing that the modifications Alsthom sought to implement at Rateau could be done without reducing the workforce. Piaget was not alone in seeing that "Rateau is impregnated with the fact of Lip, even if [the CGT] does not want this." *L'Outil des travailleurs*, February 1974, 8.

178   *Le Monde*, April 8–9, 2007, 17. Piaget in Bertrand Gauthier, *Lip, le rêve et l'histoire* (2005).

9
Women's Lip

One finds a good old concept, still valuable, in Leninism: the uninter-
rupted revolution can only develop by steps. At this time, you cannot ask
les Lip to be as anti-capitalist and as anti-bureaucratic as they are now
and to be anti-male chauvinist [*antiphallocratiques*] at the same time.

—Pierre Victor[1]

I'm going to tell you a little what happens at Lip with respect to women.
But each time I am going to replace the word man by the word white and
the word woman by the word Arab. So, at Lip, there are half whites and
half Arabs. Naturally, the great chiefs are whites, there are no Arab great
chiefs ... The white great chiefs think, reflect and speak; we, the Arabs,
we think. Me, I know this since I am an Arab. We reflect, but the white
great chiefs cannot know that we reflect since we never have the right to
say that we have reflected ...

—Monique Piton[2]

The industrialists' association, the UIMM, described the Lip conflict
in 1973 as a "collective psychosis in which the female element played
a significant role."[3] Claude Harmel, an analyst funded by the UIMM,
explained that a "monk," Raguénès, had no trouble moving the women

---

1   Gavi et al., *On a raison de se révolter*, 274 [October 1973].

2   *Libération*, October 16–17, 1976, 14 (quoted from Roussopolous' film, *Monique
et Christiane*). Jean Genet saw the film and sought out Piton to tell her how much he
liked this comparison. Piton, *Mémoires libres*, 116.

3   BDIC F delta rés 578/41 "Lip-la-Lune," supplement to *UIMM Actualités*, October
1973.

and that the women had in turn helped lead the men astray.[4] However, Gustave Le Bon is not the best guide to understanding events at Palente. Leftists were surprised to find in Besançon the class-conscious workers willing to undertake illegal actions that they had sought. Socialist feminists in turn discovered the female workers they had been looking for in some of the women of Lip, women who came to recognize and contest patriarchal power in the household, the factory and the CFDT-Lip.

Based on the active engagement of workers, the conflict became a life-changing experience, particularly for many female employees. The clear majority of women at Lip were OS or OP1, the lowest rank of skilled workers. They worked in relative isolation from one another, closely supervised and paid at piece rates that pitted workers against one another. These women had also been segregated from female employees elsewhere at Palente. When not at work, women were responsible for raising children and running their households. This double burden left them little time for other activities outside the workplace. Participation in the conflict had challenged the confines of the women workers' world. OS Paulette Dartevel explained the change the movement had made in her: "I think that before the conflict, I was living quite egotistically, a well-ordered little life; I thought of weekends, vacations. Now, all the same, I desire something else: more human contact, sharing, understanding."[5] Women especially valued breaking down the barriers that had separated them from other workers. They got to know one another outside of a system based on competing for the managers' attentions. Fatima Demougeot reflected: "It took the conflict to discover that the one judged 'stuck-up' was talented, capable of giving to others, a fighter, and that she was simply an exploited friend."[6]

Many female workers did not want what they had experienced to end. For the OS, the job action had responded to some of the discontents of factory work—pressure, the lack of opportunity to do anything different, indignity, sexual harassment, lack of acceptance as equals by others—but the demand of the movement was work for all at Lip, rather than a transformation of the workplace. The goal of many women became to sustain the change created by the conflict itself. They now saw that another world

---

4   Claude Harmel was the name taken by Guy Lemonnier after the war to hide the fact that he had been a collaborationist journalist during the Occupation. Joseph Pinard, "De l'hitlérisme aux 'études sociales et syndicales," *La Pensée* 296 (November–December 1993): 109–24.

5   *Lip au féminin*, 22.

6   *Lip au féminin*, 57.

was possible. "The OS, when they speak, are listened to," one said. "They are no longer the pathetic thing in front of a machine. This achievement must be preserved at any price. Not feeling inferior because you are a woman, because you are an OS, before people who have had the chance to continue their studies or the luck to have gotten a good position."[7] For many female workers like the OS Alice Carpena, the first liberation was to be identified as a worker, not a woman who worked, because both men and women did the same jobs during the conflict: "In the struggle, there was no longer the label man/woman."[8]

The women workers' double burden became an issue during the conflict in 1973. Their active participation required them to make changes in their domestic life not required of men. While some husbands took on tasks like cooking to allow their spouses to participate, this issue was a source of conjugal discord, particularly when women went on the road to participate in meetings. No one was a better analyst of these developments than Demougeot. She recognized that the collectivity at Lip initially took the form of a collectivity of households, but the collectivity itself challenged forms of power within the household. Demougeot had been married only a year when the conflict began, and she immediately found herself involved "in something that pleased me more than marriage, because I had the impression that marriage was not made to aid in my development." Though her husband supported her participation, she spoke of the daily battles she had with him at home "all alone" in order pursue active engagement in the struggle.[9] The conflict led her to question the institution of marriage: "Now I am against marriage. I say that the woman has too many responsibilities. She is the one who at once takes care of the household and works at the factory. She comes home and there she is again engaged in production, and under the authority of her husband. Marriage, such as it exists, does not suit me."[10]

Many couples were unmade and made in the liberty of the 1973 conflict. Piaget told a writer: "Relations, even between man and wife, were catalyzed in truth, whether for better or worse ..."[11] In the spring of 1974, when what one *militante* referred to as the phase of "normalization" (as in post-1968 Czechoslovakia) began, there were a number of divorces

7 Reine J. in ibid., 23.
8 Le Garrec, *Les Messagères*, 109.
9 BDIC F delta rés 578/46 "La Lutte des Femmes à LIP et ailleurs. Lyon juin 1975. Texte intégral de la bande son du film vidéo," 10.
10 Macciocchi, *De la France*, 440.
11 Ibid., 149.

initiated by women whose experience in the struggle gave them a new perspective and made them feel sequestered by their husbands.[12] And, in turn, the support women gave newly single women and mothers was an important element in the communities of Lip women over the succeeding years.[13]

The return to Palente raised particular issues for women relating to their place in production. The position of OS became even more feminized, moving from 77 percent female before the conflict to 84 percent after the new firm rehired the last workers early in 1975.[14] The new jobs making watchbands were done by women who "work all day up to their necks in oil."[15] As an element of a new worker consciousness that female OS assumed in the conflict, Demougeot affirmed that "it is the OS who gives work to all, who makes the enterprise run, and not the managers who give work to the OS, as those in charge of the company repeat so often. They want to put in the heads of the OS that they are losers, real sad cases. In reality, it is they who produce."[16] However, this did not lead OS to want to remain OS. The return to work brought a return to the hierarchy of skilled over unskilled, on top of that of male over female. Demougeot noted with indignation that women often spent their career as an OS with little chance of advancement, a situation male OS rarely experienced and that she attributed to management's gender bias.[17]

Engagement in the conflict in 1973 made this situation unacceptable for many women, whether being stuck at the bottom of the job hierarchy or the life of factory work itself. One female OS who had at no time expected to be anything else, reported that since the conflict, "I have trouble living with my condition of an OS. For me, the conflict was a revelation, and now it is shattering." [18] Jeannine Pierre-Émile said she had never thought about being an OS (and therefore about not being an OS) until participation in a number of popularization activities, frequently involving journalists and intellectuals, changed her:

---

12   Le Garrec, *Les Messagères*, 103–4. "À Lip, des femmes: mille manières de lutter," 34. Militants counted twenty-three divorces among Lip workers, following the 1973 movement. *Le Monde libertaire*, February 16, 1978, 8. But there may have been more. Jean-Pierre Barou thought of the close to 100 divorces during the nine months of conflict as the unspoken story of the Lip Affair. Samuelson, *Il était une fois Libération*, 244.

13   Margaret Maruani, *Les Syndicats à l'épreuve du féminisme* (Paris, 1979), 114.

14   *Politique hebdo*, March 6, 1975, 9.

15   Le Garrec, *Les Messagères*, 109.

16   *Lip au féminin*, 12.

17   Ibid., 49.

18   Macciocchi, *De la France*, 432.

And when I went back to work in the Neuschwander era, I was once again an OS, and very conscious of my condition of OS. It was very difficult then because I preferred to not be conscious of it, as before, rather than to live it consciously … My coming to consciousness of my condition as OS was for me something terrible.

From work in the conflict she knew she could do other things, but lacked the diplomas necessary to have the opportunity to do them. If male skilled workers found the vocational education courses useless and humiliating, they were particularly frustrating for female OS, for whom "the phony 'job training'" did not prepare them for advancement or change.[19]

In the Union

As negotiations took the place of militant actions at the end of 1973, women who had played a prominent role earlier began to feel dispossessed—a term used by both Piton and Demougeot—of their struggle by the (male) leadership of the CFDT-Lip.[20] Piton came to see the situation as like that in the national liberation movements in Vietnam and Algeria; when things calmed down, men wanted to take back the power, as in Algeria after independence.[21] "In the conflict we were not women, we were *militantes*," Demougeot realized.[22] "In the struggle, I always tried to do it all, to do the same things as the men."[23] But it was as a woman, not a *militante*, that the CFDT-Lip named Demougeot to the delegation at Dole.

They had no more need for me except as an extra. When they formed a delegation, they said: there has to be a woman, good, we'll put Fatima on it. We, the women, were not there to give our views, but simply to be there. At the negotiations at Dole, I was an accessory. I found myself there, isolated in the traditional role of the woman, not as a delegate of

---

19   ADD 45J96 Interview with Pierre-Émile by Beurier [c. 1992], 23–5, 37. *Lip Actualité*, September 1978, 2. See also Pierre-Émile's reflections in Macciocchi, *De la France*, 432–3.

20   *Lip au féminin*, 29. *Politique hebdo*, March 6, 1975, 8–9.

21   Piton, *C'est possible!*, 521–2.

22   Le Garrec, *Les Messagères*, 100.

23   However, Demougeot added, even at the height of the conflict there were jobs that male leaders considered unsuitable for women and did not give them (like handing out leaflets). Werner, "La question des femmes," 2453–4.

the workers, charged with defending their interests, but as a woman, to represent female charm, etc. Bidegain acted solicitously to me and the guys did not even react. And then, this really shocked me. When I spoke to them about it, they said to me: "We didn't want to mix in your private life, we wanted to leave you your liberty" … They did not pose the problem in terms of political activism by saying: the workers are all at the same level in representing the other workers in the struggle and it is not right that there be one, because she is a woman, who is set apart, taken aside by Bidegain.[24]

With the return to work in 1974, one female worker spoke for many when she said, "During the conflict, I could discuss with a man. Now, as before the struggle, a woman cannot ask a guy a question—even a technical question, for work—without him turning what she said into a joke."[25] Many rank-and-file women came to feel they had been "the OS of the struggle."[26] In Demougeot's words, male leaders had done "the work of political analysis," while women made things happen.[27]

Whatever the democratization of the conflict, the leadership of the CFDT-Lip remained much the same as it had been before 1973—Piaget, Vittot, Burgy, Jeanningros, Jean Godard, Gérard Cugney, Jean-Pierre Jusseaume, Jean-Claude Piquard, etc.—and therefore largely male.[28] However, elections for personnel delegates and works council representatives after the conflict reflected a change in participation and several of the new delegates were women. In 1975, an unprecedented forty women came forward to stand for office. However, because women were disproportionately in the first of the three colleges (workers, not supervisors or managers) and concentrated in certain sites in the factory, the union could pick only a limited number as candidates. Seven of the twenty-four CFDT-Lip elected in 1975, including four alternates, were women.[29] While this almost doubled the number of elected women, they did not escape what some characterized as being guarantors without power for

24 Le Garrec, *Les Messagères*, 104–5.
25 Françoise Dromard in *Lip au féminin*, 49.
26 Beurier, "La Mémoire des Lip," 153–7.
27 Werner, "La Question des femmes," 2463.
28 Jeannine Pierre-Émile was an important figure in the CFDT-Lip before the conflict in 1973, but not a leader in the sense that Vittot or Burgy were or that Noëlle Dartevelle was in the CGT-Lip.
29 ADD 1812W33 RG, February 5, 1975. France Culture, "Nous les Lip" (November 22, 2003). Evelyne Le Garrec, "Women's Lip," *Tankonalasanté* (Summer 1975).

male leaders.[30] Female CFDT-Lip delegates elected before the conflict had not raised issues of particular concern to women workers, for fear, in the words of one of them, alternative Paulette Dartevel, that male delegates were going to dismiss these as "old wives' tales!," or that they in turn would lose their status as militants for that of women.[31] Demougeot laid out the consequences: "You have to be able to explain all that makes up the reality of women's problems in order to be able to fight them. But there are few elected women in the unions; the male delegates do not live this situation and do not see its importance. And all the difficulties remain unaddressed."[32]

A female employee recognized that the union culture itself worked to exclude women from leadership roles:

> A woman's individual personality is not recognized. At Lip, it is obvious: if you want to work with a team of men, you have to copy their way of expressing themselves, you have to look like them; don't wear make-up, don't dress well. Nothing at all can be changed in the style of work in the local. Otherwise, we are women who do not know how to work.[33]

Alice Carpena added, "We would have had so much more taste for playing an active role if we had felt we were really integrated in the group of buddies. They got along so well together. It seemed to me sometimes that I was an extra."[34] Even when women spoke, Demougeot contended, they did not have "the deciding word"; only what males said was taken into account.[35] Other women agreed: "Masculine power that censors is always there. They think that their approach to problems is rational, so they are thrown by ours ... They will pardon us more easily for a technical error at work, but if you write up a leaflet, you don't dare put it forward. You're afraid of being ridiculed."[36]

Demougeot spoke of the need for what she later called "a revolution in the revolution" at Lip: "It is true that thanks to the conflict, to that activity, we learned a lot. But we still have further to go. We have to get to where the women are listened to like the men, considered as responsible

---

30   "Lip aujourd'hui," 23.

31   Paulette Dartevel in *Lip au féminin*, 51 (quoted). *L'Outil des travailleurs*, February 1974, 10. *Politique hebdo*, March 6, 1975, 9.

32   *Lip au féminin*, 57.

33   Macciocchi, *De la France*, 430.

34   *Lip au féminin*, 52–4.

35   Caroline Dehedin, "À Lip, les femmes aussi ont une histoire," 74.

36   "À Lip, des femmes: mille manières de lutter," 33.

militants. The men are not used to it, but we have to force them to accept us."[37] On another occasion, she spoke more bluntly: "Indeed, the men do not want to give us certain responsibilities, for fear of seeing themselves lose their place."[38] However, Demougeot believed, while union meetings were conducted in the men's union language with their agenda, women meeting together would set the agenda and speak in their language, not that of the masculinized union hall.[39]

Women's Lip

The Lip conflict was characterized by a remarkable openness of discussion and practice, but not on issues of particular concern to women. As feminists from Paris reported after a visit in the summer of 1973, Lip women treated issues relating to their lives as women as secondary to the collective concerns of the movement: "what they especially put forward was the new consciousness of their belonging to the working class and not the place they are given in it."[40] They had experienced individual forms of liberation and acted collectively as workers, but, without a place to discuss issues particular to women, they addressed them individually.[41] "Where we are wrong," said Demougeot, "is when we think that the problems of women in the enterprise are secondary. This is still a woman's way of reacting."[42]

Although women did much of the work preparing for the colloquium on employment in December 1973, the program did not originally include a session on women, like those on vocational training, school, housing and health.[43] Danièle Kergoat of *Les Cahiers de mai* saw in (male) Lip militants at the time "a big difference between the extraordinarily refined level of reasoning about everything that concerned the struggle for the retention of jobs" and what they said about subjects like the relations of men and women or child rearing, where "their critical offensive capacity disappeared ... or was not yet formed: the discourse remained at the level of the usual stereotypes of 'the average Frenchman."[44] In this

37   *Lip au féminin*, 52.
38   Macciocchi, *De la France*, 436–7.
39   AM, Transcript of Anne-Marie Martin, *Lip au féminin*, part 4.
40   Le Garrec, *Les Messagères*, 96–7.
41   Groupe de femmes, "Lip au féminin," 6.
42   "Ce qui a changé pour la moitié des lip," *Révolution* 47 (March 8, 1975).
43   Macciocchi, *De la France*, 435.
44   Danièle Kergoat, "Les pratiques revendicatives ouvrières" (Centre de sociologie des organisations, 1978), 79–80.

void, a committee of Lip women held meetings in preparation for the colloquium. This gave a project to women who had on occasion gotten together earlier. Kergoat attended one gathering, transcribed the discussion, analyzed it, and presented the results to the women: "I have a good memory of these women sitting in a circle, at first looking at one another blankly (the 'productives' against the 'unproductives'), but who finally created a women's group."[45]

Led by Piton, the women's committee organized a session on women at the colloquium. Discussion dealt with a variety of issues at Lip, ranging from training and promotion of female workers to why solidarity characterized men's workshops and jealousy those of women, as well as female workers who slept with their bosses.[46] While feminists like Jeannette Colombel criticized the report that the committee prepared as making women's issues a manifestation of class struggle, it recognized the struggle within the struggle: when women "demanded power with respect to their condition as women, they were frightening. To whom? To men and to society. The struggle of women is subversive. It questions the whole system."[47] That there was no childcare at the conference limited women's participation and confirmed that women needed to organize autonomously to address problems specific to their situation in and out of the workplace.[48]

Feminists in the PSU in Besançon not employed by Lip provided a catalyst for the formation of a longer-lived women's group. Before the expulsion from Palente, PSU militant Madeleine Laude, active in the CCPPO, and another PSU militant, Jacqueline Betain, had gotten fellow party member Piaget to convince Demougeot to gather a few women workers to meet to discuss issues germane to women. The feminists' insistence that the women workers examine the issues from their perspective as women initially made Demougeot uncomfortable, and they met only a couple of times during the conflict.[49] After the signature of the Dole accords, and with the participation of the two PSU members and of Pascale Werner, a feminist from Paris, a cluster of close to twenty women set up the Women's Group. It included fourteen Lip manual laborers, the Lip secretary Piton and the Lip social worker Plantin. Well over

---

45   Danièle Kergoat, "Une sociologie à la croisée de trois mouvements sociaux," *L'homme et la société* 176–7 (2010): 30–1.

46   ADD 1812W27 RG, December 6, 1973.

47   The report was published in *L'Outil des travailleurs*, December 1973-January 1974, 12. Jeannette Colombel, *Les Murs de l'école* (Paris, 1975), 33.

48   Piton, *C'est possible!*, 552–3, 557–8.

49   Champeau, "Lip: le conflit et l'Affaire (1973)," 115–16.

half of the fourteen were OS. Six of the fourteen were single, divorced or widowed, about the percentage of the female workforce in these situations at Lip.[50]

Women had previously sought to get home quickly after work to take care of children and other household duties, but their experience in the conflict made many feel the need to meet outside work to maintain the solidarity they had developed. As one put it, "To have the contacts and the power to tell ourselves: 'Warning, we are going back to individualism. Return to solidarity.'"[51] The Women's Group began meeting in March 1974. It engaged in consciousness-raising and elicited the participation of all. In the words of Group member Jacqueline Betain: "There is no longer the complex of those who know and those who do not know how to speak."[52] The Group met weekly at the Maison pour Tous until December 1974, and taped their conversations. The Women's Group became a place where women went to be understood and supported when they spoke about issues affecting them at Palente, like working conditions for the OS and the lack of opportunity for advancement. The Group asked why women who raised these issues in the union were met with a patronizing "yes, you're right," but little else.[53] The Women's Group reported that the warm relations established between female workers in different parts of the factory and the offices during the conflict had continued, preventing one element from being played off against another.[54] It blamed male managers for sexual exploitation rather than women for flirting. It came to feel that solidarity among women workers was the only way to counter the abuses inherent in the individual relationships that managers sought to establish with female workers.[55] For Plantin, it was important "to find ourselves among women, because we were afraid that some would take up their old behavior, their habit of wanting to please the bosses. We'll need to support ourselves, to help one another."[56] Before, an individual woman might talk back to a boss, but this was never effective; they now

---

50   Madeleine Laude, "Lip au féminin: Solidarité et créativité ouvrières" in Les Affranchies: Franc-comtoises sans frontières, ed. Nella Arambasin (Besançon, 2013), 188.

51   "Ce qui a changé pour la moitié des lip."

52   Lip au féminin, 59.

53   Idées ouvrières, July 1977. Maruani, Les Syndicats, 104.

54   Reine J. in Lip au féminin, 24.

55   Idées ouvrières, July 1977. BDIC F delta rés 578/46 Demougeot in "La lutte des Femmes à LIP et ailleurs," 7. As Vigna points out, this was innovative at a time when the term sexual harassment was first being introduced. L'Insubordination ouvrière, 120–1.

56   Il était une fois la révolution, 215.

learned to confront him as a group.[57] Nor, Demougeot added, did the Group restrict itself to workplace issues, discussing topics they had never spoken of before, like divorce and abortion.[58]

A number of the participants in the Women's Group had been engaged in the Action Committee and the new group had many of its qualities. Like the Action Committee it was a response both to the admirable qualities that made the union leadership seem unapproachable and the resulting anti-democratic and hierarchical nature of the union that led to exclusion from the leadership of important elements of the base. Reflecting forty years later, Piaget made this connection: "As there was the Action Committee to overcome the too strong imprint of the delegates, the Women's Group was indispensable for facilitating emancipation, reflections particular to women, and promoting their best propositions for the emancipation of all women for the benefit of all."[59] The Group became the place to address issues whose importance the male-led union did not appreciate, but which, after discussion in the Group, the women fought to have the CFDT-Lip take up. One male Action Committee member lamented that after the Dole accords, women met to discuss issues, but the only male workers who did so were union delegates.[60] Newly elected female union delegates participated in the Women's Group, but some of the female delegates who had been elected before the conflict did not.[61] The Group criticized them for being totally cut off from the mass of female workers. These delegates did not raise issues particular to women, which they accepted as peripheral, out of fear of themselves being marginalized. The Group accused these women of having accepted "this submission to the dominant group, this molding. They learned the discourse of others and were integrated into the union hierarchy."[62]

When rehired by the new firm, close to 100 women were moved to new positions. Women went to see the male union delegates, but they did nothing until the Women's Group brought the issue before the union. Only then did the union take it up with management and defend the reassigned female workers' interests. "This created big tensions in the enterprise," Demougeot reported.[63] However, what was more radical, she added, was the idea that what was needed in the union was not simply

---

57 Josette in *Lip au féminin*, 11.
58 Dehedin, "À Lip, les femmes aussi ont une histoire," 94.
59 Chaillet et al., "Entretien avec Charles Piaget," 123.
60 François in *L'Outil des travailleurs*, February 1974, 10.
61 *Politique hebdo*, March 6, 1975, 9.
62 Le Garrec, "Women's Lip."
63 BDIC F delta rés 587/46, "La lutte des femmes à Lip et ailleurs," 7.

more women in leadership positions. "It is another form of militancy that the women desired and that they wished for"—democratic and non-hierarchical like the Women's Group. [64]

Annie Piaget and Fernande Vittot

All workers, male and female, lauded Piaget and the other leaders of the movement for their selflessness. One woman explained:

> I admired those like Charles Piaget and the team of women and men with whom I engaged in the struggle, who sacrificed everything—family, health—to build a better society. I had thought such generosity and such abnegation no longer existed, and only egoism and profit counted. This gave me strength and courage.[65]

The outsider Pascale Werner, neither a Lip worker nor a local PSU *militante*, prompted the Women's Group to think about what made Piaget's sacrifices possible by reflecting on the way that society accepts that a father could sacrifice care of his family for the struggle, but would condemn a mother for doing the same thing.[66] Women in the Group responded to Werner's challenge by asking if it was the sacrifices of militants' wives that made possible the admirable qualities in their husbands. If so, did this create a situation, Madeleine Laude wondered, where union leaders "defend revolutionary ideas in the enterprise, but act at home in a conservative fashion"?[67]

Demougeot praised Piaget and Vittot for helping workers take a big step: "But it is up to us now to open another door: that which will allow the wives of militants—spouses in general—to join the struggle, to avoid for them the solitude that profits only those who exploit us." [68] At first, Annie Piaget and Fernande Vittot were not enthusiastic about meeting with the Women's Group. Demougeot went to see Fernande Vittot: "it was," she said, "a woman to woman hostility, a relation of rivals."[69] "You, the women of Lip, you have taken our husbands during the struggle,"

---

64   Macciocchi, *De la France*, 433–4.
65   Reine J. in *Lip au féminin*, 23.
66   Ibid., 39–44.
67   Madeleine in ibid., 42.
68   Demougeot in ibid.
69   Le Garrec, *Les Messagères*, 108.

Fernande Vittot told her.[70] "We were [Roland Vittot's] family now," Alice Carpena Lip worker recognized.[71] Roland Vittot told his wife nothing of the conflict and the Women's Group was shocked that she did not know what he was doing. Fernande Vittot revealed:

> When, in May [1973], I saw employees in white blouses who blocked the roads to spread the word, I cried ... The first time that I went to the factory, it was August 13. At that time, I was depressed. That meant that for two months I only got a glimpse of Roland now and then and we were so tired that, though happy to see one another, we could no longer bear one another. During the three hours I spent at the factory, I stayed with Roland five minutes; then I spoke with a couple of Lip women. And the rest of the time, it really hurt me to stay in the factory without knowing anyone, looking like a stranger.[72]

Annie Piaget told the Women's Group: "Solitude, yes, I experienced it ... I would like to have participated, to be there at the important moments, so as to be with *les Lip* and understand as well."[73] Although Fernande Vittot got to know and appreciate the movement in August, while her kids were in summer camp, she recognized the cost of the movement to families like hers: "At home, traces of the conflict will take a long time to erase, for it is certain that when the father remains one year (and more) without a schedule and all the work rests on the wife's shoulders, there are a lot of things that cannot be made up for."[74]

The Vittots had five children and the Piagets had six. The inability of the union leaders' spouses to participate in the fight was attributed in part to the lack of child care. Women employed at Lip had not pursued the issue during the conflict, accepting the argument that there were more important things for the collectivity to do, and not thinking of how this excluded stay-at-home mothers. Fernande Vittot did ask her spouse about whether the movement would set up child care, but he questioned the need; male leaders did not consider how this excluded women like their wives from participation in the conflict (or perhaps they considered their absence normal). One worker in the Women's Group recognized that the exhilarating feeling of participating as equals with men in the

---

70 Le Garrec, "Women's Lip."
71 BDIC F delta rés 578/46 "La lutte des Femmes à LIP et ailleurs," 3–5.
72 *Lip au féminin*, 37–8.
73 Ibid., 42.
74 Ibid., 38.

movement led them to ignore the situation of other women, until they felt the reestablishment of earlier gender hierarchies after the conflict: "Perhaps we did not pose the problem of child care because unconsciously, we wanted to escape the family, to find ourselves in a setting where neither the husband nor the children could enter any longer. We could, like that, feel liberated."[75] The struggle was not a time of liberation for militants' wives; it was a period of increased exploitation. Working women in the Group came to feel complicit in the exclusion of women like Fernande Vittot and Annie Piaget.

Piaget and Vittot drew power and allegiance as those who sacrificed for the movement: this was the source of the many presentations of Piaget as a Christ figure. What Demougeot identified as the "phenomenon of the leader" at Lip drew on this type of authority that could not be criticized or contested because its basis was in self-sacrifice.[76] The Women's Group drew attention to the unacknowledged burdens placed on militants' wives that made the militants' championing of the collective over egoism possible; a leadership premised on women's sacrifice was not the basis of a humane social order.[77] Demougeot added that a man who cannot recognize the exploitation of his wife cannot recognize the exploitation of the women with whom he works.[78]

Annie Piaget and Fernande Vittot in turn came to see that women in the workplace and in the union were no freer of male domination than they were in the household. Both became active members of the Women's Group, causing, in Charles Piaget's words, "an upheaval in the family."[79] In the Group, Annie Piaget and Fernande Vittot were recognized for occupying what Demougeot called "a pivotal position between the exploitation of women at work and their oppression in the family." [80] In working with the wives of militants, women workers found an entry way into examining their own subordination, both as those responsible for the household and in relation to union leaders, whose saintly devotion to the cause was only possible because of their wives' unacknowledged domestic labor. And, in turn, the leaders' wives realized that doing paid labor did not free working women from the masculine domination they both experienced.[81] As Demougeot made clear, a union

---

75   Reine H. in ibid., 42.
76   *Le Nouvel observateur*, September 17, 1973, 42–3.
77   *Lip au féminin*, 43. Le Garrec, *Les Messagères*, 116.
78   AM Transcript of Martin, *Lip au féminin*, part 5.
79   Thomas, *Lip, une école de la lutte à l'usage des jeunes générations*.
80   Le Garrec, *Les Messagères*, 108.
81   Ibid., 179–80.

structure predicated on wives' labor excluded those without wives—women workers—from leadership positions in their union.[82]

Lip au féminin

From transcribed discussions of their weekly meetings and short essays written by two-thirds of the workers who were members, the Women's Group produced a small book, *Lip au féminin*. The book moves from the women's liberating experiences in 1973—the Action Committee, the General Assembly, and the commissions—to the return to work, at which time challenges to the male union leadership and the patriarchy on which it rested are presented. All had participated actively in the struggle, termed the shift from "I to us" in *Lip au féminin*, but when it ended, women remained subordinate to men in the home, in the workplace and in the union, and recognized that these subordinations were interrelated. Doing away with class oppression would not end the subordination of women; only women acting collectively could further their emancipation. The dialectic of egoism and collectivity which, more than self-management, provided an ideology for the movement, was rooted in gender relationships left unaffected by the struggle. Male union leaders could see female workers only as workers, and the position of their stay-at-home wives as a private affair, unrelated to their power in the union. *Lip au féminin* was framed in terms of deficiencies in union democracy, not the assertion of a feminine identity.

The first printing of *Lip au féminin* in March 1975 sold out quickly, with 250 copies purchased at Lip. The sociologist Margaret Maruani found that all the Lip women she interviewed identified with the book, but that male workers had not read it and saw it as the work of an unrepresentative minority. Although the Women's Group waited to publish *Lip au féminin* until all were back at work, their argument that the Lip struggle was not over, but needed to address gender issues, did, in the words of one admiring feminist, take "the risk of being accused of sabotaging the image of the Lip brand, model of the exemplary struggle copied and recopied everywhere, designated a historic monument and untouchable."[83] Piaget said that union leaders were "dressed down" in *Lip au féminin*, and recognized that now, whatever the subject, there would

82 *Lip au féminin*, 57.
83 Le Garrec, "Women's Lip."

come the "oh yes, the women" time in the discussion.[84] However, the union leadership showed "reticence" toward engaging with *Lip au féminin* itself, fearing the book as a source of division; the issues it raised were not publicly debated at Lip and, despite propositions made to the commission that produced *Lip Unité*, it took the bulletin six months to publish a small article on it.[85] Pierre-Émile, the one woman fully integrated into the CFDT-Lip union leadership (and who had not responded to invitations to participate in meetings of the Women's Group), explained tactfully that "the male delegates prefer to meet trade unionists they know, instead of groups of workers."[86] Alice Carpena was blunter: male union leaders "recognize that we have a different style, but they are so convinced of knowing everything, that they cannot admit that someone different could be as intelligent as them."[87] Demougeot commented on this situation at a meeting of women in Lyon: "we must fight as well to raise the consciousness of men, and that's not an easy job at Lip."[88]

Union leaders were concerned with issues affecting the OS—lack of advancement, working conditions and wages—and the need to develop democracy and participation in leadership positions within the union, however they refused to accept these as women's issues, saying that they affected both male and female workers.[89] Piaget could recognize that women were asserting themselves in new ways and that this was a result of the conflict, but he did not see this assertion itself as part of the struggle. With prodding, the union did pursue issues which primarily concerned women, but it interpreted these as class issues. The Women's Group challenged this position by moving from the grievances of the OS to starting with the women's situation and seeing it manifested in issues germane to women workers.

If the CGT had worried about the influence of leftists, the CFDT-Lip came to see feminists in the same light. CFDT-Lip initially dismissed the Women's Group as a product of PSU women, but it soon responded by

84   "Lip aujourd'hui," 24.
85   Collectif, *Lip: affaire non classée*, 68 [quoted]; Margaret Maruani, "Les femmes dans le conflit Lip," Laboratoire de Sociologie du Travail of the Conservatoire National des Arts et Métiers (1977), 19, 23.
86   Macciocchi, *De la France*, 437 [quoted]. Le Garrec, *Les Messagères*, 107.
87   Macciocchi, *De la France*, 432. A woman active in the Women's Group explained, "I noticed that at the last spontaneous work stoppage, we were only OS. There were two CFDT[-Lip] delegates, to whom we explained our demands. Just from their faces, we understood they were disgusted. We would certainly not have found that expression among female delegates." Ibid., 437.
88   AM "Debat avec les femmes de Lip, Lyon juin 1975."
89   Maruani, *Les Syndicats*, 122.

creating a women's commission with a place in the works council under the direction of Pierre-Émile.[90] It included Women's Group stalwarts Demougeot and Plantin among its seven members. As the CGT had tolerated the Action Committee when it saw it as a means of mobilizing workers to carry out union actions, the CFDT-Lip likewise saw the women's commission as a means to mobilize women, but not as an independent group that could challenge union hegemony. In Demougeot's words, "the leaders are unsettled," but they were doing little to make women's participation easier, continuing to show "a great misogyny."[91] Interviewed by *L'Unité*, Pierre-Émile recognized the importance of women's issues—and the fact that most women on the union's commission were, like herself, not married—but did not mention the Women's Group or *Lip au féminin*.[92] And, in turn, the Women's Group maintained its autonomy in order to assure that the union would not ignore issues of concern to women.

The Women's Group knew that the female workers at Lip had more confidence in the male-led union than in their group when it posed demands—a "deformity of the system" for Alice Carpena, but one they recognized.[93] In March 1975, at the time of the publication of *Lip au féminin*, the Women's Group came up with a list of women's demands that the women's commission created by the union presented to Neuschwander. Pierre-Émile explained that on the occasion of Women's Day, March 8, the women's commission needed to pose demands, but it had none prepared. Without mentioning the Women's Group, Pierre-Émile distributed their demands. Within five minutes, union heads came to tell her she was "completely crazy" and that with satisfaction of these kinds of demands, there would be no one at work.[94] What particularly upset the leadership was that the demands concerned women workers, not workers as a collectivity.[95] At a works council meeting, when Neuschwander announced that he would meet with the women, the union delegates "caused an uproar";[96] the CGT-Lip had always feared the Action Committee would usurp union powers, and the CFDT-Lip acted similarly in response to organized women.

90 Ibid., 117.
91 Dehedin, "À Lip, les femmes aussi ont une histoire," 96.
92 *L'Unité*, March 21, 1975, 5. AMB 5Z220 "Compte-rendu de la réunion du Comité d'Entreprise du 13 mars 75," Annexe 2.
93 AM "Debat avec les femmes de Lip, Lyon juin 1975."
94 Macciocchi, *De la France*, 437.
95 Maruani, *Les Syndicats*, 108–10.
96 AM "Debat avec les femmes de Lip, Lyon juin 1975."

The demands addressed the condition of women workers, concentrated at the bottom rungs of the factory hierarchy and working at the most tiring jobs. The Women's Group wanted an end of work that required the worker to stand. It devoted special attention to older women workers, seeking the end of production norms for them as well as one paid hour break each morning for women over age fifty. The Group also asked that the wages of women near retirement be raised and that the age of retirement be lowered to fifty-five for women (and sixty for men).[97] Many women were stuck at the rank of OS. They demanded that after five years of work all pass to the next highest job category, along with the creation of more OP positions, and equal opportunity for women to be promoted. The Women's Group showed particular concern for female heads of household, contending that they should get higher posts through job training and by taking experience on the job into account. Female health issues, maternity, and child rearing also received special attention. All women should have the hours paid that they needed to visit the gynecologist and to take an annual cancer examination. Information should be made available on family planning and contraception. Pregnant women should get three-quarters of an hour off during the work day. Maternity leave should be extended to at least six months and paid at full salary; advances should be made on the sums due for health care from social security. When children were ill, workers—whether mothers, divorced fathers or widowers—should receive their pay to stay home and care for them. A legacy of Fred Lip's paternalism, a paid day off for the parents when a child married, should be retained. And finally, the members of the women's commission should receive paid hours to meet, such as the law provided for union delegates.[98] As Demougeot explained, "Women must also be able to meet to discuss their specific problems, and it is absolutely necessary that they be able to do so during their time at work. Otherwise, we will not be able to bring women together. When they leave, there are all the domestic tasks and children who await them."[99]

Neuschwander read *Lip au féminin* with interest. He was more at ease with this feminist expression than were the union leaders, even if, the Women's Group wondered, this was perhaps to "comfort himself, to

---

97   This was a national CGT demand; the CFDT sought retirement at sixty for both men and women, with a reduction in age for mothers.

98   ADD 45J85 "Revendications féminines," March 13, 1975.

99   *Lip au féminin*, 54.

show himself that he is a socially minded boss."[100] Neuschwander told the authors of *Lip au féminin*, "your brochure is really great, 'it's a call'. In short, men are flabbergasted because they had not realized." He went on to say, "Me, I'm ready to receive a group of women, to work on the problems of women, because it is true that for twenty years you, the women, have suffered an injustice at Lip and this injustice cannot be corrected in a couple of days, in a couple of months, but I promise you I'll do something." One member of the Women's Group spoke of being caught "between a feminist boss and misogynistic trade unionists."[101] Demougeot had to tell the union delegates that they compared unfavorably to Neuschwander: "You did not listen to us. He listens to us and, in the Women's Group, they said that we had finally found a man who listened to our demands."[102]

That said, Neuschwander was a boss, even if he aspired to be a socially conscious boss of a new sort, not like the paternalist Fred Lip. It was as a boss that he had ended the right to a paid day off for both parents on the day of their child's marriage. He was most receptive to the issue of women who had spent twenty or thirty years as OS, without getting the training for promotion—an issue, however, whose resolution Neuschwander could defer because it could not be remedied immediately. As these women retired with a low salary, they received a small pension; in the absence of a plan to facilitate the promotion of OS, he agreed to raise the salaries of retiring OS such that they would receive better pensions. However, Neuschwander was less open to demands concerning the work women did at Palente. At Lip, female workers over fifty had once been given a paid hour off each morning; the new firm gave this only to women starting at fifty-five or sixty, depending on the job they did. When women asked for the end of production norms for women over fifty, they were told that there were no such norms at the CEH. This may have been true for the men, but supervisors would go to women on the line and, record sheet in hand, tell them, "hold on, you didn't do your work today." Equally unsatisfactory to women workers was the provision of stools in response to the request for the end of work while standing.[103]

Neuschwander came from the same political culture as the CFDT-Lip leadership. Although he accepted some demands like the prolongation of maternity leave with full pay and paid time for an annual gynecological

100   Ibid., 11.
101   Maruani, *Les Syndicats*, 110–11.
102   Jacquin, "Lip 1973–1981," 290.
103   AM "Debat avec les femmes de Lip, Lyon juin 1975."

exam, he was resistant to many demands specific to women, contending that these would lead to hiring fewer women.[104] Neuschwander rejected paid time for the women's commission to meet and to allow women workers to meet with it. While the union leaders were concerned about women meeting with the director general, he shared an understanding of the workplace with them.

Closed Doors

Once the issue of jobs came to the fore again with the collapse of the enterprise, the Women's Group and the women's commission stopped meeting.[105] On May 8–9, 1976, workers held an open house at Palente to make the case for the continued viability of the enterprise. The Women's Group was denied the right to sell *Lip au féminin* at the event to raise funds for the movement at Lip, on the grounds that the book, published as a supplement to a PSU journal, had the PSU emblem on it. As the CGT-Lip had refused to allow the Action Committee to speak at the September 29, 1973 march, the CFDT-Lip took a similar stance with respect to the Women's Group at the open house a couple of years later. It had to sell *Lip au féminin* outside the factory gates. Although the Women's Group resembled the Action Committee in developing the voices of the unheard, Raguénès took the lead in opposing sale of *Lip au féminin* at the open house, suggesting that recognition of women would be like recognizing the marginal individuals with whom he had worked: "'No Question'. Otherwise 'I am going to look for prisoners, hooligans, the dysfunctional.'" Saying the brochure did not represent all the Lip women, Raguénès adding mockingly, "There are gulags everywhere," suggesting this was not one that concerned him.[106]

The issue was clearly the presence of a women's group among Lip workers. At the open house, stands addressing women's struggles, reproductive rights, and abortion were refused, while stands not directly related to workers' conflicts, like those of regionalist and student movements, were permitted within the factory gates. At the same event, the feminist Anne-Marie Martin filmed Demougeot and Carpena discussing the work of the Women's Group with women from other firms fighting layoffs and closures; they too contested the Group's exclusion. In

---

104   Ibid.; Neuschwander, *Patron, mais …*, 151–2. Maruani, *Les Syndicats*, 110–11.
105   *Le Monde libertaire*, February 16, 1978, 8.
106   *Libération*, May 10, 1976, 8.

contrast, Pierre-Émile is shown talking with two male union leaders, but she speaks less and less and ends by deferring to them. Eager to show that Lip was viable, the leadership presented Palente as a site of technological advances, gendered male in their presentations by (male) engineers, rather than in terms of the culture of liberation that had developed in 1973. Martin's film has several scenes of a woman working at a machine, while a male supervisor answers questions asked of the woman.[107] In response, 100 women met and wrote a letter that Demougeot read to the General Assembly a few days later:

> the visits were made by managers and technicians only and with the sole goal of showing that the "Lip tool" could work well, with technical explanations about quartz and the binocular. But there was not a single OS to explain how much these binocular glasses tire the eyes, especially when one has to use these for hours at a time for years.[108]

On the second day of the open house, the car that workers had outfitted with loudspeakers had to broadcast an appeal for men to replace women at the bar and the child-care area, since they were threatening to go on strike in order to participate in discussions in the factory.[109]

In the years following the bankruptcy of the SEHEM, women remained active in the movement, but still rarely held leadership positions. In September 1976, women established the child-care center that the leadership had passed over in 1973. Although they could not get men to work regularly in it, the center did bring together female employees and the wives of militants and of participating managers.[110] A group drawing on women from Lip and sixteen other businesses in Besançon organized in October 1976 around women's issues and fights against layoffs. Members spoke elsewhere in France and the group got permission to set up a stand inside the open house held at Palente in November 1976, although the collective led by the CFDT-Lip stipulated that it could not address directly issues like contraception and abortion.[111] However,

---

107   Anne-Marie Martin, *Lip Formation; Portes ouvertes à Lip, 8–9 mai 1976*, Association de Diffusion Populaire.

108   *Libération*, May 11, 1976, 6.

109   *Libération*, May 10, 1976, 8.

110   *Lip Unité*, no. 7, November 1976, 3. Plantin, "L'Accompagnement du service social," 48.

111   *Lip Unité*, no. 7, November 1976, 3. Dehedin, "À Lip, les femmes aussi ont une histoire," 98–9.

women used the occasion to raise the question of the gendered hierarchy in the movement at Lip. Piaget recognized that "it is true, we are dreadful conservatives"; whatever changes occurred were the result of women's initiatives.[112]

The sociologist Maruani found when she visited Palente in July 1977 that women took a more active role in the General Assembly and on the commissions than in 1973. She was impressed to find men on the teams that did the cooking, dishes, and cleaning. Although the Women's Group no longer met, she believed the experience "had spread." Lip women now formed a community, creating groups of women in individual workshops who went out together after work. Their support extended to issues like divorces and other family problems.[113] However, there were limits. Maruani thought there were more women in the CFDT-Lip than men in July 1977, but women explained that the delegations that met with the authorities often included only a token female. The male leaders rotated their choice from Pierre-Émile to Carpena to Demougeot, without including them in planning: "The men want us to participate, but there is one thing they do not want us to touch, that is the strategy." The place of women in the movement was a legacy of the French republican inability to think difference and equality together, and another face of the Catholic culture that informed the leaders' radicalism than Claude Harmel had seen.[114]

Conclusion

In the CEH, women had increasingly became the public face of Lip. In an advertisement, Neuschwander evoked "the preservation of an old trade," the male skilled artisanal craft of making watches, with the slogan "Lip: We hope that you love your trade as much as we love ours."[115] Yet the accompanying photo taken by Marc Riboud was of a female unskilled worker with a binocular strapped to her forehead. The republication of *Lip au féminin* by Syros in 1977 featured Riboud's photo on its cover and the aphorism from the advertisement, "Lip: Nothing is done well without passion"—a slogan suggested to Neuschwander by his reading

---

112   *Libération*, November 8, 1976, 7.

113   Maruani, *Les Syndicats*, 112–15.

114   Ibid., 122; Macciocchi, *De la France*, 436–7 [quoted].Joan Scott, *The Politics of the Veil* (Princeton, 2007).

115   BDIC F delta rés 702/22/4 CEH 1975 catalogue.

of Saint Augustine—but added "our passion: it is the struggle."[116] The ex-GP leader Pierre Victor initially thought that the "the struggle of the women" was "secondary" at Lip, "a little peripheral" to the main concerns of the movement.[117] However, the couple of feminists exterior to Lip who joined the Women's Group served as a spark that led women at Lip to develop their consciousness of exploitation and exclusion at the intersections of the household, the union and the workplace. They had done for women workers what the ex-GP had not done for the working class at Lip.

After dissolution of the ex-GP, Pierre Victor and other ex-GP members took a new view of women's activism. They celebrated precisely what the male CFDT-Lip leadership had feared the Women's Group would bring. When Pierre Victor said a few years later that "the [working] class must open up [*se diasporiser*]," ex-GP Denis Clodic pointed to the women of Lip as "a precise example": "the women spoke their life, their itinerary, and their desire to tear themselves from that misery. It was envisaging this possible tearing away that announced the destruction of the worker as a habitué of the factory." When they come together, "it is not to regroup on the basis of the discourse of the movement, which is the discourse of a military command." Pierre Victor replied enthusiastically, "Wouldn't this be to knock down that idol that has the name 'workers' movement'?," the project of liberation he now took from Lip.[118]

The Women's Group was not large. The male leadership of the CFDT-Lip had no interest in seeing a public discussion in the General Assembly or elsewhere of the issues *Lip au féminin* raised. In the years after Neuschwander's departure, many more female workers than had criticized the union earlier came to feel that they had been "the OS of the struggle"; this suggests their exposure to and embrace of elements of the positions of the Women's Group.[119] The Group was important not only for such long-term effects on *les Lip*, but for its role, well after the summer of 1973, in nurturing the sense throughout France that Palente was the site of a new world aborning.[120] *Lip au féminin* and several videos on women at Lip,

---

116   Neuschwander, *Claude Neuschwander*, 44.

117   Gavi et al., *On a raison de se révolter*, 277 (October 1973).

118   Raguénès et al., "Lip 1973–1976," 1256–7.

119   Joëlle Beurier, "La mémoire Lip ou la fin du mythe autogestionaire?" in *Autogestion. La dernière utopie?*, ed. Frank Georgi (Paris, 2003), 458. Thomas Faverjon discusses his mother, a worker at Lip, in these terms. Éva Ségal, "Lip, l'impossible héritage," *Images de la culture* 23 (August 2008), 49.

120   See extracts from a discussion with Lip women and other women workers at a bookstore in Paris on April 26, 1975 in *Idées ouvrières*, July 1977. These dialogues went

as well as visits with women's groups elsewhere, made their experience known.[121] The Women's Group participated in International Women's Day in Besançon on March 8, 1975 and expressed solidarity with the États-Généraux of prostitutes held in Lyon in July that year.[122] Later, when women workers went to the "festival of women" at Bordeaux to popularize the Lip movement, Christiane André shocked the CFDT-Lip when she spoke of discussions of contraception, rape and homosexuality at the festival and their success selling watches at meetings of gay organizations.[123]

Lip au féminin may have had a greater impact in union and feminist circles outside of Palente than in its place of origin. The book was translated into a number of languages and sold thousands of copies worldwide.[124] Simone de Beauvoir found the women of Lip exemplary for revealing that "the class struggle can and does encourage and develop the sex struggle."[125] The feminist Évelyne Le Garrec, wife of the PSU national secretary Jean Le Garrec, welcomed the publication of *Lip au féminin* in March 1975: "the only important event of the International Year of the Woman, it will remain a major date in the history of the women's liberation movement"; "If you want to know what the 'feminine class of 1975' is, you will have to ask the women of Lip." *Lip au féminin*, she added, would do more to advance women than 100,000 female lawyers could do. Le Garrec's enthusiasm came from the affirmation of autonomy by working-class women and their examination of the relation of women's domestic life to their public activities and the ways the former impeded participation in the latter. Le Garrec celebrated the presence of

---

in two directions. Although many Lip women wanted to hear nothing about contraception or abortion, discussion with women Alice Carpena met led her to change her views on these subjects. AM *Lip au féminin*, part 5.

121   Anne-Marie Martin's video, *La Lutte des femmes à Lip et ailleurs*, shot in Lyon in June 1975, featured five women from Lip, who discussed changes created by participation in a labor conflict. On the screening of this film to striking women elsewhere, see Anne-Marie Duguet, *Vidéo, la mémoire au poing* (Paris, 1981), 53. Carole Roussopoulos returned to Besançon and filmed the videos *Monique et Christiane* and *Jacqueline et Marcel* in August 1976. Her films voiced these employees' grievances with the male leadership of the union. These too were screened to women's groups throughout France. All four of the worker subjects in Roussopoulos' films left Lip in 1978.

122   Le Garrec, *Les Messagères*, 179–80.

123   *Libération*, October 16–17, 1976, 14. AB Interview with Burtz by Beurier [1992], 31–2.

124   Le Garrec, *Les Messagères*, 120–2. With publication of an edition by Syros, the figure of 9,000 copies sold was given. ADD 45J55 'Lip au féminin,' *L'Étincelle* 36 (November 3, 1977).

125   John Gerassi, "Simone de Beauvoir: The Second Sex 25 years later," *Society* 13:2 (January 1976): 84–5.

Annie Piaget and Fernande Vittot in *Lip au féminin* because this marked the coming together of female workers and housewives, often seen as being in opposition, and the recognition of the common factors that kept women subordinate in domestic life and in the workplace and the union.[126] These were the working-class women whom socialist feminists had long sought. No longer, she said, could women's liberation be called petty bourgeois as it had been after May 1968.[127] *Lip au féminin* fostered recognition of the collective nature of male oppression in private and public life; doing away with class oppression would not do away with it. Only women acting collectively could further their emancipation. But, to use the title of a film that Richard Copans of Cinélutte made at the time—a film in which the lived experience of women in the Women's Group takes precedence over the fight for jobs—women's advance at Palente would be slow, à *pas lent(e)s*.[128]

---

126   Geneviève Colas, a professor of urban design at Vincennes in the 1970s, reported receiving a request from the Women's Group, including Annie Piaget, for assistance in the construction of a place where wives of union leaders could meet one another "and speak of their difficulties as wives of union leaders, reduced to the role of servants in their family and not able to obtain information on the struggle of *les Lip* except through the media, as their husbands did not keep them informed of what was happening with them. They did not have a place to meet where they could escape the power of their husbands and envisaged constructing one themselves." Geneviève Colas, "Les femmes des militants de Lip après 68" (May 13, 2008), at sites.radiofrance.fr.

127   Le Garrec, *Les Messagères*, 95, 97, 139, 179–80. Not all feminists were as enthusiastic. They recognized the movement was still male-dominated. "At Lip the women always seemed to struggle to catch up with a discourse they mastered poorly, in the shadow of Piaget." Christine Fauré, "Grèves de femmes—autogestion," *Autogestion et Socialisme* 28–9 (October 1974-January 1975): 64–5.

128   Because of production problems, *À pas lentes* was not released until much later. It is on volume 2 of the DVD, *Le Cinéma de mai 68* (Paris, 2009). See Paul Douglas Grant, *Cinéma Militant. Political Filmmaking & May 1968* (New York, 2016), 110–17.

10

Like the Bodies of the Hanged at the Place de Grève

Government and business are not interested in Lip. It must, like the bodies of the hanged at the Place de Grève, rot before the gawkers in order to inspire healthy reflections in those who would contemplate imitating the leftists, the dreamers, the fanciful workers of Palente and all those who want to fight to affirm their rights.

—*Lip Unité* [1]

Lip 73 is the easy conquest of a public opinion surprised to see workers resisting a power grab. Lip 76 is the slow investigation of a cadaver that wants to lift the lid of the coffin abruptly closed on it; [the authorities] do not worry about its fate. They take care only to show the coffin to the people, who must understand that resistance to the decisions of financial powers cannot be appealed. The ultimate verdict is viability; non-viability—whatever the cause—is mortal sin.

—Jean Raguénès[2]

What a collective of Lip employees referred to as their second "long march" began with the bankruptcy of the SEHEM in April 1976.[3] But this conflict would be very different than the first. The secretary of the Besançon CFDT had scoffed at the idea of another 1973-style movement

---

1   *Lip Unité*, no. 6, November 1976, 8. The Place de Grève, now the location of the town hall in Paris, was in the past the site of public executions and a place where people looking for work gathered. The is the origin of the French for "to strike," *faire grève*.

2   BDIC F delta rés 702/4/4 Transcript of discussion of Lip employees [1978].

3   Collectif, *Lip: affaire non classée*, 88.

at Lip in 1976: "That would be absurd. Lip was a factory in a struggle with fantastic support; there cannot be national support when there are 500 factories engaged in struggles."[4] Piaget reflected that in a nation with widespread unemployment, "our fight is not destined to be a 'beacon' struggle that captures the attention of all public opinion."[5] Although legislation passed in response to the earlier Lip conflict afforded those laid off for economic reasons 90 percent of their salary for a year as they looked for work, this too was problematic. For Vittot, it "is not a social measure, but an incentive to demobilize, individualize, depersonalize workers, to prevent them from fighting."[6]

Lip workers had always rejected the label of job seekers. They had a factory and they had jobs; what they needed was an employer. Through their years of struggle, they had built a community that went well beyond that fostered by Fred Lip's paternalism. The right to live in this community became inseparable from the demand for employment that would make it possible. *Les Lip* refused to accept, in Piaget's words, the logic of capitalism that deems labor "this herd in perpetual transhumance." As the confederations and parties that helped make Lip a national affair absented themselves, Piaget affirmed the demand common to movements across France in the 1970s to "live and work in one's land."[7] Lip workers were from Franche-Comté and placed their battle in the collective memory of its struggles. They identified with the besieged inhabitants of Dole in 1636. When the French commander had told them their situation was hopeless and they must surrender—"*Comtois, rends toi*"—they had refused: "*Nenni, ma foi*." He then asked who their leaders were and they responded, "We are all leaders." Lip workers made "*Comtois, rends toi. Nenni, ma foi*" their own, writing it on the factory walls and on pottery they made and sold.

Workers saw that the state and the labor market treated the unemployed as individuals without the benefits and power that acting as a collective provided organized workers in the workplace. The national confederations were unprepared for the mass unemployment that succeeded the "thirty glorious years" of growth. They fought for individual benefits for laid-off workers, but did not organize the unemployed, accepting that unemployment was synonymous with powerlessness

4   *L'Outil des travailleurs*, February 12, 1976, 10.
5   *Témoignage chrétien*, August 5, 1976, 5.
6   Roland Vittot, "La longue marche des Lip!," *Notre combat* 191 (December 1977–January 1978): 8.
7   *Le Monde*, August 2, 1977, 18.

and passivity. Throughout their years of struggle, the Lip workers saw themselves contesting this by "staying together at the same place, refusing the paralyzing idea of fatality."[8] "For us," Piaget explained, "to be unemployed is to organize collectively"; he would later refer to himself as having been in a "collective of the unemployed."[9]

Their experience of a long period of insecurity and conflict differentiated Lip workers from other inhabitants of Besançon, making them more dependent on one another, giving them the qualities of a community that unemployment by its nature destroyed. Workers spoke of the shame and humiliation they felt in the city and within their extended families, where family councils convened to tell them to leave Lip and seek work elsewhere.[10] If the state would not intervene on its own, *les Lip* thought, perhaps it would respond to disruption in Besançon. "We are going to make ourselves unbearable," said a CFDT-Lip militant in June 1976, "in such a way that the authorities will have had enough of seeing and hearing us and will take the necessary measures for there to be 900 jobs at Palente."[11] But such acts only increased their unpopularity in Besançon, making them all the more dependent on one another.[12] In May 1976, they had glued their termination letters to the door of the préfecture.[13] The next month, workers boarded the Besançon–Paris train and spent the fifteen minutes before they were chased off explaining their cause to the passengers and gluing "LIP WILL LIVE" posters on the cars. However, the police reported, "The cars decked out with signs were replaced at Dijon by new cars, which neutralized the sought-after advertising effect."[14] A few days later, sixty workers rendered 800 parking meters unusable by gluing slogans to them, but a disappointed Piaget had to tell the General Assembly that the city had an effective thinner that allowed for a rapid clean-up.[15] In February 1977, *les Lip* put handouts

---

8   BDIC 702–14–1 Lip Collectif, "Création d'emplois d'utilité collective dans les locaux de l'usine de Palente à Besançon" (1978).

9   Piaget in an undated handout, "Vous qui venez à Lip," at franc-comtois.fr. *Le Républicain lorrain*, January 14, 2011.

10   Collectif Femmes, *18 Millions de bonnes à tout faire* (Paris, 1978), 23–8, 116–21. Charles Piaget, "'Des trésors d'imagination quand on est partie prenante ...'," *Autrement* 20 (September 1979): 168.

11   *Le Monde*, June 30, 1976, 32.

12   The police carried out a poll of eighty inhabitants of Besançon and found 15 percent favorable to *les Lip* and 72.5 percent unfavorable, with the remainder undecided. ADD 1812W30 RG, June 1, 1977.

13   Collectif, *Lip: affaire non classée*, 101.

14   ADD 1812W29 RG, June 18, 1976.

15   ADD 1812W29 RG June 22, 1976; June 24, 1976.

under the windshield wipers of cars with a reproduction of a parking ticket facing up and an explanation of their fight on the back, which the driver would read with relief.[16] Less disruptive was the distribution later that spring of 50,000 copies of *Lip républicain*, a pirated edition of *L'Est républicain*, which placed the conflict in a regional context.[17]

To receive unemployment benefits, workers had to check in every two weeks with the ANPE. They were also required to visit potential employers in order to maintain their benefits, but when they did so each was accompanied by a group, in the expectation that this would discourage the employer and that the job seeker would be sent away with papers showing that he or she had looked for work.[18] In any case, the authorities reported, the employers' reluctance to hire Lip workers led them to cooperate with *les Lip* by putting on the ANPE forms "an evasive reason such as 'does not fit', that prevents the ANPE from recording a refusal of work."[19] Laid off collectively, workers led by the CFDT-Lip rejected the CGT-Lip call for workers to look for work as individuals and to check in at the ANPE individually. They sought to check in collectively, and the union used the occasion to rally workers who were not coming regularly to Palente.[20]

Workers' engagement had been the key to success in 1973–4. In 1976–7, it was clearly harder to mobilize workers who were being paid 90 percent of their salary by the state. There were varying degrees of participation among the 630 workers who remained of the 880 that had been employed at liquidation. Virtually all who stayed on participated in security and maintenance tasks. But by February 1977, the number at the General Assembly was closer to two-thirds of the total (although many of those missing had responsibilities that excused them on any particular day); about one-third took an active role in the work of the commissions.[21] Union leaders set the agenda for the General Assembly. The number of assemblies held each week was reduced to two. In December 1976, the CFDT-Lip began organizing individual meetings in each area of the

16 *Libération*, February 5, 1977, 6.
17 *Libération*, June 1, 1977, 4.
18 ADD 1026W26 Chef du centre régional de Franche-Comté (ANPE) to Directeur départemental du travail, August 29, 1977. ADD 1026W21 RG, December 14, 1977; December 16, 1977. Plantin, "L'accompagnement du service social," 48.
19 ADD 2032W333, Directeur régional du travail to MT, January 19, 1977.
20 BDIC F delta rés 702/6/1 CFDT-Lip, "La bataille pour l'emploi, c'est aussi la bataille du pointage et des 90%." ADD 2032W333, Directeur départemental du travail to MT, May 31, 1976 ; Directeur régional du travail to MT, September 2, 1976. ADD 1812W30 RG, September 15, 1976.
21 *Libération*, February 7, 1977, 6. *Tribune socialiste*, February 10, 1977, 10.

factory, one per week, finding that it was easier to elicit participation, and later the discussion of production issues, in smaller workplace groups and commissions.[22] Arguing "that there is the same relationship between prolonged struggles and the 'classic' strike as between the marathon and the 100 meters,"[23] the union leadership asserted itself. There had always been a "guiding nucleus [*noyau dirigeant*]" of the struggle,[24] but now it emerged more clearly in the form of a "collective" which reported weekly to the General Assembly. It conceived of itself as a catalyst for "an energy that precedes it," that of the workers.[25] Initially open to all, the collective limited itself in January 1977 to about thirty-five, primarily self-selected CFDT-Lip members. A five-person secretariat met daily to handle both day-to-day and urgent matters. Issues of participation and democracy would be increasingly important for the remainder of the struggle.

4M and SCEIP

In the occupied factory in 1976 and succeeding years, workers produced goods other than watches for three reasons. The first was to show Palente remained a viable economic enterprise, a site of imagination and creativity in the economic as well as the social sphere. The second was to keep workers engaged. Lastly, when the 90 percent unemployment pay ended, workers could use sales to help support themselves.

4M—Micro-mécanique et matériel médical—was a particular example of employee entrepreneurship at Lip. What set the situation in 1976 apart from 1973 was the engagement of a number of engineers and managers. 4M began operations in the summer of 1976, registering as a non-profit so that employees could keep their unemployment benefits. Eight engineers and managers, drawn from those hired or promoted by Neuschwander, and a dozen skilled workers and other employees in the armaments division, worked with doctors from Information et actions santé. This group of leftist physicians was itself engaged in a conflict with the Conseil de l'Ordre, the hegemonic conservative association which governed the medical profession. They worked with the team from Lip to discuss with doctors their requirements for specialized equipment.

---

22   BDIC F delta rés 702/6/1 CFDT-Lip, "Information," December 8, 1976. *Tribune socialiste*, May 18, 1978, 11.

23   Collectif, *Lip: affaire non classé*, 141.

24   "Lip Larzac," 33.

25   BDIC F delta rés 702/6/2 "Réunion du 11 janvier [1977]-Collectif élargi."

Close to 90 percent of the medical devices used in France were imported. Designed with profit and not human needs in mind, they were expensive and often more complex than necessary. 4M developed surgical instruments and other new medical products; workers drew on their skills in precision mechanics to make prototypes. Early projects leading to patents included a machine to measure blood circulation under the skin and another that used magnetic forces to allow individuals with facial paralysis to close their eyelids. 4M was particularly interested in developing technology that patients themselves could operate and monitor, thus taking an active role in the management of their condition, like workers in an ailing business.[26] As one worker explained: "There exists a parallel between a sick person and a factory like ours. The situation is presented as a fatality and we are asked to be forbearing while they take charge. In refusing the fatality of unemployment, we were led to think of medical equipment that frees the sick person of the handicap of being a patient."[27]

Les Lip were deeply disappointed when, in 1977, the 4M engineers, who had already applied for four patents for new medical devices, left the occupied factory to form their own business, Statice. They did this in order to begin production and sales, which they could not legally do in the occupied factory. Workers had been actively involved in making prototypes of some thirty devices, but they were unwilling to leave the community at Palente. Although workers continued to repair medical devices for clinics and hospitals in the region after the engineers' departure, with them went their vision of Lip as a site whose future was built on the innovative research done there. If the state had allowed the workers to establish themselves legally at Palente, 4M would have become an important element of a new Lip.

The prefect understood this and played a role in the engineers' departure from Palente. In June 1977, he wrote triumphantly to the president of the pharmaceutical firm Sanofi that 4M "is now separating itself from the rest of Lip where it was entangled until now and to which it gave a moral and intellectual backing." He asked that Sanofi consider the engineers' position: "They are somewhat in the situation of those who prepare to

26   *Tribune socialiste*, October 14, 1976, 7. *Lip Unité*, no. 6, November 1976, 4–5; December 1978, 9. *Libération*, November 6–7, 1976, 6. Collectif, *Lip: affaire non classée*, 116–21. "Vivre sans trahir," *Rouge* 5 (December 1977). Auschitzky Coustans, *Lip*, 61–2. Michel Jeanningros, "LIP 1973–1981: côté armements," *Alternatives non-violentes* 41 (1981): 20. ADD 1026W18 Dossier No. 2, includes an extensive report on 4M's medical devices.

27   *Libération*, December 3–4, 1977, 5.

jump the Berlin Wall to take refuge in the West."[28] Nothing came of this introduction to Sanofi, but in October 1977, the prefect was pleased to inform Paris that the 4M engineers had moved to offices provided them by the Chamber of Commerce at his request and that they were negotiating with the French branch of a German medical supply company to establish a new business. His only concern was the media's failure to spread the news: "This blow to the credibility of *les Lip* was carefully concealed by the unions, aided in this by the silence of *L'Est républicain* and regional television."[29] Statice became and remains today an innovative manufacturer of micro-mechanical medical devices and other technologies, successful in a European-wide market.[30] It retained the democratic participatory culture of Lip and, decades later, Raguénès wondered if the engineers of Statice were the only ones who knew how to "translate into facts something of our utopia of yesterday."[31]

A second project created at the time that drew on the politically committed senior managers who came to work at the SEHEM and the expertise of Lip employees was what eventually took the name, Société Coopérative des Études Industrielles de Palente—Service, Conseil, Études Industrielles, Promotion (SCEIP). Michel Garcin and a half-dozen Lip employees, with others associated in particular projects, created a consulting group that sought to "act as anti-colonizers" in effecting technology transfers to the developing world.[32] Instead of overseeing the provision of a completed factory, the usual practice of private firms or governments, the SCEIP goal was, in the words of SCEIP employee and CFDT-Lip militant Bernard Girardot, "to put at [Third World clients'] disposal our know-how and technological capacities and to accompany them until they had complete mastery of their industries and their productions," rather than furthering forms of neo-colonial dependence.[33]

A delegation from Algeria came to Palente in February 1977 and two months later a Lip delegation went to Algiers. This led to the first

---

28   ADD 1026W22 PR to Jean-René Sautier, president of Sanofi, June 2, 1977.

29   ADD 1026W18 PR to MI, October 26, 1977.

30   "Statice: deux produits en pointe," *Besançon Votre Ville*, December 1984, 18. *Le Nouvel observateur*, May 16, 2013, VI.

31   Raguénès, *De Mai 68 à Lip*, 201. The departure of the engineers was deeply resented by *les Lip* at the time, but Beurier noted in 1992 that although the engineers of Statice told their story without mention of Lip, many Lip workers included it in their narration, because it gave the conflict an air of modernity and success. "La mémoire des Lip," 162–3.

32   *Lip Unité*, January–February 1978, 5. *Lip Actualité*, October 1978. *Le Monde libertaire*, February 16, 1978, 5.

33   *Politique hebdo*, September 25, 1977, 13.

contracts to examine what it would take to establish a watchmaking industry in Algeria and to train employees to staff it. After several years of research the SCEIP determined that the importance of micro-electronics in watchmaking no longer made this feasible in Algeria.[34] However, the SCEIP provided advice on the transfer of a number of other economic projects to Algeria, ranging from herds of Montbéliard cows to French tobacco. The SCEIP then shifted its emphasis to work in Francophone sub-Saharan Africa. In 1982, it helped arrange a visit of a dozen "authentic peasants—who dug the earth—not dignitaries," from the Sahel to Franche-Comté and nearby regions to talk with other "peasants" where they lived and worked about subjects like small-scale technology, the sharing of machines, and the role of women in production. The visitors were taken aback by European farmers' indebtedness, use of chemicals, and how the quest for increased productivity led to work without respite. The African farmers concluded that there were good elements to take from France, but this way of life was not for them.[35] Taken on a visit to the abandoned Palente factory, they saw in "the combat of *les Lip*," Jeanningros reported, "an analogy with what they engaged in as Third World peasants, faced with those who held the levers of world commerce in the products they cultivated each day and that made them more and more dependent."[36]

Work of Liberation

4M and the SCEIP were projects born of the new left politics of self-management among patients, physicians, and the citizens of Third World countries. They were the work of the educated elite drawn to the SEHEM by the Lip Affair. However, there is also a long tradition in France of workers using company machines to make objects for themselves—*la perruque*—and on June 18, 1973, when watch production began, the police expected the mechanics workshop to start turning out "trinkets

---

34   Ibid. Girardot talked of training in micro-mechanics for work in oil production and telecommunications, but Garcin later suggested that watchmaking was a pretext for Algeria to develop the expertise necessary for armaments production. "L'affaire Lip. Entretien avec Michel Garcin," May 17, 2010, at del-ly.over-blog.com.

35   The SCEIP participated in the creation of the Innovations et réseaux pour le développement in Geneva, an association dedicated to the introduction of new technologies in the Third World, while respecting existing cultures and communitarian practices. The SCEIP arranged the Africans' visit with this group.

36   *Lip Unité*, First Trimester 1983, 20.

and gadgets" for works councils at other firms to sell.[37] This did not happen then, but in 1976–7 the workers' receipt of 90 percent of their pay allowed them to explore another relation to work and to develop new forms of engagement. These took the form of production and provision of services that lacked the prestige of manufacture, but broke the workers' predilection for recreating the organization of work they had known in the factory, as when they had started up the assembly lines in 1973.[38] "The creativity aspect must find all of its expression inside an occupied enterprise."[39] The community that emerged from the conflict took precedence in these activities, in which women often played a prominent role, in contrast to their subordinate position in the direction of the factory or the union.

Each of the new workshops was run by a commission. Goods were sold and the proceeds went to the community, but this work was primarily an act of popularization. For one observer, these workshops were the antithesis of a factory like Lip: "the 'warm and relaxed' atmosphere of the commissions in no way resembles a classic workshop. No hierarchy exists. Decisions are made in common and work is somehow done."[40] Sometimes involving only a handful of workers, the workshops made a variety of wooden objects, including frames, napkin rings, toys, bedside and office lamps, and travel clocks. Some workers made embroidery, silk-screened cloth, and clothes; others decorated wall plates with political and regional themes. Employees also set up a pyrography workshop. Emblematic is the history of La Chiffonnière, which began with women collecting pieces of cloth and wool. They used this material to make a variety of goods from baby garments to scarfs. At first women worked alone, but soon a dozen, primarily OS from armaments, formed a sewing commission and worked together in a room at Palente.[41] Later, they began buying fabrics in Paris and making collective decisions about production.[42] The most popular item created by any commission were kitchen timers made from the disarmed heads of cannon shells, produced in the armaments section. *Les Lip* sold several thousand. General

37   ADD 1812W25 RG, June 18, 1973.

38   Jeanningros in Saint-Germain and Souletie, "Le voyage à Palente," 80.

39   *Lip Unité*, no. 6, November 1976, 3. Michel Garcin, "Lutte contre le chômage et création d'entreprise: l'exemple de Lip," *Rencontre: cahiers du travailleur social* 37 (Spring 1981): 45. In ADD 45J55 there is a list of list of the forty-three commissions at Palente in the autumn of 1977.

40   *Libération*, March 26, 1980, 14–15.

41   *Libération*, February 7, 1977, 6. Bondu, "De l'usine à la communauté," 436.

42   ADD 45AJ68 Raguénès in *Parti Pris*, February 1979.

Jacques Pâris de La Bollardière, imprisoned for his opposition to the use of torture in the Algerian War, and later a pacifist and supporter of the Larzac farmers in their confrontation with the army, visited Palente and was given one as a gift.[43]

In the open house in May 1976, *les Lip* sought to show that the enterprise was technologically advanced. When they held an open house in November that year, the atmosphere was different. Thirteen thousand came. Discussion was no longer of quartz watches, but of Lip as the community of the future: "Lip is already tomorrow," a slogan thought up by Clavel that echoed the CFDT call to "Live tomorrow in today's struggles" at a time when the CFDT was beginning to think in more mundane terms.[44] Rather than economic viability in a capitalist system, *les Lip* talked about living and producing in a different way. This was, after all, the source of their support among '68ers. While Piaget worried that these artisanal projects could generate an "autonomous mentality" that threatened the collectivity found in a factory,[45] Raguénès—himself an OS in armaments, site of many of the new ventures—told those who came to the open house in November 1976:

> We produce to express ourselves. When we see OS, women who usually spend all day making two or three thousand holes in parts, who now create designs, embroider, it's fantastic. We work to create other spaces and to initiate today the project of liberation and of a revolutionary socialist society of which we dream.[46]

At the beginning of 1979, a journalist portrayed Palente as having "the appearance of a community tending to autarky," in the form of services the Lip workers provided to one another.[47] Another reporter saw Palente becoming "a supermarket of services"; it included a car repair shop, a hairdressing salon, a printshop, and a child-care facility.[48] A commission purchased consumer goods wholesale, produce from local farmers, and meat from slaughterhouses; it passed the savings on to workers.[49] In December 1977, the commission sold in the range of 5,000 steaks

---

43　Jeanningros, "LIP 1973–1981," 20. *Libération*, December 5, 1977, 6.

44　Bondu, "De l'usine à la communauté," 436 n1.

45　*La Gueule ouverte*, June 7, 1978, 13.

46　*Libération*, November 8, 1976, 7.

47　*Libération*, January 12, 1979, 6.

48　*La Croix*, December 15, 1978.

49　*Lip Unité*, June 1977, 5.

per week.[50] The worker-run restaurant Au Chemin de Palente served lunch every day. For Bondu, the activities at Palente were "to a certain extent the unpremeditated implementation of the 'passionate series' dear to Fourier, where individuals associate according to their affinities and interests."[51] Sustained initially by the 90 percent unemployment pay, the May 1968 dreams of an alternative way of life took root.

Enterprises in Struggle

The live-and-work-differently community of Palente was one form of 1968 activism. Equally radical was the attention Lip workers paid to the unemployed and to workers fighting for their jobs in occupied factories throughout France. *Les Lip* criticized unions for doing little to address the isolation and powerlessness of the unemployed, beginning with those in Besançon.[52] In response to their own disappointment with state-funded job training, Lip workers established "short internships" at Palente in occupations like milling and lathe operation for youths and the unemployed of the region.[53] They sought to make the occupied factory a place where the unemployed could discuss issues and act collectively. The community offered assistance in navigating the social welfare bureaucracy and extended its activities at Palente to the unemployed of Besançon at a cost they could afford, including hairdressing, child care and legal services; the unemployed were charged for parts only when their cars needed repair. They could also purchase the low-priced goods the Lip community bought in bulk.[54] Au Chemin de Palente drew on a subsidy from the city to offer the unemployed an inexpensive lunch. It sought, in the words of the Lip workers, "to create a hub for the unemployed of Besançon."[55]

Lip workers were particularly concerned with the long conflicts of workers in occupied factories elsewhere at a time of mass unemployment. *Lip Unité* explained that the unemployed of enterprises in struggle (*entreprises en lutte*) are conscious of belonging to an enterprise. They

---

50   *Le Nouvel observateur*, December 5, 1977, 50.

51   Bondu, "De l'usine à la communauté," 430–1.

52   Collectif, *Lip: affaire non classée*, 126.

53   *Lip Unité*, no. 6, November 1976, 3.

54   ADD 45J50 "'Il faut faire craquer les murs de l'usine,'" *L'Étincelle* 26 (June 16, 1977). BDIC delta rés 578/41 *L'Heure*, p. 3 [supplement to *Lip Unité*, December 1977].

55   "A LIP, un restaurant pour chômeurs," *Lutte ouvrière* 470 (September 3, 1977).

are not the jobless; they have jobs and are fighting for employment.[56] *Les Lip* believed that the growing number of enterprises in struggle could "become an asset, an arm if they are channeled, amplified, echoed, contributing to the fight against the silence consciously maintained by business."[57]

Between July 1974 and July 1975 there were some 200 factory occupations across France, most in small to mid-sized firms with the goal of attracting public support; there were at least thirty at any one time. Twenty took the form of "productive strikes," including a diversity of machine shops and factories, clothing makers, foodstuff businesses, as well as the Caron-Ozanne printshop (Caen) and the Manuest furniture factory in Châtenois (Vosges). One of the earliest actions was undertaken by ninety-five female textile workers locked out of their factory at Cerizay (Deux-Sèvres); they set up their own workshop in August 1973 and made and sold blouses under the name PIL (Populaires Inventés Localement).[58] They learned from *les Lip* not just that they could produce and sell what they produced, but the importance of public relations. The workers at Cerizay wrote and sang anti-authoritarian songs and became the subjects of militant films.

As at Lip, these movements that were aimed primarily at protecting employment gained support because they were interpreted in terms of self-management. Production ranged from the products for which the closed firm was known to a variety of artisanal goods like those produced at Palente. In the spring of 1975, supporters could purchase from workers in the occupied factories "Konen-Westinghouse" metal hatchets (in place of the elevators manufactured there previously), "Everwear" bedspreads, "CIP" children's clothes, "Buda" jeans and cloth bags, "Isotube" plastic objects, "Annonay" leather goods; "Bretoncelles" lamps, "Idéal-Standard" cast-iron fireplace plates, "Délice des Cévennes" patisserie, and "Abattoirs de Pleynet" poultry. [59]

In some occupied factories, workers rethought production: at Manuest, workers redesigned models of furniture the owner had canceled and had

---

56 *Lip Unité*, July 1976, 6.

57 Collectif, *Lip: affaire non classée*, 131. For the results of long-duration conflicts, see Gérard Adam and Jean-Daniel Reynaud, *Conflits du travail et changement social* (Paris, 1978), 318.

58 "Lutter et chanter à Cerizay," *C.F.D.T. Aujourd'hui* 5 (January–February 1974): 3–12. Xavier Vigna, "Le mot de la lutte? L'Autogestion et les ouvrières de PIL à Cerizay en 1973" in *Autogestion*, ed. Georgi, 381–94.

59 Vigna, *L'Insubordination ouvrière*, 107–11. Adam and Reynaud, *Conflits du travail*, 310.

success selling them; at Teppaz, workers created a new model of record player; and at Bailleul, the workers designed and made new children's garments. Far from the "worker fortresses" like Renault-Billancourt, workers were learning from one another's experiences. In this period of transition within the CFDT, analysts in the confederation initially discussed these experiences in terms of liberation as well as employment. "Here perhaps is the constitution of a collective intellectual, where one sees the working class come up with ideas for itself. It is the discovery and the concrete experimentation of the wealth of experiences and practices of union organization."[60] The production and sale of watches at Lip in 1973 had been primarily a means to build support for the movement. In the economic recession that followed, however, the new generation of factories engaged in productive strikes were often closer to autonomous economic enterprises. As long as production and sales were primarily a means of advancing the struggle, the CFDT could tolerate this strategy. However, as the state chose to let these conflicts "rot," the CFDT became less supportive and in turn the enterprises in struggle came to see that their interests and experiences had no place in the confederation.

Well before the spring of 1973, the CFDT-Lip leadership had closely followed conflicts over employment elsewhere in France, writing to locals to get a full picture of what had happened and what they could take from it. They drew on what they had learned in developing their own movement.[61] Palente in turn came to see itself as a catalyst and source of experiences of value to workers elsewhere who were fighting to save their jobs. Before the September 29 march, Piaget had said that even if an agreement was reached with Giraud before then, the demonstration would still go on. It would provide an opportunity for workers at enterprises faced with job losses and factory closings to exchange experiences, "because at the same time it will be the celebration of all that was a little Lip and of what is already going on in other enterprises."[62] That such exchanges were restricted on September 29—and thwarted by the CGT that fall in the cases of the shoemakers at Romans and the printers at Larousse—was the impetus for the colloquium in December 1973 and the mobilization of the nationwide network of Lip mini-commissions to support struggles elsewhere after the signing of the Dole accords.[63] At

---

60   "Les enfants de Lip," *CFDT aujourd'hui* (September–October 1975): 24.

61   *Politique hebdo*, December 20, 1973, 16.

62   *Le Monde*, September 18, 1973, 40.

63   "Un pas vers la révolution," 30. BDIC F delta rés 578/48 Commissions Lip de Lyon, February 9, 1974.

the beginning of February 1974, the popularization commission met to discuss how Lip could bring the practices of transparency and permanent dialogue between leaders and workers to enterprises in struggle, without becoming an organization that told others what to do.[64] A group of Lip workers—reflecting in 1975 on the development of new capacities that resulted from sharing what worked in different enterprises in struggle—spoke of the "self-formation of the working class" in contrast to the job training (*formation*) that left unexamined the workplace and what took place there.[65] Lip workers and others in enterprises in struggle increasingly referred to coordination as a means to "break together the wall of silence around these struggles" by passing on experiences and insights for which there was no other source, practicing solidarity, and organizing common actions in order to develop a presence and power on the national level that they could never achieve by working through the confederations.[66]

In late October 1975, when the SEHEM was still a going concern, Lip workers in conjunction with the PSU in Besançon organized a national conference that brought together representatives from thirty factories, called "mini-Lips" by the press, where workers faced with layoffs had occupied their workplaces and in some cases launched production. They were joined by representatives from other sectors like steelmaking and the public services, where layoffs and early retirements without replacements raised employment issues. In Piaget's words, workers needed to "exchange their experiences, to reflect together and to envisage together what responses to make." They had initially tried to do so through the confederations, but "the needs [those attending] expressed show precisely that there is a void, a void that the union and political organizations do not fill." The conference was "horizontal" in nature, without the vertical ascent and descent of information characteristic of a national union structure.[67] Although the CFDT made clear to Piaget that it expected all communication between unions in enterprises in struggle to go through the union hierarchy, he found this contradictory

---

64 F delta rés 578/36 "Transcription de la Discussion du 1e Février 74 d'un collectif de la commission popularisation Lip sur ce que peut être le travail des mini-commissions dans cette nouvelle phase de la lutte des Lip," 3.

65 Piaget, "LIP. Les effets formateurs," 153.

66 *Politique hebdo*, July 28, 1976, 11–12. "Interview de Charles Piaget délégué CFDT Lip," *Révolution* 141 (June 11, 1976): 14 [quoted].

67 Lip called the meeting in July 1975, before the beginning of the crisis that led to the closing of the CEH. *Politique hebdo*, October 20, 1975. See also *Tribune socialiste*, October 25, 1975.

to his idea of working-class solidarity as the sharing of ideas and experiences, especially as the workers involved were no longer employed.[68] The confederation was particularly critical of cooperation between locals from different federations involved in long conflicts in occupied factories. It saw this as "extra-syndical" or even "anti-syndical," explicable only as the work of leftists.[69] However, as CFDT-Lip militants Raguénès and Michel Cugney pointed out in response, what these conflicts shared was more important than what differentiated them: "these enterprises are like twin sisters. Sisters, they differ. Twins, they resemble one another. But what a resemblance!"[70]

At the open house of May 8–9, 1976, visitors met representatives not only from Lip, but from some thirty other enterprises in struggle as well. The following month, Lip took the lead in organizing a meeting of these enterprises and served as the secretariat of the association they formed, becoming, in Piaget's words, "a hub for the exchange of information" on a wide variety of legal and organizational issues particular to occupied factories.[71] As far as the prefect was concerned, *les Lip* were seeking to make Palente "a kind of workers' university" to train union leaders.[72] With a dozen enterprises at its core, other meetings of the network were held in September and October 1976. *Lip Unité* became increasingly devoted to coverage of layoffs and occupations throughout France. In the spring of 1977, it cited 200 occupied enterprises with 15,000 employees; the secretariat had ties to sixty of them and close relations with a core of fifteen.[73]

The workers of Lip challenged parties and union confederations, the central state, as well as global capitalism by creating, in a pathbreaking instance of social networking, a national autonomous sphere of debate and exchange among workers engaged in battles in a deindustrializing France. Talking to Communists in Besançon in 1977, Piaget said that each firm with employment issues "felt such a leaden weight on it" that, unlike the situation at Lip four years earlier, workers in a single firm

---

68   *Témoignage chrétien*, August 5, 1976, 5.

69   *Le Monde*, June 27–8, 1976, 30.

70   *Politique hebdo*, July 28, 1976, 11–12. See also Raguénès in Jean-Marcel Bouguereau, "Quelque chose est en train de naître," *Action* 774 (July 6, 1976).

71   "Interview de Charles Piaget délégué CFDT Lip," 14.

72   ADD 2377W182 PR to MI, July 30, 1976. ADD 45J39 "Première réunion des entreprises en lutte pour l'emploi" (June 6, 1976 at Besançon).

73   *Lip Unité*, April–May 1975, 2; September 1976, 1; October 1976, 3; February–March 1977, 4–5. *Lip républicain*, supplement to *Lip Unité*, April 1977. BDIC F delta rés 702/5/1 "Seconde réunion de travail des enterprises en lutte sur l'emploi et en occupation à Besançon les 10 et 11 septembre 1976." Jean Lajonchère, *Le Curé rouge* (Paris, 2002), 95–6, 125–6.

could no longer think of fighting on their own. "In '73 there could be a few struggles with sabers drawn and white gloves. Now you can't. You need armies ..."[74] Thinking in terms of the regions particularly affected, Piaget said, "It would be a matter, in some sense, of instituting a tradition of immediate and common response each time that the authorities attack an enterprise in struggle."[75] Furthermore, enterprises in struggle could coordinate activities. Banners and handouts distributed at the beginning of the vacation season in 1976 read: 'You are going on vacation ... but there are struggles that continue."[76]

Chômageopoly

On July 26, 1976, the hundred or so Lip workers who had not gone on vacation decided to take and hide the stock of 120,000 watches held at Palente. This was a CFDT-Lip operation; the CGT-Lip was told (and gave its approval) after the fact. At the time, *les Lip* did not need to sell the watches to pay their salaries and planned to return them if serious national negotiations were held. Their goal was to prevent the sale of "the Lip brand" to Ébauches SA, "a foreign business." If this happened, they planned to flood the market with the sequestered watches. They saw the strategy as an assurance against expulsion from the factory.[77]

To prevent word getting out about the seizure of the watches and to ward off an attack by the police, workers held two senior managers at Palente until the next morning, "a useful 'staging,'" the prefect quickly realized.[78] One of them was Michel Garcin, a socialist drawn to the "tomorrow already" element of the aspirations of Lip. As a youth, Garcin had been marked by Johan David Wyss' novel *Swiss Family Robinson*, about a band of youths lost in the wild who set out to construct a new society. He had gone to Sciences Po and had been the co-president of the chaplaincy (*l'aumônerie*) there, at the time Raguénès was chaplain for law students in Paris. Although this was not what brought Garcin to Besançon, it provided Garcin and Raguénès with an important shared

---

74   ADD 177J13 Transcript of a discussion between Lip leadership and local PCF leaders at Palente (1977).

75   *Libération*, June 28, 1976, 1, 6.

76   "Interview de Charles Piaget délégué CFDT Lip," 14–15.

77   ADD 1812W29 RG, July 27, 1976. *L'Est républicain*, July 28, 1976, 1. Jeannin-gros to Reid, August 19, 2016.

78   ADD 2377W182 PR to MI, July 30, 1976.

experience.[79] Garcin had worked for four years in a training program in Cameroon and had then gone to New York as assistant director of the Banque Nationale de Paris. In the fall of 1974, he met Neuschwander, who was looking into developing a subsidiary in the United States. Named president of the short-lived American division of the CEH, he told *Time* magazine late in 1975, "There is no better store to start marketing a French product than Bloomingdale's."[80] But Christmas sales at Bloomingdale's never materialized, and he returned to France to take the position of secretary-general of the CEH.[81]

Charged by the syndics with overseeing the enterprise after the bankruptcy, Garcin said: "I had to stay to contribute to finding a solution or to pursue the struggle so that the bad blow directed at Lip would go badly." Some workers questioned his situation—paid by the bankrupt firm, but an active partisan of the workers—and compared the conflict in 1973 to one in which he would have a role: "You speak like a technocrat. Isn't that the reason for the loss of support in '76? They don't understand us anymore. We are with the managers. We practice class collaboration."[82] However, Garcin sought to use his intermediary position to help resolve the conflict in the workers' interest. A couple of days after he was kept in his office while the watches were taken, Garcin told the prefect in private that he would like to serve on a small group to examine offers to purchase the enterprise, saying he could use his position to keep a lid on things at Palente for a month or two while it did its work. Whatever union leaders said publicly, Garcin thought they were moving toward acceptance of employment elsewhere in Besançon for workers not offered positions by a new firm if they received the same level of work and pay as they had previously, and were promised priority in future hiring at Palente.[83] Although nothing came of these secret interactions, he stayed committed to the struggle at Palente.

Garcin spoke frequently with workers of the Catholic humanism they shared, "of the redemption by struggle that was present in the conflict."[84] Asked why he stayed after the bankruptcy, he answered:

79   AB Interview with Garcin by Beurier [1992], 54.
80   "Leading Toward a Green Christmas," *Time*, December 1, 1975, 82.
81   *Le Monde*, March 12, 1996.
82   BDIC F delta rés 702/4/4 Transcript of discussion of Lip employees [1978].
83   ADD 2377W182 PD, July 29, 1976. G. Michaud, "Note à l'attention de Monsieur le préfet de région," August 18, 1976.
84   AB Interview with Garcin by Beurier [1992], 53.

For me, Christianity is the permanent effort to put into the life of each day, here and now, an element of evangelical life. But, in my view, this life is characterized by the fact that it addresses the whole man, inseparably 'social and economic'. The evangelical project is that effort: to reconcile the economic and the social.[85]

However, the place of Lip in a France in which the left could come to power interested Garcin as well. Early in 1978, he spoke about why he had rejected a friend's advice not to go work at the CEH: "I believe that a government of the left, if it comes to power, will not keep it unless there develops in each enterprise nuclei [noyaux] that seek a rapid change in society, but can forestall a fascist reaction. At Lip this nucleus [noyau] exists. I wanted to get to know it." Yet many workers at Lip had trouble understanding why an individual like Garcin would join their fight: "you went to the school of those in charge and you speak like one of them. You are like a white black of the African colonies. Black skin and white mask." He responded that he was fighting to change the society that enshrined these differences.[86]

Garcin agreed with the workers' decision to take the watches in July 1976, but so as not to interfere with the search for investors, he could not be involved. The telephone lines were cut and he was held in his office until the next morning to allow the removal and disposal of the stock. Garcin's secretary was made his guard. Hired by Neuschwander in June 1974 because she was bilingual, Françoise Verderre had become active in the movement, going to Paris and to Marseille with other employees to drum up support. Left inside Palente with nothing to do that night, Garcin and Verderre thought up the idea for what became *Chômageopoly*, a reworking of *Monopoly* in terms of *chômage*, unemployment, in which players assume the roles of workforces of bankrupt firms fighting to save their jobs. As the rolls of dice and Chance cards permit, they occupy the plant and pursue a movement to reopen the business with employment for all.[87] While the game drew on what happened at Lip,

---

85 *Lip Unité*, February–March 1980, 7.

86 BDIC F delta rés 702/4/4 Transcript of discussion of Lip employees [1978]. However, when Vittot and Burgy later explained to workers the range of salaries in the newly established cooperative, Christiane André said that the women had not dared say anything to the union leaders, but sought out Garcin, "their papa, their leader," to express their discontent. "Lip la coopérative en question 'dans le socialisme, est-ce qu'il y aura le droit de grève?'," *Commune* 21 (June 30, 1978): 9.

87 ADD 45J96 "Juin 1974–Mai 1981, le parcours de Françoise Verderre, secrétaire bilingue au service export de Lip," entry of November 25, 1976.

workers there, pursuing the strategy of coordination, enriched the game by drawing on the experiences of workers in other occupied enterprises.[88] Players drew cards with messages like "The police invade, force workers to evacuate and occupy your factory. You win in popularization, but you are restrained in your activities. Take 2 power relations points and wait two turns"; or the ironic "The prefect says that he is going to take care of your struggle, and that he is going to help you. No question, you lose two power relations." The game could end with situations ranging from the dismantling of the firm and layoffs to the rehiring of all workers.

Chômageopoly was intended to familiarize players with the problems of unemployment and of a factory occupied by workers, as well as the forms of support they could provide and receive. "A good means of popularization," *Lip Unité* wrote, "it is also an excellent training tool."[89] To counter the competition that divides workers, the game could be won only by players who cooperate rather than compete with one another.[90] For Pierre Victor, *Chômageopoly* embodied the "headless totality" whose development at Lip he so valued. Party and union leaders speak in terms of the "power relations" that their august position allows them to interpret and therefore to justify their taking decisions in the place of the workers. However, the Lip struggle taught Pierre Victor that "Everyone has their small power relations. In the game of *Chômageopoly*, you can even win 10, 20, 30 ... power relations: a game accessible to all" in which power relations, not money, are the currency.[91]

Chômageopoly itself was a product of the coordination of enterprises in struggle. A commission at Palente set up to produce and sell the game called on occupied factories to make the different parts: Sitrab (Remiremont [Vosges]) made the box; the Société Centrale de Plastique et de Caoutchouc, a manufacturer of plastic bottles in Clermont-Ferrand, made the plastic pieces; and CIP (Haisnes-lez-la-Bassée [Pas-de-Calais]) made a cloth bag to hold the pieces. Well-known left artists Wiaz, Kerleroux, Forcadell, and Daullé provided illustrations for the box and the board.[92] *Les Lip* assembled and distributed the games. By early

88   *Libération*, July 31, 1976. *Chômageopoly* was in line with the original game of *Monopoly*, designed at the turn of the century to promote anti-monopoly politics. Mary Pilon, *The Monopolists* (New York, 2015).

89   *Lip Unité*, no. 6, November 1976, 3.

90   AMB 5Z224 "Philosophie du Jeu" [Chômageopoly].

91   Pierre Victor, "Lip acéphale," *Les Temps modernes* 367 (February 1977): 1266–7.

92   *Lip Unité*, no. 6, November 1976, 3.

1977, 1,000 games had been produced and plans were made to make 5,000 more: "We would like for *Chômageopoly* to be in every home, that each family plays it, so that the problem of unemployment would not be so marginal and that full employment becomes the watchword of all the French."[93] In September 1978, *Lip Unité* reported that close to 10,000 games had been sold.[94] Several thousand more were marketed, largely through the consumer cooperative of the teachers insurance fund, the Coopérative des adhérents à la mutuelle des instituteurs de France (CAMIF).[95] *Chômageopoly* was emblematic of the coordination of enterprises in struggle and the appeal of an alternative community at Palente. However, those enterprises never escaped being in struggle and the efforts to build a collective movement faltered in the late 1970s, leaving the workers of Lip increasingly on their own.

Production and the Prefect

In mid-May 1977, the collective distributed a leaflet telling the story of Robert Surcouf, the audacious Napoleonic naval officer who developed a plan to escape the naval blockade at Saint-Malo in order to get into the open sea where his boat could take advantage of its maneuverability.[96] With that goal in mind, at the end of May 1977, the General Assembly voted 390 to twenty to accept the collective's proposal to start watch production and sales in anticipation of the end of the 90 percent salary coverage for one group of workers in mid-June and for the rest in mid-July.[97] In so doing, they reiterated the belief that had inspired the campaign for a Piaget candidacy. Elections and nationalizations would not bring socialism. It would come only from struggles and their transformative

---

93   *Lip Unité*, February–March 1977, 8.

94   Workers at Lip developed ideas for other games, never realized, including one involving fifteen or twenty persons intended to prepare groups like works councils for the challenges they confront. *Lip Actualité*, September 1978, 2. The Société Centrale de Plastique et de Caoutchouc invented, had the occupied factory Copono-Book produce, and sold 2,000 copies of a board game, *Le Jeu de la solidarité*, based on the experiences of Lip, Larzac and other conflicts, and the difficulties and acts of solidarity they experienced. Lajonchère, *Le Curé rouge*, 125–6.

95   *Lip Unité*, December 1978, 7.

96   *Libération*, June 1, 1977, 4. Surcouf was also a pirate who engaged in slave-trading.

97   ADD 1026W21 RG, May 31, 1977. The CGT and PCF gave their support to the measure, although, as in 1973, they opposed sale of the sequestered watches. ADD 45J50 CGT-Lip letter to members, May 26, 1977. *Libération*, July 19, 1977, 9.

effect on society and on participants. For Garcin, the very impediments to production brought new opportunities: "When management vanishes, this permits promotions, training, new organization …"[98] Female OS who assembled watches organized semi-autonomous production groups and job rotations; they told the sociologist Daniel Jacquin that "this type of organization allows them to find dignity in their work."[99] *Lip Unité* spoke of the decision to launch production in May 1977, and of those the workers would make in the future, as "at our level—[a means to] forge Socialism in the present day."[100]

There were 10,000 watches near completion and, as in 1973, workers began on May 31, 1977 with these, running three hours a day with the goal of producing sufficient watches for an open house on June 18–19.[101] The 5,000 visitors bought more than 3,000 watches, enough to fund the first pay on July 15.[102] The open house had "the appearance of a souk," with the watches being sold alongside the variety of other goods produced at Palente. The large department store La Samaritaine was what came to the police inspector's mind, and he was pleased that sales attracted more attention than the political stands.[103] Sales were not limited to open houses. By August 1977, *les Lip* had sold 13,000 watches, for the most part completed ones they had sequestered in July 1976 (although once again, they did not make this clear to buyers);[104] by October sales had reached 24,000.[105] In succeeding years, artisanal products took on more importance. In 1979, 500 to 700 clocks were sold each month, but watch sales were always the community's primary source of income.[106]

In anticipation of paying salaries in a fight with no clear end in sight, the General Assembly approved a contract to assure participation. It required a minimum of three hours presence at the factory each day, an hour at the General Assembly and two hours on one of the forty-some commissions. Workers had to sign in each morning and have no more than five absences in a month. In addition, all had to sign up for jobs such as night guard, clean-up and landscaping, and work in the restaurant. When the General Assembly so decided, participation in demonstrations

98   Bondu, "De l'usine à la communauté," 442.
99   Jacquin, "Lip 1973–1981," 376–7.
100 *Lip Unité*, June 1977, 1.
101 *L'Unité*, June 3, 1977. *Rouge*, June 18, 1977.
102 *Le Monde*, June 21, 1977.
103 ADD 1812W30 RG, June 20, 1977. *Libération*, December 3–4, 1977, 5.
104 *Lip Unité*, August 1977, 4.
105 ADD 1026W18 PR to MI, October 26, 1977.
106 ADD 1026W20, "Situation actuelle de l'ex-Société Lip," November 13, 1979.

was an obligation. After six months *Lip Unité* reported that the Assembly had as yet not had to cut off anyone's salary.[107]

Afraid of losing their benefits, *les Lip* harassed the Association pour l'emploi dans l'industrie et le commerce (ASSEDIC) in Besançon, the agency in charge of unemployment insurance and a complement to the ANPE, which handled employment. The Besançon ASSEDIC was forced to meet in Paris in April 1977 and in June it decided to make a special allocation for three months of 35 percent of their wages to Lip workers who lost the 90 percent coverage. In addition, workers received about 400 francs per month each in public assistance.[108] However, this total was far from their regular pay and workers made plans to supplement it, starting in mid-July.[109] The General Assembly decided to maintain wage differentials, but, unlike in 1973, limited these. After taking into account the 35 percent unemployment benefit and the public assistance, the pay commission computed the amount from the sale of goods needed to bring the salary of an individual up to 90 percent of the January 1976 pay. Monthly salaries above 2,000 francs would be diminished proportionately from 10 percent (i.e., a 4,000 francs per month employee would receive 3,600 francs) to 2 percent (a 2,200 francs per month employee would receive 2,156 francs). The General Assembly established a minimum salary of 2,000 francs (or 1,800 francs for two-income families) as well as a maximum salary of 4,000 (in practice 3,600) francs. Workers with a single salary and two or more children received their full 90 percent salary up to 3,000 francs.[110] Skilled workers, supervisors, and the few remaining managers like Garcin took the biggest hit. "Impossible to go further in leveling," Piaget said the next year.[111] The element of "from each according to his abilities, to each according to his needs" in these salary decisions broke with the practice in 1973 of paying the full salaries individuals had earned when last employed by the firm. This was a product of the recognition that the conflict

---

107 Within a day of the start of production 550 Lip workers had signed on and more continued to do so. *Lip Unité*, August 1977, 2–3. *Politique hebdo*, February 20, 1978, 18–19.

108 ADD 1485W240 RG, June 22, 1977. However, social security employees came to the factory on a voluntary basis as they had in 1973 and arranged for workers to continue to receive services.

109 *Lip Unité*, June 1977, 1.

110 ADD 177J13, Section CFDT et Collectif LIP, "Vers quel type d'organisation devons-nous aller?," May 23, 1977. *Libération*, June 1, 1977, 4. *Politique hebdo*, June 6, 1977, 19. *Lip Unité*, August 1977, 2–3.

111 ADD 45J70 "Une vie intense dans la mort légale," *L'Impartial*, September 29, 1978.

could be long and of a sense of living in and taking responsibility for a community.[112]

The vote to start up production took place in the context of the legislative elections coming up in March 1978. With these in mind, the prefect instructed the police to do what they could to stop production and sales. He had no doubt that Lip workers would fail eventually, but he could not wait for others to realize this. He needed to make sure it happened now. It was important to quell the mobilizing myth that *les Lip* could succeed, just as the bankruptcy of the SEHEM had shown the futility of progressive capitalists. Lip was, the prefect contended in late June 1977, "a national problem that merits attention." He favored action to deal with the "contagious and perilous rot" of the body of Lip left hanging rather than risk the spread of social disease.[113] Two weeks later, on July 9, he asked the sub-prefect to accompany several hundred police when they went to Palente. There they disabled the transformer and seized 388 watches. However, the desired effect was limited. The prefect continued to complain that the local and national press coverage only used the unions and the Socialists who governed Besançon as sources. The police maintained a presence outside the factory in July, seeking to intimidate the 300 people who visited the factory and bought watches each day.

Realizing that the passage of the Tour de France in mid-July 1977 would give workers an opportunity to display their banners for the television cameras and to offer cyclists "stolen watches," the prefect convinced the Minister of the Interior to use the large police contingent present for the Tour to do an extensive search of Palente, to show it was not a "'sanctuary' in the strategic sense of the word."[114] When the Tour de France went through Besançon, these police, supplemented by riot police sent by the prefect, circled the factory, about one every ten meters. This did not stop the Lip workers from awarding three quartz watches, despite the prefect's request to Tour organizers to prevent this: one to the winner of the *stage* in the region, a second to the "most combative" cyclist, and the third to the one who came in last. However, the next day, when the

---

112   The following year, the General Assembly recognized that the community's ability to continue the fight required employees who were not totally worn down. It voted that all would receive paid two-week vacations in July and August 1978, with one-quarter of the workforce off at a time, leaving the others to maintain production and guard the factory as well as to handle supporters' visits and other aspects of popularization. ADD 1026W21 RG, June 1, 1978.

113   ADD 2377W185 PD, "L'affaire Lip en 1977," June 22, 1977.

114   ADD 1026W18 PD, "Note confidentielle à l'attention personnelle de M. Jean Paolini, director du Cabinet du Ministre" [July 1977]. *Libération*, July 19, 1977, 9.

cyclists left, several buses of CRS in the security force for the Tour were detached and followed a group of state police which had gotten into Palente wearing street clothes and pretending to be tourists from Alsace. They searched the factory and seized 1,438 watches, although many were random pieces that the workers had not intended to sell.[115]

The state's primary means to impede production was to cut the water, gas, electricity and telephone lines. Along with unionized public service employees, the Union de la Gauche municipal government in Besançon elected in March 1977 responded by helping Lip workers cobble together needed services. When the police disabled the transformer, the city lent Palente an electric power generator. It also provided an electric power line for the restaurant. The EDF cut the power four times—a particular problem because watch parts were kept in a refrigerated room and pumps were needed to prevent the basement of Palente from flooding— but each time Lip workers were able to reconnect and the EDF gave up. The frustrated prefect castigated "the prevarications of the EDF ... that [it] is unable to assert state authority is greatly resented."[116] After the phone lines were cut, the city used an abandoned public school to provide telephone service to *les Lip*. When the state interrupted the gas supply, workers dug up the gas lines, reconnected them and covered them over in cement. When gas was cut off again in October 1977, workers installed oil-fired stoves. In the winter, they wore warm clothing and worked in the places easiest to heat, keeping the temperature at the minimum necessary to maintain the high-precision machinery.[117] The assembly line devolved into workers carrying elements to one another.[118] The prefect was unimpressed that workers could continue the diversity of operations at Palente. He imagined that with the cuts in utilities, "one can hardly work or not work at all at Palente, which resembles more a permanent forum, attached to an episodic sales counter, than a factory displaying a coherent industrial purpose."[119]

In the summer of 1977, the prefect also began looking into the possibility of removing the machines from Palente. However, he opposed the syndics' plan to take them to the Paris region to sell. Saying that "a

---

115   ADD 1026W21 RG, July 12, 1977. *Lip Unité*, August 1977, 3–4. *Libération*, July 18, 1977, 7. *Le Monde*, July 18, 1977.

116   ADD 2377W185 PD, "L'affaire Lip en 1977," June 22, 1977.

117   For extensive material on the efforts to cut utilities, see ADD 1026W24. For the workers' responses, see *L'Est républicain*, May 2, 1977. *Libération*, July 27, 1977, 7. *Lip Unité*, August 1977, 3–5; May 1982, 6–7. *La Croix*, June 14–15, 2001, 8.

118   ADD 1026W21 RG, December 5, 1977.

119   ADD 1026W18 PR to MI, October 26, 1977.

dismantling 'Germany Year Zero' style" would be resented in Franche-Comté, the prefect favored warehousing what was taken in the region for now.[120] In response to rumors that machinery would be seized in July 1977, workers built what the police described as a "blockade of stakes on iron stands lined with tires destined to be set on fire" to create a smoke screen. Cans of gas were stocked near the barricades of tires. The workers soldered the entry gates, though visitors could still get in. Thirty meters behind the initial barrier on the way to the workshops, workers dug a trench and filled it with concrete into which they inserted metal stakes. These were wrapped in barbed wire.[121] The prefect referred to a "trench war" against the "'entrenched' of Palente."[122] Workers removed parts from the machines to render them unusable and therefore unsaleable. They also planned a set of "*gags*", like spreading oil on the floor and the machinery. Some watchmaking machines were moved out of Palente and hidden so they could be used if the workers were expelled from the factory.[123] The seizures of watches did not stop workers from holding periodic open houses in which watches were sold, though these sales no longer had the "'village fair' appearance" of their predecessors.[124] The prefect was particularly frustrated that police were ineffective in stopping sales elsewhere, because these gave "the misleading impression of a return of *les Lip* to legality"—since, agents believed, some bought watches not to express support, but because they were a good deal.[125]

With no hope that a new owner would appear, *les Lip* looked to the Union de la Gauche municipal government, which included Garcin and another Lip employee on the city council. Initially the Socialist mayor-senator Robert Schwint may have wanted the workers to leave Palente. At the time of the raid in mid-July 1977, the police reported that he told other politicians that he wished the CRS had used the opportunity to expel the workers from the factory, a step he saw as necessary for any industrial solution with a chance of success.[126] Whatever the accuracy of this account, Schwint did look to end the conflict, which he saw as wearing on city residents and giving an unfavorable impression of Besançon to

120 ADD 2377W185 PD, "L'affaire Lip en 1977," June 22, 1977.
121 ADD 1026W21 RG, January 11, 1978.
122 ADD 1026W18 PR to MI, October 26, 1977.
123 *Lip Unité*, August 1977, 5. Gaston Bordet, "Les Lip de l'utopie à la réalité," *Esprit* 45 (September 1980): 152. Burgy and Piaget, "L'aventure des Coopératives LIP." *Le Matin*, July 27, 1977. *Le Monde*, August 2, 1977, 18.
124 *Libération*, December 5, 1977, 6.
125 ADD 1026W18 PD to MI, December 7, 1977.
126 ADD 1026W21 RG, July 18, 1977.

outsiders.[127] However, he did not want to do so on the prefect's terms. The municipality pursued efforts to buy the land and buildings of Palente in order to rent them to Lip workers, a plan for which the city garnered a pledge of funding from the Conseil Régional.[128]

Although the Lip workers knew that the Union de la Gauche and the Common Program did not directly address their situation, they could not help looking to them. In the summer of 1977, Piaget told the General Assembly: "We can hold on until the legislatives [1978] and until the presidential election [1981] by drawing on the stock of watches."[129] Near the end of July 1977, Mayor Schwint sought to temper such expectations. Speaking at the General Assembly, he agreed with the worker who said that Lip "has too much the military conception of the Maginot Line" (though not with this worker's alternative of calling out the population to defend Palente).[130] However, he said that workers should think not only of defending Palente, but of initiatives to take as well, including the best use to be made of the factory if the city acquired it: "The construction of barricades in steel and concrete reminded me of the operations that I knew in '40 at the time of the phony war and the defeat. But then there was the Resistance and the victory in '45. So, think above all of forging your victory." But, Schwint added, workers should have no illusions. Saying he had met no investor who proposed a global solution to the provision of employment for all, the mayor asked Lip workers to think what they would do if an investor could propose only 100 to 200 jobs at first. They could not just wait for a victory of the left in the parliamentary elections of 1978. This would not bring an immediate resolution: "it will not become Cockaigne from one day to the next."[131]

As the elections approached in March 1978, the prefect did all he could to put an end to the affair, seeing the workers' goal as hanging on until then, "in the hope of a mythic nationalization."[132] In May 1977, the Minister of Labor figured that the total of public funds, including unemployment benefits, and private funds (i.e., company financing,

127   *Libération*, July 29, 1977, 7.

128   *Libération*, February 5, 1977, 6. For the municipality's support of the workers of Lip between 1977 and 1981, see Claude Magnin, "La bataille pour la survie de Lip," *Critique socialiste* 45 (1983): 67–74.

129   *Le Nouvel observateur*, August 15, 1977, 22.

130   *Libération*, July 29, 1977, 7. The subtitle of the article was "Palente at the time of the barricades, the Maginot line and Dien Bien Phu."

131   ADD 177 J14, Notes of Mayor Schwint in speech to the General Assembly, July 25, 1977.

132   ADD 1026W18 PD, "L'affaire Lip en 1977," June 22, 1977.

outstanding bank loans) spent on Lip since June 10, 1973 was 115,740,000 francs.[133] The prefect was very pleased in October 1977 when the Gaullist deputy Georges Bolard presented information he had provided him to the Conseil Régional on "the considerable sums swallowed up in preceding efforts to rescue Lip." He felt this information was not well known to the public, but "one can expect that it will be largely taken up over the course of the next electoral campaign." The Lip workers' leadership was on the defensive and the struggle was losing its appeal, he reported. All would be well if only the media cooperated: "This effacement would be yet more evident if the written and televised press had not offered *les Lip* a sounding board at once disproportionate and oriented in a systematically favorable sense, which does not, it seems to me, respond to the general sentiment of the population."[134] In December 1977, the prefect felt certain that the Lip Affair would be "at the center" of the upcoming legislative elections. With sales of "stolen watches" throughout France, an open house on December 3–4, 1977, and Palente operating on pirated utility services, "Lip remains today the symbol of illegality." He strongly opposed helping the city to buy Palente until the watches had been restored and other legal issues settled. Otherwise, it would just "endow Besançon with a 'red base.'"[135]

Conclusion

Support for the plethora of local struggles had been Piaget's program for the PSU and what his supporters had looked to him to bring to the presidential campaign.[136] The aborted Piaget candidacy in 1974 and the efforts to coordinate enterprises in struggle were the final efforts centered on Lip to develop a national politics drawing on the transformative possibilities of the experience. Although exchanges among enterprises in struggle petered out after 1977, the idea of coordination among workers' movements outside of national union hierarchies was a legacy of the second Lip conflict just as a representation of self-management was of the first.[137] However, with the establishment left looking to the legislative

---

133   ADD 1026W26 X. Audo [cabinet du Ministèr du travail], "Note à l'attention de Monsieur Camous, chargé de mission auprès du Ministre," May 4, 1977.

134   ADD 1026W18 PR to MI, October 26, 1977.

135   ADD 1026W18 PD to PM, December 3, 1977.

136   BDIC delta rés 578/15 Projet d'Institut ouvrier pour le développement des pratiques collectives. *Cahier de discussion* 1 (December 1974): 53–5.

137   Like self-management, coordination has an ambiguous relationship to Lip

elections of 1978, the state authorities focused on quashing the workers in Palente. What the state had begun as an attempt to demonstrate that neither organized labor nor progressive capitalists could resist the dictates of the market, became an element in the effort to draw on the renown of the Lip Affair to defeat the Union de la Gauche.

With the end of the salary support at 90 percent came the end of what some in the leadership thought of as "a luxury conflict," because participants had received close to their full income every month.[138] This had provided the context for the creative practices in the Lip conflicts of 1973–4 and 1976–7. However, it also obscured the presence of two imbricated struggles at Lip.[139] The conflict began and remained a critique of capitalism as failing to operate in the human interest; the union articulated this view in its focus on employment. This was also the source of union efforts to propose a future for Lip in a capitalist economy in the absence of a will do so by the state and business. However, the nature of the tactics pursued in the conflict also responded to the alienation of individuals from their work and from one another in capitalist society. This changed the workers at Lip, particularly those who had previously been least engaged. These two struggles were in turn at the core of the national support for the movement. The establishment left CFDT thought increasingly in terms of the former, while '68ers around the country saw in *les Lip* and in their own participation in the workers' struggle a response to the disenchantment of modern life that stifled creativity and autonomy. Lip workers and their supporters rejected the role the state and business gave *les Lip*—that of bodies left hanging as a warning at the Place de Grève.

The lived critique of a hollow and inauthentic condition took new forms after the bankruptcy of the SEHEM. 4M and SCEIP brought

---

workers' practices. "Coordination" was the term used in the 1980s for forms of student and worker mobilization, external to the local unions. The Action Committee and the General Assembly of Lip in 1973 are cited as forerunners of coordination in this sense. Patrick Rozenblatt, "La forme coordination: une catégorie sociale révélatrice de sens," *Sociologie du travail* 33 (February 1991): 242, and the intervention of Rozenblatt in Jean-Michel Denis, Bruno Karsenty, and Patrick Rozenblatt, "À propos de la coordination étudiante ou l'émergence d'un sujet virtuel" in *Futur Antérieur, Les coordinations de travailleurs dans la confrontation sociale* (Paris, 1994), 181. Pierre Lantz, "Lip précurseur des coordinations?" in ibid., 23–32. However, the term "coordination" was not widely used by *les Lip* until 1976 and then not for the Action Committee or the General Assembly, but for actions external to the confederations to connect locals. The horizontal networking and coordination of the Solidaires Unitaires Démocratiques (SUD) beginning in the 1990s are akin to this experience.

138   Berry, "Lip 1978," 39.
139   Jacquin identifies a similar division in "Lip 1973–1981," 208–9.

together politically committed professionals and workers outside the traditional hierarchy of the firm in social justice projects for which there was apparently no place in capitalism. Pierre Victor interpreted the 4M project in these terms: "the approach of the managers to the doctors, this is evidently a link in the chain that began when, precisely, the gates of the factory were opened."[140] The artisanal projects and services at Palente lacked the prestige of Lip watch production or skilled mechanical work. Nor could they provide the secure well-paid jobs that workers sought. However, they did offer an alternative to factory life. Raguénès saw in artisanal production the different way to work that motivated '68ers: "The organization, the production and the product pulls you away from what came before and opens you up to other realities."[141] Neither during the conflict nor in Neuschwander's firm had workers exercised the democratic control of production that they did in the commissions governing artisanal work.[142] Drawing on the ubiquitous metaphor of the boat, Raguénès saw in the artisanal projects an escape from the search for a new authority in the form of an employer or the state: "To the self-managing island impossible in the capitalist sea must be opposed the workers' sail boat, its impetus and spirit of adventure. This alone is likely to take us to the 'haven' (self-managed or not). This is the only way to defatalize history, and therefore to create it."[143]

The complement to work differently was to live differently. In the years after 1973 there was a move among '68ers from the Paris Commune to the commune itself, evident in any number of "back to the earth" settlements. Palente came to have some of the qualities of such communes and became a way that '68ers could think the relationship between their aspirations and those of workers. Some went further, seeing in *les Lip* the fight for survival of embattled minorities subject to state and capital which adopted the practices of a harsh internal colonialism. Michel Chemin, an établi whose visit to Lip in 1973 led him to leave the factory to work for *Libération*, wrote in 1977 that "for four years, deep down in ourselves, Lip has meant something quite different than a watchmaking enterprise in struggle." He saw at Palente both a workers' fight and the demand for a "right to existence of a minority like those found in the proclamations of Black Americans or the Indians of North America."[144]

140   Raguénès et al., "Lip 1973–1976", 1240–1.
141   *Lip Unité*, Second Trimester 1983, 12–13.
142   *Lip Unité*, December 1978, 7.
143   Raguénès et al., "Lip 1973–1976," 1244–5.
144   *Libération*, December 6, 1977, 5.

Referring to "the tribe of *les Lip* and the reserve of Palente" as "the Indians of Wounded Knee," fighting for "the right to difference," he wrote of the effort to destroy the Lip community:

> Such a will where hatred and acrimony mix, takes on the appearance of a conscious and organized genocide. And if in the authorities' eyes, the Lip community was nothing other than a tribe of Indians, of savages, that it is necessary—in the name of Western civilization and the imperatives of capital—to normalize? This would be as if *les Lip* were a Sioux community and Palente a reserve to "clean up."[145]

For Chemin, *les Lip* were not squatters at Palente, but a community with the rights of a native people. "Comtois, rends toi. Nenni, ma foi."

---

145   *Libération*, June 1, 1977, 4.

11

Reentering the Atmosphere

It is without a doubt more difficult for *les Lip* to reenter legality than for a cosmonaut to reenter the atmosphere.

—Prefect of Doubs[1]

In the description of the creation of the young cooperative [L.I.P.], there are many givens that bear a resemblance to the young Soviet Republic after October 17: encirclement, supply problems, flight of specialists, transformation of militants into managers, debates on the speed of industrialization, on the method of capitalization, on relations with the outside (the struggle or the authorities).

—Richard Copans[2]

I am just thinking of the current problems of Vietnam, or of other countries that realized advances which appeared extremely important to us and afterwards … It is difficult to verify, to know, but one hears that in Vietnam, taking into account the pressure that is exerted on the country, democracy takes a hit. Finally, there is always a risk of adopting totalitarian methods when power is held by a few and escapes the population. In small, very small ways, this phenomenon has played out at Lip, these last years, compared to '73.

—Charles Piaget[3]

---

1   ADD 1026W20 PD to MI, November 23, 1978.
2   *Parti pris*, December 1979, 31.
3   *Idées ouvrières*, December 1977, 3.

By instinct, we knew we couldn't repeat the coup of '73 … You can't launch "the first Sputnik" twice!

—Jean Raguénès[4]

Thinking of the creation of the cooperative at Lip, Piaget mused in 1979 that it was "almost as hard to return to legality as to leave it."[5] This difficult return to the legality of today, not that of tomorrow, evoked by Maire in 1973, brought into play the conflicts inherent in workers' commitment to what they had achieved and dreamed, the distancing of the parties of the left and the confederations from Lip, and the efforts of the state and capital to refute the "it is possible" of the 1968 years once and for all.

Becoming a cooperative had long been presented as an option to *les Lip*. In November 1971, Saintesprit suggested that seventy employees in the mechanics workshop constitute a cooperative that could rent equipment from Lip. This was clearly an effort to get rid of the union stronghold, and the workers' representatives refused to consider it.[6] In July 1973, when Edgar Faure and Jean Charbonnel proposed the formation of a workers' cooperative to resolve the conflict, Piaget responded that "an island of greenery in a capitalist sea is impossible";[7] the CGT-Lip was blunter, calling it a way for workers to commit hari-kari.[8] For François Ceyrac, head of the CNPF, this rejection revealed that the workers did not want to "confront the problems and risks" of capitalism.[9] In early September 1973, Clavel, ever a loose cannon, said workers should overcome their fears and establish a cooperative at Lip, which he presented as another name for the self-management inherent in their spiritual revolt.[10] However, given the desire of government and business to see Lip workers fail, it would be foolish, Piaget reiterated, to launch a cooperative.[11] In line with the CFDT position that self-management was impossible in cooperatives operating in a capitalist economy, he explained that "if we were to create a cooperative in the current industrial society, we would inevitably be caught in the same

4   Raguénès et al., "Lip 1973–1976," 1239.
5   Piaget, "'Des trésors d'imagination,'" 166.
6   De Virieu, *Lip*, 61.
7   Émile Lejeune, *L'Autogestion* (Verviers, 1974), 45.
8   ACGT Lip Box 5 *L'Heure*, bulletin of cellule LIP no. 17 [July 1973].
9   *Le Figaro*, August 23, 1973.
10   *Le Nouvel observateur*, September 3, 1973, 26. Anouar Khaled, who will appear in Clavel's *Les Paroissiens* as the journalist who was a catalyst for workers to begin manufacturing watches in June 1973, lashed out at this "class collaboration miraculously baptized as self-management." *Politique hebdo*, September 13, 1973, 11.
11   *Le Nouvel observateur*, October 1, 1973.

system of constraints as capitalist employers. We would be quickly led to have the same reactions [to situations] as them."[12] This did not stop the PSU from promoting the cooperative as a solution to the impasse at Lip a few months later. However, the workers of Lip were no more interested in the idea when it came from the left than when it came from the right. "They wanted a boss," a frustrated Rocard would later say.[13]

With the closing of the CEH, Lip workers had originally looked to investment by business or the state. Yet with the end of the 90 percent unemployment pay in the summer of 1977, it was clear that no capitalist would be coming forward to operate the firm and that the state was unwilling to invest in Lip as a center of technical innovation. "Alas for us!," Piaget lamented. "In this country we do not pardon those who are correct too early: how many politicians (de Gaulle in 1940, Mendès France in 1954, to cite just two ...) have had this bitter experience."[14] The economic crisis gave the state the leeway to resist worker demands that it had lacked in 1973. And it made the state even more wary of doing anything that could encourage workers elsewhere to resist layoffs. *Les Lip* explained that this led them to reconsider establishing a cooperative in the fall of 1977:

In '77, the authorities believe themselves strong; they resist workers' demands and will resist them until the last minute. Remember Guizot and the Revolution of [18]48. He repeated "enrich yourself" and did not give in to a single demand. Likewise, the government of [Nguyen Van] Thieu in Vietnam discusses protocol until the Vietcong arrive at the doors of his palace. Currently, the authorities in France are doing the same thing. They do not want to give an inch. Other means must therefore be found.[15]

---

12   *Le Monde*, September 18, 1973, 40. See Edmond Maire, Alfred Krumnow, and Albert Detraz, *La CFDT et l'autogestion*, 2nd edition (Paris, 1975), 38. One sees this issue at Manuest where 95 percent of the workers were CFDT members. When the firm went bankrupt in October 1974, workers occupied the factory and launched production, and in December began selling what they had made. The next month the workers voted to form a workers' cooperative in the face of opposition from their federation in the CFDT. The Manuest CFDT leader Pierre Montesinos remarked: "Either the Federation brings Neuschwanders to all whose firms are closing, or if it can't do that, then it doesn't excommunicate those for whom the revolutionary catechism is not enough to find a job." Bondu, "De l'usine à la communauté," 377.

13   *Le Monde*, March 21, 2007, 28.

14   *Le Monde*, August 2, 1977, 17.

15   *L'Heure*, 2 [supplement to *Lip Unité*, December 1977].

Not all Lip workers agreed. "There is no reason to remove the thorn that is Lip in the foot of French capitalism."[16] Opponents believed that creating a cooperative would let the state, the confederations and political parties on the left "get away Pontius Pilate style," making workers their own gravediggers.[17] The CFDT was always looking for a settlement of affairs at Lip. Syndex, the consulting firm with close ties to the CFDT, expressed support for the establishment of a cooperative at Palente.[18] As in 1973, it sent experts to Palente for what Piaget termed a very successful "economic school": 120 or 130 watch workers examined contemporary developments in the trade, and how, through a cooperative, to create a place for themselves in the market; mechanics held a workshop with the same goal.[19]

For some, the impetus to create a cooperative was the expectation that the left would win the parliamentary elections in March 1978, despite the split between Communists and Socialists in the fall of 1977. Creating a cooperative would impede the bankruptcy trustee from selling machinery before the elections.[20] Raguénès added that the cooperative would give the left in power something to work with, not a factory that had been largely dormant for two years: "if we let the machines rust for example, it is not worth it to wait for a political solution." Having a structure in place would create the conditions for the left to do what conservatives had been unwilling to do. Palente could in turn infuse a national left government with the socialist culture born of grassroots struggles.[21]

A group of Lip workers issued a declaration in *Politique hebdo* in February 1978 saying that if there was no real will to innovate and to confront inequalities and hierarchies at the base, a left victory would not make a significant change in society.[22] The victorious left could make Lip "the cutting edge of the new politics" in a plan to save the French watch industry. A nationalization under workers' control would legalize the occupation of the factory and put the enterprise under the joint control of the workers and public authority, end legal actions against the workers, and allow the city to buy Palente and the machines, stock and brand name; the (to be nationalized) Thomson-CSF could invest in research

16   *Libération*, October 12, 1977, 5.
17   "Lip: la coop contestée," *La Commune* 20 (June 15, 1978): 20.
18   ADD 1026W21 RG, October 17, 1977.
19   AR Interview with Piaget by Rouaud, December 2, 2003, 16.
20   ADD 1026W21 RG, April 26, 1978.
21   *Libération*, October 12, 1977, 5.
22   *Politique hebdo*, February 20, 1978, 17–18.

at Lip to develop technology for the manufacture of quartz watches and other products.[23] In so doing, and in line with the impetus of the Piaget presidential bid in 1974, this would be a step toward constructing socialism the only way possible, from the bottom up. Widespread support for communities pursuing social change would create the conditions for national transformation. As *Lip Unité* put it before the election: "It is often said: 'no island of self-management in a capitalist world.' Perhaps, on the condition of adding: 'no in-depth change'—and therefore, never a self-managed society—if 'the seeds of change' are not cultivated now ... Seeds that are perhaps going to flourish at Palente."[24] Along these lines, Raguénès later said, capitalist firms have "contradictions," but these are masked by authority. What would make Lip "a valuable experiment, a test of a model of the socialist enterprise," was the open expression of these contradictions and their resolution through debate and consensus, without recourse to assertions of order and authority.[25] The effort to realize this project marked the remaining years at Palente.

Yet, as the elections approached, few in the Lip leadership believed the left would win or, if it did, that it would commit itself to Lip. The CFDT-Lip, represented by Piaget and Vittot, came around reluctantly to supporting the creation of a cooperative to keep the community alive. Piaget told the General Assembly in October 1977 that he only overcame his past opposition to establishing a cooperative because the "war treasure" could not last forever and he saw no other solution.[26] He was skeptical that a victory of the left in the legislative elections would bring the desired investments in Palente, but he feared that a victory of the right would bring an offensive against Lip and other occupied factories, leading to asphyxiation or expulsion.[27]

However, with the disappearance of the possibility of a capitalist firm, the environment in which unions operate, the CFDT-Lip leadership proved reluctant to act. Raguénès and Garcin, joined by Gérard Cugney—a mechanic and former secretary of the works council who would, with Garcin, later be elected to the management board (*directoire*) of the cooperative—held a retreat to discuss the issue. They decided

---

23   BDIC F delta rés 702/12/1 "Qu'attendent les 'Lip 'd'une victoire de la gauche?...'" [early 1978].

24   *Lip Unité*, January–February 1978, 3.

25   BDIC 702/14/4, "Compte-rendu du conseil d'administration de la 2AL," April 26, 1980.

26   ADD 1026W21 RG, October 24, 1977.

27   ADD 1026W21 RG, February 23, 1978.

that the cooperative was the only viable option, one that expressed "'our passion for life in this factory," whatever the outcome of the elections.[28] Raguénès affirmed that "this is not to lay to rest the conflict. It is up to us to take charge without waiting for the miraculous solution of the authorities, to conserve in its entirety the 'communal' aspect of the conflict."[29] Piaget expressed his lukewarm support in terms of the community as well: "if we lose, we will die, but we will die together."[30]

An all-day "exploded" General Assembly was held in which groups of fifteen to twenty workers debated the issues confronting *les Lip*.[31] The reconstituted General Assembly voted to launch a cooperative in November 1977. Les Industries de Palente (L.I.P.) was established in January 1978. Garcin explained his vote with reference to the search for security that motivated *les Lip*, saying "Today we feel we are in a truck, aimless and without breaks, which will take us into an abyss."[32] Five hundred thousand copies of *L'Heure*, a supplement to *Lip Unité* distributed nationally, stated bluntly that in voting for a cooperative, "Our project is not to create a cooperative"—it was to create the legal structure necessary to sign contracts to provide work for all.[33] Yet the overriding problem that *les Lip* faced for the next several years was that a cooperative in an occupied factory was illegal. Furthermore, as Jeanningros recognized, L.I.P. was "the opposite of a normally constituted cooperative," for it started without capital, but with a large workforce whose employment was its *raison d'être*; most cooperatives begin with capital and a small workforce and gradually develop.[34] The prefect interpreted the vote to create a cooperative as a major setback for the movement. Reentering the economic system would reduce "to almost nothing the example, which could have been contagious, of a radical contestation by *les Lip* of the fundamental mechanisms of market economics." As always, his concern was that press coverage had "erased that aspect of the question." In any case, the prefect saw in the decision "the seeds of failure," since it was premised

28   Presentation to the General Assembly by Raguénès, Garcin, and Gérard Cugney in Bondu, "De l'usine à la communauté," 451–2. See also Beurier, "La mémoire des Lip," 122–3.

29   *Libération*, October 12, 1977, 5.

30   *Libération*, November 10, 1977, 7.

31   Bondu, "De l'usine à la communauté," 447–9.

32   *Libération*, November 9, 1977, 3.

33   *L'Heure*, 2. The CFDT was asked to distribute 200,000 copies of *L'Heure* across the country and 40,000 were put in mailboxes in Besançon. *Lip Actualité*, October 1978, 2. ADD 1812W31 RG, December 6, 1977.

34   Saint-Germain and Souletie, "Le voyage à Palente," 73.

on the sale of Palente and its machinery to the municipality, an act he was determined to thwart.[35]

The decision to establish a cooperative was an effort to preserve the community born of the struggle. Unable to get the state or business to act, "we had only one alternative," said Piaget: "either die with dignity on a barricade or try to create a cooperative."[36] There were 425 workers in the cooperative in the spring of 1978—233 women (about half of whom were heads of household) and 192 men—but the number dropped to about 300 two years later and 250 in the spring of 1981.[37] The cooperative made its first hires in March 1978 and had about twenty-five employees in watchmaking and mechanics in the fall of 1978 and about sixty in the fall of 1979.[38] However, all members of the cooperative worked on the commissions engaged in artisanal and industrial production, the maintenance of Palente, work with the unemployed in Besançon, and popularization of the struggle; they were all paid through contraband watch sales. The police noted in February 1978 that there were always five militants on the road, talking with workers in firms across the nation.[39]

The creation of the cooperative challenged the consensual governance without formal hierarchies at Palente by introducing systems of governance like those that would be required for legalization and by implementing regulations governing participation. The General Assembly addressed the hybrid nature of the cooperative by electing a twelve-person supervisory council composed of six representatives of the personnel and six employees drawn from the technical and managerial staff. This body in turn selected a three-person management board, each of whom had a four-year term.[40] Many of those who would direct the cooperative had benefited from the CESI classes for managerial

---

35   ADD 1026W18 PD to MI, November 14, 1977.

36   L'Est républicain, May 12, 1978.

37   Le Matin, December 8, 1977. In February 1978, the General Assembly voted narrowly to refuse to accept back anyone who took a job elsewhere, even if they asked to return to Lip. ADD 1026W21 RG, February 22, 1978. What happened to those who left? One incomplete accounting in 1978 had sixty-two no longer living in Besançon, more than 100 retired or no longer looking for work (primarily women workers), twenty on long-term disability support, and another 150 working at other jobs in Besançon. La Croix, December 15, 1978. See also ADD 45J66 "Lip vit encore," Imprimatur 208 (November 29, 1978): 4.

38   Lip actualité, September 1978. Jean-Marc Holz, "Crise, restructuration et adaptation du capital industriel à Besançon," Revue géographique de l'est 21 (1981): 72.

39   Bernard Pingaud, "Le nouveau pari des LIP," Faire 27 (January 1978): 23. ADD 1026W21 RG, February 16, 1978.

40   BDIC F delta rés 702/4/4 2AL, "Une lutte pour aujourd'hui et demain ..." "À Lip, des femmes: mille manières de lutter," 32–4.

personnel and from Neuschwander's encouragement of dialogue between leaders of the workers and his managers, both activities which had been recognized at the time as creating forms of expertise in a minority not consonant with the democratic, egalitarian culture of the struggle. The autonomy of the supervisory council and the management board made it difficult for the General Assembly to exercise democratic control of the cooperative.[41] To one worker it appeared that "between a joint-stock company and a cooperative there aren't many differences."[42]

Furthermore, a community based on work placed different demands on individuals than one based on active participation in a social movement. The eighteen months between the reoccupation of Palente and the vote in favor of a cooperative in November 1977 had seen a split between those who remained active in the struggle and those who followed it from a distance.[43] Launching the cooperative threatened to maintain this division. Burgy and Piaget commented later that because the cooperative paid salaries to everyone, though it did not have work in the factory for most of them, "to be hired [by the cooperative] means a different rhythm, different constraints, the loss of 'the space of liberty' of the struggle, for the same salary."[44] The CFDT-Lip responded by reworking the language of class struggle to say that those who let other workers take on responsibilities in the cooperative without doing their own share were practicing a form of "exploitation."[45] One of the cooperative's first steps in December 1977 was to require each of the 450 members to sign a "collective contract," which built upon the contract introduced when production had started six months earlier.

The contract stipulated that pay was not a right. Those whom L.I.P. (and later, the cooperative of artisanal producers) hired received the same "survival pay" as those who were not yet hired. Attendance at the General Assembly was mandatory; all had to punch in (and time cards would be removed fifteen minutes after the meeting began to control tardiness). The goal was to re-accustom workers, whether they had jobs yet or not, to the practices associated with work in the factory lost in 1973 and again in 1976, not the creation of a factory radically transformed by the struggle to save that lost factory.[46] In addition to participation in services like

---

41   *Lip Unité*, January–February 1978, 5.
42   *L'Heure*, 2.
43   Saint-Germain and Souletie, "Le voyage à Palente," 77.
44   Burgy and Piaget, "L'aventure des coopératives LIP."
45   CFDT-Lip tract of October 21, 1977 in Bondu, "De l'usine à la communauté," 445.
46   In mid-October 1979, the management board required workers to maintain

guarding the factory at night and working in the restaurant, the contract required all to work on their commissions at least twenty-five hours per week with fixed hours in the morning and the afternoon. Workers who were repeatedly late to work were fined and those with absences of more than four days for health reasons had to produce a medical certificate.[47] Shaming was used as well; the names of those who did not follow the rules were read to the General Assembly.[48] After the bankruptcy of the CEH, many female employees had become accustomed to having their afternoons off and would have preferred starting work earlier in order to put in the same number of hours without what was initially a two-and-one-half-hour midday break, as this took the work day into the late afternoon. Piaget responded that "The choice must be made between routines and the conflict," where routines were practices developed during the fight and the conflict now meant preparation for a return to work.[49] In 1979, the work week was brought up to forty "hours of struggle" per week, the term for the daily hours fixed for all workers, 7 a.m. to noon; 1 p.m. to 4 p.m. Although there were no time clocks, each work group monitored workers and those who were systematically late had a portion of their wages retained.[50]

A worker representative explained the importance of fixed hours for all: "It is a constraint that we have all accepted in order to have a presence in the factory that resembles the presence in a normal factory, to have an activity that resembles that which a normal factory displays vis-à-vis the neighborhood and the population."[51] "We will not be able to maintain the co-op without being very strict," Piaget contended. While waiting to hear if the state would grant legal status to the cooperative, it moved to a full day of work, although the cooperative itself could initially employ only a handful of workers. "If the industrial plan [for the cooperative

---

daily production reports, including the time taken to complete each job, in order to justify their pay. This was not popular. The next month Burgy, a member of the management board, announced to the General Assembly that sixty workers would be laid off for lack of diligence at work. However, he gave no names and the threat was apparently not carried out. ADD 1026W20 RG, October 19, 1979; November 9, 1979.

47 BDIC F delta rés 702/6/2 Collectif Animation, "Contrat collectif des Lip, application du 14 novembre 1977," December 13, 1977. Bondu, "De l'usine à la communauté," 463. If a worker refused to do commission work and could not settle the issue with the commission, the issue would be decided by the General Assembly. ACFDT 8H562 Contrat collectif des Lip, November 14, 1977.

48 Berry, "Lip 1978," 56.

49 *Rouge*, November 1977.

50 Terrieux, "L'Expérience Lip," 116.

51 "À force d'y croire … ils inventent l'avenir," *Pour* 195 (February 23, 1978): 11–14.

presented to the state] is accepted," Piaget said in May 1978, "this would be the referee's whistle, so we have to be well trained."[52]

There were times that coming to the factory was particularly import-ant. Workers were constructing both watches and, equally important, the image of conscientious workers. Piaget emphasized the latter in explaining to workers in mid-November 1977 why the collective would be strict in applying new work hours.[53] When Maire, secretary-general of the CFDT, came to Palente in February 1978, the CFDT-Lip sought to show by means of "the restored orthodoxy of its forms of action" that it was no longer the refractory outlier and should now receive the full support of the confederation. Vittot told the General Assembly that to assure that all were present in the factory, maximum penalties would be imposed on any who were late or missed work the day Maire was there.[54] When visitors came, workers were told to reply to their queries and not play cards in the workshops, even if they had no work to do.[55] However, accompanying the appearance of a productive factory was the need to pursue actions to create the conditions to become one. At a General Assembly in March 1978, Demougeot apostrophized the leaders: "We have to know what you want us to do ... You tell us that we must work. We agree. And then five minutes later, we aren't working anymore, because we have to go into the city to put up posters or hold a demo—It's not logical!"[56] And as the cooperative sought business, demonstrations were in turn questioned as discouraging potential clients.[57]

Many workers resented what they interpreted as efforts to make the cooperative appear to potential clients to be a "normal" factory: "they already wanted to remove all the posters in the hallways."[58] Despite the contract all signed, leaders had to harangue workers to get them to fulfill the jobs necessary to maintain the community. In June 1978, the prefec-ture reported that virtually every Monday, Piaget vituperated workers at the General Assembly for slipping away so as not to have to stand guard duty. He had to threaten that the pay of those who missed two turns as guards in a month would be withheld.[59] Six months later, Piaget

---

52   *Libération*, May 17, 1978, 4.
53   ADD 1026W21 RG, November 15, 1977.
54   ADD 1026W21 RG, February 8, 1978; February 10, 1978 [quoted].
55   ADD 1026W21 RG, December 20, 1977.
56   ADD 1026W21 RG, March 20, 1978.
57   *Libération*, May 30, 1979, 3–4.
58   ADD 45J61 "La face cachée de Lip," *Drapeau rouge* 37 (May 6, 1978): 8–9.
59   ADD 1026W23 Dossier: coopérative Lip "Note d'exploitation," June 5, 1978. As the conflict dragged on, it became difficult to get workers to accept responsibilities like guard duty. ADD 1026W20 RG, August 20, 1979.

found himself warning the General Assembly that many workers were punching in and then leaving the factory and that supervision would be heightened to prevent this.[60]

The imposition of penalties for those who missed the General Assembly, commission meetings, work, and guard duty was hotly debated.[61] It appeared to undercut the voluntary nature of workers' activism since for most what was being missed was not what they associated with paid labor. Some workers saw the enforcement of discipline as an effort to discourage them from staying on at Palente.[62] In a series of close votes in February 1978, the General Assembly agreed to penalize offenders in certain situations, but to extend a degree of tolerance in others.[63] In March, 100 workers had deductions in their pay for cutting work hours; the next month, some thirty workers with repeated absences were again denied a portion of their pay.[64] In November 1978 deductions were still being made for missed tours of guard duty and factory absences.[65] When only 160 showed up at a General Assembly in June 1979, Piaget reiterated that "The General Assembly is as important as attendance at work"; the equivalent of two hours of pay would be deducted for those who were absent.[66]

Watch production reached about 500 per day in the fall of 1978 and continued at this pace over the course of 1979, resulting in a monthly production of about 10,000.[67] Limits were set by the availability of watch parts. These needed to be maintained at a fixed temperature and humidity. Cuts in electrical power affected parts that had been sequestered at Palente in 1976.[68] Lip had always prided itself on the quality of its watches, but the deterioration of parts contributed to an increase in defective products.[69] In any case, continued production required access to more parts. Large firms like France Ébauches SA would not sell parts to L.I.P. until it had legal status and bank credit. There were limits to

60   ADD 1026W20 RG, January 11, 1979.
61   ADD 1026W21 RG, January 31, 1978.
62   ADD 1026W21 RG, June 1, 1978.
63   ADD 1026W21 RG, February 20, 1978; February 23, 1978.
64   ADD 1026W21 RG, March 16, 1978, April 14, 1978.
65   ADD 1026W21 RG, November 2, 1978.
66   ADD 1026W20 RG, June 8, 1979. However, Piaget had made this threat before and it is not clear if it was ever carried out.
67   ADD 1026W20, "Situation actuelle de l'ex-Société Lip," November 13, 1979; PD to MI, November 23, 1978.
68   ADD 1026W21 L.I.P., "Propositions pour une liquidation générale des actifs de l'ancienne enterprise Lip," 18–19 [September 1978] (notes of RG).
69   ADD 1026W21 RG, January 31, 1978.

what smaller firms in Besançon could provide, but the cooperative perse-vered. In December 1979, frustrated police reported that the cooperative was buying watch movements and diverse parts from Swiss and French firms.[70]

When the CEH went bankrupt in 1976, France may still have had an opportunity to take advantage of the research expertise of Lip to maintain and develop its watchmaking industry. Loss of this opportu-nity was reflected in developments following the vote to establish the cooperative in November 1977. The conflict in 1973 had been over the future of the mechanics workshop, but by 1977 it was becoming clear that precision mechanics was the future of the enterprise. In the summer of 1979, L.I.P. reported that, as subcontractors, the mechanics had done work for sixty-eight businesses, making parts for automobiles, planes, and satellites for major industries like SNIAS, Air Industrie, Thomson-CSF, Alcatel, Schlumberger, Bugatti, Kodak, EDF, and Alsthom Air, even making pieces for the landing gear of the Concorde and the Airbus. Although the PTT cut the telephone service to Palente, L.I.P. made elec-tronic components and fiber optics for the PTT through the screen of subcontracting. For Vittot, "when there is profit, our illegality no longer has importance."[71]

Watch Sales

Funds to pay salaries, however, came largely from watch sales. Between June 17, 1977 and August 12, 1979, *les Lip* sold 110,000 watches. In order to pay the salaries of 340 employees in November 1979, the police believed that the cooperative needed to sell about 4,000 watches per month. The following month, the police, taking into account seizures they had made, estimated that about 35,000 watches remained hidden.[72]

In 1978, Piaget echoed comments made in 1973 about the Lip workers' sales success, saying that the watch sales necessary to pay salaries could

70 ADD 1026W21 RG, April 3, 1978; September 5, 1978. ADD 1026W20 RG, December 12, 1979. Burtz tells of going to Germany to buy watch parts. Interview with Burtz by Reid, June 13, 2017. When the factory ran low on parts like watch cases, the women assembling watches took care of the grounds of Palente. ADD 1026W21 RG, June 1, 1978.

71 *Lip Actualité*, September 1978. *Lip Unité*, July–August 1979, 13. ADD 45J72 *Information SCOP 'Les Industries de Palente'* no. 4, November 9, 1979. *Libération*, March 26, 1980, 14 [quoted]. Terrieux, "L'expérience Lip," 100–10.

72 ADD 1026W20 RG, December 12, 1979.

also provide a way of testing markets for watch sales by the cooperative when it gained legal status.[73] In November 1977, Garcin reported that while the new cooperative had 100,000 watches, these could not be sold by the watch seller-jewelers because they were "models a little shopworn and out of fashion" (let alone the watch seller-jewelers' antipathy to *les Lip*).[74] How then did they sell watches? Visitors to Palente were one market. In the summer of 1978, workers encouraged a "Go to Lip" campaign to forestall expulsion.[75] However, although workers did make watches with "Atomkraft? Nein danke" on the face for German ecologists in 1979, Lip was no longer the subject of interest it had once been. The police reported in August 1979, at the highpoint of the tourist season, that only about twenty visitors a day came to Palente.[76] As for interested works councils around the country, they were asked to come to Palente and buy a sample of the different watches available to show their workers, who could then place orders. Payment (in cash) would not need to be made until receipt of the watches; *les Lip* would handle deliveries on orders of more than 100 watches. Individuals could place orders as well and pay when they got the watch.[77] However, the cooperative came to depend more and more on a network of fifteen to twenty Lip workers who sold at PS and PSU festivals, demonstrations like Larzac, and through networks based in workplaces and the earlier mini-commissions.[78]

Not all sales were explicitly political acts. A L.I.P. brochure from the spring of 1979 read: "Before long! … communions, Mother's Day, Father's Day; a chance to please; choose a gift from among our watches!"[79] No effort was made, as had been done in 1973, to collect the value-added tax and other charges made in legal transactions. The pricing was such that militants debated whether purchasers were acting out of solidarity or to get a good deal. Most disturbing to the prefect were arrangements made in 1978 with CAMIF. In the spring of 1978, L.I.P. delivered 1,000 watches without the Lip brand name to the teachers' cooperative, made

---

73   *Idées ouvrières*, November 1978, 8.
74   AFGM-CFDT1B577 Michel Garcin to M. Ruati, November 17, 1977.
75   *Lip Unité*, September 1978, 3.
76   Terrieux, "L'expérience Lip," 106. ADD 1026W20 RG, August 20, 1979.
77   ADD 1812W35 RG, December 14, 1978. ACFDT 8H562 L.I.P. to Comités d'Entreprise, "Vente des montres" [1978].
78   *Idées ouvrières*, November 1978, 7. ADD 1026W21 RG, August 25, 1977; November 2, 1978. ADD 1026W20 PD to MI, November 23, 1978.
79   BDIC F delta rés 702/22/4 "Les industries de Palente, brochure valable jusqu'au 31.7.79."

with parts purchased from the syndic responsible for liquidation of the CEH.[80] In September 1978, the prefect voiced concern that the sale of watches "is making itself official" in the form of advertisements in the CAMIF magazine "that do not hesitate to emphasize the benefit for the buyer of sale without invoice or the valued-added tax."[81]

The workers were not the only ones with caches of Lip watches. In early December 1977, the syndic sold a watch lot to the highest bidders, who planned to offer them in markets and boutiques. These watches had been stored for two years and had not been examined and prepared for sale. The Lip workers put out the word that they were therefore of questionable quality; Lip workers had the serial numbers of these watches and would never repair them.[82] Yet, after the elections in March 1978, *les Lip* themselves bought these watches, prepared them and were able to sell 3,000 legally the following month at the Foire Exposition of Besançon, in time for First Communion ceremonies.[83] This venture into legal sales, however, was short-lived, and vendors from Palente returned to the cat-and-mouse game of seeking to avoid the police.

The Sword of Damocles

The state did all it could to put an end to the living legacy of 1968 at Palente. In the summer of 1976, the prefect reviewed sixteen studies done of the bankrupt enterprise; his reading was that there was no chance of the revival of the SEHEM and he doubted that even individual elements of it could reappear at Palente.[84] However, the state had an important role to play to make certain that this came true. The prefect sought to ensure that the municipality did not create conditions for the workers' success and he continued trying to choke off the movement by ending watch sales. At the national level, relevant ministries impeded workers' efforts to get the legal status the cooperative needed to sign contracts and to get loans, first by ignoring L.I.P. and then by setting conditions that assured that much of what made Lip a community would not survive in a cooperative they sanctioned.

---

80 BDIC F delta rés 702/14/4 2AL, "Compte-rendu du conseil d'administration," March 4, 1978; May 20, 1978.
81 ADD 1026W18 PD to MI, September 4, 1978.
82 AMB 5Z224 Les travailleurs de LIP to Bruno Ricquebourg, December 11, 1977.
83 ADD 1026W21 RG, April 13, 1978.
84 ADD 2377W182 PR to MI, August 2, 1976.

Since July 1977 the mayor, Robert Schwint, had been in negotiations with the trustee of the bankrupt firm to buy Palente. The municipality would rent a portion to L.I.P. for a symbolic price and the remainder to other businesses. Although the prefect considered the plan unrealistic because he could not imagine other businesses would want to share a building with *les Lip*, he became concerned in late January 1978. The day after telling representatives of the cooperative that he would not sell Palente, the syndic reversed his position in a meeting with Schwint and Garcin. However, the relieved prefect was able to report that opposition from the largest stockholders had quashed the plan for the moment. With an eye to the elections in March, he noted that this "delivered a substantial blow" to the Socialist municipal council and in particular to Joseph Pinard, a councilor who was a Socialist candidate for the National Assembly.[85]

The experience was revelatory for the new prefect, Michel Denieul, who, since his appointment in May 1977, had devoted himself to ending the "contagious character of the self-managing experience." Besançon was the site of major layoffs in textiles, watchmaking and construction. "If it has lost its virulence in the country as a whole, the Lip microbe none the less remains quite dangerous for Besançon." Yet, as far as he was concerned, Lip also brought out the worst in the city's elites. On the subject of the sale of Palente, he said the syndic "has several times changed course 180 degrees." "These palinodes illustrate well the congenital irresolution of a number of representatives of the Besançon middle classes and businessmen, as well as the tenuous lucidity of some of those who speak in their name." However, he thought the left was worse: for the mayor, as well as the workers, the sale "assumes a priority not at all industrial or technical, but properly psychological and political."[86]

The survival of the cooperative while awaiting legalization was dependent on watch sales. Stopping these by confiscating watches was a central concern for the prefect. In June 1978, he reported that a car with 155 watches to sell in Belgium had been stopped at the border with Luxembourg. From his perspective, this brought out the contradiction of workers asking for public assistance while committing illegal acts, and he, perhaps naively, hoped that it would scare workers: "Among *les Lip*, this action by the police revived the concerns of those who would tend to flout the sword of Damocles that hangs over their serious and repeated

---

85   ADD 1812W31 RG, January 28, 1978. ADD 1026W18 PD to MI, February 8, 1978.

86   ADD 1026W18, PR to MI, February 4, 1978.

violations of legality."[87] A couple of days later, the prefect scored a much bigger coup when police in Besançon seized more than 7,000 watches recently made at Palente, but which had been moved to an employee's garage for fear the police were planning to invade the factory.[88] And in November 1978, state police inspectors, accompanied by several dozen municipal police officers overcame the workers standing guard at night and forced their way into Palente with two locksmiths. They left a half hour later with 3,886 watches from the stock sequestered in 1976 and kept in the refrigerated room; this raised to 12,000 the number of these watches that had been recovered. "This episode," the prefect reported, "confirms that the factory of Palente has nothing of a sanctuary about it, and that Justice and the police were not reduced to impotence." Commerce continued, but with new precautions. The next month workers involved in sales were instructed to communicate in writing rather than by telephone.[89]

Yet, where there was a will, there continued to be a way. A fellow priest and close friend of Raguénès inherited his father's building business. He gave part of the fortune to his order and used the rest to aid just causes, including the workers of Lip, to whom he gave fifteen lingots of gold. Raguénès found himself checking the price of gold to see when it would be best to sell. The operation brought in some 100,000 francs. This led Piaget to think about the gold in the form of watch cases at Palente. He had it melted down and Raguénès went to another priest in Paris who sold it for *les Lip*, explaining that it was gold from liturgical items no longer in use.[90] And perhaps one could say that is what these watches were. But such acts were not the basis of a future for *les Lip*.

The Plan

The vote for the cooperative in November 1977 had been driven by the workers' desire to make their case if the left won the legislative elections in March 1978. Defeat forced workers to think about the viability of the cooperative as an institution. If the municipality bought Palente, it could

87   ADD 1026W18 PD to MI, June 19, 1978.
88   This was one of three sites of recently manufactured watches of this size. Each had a value approaching 1.5 million francs, the equivalent of two months of wages. ADD 1026W21 "Audition de Mme. Gourmand," June 22, 1978; RG, June 26, 1978.
89   ADD 1026W18 PD to MI, November 23, 1978. *Lip Unité*, December 1978, 9.
90   Interview with Bondu by Reid, June 20, 2011.

rent it only to a legal entity. Legal status would also put an end to the cuts in public services and give the cooperative the ability to borrow money and to sign contracts with clients. By the end of 1978, a group of cooperatives had offered to loan L.I.P. 4 million francs and the CAMIF had offered another 8 million, but to carry out these transactions, they required the authorization of the Minister for the Economy and Finance. He would not consider this unless the cooperative was legally constituted, a decision that fell under his purview as well.[91] Other elements of L.I.P. were also affected. In early 1978, it negotiated a contract with Algeria for the production of gasoline pump meters; this would have provided two months of work for thirty to forty workers, but the state blocked the payment made through the Banque d'Algérie.[92]

Legalization required state approval of an economic plan for the cooperative. In December 1977, Syndex followed up its earlier support for the constitution of a cooperative by sending two engineers, D. Marre and Bruno Parmentier, to develop a plan in cooperation with a workers' commission.[93] Parmentier stayed on with the cooperative until 1981. He had graduated from the École des mines in 1972 and worked for several years with an agricultural cooperative in rural Mexico. Chile had asked him to participate in the nationalization of the copper mines in 1973, but the coup that overthrew Allende took place a week before he was to arrive.[94]

The Syndex plan began with the recognition that the potential offered by CEH research on the quartz watch had largely vanished. As things stood, the future of watchmaking in the cooperative was in assembly. The cooperative would make watch cases, but not pieces and watch movements. These would be purchased from a German firm. The watch seller-jewelers were uninterested in selling Lip watches and, without a large advertising budget, department stores would not stock them either. Even once legal, the cooperative would continue to need to sell watches through other circuits. The mechanics workshop would rely on subcontracting, but now done aboveboard.[95] Continuing the work of the SCEIP,

91   ADD 1026W21 RG, December 1, 1978. ADD 45AJ68 Compte-rendu réunion conseil de surveillance [of L.I.P.] du 8 Jan 1979."

92   ADD 1026W21 RG, February 23, 1978.

93   BDIC F delta rés 702/6/2 Syndex to Chers Camarades at Lip, December 6, 1977. The consulting firm Orgex helped put together the plan. BDIC F delta rés 702/14/4 2AL, Compte-rendu du conseil d'administration des 2AL, May 20, 1978.

94   "Portrait de François Gèze," Faits & Documents 122 (December 1, 2001): 2.

95   ADD 1026W21 RG, July 12, 1978. BDIC F delta rés 702/14/1 D. Marre, "Projet industriel horloger. Première synthèse, 22 fév 1978."

the cooperative would also consult on technology transfer, serving as a "donor of know-how."[96] Of the 400 employees still at Palente, 200 would be hired initially (of whom eighty would be first put in job-training classes). Although the plan projected employment of more than 600 in four years, 200 members of the cooperative in 1978 would not be employed in the factory for a couple of years;[97] they would work at artisanal jobs, *Lip Unité*, etc., and would be paid by the cooperative.[98]

The plan was developed to make a convincing argument to the state, but many workers felt it was an alien project, created by Syndex in consultation with the management board without workers' input. It abandoned the strategy of coordination with enterprises in struggle and any effort to put pressure on the state, leaving "on the table a greater number [of workers without jobs] than the Giraud Plan."[99] However, nothing raised as much opposition when the plan was first discussed in July 1978 as workers' responsibility for a portion of the financing of the cooperative in order to meet state requirements for a cooperative and the expectations of potential lenders. The workers' investment would have to precede exterior financing. Each worker, including eighty who had not signed on as shareholders when the General Assembly had voted for the cooperative, would have to make a payment of 750 francs immediately, at a time when only a handful of employees made more than 3,000 francs per month.[100] This was the first portion of an obligation for each worker to purchase 2,450 francs in shares (49 shares at 50 francs per share)—more than the salary many cooperative members received each month—in order to constitute an investment by workers of 1 million francs, sufficient to permit exterior parties to make loans to the cooperative.

However, no one was more critical of the plan than the prefect, who had been working for years to stifle operations at Palente. He did not believe that the cooperative could survive a start-up period without illegal sales. And he thought the plan itself was too ambitious. Not only would staying at Palente entail purchase of the site, the machines, and the stock of watches and parts taken in 1976, but Palente itself was too

---

96   *Lip Actualité*, August 1978.

97   *Libération*, September 14, 1978, 3. The number of LIP employees was projected to be eighty-seven in 1978 and 322 in 1982. ADD 1026W21 RG, July 12, 1978.

98   AMB 5Z224 "Compte-rendu de la réunion du vendredi 23 juin 1978."

99   ADD 1026W23 "Coopérative Lip note d'exploitation," June 5, 1978 (quoted). ADD 1026W21 RG, July 11, 1978. ADD 102W18, CFDT militants' untitled tract, July 10, 1978, attached to PD to MI, July 12, 1978. Terrieux, "L'expérience Lip," 85–6.

100   ADD 1026W21 RG, July 6, 1978.

large and too costly to heat for the projected size of the cooperative—and would require development funds from the state on a scale for which Besançon was not eligible.[101] In any case, departmental and regional authorities had made their willingness to participate in the purchase of Palente conditional on the Ministry of Industry's commitment of funds to the cooperative first.[102] This brought the prefect to his real concern that Paris would not follow his hard line. He doubted the resolve of the Ministry of Industry, which he saw as "always strongly imbued with the state of mind that had once led Charbonnel to support the Neuschwander project." Ministry bureaucrats "partially underestimate the technical difficulties of the realization of the Lip project, and totally its overarching psychological and political aspects."[103]

Convinced that the presence of the workers at Palente "still continues to harm the reputation" of Besançon, the prefect envisaged getting them out of the factory and using modest public and private financing to set up a cooperative with 100 (not 400) employees to do subcontracting work for other watch companies. But this, the frustrated prefect wrote to the Minister of the Interior in November 1978, would require other ministries to stop putting off dealing with the workers, which only served to lead them on. It was time to be "at once clearer and firmer. Illegality must be punished, in whatever way and wherever it manifests itself." He concluded that this is what he had done with good results: "At least, all was done on the local level for [Lip] to lose its virulence and its exemplarity; the election last March of a candidate of the Right in the first district of Doubs [versus the Socialist Pinard] showed that *les Lip* were no longer prophets in their own country ..."[104]

Negotiations

The plan for the cooperative had been developed for a government with little reason to want to oversee the revival of Lip in any form. However, now that the workers at Palente were taking steps to return to the fold,

---

101   ADD 1026W20 PD to MI, November 23, 1978.

102   ADD 1026W18 PD to MI, July 12, 1978.

103   ADD 1026W18 PD to Ministre de Commerce et l'Artisanat, October 19, 1978.

104   ADD 1026W20 PD to MI, November 23, 1978. And, in fact, internal communications show that the Minister for the Economy and Finance found the L.I.P. plans to develop Palente unrealistic, but did not make this public. See the undated (c. 1978) note from this ministry rejecting the L.I.P. plan to create 400 jobs at Palente, saying that 40 in 1979 and 80–100 in the future was what was possible. ADD 1026W25 Note in the dossier, "Procédures judiciares," January 31, 1979.

the CFDT offered to help. In May 1978, Jacques Chérèque said that "the Lip dossier is charged with political explosives; as a first step the CFDT seems to be the preferred interlocutor for entering into negotiations with government authorities."[105] But neither the confederation nor the prefect were able to get Paris to abandon the strategy of leaving Lip to rot away. It was a few intellectuals, with whom President Giscard d'Estaing sought to establish relations, who played the crucial role in getting the state to respond to the plan the cooperative had submitted to the Ministry of Industry in July 1978. They made the case that taking action on L.I.P. was how Giscard d'Estaing could show that he was different from the old right of Pompidou and Messmer. Once the icon of the new left, perhaps Lip could serve this function for Giscard d'Estaing's conception of a modern right. Clavel used the occasion of a reception in September 1978 for a colloquium on "liberalism and the [19]80 horizon"—organized by Giscard d'Estaing and several "New Philosophers"—to talk to Lionel Stoléru of the Ministry of Labor. Clavel made the case for the workers of L.I.P., emphasizing that they planned to start with industrial employment for half the workers, who would help support the others.[106] In a letter to the Minister of Commerce, he situated their fight in moral terms: "I cannot say—but all know—just how dear for five years this cause has been to me by its spirit worthy of Proudhon and of [Charles] Péguy, by the steadfastness, the self-sacrifice, the true love, by a spirituality that disturbs and disconcerts ..."[107] Important as well were the efforts of André Frossard, who presented the plan personally to Prime Minister Raymond Barre.[108] The intellectuals got a response from Giscard d'Estaing's government, but it took the form of conditions for its participation in negotiations on the legal status of the cooperative. In a meeting at the Hôtel Matignon in Paris in November 1978, representatives of the cooperative were told that it had to choose as a director someone with industrial experience who had not been involved in the conflict at Lip and accept that plans for eventually hiring all members of the cooperative were conditional on its economic performance.

The prefect sought to bolster the government's obduracy. Besançon had not given up trying to buy Palente and the prefect continued to

---

105   BDIC F delta rés 702/14/4 2AL, "Compte-rendu du conseil d'administration," May 20, 1978.

106   *Libération*, September 14, 1978, 3. Terrieux, "L'expérience Lip," 90.

107   ADD1026W18 Clavel to Ministère du Commerce et de l'Artisanat, September 11, 1978.

108   AR, Interview with Raguénès by Rouaud [2005], 3.

worry that Paris would not hold the line. In January 1979, he wrote to the Minister of the Interior that it was not the time to let "the high officials of certain ministerial departments," "victims of a complex that I do not share," compromise his efforts to "'cool down' the Lip affair" and stop the Socialist municipality from ushering in a new Lip Affair by purchasing Palente. The prefect reiterated that the state should make no financial or administrative arrangements until the end of the occupation of Palente, "the symbolic aspect of which is evident for all." No good could come from this. "Will we take the risk of a new Lip Affair-Neuschwander?" Or "the continuation of a sort of 'red base' animated by Piaget and Raguénès"?[109]

The prefect need not have worried. The cooperative agreed to satisfy the initial conditions the state set for negotiations on its future. Not surprisingly, there was deep mistrust of bringing in someone from the outside as director. In January 1979, when one candidate suggested that the mechanics workshop would need to be smaller than projected in the plan, the mechanics went on strike and were joined by the watchworkers, who felt threatened as well.[110] The Confédération des sociétés coopéra- tives de production recommended Libero Penna, and the management board hired him in February 1979.[111] Penna had worked for a decade after the war at Boimondau, Marcel Barbu's community in Valence, but he came to L.I.P. as a director. The cooperative had not raised salaries, even though a number of members had taken on new responsibilities. The pay range from the lowest-paid OS to engineer remained close to one to two. Penna came in with a salary about six times that of the lowest paid employee at Lip. He was a constant source of dissatisfaction. The workers recognized the technical expertise of engineers, but questioned managerial expertise, which in Penna's case took the form of delivering a string of reprimands to those engaged in all facets of operations.[112] When Penna sought to excuse himself by saying that he had no power, Bondu asked why he retained the trappings of power: "It is not surprising that no one understands anything anymore and it is the reign of Ubu-Roi."[113]

The plan recognized that not all workers could be hired immediately, but the requirement that not all could be promised employment went

109   ADD 1026W18 PD to MI, January 16, 1979.

110   ADD 1026W25 Note in the dossier, "Procédures judiciaires," January 31, 1979.

111   *Le Monde*, March 11, 1980, 45. Other cooperatives made loans conditional on the hiring of a "manager" to direct L.I.P. ADD 1026W21 RG, December 1, 1978.

112   ADD 1026W20 *Information SCOP 'Les Industries de Palente'* no. 16, Decem- ber 2, 1980.

113   *Lip Unité*, April-May 1980, 3.

against the commitment of a community whose identity was rooted in the memory of the vote of October 12, 1973. However, in February 1979, needing the approval of the state, the management board made public three lists that designated employment status in the cooperative. It made choices workshop by workshop, with competence and potential economic contribution taking precedence over participation in the conflict. The 160–170 on list A would be hired by L.I.P. in the first year. The 90–100 on list B would work in the diversity of activities that had developed alongside the factory at Palente. The 108 on list C were given no definite activity the first year, only the possibility that they would be hired later. Piaget told those on the List C that while they should continue to come to Palente and would receive their pay from the cooperative as before, they should look for work elsewhere. For years, workers had expressed the fear that their leadership was creating situations that would get them to leave voluntarily so that the factory would not need to find them jobs. List C now seemed to confirm their suspicions. Jacky Burtz, a staunch opponent of sacrificing the community to the establishment of the cooperative, referred to this suggestion to seek employment while waiting to be called back to work, as "the diaspora of *les Lip* … a little bit like the Jews."[114] To add insult to injury, the 108 on list C had to fulfill their commitment to purchase stock through monthly payments of 110 francs—capital which was to be used to buy from the trustee the trademark rights and machines from which they would likely never benefit.[115]

The lists gave precedence to skilled workers and technical staff, men who were at the core of the CFDT-Lip. Although the size of the CFDT-Lip had dropped precipitously, on list A, the CFDT-Lip members were in a majority; there were fewer on list B, and even fewer on list C. List C was composed disproportionately of female OS, particularly older women, including many who had put body and soul into the conflict. They had been, in Demougeot's words, "'selected', then ousted, from a struggle that was theirs."[116] Piaget was committed to the cooperative as the only viable possibility, and workers on list C found his role in presenting the lists particularly disturbing. For Paule on list C, "When *le Charles* said that the struggle no longer counted [in making the lists], it was like you got stabbed in the back."[117] The cooperative had been seen as the choice

---

114   AB Interview with Burtz by Beurier [1992], 13–14.
115   ADD 1026W20 RG, February 16, 1979.
116   *Parti pris*, January 15, 1982, 13.
117   *Lip Unité*, July-August 1979, 24.

for a community where all could be employed—that it would be governed by economic criteria set by the state was a shock. A movement that had begun with male skilled workers rallying female OS to support the retention of their jobs now planned the release of female OS and the employment of the male skilled workers.

The hiring of an external director with whom the state felt it could work, and the publication of lists of workers who would and would not be immediately rehired, eventually elicited a response from Paris. The prefect could block funds from the municipality to buy the factory, but remained ever fearful that the holdouts in Palente would get their way. Casting his action in a conciliatory tone, he wrote the prime minister in April 1979 that Lip was "a wound that can without a doubt still heal today," and it was important not to let the opportunity pass: "This is why I committed myself to trying to master its evolution with all the vigilance possible, on the local level as well as that of the different ministerial departments concerned."[118] In September 1979 he wrote again, warning that financial support for the cooperative would likely generate protests of watchmakers and municipalities, like those in 1976.[119] But, once again, his apprehensions were unwarranted.

The Minister of Industry turned to CIASI, which offered prescriptions in line with the tough stance of the prefect. A year after the cooperative had submitted its plan, the government addressed it directly for the first time. Without the legal status necessary to compete on the market, L.I.P. had been able to create only about forty-five jobs each in watchmaking and mechanics.[120] In meetings on the plan in June and July 1979, with a delegation composed of two representatives of the management board as well as one each from CFDT-Lip, FGM-CFDT, and Syndex, the CIASI eliminated watchcase production and cut the ultimate size of the workforce by more than one-half, from 650 to 320. And it set stringent conditions for even this to be achieved. To attain this level of employment, L.I.P. would have to break even in the first year, make 2.5 percent profit in the second year, and take turnover from the 6 million francs it would be in 1979 to 42 million francs in 1982.[121] But the government was not yet through. The FGM-CFDT was, as always, interested in moving on. Representatives of the federation and of the prime minister met and

118   ADD 1026W18 PD to PM, April 3, 1979.
119   ADD 1026W23 PD to PM, September 13, 1979.
120   Burgy and Piaget, "L'aventure des Coopératives LIP."
121   *Le Monde*, March 11, 1980, 45. These conditions were finalized in November 1979.

the state set two more preconditions for negotiations: departure from Palente, and acceptance of work elsewhere by a portion of the labor force. Details concerning issues like early retirement and job training for those who would not work at L.I.P. were left unresolved. Reviewing the concessions required by the government, a reporter from *Libération* wrote, "the co-op makes one think more and more of a satellite ready to jettison its launch vehicle."[122]

On October 3, 1979, the General Assembly met to hold a vote of confidence in the management board to bring to completion the negotiations for the cooperative to receive legal status. That the resolutions were read out to the General Assembly, but its members did not receive copies, and that a secret ballot was used, suggests the "tense atmosphere," in the prefect's words, in which the vote was held.[123] In joining the management board and the FGM-CFDT in favor of a yes vote, the CFDT-Lip recognized that the state had made it clear this would mean leaving Palente and accepting that many workers would not get jobs in the cooperative. In their statement recommending support, the union did not avoid the shadow cast by the vote of October 12, 1973: "[I]t will once again be the unskilled who are going to have to go elsewhere. Will you dare say face to face to someone who fought in the struggle, 'YOU MUST GO WORK SOMEWHERE ELSE'?"[124] Those who favored accepting the conditions to pursue negotiations suggested that staying at Palente was like putting 100 in a boat that could safely hold only fifty, thereby risking drowning everyone.[125]

Opponents saw in this call to accept the state's conditions the FGM-CFDT's effort to make Lip go away, whatever the price. It violated the covenant that made them *les Lip*. "To govern the life of a people didn't Moses receive from God ten fundamental laws?," Géhin asked.[126] The dissenters affirmed: "I vote against the reclassifications. Lip belongs to all who struggle. To sacrifice a part of the workers to the profitability of the enterprise—even a cooperative—is not acceptable. I did not fight for that. I refuse that we ourselves make the list of buddies whom we abandon to unemployment."[127] Action Committee veterans Jacky Burtz and François Laurent led the opposition. They were joined by Bondu,

---

122   *Libération*, October 4, 1979, 5.
123   ADD 1026W23 PD to PM, October 4, 1979.
124   ADD 45J71 "Aujourd'hui, répondre 'Oui'" (Section CFDT)," October 1, 1979.
125   AFGM-CFDT 1B577 J. Burtz et al., "Deux projets industriels mais des conséquences différentes."
126   ADD 45J108 Lip Livre Part 3/Géhin, 15–16.
127   *Le Monde*, October 4, 1979, 33.

Géhin, and Raguénès in circulating a tract, "To condemn oneself before being judged ..." The state was stipulating that the workers leave Palente and that they accept the departure of a significant portion of the labor force without addressing crucial issues concerning personnel whose future would likely not be at L.I.P.: "Can someone accept the principle of pronouncing his own death sentence? Can an innocent accept cutting off his own hand before being judged?":

> In other words, as in the USSR, the presumed 'guilty' (since they are 'plaintiffs'?) are asked to pronounce their own judgment, to confess to their mistakes and assess them. So we too must pronounce ourselves guilty of keeping 50, 100 persons among us, of wanting to remain all together. So we too must pronounce our own punishment, which is to get rid of 50, 100 persons.

Sticking to their demand for no placements outside of Lip and a job for all at Palente, the opponents also recalled the vote of October 12: "We think that the collectivity can still do better. We have done it, we will do it again!"[128]

The vote to continue negotiations was 193 in favor to 121 against, with most workers on lists A and B voting for it and those on list C voting against. Laurent would remember women tearing down banners at Palente that proclaimed a job for all.[129] All knew that workers in a capitalist economy can be laid off, but even before the first struggle in 1973, the employees of Lip, as evidenced in the case of Ouaked Areski, had made clear that to be a *Lip* was never to be party to these dismissals. The vote on the lists was so devastating because the collectivity treated list C as labor, not *les Lip*. That so many on list C were women led *Libération* to observe: "The men of the management board decide and the women suffer the consequences."[130]

In November 1979, the management board and representatives from the FGM-CFDT met at the Hôtel de Matignon with representatives of the prime minister to finalize terms to attain legal status. The CFDT-Lip had given mandates to participate in the negotiations to both the majority

---

128 BDIC F delta rés 702/6/4 D. Bondu, J. Burtz, M. Géhin, J. Raguénès, F. Laurant, and E. Fayard, 'Se condamner avant d'être jugé ...," tract distributed to CFDT-Lip members before the vote on October 3, 1979.

129 Laurent in Thomas Faverjon, *Fils de Lip* [quoted]. *Lip Unité*, February–March 1980, 2–3.

130 *Libération*, October 4, 1979.

that accepted the state's conditions and the minority, led by Burtz and Laurent, that demanded that the provisions for early retirement and other issues be settled first. However, the FGM-CFDT effectively eliminated the opponents by saying that if Burtz participated, the federation would not. The representative of the majority then withdrew. As a result, the FGM-CFDT negotiated at Matignon, not the CFDT-Lip.[131] The government maintained its hard line on limits to the size of the current and projected labor force and on leaving Palente. The municipality had seen the writing on the wall. With the Chamber of Commerce, it bought an abandoned factory in the Montarmots neighborhood of Besançon to house the cooperative in a lease purchase agreement. Knowing that the public aid for a little over half of them would be cut in December 1979, the workers got together in their workshops in late November to talk about whether to seal the deal, aware that the issues raised by Laurent and Burtz would be dealt with only later in negotiations with the CIASI and the prefect. These discussions were followed by three meetings of the General Assembly in two days; the next morning the CFDT-Lip met and split evenly on the issue, 33 to 33. The General Assembly then reconvened and opted by a narrow majority for use of the secret ballot: the vote was two to one to accept the state's terms.[132]

The state-authorized cooperative received final approval in June 1980, and moved from Palente to the new factory in March 1981. Legalization opened the way to the constitution of 12 million francs in capital, but under the draconian conditions set by the CIASI.[133] Two-thirds of these funds came from the teachers' mutual health insurance fund; nine-tenths of the rest came from the municipality and from the association of cooperatives, with the remainder from supporters and the workers' investment.[134] The supervisory council was composed of individuals

131   AFGM-CFDT 1B578, CFDT-Lip to FGM-CFDT, December 10, 1979. AB Interview with Burtz by Beurier [1992], 16. *Libération*, November 22, 1979, 7.

132   ADD 1026W20, "Situation actuelle de l'ex-Société Lip," November 13, 1979; RG, November 30, 1979. ADD 45J72 Tract de 'dissidents' CFDT, "Approuver la poursuite des négociations en sachant que cela va demander cohésion, vigilance et lutte," November 22, 1979. *Libération*, March 25, 1980. Burgy confided to the leadership of the cooperative that the impossible conditions set by the state made it a "poisoned gift." ADD 1026W23 "Note d'exploitation," written after the meeting at the Matignon on November 19, 1979.

133   AFGM-CFDT 1B578 Ministère d'Economie to Directeur General of Caisse Centrale de Crédit Coopératif, July 17, 1980.

134   Holz, "Crise, restructuration et adaptation du capital industriel," 72. Banks provided an additional 3 million francs in loans. *Libération*, March 26, 1980. 15.

elected by the members and representatives of the government and of the teachers' mutual health insurance fund.[135]

With the establishment of the cooperative in 1980, those without jobs were termed "'the reclassified,'" commented a group of workers and supporters, "as one spoke of 'the untouchables' in India or 'the lepers' in the Middle Ages."[136] That same year, a commission including Vittot, Bondu and Raguénès addressed this situation by devising a solidarity contract between those employed in the cooperative and those who would need to look for work elsewhere.[137] "It is a matter here of affirming our will to not see our activities and who we are dismantled, disseminated to the four winds!" All had participated in the creation of jobs in the cooperative; those with jobs pledged to work to create the conditions for more hires. Those who were designated to find work elsewhere would be paid by the Lip community as long as they actively sought a job and worked forty hours per week within the community, including time spent fulfilling obligations required by the ANPE, the state employment office. If a worker was offered a position, but found it unacceptable in terms of location, a minimum guarantee of stability, working conditions or pay, the worker had the right to present his or her case to a commission of Lip employees. If the commission agreed, the worker would continue to be paid, with funds coming from sales of watches, until all elements of the transition had been implemented. However, if the commission disagreed, the worker lost the right to support from the Lip community.[138]

Although only fifty or so workers signed the contract, the cooperative sought in other ways to address the situation of the nearly half of the members of the cooperative who did not have work in L.I.P. or one of the other enterprises that came out of Lip. Close to fifty took early retirement. Others took jobs with the municipality or received a

---

135   *Revue française des bijoutiers horlogers*, November 1981, 103–4.

136   BDIC F delta rés 702/14/3 "Compte-rendu de la réunion du 9 décembre 1980—Bureau de la 2AL."

137   BDIC F delta rés 702/6/5 Letter to Cher(e)s Camarades, August 11 [1980], sent by Commission de contrôle. A set of twenty pledges—e.g., the willingness to accept a lower than market wage, to do unpaid work when necessary, to accept a more egalitarian wage scale that took into account family obligations and participation in the struggle, as well as ability at work—accompanied this contract. BDIC F delta rés 702/6/5 "Critères d'engagement personnel dans le projet communautaire" [c. 1980].

138   Those who left to work elsewhere and were laid off within three months could return to the Lip community and its pay. There are several drafts of the contract [April 1980], as well as the final version [August 1980] in BDIC F delta rés 702/4/1, BDIC F delta rés 702/6/5, and Archives Bondu, "Contrat de Solidarité." For the forty hours per week provision, see BDIC F delta rés 702/6/5 CFDT-LIP, "Pour tous les Lip," April 29, 1980. Raguénès, *De Mai 68 à Lip*, 208.

separation payment from the cooperative and left to look for work on their own. Women who had gone to work at Lip after the war were in the most difficult situation. They had never worked anywhere else and "panicked at the thought of leaving."[139] At Montarmots, L.I.P. started with 170 employees, with more in mechanics than watchmaking, but slipped to 125 (seventy-two men and fifty-three women) by 1984. There were more members of the cooperative (295 in 1985) than L.I.P. employees because these included former workers who were shareholders, many of whom continued to attend the General Assembly of the cooperative.[140] The CIASI negotiated a deal for L.I.P. to acquire the brand name and machines from the syndics. However, the cooperative limited itself to assembling watches from parts and movements purchased elsewhere, much to the disappointment and incomprehension of the largely female workforce which had once made these pieces.[141]

That L.I.P. was never in a situation to hire workers from the outside helped maintain old practices. The workforce aged; the average age of a worker in 1980 was forty-six.[142] Piaget spoke figuratively of the Lip war veterans gathered around a plaque commemorating their combat.[143] He believed that new workers might have brought to L.I.P. the production norms of the firms with which it competed for work; "we are in a very diminished state of activity and I know people at L.I.P. who find their work extraordinarily difficult, while what three of them do is done by one-half a person in another factory!"[144] The organization of work remained unchanged. "The old Taylorist and hierarchical culture in effect under Fred Lip reestablished itself in the workshops," Jeannine Pierre-Émile told a reporter in 1983.[145] When Maurice Chaniot, classmate of Neuschwander at the École centrale, replaced Penna and was named president-director general in 1983 (at the same exorbitant salary in relation to other members of the cooperative as his predecessor), he expressed surprise that, although the assembly line no longer operated, workers practiced the division of labor of the assembly line—simply

139   Plantin, "L'accompagnement du service social," 49.

140   AMB 86W43 AG of L.I.P., July 9, 1987.

141   ADD 45J77 "Lip: le cadavre," *Forum* 27–8 (July–August 1980): 35–7. Jacquin, "Lip 1973–1981," 353–4.

142   *Libération*, March 26, 1980, 15. The cooperative responded to the departure of engineers by putting out the call for those with the necessary expertise to address particular problems. The appeal of the Lip project brought individuals who would spend a couple of days and resolve the problem at hand. Piaget, "'Des trésors d'imagination,'" 167.

143   Beurier, "La mémoire des Lip," Annexe VIII.

144   *Lip Unité*, April–May 1980, 8.

145   *Le Matin*, June 23, 1983, 14.

putting in three or four pieces rather than one—when the reduced production could have allowed each worker to assemble a complete watch.[146]

The continued sale of sequestered watches to pay salaries until 1981
was done without payment of the value-added tax; the resulting lower
price undercut legal sales by the cooperative. The competing offerings
of Lip watches, explained a representative of the cooperative, were
"very bad for our image." Furthermore, L.I.P. found that works councils were less enthusiastic about selling watches for a cooperative than
they had been for workers engaged in a job action.[147] Most damaging
for the cooperative was the continued refusal to stock their watches by
the watch seller-jewelers, whose grievances about illegal sales were now
compounded by legal sales to works councils and cooperatives, which
they felt constituted unfair competition.[148] L.I.P. put out a catalogue for a
new collection "more attractive for 1980," to sell watches by mail. It sent a
letter to readers of Le Nouvel observateur and put out a brochure in April
1980. The cooperative explained that it was counting on supporters to
sell watches legally while it established itself on a new footing. It offered
a discount of 10 percent on all orders of three to twenty watches, and
higher discounts on larger purchases.[149] But these efforts did not solve
the problem of marketing.

In 1982, the cooperative contracted with Kiplé to sell its watches
in supermarkets and department stores. Kiplé acquired the Lip brand
name in 1984, but paid royalties to the cooperative. L.I.P. made watches
for Kiplé until 1986, when it stopped watch production altogether.[150] In
1990, the Groupe Sensemat bought the brand name from the bankrupt
Kiplé and set up a factory to produce "Lip" watches in the Gers. The
director Jean-Claude Sensemat established a close relationship with Fred
Lip, whom he praised as a "legal delinquent" and as the model head of
a business.[151] In 2013, the firm made watches in conjunction with the
clothing line "Commune de Paris 1871" with both this logo and the Lip
logo on the watch face. Two years later, Sensemat leased the brand to the

146   Libération, June 22, 1983, 12.

147   Libération, March 26, 1980, 15. AR Interview with Burtz by Rouaud, May 6,
2004, 5.

148   L.I.P. proposed to "occulter" regions—not sell to organizations there—where
watch seller–jewelers agreed to buy from them, but this did not resolve the issue. Revue
française des bijoutiers horlogers, November 1981, 103–4. Lip Unité, December 1981, 5–6.

149   ADD 45J72 Information SCOP 'Les Industries de Palente' no. 4, November 9,
1979. ADD 45J75 Lip Spécial Amitié no. 3, April 15, 1980.

150   BDIC F delta rés 702/22/2 Directoire, "SCOP-Information "Les industries de
Palente" 25 (May 3, 1982). Libération, June 22, 1983, 12. Le Monde, May 3, 1986, 28.

151   Jean-Claude Sensemat, La Patronade (Paris, 1988), 9.

Société de montres de Besançon, a small firm that began producing Lip watches in Besançon with plans to offer them at watch seller-jewelers and department stores.[152]

With the decline of the watch industry, Besançon became a center of micro-technology. It drew upon the skills of mechanics who had worked in watchmaking and related activities at Lip and other firms.[153] After moving from Palente, L.I.P. mechanics continued to do subcontracting work in precision mechanics.[154] However, even after dropping watch assembly, L.I.P. had trouble keeping its head above water because it could not shed so easily the deficits watch production had incurred, despite an infusion of funds in 1984 from many of the same sources as before. The board of directors, which had replaced the supervisory council in the cooperative, spoke that year of having to "conquer a double independence," from creditors and from its past. With the retirement in 1983 of "the heroes," Piaget, Vittot, Burgy, and others, the board made its project to open up to those who, when the subject of Lip was raised, would say "'The struggle'? Never heard of it."[155]

Yet, even those who remembered the struggle had their limits. Its loans unpaid, the teachers' mutual fund went head to head with workers defending their machines from seizure.[156] L.I.P. went bankrupt in 1987; it then had ninety-five employees, 60 percent of whom had worked for Lip. In a familiar story, Chaniot sought to start a new firm in its place with the backing of a Swiss firm and termination of the sector where most union leaders worked. The CFDT-Lip had accepted salary cuts, unpaid hours of work, and layoffs in order to give the enterprise breathing room, but it insisted on replacing Chaniot. In conjunction with the confederation in Doubs, the local looked for other investors and a different boss. The union convinced the Tribunal de Commerce to reject Chaniot and his backers in favor of their choice of owners and a director. The joint stock company Lip Précision Industrie, SA (LPI) launched in 1988 with about seventy employees.[157]

152   L'Est républicain, May 12, 2015, 12. L'Usine nouvelle, May 13, 2015.

153   Emmanuelle Cournarie, 'De l'horlogerie aux microtechniques: approche socio-anthropologique de la reconversion industrielle bisontine,' Prix A'Doc de la jeune recherche en Franche-Comté (2010): 9–21.

154   Jonah D. Levy suggests that these contracts were the result of government pressure. Tocqueville's Revenge (Cambridge, 1999), 128.

155   ADD 86W43 "Rapport du Conseil d'Administration" of L.I.P. for 1983 [1984].

156   Interview with Burtz by Reid, June 13, 2017.

157   ADD 1812W36 RA, March 2, 1988. Libération, August 27, 1987. L'Est républicain, March 11, 1988.

After a decade, this firm too hit the rocks. Burtz, one of the few workers from Lip still at LPI, recognized that workers there called on the methods of Lip: "we too took the boss's briefcase, in which we found a plan for downsizing."[158] LPI declared bankruptcy and in 1999 the workers pooled their severance pay to create a worker-owned cooperative that Burtz initially directed. It moved from the factory at Montarmots to the site where the Lip restaurant had been at Palente. Today, fifteen employees work in the cooperative, primarily on quick turnaround work in precision mechanics. The proportion of the highest to the lowest salary is two to one. Faced with the recession in 2009, each worker took a cut in hours to assure there would be no layoffs.[159] The equipment includes a half-dozen seventy-year-old lathes taken from the original Lip factory at Palente and now back home: they are, the mechanics find, more accurate than contemporary digitally controlled machines.[160]

Bons Jours

The artisanal ventures and the restaurant born of the struggle co-existed with L.I.P. In December 1978, these employed fifty to sixty workers.[161] Although the plan for the cooperative presented to the authorities in 1978 projected full employment in a couple of years, Lip workers recognized that the "intermediary period" could "wrong individuals and cause the break-up of the community." The search for solutions to this situation preoccupied them.[162] Attention focused on the artisanal enterprises at Palente. These were the site of a live differently/work differently culture, places where workers made what they wanted under their own control and where women played a leading role. Sale of the goods produced in them developed ties with supporters, but garnered only a small fraction of the funds needed to pay the wages of those they employed. They were supported by workers' watch sales which would end when L.I.P. acquired legal status. Would the particular qualities of the artisanal workshops survive the transition?

---

158   *Témoignage chrétien*, October 22, 1998, 13.
159   *Réforme*, October 6, 2011, 10.
160   *L'Est républicain*, November 14, 2013. Lipemec, the descendant of the Lip machine tools factory in Ornans, also operates as a worker-owned cooperative.
161   *Lip Unité*, December 1978, 4.
162   *Lip Unité*, September 1978, 2–3.

In early July 1979, the Commissions Artisanales de Palente (CAP) was created as a cooperative (without legal status until 1981) at the impetus of the women's commission, one of the dozens of commissions at Palente (though not a revivified Women's Group). The CAP brought together La Chiffonnière with other commissions working in fabric, wood-working, and decorative plates. The CAP quickly grouped close to 300 members, most but not all of whom were Lip workers who purchased shares, though only a minority were employed in the CAP projects. Each member contributed 100 francs to constitute the capital for the coop-erative. Members elected a supervisory council of twelve, that in turn selected a management board in line with the legal requirements for a cooperative.[163] Three-quarters of those who worked in the CAP enter-prises were women, but the leadership was largely male. Those in charge of the CAP found that commercial imperatives forced it to go against what they found to be "the discrete intimacy of the old commissions of the struggle that had become over time little untouchable fiefdoms, crys-tallized in micro-powers."[164] These commissions had previously practiced the self-organization of production, with a distribution of power among workers. However, "the day the commissions are regrouped to make an enterprise [the CAP]," explained Marc Géhin, "and it is necessary to take into account economic imperatives, this new and indispensable 'knowl-edge' escapes the commissions. They are passed over. Another power is born, that of the management board which 'knows.'"[165]

For the CAP director Dominique Enfraze, the dispersal of power in the commissions during the conflict was difficult to reproduce in the cooper-atives because workers feared becoming "little bosses." Like the workers chosen to direct L.I.P., those selected to head the CAP found that workers responded to them as bosses, rather than assuming responsibility in the new economic environment themselves.[166] In May 1981, the CAP General Assembly was told that too few members thought about the relation of production to commercialization: "Indeed, they continue to act as if they were making products for the struggle, not giving much consideration to timing and delays, without concerning themselves if goods were or were not sold, delegating responsibility for such matters to a few people

---

163   *Lip Unité*, July–August 1979, 14–15.
164   Dominique Bondu, "LIP, dix ans après," *Autogestion* 14 (1983): 87–8.
165   *Lip Unité*, April–May 1980, 10.
166   BDIC F delta rés 702/21/3 CAP, "Compte-rendu des 2 réunions de travail. Conseil de surveillance et Directoire des 8 et 29 octobre 79." *Lip Unité*, April–May 1980, 6, 9; First Trimester 1983, 16.

in charge." This was a mindset developed in a large factory, but in a small enterprise, "each individual must feel concerned by the totality of the problems."[167] Another director of the CAP, Jean-Claude Piquard, observed: "[Previously], we thought that all decisions could be collective with a big 'C'. This situation led us to observe that the collective took responsibility away from individuals. For the necessary operations of the [CAP], we prefer to give individuals responsibility within a living collectivity."[168]

The vote to pursue negotiations in October 1979 forced the CAP to make difficult adjustments. For members to live differently, the CAP had to succeed in staying alive. It put new criteria for hiring in this order: ability to make an economic contribution (i.e., production of market-able items), participation in the struggle, and social factors (i.e., family situation).[169] Working in the CAP, Demougeot said the vote to accept the Matignon terms was experienced as "an enormous violence and like a fatality."[170] With the departure over time of many who had been active on the commissions, the CAP ended up with twenty to thirty salaried employees.[171] Palente had fostered a sense of unity among dif-ferent groups of workers. Demougeot referred to a "fragmentation of the collectivity" when the CAP moved to Besançon in 1981, although the space the municipality provided it was only 300 meters down the Rue de l'Espérance from L.I.P.[172] Raguénès spoke of the forced exile of the artis-anal enterprises from Palente to "strange residences" in Besançon where "the communal dynamic frittered away," leaving them incomprehensible, in a "kind of Babel!"[173]

The CAP had particular problems making the transition from pro-ducing objects in the context of the conflict to marketing consumer goods. "Before," the CAP explained, "when we were in commissions 'of struggle', we were making objects for us, according to our taste, without being too concerned to know if they pleased a public. Today we have to question ourselves about the quality of our products, and this faced with a public that is not necessarily activist!" Selling at political festivals and rallies, where purchasers were participating in the struggle, was one

---

167   BDIC F delta rés 702/21/1 "Pour l'AG des coopérateurs de CAP," May 21, 1981.
168   *Lip Unité*, December 1981, 11.
169   ADD 45J71 CAP, "Embauches," October 9, 1979.
170   Faucoup, "Que sont devenus les LIP?," 20:25.
171   As at L.I.P., members of the CAP gave 5 percent of their salary to the cooper-ative. The CAP salary spread was even less than the one to two in L.I.P. *Le Matin*, June 23, 1983, 14.
172   *Parti pris*, January 15, 1982, 12–13.
173   Raguénès, "Oublier Lip?," 191.

thing; offering goods to customers thinking in terms of style and cost was quite another.[174] As Demougeot recognized in 1980, "At L.I.P., people returned to their work, their machine and it is a place familiar to them. On the other hand, at the CAP people are helpless because they are asked to go from the pleasure of creating something to the profitability of this activity in terms of jobs."[175]

Members of the supervisory council took products of the CAP to potential vendors.[176] To make money, the CAP recognized, was a matter of "addressing a public with cash instead of making cheaper products for the less fortunate."[177] But this was easier said than done. The representatives they sent to the Salon des Arts Décoratifs in Paris in 1979 concluded that "it will be necessary to upgrade our products if we want to participate in the Salon next year."[178] La Chiffonnière had made objects that expressed the creativity of its members. They worked without a hierarchy and made decisions by consensus—the opposite of their lives as OS. The cooperative changed this. Production had to be of high quality, of interest to a market not composed of militants, and made inexpensively enough to assure a profit on sales. Over the protests of the women in La Chiffonnière—"We aren't Thailand here!"—the three men on the CAP management board replaced domestic sewing machines with industrial ones.[179] In any case, woodworking was more profitable. The CAP purchased a half-dozen machines and these were used to construct furniture.[180] To make itself commercially successful, the CAP did away with its heterogeneous production and completely rethought the catalogue. The directors had the unenviable task of selecting among the variety of creative activities to develop a marketable collection of fabric and wooden household goods of high quality and low production cost. This was difficult. Director of the CAP Enfraze recognized this: "The value and the conception of our products often had to be questioned, certain ones eliminated. But these products of the struggle had been made with love, and, in some cases, ingenuity."[181]

---

174 *Lip Unité*, November–December 1980, 4.

175 *Lip Unité*, April–May 1980, 11.

176 BDIC F delta rés 702/21/3 CAP, "Compte-rendu des 2 réunions de travail."

177 *Lip Unité*, December 1981, 11.

178 ADD 45J71 "Compte-rendu du conseil de surveillance" [CAP], September 9, 1979.

179 AB Interview with Alice Carpena by Beurier [1992], 14–15.

180 The management board arranged to make 300–400 doors per month for the Manuest cooperative. *Lip Unité*, December 1982, 6–9.

181 *Lip Unité*, First Trimester 1983, 14.

On the advice of a Syndex consultant, the management board had a specialist assess the commercial possibilities of making gifts for promotional sales campaigns, as well as for companies, clubs giving seminars, and for wholesalers who supplied fancy tobacco shops.[182] To prepare a collection to present to wholesalers, the management board hired "a creator" to design a line of fabric and wood household products under the name "Bons Jours." Not surprisingly, he had difficulty gaining acceptance from commissions used to making their own decisions, but the management board followed his advice, produced a catalogue, and hired sales representatives to get the new goods into boutiques: "Our collection is composed of objects for homes, or to be more exact, for the kitchen and the living room. It is aimed at a young public (by age or in spirit) that likes to entertain, to give gifts to others or themselves, looking for design and quality."[183] But the CAP never mastered the move from liberation through production to consumer commerce. Unable to get Bons Jours products into department stores, the CAP folded within a couple of years.[184]

At various points, cooperatives born of the experience of Palente, in addition to L.I.P. and the CAP, employed fifty to sixty individuals, initially drawn largely from *les Lip*. Syndex thought that small cooperatives were more likely to succeed than a single, all-embracing one. The cooperatives were interwoven. Individual workers were members of several; the governing supervisory councils had representatives of other cooperatives on them; they shared economic and commercial services.[185] However, this did not prevent these other cooperatives from eventually going under as well. These included Au Chemin de Palente restaurant (in part because not enough workers from other cooperatives fulfilled what the L.I.P. management board referred to in September 1981 as their "effort of solidarity" by eating there), and the printshop La Lilliputienne, which lasted until 1994. The Collectif de liaison études et formation (CLEF), an association of former Lip employees engaged in cultural activities and which ran vacation sites in Doubs, dissolved in 1998.

In the early 1980s, the SCEIP grew in size to twenty employees, half of whom had worked for Lip. Faced with a decline in business in the

---

182 ADD 45J73 "Compte-rendu du conseil de surveillance du 11 janvier 1980" [CAP].

183 *Libération*, March 26, 1980, 14–15. *Lip Unité*, December 1982, 6–9, 10–11 [quoted].

184 BDIC F delta rés 702/21/1 "Rapport du directoire sur le 3ème exercice de CAP, 1 décembre 81 au 30 novembre 82."

185 Bondu, "De l'usine à la communauté," 499–500.

Global South, the SCEIP turned its attention to all facets of the life of enterprises in France.[186] It took a particular interest in enabling firms in micro-mechanics and micro-electronics to take an idea to production and market. The SCEIP contracted with L.I.P. to make prototypes and test designs. In November 1979, its technicians built and delivered a prototype of a saw to cut optical fibers. It was adopted and made by L.I.P.; between sixty and 100 were sold in the first year, primarily to the Centre National d'Études de Télécommunications at Lannion and to telecommunications firms. Working for the Laboratoire d'Astronomie Spatiale in Marseille, the SCEIP designed and L.I.P. mechanics made the electronic dating system for the camera of the Soviet Soyuz spacecraft that carried the first French cosmonaut in June 1982.[187] The SCEIP worked for the General Commissariat of the Republic in charge of economic planning as well, preparing struggling enterprises for change, paying particular attention to the labor force and its variety of expertise. This was a new manifestation of the Lip workers' longstanding belief that reflection on their experience could benefit other troubled enterprises. Between 1981 and 1983, the SCEIP participated in the revival of seven firms, recreating 1,000 jobs.[188] However, in 1987, the SCEIP too closed.

Conclusion

The fate of the long 1968 in the late 1970s is often explained by the recession or the New Philosophers' rejection of Marxism. However, the state played an important role as well. As president, Giscard d'Estaing endeavored at once to move the Fifth Republic away from Gaullist technocracy and from the alternatives to it that workers like those at Palente offered. He sought to foster the capitalist entrepreneurs he thought state intervention hampered, but he saw impeding the entrepreneurship shown by worker collectivities as an important element of this project.

Many in the 1968 left believed that participation in struggles like Lip was the path to a socialist future. However, *les Lip* came to feel that

---

186   ADD 45J112 Michel Jeanningros, "SCEIP: une expérience de transfert technologique 1977–1982" [November 1982].

187   *L'Est républicain*, May 25, 1982, 13. ADD 45J112 Folder on SCEIP.

188   *Lip Unité*, November-December 1980, 8. SCEIP brochure in ADD 45J87. Michel Garcin, "Lutte contre le chômage et création d'entreprise: l'exemple de Lip," *Rencontre: cahiers du travailleur social* 37 (Spring 1981): 45. Florence Clauzel, "Faillites d'entreprises: les charognards ou les Saint-Bernard?," *Autrement* 40 (May 1982): 149–50. Terrieux, "L'expérience Lip," 162–74.

reflection on the problems they encountered could be as valuable for the French left as their successes. To construct a socialist France, the French left needed to examine what the difficulties confronted in conflicts like Lip revealed, not just in dealings with the state and capital, but within workers' communities themselves. If only communities forged in conflicts could construct a new society, the characteristics of such communities could present conundrums. This was all the more true when the communities rooted in struggle were asked to become sites of production in the old society—and when the old society mobilized to keep itself that way.

12

The Onions of Egypt

This privileged site of witnessing, this people, I compare to the people of Israel who were crossing the desert and [thinking about the place they had left] where there had been, despite slavery, security. It is the history of the onions. When the people set out into the desert they bemoaned the onions of Egypt. They no longer remembered slavery, but they said: "Before at least, we had something." The same as us saying, before, in the time of the boss, it wasn't great, it is true the boss is a bastard, but the moment you could visualize him, could name him, you could distance yourself from him and you could attack him. Even with production rates, the organization of work, through all we lived and that made us slaves, there was a certain form of security. Today, we have embarked on an adventure of almost total instability that we could name through things like the land and the buildings, the intervention of cops all the time, the incapacity to reflect on this, etc., etc. It is truly the crossing of the desert. One could imagine the golden calf, Moses, Aaron …

—Jean Raguénès[1]

No doubt the Lip collectivity is unable to go further in the current situation. They also say Stalinism came from the fact that the most advanced society in collective terms—the Russian working class—had trouble making that important step forward, 'to root democracy'. We have also reached our limits. We feel this in the conflicts among us.

—Charles Piaget[2]

1   BDIC F delta rés 702/15/1 "Débat du 20 janvier 1979," 8.
2   *Lip Unité*, July–August 1979, 8.

During the crisis, Lip practiced a self-management of the notarial type, thanks to the war treasure that procured them a certain security. Now we are putting in place, in sadness and in tears, an entrepreneurial self-management.

—Maurice Chaniot[3]

Raguénès spoke of "the before and the after November 8, 1977," of the change from the "struggle against" to the "struggle for," of moving from "the bursting forth," characterized by the Action Committee, to the "time of management" of the cooperative.[4] Piaget had held back in the debate on accepting the government's onerous terms for the cooperative at the beginning of October 1979, but ended up giving his assent: "of course we could have decided as in Guyana to inject ourselves all together, then, no more problem, we would die together, but for goodness sake, we want to continue to live. In a social conflict, there is no honorable death." In response to a worker who said that "our individual life and Lip are connected," Piaget responded, "no, our life is not that of Lip, that is the dream, the myth."[5] The community born in 1973 was the *raison d'être* of the cooperatives, but it could make their operation difficult.

Bondu captured one source of this tension in differentiating "the collectivity of the struggle," the embracing concept for Piaget and the union leadership, from "the community of labor."[6] The collectivity referred to the union culture, concerned with securing employment and organizing workers to achieve this. Community embraced networks created by workers during the struggle. Participation in the struggle transformed individuals and introduced new forms of liberation, of aspirations to live and to work differently, particularly among the young, the unskilled and female workers. A critique developed of "the 'collective in the extreme' aspect of the movement," in which the individual was suspect, haunted by the specter of egoism—"You did not have the right to say 'I', to think as an individual," in the words of one worker.[7] For many, community came to be understood as an alternative to the submission and authority in the existing workplace, and for some to the workplace itself. Visitors came to Palente to see those who showed "it is possible," and interactions with them in turn gave many workers new ideas of what was desirable

---

3   AMB 86W43 *Le Pays*, December 14, 1985.
4   ADD 45J108 Lip Livre Part 1/Conversation 1, 7.
5   *Libération*, October 4, 1979, 5.
6   Bondu, "LIP, dix ans après," 84–5.
7   Jacquin, "Lip 1973–1981," 229.

and attainable. The community these exchanges created became another legacy, crucial to the future of Lip both internally and as the recipient of external assistance: the image of Lip for supporters, Raguénès believed, was the beloved community, more than the site of production or the sale of watches.[8]

In 1973, collectivity and community at Palente were complementary, building upon one another, and they retained this imbrication: the same phenomena were interpretable as instances of both collectivity and community. However, strains emerged with the creation of the cooperative, an unfamiliar project in an inhospitable environment. In conversations among *les Lip* in 1981, Vittot spoke of capitalist exploitation of work, but did not question the work itself; he appreciated the professional identity he confirmed in doing it. Vittot did not see Lip as a community in the sense some others did, whereas Demougeot valued the individual self-realization and the community forged through practices born of the conflict, not the idea of the collectivity anchored in industry, work or demands themselves.[9] On another occasion, Demougeot spoke of believing "less and less in self-management, and much more in a collectivity that lives together"—the community—"where people, at whatever level they are, mix and exchange."[10] In January 1979, Jeanningros characterized the split as one between union leaders and those he identified as partisans of "hope," many of whom worked in the artisanal enterprises or who, like Géhin, spoke of tearing down the factory walls as he had done for himself, by establishing the printshop cooperative, La Lilliputienne.[11]

Moving from the "struggle against" to the cooperative was, for Raguénès, akin to "the passage from the Resistance at Liberation" to the Fourth Republic.[12] Stymied by the failure of the state to engage after the collapse of the SEHEM, Palente became, in the workers' words in the summer of 1977, "little by little a ghetto of resistance."[13] Piaget reflected that the second occupation at Palente (1976–81) lasted longer than the German occupation of France.[14] However, the cooperative challenged the purity of a culture of resistance. Sartre's group-in-fusion created by

8   *Lip Unité*, July–August 1979, 9.
9   Jacquin, "Lip 1973–1981," 134–6, 167–70, 197–8.
10   Macciocchi, *De la France*, 442–3.
11   Bondu, "De l'usine à la communauté," 490 [Jeanningros]. Jacquin, "Lip 1973–1981," 277.
12   Faucoup, "Que sont devenues les LIP?," 20:26.
13   ADD 85J56 Les travailleurs de Lip, "Refuser la fatalité et vivre ensemble au pays" [Summer 1977]. Bondu, "De l'usine à la communauté," 439.
14   AB Interview with Piaget by Beurier [1992], 44.

fighting an enemy that threatened death—the Germans in the war or the state and capital for Lip workers—was lost when faced with establishing the Fourth Republic or the cooperative.[15] Valorization of the struggle led leaders to rethink it in light of the challenges posed by construction of the cooperative. Raguénès came to believe that there had been a number of conflicts within the nascent community in 1973, but, as resisters in the face of an invader, they had not felt the need to deal with them, believing too easily in "the great unity, the taste for the collective, communion realized."[16] Yet, it was not "a community that chose itself, since it is events, unemployment, that made it such that community came into existence; we constantly run into problems that this state of things brings."[17] In the "struggle for" that followed, *les Lip* would need to recognize and accept "contradictions" in exchanges with one another or they would split apart.[18] In 1973, Raguénès had characterized his relation to Piaget as that of the wise mad man rooted in the festival to the mad wise man with his taste for the collective. In the cooperative, "The dream of '73 is realized today, concretely, in reality. What existed in the festival must be prolonged. It is the week with respect to Sunday."[19] But this was easier said than done. Raguénès lamented in 1980 that the community had become a site of "wise men who collapse (and close themselves to all madness) and mad men who rave. One gets to a Manichean world."[20]

This took Bondu back to the Resistance. In her madness, Jeanne d'Arc had awakened the need for community, but madness could not preserve it and it had taken the form of the oppressive nation. "To resist in 1940, this was a moment of madness for the first resisters in terms of power relations," but it had led to the Fourth Republic, purged of the resisters' madness. "Then, I ask myself if wanting to refuse structured organization and thinking madness in order to develop it over time does not lead to finding oneself dispossessed someday. And unhappy in the end."[21] Was there a place for madness in the construction of the cooperative? "The economic ... is it the devil?," *Lip Unité* asked.[22] In January 1979, Jeannin-gros spoke of his "impression that through the co-op, through economic

15   Bondu, "LIP, dix ans après," 90.
16   BDIC F delta rés 702/15/1 "Débat du 20 janvier 1979," 21.
17   *La Gueule ouverte*, June 7, 1978, 11.
18   BDIC F delta rés 702/15/1 "Débat du 20 janvier 1979," 21.
19   Faucoup, "Que sont devenues les LIP?," 20:26.
20   ADD 45J108 Lip Livre Part 1/D, 12–13.
21   Ibid., 17.
22   *Lip Unité*, February–March 1980, 1.

relations, the dream is not allowed. I think this is really serious."[23] For Géhin, "the confrontation of the 'economists' and the 'dreamers'" led to the construction of "our Tower of Babel. We no longer recognized one another, we did not speak the same language."[24]

All engaged *Lip* lived with these contradictions. Michel Cugney, a member of the L.I.P. management board, had a more critical view of work than Piaget and Vittot. Cugney had entered the factory in 1966. Work then and in 1979 "was a shitty thing, with production cadences ..." Thinking of the cooperative, he asked himself "if, in fact, we were not in the process of establishing an ambitious project on a bygone concept."[25] He conceived of the cooperative as offering two possibilities to live differently. For some the fight was for a minimum of industrial work and responsibilities in the cooperative in order to allow for the blossoming of the individual outside of the workplace; for others the cooperative could be a place where individuals would experience not just economic, but cultural and social development as well.[26] Cugney explained that "what made [him] join [the struggle] was not the matter of a job for all but much more that of living differently."[27] This was also the case for individuals who had made the choice of coming to work at Palente during the conflict, like the engineer Bruno Parmentier, commercial director of the mechanics department from 1978 to 1981. He explained that "to live differently, starting from other values," was what motivated him, rather than "a job for all."[28] However, Cugney and Parmentier spoke from within the leadership of the cooperative. In 1980, Cugney reflected that when it had become clear that neither the state nor business would offer a solution, "we could have ended the conflict with flag held high, on the barricade," or they could pursue the cooperative, knowing that it would present problems.[29] Cugney chose the latter, but he was aware of the appeal of leaving the struggle in its purity: "Therefore we took responsibilities that I feel led to dangerous modifications in behavior and we were pushed on a kind of toboggan."[30]

23 BDIC F delta rés 702/15/1 "Débat du 20 janvier 1979," 19.

24 ADD 45J108 Lip Livre Part 3/Géhin, 10–11, 36. For an earlier expression of this conflict, see "Le conflit Lip: lutter pour quel travail?," 119–20. See also Jacquin, "Lip 1973–1981," 355.

25 BDIC F delta rés 702/15/1 "Débat du 20 janvier 1979," 18–19.

26 BDIC F delta rés 702/14/4 Notes on conseil d'adminstration of 2AL [March 1979].

27 *Lip Unité*, February–March 1980, 7. Dominique Enfraze concurred. Ibid., 6.

28 Ibid., 7.

29 Ibid., 18.

30 *Lip Unité*, April–May 1980, 6.

Le Noyau Impulseur

But it was not of toboggans that many at Lip spoke, but of *le noyau impulseur*—the propulsive nucleus. That this is a term not used very often in other social movements suggests that it refers to qualities particular to Lip. Although all recognized a leadership central to the "struggle against" of 1973 and 1976, the term *noyau impulseur* was not used until 1977, when the leadership that had earlier seemed natural and was unquestioned in the fight against the threat of the death of the firm was given a name. As the unity that workers felt in opposition gave way to the diversity of their situations in the "struggle for" of the cooperative, there was recognition of a group tasked with the mission of maintaining the unity of the collectivity and giving it momentum. However, the repeated affirmations of unity by the *noyau impulseur* left *les Lip* without a forum where diverse views could be presented and discussed.[31] Itself always referred to as a collective entity, the *noyau impulseur* was not a formal group, whose members were named. It was the leadership of the movement conceived without reference to the institutional positions individuals held. Everyone knew who they were and that the group rarely incorporated new members.[32] A manager active in the conflict estimated that at the time the cooperative was approved in 1977 there were around fifty individuals, almost all male, in the *noyau impulseur*, some with positions in the CFDT-Lip or cooperative and others not, but all engaged in the struggle twenty-four hours a day.[33]

The term *impulseur* can refer to small rocket engines used to make adjustments in the flight path. Lip workers were understood to be self-propelled, not responding to the dictates of a vanguard party, but the *noyau impulseur* strategically guided their movement. The *noyau impulseur* did not have a governing structure, and those whom the workers recognized as being in it had recourse to a different kind of power than that conferred by the offices they may have held in the union or the workplace. Lip was a world where everything was discussed at length. "Discourse has in effect replaced, in inter-personnel relations, the role previously played by function."[34] Verbal mastery gave the *noyau*

---

31   ADD 45J108 Lip Livre Part 2/"Lip, déjà demain," 6.

32   Berry, "Lip 1978," 13.

33   Then, in levels of decreasing participation, were groups of 150, 200 and 50. Saint-Germain and Souletie, "Le voyage à Palente," 78. Bondu, "De l'usine à la communauté," 433–5.

34   Berry, "Lip 1978," 71. Demougeot recognized that union leaders, the core of the *noyau impulseur*, dominated male workers as well, saying that at a meeting of elected

impulseur, in Raguénès' words, "a sort of spiritual power."[35] Acting as the *noyau impulseur,* individuals within it saw themselves as without institutional power and therefore fully within the equality of the rank and file—as individuals defending their own points of view, not representatives of interests within the collectivity. They saw no need for formal mechanisms by which elements of the base could express their positions or for intermediaries between the base and themselves. In the words of one observer, "Paradoxically, the utopia of a spontaneous leadership that persists after 1973 leads to the contrary situation of a leadership totally isolated from its rank and file."[36]

Furthermore, as Géhin perceptively noted, the struggles of 1973 and 1976 were launched "with the maximum safeguarding of people," "an attempt" by the leadership "to eliminate anguish."[37] In 1978, the sociologist Jean-Pic Berry noted "the disturbing quantity of sedatives taken" by *les Lip.*[38] By reassuring workers and handling administrative problems that arose in the insecurity in which all lived after the vote to establish the cooperative, the *noyau impulseur* complicated later expectations that workers would assume new forms of responsibility in the cooperative.[39] A twenty-five-year-old skilled worker recognized this danger in 1978:

> A new point came to me in '76–'77; it is true that the collectivity gives strength, because we lean on it to go further, but it is also true that it serves as an umbrella for all who do not want to get wet, who do not want to take risks and who like being dragged along. But, when the infection reaches the foot, I am afraid the gangrene unfortunately pursues its way to the heart.[40]

All saw that Palente was bound by a high degree of affectivity. Michel Cugney spoke of this in 1979: "I must say that I react less and less in union terms and more and more in an affective mode. When you do things by friendship, by love, there is no longer the need to explain oneself."[41] The next year, Pierre Besançon, president of the support group for

---

union delegates she attended as a delegate, there were twenty-seven men, only four of whom spoke. AM, Transcript of Anne-Marie Martin, *Lip au féminin,* part 3.

35   BDIC F delta rés 702/15/1 "Débat du 20 janvier 1979," 17.
36   Berry, "Lip 1978," 12–16, 39, 67 [quoted], 82.
37   ADD 45J108 Lip Livre Part 1/Conversation 1, 15.
38   Berry, "Lip 1978," 72.
39   Bondu, "De l'usine à la communauté," 446–7.
40   Ibid., 475.
41   BDIC F delta rés 702/15/1 "Débat du 20 janvier 1979," 19.

the cooperative, recognized that "the enormous weight of the affective bonds that are woven" made the Lip conflict "a struggle unlike others" and "made it such that all analysis of the situation is strongly influenced by the relations" among employees.[42] Garcin too was struck "by the weight of affectivity at Lip. It is a wealth, but it is important to see the consequences. Many things that should not pose problems are immediately retranscribed in the affective domain, which ends up, on certain occasions, becoming negative."[43]

Debate over the concessions that legalization of the cooperative required brought fears that the affective relations that bound individuals within the *noyau impulseur* would come undone. In October 1979, the L.I.P. management board said it would step down if the General Assembly did not vote to pursue negotiations.[44] The *noyau impulseur* itself was divided. In September 1979, Raguénès had opposed accepting the conditions set by the state. However, he switched and spoke out in favor of their acceptance in October: "I voted for the unitary text though for five years I was fighting for the opposite."[45] Raguénès explained that he recognized that the success of Lip had been rooted in the close relations among members of the *noyau impulseur*, and saw his vote as affirming these:

> Finally, my comrades and I had the feeling that the *noyau impulseur* itself risked a breakup, mortal for it and consequently for the whole of the collectivity. You undoubtedly know that many things were made possible at Lip thanks, in part, to the quality of relations that certain persons, and notably the *animateurs*, had with one another. If this relationship breaks up, that is the end of the *noyau impulseur* and of the whole community.[46]

For Raguénès, then, it was imperative to maintain the *noyau impulseur*; it had become a precondition of the collectivity rather than a product of it. But the vote ironically led, in his words, to the "quasi-total disappearance of the '*noyau impulseur*.'"[47] In March 1980, many who made up one configuration or another of the *noyau impulseur* met. They projected

42   BDIC 702/14/4 Pierre Besançon, "Et pour que Lip vive" [attached to an invitation to a 2AL meeting, April 26, 1980].

43   *Lip Unité*, April-May 1980, 11.

44   Jacquin, "Lip 1973–1981," 372–3.

45   *L'Est républicain*, October 4, 1979.

46   ADD 85J56 "Réunion du conseil d'administration de la 2AL," April 26, 1980.

47   BDIC F delta rés 702/14/4 "Le Pouvoir. 2ème débat du 2.2.1980."

the existence of the *noyau impulseur* back to the first conflict, before it was named and recognized as such, and decided that it had, in fact, been absent for the last two years—since the cooperative had been initially established—during precisely the period when it was recognized and discussed. They concluded that the role the *noyau impulseur* played would need to be performed or Lip would be "'mathematically' exact as to the meaning of Lip," but just "a sympathetic phantasmagoria," with no hope of practical realization.[48] The fate of the *noyau impulseur*, a product of the struggle, but apparently not transferable to the management of the cooperative, had immediate consequences.

The *noyau impulseur* had no officers, but the cooperative did have directors and they were subject to vicious attacks. Workers despised the director brought in from the outside, Libero Penna, but this shared dislike was a unifying factor. However, hierarchical authority exercised by anyone within the collectivity was a source of heated conflict, and undermined the *noyau impulseur* from which these figures were drawn. Garcin refers to "a kind of popular tribunal" held at Palente in December 1980 to judge the pay of members of the management board, though it was in the range of twice the pay of a veteran skilled mechanic in the cooperative, where it had been set when these positions were created. The failure to recognize with pay rises individuals who had taken on new responsibilities in the management boards of the cooperatives was, Garcin affirmed, "as if during the revolution, the generals could become generals without changing their place in the ranks." A slew of unsubstantiated charges of directors selling watches and using the proceeds to take trips and buy cars were aired. Purchase of a hi-fi became evidence of corruption.[49]

Rather than being seen as necessary to maintain and develop the cooperative, individuals in positions of authority, even modestly remunerated, were difficult to accept. No one suffered more than Burgy, whose organizational and administrative skills had been a key to success in 1973. He agreed to take on the thankless job of president of L.I.P. after it received legal status. Within days, a delegation of female OS came to say that they would no longer work at the pace they had previously. A couple of months later, workers sequestered Burgy in his office for twenty-four hours to demand an across-the-board raise for all employees. Others

---

48   BDIC F delta rés 702/6/5 2AL, "Synthèse de la réunion du 'groupe des onze' qui ne demandant pas mieux que d'être plus nombreux … en date du 5 mars 1980."

49   Beurier, "La mémoire des Lip," 130–1, Annexe VIII. AB Interview with Garcin by Beurier [1992], 42–3.

could not forgive him for not hiring their relatives.[50] The *noyau impulseur* and its aura were gone.

Female Workers and the Cooperative

The state's efforts to crush the Palente community accentuated conflicts between *militantes* and the predominantly male union leadership, whether acting as officers or as the *noyau impulseur*. The CFDT-Lip was the element of the workers' culture that changed the least over the course of the conflict. It remained uncomfortable with the activism of women who had come into their own in the struggle, and who expressed interests as women in the workplace that, in the union's view, were subordinate to the interests of the workers as a whole. When the cooperative was launched, some skilled male workers had left for other factories in Besançon; in mid-March 1978, the police commented that "the factories of Palente tend more and more to transform themselves into gynaeceum."[51] In December 1979, of the 342 Lip workers remaining, 55 percent were women.[52]

From the origins of the cooperative, female leaders saw that women were likely to get the short end of the stick. When the statutes of the nascent cooperative were discussed in early December 1977, women posed three-quarters of the questions.[53] In conversation the following spring, a half-dozen female workers recognized that women provided "the backbone of the conflict": "Whether it be for guards at night, demonstrations, distribution of tracts, there are always more women than men." They suggested that the men "were a little ashamed," though this did not lead them to include women in discussing strategy.[54] Demougeot and Piton criticized the authoritarian, undemocratic methods employed by the union leaders when the governing structure of L.I.P. was established in January 1978. They raised further debate when they put forth the idea of designating a woman's representative in the management. A frustrated Piaget—who, the prefecture reported, "contrary to his usual behavior, was furious"—expressed his "deep disappointment at the behavior of the assembly" and threatened to quit. The warning was effective. The

50   Interview with Burgy by Reid, June 7, 2011.
51   ADD 1026W21 RG, March 15, 1978.
52   *Parti pris*, December 1979, 27–8.
53   *Le Matin*, December 8, 1977.
54   "À Lip, des femmes: mille manières de lutter," 33.

next meeting of the General Assembly put this idea aside and instituted the union's proposed governance of the cooperative with little debate.[55] Although Demougeot eventually served as president of the supervisory council of the CAP, she never lost her sense that the all-male management boards of both L.I.P. and the CAP constituted "a sort of aristocracy of militants that had little by little seized the right to speak from the rank and file in order to assure its power."[56]

Demougeot summed up women's experience in the cooperative as a lost opportunity. She contended that women suffered from the absence of a Women's Group, particularly in the negotiations for legalization. In its absence, they had "the feeling of failure," not even getting a retraining program to prepare them for other work in the cooperative. Demougeot believed that the cooperative itself paid the price. She now spoke of particular qualities women could have brought to the enterprise: "The constitution of a woman's group at Lip would have helped to envisage a different cooperative, excluding hierarchy, based on solidarity, sharing, the recognition of the value of each and therefore of 'complementarity'. In fact, we [the workers of Lip] did not know how to innovate and we returned, perhaps for security, to the traditional economic schema."[57]

In 1983, close to half the workers at L.I.P., the CAP, and the CLEF were women, and more than half at Au Chemin de Palente.[58] However, watch assembly and the artisanal projects in which they predominated were on their way out. That year, when Raguénès attributed a lack of workers' participation in the affairs of the cooperatives to "the years of handouts (for there were never more than 100 or so who were active)," Demougeot responded that it would be more accurate to attribute this to the situation of the OS and women in the cooperative:

> It is true that folks remained in the conflict just for the pay that the watch sales allowed, but it is too easy to put the blame on others. Many were at the forefront of the fight, discreetly without being leaders. They found themselves OS again, without anything having changed in relations with the hierarchy. This is particularly the fate of women. There is a lot to be bitter about.[59]

---

55   Three of the twelve members elected to the first supervisory council were women. ADD 1026W23 "Coopérative Lip Note d'exploitation," January 6, 1978.

56   *Le Matin*, March 4, 1986.

57   *Parti pris*, January 15, 1982, 12–13.

58   Faucoup, "Que sont devenus les LIP?," 21:4.

59   Ibid., 20:26. Renaud Sainsaulieu explained the difficulty of maintaining "effective participation" by the failure to recognize the changes the struggle had created

Women remained the OS of the struggle as they remained OS on the shopfloor, with limited opportunities to develop or advance.

The Union and the Cooperative

Referring to individuals like Piton, who charged that L.I.P. had become "a little Gulag"—she refused to punch in and was therefore denied pay— and Christiane André, who walked around the factory in June 1978 with a placard announcing that she was on strike, Piaget said of the conflicts among *les Lip* after the second bankruptcy: "We suffered from a whole group that began to dream without changing their vision of things, directly issued from '73. They still dreamed of a serious confrontation with the system while the whole surrounding context had changed."[60] With the establishment of the cooperative, Piaget recalled the efforts in the spring of 1973 to get workers to think about the situation and not production: "It had been very long and very difficult to get to eventually leaving the slavery [of production] records. And the same thing: it was very difficult to leave the slavery of the struggle."[61] In the era of the "struggle against," Lip workers were frequently spoken of as mutinying sailors. But the situation had changed, Piaget contended. Evoking the end of postwar prosperity and the film *On the Beach*, Piaget reflected in 1980: "The union lived in osmosis with a capitalism in expansion. It is over, but we have trouble admitting it: a little like the submarine crew that demands 'leaves' on the surface when half the planet has exploded … True: twenty years of struggles has turned us into robots."[62] At this point, Piaget was thinking of workers like Burtz, who had no faith that acquiescence to the state would ever lead to jobs for all. He believed that Lip workers should not abandon their demands. In the tradition of the campaign of 1973, he saw *les Lip* fighting for workers throughout France. "People support us because we are—for them—one of the last struggles," he said in the summer of 1979, "one of the last bulwarks against layoffs, dismantlement. One of the last revolts."[63]

---

among women. BDIC F delta rés 702/6/3 Sainsaulieu, "Première étape de réflexion sur les résultats de l'enquête de sociologues" [1978].

60   *Lip Unité*, Second Trimester 1983, 9. "Monique Pitton [*sic*]: "LIP 73, oui! Lip 78 … C'est plutôt moche …," *Commune* 20 (June 15, 1978): 22. Christiane André, "Grève à Lip ou comment on démontre les mécanismes de la soumission," *front libertaire* 94/95 (Summer 1978): 13.

61   Beurier, "La mémoire des Lip," Annexe VIII.

62   *Le Monde*, March 5, 1980, 44.

63   *Lip Unité*, July–August 1979, 9.

Burtz and Laurent were in charge of illegal watch sales after the end of the 90 percent salary coverage. Their commission developed an effective network of dealers in factories and hospitals, and among supporters in Paris and elsewhere. When they ran low on watches, they bought them from wholesalers and labeled them Lip. Unlike the commission in charge of watch sales after the cooperative achieved legal status, they were not dependent on works councils and did not pay the valued-added tax and other charges.[64] At the time of the votes for acceptance of the conditions for legalization of the cooperative in the fall of 1979, illegal sales accounted for more than half the turnover and perhaps three-quarters of Lip income.[65] They funded a significant portion of the salaries workers paid themselves. If selling contraband watches had originally provided the basis for resistance to state and capital, it came to do so for resistance to the management of the cooperative. The young militants who carried out the illegal sales across France sought to get more workers assigned to the job, but L.I.P. directors refused, saying that the rest of the personnel were necessary to effect the transition to legal operations.[66] Piaget saw the necessity of these sales as *les Lip* pursued negotiations, but in the summer of 1979, he spoke of fearing that their continuation would become a way to avoid facing up to the situation confronting the cooperative: "Currently, we hide behind the watch sales and this permits a saving of effort, indispensable nevertheless, if, by the development of economic activities, we want to create the necessary jobs."[67]

Burtz's crew believed the cooperative was a Lip purged of the struggle that had made the Lip for which they fought; they saw L.I.P. seeking reintegration into a system it had refused to accept and that could not accept it. In January 1978, Burtz had joined Demougeot, Enfraze, Géhin, and Laurent in writing and circulating a letter expressing their fear that the cooperative would become an end in itself with no place for the new ideas and institutions developed during the conflict. They sought to have the governing institutions of the cooperative clearly differentiated from those of the struggle.[68] Although they were not successful in keeping the cooperative fully distinct, the police noted in March 1978 that after the leadership of the cooperative reduced the number of general assemblies

64   Interview with Burtz by Reid, June 13, 2017. AB Interview with Burtz by Beurier [1992], 14–15. ADD 1026W21 RG, May 11, 1978.

65   *Libération*, October 4, 1979, 5; November 19, 1979, 19.

66   *Parti pris*, December 1979, 30.

67   *Lip Unité*, July–August 1979, 11.

68   BDIC F delta rés 702/6/3 "Lip: lutter, vivre, construire," January 10, 1978.

per week to two, these changed in character. Workers had always spoken in meetings, but from their place and "tersely." Now, however, workers left the audience to take the microphone previously reserved for those running the meeting.[69]

But as economic issues came to loom over all, workers began to withdraw. Some created tensions by working rather than attending the General Assembly.[70] The number of assemblies held was reduced to one per week and then to one every two weeks. In this context, the success of the sales crew gave it a certain independence within the cooperative. At the time of the debates over the conditions set by the state for the legalization of the cooperative in the fall of 1979, Burtz's group sought to convoke a General Assembly. Management of the cooperative and CFDT-Lip leaders went to the workshops, saying that such a meeting was not official and the lost time would not be paid. The sales crew then came through, affirming that this time would be paid with funds from watch sales. The General Assembly was held and close to half the L.I.P. employees came.[71] Emblematic of the fragmentation and demise of the *noyau impulseur* was the end of the practice of unsigned articles in *Lip Unité* after the vote in October 1979; signed articles laying out the positions of Burtz, Demougeot, and others began to appear.[72]

In the early years of L.I.P., the CFDT-Lip had trouble determining its place. In 1978 union delegates decided not to participate in management of the cooperative.[73] However, as Raguénès said the following year, at the time of the decision to accept the state's terms for legalization, this had not changed things:

In fact, on new grounds, we have kept all—or almost all!—the old habits and ways of thinking. The workers have a tendency to consider the union leaders as employers and the union leaders don't always distinguish themselves from their old bosses! As for the union as an entity, it has practically disappeared. It is no longer the union that impels [*impulse*] and guides the project … This is controlled by economic and technical imperatives, hence an ambient anarchism and *laisser-aller*.[74]

---

69   ADD 1026W21 RG, March 20, 1978.
70   Bondu, "De l'usine à la communauté," 489.
71   *Parti pris*, December 1979, 30.
72   Ségal, "Lip, l'impossible héritage," 49.
73   ADD 1812W31 *La Voix du nord*, October 28, 1978.
74   BDIC delta rés 702/14/4 Raguénès, "Réflexions sur la situation actuelle, le projet et sur la nécessité d'aboutir à une charte" (November–December 1979).

Burtz had led the opposition to the votes in October and November 1979. He argued against leaving Palente, where the variety of activities "constitute the Project and lead us little by little to 'live differently.'"[75] He favored waiting for a victory of the left in 1981, with the expectation the firm would be nationalized. At a minimum, workers should stay until issues like the conditions for early retirement had been resolved in the workers' interest: "the sole real political power relationship at our disposal is Palente."[76] In January 1980, after the vote for acceptance of the terms for legalization, Burtz told the General Assembly that the watch sales could provide the basis for a continuation of the struggle.[77] In the spring of 1980, as legalization was being finalized, he explained: "For our part, we never promised a job for all, but a salary through watch sales. This is an effort that we are going to continue to do and we will not agree to stop this activity, even if we are asked."[78]

Burtz did not believe that the cooperative was viable: sales of legally made watches and artisanal goods and subcontracting jobs in mechanics would not generate enough funds to pay workers. *Les Lip* should continue to sell watches through their network of workers and leftist supporters, while fighting for a permanent solution. They should not give in without assurance of a future that included provisions like state support for research in the watch industry.[79] In a round table in January 1980, Burtz lamented that "the economic took precedence little by little over the social. A new power appeared. We were dispossessed":

> The project of Lip became that of a classic enterprise (L.I.P.) and they wanted this to concern and involve everyone! Look around us: Lip rebuilds itself with its leaders, its hierarchy, its division of labor ... What is needed today is a good local union. Good demands. If not, life will become impossible![80]

Burtz and his group would have nothing to do with the solidarity contract, which they thought should be incumbent only on those who had negotiated the creation of a group of workers without a future at Lip. They reiterated that workers should not leave Palente. No one

---

75 *Lip Unité*, February–March 1980, 7.
76 ADD 45J76 "Lip: le déchirement?," *L'Étincelle* 107 (June 15, 1980): 13. Interview with Burtz by Reid, June 13, 2017.
77 ADD 1026W20 RG, January 11, 1980.
78 *Lip Unité*, February–March 1980, 17.
79 AR Interview with Burtz by Rouaud, May 6, 2004, 3–4, 8–9.
80 *Lip Unité*, February–March 1980, 6, 14.

should have to search for employment elsewhere; the only responsibility of a Lip worker was to fight for employment at Lip. They added that no commission had the right to tell a Lip worker to accept a job elsewhere; if the position was secure and well-paid the worker would take it. The solidarity contract and the commission to supervise it were just a way to force workers to assent to unacceptable jobs.[81] In a final effort, Burtz and Laurent distributed a tract before the General Assembly of June 26, 1980 that blamed the FGM-CFDT for imposing a quietist strategy: abandon the demand of jobs for all and hope that working and not making themselves heard would bring a final settlement. The militants asked: "Why would the authorities pay for what we give them for free: PEACE!" and reiterated their demand: "We will not leave Palente as long as there remains a single Lip without a job." However, their motion to stay at Palente until issues concerning early retirement, job training and placements were addressed received only forty votes from the 281 at the General Assembly.[82] Contraband watch sales stopped after the departure from Palente on March 20, 1981.

Piaget had not participated in the negotiations over the cooperative and was not on the management board, but with legalization of the cooperative, he spoke frequently about the need to work hard to assure its success.[83] He, after all, had been a shop supervisor as well as a union leader. He could be a demanding boss. Géhin heard in Piaget and others the productivist exhortations of the Communists at the dawn of the Fourth Republic: "we must roll up our sleeves" coming from union leaders, whose mission, he believed, should be to protect workers.[84] Burtz and Laurent criticized the CFDT-Lip for failing to defend workers' interests. They did not see it as their responsibility to make the "company," in the form of the cooperative, a more successful exploiter. "It is urgent to demystify Lip '80, this will hurt solidarity, but we must stop. Today, by the choices made, Lip has become worse than a normal factory."[85] Unsuccessful at halting the creation of the cooperative supported by a number of those who had long led the CFDT-Lip, Burtz and Laurent emerged as leaders of the CFDT-Lip in the state-authorized cooperative. Burtz pushed to create a works council in the cooperative because the

81   BDIC F delta rés 702/6/5 Des militants et des syndiqués de CFDT Lip, "Analysons ensemble le contrat," April 22, 1980.

82   ADD 1026W20 RG, June 27, 1980.

83   ADD 1026W20 RG, January 11, 1980. BDIC F delta rés 702/22/1 "Compte rendu de l'AG extraordinaire et de l'AG ordinaire du 26 juin 1980."

84   Jacquin, "Lip 1973–1981," 307–8.

85   *Libération*, March 25, 1980.

supervisory council was not there to protect workers as workers, but as members of the cooperative. He pointed out that a works council was needed to call in a labor inspector to get rules on hours and pay respected since, he thought, those in charge of the cooperative expected workers to exploit themselves.[86]

Burtz, Laurent, and their supporters did what they felt unions should do, such as defend job classifications, contest new regulations concerning hours of work, and demand better pay.[87] This brought them into opposition with Piaget and Raguénès, who saw them as threatening the future of the cooperative. In 1983, the CFDT-Lip was in the uncomfortable position of having *Lip Unité* edited by Raguénès operating out of the confederation's offices in Besançon, while Laurent, a leader of CFDT-Lip in the cooperative, complained that he could not write for *Lip Unité* because his views were not those of the people in charge of it.[88] If, Piaget said in 1980, Lip workers once had the time to debate issues and reach consensus, the need to address the economic survival of the community had now taken its place. Piaget had always been above personal criticism. It was a sign of the collapse of the unity of *les Lip* he had embodied that the regional council of the CFDT felt the need to intervene to repudiate the personal attacks Burtz and Laurent were making on Piaget and Vittot.[89]

Not surprisingly, one site of conflict in the cooperative was the precision mechanics workshop. In February 1980, a dozen of the most highly qualified mechanics had threatened to walk out if their salaries were not raised significantly, saying that they had offers to work elsewhere. They received satisfaction. The affair was handled by the management board and the supervisory council; the General Assembly was not consulted.[90] This precedent concerned Piaget because he believed it was dealt with as a hierarchical capitalist firm would have done, contrary to the democratic project of the cooperative. He saw workers focusing on what they believed they had lost over the years of the conflict, engaging in "paralyzing and dangerous backward-looking thought."[91] The mechanics' demand for a pay rise shocked Raguénès as well: "For seven years we have been living in a dynamic that has little in common with a classic enterprise." That workers would ask for a raise when the future of many

---

86   AB Interview with Burtz by Beurier [1992], 18–20.
87   Beurier, "La mémoire des Lip," 157–8.
88   Faucoup, "Que sont devenus les LIP?," 20:27.
89   ADD 45J80 Records of CFDT Union régionale Franche-Comté, March 5, 1981.
90   *Libération*, March 26, 1980, 14.
91   *Lip Unité*, Third-Fourth Trimester 1983, 13–14.

L.I.P. workers was unresolved "poses for me a serious question about the future of humanity."[92] He believed the workers' demand was based on the traditional union logic of shared individual interests rather than a communal interest. This was encouraged by a return to the diversity of individual jobs in the factory, "where each has a tendency to stick to their own domain and to refuse to look at what is going on elsewhere."[93] Raguénès saw in acts like the mechanics' demand for a raise a betrayal of what had been new in Lip, the community forged in the struggle.

Should Raguénès have been surprised? Parmentier reflected that because many in the *noyau impulseur* were rooted in the ACO, they were more idealist than the more materialist rank and file:

> At first, you succeeded in getting across this idealism to the mass. The satisfactions of all sorts that the whole of *les Lip* received from the aspect of stardom, the marked interest of the media for what you were then doing, made it such that everyone in the rank and file got something out of it. Each Lip worker could say something like this: "what I experience right now is more enriching than what I experienced yesterday" … This masks a fundamental fact: people are not motivated by an ideal, but by a material interest. When the stardom aspect disappeared and there remained only material interest, then it is the 'individual and immediate interest' that takes precedence.[94]

Piaget had recognized this when he told local PCF leaders in a meeting at Palente in 1977:

> A Christian background does not always prepare one to gauge how much time is needed to change man. We believed we had changed. All of a sudden we see that we have changed little. There are our dreams. And the reality that reminds you that it takes a long time … our experience, it helped us to gauge how much time is needed, in a nation like the USSR or China for example, to change things.[95]

---

92   BDIC F delta rés 702/14/4, "Compte-rendu du conseil d'administration de la 2AL," April 26, 1980.

93   BDIC F delta rés 702/15/1 "Débat du 20 janvier 1979," 17.

94   *Lip Unité*, February–March 1980, 12.

95   ADD 177J13 Transcript of a discussion between Lip leadership and local PCF leaders at Palente [1977].

The recognition that change takes time could lead *les Lip* back to the past. When Chaniot assumed direction of the cooperative in 1983, he found that workers rarely spoke to him of the past ten years, but referred constantly to Fred Lip.[96] Piaget himself wrote to his old boss in 1982 "about this adventure that consists in constructing an enterprise":

> What is certain is that you will remain among us today when we are trying more or less awkwardly to construct a cooperative. You remain among us and you are a reference all the time … Very often during the week, we hear: Fred Lip would not have accepted that, he would not put up with this mess (in thinking for example of the awkward management that we have had).[97]

Faced with the difficulties of making L.I.P. a functioning enterprise, Piaget may have thought of the standards Fred Lip set, but to achieve them he returned to efforts to develop participation that had roots in the conflicts with his old boss.

Workshop Councils and Entrepreneurs

"We created the cooperatives from the top. Now we need to recreate them from the bottom," Parmentier said in February 1980.[98] Why was this so difficult? In the long struggles of 1973 and 1976, workers had valued the apparent equality of all and the relative lack of hierarchical structures. What had worked then was more difficult to sustain in the cooperative. Workers had fought for their jobs, and now those who had them craved the security and stability they provided. They wanted to "hang on to their familiar spot and withdraw into the reassuring cocoon of their work station, like shells that embed themselves on the solid structure of the rock."[99] Workers were particularly resistant to changes in their work that could require the exercise of authority over others. A frustrated Piaget summed up the situation: "The workers' mentality is turned toward: you give the orders, and me, I execute. They repeated the schemas they had

---

96   *Libération*, June 22, 1983, 12
97   Charles Piaget to Fred Lip, March 9, 1982 in *M Le Magazine du Monde*, October 21, 1989, 11.
98   BDIC F delta rés 702/14/4 "Le pouvoir. 2ème débat du 2.2.1980."
99   Bondu, "De l'usine à la communauté," 468.

already learned."[100] Change, they feared, would break the valued bonds created in the workplace by opposition to authority.

The cooperative raised a fundamental issue at the heart of the movement in 1973. Was participation a value in itself or simply a means of making their efforts more effective? In 1979, Piaget explained that the "taste for democracy" remained very strong, but manifested itself in the cooperative too much in "contestation" and not enough in "participation." The cooperative did not as yet have personnel delegates, but when introduced, Piaget said that they should remain "the conscience, but that conscience will not be of contestation as in enterprises where there is not participation; it must be a struggle to animate discussion about participation, about self-management."[101] He looked for other ways to challenge the concentration of power in the cooperative than by recourse to the counter-power of the union.

For Piaget, the democracy of the struggle centered in the General Assembly impeded development in the cooperative. He questioned the effects of a dependence on the collectivity that he and the *noyau impulseur* had nurtured and evoked to garner support for their decisions from workers:

> [W]e brought problems to the General Assembly, but without ever arriving at individual responsibility with respect to the objectives ... In fact, we were building on the momentum of the struggle when we did not individualize and it sufficed to make calls to the collectivity. Starting with the construction [of the cooperative], our meetings ended without anyone feeling personally responsible with respect to specific points. In this situation, it is indeed a matter of collective decisions, but they must necessarily result in individuals taking responsibility.[102]

As for the supervisory council of the cooperative, Piaget believed it had fallen under the control of two or three workers. In November 1978, he compared the situation to the control by small groups of ostensibly democratic communes in the People's Republic of China.[103]

Piaget responded by seeking to shift discussion and decision-making as much as possible to workshop councils, which would have the qualities

---

100   Piaget, "'Des trésors d'imagination,'" 163.
101   Ibid., 167–9.
102   *Lip Unité,* Second Trimester 1983, 11.
103   *Idées ouvrières,* November 1978, 3–5.

of the commissions at the heart of the struggle in 1973. He wanted the supervisory council itself to be composed of representatives of work-shop councils and to take a more important role as an intermediary with the management board.[104] Piaget worked with Parmentier in the mechanics workshop to develop the first and most successful of these councils. Faced with the union, which Piaget now saw as a "counter-power that acted more in the mode of systematic obstruction," and a management board distanced from the shopfloor, he believed that Par-mentier, drawing on his experience far from Lip, could be instrumental in effecting change: "Someone was needed to shake this kind of general lymphatism."[105] At first, Parmentier noted, the mechanics did not see the need for the workshop council and had to be assigned to attend meet-ings. Piaget and Parmentier raised the issues of job rotation, planning, and workers' control of their work; the mechanics initially responded by going to management and demanding a raise. However, Parmentier soon recognized a change: "Starting from a very trade unionist conception of work as in principle a pain in the ass and that it is right to do as little as possible, they begin now to ask if work could not become interesting if one saw it differently."[106] Groups of eight to ten met for an hour each week in a workshop to discuss all elements of production, and once a month all the groups in a sector got together to talk through issues.[107] In this way, the councils took shape, doing away with foremen and setting up teams to handle maintenance issues.[108] Piaget put his faith in the development of workshop councils—which he saw as going beyond the goals unions had traditionally set for themselves—to respond to the issues raised by the development of a cooperative:

> It is a new role for a trade unionism that must no longer identify itself with a monolithic counter-power, but recognize advancing toward other objectives than simply to make money. We hold that, in the workshop councils, the problems that touch on the life, the future, the desire to be together also be discussed.[109]

---

104 Ibid.
105 *Lip Unité*, Second Trimester 1983, 10.
106 BDIC F delta rés 702/14/4, "Le pouvoir. 2ème débat du 2.2.1980."
107 *Parti Pris*, February 1979, 22.
108 *Libération*, March 26, 1980, 14.
109 This text draws on BDIC 702/14/4 "Le pouvoir. 2ème débat du 2.2.1980," and the slightly edited version in *Lip Unité*, April–May 1980, 6.

The workshop council in precision mechanics was particularly innovative in breaking down the division between production and sales. At
first, workers were quite reticent and the management board skeptical of
the mechanics' ability to secure business. But the project was a success.
"Brave improvised door-to-door salesmen," in Jeanningros' words, they
visited hundreds of small businesses and obtained a number of jobs.[110]
The mechanics knew what the machinery at their disposal could do, and
proved, in the words of one observer, to be "steadfast and imaginative
negotiators."[111] Each week Piaget posted for all to see the fixed charges
like rent and electricity and the wages and billable hours. By the time
he retired in 1983, the mechanics workshop was close to breaking even
in a L.I.P. being bled by losses in watch production.[112] It developed a
procedure to govern new hires. Each time turnover rose 15,000 francs
per month for three consecutive months it brought in a new employee,
using criteria set by the management board.[113] The self-management
of the workshop council was limited, but its successes were rooted in
important elements learned during the conflict itself—the dissemination of information about the situation of the workshop and the practice
of sending workers outside the factory, this time to make their case to
clients rather than supporters.

Yet there were limits. The management board did not involve the
workshops in decision-making, leading to a "'sheep-like' participation"
in the direction of the cooperative.[114] This in turn encouraged workshop
councils to continue to think in terms of a boss/worker relationship.[115]
However, it is significant that at L.I.P. important elements of the self-
management from which the movement had always differentiated itself
emerged as a response to market and union pressures. This, in turn,
led Piaget to recognize a limit on the self-management project at L.I.P.
Mechanics clearly preferred sales work to taking responsibility as "little
bosses."[116] In this they were no different than workers in the CAP. Self-
management of production was designed to counter bureaucracy and

110   Jeanningros, "LIP 1973–1981: côté armements," 20–1.
111   Libération, March 26, 1980, 14.
112   Interview with Piaget by Reid, June 7, 2011.
113   ADD 45J71 "Compte-rendu du conseil de surveillance," August 21, 1979.
114   BDIC F delta rés 702/22/5 Bureau de 2AL to François Espagne, secrétaire
genéral de la Confédération des SCOP, June 2, 1981.
115   BDIC F delta rés 702/6/5 "Propositions pour un shema [sic] de fonctionne-
ment possible …" [no author, c. 1980]. Piaget, "'Des trésors d'imagination,'" 167. Bondu,
"De l'usine à la communauté," 490. Jacquin, "Lip 1973–1981," 371–2, 376–7.
116   Burgy and Piaget, "L'aventure des Coopératives LIP."

hierarchy, whose most immediate manifestation was the shopfloor supervisor, the very position Piaget had occupied while leading the union. The
cooperative led Piaget to think about those needed to take the place of
the "little boss." What L.I.P. and the other cooperatives lacked, Piaget
believed, were what he termed *animateurs* and entrepreneurs.

All union leaders lamented the paucity of *animateurs*, in both "struggles against" and "struggles for." In discussion with Action Committee
members in November 1973, Piaget recognized that however much the
struggle had changed workers, "we lacked *animateurs*, guys who take
charge of the life [*animation*] of the struggle, and I believe that this is
one of the afflictions of the working class."[117] In the period of the cooperative, Piaget recalled, "We launched the idea à la Mao Zedong, launch
fifty cooperatives," but the great leap forward did not take place.[118] Piaget
and Burgy saw this lack of *animateurs*, rather than of ideas, as the reason
why Lip did not develop more cooperatives that could have provided
employment to those workers, almost half of the total, who did not get
jobs in the six cooperatives that were created.[119] The cooperative experience led Piaget to think that the goal should be a society in which all
become *animateurs* of the possible in the collectivity, that is to say "entrepreneurs," purged of the egoism and "cupidity" that the term conveyed
in capitalism.[120]

This was the time that prominent Second Left intellectuals and
exponents of self-management—including Pierre Rosanvallon and the
JEC and *Les Cahiers de mai* veteran Patrick Viveret, who had played a
leading role in the PSU working with Lip workers in 1973[121]—looked at
the experience of Lip and recognized that Sartre's group-in-fusion could
not persist there as such. For such struggles to avoid dependence on the
state, they needed to turn to the "entrepreneur, freed of the pejorative
reference to capitalism."[122] Those who took responsibility in the Lip cooperatives spoke this language of the entrepreneur as well. Jean-Claude
Piquard, president of the CAP, referred in 1981 to the need for workers

---

117   "Un pas vers la révolution," 30.
118   Brangolo, "Les filles de Lip (1968–1981)," 388.
119   Burgy and Piaget, "L'aventure des Coopératives LIP."
120   Interview with Piaget by Féret, "A voix nue," France Culture (2011).
121   Hervé Hamon and Patrick Rotman, *L'Effet Rocard* (Paris: Stock, 1980), 110.
122   Pierre Rosanvallon, "Mais où est donc passé l'autogestion?," *Passé présent* 4
(1984): 188. Rosanvallon and Viveret rehabilitated the term "entrepreneur" as part of
the socialist and self-management project. *Pour une nouvelle culture politique* (Paris,
1977), 124–5. This was an element of a broader movement on the "Rocardian" left. Frank
Georgi, "'Le moment Lip' dans l'histoire de l'autogestion en France," *Semaine sociale
Lamy* supplement to no. 1631 (May 19, 2014): 70.

416 OPENING THE GATES

to understand the cooperative's decisions "so that everyone, bit by bit, can take the role of entrepreneur."[123] His successor, Dominique Enfraze, contended that "in an enterprise—in any case a cooperative—we must all become responsible and entrepreneurs."[124] Jeanningros spoke of the first fifteen months after the departure from Palente as a time when *les Lip* "became entrepreneurs, on their own account."[125]

If there could not be self-management without socialism, what had been the *noyau impulseur* came to believe that self-management would also require that workers be entrepreneurs. The notion of the entrepreneur embedded in the community became the way to think the responsibility that self-management allowed and on which it depended. Work as they knew it, Piaget lamented, made workers wary of change, fostering a "worker conservatism" that was the opposite of what the worker should be: "an entrepreneur of one's life," capable of working and living differently.[126] However, he believed "all are capable of a treasure of imagination when they are actively involved and are deprogrammed from stultifying work."[127] The answer to unemployment was people with ideas, people "who want to undertake [*entreprendre*]: 'I want to be an entrepreneur'"—"each must create his employment."[128] Using the term entrepreneur, Piaget addressed the way that capitalism (and the security the union leadership could be seen to have offered) had created workers who were not prepared to take power and responsibility—the precondition for self-management. His goal was not the individualization of self-management at the heart of contemporary capitalist creeds, but to bring the qualities revealed in the "self-management of the struggle" to the workplace. The Lip conflict in 1973 was born of the "thirty glorious years," an economic prosperity that generated a sensibility that made it possible and incumbent upon all to think how work could be made more humane. However, in the recession that followed, the idea that this was not possible unless the entrepreneur latent in each worker took the place of the *noyau impulseur* became Piaget's way of

---

123   *Lip Unité*, December 1981, 11.

124   *Lip Unité*, First Trimester 1983, 17.

125   "Les Nouveaux Lips: Des Entrepreneurs," *Gardarem lo Larzac* 74 (June 1982). Jacquin noted the appearance of the figure of the entrepreneur at Lip as well. "Lip 1973–1981," 392-3.

126   *Parti Pris*, February 1979, 23.

127   Piaget, "'Des trésors d'imagination,'" 166-7.

128   AB Interview with Piaget by Beurier [1992], 4, 46. Reference to the engineers who founded 4M recur in these discussions. When workers demanded wage increases from the cooperative, Piaget contrasted them to the 4M engineers who paid themselves a minimum wage. Ibid., pp. 48-9.

reconceptualizing in a new situation the initiatives *les Lip* had shown in their earlier struggle.

Conclusion

Les Lip faced the difficulty of sustaining the community they had made in 1973 while addressing the problems that arose in the afterlife of this "revolution." Piaget found himself thinking about the Soviet Union under Stalin, the Cultural Revolution in China, and Vietnam after the Communist victory. He had long recognized the importance for those engaged in struggles of learning from the exchange of experiences. With creation of the cooperative at Lip, such experiences included the relations of the collectivity in the name of which the struggle was fought to the community born of the struggle with aspirations to live and work differently; of the *noyau impulseur* to workplace democracy; of a male-led union to expressions of a working-class feminism; and of self-exploitation to self-management in the cooperative. Such "contradictions," to use Raguénès' term, and the efforts to address them, were experiences that, in their ambiguity and irresolution, demanded the attention of all those pursuing social change. Lip remained a site where the opening of the gates brought life to the aspirations of '68ers within and without Palente. The cooperative rallied supporters, who saw in the difficulties it confronted a place they could pursue the projects of 1968 in the increasingly hostile environment a decade later.

13

From Besançon to Gdansk

A majority of Lip wanted, willingly or unwillingly, lightheartedly or all
torn apart, to shed the Spirit of Lip; the force of things had become so
heavy that many had the impression of walking with lead weights.

Yet History shows that sometimes the Spirit becomes a homebody
and decides not to leave those it inhabited.

An angel passes, hope remains, as long as something remains.

—Conseil d'administration du CLEF[1]

There is something that is happening, developing, that makes it such that
Lip is a site not directly assimilable to the whole of society such as it is
at the current time with its mediocrity, its emptiness and the fact that
there are no longer many places where hope can really catch hold. For
example, at the current time in social thought (that is to say, in the labor
movement), there is a complete void. It is not in the classical social field
that one can find points of attachment to enable our hope to live and to
see how it can advance. On the other hand, at Lip, there is something
… Furthermore, what happened and what is going to happen soon at
Lip is decisive to knowing where to put one's hopes. For if Lip produces
something that completely deviates from what we had thought, if it produces a normalized enterprise (therefore nothing interesting) … it will
no longer be necessary to nourish ourselves with speeches or to bury
our heads in the sand as we have done for fifty or 100 years. It will no

---

1   ADD 45J72 "Compte-rendu du conseil d'administration du CLEF," December
12, 1979.

longer be possible to say "socialism … self-management … we have not achieved it because of conditioning … we did it the wrong way … we'll do better the next time … those who came before us did it the wrong way, but we are going to do better …" This is what we have done for 100 years. We replaced the word socialism with self-management, saying that was better, that we see more clearly now, when it is the same thing. But Lip has lasted five years and we can no longer honestly invoke the pretext of confinement by the system to say "we failed, we will do better next time." If it fails, that will say that our hopes should no longer concentrate on this. Even so, it is not necessary to lose all reason to hope: but it will be necessary to go someplace radically different, I do not know where. Without a doubt, not religion. In contrast, if this gives something, we can say that there are perhaps reasons to continue and to hope a little for society, for the human community.

—Dominique Bondu[2]

A distinguishing characteristic of the Lip movement in 1973, and of the way it became a primary site for the expression and development of aspirations associated with May 1968, was the cooperation and dialogue it established and maintained between workers and intellectuals and politicized youth, whether in the visits, the mini-commissions, or the Women's Group. This "'opening of the gates' … is what permitted the expression of a true concrete utopia in the enclosure of a provincial factory."[3] The effort was made to renew this experience in the second struggle. In late July 1977, members of the CFDT-Lip, anchored by Raguénès, published an open letter to intellectuals, saying that the syndics were threatening to remove the machines from Palente. This would lead to the destruction of "the human community":

The departure of the machines would correspond to "their will" to reduce us to unemployment, to despair, to deportation. This in a world where, in the name of economic pseudo-imperatives, man is swept from trade to trade, from city to city, from place to place, thus losing all personal and collective identity. Our fight for employment is fundamentally a "quest for that identity." We know your relentlessness to denounce "all forms of Gulag." This is one, new, less dramatic, but, without a doubt, effective.[4]

2   BDIC F delta rés 702/15/1 "Débat du 20 janvier 1979," 8.
3   ADD 45J108 Lip Livre Part 3/Bondu, 3–4.
4   Libération, July 30–1, 1977, 7.

The reference to the Gulag was an appeal to the New Philosophers. New Philosopher André Glucksmann, along with Sartre and a few other intellectuals, intervened with the Minister of Justice to put a stop to the syndics' action.[5]

In August 1977, Raguénès suggested that an association be formed to collect funds to buy Palente from the syndics.[6] Nothing came of this at the time, but in December 1977, after the workers had voted to launch a cooperative, Raguénès took the lead in organizing the Association des Amis de Lip (2AL), with the initial goals of popularization and fund raising: "We were 100,000 for the 'great march' of 1973. So why not 100,000 today?!! We are betting that all these friends of Lip are still there and ready, once again, to respond to our call."[7] Initially, the 2AL drew on individuals mobilized by the earlier conflict. Pierre Rosanvallon, for example, recruited in his circle.[8] By the summer of 1979, the 2AL had 8,000 members, drawn primarily from the liberal professions, teachers and retirees; two years later, it reached a peak of 10,000 members.[9] The 2AL drew intellectuals from across the spectrum, making contact with Frossard and Glucksmann. It was particularly pleased when Glucksmann, in a "spectacular intervention" on television, gave out the contact information for the 2AL.[10] Michel Jeanningros suggested that the 2AL contact the left Gaullists through Charbonnel, who responded with a strong letter of support.[11]

The 2AL fund-raising mission changed as the cooperative evolved. It began with a call for funds to purchase the machines, the stock, and the brand name for the new venture.[12] However, it quickly recognized that

---

5   Saint-Germain and Souletie, "Le voyage à Palente," 72.

6   *Le Matin*, August 3, 1977.

7   BDIC F delta rés 702/4/4 2AL, "Une lutte pour aujourd'hui et demain ..." [1978]. At the end of November 1977, when *les Lip* voted to form a cooperative, Neuschwander commissioned a poll with a sample size of 1,000 weighted to reflect the population of France: 65 percent were sympathetic to the actions of Lip workers while 6 percent were hostile. If a public subscription for Lip (perhaps accompanied by a discount on watches) were launched, 45 percent would participate and 35 percent would refuse. The remainder in both cases had no opinion. AFGM-CFDT 1B577 SOFRES "Les réactions des Français face à l'action du personnel de Lip. Décembre 1977."

8   BDIC F delta rés 702/12/4 Pierre Rosanvallon to 2AL, March 25, 1978.

9   BDIC F delta rés 702/14/4 Notes on the meeting of the conseil d'administration of the 2AL [March 1979]. *Lip Unité*, July–August 1979, 5. ADD 45AJ68 "Rapport d'activité: A.A.L. Janvier 78 à Janvier 79." BDIC F delta rés 702/22/5 Bureau de 2AL to François Espagne, secrétaire genéral de la Confédération des SCOP, June 2, 1981.

10   ADD 85J56 2AL, "Compte-rendu du conseil d'administration du 20 mai 1978."

11   ADD 85J56 2AL, "Compte-rendu du conseil d'administration du 4 mars 1978." ADD 45J62 2AL to Jean Charbonnel, June 21, 1978.

12   BDIC F delta rés 702/14/4 2AL letter to recruit members, January 1978.

this was too ambitious and set its sights on securing financial backing for starting up the cooperative, which could not borrow funds on its own. If it could gather at least 1 million francs, the 2AL believed this would give it the credibility needed to play the role of go-between in financial transactions. In particular, it thought this would allow it to obtain advances from municipalities, which could not provide funds to enterprises, but could to associations. In March 1978, the 2AL spoke of Besançon quite possibly providing an advance of 500,000 francs. This was seen as important to ensure the cooperative would be included if a state plan for watchmaking were to emerge from a victory of the left in the legislative elections: "The role of the 2AL could be to contribute to making the cooperative credible as an enterprise in a system that is still, for the time being, capitalism. This can be important as well insofar as the cooperative must absolutely become industrially operational in order to inscribe itself full-blown in the plan for restructuring the watch industry." However, that said, the 2AL did not want to be the handmaiden of a state socialism. It sought to ensure that whether or not the left controlled the state, workers' creativity and control remained the key to the fight for jobs: the role the 2AL saw itself playing was to "adjust (dialectically)" workers' control on the one hand and state and capital on the other.[13]

When the left lost the elections of March 1978 and the possibility of a state plan to restructure the watch industry disappeared, *les Lip* found themselves engaged in creating a cooperative that they had approved without considering what this would entail. The 2AL played an integral role in the development of the cooperative and in building national support for it, although it never formed mini-commissions like those active in cities throughout France in 1973.[14] The 2AL encouraged all to visit the workshops at Palente and to purchase goods the workers made: "You will certainly find among all our products the little gift that will please your friends on your return." In June 1979, the 2AL asked members to invite Lip workers to social gatherings so that they could spread the word and sell their goods. As part of a campaign dubbed "Special Friendship," 100,000 catalogs of Lip products were sent to 2AL members to distribute. Volunteers were solicited who would take two or three watches to sell in their circle of friends.[15] In 1981, the CAP sent 2AL volunteers packages of products made by *les Lip* with more than three dozen different silk scarves, pillows, sacks, wall clocks, and wooden

13   BDIC F delta rés 702/14/4 2AL "Discussion sur les buts de la 2AL," March 1978.
14   *Lip Actualité*, December 1978, 1.
15   *Lip Actualité*, June 1979, unpaginated.

products, including toys and puzzles. For selling them at a discounted price for three months, supporters received a quartz clock named the "Spéciale 2AL."[16] The 2AL also solicited funds for particular projects. In December 1980, for instance, it discussed constructing a building for the restaurant and decided that 2AL bureau members "will take their 'pilgrim's staff' to visit a certain number of people 'who could be interested.'"[17]

Created in December 1977 to support the nascent industrial cooperative L.I.P., the 2AL increasingly devoted its efforts to activities "outside-the-plan," referring to the plan created in the effort to achieve legalization of the cooperative; these included the artisanal groups, the printing press, and projects of the CLEF.[18] In the words of 2AL president Pierre Besançon, "Imagination is here again: it has to be given the means to become a reality."[19] In February 1979, the 2AL explained that the artisanal and non-industrial activities at Palente were where a difference in line with the aspirations of 1968 to live and work differently could be found:

> It appears indispensable to add that these activities outside-the-plan not be perceived by the workers as 'a wage while waiting', before entering the cooperative, but as a space of creativity and communication. The project of *les Lip* will not retain all its significance unless the workers earn their bread in such a way as to make the industrial logic co-habit closely with another way of experiencing the enterprise, in its full human dimension.[20]

Between 1978 and 1981, the 2AL collected 1,200,000 francs that it used to invest in new cooperatives when they were launched by Lip workers or for the specific needs of operating cooperatives. It set up a revolving fund that made loans to L.I.P. and the CAP cooperatives. As these were paid back, it made new loans. The cooperative printshop La Lilliputienne, which printed *Lip Unité*, joined the CAP after the move from Palente. Under the direction of Lip militant Marc Géhin, it purchased machines—"the 2AL hit us with some bread"—and set up

---

16   *Lip Unité*, January–February 1981, 2.

17   BDIC F delta rés 702/14/3 "Compte-rendu de la réunion du 9 décembre 1980—Bureau de la 2AL."

18   ADD 45J112 "Rapport d'activité: AAL janvier 78 à janvier 79." For the CLEF, see below.

19   *Lip Unité*, December 1978, 10–11.

20   *Lip Unité*, February 1979, 2.

"a super cool printing press" as a cooperative separate from the CAP in November 1981; all workers received the same salary and shared work responsibilities.[21] In 1981, the 2AL bought health insurance for sixty workers, "the marathoners of unemployment," for whom positions had not yet been found in the cooperatives and who had been on unemployment too long to receive coverage.[22]

In the depression on the left after March 1978, the 2AL saw Lip as having a particular role to play as a site of national reflection:

> It seems necessary to move beyond the time of the slogan to find the routes of coherent and effective actions through which the workers' movement can advance. In effect, since the loss of the elections, there are no more political perspectives on the left to energize the working class. The cooperative at Lip is certainly not the global means of responding to this complex set of questions. But the new fight for employment that the workers are beginning through the cooperative can serve by its questions, by its contradictions, as a basis for a new reflection on the politics of employment and of industrial redeployment.

Picking up a theme repeated throughout Lip's history, the 2AL presented Lip's open engagement with the difficulties it confronted as of particular value to the left:

> We must speak of ambiguities, contradictions, and not enclose this conflict in a political, trade union and economic language ... The Lip conflict has an advantage, that it is not closed in on itself; it opens itself continually and accepts being challenged. This allows diverse strata to feel concerned by this fight and to intervene.[23]

The 2AL saw working for the renaissance of Lip as therapy for the left. It realized that media interest in the sensational that had been a key to the success of the movement in 1973 had little place for such discussion. The 2AL envisaged meetings in cities outside of Besançon in which workers and Association board members would discuss issues of concern to Lip now. The members of the 2AL could then step in. "The

---

21   *Lip Unité*, December 1981, 23. ADD 45J108 Lip Livre Part 3/Géhin, 29.

22   *Lip Unité*, January–February 1981, 1, 3, 8 [quoted]; December 1981, 17; May 1982, 25.

23   ADD 85J56 2AL, "Compte-rendu du conseil d'administration du 20 mai 1978."

424 OPENING THE GATES

friends on the outside who are 'well placed' could also send word back, write, because we now have a lot of trouble getting past the media blockade. What appears in the press is the dramatic event (sales of watches, police raids, suicide of a worker …) and much less what is happening deep down."[24]

The 2AL presented realization of the goals of *les Lip* as instrumental to realizing their own:

> Let us be clear: our participation constitutes neither an "act of charity" nor a "good act" and still less the walk-on parts given a few names inscribed as moral backing on a list of big name [supporters]! In reality, and this is fundamental, if we are, evidently, exterior to the Lip enterprise, we are not, for all that, exterior to their struggle. We identify with this fight that, for the majority of us, connects in substance and form with that which we conduct on other terrains … We make sure that in no case does the control of the struggle escape them [Lip workers]. We doubtless have a specific role to play: on two fronts: operational and, perhaps, prophetic.

The 2AL appealed to those looking for an alternative in a "blocked society":

> We take note that the Lip struggle, since '73, has an important resonance in all social classes (the working class, of course, but also middle classes, intellectuals, etc. …). Likewise, recognizing themselves in it are numerous militants looking for new forms of intervention and organization in a blocked society. For them, and this is the prophetism, the imagination, the creativity of *les Lip* prefigure another possible way to live new social relations in the enterprise.[25]

As Pierre Besançon explained in the summer of 1979: "For the 2AL that brings together 8,000 people, it is not only employment that excites the gathering around Lip, it is a philosophical, social, human project."[26]

---

24   ADD 85J56 "Compte-rendu du conseil d'administration de la 2AL. Samedi 26 avril 1980."
25   BDIC F delta rés 702/4/4 2AL, "Une lutte pour aujourd'hui et demain …"
26   *Lip Unité*, July–August 1979, 5.

The Mirror

External support was at once necessary and problematic. In 1979, the General Assembly and then the union leadership of the CFDT-Lip, after meeting with a representative of the FGM-CFDT, agreed that the cooperative would accept armaments contracts. These could provide employment for workers on list C.[27] Although some sought to be named conscientious objectors and exempted from work making weapons, the issue was more problematic outside of Palente.[28] Parmentier explained that supporters particularly valued the difference they saw in Lip:

> The image of Lip that interests the external militant is not the same [as for *les Lip*]: the exemplary struggle for employment, of course, but it is also the proof that things can be done and lived differently, an enterprise created differently. With regard to 1.5 million unemployed, the objective that each and every one of the 380 Lip has a job is not essential for the exterior. The interpretation of success on the inside and on the outside differs. To make armaments will appear a more serious affair for the friends than the problem of full employment at Lip.[29]

The contract never came through—the cooperative was, after all, still operating illegally and it may have been a gambit to get the workers to reject the state's terms for attaining legality—but the conflict Parmentier discussed was real.

Questions raised by the relation to the world outside the gates took many forms. On the one hand, the goal of providing employment for all made new hires from the outside difficult. Piaget framed the question in terms of the importance of supporters in the earlier conflict: "We should have sprinkled the enterprise with people from the outside, a little like in '73 ... We could have thus seen ourselves in another mirror, found points of reference. That sprinkling would have been necessary at all echelons and would have allowed us to stop navel-gazing."[30] The issue played out most clearly, however, in the workers' identification with the

---

27   Ibid., 3, 16–17. Jacquin, "Lip 1973–1981," 364–5.
28   Jeanningros, "LIP 1973–1981: côté armements," 22. In response to the request of anti-militarists on the works council, Neuschwander had earlier shifted thirty jobs in armaments to the production of civilian goods like deluxe cigarette lighters. Ibid., 18–19.
29   *Lip Unité*, July–August 1979, 7.
30   *Lip Unité*, Second Trimester 1983, 10.

images that supporters and the media created of them. Raguénès asked if, in 1973, "we opened up [to the outside] because we knew we were going to be admired, because we sensed that we would be applauded?"[31] The representations of the workers reinforced the "myth of uniformity and of unity" among them that made awareness of internal differences with the creation of cooperatives appear "as so many ruptures."[32] Géhin recognized that when there was conflict within the community, it closed itself off, fearful that outsiders would take sides.[33] Bondu brought these insights together. Closure to outsiders, he wrote:

> comes from a detrimental evolution of the collectivity. At a certain point, the opening became an illusion because the other (the exterior) was transformed into a mirror in which [les Lip] looked at themselves. As long as they find themselves attractive in the mirror, they accept opening up, but when they find themselves ugly, they refuse the mirror! The first point is therefore that they do not want to look at themselves … It is an 'I-Collective' that was built up and that no longer accepts referrals to the exterior … this group forged such an identity that it finished by driving out the dimension of the other in itself (the opening) … It is the sign that the group is hardening into an identity institution.[34]

"I would call this," said Bondu, "in a (little too) provocative fashion, alienation. Playing on the word—one says an asylum of the mad [aliénés], of the crazy—but this wordplay is not innocent …"[35]

When the difficult decisions that the cooperative saw itself as having to make were labeled by its supporters as unjust toward a portion of the community, its leadership rejected the criticism. From Géhin's perspective, the failure to address these critiques and the alternative courses of action proposed from the outside ultimately led the cooperative to an impasse.[36] Outsiders, he believed, could help Lip deal with the conflicts within. Bondu too felt that Lip had seen an "insidious" closing off to the outside and a consequent degradation of the community: "a community in which the other lives is real … otherwise it degenerates."[37] A gated community is not a community. Raguénès agreed: "There is a moment of

31   ADD 45J108 Lip Livre Part 1/Conversation 2, 14.
32   BDIC F delta rés 702/14/4 Pierre Besançon, "Et pour que Lip vive" [1980].
33   ADD 45J108 Lip Livre Part 1/Conversation 2, 15; Part 2/"Lip, déjà demain," 38.
34   Ibid., Part 2/"Lip, déjà demain," 38bis.
35   Ibid., Part 1/3, 10.
36   Ibid., Part 3/Géhin, 18.
37   Ibid., Part 1/B, 13.

uprising—the open gates of '73—when men are, as it were, transcended, carried by grace, and this we must fully restore even if it is sullied afterward. If we take away this impetus of grace, there remains a reality quite flat and fixed, especially as we consider the future."[38] The 2AL was rooted in Raguénès' ties to left Catholics and ex-Maoists, including Benny Lévy and Alain Geismar. Its goal was to maintain Palente as a site where 1968 activism and elements of Raguénès' wise mad man remained alive in an otherwise inhospitable world.

Keeping the Gates Open

The 2AL became a place where supporters could engage with *les Lip* who sought to live and work differently. The fifty-person board of directors of the 2AL was composed half by workers in L.I.P. and the artisanal and other projects at Palente and half by external supporters. Although the General Assembly still debated and approved all major decisions, the 2AL, as the representative of external support, was a greater presence at Palente than the mini-commissions had been in 1973. The 2AL sought to keep the Lip community from turning in on itself. In Bondu's words, "the Association assures in a meaningful way the maintenance of the 'opening of the gates' of the community of Palente, which has permitted impressive social intermixing, fertilizing so many ingenious initiatives and original ideas."[39] In addition to popularization—it financed the production of *Lip Unité*—and fund raising, the 2AL fairly quickly assumed another function as a place "from which a reflection is elaborated, an audit of the project and a tool to make it known to the exterior [*Lip Unité*]": "an attempt to make a dialectical connection (rarely expressed) between the realities of organization and the profound experience of *les Lip*."[40]

The 2AL saw its mission as both to foster exchange among *les Lip* and to break the insular nature of the cooperative: "Before this kind of Tower of Babel, in which the languages are economic, union, communitarian, etc. ... the 2AL has taken a certain number of initiatives directed toward the reconstruction of a dialogue inside Lip and a diffusion toward the exterior through [transcribed discussions of *les Lip* in] the last numbers of *Lip Unité* [1979–1980]."[41] The 2AL sought to ensure that the struggle

---

38   Ibid., Part 1/3, 10.
39   Bondu, "LIP, dix ans après," 84.
40   *Lip Unité*, December 1978, 10–11.
41   ADD 45J75 "Compte-rendu de 2AL, 26.4.80."

at Palente spoke to a wide audience, as it had in 1973: the fight for jobs "must be accompanied by speech in another language adapted to workers in other spheres, including non-manual workers."[42] Raguénès lamented a "fixedness" on class struggle that "most often conveys an incapacity to invent the present and the future." Thinking of the individuals from a diversity of professions who had participated in the struggle since 1973, he said: "Through Lip, we can show that it is possible, because we brought together people socially and culturally different and this grouping permitted construction of something quite original."[43]

The 2AL sought to respond to the weight that the Lip conflict of 1973 placed on workers. There was, in the words of the popularization commission, "a permanent ambiguity to assume" in the creation of the cooperative.[44] "Until now," the 2AL board said in May 1978, "*les Lip* have blamed themselves for choosing the cooperative, as if it was in opposition to their open struggle against political and business leaders. Their popularization as well as that of the 2AL appeared a commercial request or an appeal to public charity."[45] Unlike most Lip workers, the 2AL did not frame the creation of the cooperative as a retreat. For the Association, rejection of a cooperative in 1973 had been evidence of the "profound wisdom and lucidity of the workers of Lip." The 2AL differentiated engagement of workers in the conflict in 1973 from the "the stronger communal maturity" of the smaller group of *les Lip* in 1977–8 and succeeding years: "the collectivity of the struggle [of 1973] unquestionably lacked social maturity, that is to say that the average level of communal consciousness of *les Lip* was probably insufficient to allow it to embark with certainty in a cooperative."[46] The cooperative was the product of community consciousness, not of a retreat in the class struggle. As such, the 2AL believed it spoke to a population in France activated in May 1968, seeking its way a decade later: "Basically, we think that Lip is, in any case, a valuable element to bring to the contemporary dossier that should fuel the reflection of people today on their social future. And even more: we have the profound conviction that this history of Lip prepares new routes toward a society worthy of the name."[47]

---

42   BDIC F delta rés 702/14/4 2AL, "Discussion sur les buts de la 2AL," March 1978.

43   ADD 45J108 Lip Livre Part 2/"Lip, déjà demain," 21.

44   BDIC F delta rés 578/44 Booklet on 2AL.

45   ADD 85J56 2AL "Compte-rendu du 20 mai 1978."

46   BDIC F delta rés 702/22/5 Bureau de 2AL to François Espagne, June 2, 1981.

47   BDIC F delta rés 702/13/1 Bureau de 2AL to cher ami [personnalités diverses], June 11, 1980.

Looking at the history of cooperatives, Bondu, a 2AL board member, said in June 1979 that whatever goals a cooperative begins with, it gradually becomes "a normalized enterprise." However, he went on, he thought that the 2AL could help prevent L.I.P. from simply bowing to economic imperatives. 2AL president Pierre Besançon wanted discussion between the Association and *les Lip*, at a time when he saw L.I.P. as focused on the economic and the 2AL as what the L.I.P. leadership saw as "the flow of the dream."[48] The 2AL helped give the concept of the *noyau impulseur* wide currency among *les Lip*, but saw itself performing a role quite different in nature at Palente. This in turn reinforced its mission to the exterior. It did not see L.I.P. as simply an "interesting 'social experience,'" something to make life tolerable in a France where the aspirations of May 1968 were ebbing. "On the contrary, for us, Lip constitutes the concrete outline of a strong Hope: the possibility of a salutary reconciliation between the necessary economic survival of men at work and a human and therefore communal logic." The success of the Lip cooperatives was important to sustain this Hope, "the human project originating in the struggle."[49] What forms did this Hope take?

Palente and the Sorbonne

In line with Mao's call for intellectuals to live for several years with the proletariat, the GP and ex-GP sent members to "establish" themselves as workers. Bondu had joined the GP as a *lycée* student and had been an *établi* for a couple of months at the baggage handling center at the Austerlitz station in Paris. As *les Lip* sought to find their way after the second bankruptcy, Benny Lévy suggested to Bondu that he become an *établi* at Lip. There he expected to work as a manual laborer. However, when Bondu arrived at Palente, he was told his "knowledge and skills"—he had developed an interest in workers' cooperatives—would be much more useful to the community.[50] It wanted him to develop the "live differently"

48   BDIC F delta rés 702/14/4 Notes on conseil d'administration de la 2 AL [March 1979]. Pierre Besançon would himself oppose voting for acceptance of the state conditions in November 1979 as an abandonment by Lip of its history. He saw this leading to new hierarchies and a division among workers between those in power and in the opposition, with a risk of rupture. BDIC F delta rés 702/14/4 Besançon, "Et pour que Lip vive" [attached to invitation to AG of 2AL, April 26, 1980].

49   BDIC F delta rés 702/22/5 Bureau de 2AL to François Espagne, June 2, 1981.

50   Dominique Bondu, "Il y a quarante ans, j'ai quitté l'université pour l'usine," July 26, 2016, at bibliobs.nouvelobs.com. Bondu, "L'élaboration d'une langue commune," 69–80.

project: "not to become a worker, but so that the workers become intellectuals." Bondu lived as did other members of the cooperative. He received the state unemployment stipend supplemented by funds from the sale of watches and participated in the activities required of all, including selling watches and spending nights guarding the factory, which he remembers warmly, drinking wine, playing cards and talking for hours about the future of Lip.[51] Bondu was active in the 2AL and stayed at Lip until 1990. He became, in Géhin's words, "the guy from the exterior who embraced Lip by love and by passion."[52] Bondu told the Polish intellectual Stefan Wilkanowicz that "initially there is great mistrust of intellectuals on the part of the workers. [In France] the intellectual is restricted to two behaviors: take refuge in the ivory tower or be workerist."[53] Bondu's goal, and that of the 2AL, was to develop another relationship, but not that of "the simple status of external intellectual, advice giver."[54]

Since childhood, Bondu had had what he called "a kind of 'existential obsession with community'." This had led him to Maoism and, later, it was "this search for communal life" that attracted him to Lip: "I recovered the intuition of my youth."[55] Bondu moved on from Maoism, but the experience left him wary of the exercise of "collective power":

> I think of Sartre in a book on China that describes the individual finding himself alone facing a group of militants who are settling accounts with him ... For me, this is what is worst. I experienced it at different levels, notably in the GP. I witnessed particular instances of the settling of accounts. Each time, the individual was alone, isolated, without defense, in front of a group, inevitably stronger.[56]

Bondu found some of these qualities in the relation of the *noyau impulseur* to the base. He felt that its practice of proclaiming "day in and day out in a holier than thou way, 'the mass must take charge'," was at the core of the external support for Lip, but was in turn a source of internal problems at Lip. Bondu saw in the *noyau impulseur* the familiar story of a vanguard

---

51 Interview with Bondu by Reid, June 20, 2011. Linhart, *Volontaires pour l'usine*, 196.

52 *Lip Unité*, December 1981, 22.

53 BDIC F delta rés 702/15/5 Bondu and Raguénès, "Entretien avec Stefan Wilkanowicz, Cracovie."

54 Linhart, *Volontaires pour l'usine*, 200.

55 *Lip Unité*, February–March 1980, 9–10.

56 BDIC 702/14/4, "Le Pouvoir. 2ème débat du 2.2.1980."

party and "the 'massified' people" that it sees as mute:[57] "All who claimed to love the people or the mass proved to be the worst of the bastards ... This took me back to that Maoist terminology where, under the pretext of loving the people, you discover, in the end, that you make use of the people."[58] At Lip, Bondu sought ways out of this contradiction.

By opening the factory gates to all, including intellectuals, Lip had led Benny Lévy to rethink the relation of intellectuals and workers in the creation of a socialist society. Shortly after the October 12, 1973 vote, at the time of the dissolution of the ex-GP, Lévy (writing as Pierre Victor) published an open letter to Lip workers saying that they had shown "that workers have all sorts of talents, skills, but these are ransacked by capitalism." The Minister of Labor had proposed job training for *les Lip* who lost their jobs, but, Lévy believed, Lip workers could build a school in the factory and handle this themselves. "Call on intellectuals, teachers, students, magistrates, engineers, to help you in the construction of this school. In May '68 intellectuals put in question the old school, separate from life, from production, from workers. Yes, it would be possible: we produce, we sell, we pay ourselves, we train ourselves."[59]

Bondu's goal became to "live differently" the radical intellectual's relation to the workers' community in order to allow the community itself to live differently. In 1978, he set up the Collectif de Liaison, Études et Formation (CLEF) with the idea of "giving the Sorbonne to the workers" by taking advantage of a state-funded vocational training program for workers to go to college. For three months, Bondu helped prepare a couple of dozen Lip employees, about half of whom were women aged between forty-five and fifty, for the entrance exam to pursue study at the Sorbonne for a two-year DEUG degree in "economic and social administration," and training as "personnel staff."[60] Funded by scholarships, workers would not need to be paid by the cooperative. Exemplifying the appeal that Lip still held for many outside the left, a young Giscardian bureaucrat in Paris allocated virtually all of the scholarships under his control to the workers from Lip.[61]

Not all those who took the entrance exam were admitted to the Sorbonne, but many of those who did not pass the exam remained in

---

57   ADD 45J108 Lip Livre Part 2/"Lip, déjà demain," 18.
58   Ibid., Part 1/Conversation 4, 7.
59   *Libération*, October 19, 1973, 3.
60   ADD 45J112 "Rapport d'activité AAL janvier 78 à janvier 79."
61   Interview with Bondu by Reid, June 20, 2011. For the program itself, Bondu to Reid, July 25, 2016.

the group, working through the Collège Coopératif, an innovative institution that gave workers credit for their experience. Bondu arranged
for those going to the Sorbonne to have their required courses grouped
on one day. They boarded the train to Paris early each Friday morning
and came back very late the same night. Their other work was done as
tutorials at Palente because their obligations to the cooperative would
not allow them to take classes during the week. They engaged in "collective instruction"—cooperative learning involving some teaching by Lip
workers to others, and calling on experts in particular disciplines when
needed, not unlike what Lévy had conceived. Students who were going
to the Sorbonne taught what they were learning to other students in the
group.[62] "The lesson of 1974 [the state job-training classes] has borne its
fruits," *Lip Actualité* told readers, "and at Lip 'garbage' training is dead
and gone!"[63]

Including the time spent preparing for the entrance exams, the
venture lasted three years. Workers studied in a room at the end of
the passerelle in the occupied factory. They could be seen through the
windows, working their way through a text by Marcel Mauss or debating
Jacobinism.[64] Piaget referred to the "extreme emotion" accompanying the
announcement of the results of the end-of-course exams.[65] A worker who
took one of the exams recalled how surprised they were, as veterans of
the conflict at Lip, to find out that on the exam subject "The individual
and the collective in labor conflicts within the enterprise" half of them
were judged not to know it well enough.[66] Engagement in the start up
of the cooperatives prevented a number of workers from completing
the full two years of the program, and only a small number received
degrees. However, some who wanted to pursue their education financed
their studies by speaking to groups that wanted to hear about Lip. They
did not do this as an act of popularization. While the 2AL provided their
first clients, these workers also spoke at institutions like business schools
on the economics of the conflict and the operation of the cooperative.[67]

62   Kilin, "A chacun son LIP," at liplefilm.com. This is drawn from an entry in the
journal of Françoise Verderre, available in part in ADD 45J96.
63   *Lip Actualité*, September 1978, 2.
64   *Lip Unité*, December 1978, 8.
65   AMB 5Z222 Piaget to M. et Mme. David, October 28, 1978. Although Marcel
David was a pioneer in opening universities to workers, even he was daunted by the reputation of *les Lip*. Bondu reports that David feared being attacked when he announced
that not all had passed the entrance exam. Interview with Bondu by Reid, June 20, 2011.
66   *Lip Actualité*, October 1978, 2.
67   AB Interview with Denise Tournier by Beurier [1992], 14–20.

The CLEF also formed a research group on industry and craft trades in Franche-Comté.[68]

In discussing the relation of the cooperative to the Sorbonne project in October 1978, Piaget explained that it was "indispensable to pair the economic plan with a social project envisaging another organization of the enterprise. In this sense, it is necessary that the project be realized by drawing on individuals who have reflected in peace a little more on these questions." The cooperative planned to hire the graduates to perform "the functions of *animateurs* of work groups"—what Piaget saw as the primary need at Palente.[69] Although none ended up being employed by L.I.P., a number played important roles in the CAP.[70] The CLEF participated in the development of the CAP and at times played the role of a think tank for the cooperative, "an active site of reflection possible on the global project of Lip."[71] Two workers who went to the Sorbonne— Dominique Enfraze, a mechanic who had been close to the GP militants who came to Besançon, and Jean-Claude Piquard, a factory foreman when the conflict began in 1973—served as directors of the CAP.

The CLEF continued to function after the workers had finished their studies. It acted as a consulting firm, offering a diversity of social and cultural services to public and private institutions.[72] In 1983, six of the CLEF staff were employed by works councils around the country.[73] The CLEF entered the field of social tourism in 1981, with the goal of fostering "the meeting with others, exchanges between different categories of the population generally isolated from one another, and the constitution of multiple social bonds between individuals": of creating sites where "the hand of the man who kneads the clay will no longer ignore the brain of the one who studies philosophy." In the early 1980s, some forty works councils, municipalities, clubs and associations worked with the CLEF to plan and carry out vacation programs.[74] For a decade, beginning in 1983, it also operated two year-round lodges in Franche-Comté and the Jura

68   Terrieux, "L'expérience Lip," 115.

69   AMB 5Z222 Piaget to M. et Mme. David, October 28, 1978.

70   Terrieux, "L'expérience Lip," 190–3.

71   *Lip Unité*, December 1978, 8. Kilin, for instance, went to work for the SCEIP. Kilin, "A chacun son LIP."

72   BDIC F delta rés 702/15/3 "Centre de Restauration et d'Activités Culturelles Lip: novembre 1980."

73   Bondu, "LIP, dix ans après," 88–9.

74   ADD 45J112 "Le projet philosophique du CLEF." One CLEF employee remembered CLEF picking through the 2AL lists for teachers to contact. AB Interview with Françoise Dromard by Beurier [1992], 64.

with a total of 136 beds. *Lip Unité* referred to "these two places where the 'communal' project of Lip must live."[75]

Travail

Bondu spoke of his admiration for Herman Melville's *Bartleby the Scrivener*, which he termed "an enigmatic book, on the elusive enigma that is the other."[76] Bartleby worked in a dead letter office. A lawyer hires him as a scrivener, but he refuses to adapt to the new demands of working in an office with others and ultimately stops working altogether. He responds to all requests with the words "I would prefer not to." After his efforts to help Bartleby are spurned, the lawyer moves out of the office; but Bartleby has made it his home and remains rooted there. When a new business arrives and cannot remove him, Bartleby is sent to prison, where he wastes away and dies. Was Bondu reflecting on the enigma of workers he knew who had occupied their place of work and would prefer not to do what they were instructed to do?

If so, *Bartleby the Scrivener* was not the only novel to which Bondu turned to understand the experience at Lip. He created a "philosophy workshop," and in a project rooted in the Collège Coopératif, around twenty of the worker-students at the Sorbonne and the Collège read and in May 1979 discussed Emile Zola's *Travail*, a fictionalized account of the Fourierist Jean-Baptiste Godin's *familistère* in Guise—a "glass house" (like Palente), as Zola called it in his notes.[77] In the novel, Luc imagines and builds a company called La Crêcherie. He manages the firm for an owner-scientist on the verge of discoveries that will revolutionize the steel industry. La Crêcherie competes successfully with the long-established L'Abîme, a family firm that has been bought by outsiders to generate profits. It is a site of physical and moral corruption, of brutality and alcoholism. Luc believes that a new social environment will bring out the new man in his workers. La Crêcherie is an economic success, a community with profit sharing, worker participation in management, job rotation, consumer cooperatives, and its own housing and schools.

---

75   *Lip Unité*, Third–Fourth Trimester 1983, 3–7. However, CLEF publicity materials did not mention Lip.

76   Catherine Chaillet and Pierre Laurent, *Besançon. Un temps d'avance* (Paris, 2007), 100.

77   Bondu, "De l'usine à la communauté," 273, 544. Bondu to Reid, July 26, 2016. Neuschwander had been taken with Godin and his *familistère* as a young man.

Raguénès could adamantly assert that "At no time did we want to revive the phalanstery of Fourier. Lip should have no 'Lipanstères'!,"[78] but the philosophy workshop at Palente recognized similar ambitions and experiences in the novel and in their cooperatives, the difference being, as Lip workers Serge and Louis recognized, that Luc alone assumed responsibility at La Crêcherie, whereas at Palente all workers did, in theory at least.[79] *Les Lip* discussed the conflicts between community and egoism at Palente and La Crêcherie. They set "the festivals" of 1973, when "power disappeared, there is fusion, communion," against "egoism, the framework that encloses us," "the source of all our current problems."[80] Participants in the discussion of *Travail* recognized that in the cooperative there were some workers formed in the existing world who were frightened of doing something new: "*Entreprendre*, that scares them."[81] They expressed surprise at the workers' acceptance of job rotation at La Crêcherie, which ran contrary to the desire of many workers at L.I.P. to stay in their particular posts. However, the participants were quite cognizant that they had made a choice to commit to the Lip community and believed that this choice was a stronger bond than the security they craved, and which Luc gave to his workers: "Lip is thus more profound, richer than La Crêcherie," Serge explains. "We are not doing an experiment for anyone to prove something, whether self-management or something else. We have undertaken to live together, for that is our choice whose origin was our absence of choice" when faced with the planned dismantling of Lip done behind their backs.[82]

In discussing *Travail*, the workers reflected on affectivity at Palente. La Crêcherie is a community structured by Love and this led them to think about Love at Palente. Vincent recognizes that "Love today at L.I.P., it is hard ... People assimilate love to power because by love I embrace and in embracing I enclose, I constrain them." Anne elaborated: "In fact when you love, you expect something back. You demand as your due that the other recognizes you or that he conform to your image. And it is then that you are deceived and you are no longer capable of loving."[83] Clément then responded that the very nature of L.I.P. had developed this economy of sentiments:

---

78   *Lip Unité*, April–May 1980, 23
79   "Préface des ouvriers de Lip," 19.
80   Ibid., 15.
81   Ibid., 25.
82   Ibid., 28.
83   Ibid., 20.

[There are those who believe that] the one who is just must always give, spend without counting the cost. But, in any case, he must not become intrusive! Otherwise, he becomes an unbearable boss. They receive hands outstretched, and then they coldly evaluate, they weigh, they compare. The wage scale is no longer significant, so they establish another hierarchy. They want someone like the rich man—intellectually, spiritually—and call on him to spend with generosity. Them, they wait. This hierarchy does not appear as in the classical enterprise. But it exists, terribly cumbersome.

Anne added: "It is more complicated! If I have nothing to say, nothing to give, I remain silent, stingy; at root I am unhappy and he who I see rich, verbose, generous, I am going to judge him with envy and frustration. I am going to say that he does not give me enough."[84] Those who sacrifice themselves in seeking to pursue a collective project exert a power contrary to the non-hierarchical, egalitarian community: a love exists with the expectation of a response from the other that can feel like a form of confinement. This exchange can create a hierarchy conceived in emotional terms that takes the place of the forms of hierarchy found in other workplaces. Through their discussion of *Travail*, the workers who analyzed power and authority in the way the *noyau impulseur* operated at Lip were quite insightful and self-analytical, representative of what the 2AL recognized *les Lip* had to offer.

Bondu's projects are evidence of a fruitful exchange of worker-philosophers and philosopher-workers, both going where they had not gone before—the antithesis of the stalemate of Bartleby. In 1973, one reporter had referred to Palente as "a summer trade union university. The factory in the greenery of Besançon has become a campus."[85] Three years later, after visiting Palente, Maria-Antonietta Macciocchi would say, "*Les Lip*, on the grounds of Palente, have created a kind of workers' technical and political university."[86] Writing in 1980, Gaston Bordet called Palente "one of the high points of culture in Europe during this decade," "a sort of proletarian Vincennes."[87] Yet this was a telling reference. Vincennes was the university established in response to May 1968 by Edgar Faure, Minister of Education and deputy of Doubs. It quickly became a center of

---

84   Ibid., 20–1.
85   *La Croix*, August 22, 1973, 3.
86   Macciocchi, *De la France*, 171.
87   Gaston Bordet, "Les Lip de l'utopie à la réalité," *Esprit* 45 (September 1980): 156.

innovative radical thought and practice in France. As Michel Garcin recognized, a little more than a decade after May 1968 the state demanded that the centers of thought and practice rooted in that experience move, leaving behind their iconic sites: *les Lip* from Palente to Besançon, and the Vincennes campus to Saint-Denis.[88]

From Sartre to Levinas

Bondu went to Palente as an *établi*, but in pursuing his work with *les Lip*, he developed an understanding of work communities that he drew on for a thesis.[89] Saying that "social reality cannot be truly understood except from inside," he presented his work at Lip as a form of "participant observation." The individual in his position "becomes the Other who primes the dialogue, who surprises, who spurs thought. And that expression of Exteriority in the Same is at the origin of a social asset in the collectivity itself."[90] Bondu situated himself in the debates over the cooperative, aligning with Raguénès' embrace of the community and Dominique Enfraze's of diversity, thus differentiating himself from the appeal to self-interest he saw operating in L.I.P.—"become conscious of your interest tied to the cooperative and act for yourself."[91] For how those like Bondu and the 2AL who accompany workers in their struggles interpret the experience may speak to it without being what most workers and their leaders make of their situation.

Bondu believed that the Lip workers were able to come together in 1973 because their illegal acts had made them "marginal, on the margin of the social norm," creating a community that thought "we are all outlaws." Constructing a future together in an authorized cooperative proved much more difficult.[92] As had Lévy, Geismar, and Rosanvallon, Bondu thought of Lip in 1973 in terms of Sartre's group-in-fusion, at the origin of which lies the threat of destruction or death.[93] At Lip, Bondu, like Raguénès, believed that

---

88   AB Interview with Garcin by Beurier [1992], 19–22.
89   Interview with Bondu by Reid, June 20, 2011. Bondu to Reid, July 3, 2017.
90   Bondu, "De l'usine à la communauté," 9–10.
91   Bondu, "Coopération et alterité," *Revue des études coopératives* 208 (1982): 47 [quoted]. Bondu, "L'élaboration d'une langue commune," 73. For Enfraze, see Jacquin, "Lip 1973–1981," 391–2.
92   BDIC F delta rés 702/15/1 "Débat du 20 janvier 1979," 14.
93   *Le Monde*, June 12, 1974, 21. Rosanvallon, *L'Age de l'autogestion*, 64–7. Jeannette Colombel, *Sartre ou le parti de vivre* (Paris, 1983), 240–1.

the menace of death is the shutdown of the factory and unemployment
—therefore loss in social terms. There was regrouping, community, élan
and movement … But the end, is it not already contained in this origin
due to a defect at the start that constitutes a gathering whose positivity
is not evident since it is produced by a negation?[94]

Bondu asked, "Is the adversary, the boss, the chief executive, whoever,
each time the mediation we give ourselves to avoid the brutal question of
the relation with the other?"[95] "And once the enemy-catalyst is gone, the
members of the group so constituted find themselves powerless … in the
intimacy, in the face-to-face of the community."[96] Institutions created
in the initial conflict are unable to deal with a situation where workers'
individual interests, like those of the mechanics that shocked Raguénès,
are not united in opposition; all they have is "a haunting nostalgia for the
lost community."[97] In this situation, Bondu contended, workers do not
want self-management; the belief that they do is akin to the attribution of
"a messianic mission" to the working class.[98] Workers lived Sartre's "bad
faith," affirming that the bosses prevented them from changing things,
when their own desire to maintain the advantages of their situation led
them to oppose change.[99] Neither the cooperative nor self-management
would naturally emerge were state and capital to vanish.

However, Bondu saw in both the workers and their supporters the
roots of a new society in which the acknowledgment of difference and
others' interests would not be rejected as a betrayal of the group-in-
fusion. Accepting that without a universally recognized, identifiable
threat the group-in-fusion was no longer viable, Bondu worked with Lip
workers on an alternative in the form of a charter laying out the project of
the cooperative and the obligations this involved, with the idea that only
those who signed it would receive the struggle pay.[100] Like Benny Lévy,

94   ADD 45J108 Lip Livre Part 2/"Lip déjà demain," 2.
95   BDIC F delta rés 702/15/1 "Débat du 20 janvier 1979," 21.
96   Bondu, "De l'usine à la communauté," 582, 586.
97   Bondu, "Coopération et alterité," 42.
98   Bondu, "De l'usine à la communauté," 132, 144.
99   Bondu, "Coopération et alterité," 42.
100   Interview with Bondu by Reid, June 20, 2011. Although this initiative did
not take root, its logic is found in the response of Benny Lévy, a member of the 2AL
board, to the issues raised by the release of the A, B, and C lists in February 1979. He
said that that all Lip workers should have been required to take an oath to engage fully
in all the risks of the struggle. This, rather than competence and initiative, should have
determined who was placed on the A and B lists, with the understanding that those who
had taken the oath could not complain if they were placed on list C. BDIC F delta rés

he turned to the thought of Emmanuel Levinas. At one point, Bondu responded to a "hell, it is the others" moment, to use Sartre's words, by attaching to the minutes of a CLEF meeting a passage from Levinas on responsibility.[101] One sees in the workers' conversation about *Travail* the sense that the key to building another society is recognition of the humanity of the other, whose difference cannot not be dismissed solely as egoism. Bondu expressed this in terms of Levinas' concept of alterity:

> First proposition: the constitution of individuality, then the construction of the community, takes place, not first by a coming to self-consciousness, by a collective consciousness, but by the welcome of the other in oneself, "the opening of the gates," that is to say the discovery of the exteriority in one's interiority, the "visitation" of the stranger in a common dwelling. Second proposition: the meeting, the social bond, these are not identification in the Same, incorporation in the same body, abolition of the distance, but on the contrary, full recognition of this irreducible distance, of this radical exteriority of the "close," that which establishes the possible space for a society.[102]

In the very nature of the community workers had built in the "struggle against" could be found the model to build the new world of the "struggle for." Bondu saw in the "opening of the gates" that had so marked the Maoists the answer for the workers as well, starting with their own experience among themselves in the factory:

> The community, the social bond, exists then through this face-to-face encounter accepted, recognized. It is the "opening of the gates," according to the beautiful expression of *les Lip*. Before, the factory was a closed space, closed to all outsiders. In the interior, each found himself compartmentalized, arranged as a function of the layout; it is the closing within of the walls as well. The opening of the gates is the welcoming of the exterior, of the strangers to the house, to the factory, the welcome of different social classes, intellectuals, peasants, of those who do not resemble us. The opening of the gates that strengthens the community is the opposite of the autonomy of the autonomous, categorical, homogeneous group; it is the acceptance of "social heteronomy," the mixing

---

702/14/4 Notes of conseil d'adminstration of 2AL [March 1979].

101   ADD 45J112 Conseil d'administration du CLEF, December 10, 1985.

102   Bondu, "De l'usine à la communauté," 572–3.

of social groups, socio-professional categories, even of classes. Likewise, the opening of the gates happens inside the factory; it is the meeting, the relationship with the outsider to watchmaking, to the office. The destruction of barriers, of closed doors, marks the beginning of the social bond through acceptance of this heteronomy. And the truly social factory has to rest on the exchange of the intellectual and the manual, of the OS, the manager and the engineer. The only way possible requires mutual recognition.

At Lip, the regular organization of "open doors" operations found its justification other than in simple tactical necessities. It is profoundly a matter of the institution of a vital rite for the community. By these operations, in effect, the permanence of this social openness, constitutive of Lip, was established.[103]

In the words of Anne discussing *Travail*: "The game of Love is to receive the other in their difference even if you have to force yourself."[104]

To explain the necessary "fertilizing alterity" in the cooperative, Bondu turned to Marcel Mauss's "economy of the Gift, based on active recognition of the infinite debt of each toward others present: *heterogestion* and not only *autogestion* [self-management]!"[105] If the 2AL had begun with the idea that the cooperative was a means to "perhaps prepare in a certain way self-management," Bondu now saw the goal for Lip as *hétérogestion*, the practice of alterity.[106] The responsibility of each for the other, without the mediating figure of the boss or the leader like Piaget, took workers beyond the group-in-fusion. This turn to Levinas offered as well a way to rethink the *établi* experience in which the *établis* play a valuable role as the other, not trapped by the effort to efface their difference. This was the ideology of the 2AL; it made the presence and mission of the 2AL integral to Lip. 2AL board member Gaston Jouffroy spoke in January 1979 of the break with the long valorized "taste for the collective": "A couple of months ago Lip got over standardization: before, they liked to think in the same way because they had a sort of prohibition on not thinking collectively."[107] This required members of the cooperative to break with the practice of seeing solidarity as based on workers

---

103   Ibid., 576, 582.
104   "Préface des ouvriers de Lip," 21.
105   Bondu, "Coopération et alterité," 50.
106   ADD 85J56 2AL, "Compte-rendu du conseil d'administration du 20 mai 1978."
107   Archives Bondu, "Débat du 20 January 1979," 12.

having identical interests. Initially posed by female workers, difference now became a way for the 2AL to interpret the totality of relationships in the community and to address the fear that communities were by nature oppressive.

The Lip struggle was a defining moment of the legacy of 1968. Alterity became a way of reconciling both the economic and the live-and-work-differently imperatives at Lip, and the diversity of identities and the collectivities in which movements born of 1968 are interpreted, by seeing each as dependent on the other. At the time that the Socialist government of François Mitterrand was enacting numerous nationalizations, Bondu proposed Lip as a site in which to examine socialism as more than and other than solely a question of ownership of the means of production. In a leitmotif of Lip discourse, he saw that the "crossing of the Red Sea" from wage-earner, *salariat*, to cooperative member, *sociétariat*, being made by workers at Lip and elsewhere "contains treasures of teachings apropos of this crucial transformation of mentalities." This led Bondu to see the future of socialism being played out in Besançon at a time when Lip workers themselves were primarily concerned with the survival of the cooperatives and their jobs:

> In moving from the "struggle against" to the "struggle for" (in the language of *les Lip*), the new worker members [of the cooperative] made an authentic existential conversion. And pushed, in spite of themselves, to a strange land, these activists of the new break are going to become the artisans of a certain evolution of the French workers' movement, long anesthetized by ideology. In particular, they demonstrated that the transformation of a protest movement into the dynamics of social construction does not answer so easily to the supposed laws of the dialectic, and requires a radical shake up of ways of thinking, of all cultural habits, ways of living and representations of the world. Without this voluntary mental labor, all attempts at worker emancipation remain condemned to failure and the collective appropriation of the means of production remains a condition without a future.[108]

A critique of the socialist programs of another era, Lip could also be interpreted as harboring the social secrets of the enterprise at a time when the crippling of the enterprise could still be understood by capitalists as a crippling of capitalism. In 1980, Bondu began a discussion of the charter

---

108   Bondu, "Coopération et alterité," 38.

laying out the obligations of members of the cooperative to one another with a review of contemporary American and French management literature, like that Luc Boltanski and Ève Chiapello would later undertake.[109] "All of these texts unambiguously affirm the vital need to transform the enterprise into a human community" in which workers are less alienated and, feeling that they are members of a group, will contribute more. Lip workers lacked the capital, the machines, and the competitive products of capitalist firms, but, Bondu contended, they needed to realize that they had what capitalists now craved and were stymied in creating in their firms: "this human capital that must be protected, dearly cared for, like the apple of one's eye." As Lip workers developed the cooperative, they should cultivate its difference. They should not succumb to an "inferiority complex" and imitate business, "copying as closely as possible their model and their ways. That is how, by fatalism, one becomes more royalist than the king." Lip could succeed where business was failing. From seven years of struggle, Lip had what "a good number of bosses now feel to be an asset of the first order." "What, Lip is morbid? But ... 'from these bones will be resurrected the living!' This phrase of the Prophet-Hope, Jean Raguénès often repeats to us ..."[110] For Bondu and the 2AL, Lip remained, in the agony of the years of the cooperatives, a fruitful site of social thought and experimentation. Lip became an unlikely venue for the valorization of alterity, conceived in terms of and made possible by the opening of the gates of Palente.

Workers and Intellectuals

Raguénès, Bondu, and others in the 2AL contended that just as opening the gates was transformative for the ex-GP, relations with external supporters had been crucial in the development of *les Lip*. Workers and their supporters still needed one another to determine who they were and what they could do. In 1973, events at Palente had given the ex-GP a new understanding of radical political change, one in which they were not needed as a vanguard party. A different set of questions rooted in the ex-GP experience came up in the "struggle for" period of the cooperative. The 2AL looked at Palente as a means to think not only about how to make a revolution, but also the other fundamental question Piaget too

---

109   Luc Boltanski and Ève Chiapello, *Le Nouvel esprit du capitalisme* (Paris, 1999).
110   BDIC F delta rés 702/6/6 Bondu, "Contribution en vue d'une charte" [c. 1980].

had confronted: how to keep alive a political and cultural transformation initiated in a radical movement of change without becoming an oppressor.[111] A number of 1968 leftists turned New Philosophers repudiated Marxist revolution and the totalitarian regimes to which they believed it led. New Philosopher André Glucksmann was a prominent 2AL supporter. However, Raguénès and Bondu and others in 2AL approached the question from a different perspective. How, Bondu asked, can revolutionaries avoid becoming "closed and egotistical groups," a fate he saw befalling all before them, whether Guevarists, utopian socialists or the ex-GP?[112] Adopting the birth metaphor Raguénès had used in talking about the fruit of worker/supporter interactions at Lip, Bondu believed that leftism had a prophetic role in post-1968 France, but had never developed the means to realize itself within communities and had led only to "stupid little runts [*avortons stupides*]." Raguénès, probably thinking of Lip, replied that one should not "throw out the baby with the bathwater," saying that the key was how the child born of radical acts matures.[113]

How does a community survive and develop in the absence of the unifying menace of death? To counter the historical precedents—the oppressive conformity of communist equality governed by an elite, or the inhumane competition of autonomous individuals in capitalist society—Bondu and others in the 2AL looked to a critical assessment of Palente for guidance in developing communities that respect "the rhythms of each person within them."[114] Perhaps the menace of death had never explained all. The threat could lead to the affirmation by the collectivity of no layoffs and no dismantling, said Raguénès, but it did not explain how the Lip workers had responded—taking the watches, starting up production, and running commissions; all the acts of creativity and imagination at the heart of the communities at Palente.[115] To return to Raguénès' delineation of the mad wise men and the wise mad men, the collective and its demands were wise and the illegal and communitarian activities were mad; what made Lip so successful in 1973 were the ways in which the wise and the mad acts fed into one another when, in the words of Pierre Besançon, "a job for all" became understood as "a place in the group for all."[116]

---

111   ADD 45J108 Lip Livre Part2/"Lip déjà demain," 22.
112   Ibid., 20.
113   Ibid., 33.
114   Ibid., Part 1/Conversation 5, 6.
115   Ibid., Part 2/"Lip déjà demain," 5.
116   Ibid., Part 3/Pierre Besançon, 19.

What brought the mad and the wise together at Palente? For Raguénès, the story of the journalist who had been a catalyst for the starting up of production in June 1973 was crucial in the realization of the Lip project. The idea was in the air among *les Lip*, but it was the interaction with the other that led workers to take the leap. *Les Lip* were secure in who they were, but they developed when they engaged with external supporters, not simply with media representations of themselves. And, in turn, when *les Lip* closed off, their project stagnated. 2AL saw itself not only, or perhaps even primarily, as providing material assistance to the community facing the challenges of creating the cooperative. It was an alternative to the *noyau impulseur*—an external force continuing, in Bondu's words, "the relation of the I to the Other [that] provoke[d] the creation of the Lip community" in 1973.[117] Although the 2AL leadership was male and did not reflect on the development of the Women's Group, the latter was a revealing instance of this phenomenon. Lip women opened the gates to feminists who helped them express and defend what they already felt and experienced, leading to new forms of mini-community, to use Raguénès' term, with the incorporation of the leaders' wives, and in turn to an impact on feminists elsewhere through the publication of *Lip au féminin*.

Raguénès and Bondu were central figures in the development of the idea that opening the gates was crucial for *les Lip*. By their origins, they embodied the project. They were naturalized citizens of Lip, but the difference they never lost enabled them to act as catalysts. Raguénès' response to the workers who came to see him with their concerns had led to creation of the Action Committee, an expression of community in its openness, democracy, and impermanence. At the request of the cooperative, Bondu become one of *les Lip* by retaining important elements of who he was when he arrived. He helped individuals in Palente develop the tools to challenge the socialization of the existing order and their place within it, premised as it was on an acceptance of authority and an avoidance of responsibility.[118]

Although most Lip workers thought of the 2AL as a source of financial and political support more than in terms of necessary transformative relations with the other, the 2AL contended that only a community that continued to welcome outsiders and engage with them could succeed. The change to come in the France of the 1970s would not take the form of insurrections, but would look more like Lip and Larzac, what Raguénès

---

117   Ibid., Part 2/"Lip déjà demain," 36.
118   Ibid., Part 1/Conversation 5, 21.

called the fires one could see at night on the day of St. Jean. "What obstacles do we encounter?," he asked. "Why is it that we cannot render immortal the uprising, why can madness not be lived all the time and remain as grace? … Render immortal the festival," not as another kind of party, but as a functioning world turned upside down: "this is the big question today when we speak of socialism …"[119] After all, what had thrilled Pierre Victor on October 12, 1973, and led to talk of an October 12 movement, was that he saw in it the men and women of Palente continuing their uprising unabated. Although the 2AL did not reference Larzac, its position would be validated by the welcome given to and the incorporation of external support there—leading to Larzac's continued existence as the brightest of the fires of St. Jean, a mini-community open to others, as devoted to forwarding non-violence and ecology as to raising sheep.

Non, je ne regrette rien

The 2AL felt a close connection with Solidarity in Poland, seeing it as confronting the same issues Lip faced: "What at Lip we named the Community, what the Poles call Solidarity, corresponds precisely to the emergence of multiple social centers where man is truly present to man."[120] Bondu and Raguénès went with a GP veteran to Poland in 1981. Talking to the Polish Catholic intellectual and Solidarity militant Stefan Wilkanowicz in Cracow, Raguénès asked the question that preoccupied him: "How to succeed such that men are actors in a permanent way and not only episodically or at exceptional moments?"[121] With individuals who had been in the GP, Bondu and Raguénès hosted a meeting in Besançon in June 1981 for all les Lip who wanted to meet with a small group of Polish workers and intellectuals from Nowa Huta, the Committee for Social Self-Defense KOR, and Solidarity militants. Lip workers and the 2AL proposed an agenda centered on the issues they faced: "How

---

119   Ibid., Part 1/Conversation 3, 12.

120   *Lip Unité*, April-May 1981, 27. Bernard Guetta, who covered the Lip conflict, and later the Solidarity movement, for *Le Nouvel observateur*, explained that Lip workers had "such a curiosity about the world and such open-mindedness that they were touching on the universal, and our long exchanges helped me considerably later to enter fully, to feel at home, in the Catholic and worker world of Polish factories …" Bernard Guetta and Jean Lacouture, *Le Monde est mon métier* (Paris, 2007), 77.

121   BDIC F delta rés 702/15/5 Bondu and Raguénès, "Entretien avec Stefan Wilkanowicz, Cracovie."

can the construction of a society, of a community, avoid the trap of a sclerotic institutionalization?"[122]

Raguénès and Bondu saw in the engagement of intellectuals with Solidarity what the 2AL sought at Lip. Raguénès told of a conversation he and Bondu had with a Polish intellectual who had brought a letter of support signed by more than 100 intellectuals to workers in Gdansk at the time when Solidarity was coming into existence. The letter was read and applauded at the workers' general assembly, but its bearer was told that this was not enough. To create and sustain Solidarity, workers would need intellectuals' expertise in law, economics, history, and other domains: "You are, you too, indispensable to action":

In the Polish of Solidarity, "Expert" is not only one who has the knowledge.

He is first of all, the Friend. The one "in whom one has confidence."

The one who accompanies us, who fertilizes us … sometimes instructs us.

The one who extends us tenfold, a hundredfold.

The one who expands our abilities. All our abilities.[123]

Yet the 2AL recognized that the interactions of intellectuals and workers represented by the opening of the gates at Palente had only gone so far. In an article entitled "The Relations of Intellectuals and Workers at the Heart of the Polish Movement," published in *Lip Unité* in the spring of 1981, at the time of Mitterrand's election to president, 2AL wrote:

At Lip we suffer a lot now from the attitude of the majority of French intellectuals. When in 1973, and even in '76, the spotlights were aimed at Palente, it was good form to say a few words into the microphones, to pick up the most beautiful pen to write of Lip, to express one's pertinent feelings about the affair. Today, when our slow underground construction conceals so many buried treasures, hidden lessons, our intellectuals, so brilliant at the time, take refuge behind the thick walls of their offices. Discreetly, they observe from a distance what is happening with us, without taking the risk of remaining openly faithful to us.[124]

---

122 BDIC F delta rés 702/15/5 "Propositions des travailleurs de LIP et des amis pour le séminaire Franco-Polonais, à Besançon," April 6, 1981. Bondu to Reid, July 3, 2017.

123 ADD 45J108 Lip Livre Part 3/Raguénès, 40–1.

124 *Lip Unité*, April–May 1981, 14.

In December 1980, the 2AL board had met and, after a feast prepared by Raguénès, sung several verses of Édith Piaf's "Non, je ne regrette rien."[125] But that did not prevent the 2AL from collapsing as the long 1968 gave way to a longing. In December 1982, the Association reported that of its 10,000 members (and recipients of *Lip Unité*) only 400 had responded to the call to resubscribe.[126] The 2AL would linger for a while before folding, but the Lip experience, in the words of Claude Lévi-Strauss, has remained good to think with.

---

125   BDIC 702/14/3 "Compte-rendu de la réunion du 9 décembre 1980—Bureau de la 2AL." Géhin recounts a conversation with Raguénès in 1983 that ends with Géhin putting on a record. Raguénès guesses it will be Jacques Brel. Told it is by Édith Piaf, he says "La Foule," but Géhin has chosen "Non, je ne regrette rien." ADD 45J108 Lip Livre Part 3/Géhin, 37. Yet Raguénès is not wrong. Played in order, the three selections are the soundtrack of their experience at Lip.

126   *Lip Unité*, December 1982, 3.

14

In the Musée Grévin

The Lip Affair is the story of the Raft of the *Medusa*, awaiting eternal submersion and where the shipwrecked, abandoned by all of their captains, reveal to themselves a moving friendship instead of devouring one another.

We can always be told that they do not know how to count. There were doubts. This accounting ignorance only increases the sympathy we have for them and the gratitude we owe them. I do mean gratitude, for if one day a profound change is made in social relations, we will owe it in large part to their example of solidarity without hatred.

It is possible that this mustard seed dies. It will become, none the less, as in the parable, a great tree. That in any case is the hope of those who do not resign themselves to injustice or the gulag.

—André Frossard[1]

Lip must enter meekly into the Musée Grévin of their strikes.

—Quatre Millions de Jeunes Travailleurs[2]

---

1 *Le Figaro*, April 7, 1976, 1. The naval frigate *Medusa* ran aground in 1816. Survivors embarked on a raft they built and practiced cannibalism to survive. The raft is the subject of an iconic painting by Théodore Géricault. Frossard saw those who sold watches to support themselves as like the survivors of the *Medusa*, shipwrecked as a result of the captain's incompetence, and surviving on what remained of the ship's cargo. Those who condemn the Lip workers, he adds, would have put the survivors on trial for eating the ship's supplies without the shipowner's permission. *Le Point*, July 18, 1977, 55.

2 "Contribution à une critique radicale du conflit de Lip," the long version of the faux *Lip Unité*.

One error consists in already wanting to absolutize this moment [May '68; Lip '73], to want to make it an Event. This does not prepare it to last, but at most to be nostalgia.

—Dominique Bondu[3]

In July 1973, Sartre called the Lip conflict "the achievement of a socialist design that will fail ... but which at the same time marks a kind of ideal that other workers will seek to attain." Pierre Victor responded that Lip "as a material power of the working class will come to an end, but will remain as a symbolic power," by which he meant that the Lip Affair led workers to question what Marx called the eternalization of capitalist relations of production.[4] Philippe Gavi chimed in that the Communists sought a victory at Lip that would maintain the world as it was. Gavi's Lip was about making a different world. It could not be successful in the way the world in which he lived measured success, but it would move society toward a new world.[5] Sartre returned to this subject in November 1973, saying that the end of Lip in perhaps six months will be "catastrophic": "It will not provide a real gain for the working class which, in the end, will get nothing ... Once Lip is over ... we must preserve its memory, recall it constantly, and stress the possibilities that Lip revealed to us."[6] From its entry on the national stage, supporters talked about how to make memory of its defeat further the cause.

This is the nature of history written from a critical left perspective. What strength and meaning can be drawn from defeat? And in turn how to relate this experience to other orphaned radical sites past? While Benny Lévy celebrated the headless statues of Fred Lip's forebears as emblematic of the liberation at Palente, he also saw in Palente a "decapitated concept," a term he took from Sartre's *Being and Nothingness*. This "acephalism" revealed "a kind of desire of parthenogenesis, of self-begetting," that marked social movements, leaving a "blind spot, like a scar (a mark where the head was cut off)." In 1976 Lévy saw Lip 1973 as forgetting that May 1968 was one of its "real origins," and his active participation in the 2AL was an effort to support aspirations of May that needed support, even if *les Lip* of the workers' republic of Palente did not themselves trace them back to the student republic of the Sorbonne.[7] Piaget recalled that he

---

3 ADD 45J108 Lip Livre Part1/Conversation 4, 38.

4 Gavi et al., *On a raison de se révolter*, 234 (July 1973).

5 Ibid., 237 (July 1973).

6 Ibid., 315–16 (November 1973).

7 Benny Lévy, *Pouvoir et liberté* (Lagrasse, 2007), 73 (December 22, 1976). "De Besançon aux Monts Tsingkiang," *Cahiers prolétariens* 2 (January 1974): 39.

would go to meetings and be asked if he had ever read Antonio Gramsci. He had not, but the Italian leftist Maria-Antonietta Macciocchi visited Lip in 1976 and read Gramsci's essays on factory councils to Piaget and other militants. She was pleased they could that see the battles Gramsci had lost fifty years before were relevant to their struggle.[8]

However, the most common touchstone for the radical left was the Paris Commune, whose hundredth anniversary had been marked in 1971. When Maire came to Besançon after the expulsion from Palente, he referred to the CRS as "these modern Versailles troops" that had attacked the Paris Commune of today.[9] For the Maoist *La Cause du peuple* in July 1973, the Lip movement had that symbolic power to which Pierre Victor referred. It would not last, "but, in fact, the Paris Commune did not last a long time either. Nevertheless, it gave ideas to the workers' movement for a long time."[10] That same month Gavi told Sartre and Pierre Victor: "Five years after May 1968, a bunch of ideas ripened in the factories and suddenly they materialized in this factory that becomes a kind of 'BATEAU IVRE'. In this sense ... *les Lip* discovered the extraordinary in a natural way."[11] In Arthur Rimbaud's poem, written a few months after the Commune fell, the *bateau ivre*, a boat drunk on the water it takes in, itself tells of the many wondrous things it witnesses as it wanders the seas. But unlike Rimbaud's boat, Palente has a crew. They keep it moored and themselves produce the extraordinary possibilities that admirers recount.

Sociologists' Prescriptions

Rimbaud concludes *Le Bateau ivre* with the boat exhausted, its marvelous visions receding, and asking for its voyage to end, but the sailors at Palente would not succumb easily. In the years after the launch of the cooperative in 1977, the sociologists who came to Palente examined the steadfast crew. Gone was the astonishment of visitors in 1973 and the *Les Cahiers de mai* project of enabling Lip workers to take their insights and practices to others directly. Entering the gates opened to them, the sociologists did not find the exceptional experience at the heart of the

---

8   Féret, *Les Yeux rouges*, 67–8. Macciocchi, *De la France*, 144.

9   AFGM-CFDT 1B570 "Intervention d'Edmond Maire," August 16, 1973.

10   *La Cause du peuple*, July 6, 1973, 8–9.

11   Gavi et al., *On a raison de se révolter*, 228 (July 1973). Clavel refers to the *bateau ivre* of Palente as well. *Les Paroissiens de Palente*, 195.

2AL project. Their research served as a prologue to the decade or two after 1981, when Lip lost its place in the public sphere before returning as history and as a national memory.

In the summer of 1978, "the 'humanist' fraction of the leadership," in the person of Raguénès, asked Renaud Sainsaulieu to do a study of Lip so as to "grasp exactly" the distance between the leaders and the base.[12] His student Jean-Pic Berry drew on a number of interviews for a perceptive master's thesis that analyzed the relation of the *noyau impulseur* to the rank and file. *Lip Unité* responded that, "in sending us back to our own image," such studies "permitted numerous discussions to situate calmly our limits, our strengths and weaknesses at the time" (though Raguénès himself dismissed Berry's study six months later).[13]

Sainsaulieu, accompanied by Philippe Bernoux, another influential young industrial sociologist, and Berry, came to Palente and met with Raguénès and Parmentier. They recommended the creation of "communal sub-groups" to provide intermediaries between the *noyau impulseur* and the base.[14] However, what struck Berry was Sainsaulieu's bearing in the meeting: he "went deliberately from a sociological analysis of the situation to an attitude of counselor, bordering on 'comrades, we will do all we can to help you.'"[15] Sainsaulieu thought *les Lip* remained too fixated on 1973. They should break with the dramatic earlier conflict and draw on the capacities that workers had revealed since 1976 to create small enterprises, the best source of new jobs.[16] In November 1978, Sainsaulieu dropped a note to Raguénès to say that there was a government program to provide funds to groups to create jobs and he thought that the artisanal work at Palente fit the criteria. The Minister of Labor wanted Sainsaulieu to be on the committee that allocated funds, and Sainsaulieu said that he could not refuse, "given the service this can render." "Your dossier," he told Raguénès, "will get absolute priority."[17] However, Berry's thesis itself served other purposes. In October 1979, when workers were faced with whether to accept the draconian conditions for legalization of the cooperative, Michel Crozier—a friend of the Berry family—sent Berry's

---

12   Berry, "Lip 1978," 38–9.
13   *Lip Unité*, September 1978, 3. BDIC F delta rés 702/15/1 "Débat du 20 janvier 1979."
14   BDIC F delta rés 702/6/3 "Réunion du 26 juillet 1978"; "Réunion du 27 juillet 1978."
15   Berry, "Lip 1978," 4.
16   BDIC F delta rés 702/6/3 Sainsaulieu, "Première étape de réflexion sur les résultats de l'enquête de sociologues" [1978].
17   BDIC F delta rés 702/14/1, Sainsaulieu to Raguénès, November 15, 1978.

thesis to the prefect with a cover letter written by an ENA student under-scoring the division between leaders and led at Lip and saying that the workers, although enamored with their mythic past, would accept that not all would be rehired.[18]

A few years later, in an insightful thesis on *les Lip*, Daniel Jacquin used his adviser Alain Touraine's method of bringing together a group of workers to pursue a self-analysis of their situation. As a means of giving participants distance from their experience, the researcher constructs hypotheses from the initial group discussion and presents these to the group for further discussion; this analysis in turn is presented to other groups of employees.[19] Jacquin's study of Lip confirmed for Touraine that he was witnessing "the end of the workers' movement as such," not a journey back to the future of the Commune.[20]

Painful Memories

Although not conceived in these terms, there was a sense of loss among *les Lip* in the early 1980s that no one at the time caught better than Bondu:

> A long time ago our adventure turned its back on Happiness. Our long march toward the Kingdom seems to have transformed itself into a descent to the bottom of a dark mine, where each lost their mantle of light, resplendent smile and magnificence. The majority of us live like vagabonds in rags, aspiring to the security of an asylum.[21]

The Communards had experienced a decade of exile, and efforts to explore the meaning and memory of the Lip Affair began only a decade after the departure from Palente in 1981.

Neuschwander wrote in 1993 that *les Lip* "were marginalized; victims of an unscrupulous ostracism," and their story was rarely evoked in

---

18   ADD 1026W22 Robert de Nicolay to PD, October 2, 1979.

19   Alain Touraine, "Note sur l'intervention sociologique" in *Mouvements sociaux d'aujourd'hui. Acteurs et analystes*, ed. Alain Touraine (Paris, 1982), 14–16. Jacquin, "Lip 1973–1981," 7–8, 12. Jacquin drew the initial group of nine largely from skilled workers or supervisors and militants like Vittot, Géhin, and Demougeot, but their analyses were later presented to female OS and to directors of the cooperative.

20   Alain Touraine, Michel Wieviorka, and François Dubet, *Le Mouvement ouvrier* (Paris, 1984), 209.

21   ADD 45J108 Lip Livre Part 3/Bondu, unpaginated.

France except as an instance of 1968-era disorder: "An incredible magma composed of badly formulated accusations, an irrational catch-all where unchecked fears are heaped, a whole slew of failings are dumped, in bulk, without sorting, in the Lip trashcan," in the words of Neuschwander's co-author Gaston Bordet.[22] This was the mirror offered *les Lip* at the time Joëlle Beurier interviewed thirty Lip workers and cadres in 1992 for her pathbreaking master's thesis on the memories of the conflict among *les Lip*. Beurier's father was a manager in the CFDT bastion of mechanics. He was a member of the CGC, though not particularly active in it, and he left Lip after the vote of October 12, 1973.[23] She was a child of what Marc Géhin, like Burtz, referred to as the "diaspora," those who shared a past, but had left for one reason or another over the course of the conflict.[24] In her interviews, she found a widespread, positive memory of Lip before 1973, in particular of the human and professional qualities of the person-nel and the important innovative research sector, and of the conflict in 1973.[25] However the difficult years of the cooperative fostered accusations among some that CFDT-Lip leaders had misled workers and profited from their hardships. Édith Piaf did not sing their song. They did regret quite a bit. No one captured this sense of betrayal better than another child of Lip, Thomas Faverjon.

A decade after Beurier did her research, Thomas Faverjon began filming interviews that became the basis for *Le Fils de Lip* ("The Son of Lip"), released in 2007. His mother Liliane Faverjon had been a secretary at Lip and his father André Faverjon a mechanic there. When the workers voted to accept the conditions for state recognition of the cooperative in October 1979, his father was on list A, but his mother was on list C, excluded from Lip after more than six years in the struggle. Thomas had been a small child during these years and his memories were of a community whose uniqueness he could not see. When asked as a child what a factory was, he responded, "it is a place where there is a nursery, a grocery, a butcher's shop, you can eat with the workers, there are a lot of people there and you can see your mother and your father work, it is very happy!";[26] "I believed that it was normal that workers took turns

---

22   Neuschwander and Bordet, *Lip 20 ans après*, 21, 33.
23   *L'Est républicain*, April 20, 1993. AB Interview with Louis Soulet by Beurier [1992], 39. Interview with Vittot by Beurier [1992], 15.
24   ADD 45J108 Lip Livre Part 3/Géhin, 36.
25   The centrality that union leaders like Vittot give to mobilizations before 1973 offers a variant of this.
26   "Discussion avec Thomas Faverjon sur la pelouse du stade de Lussas" (August 22, 2007), at arkeprix.com.

guarding the factory on Sundays."[27] But Faverjon's parents did not speak to him of the trauma of exclusion and it remained the unspoken sadness that weighed on his family and on him when he undertook his project on the thirtieth anniversary of the summer of 1973. The collective at the heart of the struggle could still act as a censor. When asked to talk about Lip in the film, his mother leaves the room and mutters to her husband that it had been a waste of time. When her son hears her, she tells him not to tell others what she had said; they will yell at her.

Faverjon set out initially to respond to his mother's depression by making a film that would show her that what she had experienced "was positive, glorious, epic." But he recognized this story had no place for what his parents were telling him in their refusal or inability to talk about the conflict, in silences movingly recorded in *Le Fils de Lip*. Faverjon asks if there was something of value in the struggle of *les Lip*. His father responds, "You tell us." Then Faverjon recounts the workers' fight, using footage from contemporary films. But if redeeming recollections are what he had expected and perhaps longed to hear from his parents, he understands that they interpret their memory through a set of experiences and sentiments for which there is no place in this celebratory narrative. "I would dream of making films of heroic, romantic struggles, like those of Chris Marker, but I was incapable as I had lived the defeat of struggles from the inside."[28]

Recognizing that he cannot tell the story that has led to his parents' silence, he turns to three sets of figures. The film begins with Demougeot, the one figure with whom all who devoted themselves to the struggle continue to feel kinship: "perhaps the most successful product of the Lip culture," in the words on one journalist.[29] Because she insists on not being filmed, only recorded as she walks along the Doubs, she provides a complement to footage of Faverjon's silent parents. A second perspective is provided by Piton and Burtz, Action Committee activists who frequently challenged the CFDT-Lip leadership. The film ends with Piton reading an essay she had published in 1978, explaining why she was leaving the struggle and predicting that it would betray itself by excluding a number of those who had been involved since the beginning. Viewers have already seen Piton in footage from 1973 attesting to the inclusiveness of the struggle. Faverjon shows this same footage again, as she is heard reading the article from 1978, until she breaks down and

---

27   Ségal, "Lip, l'impossible héritage," 46.
28   Ibid., 46, 48.
29   *L'Unité*, March 14, 1986, 22.

Faverjon finishes reading it. Burtz was the leader of the opposition to acceptance of the state's conditions for legalization of the cooperative in 1979, and condemns it by saying that the cooperative acted like a despicable boss, keeping the workers from whom a profit could be drawn, along with a few of the vulnerable valued for their political positions, but letting "the most fragile" go, one of whom committed suicide. The exclusion of Faverjon's mother from the community, which Faverjon believes had felt to her like a family,[30] in turn excluded his parents from the discourse in which the community articulated itself, without giving them the tools to criticize it. Faverjon interviews a third group, workers on list C like his mother, but who were more politically articulate before their exclusion—one had been quoted frequently in *Lip. Charles Piaget et les Lip racontent* (1973), though she says she would no longer say those things. Another list C worker lays it on the line, saying that they lived the dreams of others, but suffered the consequences themselves. And in turn, she feels that to assuage their guilt, the collectivity found reasons to denigrate those they would be excluding.

Reunions

Le Fils de Lip captures brilliantly an important legacy of the struggle among the rank and file. However, many Lip workers had individual memories of a common past and sustained close relationships. Yet there was no group of the sort needed to develop and carry on a collective memory.[31] Their revered collectivity could become a resented confinement. In 1979 Raguénès had recognized that "The particularity of Lip is that people who did not choose to do so live things until the end and, something that is not trivial, in a very imprisoning environment. As it were, we Lip could not escape Lip …"[32] And, in turn, Besançon and its inhabitants wanted nothing to do with remembering the conflict. At the time of the fortieth anniversary of 1973, the municipal government continued to refuse to mark the conflict at Lip, fearing that this would keep business away.[33]

When Lip employees did get together, it was not to commemorate the Lip Affair. Researching in 1992, Beurier found that each year the CGT-Lip

30   Ségal, "Lip, l'impossible héritage," 47.
31   Beurier, "La mémoire des Lip," 181, 191.
32   Archives Bondu, "Débat du 20 January 1979," 5.
33   Paulette Pernin, "LIP quarante ans après, des commémorations en tensions." Mémoire, Université de Lille II, 2014.

held a supper and a dance; the CGC-Lip had a dinner to which forty-five to fifty managerial personnel came. These were social gatherings. What drew participants together were memories of Lip before 1973 as well as elements of the struggle in 1973 for the CGT-Lip. The CGC-Lip and CGT-Lip had withdrawn from the conflict after 1976. That the CFDT-Lip did not hold a reunion until 1993 was, Beurier believed, because the years after 1976 had left workers divided and many resentful of elements of the union leadership.[34] In 1993 Jeanningros organized the first of a series of CFDT-Lip decennial dinners, to which CGT-Lip members were also invited. Close to 200 came. Ten years later, all who had worked at Lip were invited, whether or not they had participated in the conflict, including managers (despite the opposition of Piaget and Vittot to their inclusion). Two hundred and fifty attended. In 2013, 120 showed up.[35] These meals drew on social bonds dating from before 1973; participants backed away from recalling the divisive events of later years.[36]

Red Eyes

When the Lip experience returned to the national stage at the end of the 1990s in the form of Dominique Féret's play Les Yeux rouges ("Red Eyes"), it was recounted in terms of individual transformations, rather than the Lip communities or collectivity that had been focal points in interviews with the workers twenty-five years earlier. Performed first in Besançon in 1998, Les Yeux rouges toured twenty-two cities in France in 1999–2000.[37] Féret's original idea had been to present a conversation with Piaget, but he found that Piaget's "language is not 'theatrical' enough. And how do you make the central character of the piece a man who does not use 'I', but always says 'we' or 'buddies'?"[38] Féret interviewed about thirty Lip workers in 1997–8. He drew on conversations with three women and with Piaget to recreate four separate interviews in Les Yeux rouges. The cumulative effect is to see the struggle of these three women not so much

---

34   Beurier, "La mémoire des Lip," 182–91.

35   *Libération*, September 22, 2003. *Le Monde*, August 6, 2003. AR Interview with Jeanningros by Rouaud, December 4, 2003. Rachida El Azzouzi, "Charles Piaget: une leçon de liberté" (July 6, 2013), at mediapart.fr.

36   Many stayed away altogether. Burgy, burned by his experience directing L.I.P., does not go to the Lip reunions. Interview with Burgy by Reid, June 7, 2011.

37   For Beurier's critique of *Les Yeux rouges*, see her "La mémoire Lip ou la fin du mythe autogestionnaire?," 456–61.

38   *L'Est républicain*, October 7, 1998.

through the lens of a betrayal, as do Beurier's and Faverjon's subjects, but in acts of individual self-realization. Féret values the individuals who lived the struggle of 1973 over the aspirations they had then inspired in his twenty-two-year-old self:

> To go back to places, in Besançon, twenty-four years later, is to find again the men and the women, it is to discover biographies more beautiful than our long-gone dream. A little like the statues of the Middle Ages that, having lost their original radiance, have faded colors and bruises, making them more moving and more alive.[39]

By comparing *les Lip* to statues of the Middle Ages, Féret underscores a sense that the Lip Affair itself belongs to an age past.

For the three women in *Les Yeux rouges*, the conflict is presented in terms of opening up to a new world. All mention the hostility of the inhabitants of Besançon during and after the movement. Lip employees remained the group set apart they had always been. "We had the brand on our forehead: Lip," Paulette Dartevel says.[40] This makes the women all the more receptive to the new vistas revealed by the broaching of the social divide between workers and intellectuals, artists, and leftists, and especially by the experience of going elsewhere to talk of Lip, an act the drama can be seen as replicating. But, to the disappointment of many Lip workers who saw *Les Yeux rouges*, Féret included material with no place in the past as they wanted it told. Renée Ducey is a divorced middle-aged OS, who saw herself as the lowest of the low, shunted from one workshop to another to do the work others did not want to do. Although the strike released her—"Then, I was able to burst forth, I could say *merde* to those who poisoned our life"—she speaks movingly of her six-year affair with a married engineer brought in by Neuschwander. This challenges both workerist narratives of collectivity and feminist narratives of liberation.[41]

The most sustained, detailed elements of the interviews are devoted to individuals' efforts to overcome self-imposed limits, gratifying desires they would not have expressed before, and challenging ingrained behaviors, all acts made possible by participation in the struggle. This is true even for Piaget in his grappling with perfectionism and sexism. The play closes with Piaget talking about how he is trying to change and now does

---

39   Féret, *Les Yeux rouges*, 7.
40   Ibid., 11.
41   Ibid., 41. At the end of Copans' film *À pas lentes*, Renée speaks of a manager whom she loved as a person, but hated as a manager.

the dishes and sometimes the washing. Paulette Dartevel, who contributed to *Lip au féminin*, notes that men "put on their chiefs' hats" during the conflict. She speaks of a number of "disappointments," beginning with the nature of work in the CEH and continuing with the emphasis on production in the cooperative ("we were had"), but she opens up and stops asking the interviewer what he would like her to say when she talks about her work since retirement with families who come to visit prisoners in Besançon.[42] Féret presents the workers in *Les Yeux rouges* as individuals engaged in self-discovery, not as embodiments of a collectivity at the heart of the idea of *les Lip* popularized in 1973.

Imagination in Power

Beurier and Faverjon based their works on the idea that a national memory of the Lip Affair as it was popularized in 1973 remained a presence in the French social imagination and that this made living with the perceived injustices of the cooperative all the more difficult. But it may have been that this representation was known, if not embraced, by a number of Lip veterans in Besançon, but was becoming less resonant in the national political culture. Féret too depended on the audience's investment in a memory against the background of which individual workers' accounts assume meaning. In 1973, an important source of the national image of the Lip conflict were contemporary films. But fewer films on Lip were made and seen in succeeding years. Dubosc worked with the popularization commission in the fall of 1974 on a film about the conflict the preceding year, not, they agreed, as an "album of memories," but to spur viewers to reflect on the development of practices of the collectivity.[43] However, the commission lost interest in the project, leaving Dubosc and Piaget to complete *LIP ou le goût du collectif* ("LIP or the Taste for the Collective") with a grant from the Institut national d'audiovisuel (INA).[44] Though coproduced by the INA, the film was not shown on television—the purpose of the INA—as the state was doing all it could to discourage laid-off workers from following the precedent set by Lip.[45] *LIP ou le goût du collectif* was finished at the end of 1976 and

---

42   Ibid., 15–16.

43   *Lip Unité*, October 1974, 4.

44   BDIC F delta rés 578/50 B. Fromentin (Association de Diffusion des Idées Ouvrières) to Guilio Girardi, January 17, 1977.

45   "Faire voir, ceci et rien d'autre," Interview with Dominique Dubosc by Christine

taken on the road the following spring, accompanied by workers now engaged in the renewed fight to save Palente. Released at a time when the New Philosophers were pointing to dangers inherent in collectivity, the absence in the film of any attempt to have the viewer identify with an individual—"no interviews, nothing but public declarations"—made *LIP ou le goût du collectif* "at once exhilarating and terrorizing," in the words of one reviewer.[46]

When Dubosc was soliciting funds from the INA, Richard Copans also had to get state support to complete his film on Lip women, *À pas lentes* ("Slow Steps"). In the late 1970s, films made with the aim of contributing to the overthrow of the system received funding from that system, an initial step in distancing 1968 as history, while preserving it as an aesthetic experience. By the time *À pas lentes* was completed in 1979, the circuit of radical film showings had disappeared and it was not made available to the public until 2009.[47] However, Copans was not done with Lip. Faverjon had dug up a copy of *À pas lentes* in a film studio basement. He found it "magnificent" and was influenced by it.[48] And at the time Faverjon was working on *Le Fils de Lip*, Christian Rouaud went to see Copans, now a successful film producer, with a different experience of Lip and a different idea for a film.

Rouaud came from a practicing Catholic working-class family, members of the ACO. He began studies at the Sorbonne and there he participated in the events of May 1968. This led him to the new university at Vincennes where he studied film. As a PSU militant, Rouaud and fellow party members considered Lip in 1973 as "our strike"; he saw in the General Assembly "the justification of my daily militant action."[49] From his perspective, 1968 has been wrongly identified solely with the student movement in May. Rouaud thought of 1968 in terms of the decade of struggles that followed, which mobilized workers, farmers, women and

Martin, September 2004, at dominiquedubosc.org.

46   *Le Matin*, March 30, 1977. Three decades later, when Dubosc edited the film for a new release, he changed the title to *Le Conflit LIP, 1973–1974*, to prevent anyone from thinking of "*LIP ou le coût du collectif*" (i.e., the cost of [*le coût du*], rather than the taste for [*le goût du*], the collective). Dominique Dubosc, "Un Itinéraire militant" in *Jeune, dure et pure!: une histoire de cinéma d'avant-garde et expérimental en France*, ed. Nicole Brenez and Cristian Lebrat (Paris, 2001), 340–1. *LIP ou le goût du collectif* is available with English subtitles at vimeo.com.

47   Richard Copans, "*À pas lentes* de Collectif Cinélutte," at peripherie.ass.fr.

48   Ségal, "Lip, l'impossible héritage," 46.

49   Patrick Richet, "Vers un nouveau syndicalisme?," 37, 39, at cinema-histoire-pessac.org. ADD BC 20893 "*Les sages fous et les fous sages*. Un film documentaire de Christian Rouaud," 3.

gays to pursue liberation and new forms of power. He could remember when Lip "carried the dreams of a whole generation," in the words that open his film, *Les Lip. L'Imagination au pouvoir* ("*Les Lip*. Imagination in Power"). So could Copans, who agreed to produce the film. Rouaud felt that Lip and Larzac, about which he also made a film, and what they represented had been lost to succeeding generations. "I would like this film to address the generation that did not know the 1970s, but which lives the myth of 1968."[50] Faverjon described *Le Fils de Lip* as "a film on my generation, to try to understand its difficulty in engaging in struggles."[51] Faverjon saw in his parents' sense of betrayal at Lip not a tale limited to one family, but a key to understanding the quiescence of his own generation. Rouaud, however, envisaged telling the story of Lip as an encouragement for later generations to act. The release of *Les Lip. L'Imagination au pouvoir* shortly before the presidential elections in 2007, he explained, "is, as a matter of fact, not totally fortuitous, because the combat of *les Lip* can shed light on debates that concern us today."[52] In the film, Neuschwander tells of asking workers twenty years after 1973 if they would reveal the hiding places of the watches, and being told "No, they can be used again!"

In content and style, *Les Lip. L'Imagination au pouvoir* is consonant with the interviews in *Libération*, the films, and the popularization campaigns of 1973. The film was screened in 2007 in more than 300 cities in France, followed by a discussion with the audience in a style reminiscent of the "6 Heures avec Lip," in which Rouaud had participated in 1973. Rouaud engaged in 200 of these discussions and Piaget in 110. Neuschwander and Jeanningros were particularly active participants as well.[53] But now it was not a question of generating support for an ongoing struggle, but of making a past conflict come alive to inspire people in the future.

Les Lip. L'Imagination au Pouvoir tells the story of the first struggle, though as Vittot rightly points out, May 1968 and what preceded 1973 at

50   Guillaume Monier, Interview with Christian Rouaud [March 2007], at even.fr.

51   Ségal, "Lip, l'impossible héritage," 48.

52   Edith Meaume and Alain André, Interview with Christian Rouaud in *Profession Éducation* (March 2007), at liplefilm.com. See Julian Bourg's thoughtful "Tempered Nostalgia in Recent French Films on the '68 Years" in *The Long 1968: Revisions and New Perspectives*, ed. Daniel Sherman (Bloomington, 2013), 327–35.

53   Pernin, "LIP quarante ans après," 22, 37–8. For a discussion of presentations of "screenings-discussions in the style of '6 Heures avec Lip'" by the firm in charge of publicity for the film, see ADD 45J95 Philippe Hague of Pierre Grise Productions, December 2006.

Lip and that made it possible are not shown.[54] The film ends in 1976. In the style of the texts and films from 1973, those involved narrate the story; viewers do not hear or see Rouaud, whose editing recalls Clavel's polyphonic narration. With this in mind, Piaget said that of all the films on Lip, "this is the only one that tries to show what it is to live together, to struggle together."[55] Although the viewer sees only leaders, they seek to preserve the ethos of 1973, speaking on a number of occasions in the film of ideas that came from the base, not the leadership: real success, says Piaget, would be "to no longer need leaders."

Charbonnel and Neuschwander are the dominant figures in the final section of the film, the most original in historical terms in making the fate of Neuschwander's firm central to the narrative of the Lip Affair. Charbonnel says that Rouaud stands alone among chroniclers of the Lip Affair in recognizing his crucial role in bringing to fruition Riboud's project to create a successor firm to Lip. There was no place, he believed, in the "censorship coming from the orthodox left" for a Gaullist with a social vocation who could take such an initiative.[56] Of course, there was soon no place for Charbonnel in Messmer's cabinet either. Neuschwander, in turn, had long lived with Riboud's accusation that his mismanagement had doomed Lip, when in fact the state bore an important responsibility. In the film, Charbonnel says that Riboud and other patrons told him that they could not resist government pressure to put an end to Lip. Neuschwander is the one interviewee in the film who speaks in anger, at one point giving the *bras d'honneur* to Antoine Riboud and evoking "the quasi-Stalinist diktat that it must be killed," directed by the state against his firm. *Les Lip. L'Imagination au pouvoir* gives Neuschwander the opportunity to vindicate himself. For Neuschwander, Rouaud's film "breaks the stream of reproaches that, for thirty years, were addressed [to him]. For [him], it is a rehabilitation."[57] If some viewers found a film on a workers' struggle that vindicates bourgeois figures problematic, it allowed Rouaud to explain that "it is possible" was a victim of politics,

---

54 Interview with Vittot by Reid, June 3, 2011.

55 Paris and Genest, "Ce que démontre Lip," 19. Rouaud had initially thought of doing a film on Piaget, like an earlier film he had done on Bernard Lambert (*Paysan et rebelle*), but Piaget had refused to be the lone raconteur of the Lip story. Emmanuel Dreux and Didier Blain, Interview with Christian Rouaud in *CFDT Magazine* (March 2007).

56 Jean Charbonnel, *Dictionnaire raisonné d'un gaulliste rebelle* (Chaintreaux, 2014), 146. However, Piaget was not alone in saying that he had never heard Charbonnel say what he said in Rouaud's film until 2005, and certainly not in 1973-4. Piaget in Thomas, *Lip, une école de la lutte*.

57 *Libération*, May 3, 2007.

and thus counter the conservative narrative that 1968-era projects were by nature unrealizable.

The individual memories of many Lip workers who continued the struggle in the years after 1976 are those of conflicts and injustices. *Les Lip. L'Imagination au pouvoir* articulates what Beurier terms a PSU memory of self-management and women's liberation, not the failed fight for jobs in the cooperative. The position articulated by Neuschwander, and adopted in the film by Piaget and Raguénès, is that of a defeat at the hands of political opposition, not market inexorability. There has in turn been a move in the narrative of Lip, first evident in Rouaud's film, toward examination of the viability of the CEH in 1976.[58] If Rouaud began with the "it is possible" of workers paying themselves, he ends with the "it is possible" of a capitalist firm. This is one way that the events of the 1970s speak to millennials. It may also be evidence of the society the PCF always feared: one that weighs choices between good and bad capitalism, between La Crêcherie and L'Abîme of the contemporary world.

Imagining *les Lip* today

Les Lip. L'Imagination au pouvoir is focused on worker power and state efforts to quell it, and why "it is possible" was thwarted in this historical situation. Lip is still a living set of possibilities for Rouaud. More recent works, however, have made the interpretation in Rouaud's film the context for coming-of-age narratives and liberation stories of individual young women. The struggle is the backdrop of these stories, not the site of liberation itself. The personal is the political, but the political in which personal change takes place is not the struggle narrated in *Les Lip. L'Imagination au pouvoir*. Characters participate in the movement, but conflicts and resolutions take place in the family and elsewhere in society. Where there is liberation, it is individual, not collective. Liberation in these works is not about transforming society, but about finding one's place within it. They at once salute the struggle at Lip, but evince a farewell to the 1968-era aspirations of labor.

L'Été des Lip ("The Summer of *les Lip*"), released in 2012, is a telefilm set in 1973–4 directed by Dominique Ladoge. The film is quite sympathetic to the workers and quite critical of the prefect, presented as an arrogant and uncaring technocrat, and of the national government. However,

---

58   Pernin, "LIP quarante ans après," 48.

capitalism itself is not criticized. In the film Charbonnel explains that he brought in Neuschwander because self-management is impossible. *L'Été des Lip* ends with a voiceover explaining that the firm closed again in 1976 when the state withdrew orders because it could not allow the revival of Lip to offer an alternative to workers in a period of large-scale unemployment. In this it follows Rouaud's *Les Lip. L'Imagination au Pouvoir*. However, the story told in the film takes viewers elsewhere.

L'Été des Lip is the tale of the felicitously named Tulipe, a twenty-year-old OS at Lip. Pauline Brangolo has astutely noted that the press coverage of the conflict in 1973 featured the photos, if not the voices, of a disproportionate number of attractive young female workers;[59] they stand in for *tous-les-lip*. Tulipe is the daughter of a skilled watch worker at Lip who initially opposed the strike, but later turns his apartment into a clandestine workshop. She joins the CFDT-Lip in the spring of 1973 and is very quickly brought in as the only woman in small meetings of the union leadership. Tulipe is the one who suggests that the workers take the watches on the night of June 12. She falls in love with Sébastien, a student making a film of the strike (though he is shown filming Tulipe, rather than the demonstration in which she participates), and becomes pregnant with his child. After being arrested during the demonstrations following the expulsion from Palente, Sébastien, the figure representing the support of radical youth, abandons her. She rejects her friend's talk of an abortion.[60] When work resumes, Tulipe decides to leave the factory and return to school to pursue a career working with children. In the Women's Group that produced *Lip au féminin*, Suzy had said that as a single mother she had felt an isolated social pariah, but in the struggle, she had seen that bosses thought of workers as pariahs, as she was in her life.[61] Tulipe participates in acts of emancipation in the conflict and in challenging paternal authority in her romance, but her emancipation is not found in a women's group and takes her away from Palente.

The 2014 graphic novel by Laurent Galandon and Damien Vidal, *Lip des héros ordinaires* ("Lip. Ordinary Heroes"), also follows Rouaud's film

---

59   Brangolo, "Les filles de Lip (1968–1981)," 85–92.

60   Piton tells of discovering on June 12, 1973 (!) that a typist wanted to end her pregnancy and of working with other women to help her go to the Netherlands for an abortion, a procedure then illegal in France. *C'est possible*, 73–4. However, the issue divided the population. OS Jeanne Z. made this clear a few months later: "We did not occupy the factory for three months, set out to sell watches, start up production, in order to speak of contraception, of abortion, etc." "Comment 'l'affaire' nous a changés," 65.

61   *Lip au féminin*, 19–20.

and is focused on an individual woman.[62] The OS Solanges is at the heart of the struggle, but does not find her liberation within it. In the spring of 1973, it is she who suggests the switch from a slowdown in production to stopping work periodically. Solanges finds the briefcase during the sequestration on June 12, and she is the one who proposes hiding the watches. Her father had been in the army and entered a monastery a few months after returning from Algeria, traumatized by what he had lived through there. Solanges hides watches with him. She participates actively in the Action Committee and in popularization activities. Her husband is employed at another firm and is afraid of the repercussions on his own career of her involvement in the conflict. He kicks out Solanges and their child. She had taken photographs of the movement for the press, and when the conflict is resolved in 1974, she leaves Besançon to become a freelance photographer in Paris.

Audiences today look to the Lip Affair for what Piaget refers to as the "deconditioning of subordination," but this may not lead them to the collectivity in Palente.[63] For Tulipe and Solanges, women's liberation takes the form of liberation from the factory as single women navigating the existing society. Women are central to these works, unlike the "Lip au masculin" world of *Les Paroissiens de Palente*, but there is no new world imagined, as there had been in Clavel's novel.

For many in the rank and file, individual memories of the Lip conflict are marked by the trauma of betrayal. The child of disenchanted parents, Faverjon speaks of being unable to follow Chris Marker, of distrusting the "'they' who tell you it is possible." But that disenchantment became Marker's as well, who saw in *Le Fils de Lip*, "the liveliest, the fairest and the most needed film on the saga of *les Lip*," with implications well beyond that struggle.[64] Contemporary storytellers lift young Lip women out of Palente, making their individual liberation possible only outside this community. However, as the Lip conflict becomes history, there has developed a national memory of the conflict of 1973, rooted less in the individual lives of Lip workers than in what those throughout France who participated with them took from the struggle. Although this memory draws on what the supporters knew and experienced in 1973, it is presented now by leaders of the conflict themselves, whose story it is as well, in new forms of the national tours that galvanized the nation at the

---

62   Laurent Galandon and Damien Vidal, *Lip des héros ordinaires* (Paris, 2014).
63   Charles Piaget, "Preface" to Chaudy, *Faire des hommes libres*, 11.
64   "Dossier de candidature de Thomas Faverjon au CLEA," 9, at cndp.fr.

time. But when these historic figures are no longer able to perform this role, there is no large party to adopt the Lip experience as central to its identity and draw meaning or inspiration from it. There will be no *mur des fédérés* for *les Lip* as there is for the Communards, maintained and venerated by the Communist Party. However, if the Lip struggle is not a defining event in the narrative of a powerful organization, this allows individuals and groups to make it their own. The Lip Affair asks those who respond to it not just to engage in acts of individual liberation, but to reflect on how acts of collective civil disobedience can continue to challenge the limits the social order sets on the possible.

Afterword

In 1978, the Soviet dissident Leonid Plyushch came to participate in a colloquium in Besançon. Throughout the meeting, a woman from Lip who had left the community over an ideological dispute, expressed her resentment. As he listened attentively, the Russian mathematician murmured disconsolately: "You take away my last hope."

—Dominique Bondu[1]

If this conflict can be objectively analyzed, the event, on the other hand, cannot be explained. It occurred. The great lesson of Lip is how it was read and interpreted.... We hope ... that all the CFDT ... remembers the Lip struggle not as a model to imitate, but certainly as an example to meditate upon.

—Nicole Notat[2]

[I] see in Lip the genealogy of a new revolutionary discourse. One that allows us to envisage making revolution without taking power.

—Michel Onfray[3]

If [Lip] works, [historians] will say it was ripe; if it fails, they will say it was premature ... It is rare that they weary themselves more.

—Maurice Clavel[4]

---

1   Bondu, "De l'usine à la communauté," 206. In June 1977, at a reception for Plyushch and other Soviet dissidents held when Leonid Brezhnev was visiting France, Claude Mauriac sat with Raguénès, who spoke to him of the daily General Assembly at Palente. For Mauriac, Lip, not the dissidents, presented "the most enriching, the most moving moment of the evening." Claude Mauriac, entry of June 21, 1977, in *Signes, rencontres et rendez-vous* (Paris, 1983), 251.

2   ACFDT CSG/5/3 Nicole Notat, "Il y a 20 ans, LIP ...," September 29, 1993.

3   *Le Monde*, April 2–3, 2011, 26.

4   Clavel, *Les Paroissiens de Palente*, 304.

Michel Garcin recognized that the conflicts at L.I.P. participated in national debates about creating sites that could prefigure the future, while surviving in the present. Disputes in the years before 1981 over making salaries correspond with responsibilities at Palente, he believed, were of a piece with those at *Libération* in 1979, when Serge July broke with the culture premised on the same salary for all.[5] Richard Copans was a militant in Cinélutte, a group born in 1973 out of the break between Communist and leftist filmmakers. "We wanted a collective project, without hierarchy, without division of labor." No Cinélutte film had credits by name until Copans' film on Lip, *À pas lentes*, in 1979. "At that moment," he said, "leftism was finished."[6] After 1981, some leftists thought *les Lip* had enacted the end of the 1968 years in their efforts to keep the enterprise alive. They saw the cooperative's decision to accept layoffs as "the dress rehearsal of the reformist treason that will culminate in the Mitterrand years."[7]

Although drawing on their own experience and thinking in terms of participation and engagement rather than the politics of betrayal, Lip leaders too looked at France under Mitterrand and saw elements of the situation at Lip. "What France has lived with the left for two years," Bondu said in June 1983, "is quite simply what we have lived at Lip for five years."[8] Piaget saw the workers' passive optimism at L.I.P. when it replaced the director with a president-director general in 1983 as an echo of the national experience: "This resembles a little the left that assumed power."[9] For Vittot, "The image of France after May 10 [the election of Mitterrand in 1981] is also that of Lip": apathy derived from years of the right in power in the state on the one hand, and from the weight of the management boards in the Lip cooperatives on the other.[10] However, all was not lost. Vittot felt that "the collective analysis that the working class and the left so need" would be enriched if "those who made Lip and lived it daily" got together several times a year "to revive reflection"—the act at the heart of Lip worker activism since its origins.[11]

---

5   AB Interview with Garcin by Beurier [1992], 44.

6   Éva Ségal, "Richard Copans le cinélutteur de fond," *Images de la culture* 23 (August 2008): 111.

7   David Faroult, "Note sur *Fils de Lip*," *Revue documentaires* 22–3 (2010): 234.

8   *Libération*, June 22, 1983. *L'Unité*, March 14, 1986, 23. In *Lip 20 ans après*, Neuschwander argued that the failed policies that the left in power practiced in addressing unemployment were those of the right in dealing with Lip in 1975–6.

9   *Lip Unité*, Second Trimester 1983, 13.

10   *Lip Unité*, December 1982, 11.

11   *Lip Unité*, December 1981, 9.

Piaget took early retirement in 1983 and quit the CFDT over what he saw as the confederation's fatalism with regard to unemployment.[12] A decade later, he became a militant in Agir ensemble contre le chômage! (AC!), a group that worked with the unemployed left on their own by unions. In 1993, when the CFDT organized a colloquium in Besançon on unemployment to mark the twentieth anniversary of the march of September 29, 1973, Piaget saw nothing of Lip in what he termed the secretary-general Nicole Notat's imitation of the "modern language of employers" in her discussion of unemployment.[13] Piaget found himself returning to the origins of his own radicalism. In 1998, forty years after his realization that the Algerians' situation shared characteristics with that of Lip workers and his decision to support the Algerians during their war of independence, Piaget used this as an example of the kind of connections unions had to make now—and act upon—between the situation of the socially excluded and the deterioration of the workers' situation in France.[14] A decade later, he asked himself if he had been wrong not to run for president in 1974 as the candidate of struggles, seeing it as a missed opportunity to put in place a dynamic to combat unemployment that the French left has never developed.[15]

It is a testimony to both the politically radical and traumatic nature of the Lip Affair that it has left no memorial traces in the urban landscape of Besançon today: it is what in France is termed a *lieu de mémoire* (place of memory), but it is without a material place. The Palente of Fred Lip and *les Lip* is gone. In 1985, the Chamber of Commerce and the municipality were finally able to buy the nine-hectare property. They razed or rehabilitated the buildings and converted Palente into an industrial park, including a "nursery" on a little more than one-third of the space to serve as an incubator for new businesses. The Espace industriel de Palente—the president of the Chamber of Commerce wanted to name it Espace Lip, but was vetoed by the remaining watchmakers who wanted no reference to their nemeses of Fred Lip and his employees—has been successful. At the twentieth anniversary of the Lip conflict in 1993, Mayor Schwint pointed to the more than 850 jobs in the reborn Palente, saying "this is proof that beyond conflicts hope can be reborn."[16] Accounts often point out that there were more jobs created in the Espaces than had

---

12   El Azzouzi, "Charles Piaget: une leçon de liberté" (July 6, 2013), at mediapart.fr.
13   AR Interview with Piaget by Rouaud, December 2, 2003, 7.
14   "Il y a 25 ans ... Lip" [interview with Charles Piaget], *Sud* 85 (September 1998): 8.
15   ADD 45J100 Draft of Thomé, *Créateurs d'utopies*, 7–8.
16   *Besançon Votre Ville*, May 1993, 3.

been lost with the closing of Lip.[17] By 2006, a diverse group of eighty-five firms—many specializing in microtechnology, with a total of 1,030 employees, including those in LPI, the cooperative born of L.I.P.—were found at the Espaces. Seven to ten new businesses with sixty-some employees were created each year. Well over one-third of the businesses in the Espace industriel de Palente had its origins in the "nursery," which took the place of the phalanstery of Godin and Neuschwander, of Zola's La Crêcherie, and of les Lip in Bondu's philosophy workshop.[18] For some, these ventures were a refutation and for others a realization in a new environment of elements of the imagination and entrepreneurial qualities les Lip had shown in their struggle.

At the origins of the long 1968, E.P. Thompson analyzed how English commoners in the era of early industrial capitalism fought to sustain the life of their communities.[19] At a comparable point in the development of late industrial capitalism and market globalization in France, the workers of Lip mobilized to defend their community. In both cases, men and women created sites of resistance motivated by democratic, egalitarian, communal values. They opened their gates to supporters who were in turn transformed by the experience. Frank Georgi is right to call the Lip Affair "the swan song of the heroic act of the 'struggles,'" the point at which the revolutionary aspirations of 1968 and those who embraced them confronted the recession of the late 1970s.[20] The Lip Affair was a site of the ebbing of left Gaullism and the transformation of the Second Left, of an apogee and decline of French Maoism and left Catholicism, of the development of working-class women's consciousness of their position as workers and as women, and of the affirmation and challenge to the enterprise as a site of managerial capitalism and of self-management.

However, the democratic culture of les Lip, their relations with outsiders and with those who would accompany them, their efforts to organize horizontally with other workers contesting factory closures, and their radical insistence that workers' investment of their lives in their enterprise gives them expertise and rights as a democratic collectivity to participate in decisions concerning their future, also made their struggle

---

17   Le Monde, September 25, 2001.
18   Association de Palente, Palente au fil du temps, 273–4.
19   E.P. Thompson, The Making of the English Working Class (London, 1963).
20   Frank Georgi, "'Vivre demain dans les luttes d'aujourd'hui.' Le syndicat, la grève et l'autogestion en France (1968–1988)" in Les Années 68. Le temps de la contestation, ed. Geneviève Dreyfus-Armand et al. (Paris, 2000), 407.

a bridge from the aspirations and practices of the long 1968 to those of the alternative globalization (*altermondialisation*) movements today. The creation by Lip of a self-administered community in struggle, and its challenge to who determined what was possible, make it an important predecessor of contemporary Occupy movements in ideology and practice.[21] Causes which were lost in Besançon may yet be won.

21   Patrick Viveret, "L'autogestion: un mort bien vivant!," *Mouvements* 18 (2001): 38–43. Guillaume Gourgues, "L'autogestion, une idée neuve?," *Semaine Sociale Lamy* supplement to 1163 (May 19, 2014): 73–8. Matteo Albanese, "LIP: a workers' community facing globalization," *Labor History* 58 (2017): 91–105.

Bibliography

The source base for this study is large and diverse. The major archival holdings are in the BDIC, ADD, AMB, ACGT, ACFDT and AFGM-CFDT.[1] Charles Piaget, Anne-Marie Martin, Claude Neuschwander, and Dominique Bondu graciously provided access to their papers. Press coverage, ranging from national mainstream periodicals to leftist newspapers and *Lip Unité*, is a valuable source on the realities and representations of the movement as are films made at the time and more recently. This study has been deeply enriched by consultation of the transcripts of interviews done by Joëlle Beurier and Christian Rouaud, as well as interviews conducted by the author.

Joëlle Mauerhan, museum curator in Besançon, compares historians of Lip to historians of the French Resistance. In both cases, the historical actors may claim a knowledge inaccessible to those who did not participate.[2] More broadly, there is a generational element to much of the best work on the Lip Affair, which has shown that leaders' narratives of unity and equality (particularly of men and women), and supporters' narratives of workers' self-management voiced at the time of events, are incomplete or misleading. When Saoura Cassou's father showed her the Lip watch he had bought to support *les Lip* he explained that "they

---

1   Each of these archives has a good guide to materials concerning the Lip Affair. Guillaume Gourgues and Laurent Kondratuk are engaged in a project to put archival materials dealing with Lip in a digital format: http://crjfc.univ-fcomte.fr/download/crjfc/document/palente.pdf. One largely unexplored source are recordings of General Assembly meetings and negotiations at Arc et Senans in 1973–1974. See in particular ACGT Carton K7 Audio and ADD Fonds Jeanningros 12AV.

2   Pernin, "LIP quarante ans après," 75.

represented the vast and impressive aggregate, 'the workers.'"[3] That they may have represented this for Cassou's father is at the heart of the questions she poses in her study. Cassou's work is also an element of the largest and best body of work on the Lip Affair—unpublished theses.

Selected Published Works Relating to the Lip Affair

"À Lip, des femmes: mille manières de lutter," *Des femmes en mouvement* 5 (May 1978): 32–4.

Albanese, Matteo. "LIP: a workers' community facing globalization," *Labor History* 58 (2017): 91–105.

Association de Palente. *Palente au fil du temps. Du village à la cité*. Besançon, 2011.

Auschitzky Coustans, Marie-Pia. *Lip, des heures à conter*. Seyssinet, 2000.

Barou, Jean-Pierre. *Gilda je t'aime à bas le travail!* Paris, 1975.

Beurier, Joëlle. "La mémoire Lip ou la fin du mythe autogestionaire?" in *Autogestion. La dernière utopie?*, ed. Frank Georgi. Paris, 2003, 451–65.

Bondu, Dominique. "Coopération et alterité," *Revue des études coopératives* 208 (1982): 37–51.

—"L'Élaboration d'une langue commune: LIP-GP," *Les Temps modernes* 684–5 (July–October 2015): 69–80.

—"LIP, dix ans après," *Autogestion* 14 (1983): 83–96.

Burgy, Raymond and Charles Piaget. "L'aventure des Coopératives LIP" (2007), appendix to Thomé, *Créateurs d'utopies*, at genepi.blog.lemonde.fr.

Chaillet, Daniella, Marie-Odile Crabbé-Diawara, and Jacques Fontaine. "Entretien avec Charles Piaget. 'Notre lutte, nos objectifs, c'est à nous seuls de les contrôler," *Contretemps* 22 (2014): 116–27.

Chaudy, Michel. *Faire des hommes libres. Boimondau et les communautés de travail à Valence*. Valence, 2008.

Clavel, Maurice. *Les Paroissiens de Palente*. Paris, 1974.

Collectif [of Lip employees]. *Lip: affaire non classée*. Paris, 1976.

Collombat, Benoît. "Lip, 1973: la grande peur du patronat" in *Histoire secrète du patronat de 1945 à nos jours*, ed. Benoît Collombat and David Servenay. Paris, 2009, 217–25.

"Comment 'l'affaire' nous a changés," *Preuves* 16 (1973): 63–81.

Daumas, Jean-Claude. "Le système productif localisé et la manufacture.

---

3 Cassou, "Lip, la construction d'un mythe," 4.

L'industrie horlogère en Franche-Comté au début des années 1970)," *Semaine sociale Lamy* supplement to no. 1631 (May 19, 2014): 11–17.

Divo, Jean. *L'affaire Lip et les catholiques de Franche-Comté*. Saint-Gingolphe, 2003.

Faucoup, Yves. "Que sont devenus les LIP," *L'Estocade* 20 (September-October 1983): 22–9, and 21 (November-December 1983): 3–4.

Féret, Dominique. *Les Yeux rouges*. Besançon, 1998.

FTM-CGT. "La CGT et Lip," *Le Guide du militant de la métallurgie* 94 (April 1974).

Gavi, Philippe, Jean-Paul Sartre, and Pierre Victor. *On a raison de se révolter*. Paris, 1974.

Georgi, Frank, ed. *Autogestion. La dernière utopie?* Paris, 2003.

— "L'autogestion en France des 'années 1968' aux années 1980. Essor et déclin d'une utopie politique," *La Pensée* 356 (October-December 2008): 87–101.

— "L'autogestion: une utopie chrétienne?" in *À la Gauche du Christ*, eds. Denis Pelletier and Jean-Louis Schlegel. Paris, 2012, 373–98.

— *Soufflons-nous de la même forge. Une histoire de la fédération de la métallurgie CFTC-CFDT, 1920–1974*. Ivry-sur-Seine, 1997.

— "Un 'conflit autogestionnaire' sous Georges Pompidou: les pouvoirs publics face à l'affaire Lip (1973–1974)" in *Action et pensée sociales chez Georges Pompidou*, eds. Alain Beltran, Gilles Le Béguec, and Jean-Pierre Williot. Paris, 2004, 157–76.

— "'Vivre demain dans nos luttes d'aujourd'hui'. Le Syndicat, la grève et l'autogestion en France" in *Les Années 68: le temps de la contestation*, ed. Geneviève Dreyfus-Armand, Robert Frank, Marie-Françoise Lévy, and Michelle Zancarini-Fournel. Paris, 2000, 402–13.

— "Vivre la lutte, incarner l'utopie: les conflits Lip et leurs représentations, 1973–1981," *D'Ailleurs* 1 (2015): 20–35.

Giraud, Henri. *Mon été chez Lip*. Paris, 1974.

Gourgues, Guillaume. "Le débat dans la lutte. Changement et 'vérité' économique dans le conflit Lip (1973)" in *Critiques du dialogue: Discussion, traduction, participation*, ed. Sylvain Lavelle. Villeneuve d'Ascq, 2016, 245–74.

— "Occuper son usine et produire: stratégie de lutte ou survie ? La fragile politisation des occupations de l'usine Lip (1973–1977)," *Politix* 117 (2017): 117–43.

Groupe de femmes en lutte du 18ème arrondissement. "Lip au féminin," *Les Pétroleuses* 0 [1974].

Il était une fois la révolution. Paris, 1974.

Jeanningros, Michel. "LIP 1973–1981: côté armements," *Alternatives non-violentes* 41 (1981): 18–22.

Jusseaume, Pierre. "Un succès venu de loin. La 'popularisation' chez Lip," *Politique aujourd'hui* (March–April 1974): 63–70.

Lantz, Pierre. "Lip et l'utopie," *Politique aujourd'hui* 11-12 (December 1980): 97–104.

— "Lip précurseur des coordinations?" in *Les Coordinations des travailleurs dans la confrontation sociale.* Paris, 1994, 23–32.

— "'Une espèce de flou paradisiaque, un désir sorti de l'enfance': les Lip" in *La Gauche le pouvoir le socialisme,* ed. Christine Buci-Glucksmann. Paris, 1983, 172–83.

"Le conflit Lip: lutter pour quel travail?," *Frères du monde* 84–5 (1974): 117–23.

Le Garrec, Évelyne. *Les Messagères.* Paris, 1976.

Les Cahiers de mai, "The Lip Watch Strike," *Radical America* 7:6 (November–December 1973): 1–18.

Linhart, Virginie. *Volontaires pour l'usine. Vies d'établis 1967–1977.* Paris, 1994.

Lip, Fred. *Conter mes heures.* Paris, 1973.

Lip au féminin. Supplement to *Combat socialiste* 16 (1975).

"Lip aujourd'hui," *La Barre à tous* 3 (April 1975): 2–34.

"Lip des militants du comité d'action parlent," supplement to *Revolution!* 35 (1973).

"Lip Larzac," *Cahiers pour le communisme* 1 (February 1974).

Lopez, Jean. "Lip Interview [with members of the Comité d'action]" [November 1973] typescript at BDIC (Q Pièce 12.785).

Lourau, René. *L'Analyseur Lip.* Paris, 1974.

Macciocchi, Maria-Antonietta. *De la France.* Paris, 1977.

Maruani, Margaret. *Les Syndicats à l'épreuve du féminisme.* Paris, 1979.

Morawe, Bodo. *Aktiver Streik in Frankreich oder Klassenkampf bei LIP.* Reinbek, 1974.

Mothé, Daniel. "Lip: réussite de la lutte, échec de la grève," *Esprit* 430 (December 1973), 890–6.

Neuschwander, Claude. *Claude Neuschwander: une vie de militance[s].* Gap, 2011.

— and Gaston Bordet. *Lip 20 ans après (propos sur le chômage).* Paris, 1993.

Paris, Stéphane and Jean-Louis Genest, "Ce que démontre Lip," *Les Idées en mouvement* 147 (March 2007): 19.

Pelletier, Denis. *La Crise catholique. Religion, société, politique.* Paris, 2002.

Piaget, Charles. "'Des trésors d'imagination quand on est partie prenante...'," *Autrement* 20 (September 1979): 163–9.

— Interview [1998] in *La Subversion démocratique*, ed. Auguste Dubourg. Pantin, 2000, 303–28.

— "La formation par l'action collective" in *L'École à perpétuité*, eds. Heinrich Dauber and Étienne Verne. Paris, 1977, 151–84.

— "Les luttes de LIP de 1948 à 1983" [2005] at alencontre.org.

— "Lip 1973: des problématiques toujours d'actualité" in *Autogestion. Une idée toujours neuve*, ed. Guillaume Davranche. Paris, 2010, 101–10.

— *Lip. Charles Piaget et les Lip racontent.* Paris, 1973.

— "LIP. Les effets formateurs d'une lutte collective," *Entropia* 2 (Spring 2007): 141–65 [collective work (1975)].

— "Texte de l'intervention de Ch. Piaget au cours du meeting qui a eu lieu à la Bourse du Travail de Lyon, le 24 octobre 1973" [BDIC F delta rés 578/36].

— and Edmond Maire. *Lip 73.* Paris, 1973.

— and Roland Vittot. "LIP: une lutte riche d'enseignements" in *Parti et mouvement social. Le chantier ouvert par le PSU*, ed. Jean-Claude Gillet and Michel Mousel. Paris, 2011, 275–90.

Piton, Monique. *C'est possible!* Paris, 1975.

— *Mémoires libres.* Paris, 2010.

Plantin, Georgette, "L'accompagnement du service social durant les difficultés vécues par Lip et son rôle actuel," *Rencontre: cahiers du travailleur social* 37 (Spring 1981): 47-50.

Porhel, Vincent. *Ouvriers bretons. Conflits d'usines, conflits identitaires en Bretagne des années 1968.* Rennes, 2008.

"Préface des ouvriers de Lip" in Emile Zola, *Travail.* Lagrasse, 1979, 11–32.

Raguénès, Jean. *De Mai 68 à Lip. Un dominicain au coeur des luttes.* Paris, 2008.

— Pierre Victor, and Denis Clodic. "Lip 1973–1976," *Les Temps modernes* 32 (February 1977): 1235–69.

Ravenel, Bernard. "Un militant ouvrier autogestionnaire. Entretien avec Charles Piaget," *Mouvements* 8 (March-April 2000): 111–21.

Réseau Citoyens Résistants. *La Force du collectif. Entretien avec Charles Piaget.* Paris, 2012.

Rosanvallon, Pierre. *L'Âge de l'autogestion.* Paris, 1976.

Roy, Jacques. "Lip 1973: l'entreprise transformée," *Que faire aujourd'hui?* 22 (April-May 1983): 20-3.

Saint-Germain, Pierre and Michel Souletie. "Le voyage à Palente," *Les révoltes logiques* 7 (Summer 1978): 67–80.

Ségal, Éva. "Lip, l'impossible héritage," *Images de la culture* 23 (August 2008): 46–8.

Silberstein, Patrick. "Lip" in *La France des années 68*, eds. Antoine Artous, Didier Epsztajn, and Patrick Silberstein. Paris, 2008, 472–81.

Ternant, Évelyne. "L'affaiblissement du SPL horloger franc-comtois depuis le milieu des années 70: mythes et réalités historiques" in *Les Systèmes productifs dans l'Arc jurassien. Acteurs, pratiques et territoires*, ed. Jean-Claude Daumas. Besançon, 2005, 107–33.

— "Le milieu horloger français face à la mutation de la montre à quartz (1965–1975)" in *De l'horlogerie aux microtechniques: 1965–1975*. Besançon, 1996, 25–46.

Thomé, Pierre. *Créateurs d'utopies*. Paris, 2011.

"Un an de lutte chez LIP," supplement to *Critique socialiste* 5 (June 1971).

"Un pas vers la révolution," supplement to *Rouge* 231 (1973).

Vigna, Xavier. *L'Insubordination ouvrière dans les années 68. Essai d'histoire politique des usines*. Rennes, 2007.

— "Lip et Larzac. Conflits locaux et mobilisations nationales" in *68 Une Histoire collective [1962–1981]*, eds. Philippe Artières and Michelle Zancarini-Fournel. Paris, 2008, 487–93.

de Virieu, François-Henri, *Lip: 100.000 montres sans patron*. Paris, 1973.

Werner, Pascale. "La question des femmes dans la lutte des classes. L'expérience Lip (Avril 73–Mars 74)," *Les Temps modernes* 336 (July 1974): 2443–66.

Selected Unpublished Theses on the Lip Affair

Berry, Jean-Pic. "Lip 1978." Mémoire, Centre de Sociologie des Organisations, 1978.

Beurier, Joëlle. "La Mémoire des Lip." Mémoire, Université de Paris 1, 1992.

Bondu, Dominique. "De l'usine à la communauté. L'Institution du lien social dans le monde de l'usine." Thèse de 3ème cycle, École des Hautes Études en Science Sociales, 1981.

Brangolo, Pauline. "Les filles de Lip (1968–1981): trajectoires de salariées, mobilisations féminines et conflits sociaux." Mémoire, Université de Paris 1, 2015.

Cassou, Saoura. "Lip, la construction d'un mythe." Mémoire, Université de Paris 1, 2002.

Castleton, Edward. "Lip: une remise à l'heure: de l'action sociale à la gestion de production (1973–1983)." Mémoire, Institut d'Études Politiques de Paris, 1996.

Champeau, Thomas. "Lip: le conflit et l'affaire (1973)." Mémoire, École des Hautes Études en Sciences Sociales, 2007.

Cuénot, Claude. "Ouvriers et mouvement ouvrier dans le Doubs de la fin de la première guerre mondiale au début des années 1950." Thèse d'histoire, Université de Bourgogne, 2000.

Dehedin, Caroline. "À Lip, les femmes aussi ont une histoire: la lutte des ouvrières de 1973 à 1977." Mémoire, Université de Rouen, 2011.

D'Houtaud, Sophie. "L'héritage de mai 68 à Besançon vu par ses propres acteurs." Mémoire, Université de Franche Comté, 2006.

Firmin, Mathieu. "*Les Cahiers de mai* 1968/1974. Entre journalisme et syndicalisme." Mémoire, Université de Paris 1, 1998, 2 vols.

Jacquin, Daniel. "Lip 1973–1981 (Analyse sociologique)." Thèse de 3ème cycle, École des Hautes Études en Sciences Sociales, 1982.

Maradji, Marie-Claire. "Les interventions syndicales dans l'affaire Lip." Mémoire, Université de Paris I, 1978.

Molis, A. "Du conflit des Lip en 1973 à Besançon à la formation de la Commission Femmes: expression d'un féminisme ouvrier?" Mémoire de Master. Université de Picardie Jules Verne, 2011.

Pernin, Pauline. "LIP quarante ans après, des commémorations en tensions." Mémoire, Université de Lille II, 2014.

Rozenblatt, Patrick, Francine Tabaton, and Michèle Tallard. "Analyse du conflit Lip et de ses répercussions sur les pratiques ouvrières et les stratégies syndicales." Thèse de 3ème cycle, Université de Paris IX, 1980.

Ternant, Evelyne. "La dynamique longue d'un système productif localisé: l'industrie de la montre en Franche-Comté." Thèse de doctorat, Université Pierre Mendès-France, 2004.

Terrieux, Gérard. "L'expérience Lip." Thèse de 3ème cycle, Université de Panthéon-Sorbonne, 1983.

Zurbach, Thomas. "1968: le Mai des travailleurs à Besançon." Mémoire, Université de Franche-Comté, 2002.

Selected Films

À *pas lentes*. Directed by Richard Copans. 1979. Cinélutte.

Fils de Lip. Directed by Thomas Faverjon. 2007. TS Productions.

Les Lip. L'Imagination au pouvoir. Directed by Christian Rouaud. 2007. Les Films d'Ici.

L'Été des Lip. Directed by Dominque Ladoge. 2011. Jade Productions.

Lip Formation. Portes ouvertes à Lip, 8–9 mai 1976. Directed by Anne-Marie Martin. 1976. Association de Diffusion Populaire.

Lip, le rêve et l'histoire. Directed by Bernard Gauthier. 2005. Beau Comme Une Image.

LIP ou le goût du collectif. Directed by Dominique Dubosc. 1976. INA.

Lip. Réalités de la Lutte. Directed by Alain Dhouailly. 1973. Unicité.

Lip, une école de la lutte à l'usage des jeunes générations. Directed by Thomas Lacoste. 2008. La Bande Passante.

Monique (1973); *La Marche de Besançon* (1973); *Monique et Christiane* (1976); *Jacquelyn et Marcel* (1976). Directed by Carole Roussopoulos. Vidéo Out.

Non au démantèlement! Non aux licenciements! Directed by Dominique Dubosc. 1973. Commission Popularisation des travailleurs de Lip.

Puisqu'on on vous dit que c'est possible. Directed by Chris Marker. 1973. Scopcolor.

Index